Strategies for
Library Administration

STRATEGIES FOR LIBRARY ADMINISTRATION:
Concepts and Approaches

By
Charles R. McClure
and
Alan R. Samuels

1982
LIBRARIES UNLIMITED, INC.
Littleton, Colorado

Copyright © 1982 Libraries Unlimited, Inc.
All Rights Reserved
Printed in the United States of America

No part of this publication may be reproduced, stored in a retrieval system, or transmitted, in any form or by any means, electronic, mechanical, photocopying, recording, or otherwise, without the prior written permission of the publisher.

LIBRARIES UNLIMITED, INC.
P.O. Box 263
Littleton, Colorado 80160

Library of Congress Cataloging in Publication Data

Main entry under title:

Strategies for library administration.

   Includes bibliographical references and index.
   1. Library administration. I. McClure, Charles R.
II. Samuels, Alan R., 1942-
Z678.S77   025.1   81-12408
ISBN 0-87287-265-3   AACR2

Preface

The purpose of this book is to provide library administrators, staff, educators, and students with the background information they will need to make effective administrative decisions. The volume is intended to be a summary of important concepts and techniques related to library administration. Although some of the articles provide practical suggestions for improving overall library administration, this is not a "how to" book and the reader will find no quick cures for library administrative problems. In compiling this book, we have deliberately avoided the excessively narrow perspectives which often permeate a collection of articles about library administration. Instead, we have adhered to our belief that those interested in library administration must understand concepts and approaches that are basic to administrative techniques, and that they must be exposed to the widest possible number of managerial perspectives in order that an understanding of what is, and what is not, relevant to a particular set of circumstances can be acquired. To obtain such an understanding requires knowledge of theory as well as practice, and obtaining a theoretical knowledge of library administration is thematic throughout the book.

Although the emphasis of the book is on *library* administration, we believe the individual articles have wide applicability to administrative topics in other information-related organizations regardless of their formal title—Information Resource Center, Information Center, or Library and Information Center. Thus, we consider the term "library" to be a generic one that includes a broad range of organizations whose primary responsibilities are to acquire, organize, and disseminate information.

The collection of articles in this volume represents both original and reprinted works which deal with basic administrative problems affecting today's libraries. In deciding which articles should be included, we have placed ourselves in the position of administrators, students, teachers, and library staff to provide a mix of articles of interest to these various groups.

To accomplish this mix of articles, we drew equally on writings from disciplines outside library science. Because of the interdisciplinary bases of administration, inclusion of writings from a broad spectrum in the behavioral sciences will assist librarians to understand better the research and techniques being considered by other disciplines. We believe that the infusion of such writings into library science can significantly increase the quality and critical analysis of our own research and approaches.

The 34 articles have been grouped into 13 general categories that describe critical areas related to library administration. Some of the criteria used to determine the articles to be included were: currentness of the article; importance of the article as a "classic" discussion of a given topic; presentation of innovative ideas and approaches; clarity and organization of the piece; and appropriateness of the article for a library audience.

The genesis of this book can be traced to our lack of enthusiasm for the way in which administration is generally conceptualized in the library literature. As we searched the library administrative field for suitable vehicles to integrate modern management theory with current library practices it soon became apparent that no such vehicle could be identified. Many involved with library administration either seem to adopt excessively pragmatic approaches without considering the theoretical bases for such approaches or choose to treat library administration as if it were merely a temporary departure from traditional business administration. We do not wholly reject either approach. Rather, we suggest that neither approach adequately prepares librarians to assume an effective administrative role—whether that administrative role be one of director or staff.

The approach that is suggested in this volume is one that draws upon a number of administrative schools of thoughts. It is our belief that librarians must widen their administrative perspective, examine a broad base of research and writings on administration from a number of disciplines, learn how to analyze specific administrative situations carefully given individual and environmental constraints, and develop strategies based on a conceptual framework that allows each individual in the organization to be as productive as possible in helping the organization achieve its goals and objectives.

Many of the favorite administrative exhortations of librarianship will not be found in this volume. This is deliberate; those seeking such material will find it amply represented elsewhere. In the present book we have emphasized writings that point to newer, more innovative, less traditional directions. Library administrative thought still requires significant development, both in theory and practice. In this book we have tried to suggest ways in which this development can be furthered and hope to encourage others to follow similar paths.

A special note of appreciation must be given to the University of Oklahoma, University Research Council and to the School of Education, University of North Carolina at Greensboro, which assisted in the preparation of the volume by supporting copying and communication costs; to Rebecca Holland, who as a research assistant at the University of Oklahoma, School of Library Science assisted in the endless chores of record keeping related to the various permission forms and verifying bibliographic citations; and to Sheri Lambeth who did the final typing of the introductions.

Norman, Oklahoma	Charles R. McClure
Greensboro, North Carolina	Alan R. Samuels

Contents

Preface 5

Part I
ADMINISTRATIVE THEORY

Introduction 11

Toward a Theory of Library Administration
By Alan R. Samuels and Charles R. McClure 12

The Management Theory Jungle Revisited
By Harold Koontz 29

Part II
ORGANIZATION AND BUREAUCRACY

Introduction 39

Libraries as Bureaucracies
By Beverly P. Lynch 41

The Limits to Complexity: Are Bureaucracies Becoming Unmanageable?
By Duane S. Elgin and Robert A. Bushnell 50

The Columbia University Management Program
By Jerome Yavarkovsky and Warren J. Haas 63

Part III
DECISION MAKING AND LEADERSHIP

Introduction 71

An Overview of Decision Making
By E. Frank Harrison 73

Library Administration & New Management Systems
By Richard De Gennaro...90

Leader Behavior in Changing Libraries
By Andrea C. Dragon...96

Part IV
PARTICIPATION

Introduction...111

On Decision Sharing in Libraries: How Much Do We Know?
By Louis Kaplan...113

Management By Objectives and the Academic Library: A Critical Overview
By James Michalko..120

Committee Management: Guidelines from Social Science Research
By A. C. Filley..138

Part V
COMMUNICATION AND INFORMATION MANAGEMENT

Introduction...147

The Process of Communication
By Richard Emery...149

Strategies for Organizational Information Management
By Charles R. McClure..163

Part VI
FINANCIAL BASIS OF THE LIBRARY

Introduction...173

Budgeting
By Ann E. Prentice..175

Zero Base Budgeting
By Anne G. Sarndal...196

Sources and Uses of Funds of Academic Libraries
By Jacob Cohen and Kenneth W. Leeson...202

Part VII
PLANNING AND EVALUATION OF LIBRARY SERVICES

Introduction...225

The Planning Process: Strategies for Action
By Charles R. McClure..227

Purposes of Evaluation
  By Carol H. Weiss..238

Part VIII
MOTIVATION AND JOB SATISFACTION

Introduction...253

Applying Theory Y to Library Management
  By Donald J. Morton..255

Managing Motivation and Job Satisfaction
  By Maurice P. Marchant...261

Part IX
PERSONNEL

Introduction...275

Developing Human Resources: An Administrative View
  By James S. Healey...277

Job Assessment and Job Evaluation
  By B. G. Dutton..289

Library Staff Development through Performance Appraisal
  By Dimity S. Berkner...306

Part X
UNIONIZATION

Introduction...317

Problems and Strategies for Collective Bargaining in Public Libraries
  By George B. Viele...319

Professional Associations and Unions: Future Impact of Today's Decisions
  By Dora Biblarz, Margaret Capron, Linda Kennedy,
  Johanna Ross, and David Weinerth...................................329

Bargaining's Effect on Library Management and Operation
  By Carol E. Moss...337

Part XI
SYSTEMS PERSPECTIVE AND TECHNOLOGY

Introduction...357

General Systems Theory: Applications for Organization and Management
  By Fremont E. Kast and James E. Rosenzweig.........................359

Operations Research in Libraries: A Critical Assessment
By Michael Bommer..378

Humanizing Computerized Information Systems
By Theodore D. Sterling..381

Part XII
MARKETING THE LIBRARY

Introduction...391

Marketing the Library
By Andrea C. Dragon...393

Marketing Library and Information Services: The Strengths and Weaknesses of a Marketing Approach
By Christine Oldman...398

Part XIII
CHANGE

Introduction...411

Managing Innovation in Academic Libraries
By Miriam A. Drake..413

Organizational Climate and Library Change
By Alan R. Samuels..421

Contingency Theory, Values, and Change
By J. A. Millar...432

Part I
ADMINISTRATIVE THEORY

Introduction

In a book devoted to library management, the word "theory" may be thought inappropriate by some and irrelevant by others. Often, librarians are told that theory is too etherial to be discussed in the hard reality of a library's effort to make it through another day, and that, in any case, libraries are so different from other types of organizations that what may work in profit-making organizations simply won't do for libraries. The fallacy represented by this sort of perspective is that library administrators already use theory to manage their libraries, whether that theory is stated or not. Declaring that theory is not relevant to, or present in, current library administrative practice is incorrect. Librarians use theories every day, whether these theories are explicitly stated or merely implied by actions.

Those who look for library administrative theory search for it outside of librarianship. Because library administration is so pragmatically oriented, it seems impossible that a theoretical framework for viewing administrative practice *already* exists within libraries. Yet this is indeed the case. It remains only to ferret it out. This need not be a difficult task if librarians are willing to face the reality of what it is they do in administering a library and, more importantly, WHY they do it!

Two perspectives on administrative theory are presented in this section. In the first article, Alan R. Samuels and Charles R. McClure go in search of library theory. Their view is primarily historical and evolutionary, though it is tempered with forays into current library practice. Thematic in their view of administrative theory is that it can be developed from a purely library perspective. Library administrative theory does exist, although it has not yet been fully identified. The threads of a theory of library administration are already present and can provide guidelines for further investigation. While administrative theory outside of librarianship is, and should be, important to anyone who wants to manage libraries better, what already exists within the library field cannot be ignored. The integration of theoretical perspectives from within and without librarianship is thematic in Samuels' and McClure's article, as it is in the entire book.

But searching for theories of administration in every nook and cranny of library practice does have its dangers. Harold Koontz's article is a good example of the kind of fragmentation administrative theory can take. Although Koontz provides one of the best discussions of modern administrative theory "schools," his attempt at integration is only partially successful, which indicates the difficulties library administrative theorizers are likely to have. Unlike the proponents of "The One Best Way" who characterized classical management, the reductionist tendencies of modern administrative theorists must be viewed with caution. While description and reduction is important in theory development, there must always be an underlying attempt to integrate, to synthesize, to organize. We may be on the verge of developing a valid theory of library administration which is balanced and realistic; however, unless we are careful, it will be quite easy to repeat the mistakes of our predecessors in other fields. Knowledge of what has already occurred may prevent the repetition of an unsavory past.

Toward a Theory of Library Administration
By Alan R. Samuels and Charles R. McClure

INTRODUCTION

What is "library administration?" Does library administration differ from more familiar types of administration such as one might find in a profit-making organization? These types of questions are representative of the cross-fertilization to which the study of library administration has become wedded. It is as if we desperately seek frameworks from non-library contexts to strengthen our own uncertain foundations. A lack of confidence rather than strength of conviction often characterizes the way in which libraries look at the management of libraries. This can result in artificially set parameters for the content of library administration, parameters that equate libraries with either assembly lines or charitable institutions. Adherence to either metaphor is distracting at best and highly misleading at worst.

If a "theory" of library administration is to be developed, those whose interests lie in this area must seek to avoid the adoption of excessively narrow perspectives which view the library as if it existed totally apart from the mainstream of administrative thought. Theories and concepts from cognate areas need to be applied to libraries as guides to action and research. We need to become aware, not only of the existence of such theories and concepts, but also the manner in which they may operate in library contexts. But before we can study theories of administration in library contexts we must know what they are. Failure to develop this understanding often leads to a dichotomization of theory and practice, as if they were somehow different from one another and mutually exclusive. It is unfortunate that theorists are looked at with some suspicion by library practitioners; that they are said to be entirely unconcerned with the "real world" in which libraries must operate.

Such a dichotomy is false! Good theory must inevitably lead to good practice. Without theory, there can be little purpose to what we do. As Granger (1964, p. 64) succinctly puts it:

> We cannot do without theory. It will always defeat practice in the end for a quite simple reason. Practice is static. It does well what it knows. It has, however, no principle for dealing with what it doesn't know.... Practice is not well adapted for rapid adjustment to a changing environment. Theory is light footed, it can adapt itself to changed circumstances, think out fresh combinations and possibilities, peer into the future. Theory provides a clear framework, administrative practice reduces to a series of meaningless acts, without purpose or direction.

While a non-theoretical stance toward library administration may be comfortable and relatively uncomplicated, it is also a successful preventive to increasing library effectiveness.

Seeking new parameters of library administration requires that we abandon the passivity to which we have become accustomed. New and innovative perspectives must be brought to bear on library problems, not merely as suggestions but as working frameworks for action. These perspectives should not be blindly adopted, but constantly tested in library environments. It is this constant retesting of theory that will allow a true theory of library administration to emerge.

THE FORCE OF TRADITION

The development of library administrative theory should be placed in the context of library development itself and of the historical setting that influenced that development. During the latter part of the nineteenth century and the early years of the twentieth, well over 1,600 public libraries were created (Bobinski, 1969, p. 3). In addition, many academic institutions were created as a result of both the Morrill Act of 1862 and the growth in the number of private colleges and universities. Because of a concern for educational standards and "status" within the educational community, each such institution viewed the acquisition of a library as vital. However, the management of such libraries was of little concern. It was an era during which warehousing of books assumed primacy in the minds of librarians.

Relatively unnoticed by librarians responsible for the maintenance of their growing collections were two critical variables that strongly affected the profit-making organizations of that vigorous time in American history. Yet those variables were to have profound effect on library administration. The first of these was the wide adoption of Frederick Taylor's "scientific management." The second was the growing realization that "seat-of-the-pants" management of libraries was totally inadequate to meet the increasing diversity of patron demands, no matter what type of library was involved. Eventually, library directors sought guidance from current management thinking of the time, and scientific management was adopted to provide just such guidance. However, unlike the normal evolution of general administration which took place outside of libraries, evolution of library administration remained static, unchanging, and fixed in highly "process-oriented" modes.

Other important factors impacted on library administrative development. These factors were translated into what can only be called general assumptions, assumptions that affected the way in which librarians viewed their work. First, library work was considered "woman's work" since it fell into the category of cultural and community activities, clearly not relevant to the scientific and technical activities of men! There is no better representation of this attitude than in the well-known image of Dewey surrounded by the graduating class of Columbia's library school, most of which (though not all) were women. Second, the library was considered to be "a good thing." Little justification of its existence needed to be provided. If a community was considered "educated" then a library, like a fountain, park, museum, statue, or other monument needed to be present. Third, the library was to hold books. The notion of the library as integral to the development of a larger institution or community was generally ignored and held only by cultural dilettantes who had nothing better to do. Finally, the process orientation of library administration placed maximum emphasis on efficiency (allocating resources) rather than effectiveness (defining and accomplishing goals and objectives).

Only recently have these general assumptions been questioned. Yet the impact of these assumptions on the operations of libraries is still strong; library administrators have not (until recently) either felt the need for, or understood the importance of, using theoretical approaches to solve library problems. In an early (and still highly relevant) overview of library administration, Wasserman (1958) pointed out that two basic schools had developed in library administrative thought. The first, identified with Jesse H. Shera, described attempts to apply to librarianship the skills and techniques of the basic and applied sciences. The second, attributed to Lawrence Clark Powell, was more ethereal and affirmed that to administer libraries calls for the gifts of the mind and spirit. Wasserman referred to this latter approach as "humanistic," one that is used intuitively. Wasserman's approach to theory development in library administration is an excellent summary of the bimodal, either-or approach taken by many library administrators (and library researchers for that matter).

This dichotomy between science and humanism has had substantial impact on library administration—at least it did until the mid 1960s. A good example of the dialogue between proponents of the two points of view exists in the written debate between Chris Argyris (1973), the defender of the irrationality in Man, and Herbert Simon (1973), the supreme rationalist. Argyris discounts Simon's belief in "rational" administrative theory and in the advocacy of controls and organizational structures required for maintaining employee productivity. For his part, Simon justified the need for administrative power and autonomy and criticizes Argyris for expecting workers to adhere to any unmeasurable psychological ideas such as "self actualization." Simon rejected Argyris' romantic view that workers had a natural innate sense of responsibility, and, to be creative, needed an environment which nurtured creativity and responsibility. This dichotomy, until recently, has been the basis of most library administrative theory—or what there was of it. Wasserman's (1958, p. 31) analysis of library administrative theory, although harsh, expresses this dichotomy. He writes:

> The large mass of material published in the professional journals or librarianship dealing with management issues can best be characterized as a type of latter-day folklore. There is a plethora of how-we-do-it articles which describe particular techniques employed by individual libraries, with the presumption that methods which work (or seem to work) one place are sound operating principles to guide action elsewhere. The literature is deficient in contributions which attempt to theorize and very little can be generalized when the preponderance of published offerings are accounts of noncumulative, isolated experiences. Virtually no writing has attempted to distill from a study of administrative practices in a number of institutions a set of hypotheses which might provide a framework for understanding common situations in different settings.

Many of Wasserman's points are still valid. Although there have been significant developments in the application of different management theories to libraries, as yet no comprehensive distillation of these works has appeared to suggest an overall framework of what a theory of library administration ought to look like. We still concern ourselves with whether or not libraries are better managed "humanistically" or "scientifically" without worrying about the applicability of either mode to particular library contexts.

It is highly unlikely that either Max Weber or Frederick Taylor had libraries in mind when they developed their respective views of how organizations should be structured or how efficiency on the job could be maintained. Nevertheless, this "gospel of efficiency" quickly took hold of library administrators. In the process, the theoretical underpinnings of both bureaucracy (Weber) and scientific management (Taylor) were soon forgotten, to be replaced by rigid adherence to procedure, process, and form. That which could solve immediate problems, which could directly and unquestionably relate to the "here and now," become prominent in the minds of library administrators.

One early writer on library administration (himself a library director), John Adams Lowe (1928), represented much of this thinking by strongly emphasizing centralization of authority and the necessity of viewing staff participation in library decision making as a privilege, to be jealously guarded, rather than as a right. Control rather than flexibility and innovation was stressed, a view that is apparently still shared by more recent writers on library administration. The "how" of accomplishing library tasks far outweighed the "why."

The notion that management "principles" could be developed for libraries was not totally ignored. In the course of his discourse on "the one best way" to manage a library, Lowe developed principles for public library operation in keeping with the growing importance of the classical management ideas of his time. Under the influence of the University of Chicago's Graduate Library School, Paul Howard (1940) examined existing library management practice (as reflected in staff manuals) and extracted his own set of principles, which, while clearly reflecting his time, are still worth studying as precursors of more modern thinking. Unfortunately, Howard did not develop his principles into anything resembling a "theory of library administration" and his work goes largely ignored today. The traditional administrative texts emphasizing pragmatics are still quite evident in Wheeler and Goldhor (1962, 1981), Rogers and Weber (1971), Lyle (1974), Evans (1976), and Stueart and Eastlick (1981). However, a recent text by Rizzo (1980), provides greater emphasis on management theory.

One should not conclude that today's library administration is entirely devoid of theory. Since 1950 a number of monographs, articles, and studies have emerged which have used theory from other areas to illuminate library managerial problems. Emerging, in part, from the Public Library Inquiry (Leigh, 1950), with its highly interdisciplinary aspect, some insights into what a theory of library administration might consist of have been developed. This interdisciplinary approach to library management problem solving can provide a more eclectic forum in which new and innovative library administrative theories can be developed. The outline of such a theory is emerging. Themes that reflect the diversity to which modern management has become subject are gradually replacing the narrow rigidity so characteristic of library administration.

A FRAMEWORK FOR ANALYSIS

A framework for imposing some structure on what may be emerging as "library administrative theory" is presented in Figure 1 (page 16). Figure 1 assumes that, generally speaking, current library administrative theory originated in the scientific management views of Taylor and his disciples. It then branched out into two recognizable traditions, the first more reflective of the growing trend toward universalism so characteristic of classical management and the second more humanistically oriented. Various divergences from the main lines can be seen. From classical management has derived the more pragmatic forms of library administration.* The humanistic point of view has led to the growing importance of behaviorism as a means of ensuring library effectiveness through its emphasis on the worker rather than on the product. Finally, the all-encompassing role of General Systems Theory (GST) can be viewed as providing a point of convergence, which, in turn, leads to new emphasis and new ways of viewing administration. Each branch of library administrative development, the "classical" and the "humanistic," can be characterized by

---

*Although the term "management" typically applies to the profit making sector of the economy and "administration" to the not-for-profit sector of the economy, the two terms are used interchangeably in this paper.

certain widely held assumptions. The differing set of assumptions are presented in Figure 2. Together, these two sets of assumptions summarize the classical-humanistic differences identified by Wasserman (1958).

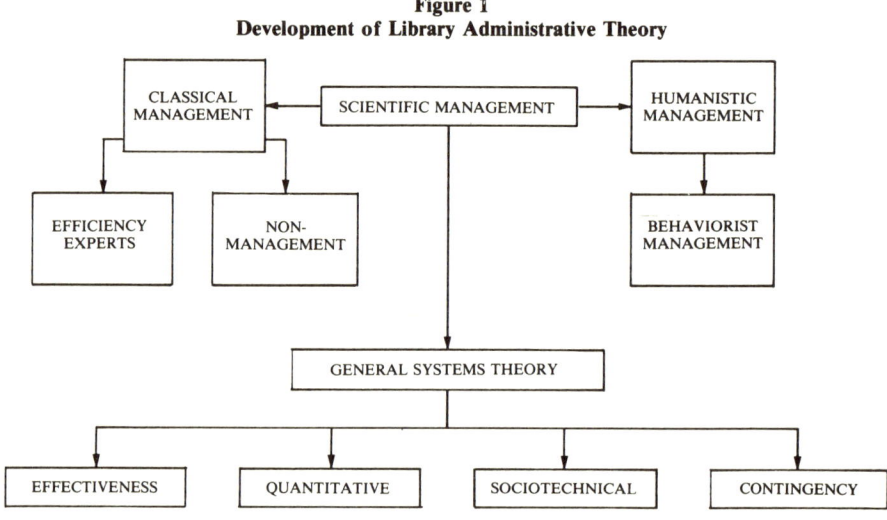

Figure 1
Development of Library Administrative Theory

Although these sets of assumptions are not entirely divorced from one another, they lack the degree of interaction necessary to develop a truly integrated theory of administration. While adhering to one set of assumptions, the library administrator may pay lip service to the other.

Apparently, two schools of thought are important in accounting for the nontheoretical stance of current library administrative thinking. One school can be best described as the "non-management" school. Adherence to this point of view relies heavily on assumptions from classical management and exhibits only a pseudo-concern for the more humanistic aspects of the workplace. This particular "school" is notable, not for its production of new theory or approaches which resolve library administrative problems, but rather for stressing that complex managerial systems and techniques are somehow inappropriate for the library.

Some writers believe that basic intuitive skills, innate intelligence, and an inborn ability to work effectively with others are likely to be the best tools the administrator can possess. As DeGennaro (1978, p. 2482) has suggested, "management systems ... offer mechanistic systems for dealing with complex realities and keep us from thinking about and solving our management problems in practical, realistic, and common sense ways." Adherents of this school of thought do not show a concern for theory development but concentrate almost exclusively on the pragmatics of administration, what is usually called (incorrectly) "practical" management. They emphasize the uselessness of management theory as applied to the library and suggest simplistic nostrums for curing library problems.

Figure 2
Administrative Assumptions

Classical	Humanist
1. Efficiency is measured in terms of productivity	1. The organization is a social system as well as a technical and economic system
2. Human Beings Act Rationally	2. The individual is motivated by diverse social and psychological factors
3. Human beings prefer security, definite tasks, and do not value freedom in determining their own approaches to problems	3. On-the-job behavior is affected by feelings, values, and attitudes
4. Management controls the formal and official activities of people	4. Increased worker satisfaction will lead to increased productivity
5. People's activities should be viewed objectively without regard to personal problems	5. Managers require social skills as well as technical skills
	6. Employees have certain psychological needs that management must consider when assigning tasks
6. Employees are motivated primarily by economic needs	7. The informal work group is a dominant influence on people's behavior
7. People do not like to work	
8. Coordination cannot be achieved without planning and direction from above	8. People must be able to participate effectively in organizational communication to accomplish organizational goals
9. Authority has its source at the top	9. The status of the employee is a reference from which he/she derives job satisfaction and social rewards
10. There are universal management principles which can be identified and should be applied	10. A complaint does not necessarily result from objective events; it is a symptom of personal disturbance, the cause of which may be deep-seated
11. Simple tasks are easier for the individual to master than broad responsibilities	
12. Employees expect administrators to make important decisions for them	11. It is at least as important for the individual to feel growth and learning on the job as it is to accomplish organizational goals

A second school of thought can be termed the "efficiency expert" school. The importance of this school (Dougherty and Heinritz, 1966) is that it served as the precursor for the highly quantitative approaches to library management so prevalent today. In addition, this school clearly demonstrated that science was indeed applicable to libraries in the form of rigorous methods of resource allocation and measurement. Finally, the efficiency experts suggested that decision making was as much a science as an art and was therefore amenable to the logic and consistency of scientific methodologies. However efficient the experts were in moving library administration away from a "crisis" mentality and toward more operations-based management, they tended to ignore the vital importance of library effectiveness, of goal accomplishment, or of asking "just what business are we in anyway?" The basic problem of doing things well ("efficiently") that need not be done in the first place ("ineffective") was not, nor has it been, resolved.

SYSTEMS THINKING AS A BASIS FOR ADMINISTRATIVE THEORY

The idea of libraries as systems is not particularly new. Many user studies that have appeared over the years have nearly always attempted to relate library services to the needs of library clientele, and to stress the importance of utilizing library inputs in ways best-suited to meet these needs. However, this is insufficient if libraries are to be viewed as "living systems," subject to growth, decay, death, and fossilization. New perspectives are needed, ones that more clearly express the theoretical aspects of systems theory as guides to library actions. Libraries do have the ability to change as their environments change. They need not remain isolated from the communities they serve. Movement and adjustment to changing conditions should be characteristic of library organizations just as they are of other organizational types. (Note that one should not confuse such process-oriented techniques as "systems analysis" and "operations research" with systems thinking, although both are derived from general systems thinking.) In our haste to find solutions to immediate problems, we cannot ignore the theoretical underpinnings that guide and direct what we do.

As Kast and Rosenzweig point out (1979, p. 18), a system consists of mutually interdependent parts. No one part exists in isolation, whether that part is a library department, a library and the institution of which it is a part, or a library and the community it serves. Examining the role of one element of the system without relating it to other elements can easily and quickly give a false picture of library operations. Failing to stress the close connection of library with community, library with other information agencies, or library with institution can create a situation in which passivity is the rule and advocacy and change are ignored.

All this may seem commonplace to libraries. But is it really? It is doubtful that the full implications of systems thinking for libraries have been investigated and tested. The realization that libraries are subject to the disease of irrelevance should guide our actions. A management stance that values the change process as normal and ongoing will require flexibility of organizational structure, the ability to revise library operations as needed, the constant testing of long-held assumptions and beliefs, and the elimination of the mythology, rites, and rituals that isolate department from department, library from library. Zweizig's (1973) notion of libraries as not occupying a central place in an individual's information seeking behavior must be accompanied by a more realistic view that develops new administrative strategies in whatever direction is necessary to meet new information demands and to avoid recurring political, economic, and societal threats.

A particularly useful feature of systems thinking lies in its emphasis on matching input to output, resources to outcomes. The transformation of the raw material of information into products that can be used by those seeking information depends in large part on the type of product actually desired. If we are to view libraries as systems, we must be fully aware of consumer preferences and be prepared to use whatever raw materials are necessary to meet those preferences. These raw materials need not be solely limited to the collection—an assumption frequently made by libraries—rather, they encompass the entire gamut of information-supplying resources, ranging from people to community agencies. What is necessary is a constant readjustment in thinking based on careful assessment and evaluation of current library services, and a willingness to encourage such change in those services as newly defined information needs dictate. The development of such an attitude among librarians requires a management stance which discourages insularity among library departments and encourages the mutual exchange of information among all elements of the library on a continuing and constant basis. This is the "theory" of systems theory.

Thus the potential of systems thinking for library administrative theory is great and can be developed further. Although there is likely to be little agreement among library administrators on this point, many of the emerging trends in administrative theory rely on systems thinking to a greater or lesser degree. Because of this, the synthesizing role of systems thinking as a means of gathering together the loose threads of an emerging library administrative theory should be more intensively investigated and more greatly stressed.

EMERGING TRENDS IN LIBRARY ADMINISTRATIVE THEORY

The growth of the literature base related to library administration has been significant in recent years. However, an analysis of the literature related to library administration during 1960-1970 indicated 1) two journals accounted for the core of articles related to library administration, 2) a preference for monographs over any other form of publication, and 3) in general, "unscholarly" literature (Mittermeyer and Houser, 1979, p. 273). In a related article covering the same topic and time span the authors concluded that "library administration is dependent on other areas for its theoretical material ..., [which] further suggests that the field is still in a descriptive phase" (Houser and Sweaney, 1979, p. 375). A study is yet to be done that analyzes the library administration literature base for 1970-1980. However, we believe that significant improvement in the scholarly quality of the literature and a movement from descriptive writing to more conceptual and research-oriented writing can be discerned since 1970.

An overview of what currently exists in writings on library administration suggests that at least five schools of thought are emerging as conceptual bases for the study and practice of library administration. It should be stressed that the boundaries between these schools are not all that clear; there is considerable overlap. Further, a cross-fertilization of ideas and techniques has occurred among these schools and with basic classical and humanistic management concepts. Only rarely are practitioners likely to be aware of which approach is being utilized since, in many instances, different schools of thought are used in response to different situations. The schools that are identified are emphasized in terms of their differences for purposes of analysis, although their interdependence is also recognized. Still, these schools of thought do approach library administration from different conceptual bases, from different underlying assumptions, and with different suggestions for action. Furthermore, the writers associated with the schools are illustrative; no attempt has been made to provide a comprehensive listing.

The Effectiveness School

Certainly one of the most encouraging trends in library administrative theory is an increasing concern for library performance. The "effectiveness school" stresses delineation, accomplishment, and evaluation of goals and objectives at both the organizational and the individual level. However, questions of efficiency (resource allocation) are not ignored, but are merely given a more balanced attention and placed in proper perspective. The development of this approach is a revision of the earlier view of the efficiency experts who emphasized cost ratios, time studies, and similar work study techniques at the expense of the less measurable aspects of goal accomplishment.

The importance of stressing organizational effectiveness continues to increase in the literature. It also continues to branch out in various directions. One important area in which this effectiveness approach has contributed to an emerging library administrative theory lies in planning. One of the more important precursors of this emphasis on library planning was Ernest DeProspo whose performance measure for public libraries (1973) and Program Planning and Evaluation (1975) are not only careful descriptions of "how to do it," but also models of how theory can be used to guide some very practical library activities. DeProspo's work demonstrated the importance of the planning process as an administrative strategy to increase library effectiveness in a very real and meaningful way.

DeProspo's work is similar to other later works on library planning. Webster (1974), in emphasizing the importance of systematic organizational analysis for academic library planning, has provided a variety of tools for conducting such analysis. Liesener (1976) has done similar work in the school media center. McClure (1978), for example, has suggested an overall planning model for use in academic library settings. Samuels (1979) in building on the work of McClure, DeProspo, and others, has suggested several psychological correlates of the planning process which can serve to increase the chances of success for such processes. Whatever the particular model emphasized, the planning/effectiveness approach is intended to stress the importance of accomplishing clearly designated goals and objectives in a climate receptive to such planning activity.

More recently, the planning approach suggested by Palmour et al. (1980), surely the most elaborate such approach yet suggested for libraries, utilizes the basic assumptions of the effectiveness approach. In the context of the public library, this approach has been expanded into an ongoing management program that includes citizen participation, staff involvement, and formal review and evaluation. Although this ALA-sponsored study has been criticized as being too complicated and time consuming for use by many public libraries, it will not be surprising to find the emergence of a number of other library-oriented planning approaches in the near future based directly on this approach.

The underlying conceptual bases of the effectiveness approach are now undergoing review. Specific effectiveness criteria have been suggested by DuMont (1980), who discusses the different criteria used by researchers to measure effectiveness. However, DuMont is somewhat vague on the meaning of these criteria. For example, three of them measure resources and various "efficiency-oriented" inputs. No approach is identified that stresses specific service outcomes or overall benefits as measures.

The effectiveness approach as a basis for library administrative theory has yet to come to grips with the relationship between efficiency and effectiveness. Writers in this area have not studied the impact of a trade-off between the two as has been done by non-library based administrative theorists (Churchman, 1968). Little true conceptual analysis of the different approaches in the effectiveness school has been accomplished. More importantly, the transference of such conceptual analysis to pragmatic guides to action has not yet emerged.

The Socio-technical Approach

Historically, the library has always been a labor intensive organization. Lacking high technology, library tasks were performed by individuals, not machines. Little attention was given to matching individuals with the technological qualifications to the job. What you didn't know, you learned on the job. And what you learned was not substantially different from what you expected.

Today's library environment is quite different. Often requiring skills beyond the scope of many librarians, library jobs may be filled with people psychologically unprepared to cope with the stresses that a mismatch between employee and task can cause. Traditional library organizational structures are frequently unable to meet the demands of increasingly sophisticated library tasks. Some library researchers (Lynch, 1974a, 1974b; Ricking, 1974; Shaughnessy, 1972) have attempted to analyze library functions in terms of the tasks to be performed, the technology to be employed, and the type of organizational structure in which the best match between task and technology can be achieved. However, outside relatively inaccessible works (mostly in dissertation form), little continuing effort has been expended in this area.

In general, one area of socio-technical theory which has received considerable attention is the development of various organizational structures to accommodate specific characteristics of that organization. Perhaps the best known of these is the study of the organization and staffing of the Columbia University libraries (Booz, Allen, and Hamilton, 1973). The organizational changes made at Columbia as a result of this study present a model of how organizational structures can impact on librarians' responsibilities and work.

Additional work on non-traditional forms of library organization as a means of better matching individual needs to organizational purposes was done by Howard (1970), with his "orbital organization," by Burgis (1971), with the "matrix" organization, and Axford (1975), with his emphasis on decentralized library organizations. However, these approaches, which are essentially non-empirically based, provide little data to evaluate the effectiveness of such structures and they do not come to terms with relationships between organizational structure and function. We still lack specific criteria to compare different library organizational types and to evaluate the impact of these organizational types on other administrative variables such as decision making, communication, motivation, and leadership.

Socio-technical theory has received considerable attention outside the library field since its initial presentation by Trist and Bamforth (1951). One might even say that the theory has reached a "decadent" state in which reappraisals and redefinitions of the concept are taking place, placing the theory in a more general contingency framework (Kelly, 1978). However, the emphasis socio-technical theory placed on diagnostic tools has not yet been fully exploited or extensively investigated in library contexts. While socio-technical approaches to library administration do exist, they have remained at a rudimentary level.

The Quantitative Approach

The quantitative approach to library administrative theory attempts to develop models of various library operations which are subject to specific measurement. Based on collected data that is related to these operations, models can be used for decision making. Many of the specific techniques utilized in this approach originated with operations research. However, a significant departure from the "efficiency experts" is the emphasis on *both* effectiveness and efficiency.

One area in which important progress has been made is in the development of performance measures and measures of the "goodness" of library service. An underlying assumption of this approach, which has far-reaching implications, is that the operation and effectiveness of the library really *can* be measured! Further, the assumption is made that these activities can be modeled and generalized as a basis of comparison among libraries. Early work in this area by Morse (1968), Orr (1973), and DeProspo (1973) demonstrated the value of measuring the overall quality of a library. Although not all researchers in this area produced generalized models describing such quality, their formulations do suggest theoretical bases through which library administrators can develop appropriate criteria for decision making in specific library environments.

A second area in which the quantitative approach has provided theoretical guides for library administration is bibliometrics. Deriving in part from other disciples, models such as Lotka's law and the Bradford/Zipf distribution have been extensively investigated. Writers such as Fussler and Simon (1969), Slote (1975), and Buckland (1975) have greatly facilitated the movement toward applying these approaches to library-related decisions.

A third area is networking and interlibrary loan. Once again, models developed by Reisman (1972), Nance (1973), and King (1979) provide valuable insights into what can be done to relate quantitative approaches for improved library effectiveness. Finally, Hamburg (1974) has devoted much space to summarizing and analyzing these models, presenting measures of his own related to "document exposure," and presenting a detailed schema for developing such models. A number of these models is presented by Lancaster (1977). The major underlying assumption of all these models is that the administration of libraries must be based on quantitative techniques by which the decision maker then can select an appropriate action to maximize both the efficiency *and* effectiveness of the organization. Although the quantitative approach has (justifiably) been criticized for emphasizing models that are highly complex mathematically and difficult to understand, it does suggest some very important directions where further library administrative theory development can take.

The Behaviorist Approach

In general, the behaviorists seek to understand the activities of organizational members by focusing on the ways in which individuals affect other individuals and on the relationship between individual behavior and organizational environment. Variables subsumed by this approach include personality, group interaction, attitudes, and a host of additional items of interest to the organizational psychologists. Unlike the humanists, the behaviorists tend to take a more scientific approach to administration, preferring to base their conclusions on empirical data carefully collected to describe specific organizational contexts.

One library administrative area in which the behaviorist approach has had great impact is participatory decision making (PDM) and job satisfaction. In this area, library administrators are reflecting a similar concern that has pervaded modern administrative thought for some time. However, while non-library administrative research has not concentrated on any one type of organization, library research into PDM has proven highly insular; academic libraries are by far the most common vehicle for investigating PDM, a trend which shows little signs of abating. Nevertheless, as research findings accumulate, some movement toward a behavioristic theory of library administration can be detected.

Recent research by Marchant (1976) has proved to be the most intensive investigation of PDM in (academic) library contexts. Marchant identified specific variables, which were postulated to explain relationships between job satisfaction and PDM. His work, although criticized on methodological grounds by Lynch (1978) among others, suggests that individual librarian behaviors can, in fact, be identified and adequately measured. The implications of Marchant's research are substantial: administrative strategies must consider the interactions of individuals and groups as intervening variables between task assignment and productivity. The psychological correlates of library operation were seen by Marchant to be essential factors to ensure library effectiveness. Others who have investigated similar variable sets are Plate and Stone (1974), Kaplan (1975), and D'Elia (1979).

One of the most difficult problems facing behaviorist views of library administration is the necessity to eliminate paternalistic, emphatic management techniques, which frequently exist as "pseudo-behaviorism." The work of B. F. Skinner is frequently cited as representative of this misuse of behaviorism. Those who use Skinner's reinforcement theory as the basis for administrating a library frequently digress into the carrot-stick, or reward/punishment technique, thus reducing a complex theory to simplistic "pragmatic" techniques to justify an action. This sort of strategy is an excellent example of taking approaches and theory from outside the library field, implementing them incorrectly, and piously citing "behaviorism" as justification.

Still, the behavioristic approach has caught the attention of library researchers. The theories of Herzberg, McGregor, Maslow and others have been, and are being, studied in many library contexts. The possibility of a library-based empirically derived organizational psychology emerging as a viable discipline in and of itself is very real. Questions such as how psychological theory can be reconciled with library reality need to be addressed. There is no lack of polemic on this matter and "pop psychology" in library administration abounds. Such well-known concepts as McGregor's "Theory X and Theory Y," Houses' path-goal theory of leadership, Likert's theories of PDM, and other similar ideas have proven quite attractive to librarians. What is lacking, however, is a unifying framework. While we are perhaps closer to developing such a framework in this area than in any other, the final transition from empiricism to theory has yet to be made.

The Contingency Management Approach

A relatively recent administrative theory introduced to management literature is the "contingency approach." Writers such as Koontz (1976), Luthans (1976), and Kast and Rosenzweig (1979) suggest that administrators are likely to modify employee behavior by developing specific administrative strategies that 1) recognize the unique strengths and weaknesses of each individual in the work place, and 2) recognize the importance of environmental characteristics to ensure individual worker productivity. Based on recognition of these two factors, administrators develop a match between situation and individual, a strategy summarized by the "if ..., then ..." construct. *If* the individual has a certain set of skills or certain strengths and weaknesses, *then* the administrator's role is to create an environment in which these skills, strengths, and weaknesses can best be exploited for the good of *both* the individual and the organization.

Contingency approaches in library administration are only now emerging. Several studies have applied this approach to library administrative research. D'Elia (1979) indicated that the variable "ability utilization" is related to job satisfaction, at least for beginning librarians. Unfortunately, as it now stands, the variable cannot be generalized beyond D'Elia's research environment. D'Elia's study, which deserves a further investigation in a much wider context, suggests *contingencies* in which a librarian is likely to have greater job satisfaction, *if* the administrator can match that librarian's abilities to specific job requirements.

In another study that examined the information handling ability of academic librarians, McClure (1980) found that there is a wide variance among librarians as to 1) their number of contacts with information sources, 2) their perceived evaluation of the worth of information sources as bases for specific decision situations, and 3) their corresponding involvement in library decision making. McClure suggests a number of contingencies that could form the basis of theory (at least as far as library decision making is concerned). McClure identified four different contingencies to describe the information handling abilities of librarians and further suggested a relationship between the types of information contacted and the perceived importance of the decision.

In one of the few forays into organizational psychology in libraries, Samuels (1979) investigated the concept of organizational climate in public libraries in an effort to develop a typology of climates within which certain library activities could most productively be carried out. His research suggested that organizational climate does indeed vary among libraries. Libraries with certain types of climates may be better able to respond to one set of environmental stimuli rather than another (Samuels, 1981). As with that of McClure, research of this type appears to be useful to understanding why some library organizations are more effective than others.

In another area, Dragon (1979) utilized non-library based leadership theory to describe the library environment. This research, utilizing the leadership variables "consideration" and "initiating structure," showed that in some situations individuals with certain skills will be more effective than individuals without such skills, a finding which is not nearly so obvious as it may seem.

Contingency views of library administration assume that library administrators are perhaps more sophisticated than they really are in their ability to analyze the assumptions of organizational employees, their ability to develop specific strategies to meet individual situations, and their ability to identify key environmental characteristics that may affect either the individual or the organization. Of key importance in this point of view is the ability to develop administrative strategies based on a range of matrix-like contingencies of the "if ..., then ..." variety.

Contingency approaches in the management literature have been criticized because they seem simplistic and provide no underlying laws from which an understanding of organizational activities can be derived. However, in library administration at least, contingency views are only now being developed and becoming available for study. More research must be done and, even more important, must be widely disseminated, to determine specific "if ..., then ..." relationships in different libraries using different organizational and behavioral variables.

ADMINISTRATIVE THEORY AND PRACTICE

Argyris (1978) has pointed out that all administrators operate under some sort of "theory," whether formally stated or not. These "theories in use" guide the way in which administrators actually behave and are not necessarily consistent with the way in which they say they are behaving. Realization that a substantial number of theories are already in use by library administrators should help to remove any hostilities between practitioner and theorist. A reconciliation between library administrator, an individual existing in an almost totally experiential world, and the more abstract realm of theory is an essential step to ensure more effective management of libraries.

This reconciliation, however difficult, requires a willingness on the part of all concerned to facilitate this integrative process. Above all, library administrators should understand that theoretical frameworks are *not* universal panaceas for whatever ails the library. Nor are they absolute prescriptions for "the one best way." As in any discipline, controversy exists in administrative theory, and the library administrator must be able to select theory that seems to be most useful given his/her library environment.

Administrative theories should be seen as tools that are available to the practicing librarian to improve library efficiency and effectiveness. As such, tools can be selected correctly or incorrectly for the job to be done. Once selected, they can be implemented accurately or inaccurately. While librarians have the responsibility to identify and develop administrative theories and techniques which fit the theory, they also have the responsibility to select appropriate theories and to implement the techniques suggested by these theories correctly. It is vital that an administrative theory or technique not be discredited because of misuse.

The importance of theory development cannot be overstated. Two primary purposes exist for theory: prediction and understanding. With regard to administrative theory, both are crucial to the overall effectiveness of the library and its usefulness within the broader societal context. Prediction is necessary in order that organizational members know beforehand the probability of success of specific administrative strategies given certain contexts; understanding the administrative process through theory development is perhaps our best hope in analyzing why some administrative strategies are successful and others are not. Further, theory development in library administration increases the profession's credibility as a profession and demonstrates its concern with integrating research with practice.

The profession as a whole must recognize the importance of understanding theory as a professional responsibility. The utility of administrative theory for librarians in whatever type of library must be stressed. Regardless of title, professional librarians are decision makers: they attempt to accomplish specific goals and objectives, and they work in an organizational environment in which they must interact constantly with colleagues. As professionals, whether administrators or not, librarians have a responsibility to understand and work toward the development of improved organizational effectiveness, regardless of position. Without a knowledge of library administrative theory professionals cannot organize, structure, and manage the library for maximum efficiency and effectiveness.

In 1974 Lynch commented that "the practical art of library organization and management is far ahead of its corresponding theory" (p. 432). Clearly, practical applications and techniques have been, and are likely to be, utilized by practitioners without understanding their theoretical bases. However, the appropriateness of such use and its attendant ignorance of theory must be questioned. The claim that library administrative theory does not exist is questionable, as the authors of this paper have pointed out. To be sure, there are considerable gaps in this theoretical structure. A great deal of research and theory development, with its corresponding testing and retesting in libraries, must occur before we can truly identify a "theory of library administration."

At the present stage of library administrative theory development, there can be no final determination of precisely what such a theory should contain. We are very much in an experimentation mode in which diagnostic tools to measure the effects that library operations and organizational structures have on people, those using our services, and those whose responsibility it is to provide these services, must be developed. The result of such developmental activity can result in the library's becoming what Wildavsky (1972) called the "self-evaluating" organization, in which evolution, change, skepticism, and flexibility become valued parts of library operation. The future development of library administrative theory will depend in no small part on our ability to establish such "self-evaluation" on an ongoing basis in library organizations.

Argyris, Chris. "Some Limits of Rational Man Organizational Theory," *Public Administration Review* 33 (May-June 1973): 253-67.

Argyris, Chris, and Donald A. Schon. *Organizational Learning: A Theory of Action Perspective.* Reading, MA: Addison-Wesley, 1978.

Axford, H. William. "The Interrelations of Structure, Governance and Effective Resource Utilization in Academic Libraries," *Library Trends* 23 (April 1975): 551-71.

Bobinski, G. S. *Carnegie Libraries, Their History and Impact on America Public Library Development.* Chicago: American Library Association, 1969.

Booz, Allen & Hamilton, Inc. *Organization and Staffing of the Libraries of Columbia University.* Westport, CT: Redgrave, 1973.

Buckland, Michael K. *Book Availability and the Library User.* New York: Pergamon Press, 1975.

Burgis, Grover C. "Systems Concept of Organization and Control for Large University Libraries," *Canadian Library Journal* 28 (January 1971): 24-29.

Churchman, C. West. *The Systems Approach.* New York: Dell, 1968.

DeGennaro, Richard. "Library Administration and New Management Systems," *Library Journal* 103 (December 15, 1978): 2477-82.

D'Elia, George. "Determinants of Job Satisfaction Among Beginning Librarians," *Library Quarterly* 49 (July 1979): 283-302.

DeProspo, Ernest R., and Alan R. Samuels. *A Program Planning and Evaluation Self Instructional Manual.* New York: College Entrance Examination Board, 1975.

DeProspo, Ernest R., Ellen Altman, and Kenneth E. Beasley. *Performance Measures for Public Libraries.* Chicago: American Library Association, 1973.

Dougherty, Richard M., and Fred J. Heinritz. *Scientific Management of Library Operations.* Metuchen, NJ: Scarecrow Press, 1966.

Dragon, Andrea. "Leader Behavior in Changing Libraries," *Library Research* 1 (Spring 1979): 53-66.

DuMont, Rosemary Ruhig. "A Conceptual Basis for Library Effectiveness," *College & Research Libraries* 41 (March 1980): 103-111.

Evans, Edward, Harold Borko, and Patricia Ferguson. "Review of Criteria Used to Measure Library Effectiveness," *Bulletin of the Medical Library Association* 60 (January 1972): 102-110.

Evans, G. Edward. *Management Techniques for Librarians.* New York: Academic Press, 1976.

Fussler, H. H., and J. L. Simon. *Patterns in the Use of Books in Large Research Libraries*, 2nd ed. Chicago: University of Chicago Press, 1969.

Granger, Charles H. "The Hierarchy of Objectives," *Harvard Business Review* 42 (May-June 1964): 63-74.

Hamburg, Morris, et al. *Library Planning and Decision Making Systems.* Cambridge, MA: MIT Press, 1974.

Houser, Lloyd J., and Wilma Sweaney. "Library Administration Literature: A Bibliographic Measure of Subject Dispersion," *Library Research* 1 (1979): 359-75.

Howard, Paul. "The Functions of Library Management," *Library Quarterly* 10 (July 1940):313-49.

Kaplan, Louis. "The Literature of Participation: From Optimism to Realism," *College & Research Libraries* 36 (November 1975): 473-79.

Kast, Fremont E., and James Rosenzweig. *Organization and Management: A Systems Approach*, 3rd ed. New York: McGraw-Hill, 1979.

Kelly, John E. "A Reappraisal of Sociotechnical Systems Theory," *Human Relations* 31 (1978): 1069-99.

King, Donald W. "Some Comments on the Impact of Technology on Library Networks," in Allen Kent and Thomas Galvin, eds. *The Structure and Governance of Library Networks*. New York: Marcel Dekker, 1979.

Koontz, Harold, and Cyril O'Donnel. *Management: A Systems and Contingency Analysis of Managerial Functions*, 6th ed. New York: McGraw-Hill, 1976.

Lancaster, F. W. *The Measurement and Evaluation of Library Services*. Washington, DC: Information Resources Press, 1977.

Leigh, Robert D. *The Public Library in the United States: The General Report of the Public Library Inquiry*. New York: Columbia University, 1950.

Liesener, James W. *A Systematic Process for Planning Media Programs*. Chicago: American Library Association, 1976.

Lowe, John Adams. *Public Library Administration*. Chicago: American Library Association, 1928.

Luthans, Fred. *Introduction to Management: A Contingency Approach*. New York: McGraw-Hill, 1976.

Lyle, Guy. *The Administration of the College Library*, 4th ed. New York: Wilson, 1974.

Lynch, Beverly P. "The Academic Library and Its Environment," *College & Research Libraries* 35 (March 1974): 126-32.

Lynch, Beverly P. "Organizational Structure and the Academic Library," *Illinois Libraries* 56 (1974): 201-206.

Lynch, Beverly P. "Review of *Participative Management in Academic Libraries*," *Library Quarterly* 48 (January 1978): 77-78.

McClure, Charles R. *Information for Academic Library Decision Making: The Case for Organizational Information Management*. Westport, CT: Greenwood Press, 1980.

McClure, Charles R. "The Planning Process: Strategies for Action," *College & Research Libraries* 39 (November 1978): 456-66.

Marchant, Maurice P. *Participative Management in Academic Libraries*. Westport, CT: Greenwood Press, 1976.

Mittermeyer, Diane, and Lloyd J. Houser. "The Knowledge Base for the Administration of Libraries," *Library Research* 1 (1979): 255-76.

Morse, Philip M. *Library Effectiveness: A Systems Approach*. Cambridge, MA: MIT Press, 1968.

Mussman, Klaus. "Sociotechnical Theory and Job Design in Libraries," *College & Research Libraries* 39 (January 1978):20-28.

Nance, R. E., et al. "Information Networks: Definitions and Message Transfer Models," *Journal of the American Society for Information Science* 23 (1972):237-47.

Orr, Richard H. "Measuring the Goodness of Library Science," *Journal of Documentation* 29 (1973): 315-32.

Palmour, Vernon E., et al. *A Planning Process for Public Libraries*. Chicago: American Library Association, 1980.

Plate, Kenneth L., and Elizabeth Stone. "Factors Affecting Job Satisfaction," *Library Quarterly* 44 (April 1974): 97-110.

Reisman, A. "Timeliness of Library Materials Delivery: A Set of Priorities," *Socio-Economic Planning Sciences* 6 (1972): 145-52.

Ricking, Myrl, and R. E. Booth. *Personnel Utilization in Libraries: A System Approach*. Chicago: American Library Association, 1974.

Rizzo, John R. *Management for Librarians: Fundamentals and Issues*. Westport, CT: Greenwood Press, 1980.

Rogers, R. D., and D. C. Weber. *University Library Administration*. New York: Wilson, 1970.

Samuels, Alan R. "Assessing Organizational Climate in Public Libraries," *Library Research* 1 (1979): 237-54.

Samuels, Alan R. "Planning and Organizational Culture," *Journal of Library Administration* 2 (1981). In press.

Shaughnessy, Thomas W. "Technology and Job Design in Libraries: A Socio-technical Systems Approach," *Journal of Academic Librarianship* 3 (1977): 269-72.

Simon, Herbert A. "Organization Man: Rational or Self Actualizing?," *Public Administration Review* 33 (July-August 1973): 346-53.

Slote, Stanley J. *Weeding Library Collections*. Littleton, CO: Libraries Unlimited, 1975.

Stueart, Robert D., and John Taylor Eastlick. *Library Management*, 2nd ed. Littleton, CO: Libraries Unlimited, 1981.

Trist, E. L., and K. W. Bamforth. "Some Social and Psychological Consequences of the Long Wall Method of Coal Getting," *Human Relations* 4 (1951): 3-35.

Wasserman, Paul. "Development of Administration in Library Service," *College & Research Libraries* 19 (July 1958): 283-94; quoted from Paul Wasserman and Mary Lee Burndy, eds. *Reader in Library Administration*. Washington, DC: Microcard Editions, 1968, pp. 29-40.

Webster, Duane. "The Management Review and Analysis Program," *College & Research Libraries* 35 (March 1974): 114-25.

Wheeler, Joseph, and H. G. Goldhor. *Practical Administration of Public Libraries*. New York: Harper and Row, 1962. (Rev. ed., 1981).

Wildavsky, Aaron. "The Self-Evaluating Organization," *Public Administration Review* 32 (September-October 1972): 509-520.

Zweizig, Douglas. *Predicting Amount of Library Use: An Empirical Study of the Role of the Public Library in the Life of the Adult Public*. Unpublished Ph.D. dissertation, Syracuse University, 1973.

The Management Theory Jungle Revisited
By Harold Koontz

The various schools of or approaches to management theory that I identified nearly two decades ago, and called "the management theory jungle," are reconsidered. What is found now are eleven distinct approaches, compared to the original six, implying that the "jungle" may be getting more dense and impenetrable. However, certain developments are occurring which indicate that we may be moving more than people think toward a unified and practical theory of management.

Nearly two decades ago, I became impressed by the confusion among intelligent managers arising from the wide differences in findings and opinions among academic experts writing and doing research in the field of management. The summary of these findings I identified as "the management theory jungle" [Koontz, 1961]. Originally written to clarify for myself why obviously intelligent academic colleagues were coming up with such widely diverse conclusions and advice concerning management, my summary was published and widely referred to under this title. What I found was that the thinking of these scholars fell into six schools or approaches in their analysis of management. In some cases, it appeared that, like the proverbial blind men from Hindustan, some specialists were describing management only through the perceptions of their specialties.

Judging by its reception over the years, the article and the concept of the "jungle" must have filled a need. In fact, so many inquiries have been made over the intervening years as to whether we still have a "management theory jungle" that I now believe the "jungle" should be revisited and reexamined. What I now find is that, in place of the six specific schools identified in 1961, there are at least eleven approaches. Thus, the jungle appears to have become even more dense and impenetrable. But various developments are occurring that might in the future bring a coalescence of the various approaches and result in a more unified and useful theory of management.

The Original Management Theory Jungle

What I found nearly two decades ago was that well-meaning researchers and writers, mostly from academic halls, were attempting to explain the nature and knowledge of managing from six different points of view then referred to as "schools." These were: (1) the management process school, (2) the empirical or "case" approach, (3) the human behavior school, (4) the social system school, (5) the decision theory school, and (6) the mathematics school.

These varying schools, or approaches (as they are better called), led to a jungle of confusing thought, theory, and advice to practicing managers. The major sources of entanglement in the jungle were often due to varying meanings given common words like "organization," to differences in defining management as a body of knowledge, to widespread casting aside of the findings of early practicing managers as being "armchair" rather than what they were — the distilled experience and thought of perceptive men and women, to misunderstanding the nature and role of principles and theory, and to an inability or unwillingness of many "experts" to understand each other.

Although managing has been an important human task since the dawn of group effort, with few exceptions the serious attempt to develop a body of organized knowledge — science — underpinning practice has been a product of the present century.

Reprinted with permission from *Academy of Management Review*, vol. 5, no. 2 (April 1980), pp. 175-87.

Moreover, until the past quarter century almost all of the meaningful writing was the product of alert and perceptive practitioners — for example, French industrialist Henry Fayol, General Motors executive James Mooney, Johns-Manville vice-president Alvin Brown, British chocolate executive Oliver Sheldon, New Jersey Bell Telephone president Chester Barnard, and British management consultant Lyndall Urwick.

But the early absence of the academics from the field of management has been more than atoned for by the deluge of writing on management from our colleges and universities in the past 25 years. For example, there are now more than 100 (I can find 97 in my own library) different textbooks purporting to tell the reader — student or manager — what management is all about. And in related fields like psychology, sociology, system sciences, and mathematical modelling, the number of textbooks that can be used to teach some aspect — usually narrow — of management is at least as large.

The jungle has perhaps been made more impenetrable by the infiltration in our colleges and universities of many highly, but narrowly, trained instructors who are intelligent but know too little about the actual task of managing and the realities practicing managers face. In looking around the faculties of our business, management, and public administration schools, both undergraduate and graduate, practicing executives are impressed with the number of bright but inexperienced faculty members who are teaching management or some aspect of it. It seems to some like having professors in medical schools teaching surgery without ever having operated on a patient. As a result, many practicing managers are losing confidence in our colleges and universities and the kind of management taught.

It is certainly true that those who teach and write about basic operational management theory can use the findings and assistance of colleagues who are especially trained in psychology, sociology, mathematics, and operations research. But what dismays many is that some professors believe they are teaching management when they are only teaching these specialties.

What caused this? Basically two things. In the first place, the famous Ford Foundation (Gordon and Howell) and Carnegie Foundation (Pearson) reports in 1959 on our business school programs in American colleges and universities, authored and researched by scholars who were not trained in management, indicted the quality of business education in the United States and urged schools, including those that were already doing everything the researchers recommended, to adopt a broader and more social science approach to their curricula and faculty. As a result, many deans and other administrators went with great speed and vigor to recruit specialists in such fields as economics, mathematics, psychology, sociology, social psychology, and anthropology.

A second reason for the large number of faculty members trained in special fields, rather than in basic management theory and policy, is the fact that the rapid expansion of business and management schools occurred since 1960, during a period when there was an acute shortage of faculty candidates trained in management and with some managerial experience. This shortage was consequently filled by an increasing number of PhD's in the specialized fields noted above.

The Continuing Jungle

That the theory and science of management are far from being mature is apparent in the continuation of the management theory jungle. What has happened in the intervening years since 1961? The jungle still exists, and, in fact, there are nearly double the approaches to management that were identified nearly two decades ago. At the present time, a total of eleven approaches to the study of management science and theory may be identified. These are: (1) the empirical or case approach, (2) the interpersonal behavior approach, (3) the group behavior approach, (4) the cooperative social system approach, (5) the sociotechnical systems approach, (6) the decision theory approach, (7) the systems approach, (8) the mathematical or "management science" approach, (9) the contingency or situational approach, (10) the managerial roles approach, and (11) the operational theory approach.

Differences Between the Original and Present Jungle

What has caused this almost doubling of approaches to management theory and science? In the first place, one of the approaches found nearly two decades ago has been split into two. The original "human behavior school" has, in my judgment, divided itself into the interpersonal behavior approach (psychology) and the group behavior approach (sociology and cultural anthropology). The original social systems approach is essentially the same, but because its proponents seem to rest more heavily on the theories of Chester Barnard, it now seems more accurate to refer to it as the cooperative social systems approach.

Remaining essentially the same since my original article are (1) the empirical or case approach, (2) the decision theory approach, and (3) the mathematical or "management science" approach. Likewise, what was originally termed the "management process school" is now referred to more accurately as the operational theory approach.

New approaches that have become popular in the past two decades include the sociotechnical systems approach. This was first given birth by the research and writings of Eric Trist and his associates in the Tavistock Institute in 1951, but did not get many followers to form a clear-cut approach until the late 1960s. Also, even though the systems approach to any science or practice is not new (it was recognized in the original jungle as the "social systems" approach), its scholarly and widespread approach to management theory really occurred in the 1960s, particularly with the work of Johnson, Kast, and Rosenzweig [1963].

The managerial roles approach has gained its identification and adherents as the result of the research and writing of Henry Mintzberg [1973, 1975], who prefers to call this approach the "work activity school."

The contingency or situational approach to management theory and science is really an outgrowth of early classical, or operational, theory. Believing that most theory before the 1970s too often advocated the "one best way", and often overlooking the fact that intelligent practicing managers have always tailored their practice to the actual situation, a fairly significant number of management scholars have begun building management theory and research around what should be done in various situations, or contingencies.

Many writers who have apparently not read the so-called classicists in management carefully have come up with the inaccurate shibboleth that classical writers were prescribing the "one best way." It is true that Gilbreth in his study of bricklaying was searching for the one best way, but that was bricklaying and not managing. Fayol recognized this clearly when he said "principles are flexible and capable of adaptation to every need; it is a matter of knowing how to make use of them, which is a difficult art requiring intelligence, experience, decision, and proportion" [1949, p. 19].

The Current Approaches to Management Theory and Science

I hope the reader will realize that, in outlining the eleven approaches, I must necessarily be terse. Such conciseness may upset some adherents to the various approaches and some may even consider the treatment superficial, but space limitations make it necessary that most approaches be identified and commented on briefly.

The empirical or case approach The members of this school study management by analyzing experience, usually through cases. It is based on the premise that students and practitioners will understand the field of management and somehow come to know how to manage effectively by studying managerial successes and failures in various individual cases.

However, unless a study of experience is aimed at determining *fundamentally* why something happened or did not happen, it is likely to be a questionable and even dangerous approach to understanding management, because what happened or did not happen in the past is not likely to help in solving problems in a most certainly different future. If distillation of experience takes place with a view to finding basic generalizations, this approach can be a useful one to develop or support some principles and theory of management.

The interpersonal behavior approach This approach is apparently based on the thesis that managing involves getting things done through people, and that therefore the study of management should be centered on interpersonal relations. The writers and scholars in this school are heavily oriented to individual psychology and, indeed, most are trained as psychologists. Their focus is on the individual, and his or her motivations as a sociopsychological being. In this school are those who appear to emphasize human relations as an art that managers, even when foolishly trying to be amateur psychiatrists, can understand and practice. There are those who see the manager as a leader and may even equate managership and leadership — thus, in effect, treating all "led" activities as "managed." Others have concentrated on motivation or leadership and have cast important light on these subjects, which has been useful to managers.

That the study of human interactions, whether in the context of managing or elsewhere, is useful and important cannot be denied. But it can hardly be said that the field of interpersonal behavior encompasses all there is to management. It is entirely possible for all the managers of a company to understand psychology and its nuances and yet not be effective in managing. One major division of a large American company put their managers from top to bottom through sensitivity training (called by its critics "psychological striptease") only to find that the managers had learned much about feelings but little about how to manage. Both research and practice are finding that we must go far beyond interpersonal relations to develop a useful science of management.

The group behavior approach This approach is closely related to the interpersonal behavior approach and may be confused with it. But it is concerned primarily with behavior of people in groups rather than with interpersonal behavior. It thus tends to rely on sociology, anthropology, and social psychology rather than on individual psychology. Its emphasis is on group behavior patterns. This approach varies all the way from the study of small groups, with their cultural and behavioral patterns, to the behavioral characteristics of large groups. It is often called a study of "organization behavior" and the term "organization" may be taken to mean the system, or pattern, of any set of group relationships in a company, a government agency, a hospital, or any other kind of undertaking. Sometimes the term is used as Chester Barnard employed it, meaning "the cooperation of two or more persons," and "formal organization" as an organization with conscious, deliberate, joint purpose [1938, p. 65]. Chris Argyris has even used the term "organization" to include "*all* the behavior of *all* the participants" in a group undertaking [1957, p. 239].

It is not difficult to see that a practicing manager would not likely recognize that "organizations" cover such a broad area of group behavior patterns. At the same time, many of the problems of managers do arise from group behavior patterns, attitudes, desires, and prejudices, some of which come from the groups within an enterprise, but many come from the cultural environment of people outside of a given company, department, or agency. What is perhaps most disturbing about this school of thought is the tendency of its members to draw an artificial and inaccurate line between "organization behavior" and "managing." Group behavior is an important aspect of management. But it is not all there is to management.

The cooperative social system approach A modification of the interpersonal and group behavior approaches has been the focus of some behavioral scientists on the study of human relationships as cooperative social systems. The idea of human relationships as social systems was early perceived by the Italian sociologist Vilfredo Pareto.

His work apparently affected modern adherents to this school through his influence on Chester Barnard. In seeking to explain the work of executives, Barnard saw them operating in, and maintaining, cooperative social systems, which he referred to as "organizations" [1938, pp. 72-73]. He perceived social systems as the cooperative interaction of ideas, forces, desires, and thinking of two or more persons. An increasing number of writers have expanded this concept to apply to any system of cooperative and purposeful group interrelationships or behavior and have given it the rather general title of "organization theory."

The cooperative social systems approach does have pertinence to the study and analysis of management. All managers do operate in a cooperative social system. But we do not find what is generally referred to as managers in *all* kinds of cooperative social systems. We would hardly think of a cooperative group of shoppers in a department store or an unorganized mob as being managed. Nor would we think of a family group gathering to celebrate a birthday as being managed. Therefore, we can conclude that this approach is broader than management while still overlooking many concepts, principles, and techniques that are important to managers.

The sociotechnical systems approach One of the newer schools of management identifies itself as the sociotechnical systems approach. This development is generally credited to E. L. Trist and his associates at the Tavistock Institute of England. In studies made of production problems in long-wall coal mining, this group found that it was not enough merely to analyze social problems. Instead, in dealing with problems of mining productivity, they found that the technical system (machines and methods) had a strong influence on the social system. In other words, they discovered that personal attitudes and group behavior are strongly influenced by the technical system in which people work. It is therefore the position of this school of thought that social and technical systems must be considered together and that a major task of a manager is to make sure that these two systems are made harmonious.

Most of the work of this school has consequently concentrated on production, office operations, and other areas where the technical systems have a very close connection to people and their work. It therefore tends to be heavily oriented to industrial engineering. As an approach to management, this school has made some interesting contributions to managerial practice, even though it does not, as some of its proponents seem to believe, encompass all there is to management. Moreover, it is doubtful that any experienced manager would be surprised that the technology of the assembly line or the technology in railroad transportation or in oil companies affects individuals, groups, and their behavior patterns, the way operations are organized, and the techniques of managing required. Furthermore, as promising and helpful as this approach is in certain aspects of enterprise operations, it is safe to observe that there is much more to pertinent management knowledge than can be found in it.

The decision theory approach This approach to management theory and science has apparently been based on the belief that, because it is a major task of managers to make decisions, we should concentrate on decision making. It is not surprising that there are many scholars and theorists who believe that, because managing is characterized by decision making, the central focus of management theory should be decision making and that all of management thought can be built around it. This has a degree of reasonableness. However, it overlooks the fact that there is much more to managing than making decisions and that, for most managers, the actual making of a decision is a fairly easy thing — if goals are clear, if the environment in which the decision will operate can be fairly accurately anticipated, if adequate information is available, if the organization structure provides a clear understanding of responsibility for decisions, if competent people are available to make decisions, and if many of the other prerequisites of effective managing are present.

The systems approach During recent years, many scholars and writers in management have emphasized the systems approach to the study and analysis of management thought. They feel that this is the most effective means by which such thought can be organized, presented, and understood.

A system is essentially a set or assemblage of things interconnected, or interdependent, so as to form a complex unity. These things may be physical, as with the parts of an automobile engine; or they may be biological, as with components of the human body; or they may be theoretical, as with a well-integrated assemblage of concepts, principles, theory, and techniques in an area such as managing. All systems, except perhaps the universe, interact with and are influenced by their environments, although we define boundaries for them so that we can see and analyze them more clearly.

The long use of systems theory and analyses in physical and biological sciences has given rise to a considerable body of systems knowledge. It comes as no surprise that systems theory has been found helpfully applicable to management theory and science. Some of us have long emphasized an arbitrary boundary of management knowledge — the theory underlying the managerial job in terms of what managers do. This boundary is set for the field of management theory and science in order to make the subject "manageable," but this does not imply a closed systems approach to the subject. On the contrary, there are always many interactions with the system environment. Thus, when managers plan, they have no choice but to take into account such external variables as markets, technology, social forces, laws, and regulations. When managers design an organizational structure to provide an environment for performance, they cannot help but be influenced by the behavior patterns people bring to their jobs from the environment that is external to an enterprise.

Systems also play an important part within the area of managing itself. There are planning systems, organizational systems, and control systems. And, within these, we can perceive many subsystems, such as systems of delegation, network planning, and budgeting.

Intelligent and experienced practicing managers and many management writers with practical experience, accustomed as they are to seeing their problems and operations as a network of interrelated elements with daily interaction between environments inside or outside their companies or other enterprises, are often surprised to find that many writers regard the systems approach as something new. To be sure, conscious study of, and emphasis on, systems have forced many managers and scholars to consider more perceptively the various interacting elements affecting management theory and practice. But it can hardly be regarded as a new approach to scientific thought.

The mathematical or "management science" approach There are some theorists who see managing as primarily an exercise in mathematical processes, concepts, symbols, and models. Perhaps the most widely known of these are the operations researchers who have often given themselves the self-annointing title of "management scientists." The primary focus of this approach is the mathematical model, since, through this device, problems — whether managerial or other — can be expressed in basic relationships and, where a given goal is sought, the model can be expressed in terms which optimize that goal. Because so much of the mathematical approach is applied to problems of optimization, it could be argued that it has a strong relationship to decision theory. But, of course, mathematical modelling sometimes goes beyond decision problems.

To be sure, the journal *Management Science*, published by the Institute of Management Sciences, carries on its cover the statement that the Institute has as its purpose to "identify, extend, and unify scientific knowledge pertaining to management." But as judged by the articles published in this journal and the hundreds of papers presented by members of the Institute at its many meetings all over the world, the school seems to be almost completely preoccupied with mathematical models and elegance in simulating situations and in developing solutions to certain kinds of problems. Consequently, as many critics both inside and outside the ranks of the "management scientists" have observed, the narrow mathematical focus can hardly be called a complete approach to a true management science.

No one interested in any scientific field can overlook the great usefulness of mathematical models and analyses. But it is difficult to see mathematics as a school of management any more than it is a separate school of chemistry, physics, or biology. Mathematics and mathematical models are, of course, tools of analysis, not a school of thought.

The contingency or situational approach One of the approaches to management thought and practice that has tended to take management academicians by storm is the contingency approach to management. Essentially, this approach emphasizes the fact that what managers do in practice depends on a given set of circumstances — the situation. Contingency management is akin to situational management and the two terms are often used synonymously. Some scholars distinguish between the two on the basis that, while situational management merely implies that what managers do depends on a given situation, contingency management implies an active interrelationship between the variables in a situation and the managerial solution devised. Thus, under a contingency approach, managers might look at an assembly-line situation and conclude that a highly structured organization pattern would best fit and interact with it.

According to some scholars, contingency theory takes into account not only given situations but also the influence of given solutions on behavior patterns of an enterprise. For example, an organization structured along the lines of operating functions (such as finance, engineering, production, and marketing) might be most suitable for a given situation, but managers in such a structure should take into account the behavioral patterns that often arise because of group loyalties to the function rather than to a company.

By its very nature, managerial practice requires that managers take into account the realities of a given situation when they apply theory or techniques. It has never been and never will be the task of science and theory to prescribe what should be done in a given situation. Science and theory in management have not and do not advocate the "best way" to do things in every situation, any more than the sciences of astrophysics or mechanics tell an engineer how to design a single best instrument for all kinds of applications. How theory and science are applied in practice naturally depends on the situation.

This is saying that there is science and there is art, that there is knowledge and there is practice. These are matters that any experienced manager has long known. One does not need much experience to understand that a corner grocery store could hardly be organized like General Motors, or that the technical realities of petroleum exploration, production, and refining make impracticable autonomously organized product divisions for gasoline, jet fuel, or lubricating oils.

The managerial roles approach Perhaps the newest approach to management theory to catch the attention of academics and practitioners alike is the managerial roles approach, popularized by Henry Mintzberg [1973, 1975]. Essentially this approach is to observe what managers actually do and from such observations come to conclusions as to what managerial activities (or roles) are. Although there have been researchers who have studied the actual work of managers, from chief executives to foremen, Mintzberg has given this approach sharp visibility.

By systematically studying the activities of five chief executives in a variety of organizations, Mintzberg came to the conclusion that executives do not act out the traditional classification of managerial functions — planning, organizing, coordinating, and controlling. Instead they do a variety of other activities.

From his research and the research of others who have studied what managers actually do,

Mintzberg has come to the conclusion that managers act out a set of ten roles. These are:

A. Interpersonal Roles
 1. Figurehead (performing ceremonial and social duties as the organization's representative)
 2. Leader
 3. Liaison (particularly with outsiders)
B. Informational Roles
 1. Monitor (receiving information about the operation of an enterprise)
 2. Disseminator (passing information to subordinates)
 3. Spokesperson (transmitting information outside the organization)
C. Decision Roles
 1. Entrepreneur
 2. Disturbance handler
 3. Resource allocator
 4. Negotiator (dealing with various persons and groups of persons)

Mintzberg refers to the usual way of classifying managerial functions as "folklore." As we will see in the following discussion on the operational theory approach, operational theorists have used such managerial functions as planning, organizing, staffing, leading, and controlling. For example, what is resource allocation but planning? Likewise, the entrepreneurial role is certainly an element of the whole area of planning. And the interpersonal roles are mainly aspects of leading. In addition, the informational roles can be fitted into a number of the functional areas.

Nevertheless, looking at what managers actually do can have considerable value. In analyzing activities, an effective manager might wish to compare these to the basic functions of managers and use the latter as a kind of pilot's checklist to ascertain what actions are being overlooked. But the roles Mintzberg identifies appear to be inadequate. Where in them does one find such unquestionably important managerial activities as structuring organization, selecting and appraising managers, and determining major strategies? Omissions such as these can make one wonder whether the executives in his sample were effective managers. It certainly opens a serious question as to whether the managerial roles approach is an adequate one on which to base a practical theory of management.

The operational approach The operational approach to management theory and science, a term borrowed from the work of P. W. Bridgman [1938, pp. 2-32], attempts to draw together the pertinent knowledge of management by relating it to the functions of managers. Like other operational sciences, it endeavors to put together for the field of management the concepts, principles, theory, and techniques that underpin the actual practice of managing.

The operational approach to management recognizes that there is a central core of knowledge about managing that exists only in management: such matters as line and staff, departmentation, the limitations of the span of management, managerial appraisal, and various managerial control techniques involve concepts and theory found only where managing is involved. But, in addition, this approach is eclectic in that it draws on pertinent knowledge derived from other fields. These include the clinical study of managerial activities, problems, and solutions; applications of systems theory; decision theory; motivation and leadership findings and theory; individual and group behavior theory; and the application of mathematical modeling and techniques. All these subjects are applicable to some extent to other fields of science, such as certain of the physical and geological sciences. But our interest in them must necessarily be limited to managerial aspects and applications.

The nature of the operational approach can perhaps best be appreciated by reference to Figure 1. As this diagram shows, the operational management school of thought includes a central core of science and theory unique to management plus knowledge eclectically drawn from various other schools and approaches. As the circle is intended to show, the operational approach is not interested in all the important knowledge in these various fields, but only that which is deemed to be most useful and relevant to managing.

The question of what managers do day by day and how they do it is secondary to what makes an acceptable and useful classification of knowledge. Organizing knowledge pertinent to managing is an indispensable first step in developing a useful theory and science of management. It makes possible the separation of science and techniques used in managing and those used in such nonmanagerial activities as marketing, accounting, manufacturing, and engineering. It permits us to look at the basic aspects of management that have a high degree of universality among different enterprises and different cultures. By using the functions of managers as a first step, a logical and useful start can be made in setting up pigeonholes for classifying management knowledge.

The functions some theorists (including me) have found to be useful and meaningful as this first step in classifying knowledge are:

1. Planning: selecting objectives and means of accomplishing them.
2. Organizing: designing an intentional structure of roles for people to fill.
3. Staffing: selecting, appraising, and developing people to effectively fill organizational roles.
4. Leading: taking actions to motivate people and help them see that contributing to group objectives is in their own interest.
5. Controlling: measuring and correcting activities of people to ensure that plans are being accomplished.

As a second step in organizing management knowledge, some of us have found it useful to ask basic questions in each functional area, such as:

1. What is the nature and purpose of each functional area?
2. What structural elements exist in each functional area?
3. What processes, techniques, and approaches are there in each functional area and what are the advantages and disadvantages of each?
4. What obstructions exist in effectively accomplishing each function?
5. How can these obstructions be removed?

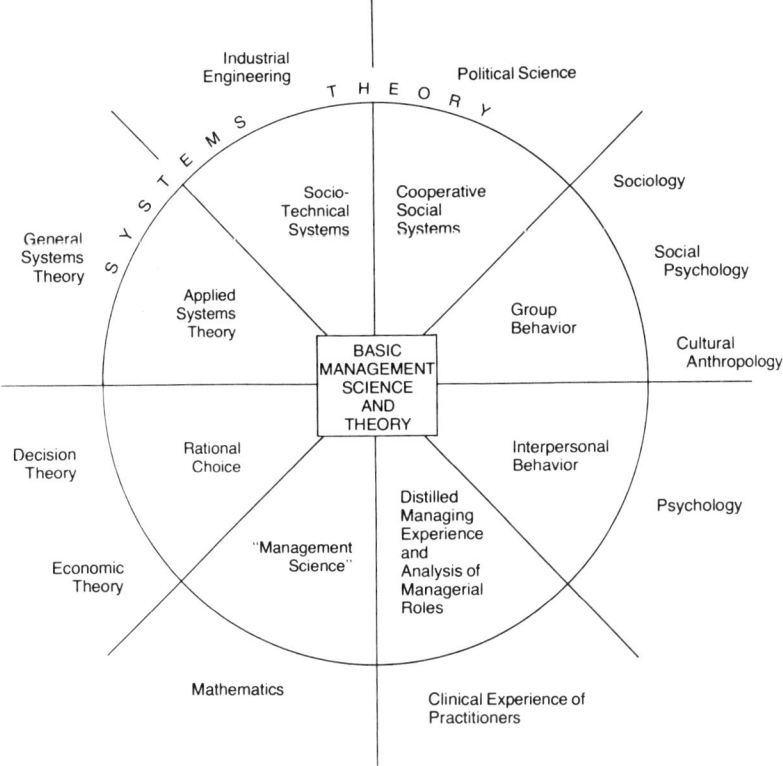

Operational management science and theory is that part of the diagram enclosed in the circle. It shows how operational management science and theory has a core of basic science and theory and draws from other fields of knowledge pertaining to management. It is thus, in part, an eclectic science and theory.

**Figure 1
The Scope of Operational Science and Theory**

Those who, like me, subscribe to the operational approach do so with the hope of developing and identifying a field of science and theory that has useful application to the practice of managing, and one that is not so broad as to encompass everything that might have any relationships, no matter how remote, to the managerial job. We realize that any field as complex as managing can never by isolated from its physical, technological, biological, or cultural environment. We also realize, however, that some partitioning of knowledge is necessary and some boundaries to this knowledge must be set if meaningful progress in summarizing and classifying pertinent knowledge is ever to be made. Yet, as in the case of all systems analyses where system boundaries are set, it must be kept in mind that there is no such thing as a totally closed system and that many environmental variables will intrude on and influence any system proposed.

The Management Theory Jungle: Promising Tendencies Toward Convergence of Theories

As can be seen from the brief discussions above of the schools and approaches to management theory and science, there is evidence that the management theory jungle continues to flourish and perhaps gets more dense, with nearly twice as many schools or approaches as were found nearly two decades ago. It is no wonder that a useful management theory and science has been so tardy in arriving. It is no wonder that we still do not have a clear notion of the scientific underpinnings of managing nor have we been able clearly to identify what we mean by competent managers.

The varying approaches, each with its own gurus, each with its own semantics, and each with a fierce pride to protect the concepts and techniques of the approach from attack or change, make the theory and science of management extremely difficult for the intelligent practitioner to understand and utilize. If the continuing jungle were only evidence of competing academic thought and research, it would not much matter. But when it retards the development of a useful theory and science and confuses practicing managers, the problem becomes serious. Effective managing at all levels and in all kinds of enterprises is too important to any society to allow it to fail through lack of available and understandable knowledge.

At the same time, there appears to be some reason to be optimistic, in that signs exist indicating tendencies for the various schools of thought to coalesce. Although the convergence is by no means yet complete, there is reason to hope that, as scholars and writers become more familiar with what managers do and the situations in which they act, more and more of these schools or approaches will adopt, and even expand, the basic thinking and concepts of the operational school of management.

While acknowledging that these are only indications and signs along the road to a more unified and practical operational theory of management, and that there is much more of this road to travel, let us briefly examine some of these tendencies toward convergence.

Greater Emphasis on Distillation of Basics within the Empirical Approach

Within the many programs utilizing cases as a means of educating managers, there are indications that there now exists a much greater emphasis on distilling fundamentals than there was two decades ago. Likewise, in the field of business policy, by which term most of these case approaches have tended to be known, there has been increased emphasis in teaching and research toward going beyond recounting what happened in a given situation to analyzing the underlying causes and reasons for what happened. One major result of all this has been a new emphasis on strategy and strategic planning. This has been nowhere more noteworthy than at the Harvard Business School, which is regarded as the cradle of the case approach. This has led many empiricists to come up with distilled knowledge that fits neatly into the operational theorist's classification of planning.

Recognizing that Systems Theory Is Not a Separate Approach

When systems theory was introduced into the management field some two decades ago, it was hailed by many as being a new way of analyzing and classifying management knowledge. But in recent years, as people have come to understand systems theory *and* the job of managing better, it has become increasingly clear that, in its essentials, there is little new about systems theory and that practicing managers as well as operational theorists had been using its basics (although not always the jargon) for a number of years. Nonetheless, as those in the field of operational management theory have more consciously and clearly employed the concepts and theory of systems, their attempts at developing a scientific field have been improved.

Recognizing that the Contingency Approach Is Not a New or Separate Approach

Although perceptive and intelligent managers and many management theorists have not been surprised by the realization, it is now clear that the contingency view is merely a way of distinguishing between science and art — knowledge and practice. As I pointed out earlier, these are two different things, albeit mutually complementary. Those writers and scholars who have emphasized contingency approaches have, to be sure, done the field of management theory and practice a great service by stressing that what the intelligent manager actually does depends on the realities of a situation. But this has long been true of the application of *any* science.

That contingency theory is really application in the light of a situation has been increasingly recognized, as is evidenced by a recent statement by one of its founders. Jay Lorsch recently admitted that the use of the term "contingency" was "misleading" [1977, pp. 2-14]. He appeared to recognize that an operational management theorist would necessarily become a situationalist when it came to applying management concepts, principles, and techniques.

Finding that Organization Theory Is Too Broad an Approach

Largely because of the influence of Chester Barnard and his broad concept of "organization" as almost any kind of interpersonal relationships, it has become customary, particularly in some academic circles, to use the term "organization theory" to refer to almost any kind of interpersonal relationships. Many scholars attempted to make this field equal to management theory, but it is now fairly well agreed that managing is a narrower activity and that management theory pertains only to theory related to managing. Management theory is often thought of as being a subset of organization theory and it is now fairly well agreed that the general concept of organization theory is too broad.

This sign offers hope of clearing away some of the underbrush of the jungle.

The New Understanding of Motivation

The more recent research into motivation of people in organizational settings has tended to emphasize the importance of the organizational climate in curbing or arousing motives. The oversimplified explanations of motives by Maslow and Herzberg may identify human needs fairly well, but much more emphasis must be given to rewards and expectations of rewards. These, along with a climate that arouses and supports motivation, will depend to a very great extent on the nature of managing in an organization.

Litwin and Stringer [1968] found that the strength of such basic motives as needs for achievement, power, and affiliation, were definitely affected by the organizational climate. In a sample of 460 managers, they found a strong relationship between highly structured organizations and arousal of the need for power, and a negative relationship with the needs for achievement and affiliation. Likewise, in a climate with high responsibility and clear standards, they observed a strong positive relationship between this climate and achievement motivation, a moderate correlation to power motivation, and an unrelated to negatively related relationship with affiliation motivation.

The interaction between motivation and organizational climate not only underscores the systems aspects of motivation but also emphasizes how motivation depends on what managers do in setting and maintaining an environment for performance. These researches move the problem of motivation from a purely behavioral matter to one closely related to and dependent on what managers do. The theory of motivation, then, fits nicely into the operational approach to management theory and science.

The melding of motivation and leadership theory Another interesting sign that we may be moving toward a unified operational theory of management is the way that research and analysis have tended to meld motivation and leadership theory. Especially in recent years, leadership research and theory have tended to emphasize the rather elementary propositions that the job of leaders is to know and appeal to things that motivate people and to recognize the simple truth that people tend to follow those in whom they see a means of satisfying their own desires. Thus, explanations of leadership have been increasingly related to motivation.

This melding of motivation and leadership theories has also emphasized the importance of organization climate and styles of leaders. Most recent studies and theories tend to underscore the importance of effective managing in making managers effective leaders. Implied by most recent research and theory is the clear message that effective leaders design a system that takes into account the expectancies of subordinates, the variability of motives between individuals and from time to time, situational factors, the need for clarity of role definition, interpersonal relations, and types of rewards.

As can be readily seen, knowledgeable and effective managers do these things when they design a climate for performance, when goals and means of achieving them are planned, when organizational roles are defined and well structured, when roles are intelligently staffed, and when control techniques and information are designed to make self-control possible. In other words, leadership theory and research are, like motivation, fitting into the scheme of operational management theory, rather than going off as a separate branch of theory.

The New Managerially Oriented "Organization Development"

Both "organization development" and the field ordinarily referred to as "organization behavior" have grown out of the interpersonal and group behavior approaches to management. For a while, it seemed that these fields were far away and separate from operational management theory. Now many of these scientists are seeing that basic management theory and techniques, such as managing by objectives and clarifying organization structure, fit well into their programs of behavioral intervention.

A review of the latest organization behavior books indicates that some authors in this field are beginning to understand that behavioral elements in group operations must be more closely integrated with organizational structure design, staffing, planning, and control. This is a promising sign. It is a recognition that analysis of individual and group behavior, at least in managed situations, easily and logically falls into place in the scheme of operational management theory.

The Impact of Technology: Researching an Old Problem

That technology has an important impact on organizational structure, behavior patterns, and other aspects of managing has been recognized by intelligent practitioners for many years. However, primarily among academic researchers, there has seemed to be in recent years a "discovery" that the impact of technology is important and real. To be sure, some of this research has been helpful to managers, especially that developed by the sociotechnical school of management. Also, while perceptive managers have known for many years that technology has important impacts, some of this research has tended to clarify and give special meaning to this impact.

The impact of technology is easily embraced by operational management theory and practice. And it should be. It is to be hoped that scholars and writers in the area of technological impacts will soon become familiar with operational management theory and incorporate their findings and ideas into that operational framework. At the very least, however, those who subscribe to the operational approach can incorporate the useful findings of those who emphasize the impact of technology.

Defections Among "Management Scientists"

It will be recalled that in the discussion of schools or approaches to management, one of them is identified as the mathematical or "management science" approach. The reader has also undoubtedly noted that "management science" was put in quotation marks; the reason for so doing is that this group does not really deal with a total science of management but rather largely with mathematical models, symbols, and elegance.

There are clear signs among the so-called management scientists that there are defectors who realize that their interests must go far beyond the use of mathematics, models, and the computer. These especially exist in the ranks of operations researchers in industry and government, where they are faced daily with practical management problems. A small but increasing number of academics are also coming to this realization. In fact, one of the leading and most respected academics, one widely regarded as a pioneer in operations research, C. West Churchman, has (in conversations with me) been highly critical of the excessive absorption with models and mathematics and, for this reason, has even resigned from the Operations Research Society.

There is no doubt that operations research and

similar mathematical and modeling techniques fit nicely in the planning and controlling areas of operational management theory and science. Most operational management theorists recognize this. All that is really needed is for the trickle of "management science" defectors to become a torrent, moving their expertise and research more closely to a practical and useful management science.

Clarifying Semantics: Some Signs of Hope

One of the greatest obstacles to disentangling the jungle has long been, and still is, the problem of semantics. Those writing and lecturing on management and related fields have tended to use common terms in different ways. This is exemplified by the variety of meanings given to such terms as "organization," "line and staff," "authority," "responsibility," and "policies," to mention a few. Although this semantics swamp still exists and we are a long way from general acceptance of meanings of key terms and concepts, there are some signs of hope on the horizon.

It has become common for the leading management texts to include a glossary of key terms and concepts and an increasing number of them are beginning to show some commonality of meaning. Of interest also is the fact that the Fellows of the International Academy of Management, composed of some 180 management scholars and leaders from 32 countries of the world, have responded to the demands of its members and have undertaken to develop a glossary of management concepts and terms, to be published in a number of languages and given wide circulation among many countries.

Although it is too early to be sure, it does appear that we may be moving in the direction necessary for the development of a science — the acceptance of clear definitions for key terms and concepts.

The Need for More Effort In Disentangling the Jungle

Despite some signs of hope, the fact is that the management theory jungle is still with us. Although some slight progress appears to be occurring, in the interest of a far better society through improved managerial practice it is to be hoped that some means can be found to accelerate this progress.

Perhaps the most effective way would be for leading managers to take a more active role in narrowing the widening gap that seems to exist between professional practice and our college and university business, management, and public administration schools. They could be far more vocal and helpful in making certain that our colleges and universities do more than they have been in developing and teaching a theory and science of management useful to practicing managers. This is not to advocate making these schools vocational schools, especially since basic operational management theory and research are among the most demanding areas of knowledge in our society. Moreover, these schools are *professional* schools and their task must be to serve the professions for which they exist.

Most of our professional schools have advisory councils or boards composed of influential and intelligent top managers and other leading citizens. Instead of these boards spending their time, as most do, in passively receiving reports from deans and faculty members of the "new" things being done, these boards should find out more of what is going on in managerially related teaching and research and insist that some of these be moved toward a more useful operational science of management.

REFERENCES

Argyris, C. *Personality and organization.* New York: Harper & Brothers, 1957.

Barnard, C. I. *The functions of the executive.* Cambridge, Mass.: Harvard University Press, 1938.

Bridgman, P. W. *The logic of modern physics.* New York: Macmillan, 1938.

Fayol, H. *General and industrial management.* New York: Pitman, 1949.

Gordon, R. A.; & Howell, J. E. *Higher education for business.* New York: Columbia University Press, 1959.

Johnson, R. A.; Kast, F. E.; & Rosenzweig, J. E. *The theory and management of systems.* New York: McGraw-Hill, 1963.

Koontz, H. The management theory jungle. *Academy of Management Journal,* 1961, *4* (3), 174-188.

Litwin, G. H.; & Stinger, R. A., Jr. *Motivation and organization climate.* Boston: Harvard Graduate School of Business Administration, 1968.

Lorsch, J. W. Organization design: A situational perspective. *Organizational Dynamics,* 1977, *6* (2), 12-14.

Mintzberg, H. *The nature of managerial work.* New York: Harper & Row, 1973.

Mintzberg, H. The manager's job: Folklore and fact. *Harvard Business Review,* 1975, *53* (4), 49-61.

Pierson, F. C. *The education of American businessmen: A study of university-college programs in business administration.* New York: McGraw-Hill, 1959.

Part II
ORGANIZATION AND BUREAUCRACY

Introduction

Even the word "bureaucracy" has a negative connotation. Yet, the concept when first developed by Weber was intended to assist an organization to develop the most efficient structure possible. What has happened in the meantime to cause such a radical change from the intended benefits of this type of organization? And why have libraries apparently adopted the bureaucratic form of organization so easily?

Historically, the formative development of library organization and administration took place in conjunction with the rise of scientific management and its promotion as "the one best way" to manage. Additionally, the endless procedures and routines associated with library work, so stressed by Dewey and other early librarians, offered a fertile ground for bureaucratic concepts. Written rules and procedures, clear levels of authority and hierarchy, and the trend toward specialization of personnel, all encouraged a bureaucratic library organization.

But is bureaucracy all that bad? In this section, Beverly P. Lynch suggests that bureaucracy and professionalism have much in common. It may be that the librarian's search for professional status, work, and authority increases the degree of bureaucracy already existing in a library. She points out that conflict can result between the apparent desirability of the bureaucratic library organization and the espoused service orientation of the staff, an orientation that can be retarded by those very elements that characterize a bureaucracy. Lynch poses the question of whether or not libraries can really be anything but bureaucratic. And if this type of organization is indeed viable, what can be done to integrate the advantages of bureaucracy with the need for professionalism among staff?

In future years this question is likely to be crucial to libraries. Staff clamor for greater input to and control over the organization, the demands of governing boards for greater efficiency in allocating resources, and the changing information needs of library consumers will place greater and greater demands on libraries. Pressures such as these will force librarians to ask whether bureaucracies are becoming unmanageable—and what are the alternatives? If one accepts Lynch's view that libraries are likely to remain bureaucratic and will continue to grow in size, the future manageability of the library must be questioned.

Looking at organizational growth in general, Duane S. Elgin and Robert A. Bushnell present 16 propositions about the growth of organizations into complex bureaucracies that should give alarm to librarians. The applicability of these propositions to library contexts is clear. Although Elgin and Bushnell talk about "large" organizations and complex systems, "large" really refers to the degree of bureaucracy existing in any size organization. Small organizations too can be highly bureaucratic.

The life cycle of an organization—from birth to death—also deserves to be considered within a bureaucratic framework. If libraries are truly tied into the bureaucratic form of organization, what future exists for the library as a responsive, service-oriented, institution? In addressing this question, Elgin and Bushnell suggest that four stages of organizational growth must be considered. Although they do not mention libraries directly, it is interesting to speculate what stage of growth libraries exhibit. Many well-informed library administrators would suggest that stage III ("severe diseconomies/era of skepticism") and stage IV ("systems crisis/era of despair") are already here!

If one accepts the arguments of Elgin and Bushnell, then a radical transformation in library organization will be required. Librarians cannot continue to build increasingly complex information handling systems and procedures and still respond to the information demands of their communities. They need to ask whether or not there exist alternative forms of organizational structures that might temper the effects of increasing bureaucratization and still encourage the service orientation so desperately needed.

One organizational alternative is described by Jerome Yavarkovsky and Warren J. Hass. This alternative is important because it assumes a radical departure from traditional service roles and responsibilities assigned to librarians. To Yavarkovsky and Hass, libraries should organize in such a manner as to better accomplish clearly identified goals and objectives; organizing is *not* an end in itself, in spite of classical management admonitions to the contrary. This point is crucial, because libraries and librarians have been accused of creating organizations and procedures which serve themselves rather than which respond to service goals. Of course, libraries must be prepared to engage in the difficult task of identifying meaningful goals and objectives, still a long way off for many.

But other approaches and organizational schemes have been presented to the library profession under such names as "orbital, matrix, decentralized," and others. These various schemes have not seen significant adoption by libraries. In general, libraries retain the traditional organizational chart that breaks the library into public and technical services, and then further by specific function within these service areas. Such an organizational approach is likely to lead only to greater and greater bureaucratization, as it has in the past.

The bureaucratic characteristics of library organizations have been identified but not studied. Little research has been done to relate specific characteristics of a bureaucracy to specific performance measures in library contexts. Thus, administrators do not know how bureaucracy really affects library operations, the provision of information to consumers, and the performance of personnel. There exist many suggestions on the impact of bureaucracy on non-library organizations. But these suggestions cannot be adopted in library environments without careful study to test their validity. We do know that many characteristics of bureaucracies are dysfunctional for implementing service goals in organizations such as libraries. Knowing these characteristics, testing them in libraries, studying their relationship to professionalism, and knowing what alternatives exist, is a first step in making libraries more manageable.

Libraries as Bureaucracies
By Beverly P. Lynch

Two MAJOR THEMES can be discerned in much of the literature on the organization and management of libraries. The first considers libraries in terms of their formal characteristics, emphasizing the relationships of hierarchy of authority, size, rules and the division of labor. The objective of the study of the formal structure of libraries is to find ways to organize the library in order to achieve maximum administrative efficiency. The study of the formal structure is guided by the concept of achieving specific objectives at minimum cost.

The second theme considers the informal processes in the library. This approach seeks to describe the experiences, attitudes and behavior of individual staff members as they participate in a complex organization. The objective of the study of informal processes and unofficial practices is to find those organizational characteristics or elements which inhibit the achievement of the library's goals of service.

Each of these approaches to the study of libraries as complex organizations complements the other. Each tells much about the organization and management of libraries. Rarely are studies of formal structure and of informal process carried out simultaneously, however, for the approaches are derived from different theoretical frameworks and require different methods of research. The management literature has sought to synthesize the two theoretical perspectives, since each contributes to the understanding of organizational behavior. The literature of librarianship, for the most part, has reflected one or the other theme with little synthesis of perspectives into a single framework.

Reprinted from *Library Trends*, vol. 27, no. 3, Winter 1979, by permission of the publisher. © 1978 Board of Trustees of the University of Illinois.

Bureaucracy as a colloquial expression means inefficiency and red tape; it is used most often in a pejorative sense. The sociological meaning of the term refers to the administrative aspects of an organization; it emphasizes those tasks that maintain the organization and coordinate the activities of its members. The tasks of maintaining the library are considered to be separate and distinct from those which relate directly to the achievement of the library's overall goals.

Max Weber's ideal type of organization is a bureaucracy characterized by a hierarchy of office, careful specification of office functions, recruitment on the basis of merit, promotion according to merit and performance, and a coherent system of discipline and control.[1] Weber is not the only theorist who finds the study of bureaucracies of interest, but it is his work on bureaucracy as an ideal type which has served as a basis for important segments of administrative theory and as a theoretical source for the study of the formal structure of organizations. Weber and others, including the leaders of the scientific management school, identify size as a fundamental characteristic of bureaucracies. Weber suggests that large size leads to greater organizational complexity, more specialization, training and professionalization of staff, an increase in rules and regulations, and an expansion of administrative staff and apparatus.

Weber's theory of increase of size as a determinant of increased bureaucracy guided Paul Spence's systematic study of libraries as bureaucracies.[2] Although there are flaws in his research design and method (for example, the independent variable, size, was controlled by selecting as libraries for study sixty-two members of the Association of Research Libraries, by definition the largest academic libraries in the United States), several conclusions drawn by Spence are similar to those reported by Peter Blau in his studies of governmental finance departments and personnel agencies.[3] Both Blau and Spence find high correlations between the professionalization of staff and the size of the organization's administrative component. It is this similarity of results which makes Spence's study of libraries as bureaucracies so interesting. Librarians often assume that the hiring of experts (defined as professionally trained librarians) should reduce the administrative component necessary to run the library. The professional's authority, stemming from his or her certification as an expert, is expected to prompt others to follow voluntarily the professional's directive, thus eliminating the need for an organizational hierarchy, authority, or specific rules and regulations. Yet Blau and Spence find that organizations which hire experts remain organized in a hierarchical fashion. The administrative components of these organizations are not reduced.

These findings are of great theoretical interest and can help in the understanding of libraries as bureaucracies.

The work of Weber has greatly influenced the study of the formal structures of organizations. Influential too are the writings of Frederick Taylor, Luther Gulick, Lyndall Urwick, and James D. Mooney, which form the basis of scientific management — an important influence in the management of libraries. Most of these writers were managers who took time to record what they did and then organized their observations into sets of principles. The major thrust of scientific management rests in the attempt to establish normal times for various production tasks through the use of job analysis and time and motion studies. Scientific management became popular in the 1930s and 1940s when large governmental and industrial organizations emerged. Plants or divisions had to be coordinated from the top. New specialists, sales executives, engineers and scientists were added to organizations. The proponents of scientific management, seeking ways to enhance the efficiency of management practices, made the first contributions to the analysis of management in these new and large organizations. Libraries also were growing during this time, and library administrators sought techniques used elsewhere which might help them to administer libraries which were becoming increasingly complex.

In an early review of scientific management in research libraries,[4] several elements are identified which characterize the application of scientific management to libraries. The first is the determination of standards of performance for specific library operations. Such standards, established by the library's administration either through time and motion studies or through less formal means, identify average levels of performance for specific library operations. Another characteristic of the use of scientific management in libraries is the careful definition and assignment of work in each department. Work definition is expected to facilitate the measurement of performance. It fixes responsibility of performance and influences the hiring and assignment of personnel. The efforts to identify and to differentiate the work of the professional from that of the clerical employee reflects this characteristic and leads to a centralization of personnel functions and a codification of personnel policies, both elements of the classical theory of bureaucracy. Work definition and organizational design require careful planning, and the separation of the planning function from the operational function is another characteristic of scientific planning and management.

Library managers seeking useful management techniques to apply in their own libraries recognize intuitively the influence of the size factor on the formal structure of libraries. In the 1950s those libraries with collections over 200,000 volumes were identified as being large enough to apply the concepts of scientific management.[5] Librarians in these libraries were interested in achieving maximum efficiency at minimum cost. They accumulated data on unit costs, particularly costs associated with the cataloging and processing of materials (which amounts to a large part of the library's budget), in order to identify ways which would reduce these costs. Time and motion studies were carried out in many libraries, textbooks were written for library managers,[6] and studies were undertaken regularly to create efficiencies in library operations through time reductions.

The work of Mayo, Barnard and others followed that of the scientific managers and brought to industry (and later, to libraries) the human relations theories, as well as the inevitable attack on the principles of scientific management and on the elements of bureaucracy, such as hierarchy of authority and formal rules and regulations. The influence of the human relations approach in the study of informal processes in organizations has been felt widely in libraries. Professionals tend to chafe under perceived bureaucratic constraints and strive for greater participation in library affairs so as to eliminate some of the constraints. The quest for efficiency and improved performance pervades the organization and does influence the work on participation in libraries. Therefore, many of the demands for greater participation are justified by the argument that the library's overall performance will improve, because greater participation by library staff members in the overall decision-making of the library will lead to greater job satisfaction and better performance.

Library managers seeking organizational efficiency and librarians seeking the best in service programs may disagree on solutions to particular library problems. Although the decisions in many academic libraries to change from old classification systems to the Library of Congress system were for the most part noncontroversial, the decision to switch to the Library of Congress system offers good examples of both the managerial approach to decision-making with a base in efficiency, and a professional expert approach with a base in a service idea. In many libraries the decision to change classification schemes was made on the grounds of greater efficiency, as managers sought ways to reduce the costs in technical services operations. The decision to change sometimes reflected the need for updating the classification schedules for scientific materials. Rarely was the decision based on an extensive analysis of classification schemes or on an assessment of how the particular library's clientele used the old scheme to find needed materials and information. The decision was made primarily on the basis of operational costs. Whether the change in classification scheme is an inhibition of any consequence to the library user is a professional concern, but not one which appears to be of any major interest. The administrator strives to achieve maximum efficiency at minimum cost. Whenever the cost of attaining a particular objective rises in terms of time, effort or money, the administrator seeks less to attain that objective.

There has been surprisingly little discussion on the impact of classification schemes. It may be that all librarians, managers or not, are in general agreement that lower technical services costs are of paramount importance and should take precedence in any decision involving cataloging and classification; or, the profession may not understand clearly enough the strengths and weaknesses of particular classification systems; or, the classification scheme may have become only a shelving device, having lost the ability to help users find a variety of materials on a particular subject. In any case, the reasons for the decision on classification schemes are of little importance to the present discussion. The example only illustrates a potential conflict which has its base in a decision influenced by managerial efficiencies instead of organizational goals. Had the decision been more controversial, the conflicts may have been more readily observed.

Bureaucracy and professionalism have several elements in common. Each requires impersonal detachment and specialized technical competence. Each bases its decision-making in a rational application of standards. There are also differences, however. Bureaucratic authority rests not so much on technical skills or competencies as on the official position. Bureaucratic authority requires subordinates to comply with directives under threat of some sanction. Professional authority rests upon possession of expertise. It requires an abstract body of knowledge to support the technical skills. Professional authority is self-governing through an association of peers, professional standards of practice and ethical conduct. Professionalism has a service orientation.[7]

The service orientation of the professional can lead to an opposite approach to work from that based in strict compliance with work procedures, a bureaucratic characteristic, and conflict can occur when these approaches are joined. Conflict can occur when decisions are made on the basis of purely professional standards, ignoring the administrative requirements of the organization. Yet large libraries, like all organizations of a certain size, are bureaucratic to some degree, even though they are staffed with professionals. There is someone at the top who decides what the library program will be and who assigns jobs. Specializations in tasks are determined and jobs are designed within the library to carry out these tasks. Rules and regulations are introduced and are useful in dealing with organizational issues such as staff turnover, consistency in performance and output. Among organizations the degree of bureaucratization does vary, and interesting questions center on why variations occur. For example, what conditions shape the organizational hierarchy? Does the work influence the division of labor or the nature of rules? How might the qualifications of the library's staff influence the structure of authority in it? Within large libraries are often found reference departments in which a high percentage of staff are professionals with expert training and experience. The catalog department, by contrast, although staffed with some professional people, generally has a higher percentage of clerical staff. These units should be expected to differ in terms of their bureaucratic characteristics, i.e., authority structures. Reference departments should exhibit a greater degree of participation in decision-making than catalog departments.

The relationship between the professional skills and competencies of the librarian and the bureaucratic authority vested in the hierarchy of office in the library occupies considerable attention and is a useful theoretical issue in the study of libraries as bureaucracies. The organization model which influences the library literature is the model of the autonomous professional. The work of the librarian is most often described in terms of a librarian/client relationship, a one-to-one relationship. Yet much of the work performed in libraries is divided into specialized tasks and is conducted outside the framework of the client relationship. Rarely does a librarian participate in all the tasks required in the selection of materials, in their cataloging and classification, or even in the answering of a reference question. The library profession itself seeks ways to divide the work into those tasks which are professional and those which are clerical in order to reduce costs, achieve greater efficiency, and utilize to the greatest extent possible the knowledge of the professional. Much effort is given to separating the routine tasks from the less routine, and then to designing jobs according to the nature of the tasks. The amount of job specialization will vary in libraries and it is to be expected that the specialization of tasks or the division of labor would be greater in large libraries than in small ones — consistent with Weber's theory that the larger the size of the organization the greater the specialization. Spence, in his library study on bureaucratic characteristics, found no support for Weber's theory of bureaucracy regarding size and specialization, but methodological problems in Spence's study make his results suspect.

Although Weber implies that professional authority, with its basis in technical competence, and bureaucratic authority, with its basis in a positional hierarchy, would exist concurrently in organizations, the prevailing attitude among librarians is that the professional's work suffers from the constraints of bureaucratic conditions. Yet much of the work in libraries is governed by written rules and regulations. The rules are more or less stable, more or less exhaustive, and can be learned. Knowledge of the rules and regulations forms the technical skills identified by Weber as a bureaucratic characteristic. Within libraries, technical knowledge and professional knowledge exist concurrrently, although variation in degree will exist.

Some of the support in libraries for the human relations approach and the study of informal processes has its basis in the inherent difference of opinion between library managers and staff members over the type of organizational structure needed to achieve organizational goals.[8] Given the different theoretical perspectives governing the knowledge available about library organization and behavior, such conflict is predictable. The library is an organization in which tasks are arranged in a rational way and one in which a marshalling of scarce resources is the responsibility of management. The literature of librarianship reflects the effort expended by librarians to find and report more efficient ways of getting work done. The library is also an organization in which professional experts seek to provide the best service possible, sometimes with little regard to cost. The recent library literature emphasizes the conditions which affect the attitudes and initiative of librarians and derides some of the bureaucratic conditions which exist in libraries. Nevertheless, every library exhibits the characteristics of a bureaucracy to a certain degree; each has a certain pattern of behavior based on specialized tasks and role design. Libraries are expected to vary in the degree to which they are bureaucratized, i.e., in structural characteristics. Some libraries will have a greater degree of job specialization than others. Some will restrict the discretion of staff members more than others in terms of required adherence to rules and regulations. Some will centralize authority in a small cadre of administrators, while others will delegate authority to the lower levels.

The research conducted so far which attempts to compare libraries or their structural characteristics is inconclusive, though tantalizing.

Research which compares organizational structure by type of library will be even more interesting. In the absence of specific research on libraries as bureaucracies, the studies of other types of organizations must be examined for insights and theories to guide one's understanding.

Although many professionally trained librarians seek work environments which are flexible, democratic and completely participatory, it is rare for libraries to be structured in this way. Such work environments are generally inefficient, and libraries are designed to be as efficient as as possible. Efficiency demands a stable and constant environment. The library is heavily influenced by its environment and much of the library manager's time is spent trying to reduce these environmental influences. Library managers commonly use both staff specialists and rules and regulations to cope with environmental problems. Some rules and regulations, of course, are designed to assist the librarians in carrying out their work. Cataloging rules and the like are examples of library rules which are related to the work of the library. Other rules are those which do not contribute to the library's goals and objectives, but are designed to maintain the library itself. Particularly important are rules and regulations related to the hiring of staff. In a completely democratic organization each individual staff member would hire his or her own replacement, since the individual staff member is in the best position to determine the knowledge, skills and abilities needed to do the job. The hiring process, being affected by such outside factors as ability to judge potential successors, union contracts, civil service requirements, affirmative action procedures, availability of a pool of qualified candidates from which to hire, is aided by organizational rules regarding appointments and by staff specialists who are responsible for determining minimum qualifications for various positions and for finding suitable candidates for the position. Libraries often reflect homogeneity in terms of personnel, partly because of geographic reasons and the self-selection on the part of applicants, and partly because of the personnel specialists' determination to hire people with similar backgrounds and characteristics in order to increase predictability, i.e., to limit the uncertainty which a variety of backgrounds inevitably brings to an organization.

Turnover in staff entails other rules and regulations. The efficient organization will codify the way a particular person does a job and make that way the "right way." The codification is designed to minimize the differences in job performance a new person will bring to a position and to reduce the uncertainty and adjustment problems the new person might have. An organization designs many rules and regulations in order to exert control over the external influences upon organizational behavior. Such rules and regulations often are described as bureaucratic red tape since they appear to be unrelated to the actual work of the organization. Nonetheless, these rules serve to control and to stabilize environmental influences, enabling the organization to deal with the environment in a more predictable and routine fashion.

The emphasis in most organizations, including libraries, is to make tasks routine, reduce uncertainty, increase predictability, and centralize authority. There is an inevitable tendency toward internal efficiency. The question of efficiency depends on a stable environment.

Libraries are bureaucracies. The bureaucratic elements which critics identify have their sources, not in the red tape or pettiness of officials, but in the attempt of the library to control its environment. The elements of bureaucracy emerge from the library's attempt to ensure its efficiency and its competency and from its attempt to minimize the impact of outside influences. Although variations will exist in the bureaucratic conditions, libraries will remain bureaucratic in form.

References

1. Weber, Max. "Bureaucracy." In *From Max Weber: Essays in Sociology.* H.H. Gerth and C. Wright Mills, trans. New York, Oxford University Press, 1962, pp. 196-244.
2. Spence, Paul H. "A Comparative Study of University Library Organizational Structure." Ph.D. diss., University of Illinois, 1969.
3. Blau, Peter M. "The Hierarchy of Authority in Organizations," *The American Journal of Sociology* 73:453-67, Jan. 1968.
4. Kipp, Laurence J. "Scientific Management in Research Libraries," *Library Trends* 2:390-400, Jan. 1954.
5. McAnally, Arthur M. "Organization of College and University Libraries," *Library Trends* 1:21-36, July 1952.
6. Dougherty, Richard M., and Heinritz, Fred J. *Scientific Management of Library Operations.* New York, Scarecrow Press, 1966.
7. Blau, op. cit.
8. Webster, Duane, et al. "Effecting Change in the Management of Libraries: The Management Review and Analysis Program." *In* "Coping with Change: The Challenge for Research Libraries," *Minutes of the Eighty-Second Meeting, Association of Research Libraries,* May 11-12, 1973, pp. 41-80.

The Limits to Complexity: Are Bureaucracies Becoming Unmanageable?

By Duane S. Elgin and Robert A. Bushnell

Social systems tend to decline in performance as they become bigger, more complex, and increasingly incomprehensible. They also become less amenable to democratic control, and more vulnerable to disruption at key points. There now appears to be evidence that we may be pressing against the relative limits of our ability to manage large bureaucracies.

Modern society must face up to the prospect that we may be reaching the limits of our capacity to manage exceedingly large and complex bureaucracies. Already there is considerable agreement regarding the details of bureaucratic malfunction, such as massive but ineffective urban governments and huge but wasteful governmental programs. Indeed, there is growing concern whether many of the largest bureaucracies can survive.

Consider a sampling of recent statements by opinion leaders:

> Ten years ago government was widely viewed as an instrument to solve problems; today government itself is widely viewed as the problem.
> Charles Schultze and Henry Owen, *Setting National Priorities*, 1976

> We're frantically trying to keep our noses above water, racing from one problem to the next.
> U.S. Senator Adlai Stevenson, *U.S. News and World Report*, November 10, 1975

> The demands on democratic government grow while the capacity of democratic government stagnates. This, it would appear, is the central dilemma of the governability of democracy which has manifested itself in Europe, North America, and Japan in the 1970s.
> Report to the Trilateral Commission on the Governability of Democracies, 1975

These statements raise the possibility that, with an enormous increase in our technological capacity, we have rushed to create bureaucracies of such extreme levels of scale, complexity, and interdependence that they now begin to exceed our capacity to comprehend and manage them. We are discovering that the

---

Reprinted from *The Futurist*, December 1977, pp. 337-49; published by the World Future Society, 4916 St. Elmo Ave., Washington, DC 20014.

power to create large, complex social bureaucracies does not automatically confer the ability to control them.

Recognition of the growing complexity of social systems as a problem worthy of attention in its own right emerged during a recent study, conducted by the Center for the Study of Social Policy, a division of SRI, Inc., in Menlo Park, California, which was seeking to identify important future problems that now are receiving insufficient attention.

Problems of Large, Complex Systems

After an extensive review of literature pertaining to the problems of bureaucracies, 16 propositions were selected as a useful sample of the problems associated with the growth of social systems. (See list.)

These propositions are not necessarily problems per se, but they become problematical in accordance to the relative *speed* of systems growth, its relative *size* (the absolute number of elements grouped together), its *complexity* (the number and diversity of elements in the system), and *interdependence* (tightness of coupling among elements both within and between bureaucracies). Thus, although the size of a social system is not the exclusive consideration in formulating these propositions, it is the primary point of reference from which the patterns of growth of large, complex systems are explored.

This article focuses on problems of large social bureaucracies as exemplified by the welfare system, the Medicare-Medicaid programs, and major metropolitan governments. These bureaucracies are very large and complex, highly interdependent, and concerned primarily with the delivery and consumption of public services. They are further characterized by high levels of human interaction and by ambiguous and sometimes conflicting objectives.

Although this article is directed principally to the problems of bureaucracies in the public sector, it also has relevance for private sector bureaucracies (such as large corporations). Crucial differences between these two categories of bureaucracies, however, prevent the direct application of this discussion to private sector bureaucracies.

The 16 problems are as follows: (Note: Each problem should be read as if it began with "When a bureaucracy grows to extreme levels of scale, complexity, and interdependence, then . . .)

1. The relative ability of any individual to comprehend the system will tend to diminish.

This proposition applies both to the public that is served by the social system and to the decision-makers who run it. To manage a social system effectively, a decision-maker must acquire knowledge at a rate at least equal to the pace at which decisions become more numerous and complex.

As a system grows in scale, the parts of the system will increase generally in an arithmetic progression but the interrelationships between the parts will tend to increase in a geometric progression. Hence, the *knowledge required* to comprehend both the discrete parts and their interrelationships will tend to increase geometrically, but due to the decision-maker's biological, mechanical, and temporal limitations, the *knowledge available* is likely to grow relatively slowly.

The importance of this problem is stated succinctly by seasoned bureaucrat Elliot Richardson in his book, *The Creative Balance* (New York: Holt, Rinehart, & Winston, 1976):

> For a free society, the ultimate challenge of the foreseeable future will consist not simply in managing complexity but in keeping it within the bounds of understanding by the society's citizens and their representatives in government.

Thus the size and complexity of social systems may jeopardize representative democracy itself. There is evidence to suggest that the relative levels of the public's comprehension of social systems may be declining significantly. For example, over a number of years, the Survey Research Center in the University of Michigan has asked people if they agreed or disagreed with the following statement: "Sometimes politics and government seem so complicated that a person like me can't really understand what's going on." In 1960, 40% of those responding disagreed with this statement and in 1974 only 26% disagreed.

The fact is that the stuff of public life seems to elude the grasp of many people. Bureaucratic processes have become specialized and professionalized. Yet, many of the larger bureaucracies are plagued with the unspoken but undeniable feeling among management and staff that no one truly is in control, that the dynamics of the organization are beyond the comprehension of any one individual.

Nor does the mere aggregation of information necessarily contribute to the understanding of the system. Although the computer revolution has vastly increased the amount of information at our disposal, its has exacerbated the difficulty of decision-making by confronting the manager with a mountain of information that he has no hope of ever assimilating given the crisis management that prevails in many of the largest bureaucracies. Thus, the ability to collect massive amounts of information does not automatically assure that it will be used or be useful in the management of large systems. It is possible to be information-rich and knowledge-poor as a manager or consumer of public services.

2. The capacity and motivation of the public to participate in decision-making processes will tend to diminish.

As discussed in Proposition 1, the relative capacity of all constituents of a social bureaucracy to participate knowledgeably in decision-making may diminish as the system grows. At larger scales, the perceived significance of an individual's participation in systems governance, especially through the act of voting, is impaired by the participation of large numbers of people in the process.

At smaller scales there is much greater opportunity for an individual citizen to have a discernible impact, but these small-scale decisions are likely to be relatively inconsequential. Robert Dahl, in an article on "The City in the Future of Democracy," concludes:

Thus for most citizens, participation in very large units becomes minimal and in very small units it becomes trivial.

To the extent that the cost (in time or money) of informing oneself for participation in the system is substantial and the perceived return from that information is trivial, then a rational response is to remain ignorant and passive. In his book, *Inside Bureaucracy*, urbanist Anthony Downs explains:

Therefore, we reach the startling conclusion that it is irrational for most citizens to acquire political information for the purposes of voting. . . . Hence, ignorance of politics is not a result of unpatriotic apathy; rather it is a highly rational response to the facts of political life in a large democracy.

An initially diminished capacity to participate as a result of mounting complexity is thus coupled with incentives that further reinforce the diminished capacity. As part of a self-fulfilling pattern, the power and willingness to make decisions are shifted from the public to the systems managers.

3. The public's access to decision-makers will tend to decline.

Regardless of the size of his constituency, there is only one mayor, one governor, one Secretary of Health, Education and Welfare, and one President. As the number of persons under his jurisdiction grows, an inevitable consequence is a reduction in the amount of time that a manager can spend with any one person. Beyond some threshold size, general access to the leader will, for all practical purposes, be eliminated.

In his discussion of the effects of scale upon a political system, Robert Dahl states:

The essential point is that nothing can overcome the dismal fact that as the number of citizens increases the proportion who can participate *directly* in discussions with their top leaders must necessarily grow smaller and smaller.

Certainly the actual degree of public access to its leaders has steadily declined as the scale of institutions has increased.

Despite this gradual erosion of access, the perception of this process by the public seems relatively recent. A 1975 Louis Harris survey reveals substantial

Blackout of New York City demonstrates how a breakdown in one part of a complex system can have enormous and widespread impacts. This photograph shows the New York skyline on July 13, 1977, during the second major blackout of the city.

Photo: UPI

changes in citizen perceptions of distance from their leadership during the period of 1966 to 1975. Although this period included the unusual events surrounding Watergate and the Viet Nam War (which exacerbated the feeling of distance between the American people and their leaders), the statistics, nonetheless, are striking.

The feeling that "What I think doesn't really count much any more" has risen from 37% to 67% since 1966; the view of the "People with power are out to take advantage of me" has jumped from 33% to 58% over the same period; the notion that "People running the country really don't care what happens to me" has gone up from 33% to 63%.

As our bureaucracies burgeon, they recede from the comprehension, the familiarity, and the control of the public.

4. Participation of experts in decision-making will tend to grow disproportionately, but this expertise will only marginally counteract the effects of geometrically mounting knowledge requirements for effective management of the bureaucracy.

It seems reasonable for a decision-maker faced with a large number of complex problems to seek expert advice in trying to grapple with those problems. Yet, as Elliot Richardson has warned in *The Creative Balance*, this apparently rational response to complexity may reduce the ability of the public to participate in decision-making:

Unless we in America can succeed in [managing complexity] . . . we shall lose our power to make intelligent—or at least deliberate—choices. We shall no longer be self-governing. We shall instead be forced to surrender more and more of our constitutional birthright—the office of citizenship—to an expert elite. We may hope it is a benevolent elite. But even if it is not, we shall be dependent on it anyway. Rather than participating in the process of choice, we shall be accepting the choices made for us.

Moreover, it is possible that exponentially growing needs for knowledge in decision-making will eventually overwhelm the expert as well as the decision-maker. The expert ultimately faces the same human limitations to his acquisition of knowledge as does the decision-maker and the general public.

Further, there appear to be intrinsic limits to the assistance that experts can render to decision-makers. Expert knowledge may be so fragmented, as a result of specialization, that it is below the necessary threshold of aggregation to be useful to the decision-maker. Also, the information may be exceedingly complex and difficult to transmit efficiently from expert to decision-maker. Accordingly, expert information may be ignored for very rational reasons.

5. The costs of coordinating and controlling the system will tend to grow disproportionately.

Initial increases in scale allow greater efficiency by facilitating specialization and division of labor and by allowing the use of more advanced technologies (which may only become cost-effective for larger organizations). Yet, at some scale of activity, the number of units in the system will grow so large that the costs of coordinating and controlling those units will more than offset any increases in efficiency that accrue from the larger scale.

As the bureaucracy grows and top management becomes increasingly divorced from day-to-day functioning of the system, decision-making responsibility and authority must be delegated to successively lower levels within the system. This, however, requires increases in staff, paper work, travel budgets, and communication costs if the plans and decisions of a vast number of separate decision-making units are going to mesh. Beyond some critical threshold of size, then, the costs of coordination grow disproportionately.

6. An attempt may be made to improve efficiency by depersonalizing the system.

Since human diversity adds enormously to a system's complexity, a potential means of coping with complexity is to reduce the diversity of human interactions within the system. Rational management techniques may attempt to depersonalize the system by standardizing human responses within the organization.

To the extent that efficiency is valued over human diversity, the human interaction with the system must acquire attributes that increasingly conform to the systemic preference for uniformity and predictability. Employees, constituents, or clients will tend thus to become increasingly depersonalized in their interactions with the system.

7. The level of alienation will tend to increase.

A 1975 Louis Harris survey reveals that in the period from 1966 to 1975, the number of people who say "I feel left out of things going on around me" has risen from 9% to 41%. These and related data suggest that the level of public alienation may be reaching pathological proportions.

Nor is the sense of alienation limited to a particular segment of society. In a 1976 *Saturday Review* article, Leonard Silk and David Vogel examined the crisis of confidence in American business and concluded that it is a part of a larger pattern of alienation:

The mood for business leadership is strikingly similar to that of other groups in one important respect: a feeling of impotence, a belief that its future is in the hands of outside forces. For business, as for other groups, frustration often turns to hostility. Feelings of alienation that began in the black community soon spread to the children of the middle class, moved into the white working class, and have affected the military and the police. This mood has now reached the business community. . . . It is a remarkable society in which so many groups, even the "Establishment," feel that "someone else" is in charge, "someone else" is to blame for whatever goes wrong.

Sociologist Melvin Seeman postulates five historical trends that may form the causal basis for the emergence of alienation. These are directly or indirectly tied to the emergence of very large social systems:

1. The expansion of scale of population and social institutions.

2. The decline of kinship and the consequential increase of anonymity and impersonality in social relations.

3. Increased physical and social mobility.

4. Social differentiation arising from specialization and division of labor.

5. Decline of traditional social forms and roles.

These observations suggest a rather direct linkage between alienation and the growth of large social systems.

8. The appropriateness of basic value premises underlying the social system will tend to be increasingly challenged.

This proposition assumes that as a system grows, the sheer *quantitative* aggregation will ultimately result in the emergence of a *qualitatively* different system. Thus, the value premises upon which the system was initially established will become increasingly incompatible with the changing demands of a quantitatively enlarged and qualitatively altered system.

To the extent that large, complex social systems have been created by value premises that have become functionally obsolete, then either the system must change to reflect the original values, or the basic value premises themselves will have to change to reflect the character of the changed system. Social conflict will increase until either the value premises or the system itself is changed so as to reestablish congruence between them.

Contemporary challenges to the legitimacy of traditional value premises have assumed such forms as women's liberation, black power, third world ethics, the antiwar movement, the hippy counterculture, the flourishing of Eastern religions, and the conservation and ecology movement. These disparate trends do not individually signify the transformation of historic value premises. Yet, considered collectively, they suggest that major challenges to traditional values are occurring.

9. The number and significance of unexpected consequences of policy actions will increase.

As a system grows, it may be subject to the "law of requisite variety" as stated by W. Ross Ashby in *An Introduction to Cybernetics*. This law asserts that the complexity of any policy solution must, in the long run, be equal to the complexity or variety of the problem. To the extent that diminished levels of systems comprehension (Proposition 1) force managers to apply relatively simple solutions to increasingly complex problems, then the law of requisite variety will not be satisfied and unexpected consequences of policy action may result.

Professor Jay Forrester of the Massachusetts Institute of Technology has suggested another reason why the behavior of large systems may result in outcomes that run counter to expectations. In social systems, political pressures often favor short-term policy measures, but when short-term actions, which previously produced favorable results, are redoubled without regard for their long-term consequences, changed circumstances within and without the system may produce both unexpected and even disastrous results.

With smaller and less interdependent bureaucracies, a wrong decision has only limited consequences because of the small scale and loose coupling between social systems. With very large and highly interdependent systems, however, a wrong decision can have far-reaching implications as its impact affects a pervasive and tightly interconnected web of socio-economic systems. Therefore, the number of unexpected outcomes of policy actions and the disruptive potential of these unexpected outcomes may be expected to expand as social systems grow in scale.

10. The system will tend to become more rigid since the form that it assumes inhibits the emergence of new forms.

Economist Kenneth Boulding has written, "Growth creates form, but form limits growth." This principle suggests that as a system grows in size, complexity and interdependence, it will seek an enduring, predictable form that will, in turn, limit the ability of the system to generate new forms. Large bureaucracies seem to exhibit this characteristic. Richard Goodwin, writing in *The New Yorker*, describes the resistance of large social systems to fundamental structural changes:

[T]he passion for size, reach, and growth is the soul of all bureaucracy. Within government, the fiercest battles are waged not over principles and ideas but over jurisdiction—control of old and new programs. Radically new pronouncements and policies are often digested with equanimity, but at the slightest hint of a threat to the existing structure, . . . the entire bureaucratic mechanism mobilizes for defense. Almost invariably, the threat is defeated or simply dissolves in fatigue, confusion, and the inevitable diversion of executive energies.

As growing bureaucracies lock themselves into relatively static and inflexible forms, creative management becomes an exercise analogous to swimming through progressively hardening concrete and the flow of social and organizational evolution is impeded.

11. The number and intensity of perturbations to the system will tend to increase disproportionately.

As a social system grows, the number of elements aggregated together also grows. As Donald Michael notes in his book, *The Unprepared Society*, if the same proportion of those elements malfunction, then the increase in absolute numbers aggregated together should yield a greater number of disturbing events within the system.

Further, as the number and diversity of activities within a system increase and relationships among the activities are established, the number of interconnections within the system will tend to increase geometrically. If a significant proportion of those connections are vulnerable to disruption, then the number of perturbations could increase more rapidly than increases in scale.

12. The diversity of innovation will tend to decline.

As a system grows, the span of diversity of innovation will tend to constrict, because innovation is confined within the narrowing boundaries of what the system can assimilate without itself undergoing fundamental change. Further, as the system acts to ensure its own survival, diversity of innovation may become confused with disorder.

Moreover, it seems plausible that as social forms become increasingly concretized, greater reliance will be placed on technological rather than social innovation to cope with social problems. Consequently, both the breadth and the depth of innovation will tend to decline.

13. The legitimacy of leadership will tend to decline.

To the extent that a system manager must draw his power to govern from the consent of the people, then, within limits, he must demonstrate to his constituency his ability to manage the system well. As the system grows in scale and complexity, relative levels of comprehension at all levels may decline, counterexpected and unexpected consequences may mount, system resilience may diminish, and, for other reasons, the performance of the system may decline. The public will hold the manager of the system responsible for the poor performance. Then, according to the rules of the game, other leaders who wish to be elected will endeavor to persuade the public that they have the "right" and "true" answers to solve the mounting problems of systems malfunction. Thus, a doubly dangerous situation is created: there is the appearance of understanding (in order to get elected or to retain power), but the reality of understanding may be diminishing. Public expectations for effective decision-making may be inordinately high at the same time that the relative capacity to make informed decisions declines. As the gap between expectation and reality grows more pronounced, the legitimacy of the decision-maker will diminish.

One of the most pervasive themes to be found in an examination of the state of health of our sociopolitical systems is the crisis of confidence in leadership and the withdrawal of legitimacy. Pollster Louis Harris described the situation this way in a 1975 talk:

The toll on confidence in the leadership of institutions has been enormous, both in the public and private sectors. . . . But perhaps the most serious drops have taken place in the case of two of our most central points of power: American business and the federal government. High confidence in business has slipped from 55% in 1966 to 18% in 1975; in the White House it has fallen from 41% to 14%; Congress from 42% to 14%; the U.S. Supreme Court from 51% to 28%. . . . Basically, however, the startling news is that the two major institutions viewed as out of touch with the reality of what people think and want are American business, which for so long has prided itself as correctly anticipating public needs, and American political leadership, which so often has claimed to head up the most responsive democratic system in the world.

Nor is this an isolated finding. The University of Michigan Survey Research Center found that the proportion of people trusting the government in Washington to do what is right "just about always" or "most of the time" dropped from 81% in 1960 to 61% in 1970, and by 1974 the proportion had dropped to 38%. A 1975 report to the Trilateral Commission stated that "Leadership is in disrepute in democratic societies."

To the extent that the capacity to govern requires the consent of those governed, then the pervasive and sustained withdrawal of legitimacy could well cripple the capacity of democracies to manage their affairs.

14. The vulnerability of the system will tend to increase.

If we assume that most of the problems of large systems move in concert or on parallel paths, then with rising scale the combined effects of the problems will render the system increasingly vulnerable to disruption. Eric Sevareid forcefully describes the vulnerability of our social systems:

We now live in and by the web of an enormously complicated, intensely interrelated technology, the whole no greater than its parts and its strongest parts at the mercy of its weakest links. This is a way of life that depends absolutely on order and continuity and predictability. But it happens that we have simultaneously reached a point of discontinuity in the political and social relations of men, where little is predictable and disorder spreads.

One hijacker can capture a multimillion dollar airplane and catapult nations into political confrontation. One defective capacitor can prevent the communication of two presidential candidates with more than 100 million constituents. The shutdown of a single brake plant can stop production at major auto assembly plants throughout the country. A localized power grid failure can plunge the entire eastern seaboard of the U.S. into darkness. The consequences of otherwise isolated and relatively insignificant events, therefore, jeopardize the continued functioning of large systems sensitive to the slightest disruption.

15. The performance of the bureaucracy will tend to decline.

If we assume that the previously stated propositions are valid, then as a social system grows to extremes of scale we would expect that the costs of coordination and control will escalate, the comprehensibility of the system will decline, the number and intensity of perturbations will increase, and so on. When these individual problems reach a critical threshold and thereby collectively and intensively reinforce each other, the decline of system performance will be accelerated.

There is no lack of opinion that the performance of many of our largest bureaucracies is rapidly deteriorating. This is graphically reflected in a statement by U.S. Representative James C. Cleveland:

There is no question that the American people are coming to the conclusion that their Government couldn't run a two-car funeral without fouling up the arrangements.

16. The full extent of declining performance of the system is not likely to be perceived.

In most large bureaucracies there are few reliable measures of systems performance. This is partially attributable to the fact that the complexity of the system obscures the operation of the system. Also, the bureaucrat, in order to acquire or retain power, may minimize the significance of malfunctions and error, and maximize the public visibility of his own achievements. Further, there may be delayed, ambiguous and conflicting feedback concerning the effectiveness of various programs. These and other forces make it difficult to monitor the performance of a massive bureaucracy and thereby make it unlikely that most persons will be able to perceive the true extent to which performance is declining.

We have briefly examined a range of problems that are hypothesized to emerge as social systems grow to extremes of scale. The question naturally arises, are these problems connected with one another or do they arise independently and randomly? Since we are considering systems problems—where, by definition, everything is connected to everything else—it seems logical that we might discern a coherent pattern of interconnection among these various problems.

Stages of Growth of Social Systems

In order to identify and describe patterns of systems problems, we require a common frame of reference from which to search for that pattern. Fortunately, a single common denominator among these 16 propositions does exist. Each is defined so that it changes with variations in scale. This is *not* to say that the scale of a social system, per se, is critical. In many instances, complexity (or the number and diversity of interactions among systems elements) seems a more serious contributor to many of these problems than does scale. However, scale or size does provide the Occam's Razor to cut through a maze of complexity and establish a consistent frame of reference from which to explore relationships between problems.

Before we can infer the patterns of problems that might emerge as a system grows in scale, we must first describe the nature of the basic pattern of systems growth itself. Indeed, the model or description of the nature of social systems growth that we select will strongly condition what pattern of problems will be perceived. Fortunately, there exists a widely used concept in economics that lends itself well to clarifying our understanding of the cycle of growth that may occur as a system grows to extremes of size.

One of the few "laws" in economics is the "law of diminishing returns." One application of this law asserts that, at some size or scale of activity, no further advantages can be derived from further increases in scale; moreover, if scale continues to increase, diseconomies of scale will emerge. In other words, the system can reach a size where efficiency fails to increase as the organization becomes larger.

The difficulty in applying the "law of diminishing returns" to the growth of bureaucracies is that economic theory assumes that the rational organization will recognize when it is growing too large (is experiencing "diseconomies of scale") and choose to halt its growth at that point. Perhaps business firms, governed by the relatively precise rule of profit, will not intrude too far or for too long into a domain of increasingly severe diseconomies of scale. However, there are a number of reasons to think that our governmental bureaucracies may grow into this region and persist there for some time. (See box [page 61] giving reasons for this "ratchet effect.")

Even if a bureaucracy were aware that its size was excessive, the "ratchet effect" could strongly inhibit retreat from that scale of activity. The notorious difficulty in eliminating or restructuring a government agency or program seems a manifestation of the ratchet effect. It seems unlikely, then, that a government bureaucracy would voluntarily shrink in size; rather, it would tend to grow smaller only when forced by the necessities of its own survival or by the superior power of a higher-order system.

With the ratchet effect inexorably driving the growth of government bureaucracy, it becomes necessary to extend the application of the "law of diminishing returns" to include the range of severe diseconomies of scale, and beyond. By extending the domain of organizational performance considered under the "law of diminishing returns," we derived a four-stage life-cycle of the growth of social systems. (See graph). The four stages in the life-cycle of social systems growth are: an initial stage of high growth, a second stage of great efficiency, a third stage plagued by diseconomies of scale, and a fourth stage of systems crisis.

Having developed this four-stage description of the life-cycle of social systems growth, we can now mesh the model with the 16 problems proposed as intrinsic to many large, complex social systems. A matrix format was used to describe how each of the 16 problems would likely become manifest in each of the four stages of growth (this synthesis was achieved through logical inference aided by computer simulations).

Where Are We Now?

Given this four-stage description of the life-cycle of bureaucracies, where might present social systems be located relative to each of the four stages? Although hard evidence is scanty and dispersed, the information gathered so far suggests that a number of the largest government bureaucracies in the U.S. are experiencing severe diseconomies of scale (a Stage III condition).

A prime example of the present plight of large bureaucracies is the massive, exceedingly complex, and highly interdependent U.S. welfare system. There seems to be general agreement that the welfare bureaucracy is plagued by high costs, wasteful administration, inadequate performance, ineffective coordination and control of programs, and so on. Many of the problems of the present welfare system seem characteristic of a system either in Stage III (severe diseconomies of scale) or, as some might argue, intruding into the Stage IV region of systems crisis.

Thus, for some social systems (such as the welfare bureaucracy), the problem of reaching limits to the manageability of systems is already assuming critical proportions. And, given the built-in momentum toward ever greater scales of activity via the "ratchet effect," an increasing proportion of our major social systems seem likely to grow into Stage IV (systems crisis). The overall criticality of systems problems will depend considerably on the proportion of our larger social systems that may *simultaneously* intrude into a stage of severe systems malfunction. If many social systems enter Stage IV (systems crisis) at about the same time, there may be little resiliency or vigor in the remaining systems for those bureaucracies in difficulty to fall back upon.

In short, the problem of institutional "limits to growth" seems increasingly critical for *some* bureaucracies at the present time and, if this model has descriptive validity, then it seems likely that these "limits" will become increasingly critical for *many* bureaucracies in the decades ahead. It is our judgment that the constellation of problems characteristic of the later stages of the cycle of growth will become increasingly critical, long-term, pervasive, and difficult to solve. In turn, if this ballpark estimate of the situation is accurate, then it seems likely that long before we reach resource and environmental "limits to growth," we will reach institutional "limits to growth" imposed by the malfunctioning of our major social systems.

In a sentence, the time available to respond creatively to increasingly severe systems problems seems very short.

Coping with Institutional "Limits to Growth"

A number of different strategies could be applied in coping with the problems of large, complex bureaucracies.

- Develop alternative models of the behavior of bureaucracies as they evolve over time to ever greater levels of scale, complexity, and interdependence.
- Conduct surveys to ascertain the present status of key social bureaucracies whose continued vigor seems central to a healthy society. Such a survey could, for example, engage the politician and bureaucrat in the process of describing the behavioral properties and problems of large, complex social bureaucracies.
- Develop a spectrum of systems indicators—patterned after economic and social indicators—that may better inform us as to the state of "health" of our central social bureaucracies.
- Encourage the President to consider the state of the social bureaucracies when examining the state of the nation.
- Fund research on the least understood of the four hypothesized outcomes from a period of "systems crisis"—namely, what the nature and form of transformational change of major social bureaucracies could be.
- Explore new individual learning modes that could increase the rate and richness of our acquisition of knowledge (the internalization of information).
- Develop new group learning processes to enable more effective knowledge aggregation and patterning.
- Fund television programs (such as *Nova*) that are educational/informational at much higher levels and across a much broader range of topics and thereby attempt to inform the public of major issues of critical national importance—including the problem of the malfunctioning bureaucracies.
- Pursue governmental reorganization designed, where reasonable and possible, to reduce the scale, interdependence, and complexity of social systems.

The foregoing responses to the problems of bureaucracies are primarily restorative—they are intended to help ameliorate the severity of these problems and to help maintain the existing form of these bureaucracies. A different kind of response would be to search for innovative alternative systems whose "performance" surpasses existing bureaucracies.

Illustrative of these kinds of activities that may engender responses to surpass rather than merely maintain bureaucracies are the following:

For example, we could:

- Fund small-scale social and technological experiments and provide "social space," relatively free of bureaucratic impingements, within which these innovations can be tested. This might take the form, for example, of a range of different types of small-scale intermediate new communities that employ different technological and social forms to cope with the new scarcity and other problems that beset our larger systems.
- Develop intermediate or appropriate technology that can increase systems

resilience by increasing the self-sufficiency of local communities.

• Encourage national opinion leaders to become informed about the role that small-scale, social innovation could play in coping with larger systems problems and begin the process of building greater social legitimacy for action of this kind.

Among these various responses, perhaps the most powerful but most neglected is that of small-scale social innovation. Consequently, it seems useful to explore briefly the present status of small-scale social innovation in our society.

We are blanketed with large-scale social innovations (e.g., social security, food stamps, medicare) and with large-scale technological innovations (e.g., mass transit, space shuttle). There are many fewer attempts at small-scale technological innovations (e.g., new agricultural technologies), and there are extremely few small-scale, diversely conceived, social innovations.

The source of creative social innovations has traditionally been the local government. However, the federal government seems to have preempted many major areas of innovation from the state and local government. Perhaps more significantly, the federal government has sapped the vitality from innovation at the local level. Richard Thompson in his book *Revenue Sharing* (Revenue Sharing Advisory Service, Washington, D.C., 1973), examined the impact of federal funding policies and observed that "the federal government has stepped in and many localities have become administrative mechanisms for implementation of national policies rather than dynamic centers of authority and creative problem solving." In a vicious circle of abdication of responsibility for local vitality, small-scale social innovation is seldom tolerated, let alone encouraged.

There seem to exist two substantial stumbling blocks to small-scale social innovation. First, our cultural "opinion leaders" (in business, government, education, and so on) perhaps do not themselves recognize the crucial role that small-scale social innovation can possibly play in responding to increasingly severe, large-scale systems problems. Consequently, small-scale social experimentation may be seen as an activity of only peripheral significance. Yet, support of the larger society appears important since truly creative innovation requires a willingness to risk the possibility of failure.

Few people at the grass roots level seem willing to engage in such risk taking without the tolerance and support of the larger community—particularly when the payoff is not windfall profits to an individual but greater resiliency of our social structures. Even if contemporary opinion leaders did no more than publicly acknowledge and affirm the importance of small-scale social experimentation, it could still result in an outpouring of creative talent.

A second barrier to innovation is that such experimentation can be viewed as a threat to existing institutions (whose participants may not perceive the larger, longer-term threat of a systems crisis). Existing institutions may act in self-defense and attempt to prevent social innovation by engulfing the process in so much "red tape" that it never gathers the momentum or the social space necessary as a precondition to success. Thus, there needs to be sufficient "institutional relaxation"—providing social space relatively free from bureaucratic impingement—to allow these small-scale, social experiments to emerge of their own accord. The advice given by Donald Michael in his book *The Unprepared Society* a decade ago seems even more relevant today in suggesting that the right place to initiate the process of social learning

. . . may very well be in a "societal interstice" where there may develop or be preserved a different standard and lifestyle. Thereby, at some later, more propitious time, this enclave or subculture could serve as a model for many other people as our larger society struggles to find its confused and dangerous way.

Evolution is not stasis. Everything alive is impermanent. If our bureaucracies are alive, they will assuredly prove to be impermanent as well. One direct way to recognize the life and vitality of our social systems is by fostering diverse social experimentation so that, in due course, existing social forms may gradually yield to the new forms they have helped to create.

Authors' Note: The conclusions in this article reflect the opinions of the authors but rely upon a diverse body of literature. References to these resources may be found in the technical paper on which this article is based, "Limits to the Management of Large, Complex Systems" by Duane S. Elgin, prepared as part of the project on *Assessment of Future National and International Problem Areas,* Project 4676, prepared for the U.S. National Science Foundation by SRI, Inc., Menlo Park, California 94025, 1977.

The "Ratchet Effect": Reasons Why Bureaucracies Grow Too Large

- **Imprecise means of measurement.** The "rule of profit" may be harsh, but for business firms it is a relatively certain yardstick against which to measure the efficiency of a given scale of activity. In contrast, governmental bureaucracies and other social systems must attempt to measure efficiency via a number of qualitative, multidimensional, often conflicting, and ambiguous measures and objectives. With virtually no measures of system health, bureaucracies can conceivably grow to excessive scales of social organization.

- **Responding to the needs of a given population.** A business firm can choose its scale of operation so as to maximize efficiency. However, many government bureaucracies are obliged by law and/or by egalitarian principles to attempt to respond to the needs of an entire population or population segment (e.g., all old people, all school-age children, all poor people who are in ill health). There may be little choice as to the size of the bureaucracy if it is largely dictated by the size of system needed to respond to a given population segment.

- **Bureaucratic imperative.** If the size of a system or subsystem is considered an important source of status and power to the managers of that system, then systems managers may attempt to foster the growth of a system in order to secure greater benefit for themselves — even at the cost of a decline in overall systems efficiency. This "tragedy of the commons" behavior within a bureaucracy may be prompted by the search for a larger staff, a larger budget, greater responsibility, and so on. If many bureaucrats pursue this behavior, the collective effect could be considerable in producing an inefficient scale of activity in social bureaucracies.

- **Technological imperative.** Technology provides the possibility to vastly expand the scale of social systems, and this possibility often seems to be translated into a necessity. Social systems may be designed so as to reap the maximum benefits from potent technologies (ranging from computers to photocopying machines) only to find that the overall system (which includes the human element) now exceeds its most efficient scale. Thus, uncritical adoption of technologies may push a system to excessive scales of social organization.

- **Growth is good.** A central value premise in the industrial world view has been that growth is good. This has created a climate in which a concern for the bigness of our social bureaucracies would be less likely to be questioned.

- **Something for everyone.** Political bureaucracies employ the art of compromise in an attempt to provide "something for everyone" so that no important constituency will be alienated or angered. The bureaucracy defends its own interest group and draws support from the many persons who depend on its continued existence. Intrinsic to democratic political processes, then, is a pattern of expectations and demands which tends to inhibit the reduction of bureaucratic activity which, once instituted, becomes the norm.

(Graph and table appear on page 62)

Problems of Large Systems Arrayed by Stages of Growth of Bureaucracies

This graph and table sum up the authors' theory of bureaucratic development.

INCREASES IN THE SOCIAL PRODUCT
INCREASES IN SCALE

- Muddle Through?
- Social Chaos?
- Authoritarianism?
- Transformation?

	STAGE I HIGH GROWTH	STAGE II GREATEST EFFICIENCY	STAGE III SEVERE DISECONOMIES	STAGE IV SYSTEMS CRISIS
1. Relative level of system's comprehension	High	Moderate	Low	Minimal / High?
2. Degree of public participation in political process	Moderate	Moderate	Low	Minimal / High?
3. Degree of public access to leaders	High	Moderate	Low	Minimal / High?
4. Role of experts in decision-making	Minimal	Substantial	Central	Peripheral / Substantial?
5. Costs of coordination and control	Low	Moderate	High	Very high / Moderate?
6. Degree to which human interactions are rationalized	Minimal	Moderate	Substantial	Very high / Moderate?
7. Level of alienation	Low	Moderate	High	Very high / Low?
8. Legitimacy of basic value premises	Unquestioned	High	Questioned	Challenged / High?
9. Degree of counter-expected systems behavior	Low	Moderate	High	Very high / Moderate?
10. Degree of system's rigidity	Low	Growing Viscosity	Rigidifying	Brittle / Fluid?
11. Number and intensity of perturbations	Low	Moderate	High	Very high / Moderate?
12. Degree of diversity of innovation	High	Moderate	Low	Very low / High?
13. Legitimacy of leadership	High	High	Low	Very low / High?
14. Degree of system's vulnerability	Low	Moderate	High	Extreme / Moderate?
15. Level of system's performance	High	Stabilizing	Declining	Dropping / High?
16. Relative capacity of system's participants to perceive systems problems	High	Moderate	Low	Very low / Moderate?

Large complex systems tend to decline in performance after they reach a certain size. Eventually they enter a stage of "systems crisis," which may lead to very different results: On the one hand, the systems may move toward total collapse; on the other, the systems may be transformed. The far right column suggests the shift in the character of a system if it is to successfully resolve the problems of Stage IV.

Note: The "social product" of a bureaucracy may be defined as the improvement in well-being of the clients of a system produced by the operation of that system. The social product might be health care, education, or some other public service.

The Columbia University Management Program*

By Jerome Yavarkovsky and Warren J. Haas

During recent years much attention has been paid to the general subject of the administration of research libraries, prompted in large part by the growing complexity and increasing costs of these important organizations. Much of this analytical work has been stimulated by the Council on Library Resources, Inc., working closely with the Association of Research Libraries. As part of the ARL program, and with CLR participation and financial support, a major review of the organization and staffing of the Columbia University Libraries was conducted by a management consulting firm, Booz, Allen & Hamilton, Inc.[1] The result of this work, a published report, has been the basis for change at Columbia and has influenced similar efforts at a number of other academic and research libraries as well. This report records in brief form the methods used in converting the consultants' report into action.

The case study performed at the Columbia University Libraries in 1971 was undertaken to improve library performance by reviewing and strengthening the organization and recasting staff composition and deployment patterns. The recommendations which emerged from that study were designed to improve operating effectiveness and to enhance individual staff performance and job satisfaction. The overall goals were to provide an organization which would be more responsive to needs generated by a changing university and which would provide improved opportunities for individuals to develop professionally.

To achieve organizational effectiveness, an administrative structure was recommended which would emphasize functional relationships and take full advantage of subject and operational specializations among the staff. The key proposal to accomplish this change was the formation of three sub-structures:

---

*The paper was originally presented at the IFLA General Council Meeting in Washington, DC 1974, Sub-Section on University Libraries.

Reprinted from *Libri* v. 25 (September 1975), pp. 230-37.

- A Resources Group, responsible for collection development, bibliographic control and specialized reference or resource application programs. A particular concern of this unit is to link resource development with resource utilization. Located here are bibliographers, catalogers, resource program development staff, and ultimately certain reference librarians.

- A Services Group, with its staff specializing in the delivery of library services and responsible for day-to-day public contact, user assistance and user facilities – in the eyes of many patrons, the most visible aspect of library operations. Here, the development of ever higher levels of expertise in providing library services is a primary objective. Circulation activities, photocopy equipment, access tools and other reader services are located in this major unit.

- A Support Group, responsible for the business and processing functions required to support all aspects of library operations. The underlying principle here was to consolidate the many activities which sustain the library as an enterprise. Here are found the acquisitions processing units, facilities and supplies maintenance, bibliographic searching, systems input preparation and quality control, and collection preservation activities.

The effect of these proposed changes and other organizational recommendations contained in the study was judged to be of such potential impact that several needs related to implementation were apparent to the Libraries' administration. First, because of the size and complexity of the Libraries, there was a need to thoroughly analyze and refine the recommendations to be sure they were realistic and viable. For the same reasons, it was necessary to specify in great detail what the new organization would be and how it would work. Finally, it was important to achieve within the staff broad comprehension of the significance of the report and its implications by engaging the maximum number of professional staff members in the analysis and determination of the new structure and operating mode. It was believed that widespread staff participation would apply to these tasks the collective intelligence and breadth of library experience represented in the staff, whether that experience derived from years of responsibility in librarianship or recent graduate study in library school. Further, it would allow scrutiny of the recommendations by library professionals intimately familiar with the Columbia library system to ensure that the proposed organization changes would work. Above all, it was believed essential to the spirit of the recommendations and to the success of the changes that the staff play an active role in determining the structure and direction of the new organization.

When the work of the consultants was complete, their report thoroughly reviewed at all levels of the Libraries' administration and staff. The Director of Libraries, with the study team, conducted a series of staff meetings to describe and explain the recommendations. These provided opportunities for the staff to understand the report and its implications, to discuss them and to respond to them. All staff members were invited to write their reactions to the report and any of its particulars. The Libraries' eight standing committees were also requested to review the report in the context of their special interests. Out of these meticulous review efforts some seventy pages of comments came as memoranda and reports. The consensus was that the concepts and recommendations of the study were fundamentally sound and logical, and that the Libraries would benefit from their application to our environment. Staff members disagreed with many specific details of the recommendations, but basically accepted and supported the general changes proposed.

It was clear when the report was issued that the study and its recommendations were thorough, but not detailed enough or of a nature to permit direct implementation. They were regarded as guidelines for the Libraries' organization and responsibilities, but not necessarily as complete or sacrosanct specifications. The initial review activities were the first steps in a careful examination of the report and delineation of organization details which could be installled in an orderly manner with minimal disruption to service and operations. The work of preparing the Libraries for the new structure and for changes in staffing was conceived as a planning process independent of the actual implementation, with the planning to proceed in three discrete but interrelated phases concerned with organization, staffing and operations.

The first phase, Organization Definition, resulted in a detailed description of each unit in terms of its objectives, functional responsibilities, reporting and working relationships, and performance criteria.[2] Phase two, Staffing Description, determined general staffing patterns and assessed the immediate impact of the new administrative structure on all professional staff responsibilities. Phase three, Operations Planning, has been a continuing effort directed toward the programs of the Libraries.

The progress which was made in planning and implementing the study recommendations was possible in large part because of events which took place within the University administration at the same time that the study team was engaged in its work. In an independent and unrelated effort, the University administration undertook a review of the organization structure of the University itself. Among other findings, it was concluded that all of the University's information resources would be more effectively coordinated with academic programs if they were better integrated into the University's academic planning and decisionmaking structure. Toward this end, a new position was created within a reorganized University administration – Vice President for Information Services and University Librarian, reporting to the Executive Vice President for Academic Affairs. This position was assigned responsibility for the University's major information and academic support resources, including the Libraries, the Computer Center, and several other diverse but related academic information units. Although the study team recommended that the University Librarian be a vice president, the action of the University went beyond that recommendation by its administrative consolidation of libraries and all other information resources. In both cases the underlying principle was the same, namely that academic programs and their information-based support are intimately related and that planning for both of them should take place in concert.

In a sense, although the University's decision was independent of the case study, it had the effect of beginning the implementation process. Several other key recommendations of the study were implemented shortly after the report was published and these were instrumental in getting the full-scale implementation started. The Planning Office was established with the designation of an Assistant University Librarian for Planning, and the Personnel Office was reoriented toward the recommendations through the designation of the Assistant University Librarian for Personnel. Two standing committees were established as a means to apply in special situations the experience and competence of professional staff members at all levels of the organization. The first of these, the ten-member Professional Advisory Committee, was charged with providing comprehensive professional advice and counsel to the University Librarian, and with conducting specific studies in professional areas. The second, the six-member Staff Development Committee, was made responsible for the review and recommendation of staff development plans and for individual professional staff performance review for purposes of recommending professional advancement. Each of these committees was to accomplish its special studies through the appointment of special task forces drawn from throughout the Libraries as well as from within the committee itself.

The designation of these positions and the appointment of the two committees to replace the former eight standing committees provided a framework within which the detailed planning for the new organization could take place.

The actual procedure followed during the Organization Definition phase of planning which produced the detailed unit descriptions was coordinated through the Professional Advisory Committee. The Committee formed the core of three major task forces. In total, about half the professional st.... the Libraries actively participated in the work. The first task force reviewed the basic premises of the study report at the highest levels of the recommended organization. It validated or modified the structure of the first and second levels of the organization and carefully described all the units comprising these levels. Based on these unit definitions, the second task force extended the descriptions to the most detailed level of the organization, making modifications to previously defined units or structural relationships based on further scrutiny and analysis. The third task force addressed itself to the so-called allied libraries. After each round of analysis and definition, the work was reviewed by the Libraries' staff, the senior administrative body of the Libraries, and the Professional Advisory Committee.

The charge to the task forces called for them to consider thoughtfully the case study recommendations and the review documents prepared by the staff in response to the study. They were urged to consult with knowledgeable staff members when necessary in order to resolve issues, but not to recreate the study. Instead, they were to work with the study report as a guide and to develop in detail for the proposed organization the elements and relationships which would achieve the principles of the report. If conflicts arose with the study recommendations or within the task force, the members were urged to seek facts and make decisions. The task forces responsibly fulfilled their charge and created an organization which adheres to the spirit of the study and delineates a realistic and effective administrative structure. Where the revised organization varies from the original recommendations, the differences are logical refinements which preserve the essence of the recommendations while contributing to more effective coordination of library activities, orderly transition to the new arrangement, and implementation within the limits of existing budgets.

When the work of definnig the organization was completed, a task force of the Staff Development Committee proceeded to reconcile existing professional staff positions with positions required in the new organization. This work disclosed that in most cases position responsibilities had not drastically changed. Instead, there was a reasonably close correspondence between most positions in the old and the new organizations. There were, however, some reconstituted positions, most of which had identifiable counterparts in the old organization. In addition, some entirely new positions were created, most of them supervisory or managerial. While the impact on responsibilities of specific positions was moderate, one primary result of the rigorous organization definition and review was the re-arrangement of the organization's component units, thus establishing new reporting relationships. The changes which took place were structural rather than procedural, so that there were minimal immediate changes in day-to-day operations. Rather, by bringing together in a new way the functionally related organization elements with common goals underlying the broad purposes of the Libraries, the capacity was established for achieving those goals more effectively. Further, by relating functional and subject specializations to library objectives and by creating mechanisms for broadened responsibilities, new opportunities were created for staff members to enrich their experience, at their choice, and to grow professionally and personally.

When positions which had been affected and newly-created positions were identified, a second task force of the Staff Development Committee prepared detailed position descriptions for them based on the description of their parent unit. These position descriptions were developed to help individuals understand the scope of their new responsibilities. They also contributed to the recruiting process and staffing of the new organization by delineating each position carefully enough to establish qualifications and seek candidates for it. Both professional and supporting positions were described in terms of function, with an indication of the relative priority and time required for each function. In addition, the authority assigned the position, required qualifications, and reporting relationships were included.

The work of defining the organization and establishing staffing requirements opened the way for implementing the revised recommendations, and that process promptly began. Concurrently, a number of new activities were initiated, and others which had begun earlier, independent of the study, were intensified, to achieve the study's longterm staffing objectives. These included the development in the Personnel Office of a two-track schedule of position categories and professional ranks as a tool to relate individual performance and professional responsibilities to salary administration and staff development. In conjunction with this, the Staff Development Committee developed a format and procedure for regular performance appraisal. Further, a Staff Development Officer was appointed to administer training and development programs for professional and supporting staff members.

The Libraries' on-going program of operational planning is taking place in the context of a fully-documented organization in which each operating unit and each position is defined in terms of its essential characteristics to permit review, evaluation and support on both the organizational and individual level. In addition, the Libraries' budget has been restructured to facilitate fiscal analysis and control within major segments of the organization, as well as across organization lines. Further, a program accounting technique of cost analysis has been developed to provide additional data and insights into library activities. A permanent planning structure has been established, based on a high-level planning and policy committee, to apply these tools to the enhancement of the Libraries and to guide the development of plans. Finally, a policy manual is in preparation to guide decision-making and to encourage the distribution of authority throughout the Libraries.

The organization description process afforded an opportunity for a thorough evaluation of the role each functional unit would play in the context of the overall mission of the Libraries, and of the criteria used to measure accomplishments. The thorough and comprehensive nature of this work was important for several reasons. The proposed organization underscored some new concepts of the place of the library in the university environment. The process of analysis provided a mechanism for each individual to reassess his personal assignment in the context of new relationships and to realize fully the potential and significance of the changes. One of the primary goals of the reorganization was to provide better opportunities for individuals to broaden their experience, take advantage of their diversity of interests and expertise, develop professionally, and consequently function more effectively and in a personally satisfying manner. The intense analytic and evaluative activity during the process of organization definition permitted staff members to develop an understanding of library service obligations and their own responsibilities in terms which could ultimately be linked to individual objectives and be made rewarding in personal terms.

Hence, the articulation of the Libraries' reason for being and the redefinition of structure was significant for its involvement of a majority of the professional staff at all levels of experience and responsibility, and for the opportunity it afforded them to influence the direction and form of the organization. However, the process was equally important for the organization plan which resulted. In addition to a set of operating relationships, it has formed the basis of a structure and procedure for the ongoing planning and review of library activities on a unit by unit basis. The unit definitions are a documentary base for the periodic examination of goals, evaluation of progress or activity relative to those goals, and adjustment of resources as conditions or objectives change. Along with policy statements, these definitions are a set of general operating guidelines and a base for program planning.

It is intended to sustain at an effective level staff participation in operational planning and review so that this initial effort will not gradually become a legendary event unrelated to the continuing service commitment of the Libraries. This work is seen as an initial and intensive experience in a movement toward a participative environment in which the staff will be personally involved in the ultimate purpose of the Libraries, by comprehension of both institutional purpose and their personal role in achieving it.

The case study was undertaken in part because the present dynamic nature of academic and research libraries dictates the need to make them more flexible and responsive to change. The study and the subsequent implementation effort have generated a climate and potential for change in the new organization. The unit definitions were prepared as a description of the organization at time zero. The change in organization and operating patterns implies change in individual staff and administrative behavior as well. It would be unrealistic and undesirable to expect these changes to occur abruptly. Rather, they will come with education, individual exploration of alternate approaches, testing of new personnel procedures, and gradual movement towards improved effectiveness. The capability and desire to change varies greatly among individuals; thus it is important that each individual be able to choose growth patterns consistent with his own personal and career objectives.

The new organization is the starting point for the evolutionary change which the case study and restructuring were intended to permit. As objectives and performance are reviewed, the results will possibly prompt changes in the details of the organization and even structural relationships, since organization forms and staffing patterns are means to ends rather than ends in themselves.

REFERENCES

1. Booz, Allen & Hamilton, Inc., *Organization and Staffing of the Libraries of Columbia University*, Redgrave Information Resource Corp., Westport, Connecticut, 1973.
2. Columbia University Libraries, *The Organization of the Libraries of Columbia University*, Columbia University Libraries, New York, 1973.

Part III
DECISION MAKING AND LEADERSHIP

Introduction

Decision making and leadership are key elements in the overall administrative makeup of an organization and have been recognized by researchers and practitioners as crucial for any organization to be effective and efficient. Regardless of job title, librarians have daily responsibilities to make decisions and demonstrate readership both in the library and in the profession. Although the importance of decision making and leadership have been recognized, disagreement on how to describe and measure these skills persists, especially in library contexts.

The study of decision making usually involves three related topics: the decision making process, the decision maker, and the decision itself. Within each of these areas, decision making involves value judgments made by a variety of people. But if one defines decision making as that process by which information is converted into action, then decision making is largely concerned with the process of acquiring, controlling, and utilizing information to accomplish some objective. Thus, a major task for the decision maker is to identify *what* information is needed to make the decision, *how* that information can be acquired and made available in a form suitable for use by the decision maker, and *how much* information is necessary to make the decision.

This task, reflected in E. Frank Harrison's contribution to this section, suggests a very rational approach to decision making. However, constraints such as lack of time to analyze the decsion, limited resources that can be applied to implementing the decision, and lack of staff to support the decision, must also figure into the decision-making process. The study of decision making can be confounded by tangible and intangible constraints such as values, attitudes, personality characteristics, and other, more psychologically oriented, elements of both the decision to be made and the decision maker.

Decision making and leadership can easily digress into what skills, personality characteristics, and experiences a "good" leader must have. Typical of this view is the statement that "a good decision maker is born, not made." Another view suggests that good decision makers tend to use specific decision-making strategies appropriate for a given situation. In other words, good decision makers are made, not born. While Richard De Gennaro tends to support the former viewpoint, Andrea C. Dragon presents evidence in support of the latter.

Of particular interest to librarians is Harrison's discussion of decision "types." The typology he presents (adopted from Herbert Simon's differentiation between programmed and non-programmed decisions), suggests that as many as 90% of all decisions made by librarians are "programmed" or routine in character. In this kind of decision-making environment, work quickly becomes boring, monotonous, and provides little opportunity for creativity and innovation.

Discussions of leadership have historically revolved around desired or exhibited traits of leaders that can be identified as either effective or ineffective. Dragon points out that there are many problems connected with this perspective. The behavioral approach Dragon suggests focuses on specific leader behaviors, attempting to relate these behaviors to particular organizational contingencies. This situational approach makes no assumption about cause and effect, but rather provides a means by which different dimensions of leadership can be measured and described. The situational approach focuses on the interaction between leaders and specific organizational environments or situations.

Dragon's research indicates that different leadership styles are demonstrated by different library leaders. Her review of leadership studies outside librarianship suggests that certain leadership skills may be more effective in achieving organizational goals in some situations than in others. In short, effective leadership skills depend on the nature of environmental impacts on the organization, the specific situation or decision area in which leadership is required, and the nature of the leader's subordinates. "Good" leadership, then, is less defined by the skills or traits of the leader than by the combination of factors, which produces a number of contingency relationships that encourage either "good" or "poor" leadership.

Yet for many, the question of "good" or "poor" leadership and decision making remains basically intuitive. Organizational members find it easier to identify a "good" or "poor" leader than to describe what makes that leader "good" or "poor." Ultimately, effective decision making and leadership facilitates the accomplishment of organizational goals and objectives. More descriptive work needs to be done or we are likely to remain with the pragmatic, seat-of-the-pants, approach described by many writers in the literature.

An Overview of Decision Making
By E. Frank Harrison

Decision making is an integral part of the management of any organization. More than anything else, competence in this activity differentiates the manager from the nonmanager and, more important, the good manager from the mediocre manager. It would be difficult to find many managers who do not consider themselves good decision makers. Any suggestion that a given manager might improve his decision-making techniques almost surely would elicit a highly defensive reaction. For example, who among the readers of this book would admit that he is not a good decision maker?

The opinions of a manager regarding his own decision-making abilities are conditioned strongly by his perception of what a satisfactory decision is. For some it is a choice arrived at by the consensus of one or more groups in the organization. For others it is a decision that does not elicit unfavorable reactions from those affected by it. Or it may simply be the choice among available alternatives that offers the highest possible payoff. Or perhaps it is a decision that promises to meet a specific objective—a decision reached only after a careful search for alternatives within discernible boundaries and one that will be implemented smoothly with maximum benefits to those affected by it.

This diversity of viewpoints regarding the goals and techniques of decision making makes it difficult to evaluate a manager's abilities in this area. There is a lack of universal agreement as to what constitutes a really good decision, and there is no generally accepted approach for managers to follow in pursuit of choices most likely to

---

Reprinted from E. Frank Harrison: *The Managerial Decision-Making Process.* Copyright © 1975 by Houghton Mifflin Company. Reprinted by permission of the publishers.

result in favorable consequences. Much is assumed but little is known about this most important managerial activity. It is hoped that this book will help illuminate the darkness that has prevailed and, through the presentation of relevant theory and viable conceptual frameworks, assist managers in organizations of all types to become more effective decision makers.

Profile of a Decision

In discussing the subject of decision making, it is customary to focus on one or more of three things: (1) the decision-making process, (2) the decision maker, or (3) the decision itself. It is interesting to note the virtual absence of a definition for the term *decision*. To illustrate, a statement of alternative definitions of this word was given by Ofstad in the following passage:

To say that a person has made a decision may mean (1) that he has started a series of behavioral reactions in favor of something, or it may mean that he has made up his mind to do a certain action, which he has no doubts that he ought to do. But perhaps the most common use of the term is this: "to make a decision" means (2) to make a judgment regarding what one ought to do in a certain situation after having deliberated on some alternative courses of action.[1]

In their book on the organizational aspects of choice, Shull and his associates define the decision-making process as

. . . a conscious and human process, involving both individual and social phenomena, based upon factual and value premises, which includes a choice of one behavioral activity from among one or more alternatives with the intention of moving toward some desired state of affairs.[2]

Herbert A. Simon in his classic work on the science of management decision treats decision making as a process synonymous with the whole process of management.[3] In Simon's words,

---

[1] H. Ofstad, *An Inquiry into the Freedom of Decision* (Oslo: Norwegian Universities Press, 1961), p. 15.
[2] Fremont A. Shull, Jr., Andre L. Delbecq, and L. L. Cummings, *Organizational Decision Making* (New York: McGraw-Hill, 1970), p. 31.
[3] Herbert A. Simon, *The New Science of Management Decision* (New York: Harper and Row, 1960).

Decision making comprises three principal phases: finding occasions for making a decision; finding possible courses of action; and choosing among courses of action.[4]

Emory and Niland view a decision as only one step in an intellectual process of differentiating among relevant alternatives. It is

... the point of selection and commitment. ... The decision maker chooses the preferred purpose, the most reasonable task statement, or the best course of action.[5]

Eilon accurately observed that most of the definitions of a decision indicate that "the decision maker has several alternatives and that his choice involves a comparison between these alternatives and an evaluation of their outcome."[6]

In this book, a decision is defined as

a moment, in an ongoing process of evaluating alternatives related to a goal, at which the expectations of the decision maker with regard to a particular course of action impel him to make a selection or commitment toward which he will direct his intellect and energies for the purpose of attaining his objective.

The process within which this moment of choice occurs is treated extensively in Chapter 2. In fact, the primary concern of this book is with decisions that are made as part of an interdisciplinary process by decision makers who are, for the most part, oriented toward the accomplishment of stated objectives.

Decision Theory

Decision theory as an academic discipline is still relatively young. It is only since the Second World War that operations research, statistical analysis, and computer programming have imparted a "scientific" aura to the process of choice and only within the last ten or fifteen years that the behavioral sciences—sociology, psychology and social psychology—have begun to contribute to the body of knowledge comprising decision theory.

[4] Ibid., p. 1.
[5] C. William Emory and Powell Niland, *Making Management Decisions* (Boston: Houghton Mifflin, 1968), p. 12.
[6] Samuel Eilon, "What Is a Decision?," *Management Science* (December 1969): B-172.

Even today the bulk of the literature in the field has a strong quantitative orientation. That is, the decision maker is assumed to have (1) a fixed objective, (2) almost unlimited time and money to spend in search and evaluation activities, (3) virtually perfect information regarding the probability of alternative outcomes, and (4) inexhaustible cognitive powers for comprehending, assimilating, and retaining an infinite number of variables. (While such assumptions may be necessary to quantify a decision-making situation, they do limit the applicability of quantitative methods in decision making and dictate extreme caution in interpreting and using quantified results.)

Some writers concede that decision making is accomplished through a process, but one that can be highly proceduralized if not actually quantified.[7] Other authors treat decision making as a complex exercise in mathematics or statistics.[8] Several books have been published in recent years that present decision making through a series of cases.[9] Other publications take some cognizance of the behavioral aspects of decision making, but usually by compiling several articles from scholarly journals.[10] In fact, there are few, if any, books that focus on decision making as an integrated process accomplished within an interdisciplinary framework.[11] And the articles in behavioral science and management journals are usually

---

[7] See Emory and Niland, *Making Management Decisions*, pp. 1–22.

[8] See John Aitchison, *Choice Against Chance: An Introduction to Statistical Decision Theory* (Reading, Mass.: Addison-Wesley, 1970); D. V. Lindley, *Making Decisions* (New York: Wiley, 1971); and Albert N. Halter and Gerald W. Dean, *Decisions Under Uncertainty with Research Applications* (Cincinnati: South-Western Publishing Co., 1971).

[9] See Rossall J. Johnson, *Executive Decisions*, 2d ed. (Cincinnati, South-Western Publishing Co., 1970); and Francis J. Bridges, Kenneth W. Olm, and J. Allison Barnhill, *Management Decisions and Organizational Policy* (Boston: Allyn and Bacon, 1971).

[10] See Marcus Alexis and Charles Z. Wilson (eds.), *Organizational Decision Making* (Englewood Cliffs, N. J.: Prentice-Hall, 1967); Alvar O. Elbing, *Behavioral Decisions in Organizations* (Glenview, Ill.: Scott, Foresman and Co., 1970); and William T. Greenwood (ed.), *Decision Theory and Information Systems* (Cincinnati: South-Western Publishing Co., 1969).

[11] One possible exception is the book by Shull, Delbecq, and Cummings, *Organizational Decision Making*, in which the authors focus mainly on the behavioral sciences, but not within a decision-making process.

concerned with the decision maker at the moment of choice in the decision-making process.[12]

The relative newness of decision theory as an academic discipline doubtless accounts for the diversity of approaches to the subject. Still there exists a need for a unified, interdisciplinary approach that would combine the behavioral and quantitative aspects of the field into a cohesive, meaningful process useful to academicians, consultants, and managers in all forms of organizational endeavor. This is an ambitious undertaking, one that will doubtless require much input of work and time. But the effort is worth making, and it is hoped that the approach set forth in this book will make a small contribution toward that end.

The Scope of Decision Making

Decision making can occur at several levels. The first and perhaps most basic level is that of the individual acting to satisfy his basic needs. According to Maslow, human beings are motivated by a hierarchy of needs, the highest being the need for self-actualization or the need to become all that one is capable of becoming.[13] However, self-actualization may take many forms and be pursued with varying degrees of intensity. The satisfaction of a lower-level need for one individual may, for example, represent a kind of ultimate fulfillment for another individual. Still the concept of a hierarchy of human needs provides a useful framework for analyzing individual decisions.

Much of the decision making accomplished by an individual relates to the solution of problems—personal, employment, or social problems. As a general statement on the decision-making or problem-solving approach of individuals, the following may be said:

1. Problem solving by individuals entails the use of strategies (plans or patterns) of searching for relevant alternatives, especially

---

[12] For example, see Henry Morlock, "The Effect of Outcome Desirability on Information Required for Decisions," *Behavioral Science* (July 1967): 296–300; and L. Williams, "Some Correlates of Risk Taking," *Personnel Psychology* 18 (1965): 297–309.

[13] See A. H. Maslow, "A Theory of Human Motivation," *Psychological Review* 50 (1943): 370–396.

when the slightest degree of complexity prevails. The greater the cognitive strain imposed by the problem constraints such as time, information availability, and recall capability, the simpler the rules of search. The individual usually tries to minimize cognitive strain in part by his choice of problem-solving strategies.
2. Problem-solving behavior is adaptive. Individuals start with a tentative solution, search for information, modify the initial solution, and continue until there is some balance between expected and realized results.
3. Even in the most restricted problem-solving situation, the individual's personality and his aversion to or preference for risk enter into his choice of strategies, his use of information, and his ultimate solution.[14]

In summary, individuals tend to employ rather simple strategies, even in the presence of complex problems, to obtain desirable solutions, which are constrained by imperfect information, time and cost factors, frequently severe cognitive limitations, and manifold psychological forces.

In our complex society individuals usually find need satisfaction as members of groups that have particular purposes. Often they must compromise their personal desires if the group is to arrive at a consensus. Therefore, group decisions represent more than just a collection of the desires of the individual members. Group choices reflect a special synthesis of compromised desires of individual members. Presumably such a synthesis is less volatile and perhaps even more viable than a similar decision made unilaterally by an individual would be. But it is not necessarily a better decision in terms of need satisfaction at the level of the individual or goal attainment at the level of the organization. It represents most simply an expansion of the scope of choice, from a single to a multiple decision maker.

It is also true that a group normally provides a broader range of knowledge and a variety of critical viewpoints that may facilitate a more penetrating analysis of a given problem. Still, the need to obtain a consensus of the members is often time-consuming and

---

[14] Alexis and Wilson, *Organizational Decision Making*, pp. 73–74.

frustrating to the individual who would much prefer the relative freedom of unilateral choice. Other individuals, of course, prefer to make decisions as members of a group because the risk of personal criticism is often lessened and the responsibility for unfavorable results is likely to be diffused. (Further discussion of individual and group decision making is presented in later chapters.)

The scope of decision making does not stop at the level of the group. After all, a group is simply an entity within a larger aggregate called an organization.[15] The organization comprises the total enterprise or institution within which numerous subunits and groups function to accomplish its objectives. A decision made by a particular group may commit the organization to a given course of action. More likely such decisions will be made by several groups, be reviewed at several levels in the formal structure, and eventually be ratified by the chief executive or the top administrator. A decision at the level of the organization is therefore much more complex than a choice made at the level of the group, because a group is simply a subset of an organization.

The following list contains some of the basic characteristics of decision making at the level of the organization:

1. Organizations make extensive use of programmed decisions, which involve reasonably well-structured patterns of search. Naturally the more complex and significant the decision, the more extensive the search process will be.
2. Organizations often use rather simple rules of thumb to make decisions as well as the complex analytical frameworks that are so often attributed to organizational decision making. Again, the complexity, uniqueness, and significance of the decision are determining factors. Obviously some decisions don't permit rule-of-thumb treatment.
3. Organizations make decisions that are bound and biased by the local rationality of the decision unit. That is, given the constraints in the situation and the uncertainties of the moment, organizations are likely to make decisions that are optimal in their spheres but suboptimal when received in the larger totality.

---

[15] See Maneck S. Wadia, "Management and the Behavioral Sciences: A Conceptual Scheme," *California Management Review* (Fall 1965):65–72, for a discussion of the relationships among individuals, groups, and organizations.

4. Organizations engage in directed search for relevant alternatives. The choice of decision rules and decision strategies is constrained by the desire to minimize uncertainties.
5. Organizations learn. To the extent that organizations are part of open systems, there is little doubt that they learn from and adapt to their environment.[16]

Decision making at the level of the organization is expressed primarily through the basic functions of the manager, which include (1) planning, (2) organizing, (3) staffing, (4) directing, and (5) controlling.[17] For example, objectives are determined only after decisions have been made regarding the basic purposes of the organization. Plans are formulated in the light of decisions made for resource requirements to accomplish the objectives within some selected period of time. A division of labor is accomplished and functional specialties and reporting relationships are established in pursuit of the objectives set forth in the plan. Candidates are identified and final selections are made based upon the requirements reflected in the positions comprising the formal structure. Progress toward fulfillment of the objectives contained in the plan is accomplished by countless daily decisions required to make the product or dispense the service provided by the organization. Control of operations is affected by choices to take or withhold corrective action when comparing actual against standard performance. As Simon has stated, "Decision making is synonymous with managing."[18] It is the dynamic element that activates and sustains the managerial process.

However, the scope of decision making extends beyond the managerial process at the level of the organization. The totality of organizations comprises the system of enterprise, which in the United States is capitalism.[19] Decisions made at the level of the system of enterprise tend to be oriented toward (1) consumer wel-

---

[16] Alexis and Wilson, *Organizational Decision Making*, pp. 76–78.
[17] See Harold Koontz and Cyril O'Donnell, *Principles of Management: An Analysis of Managerial Functions*, 5th ed. (New York: McGraw-Hill, 1972), pp. 46–49, for a description of the basic functions of the manager.
[18] Simon, *The New Science of Management Decision*, p. 1.
[19] See Wadia, "Management and the Behavioral Sciences," pp. 66–67.

fare, (2) allocation of resources, and (3) production and distribution of goods and services.[20] Although the primary focus is on macroeconomics at this level, the decision-making process is analogous to that employed at the level of the individual, the group, and the organization.

Decisions are also made at the level of the total society. Here the primary objective is social welfare with significant corollaries of (1) the good life, (2) culture, (3) civilization, (4) order, and (5) justice. The principal orientation is not, as at the level of the system of enterprise, of an economic nature. Bernthal cited the basis for decisions at this level rather well in the following excerpt:

> It is necessary to see the importance to a culture and civilization of developing not only vigor in economic activity, but also of devoting man's energies to the civilizing process, once economic survival is assured. A surplus of goods . . . makes it possible for man to devote more energy and attention to the creation of works of literature, architecture, sculpture, music . . . to the establishment of orderly societies . . . and just rules. . . .[21]

Because organizations exist within the economic system that is a part of the total society, managers need to be aware of and responsive to the decisions made and the rationale for them at these superordinate levels.

The world is comprised of nation-states reflecting particular ideologies. For example, the ideology of the Soviet Union is communism, which is based upon a totalitarian state within which the freedom of the individual is subordinate to the dictates of the political system. On the other hand, the United States is a democracy whose laws are made by and administered in the best interests of the people, with a maximum emphasis on personal freedom and the right to individual self-expression. Frequently, such ideological differences lead to tension, strain, and outright hostility between nation-states. Even where national ideologies are compatible, decision makers are interested mainly in attaining pragmatic objectives such as trade concessions and geopolitical advantages. Still, with some modifications, decisions made at this level follow essentially

---

[20] See Wilmar F. Bernthal, "Value Perspectives in Management Decisions," *Journal of the Academy of Management* (December 1962): 193, 196, for a discussion of objectives at the level of the system of enterprise.

[21] Ibid., p. 194.

the same process that characterizes choice at the subordinate levels discussed previously. It is well known, for example, that

> Presidents and premiers do sit down with their advisers and weigh alternatives, consider possible outcomes of action, explicitly assign utilities to these outcomes, and try to assess the probabilities that various outcomes will follow a given action.[22]

The scope of decision making is indeed wide. It commences at the level of the individual and extends to the deliberations of the groups that compose the organization. Organizations, in turn, make up the overall system of enterprise, which forms part of the total society; and societies make up nation-states that espouse compatible or conflicting ideologies, the sum total of which constitutes the whole world.

A Typology of Decisions

Having defined the term *decision*, presented a brief description of the field of decision theory, and articulated the scope of decision making, we set forth at this juncture a typology of decisions for use in describing the decision-making process and its interdisciplinary framework in the chapters to follow.

Various experts in the field of decision theory have advanced numerous ways of classifying decisions. Perhaps the best known of these classifications is the distinction proposed by Simon between programmed and nonprogrammed decisions. According to Simon,

> Decisions are programmed to the extent that they are repetitive and routine, to the extent that a definite procedure has been worked out for handling them. . . . If a particular problem recurs often enough, a routine procedure will usually be worked out for solving it. . . . Decisions are nonprogrammed to the extent that they are novel, unstructured, and consequential. There is no cut-and-dried method for handling the problem because it hasn't arisen before, or because its precise nature and structure are elusive or complex, or because it is so important that it deserves a custom-tailored treatment.[23]

---

[22] Martin Patchen, "Decision Theory in the Study of National Action: Problems and a Proposal," *Journal of Conflict Resolution* (June 1965): 165.
[23] Simon, *The New Science of Management Decision*, pp. 5–6.

Drucker made essentially the same distinction as Simon, but he labeled programmed decisions "generic" and nonprogrammed decisions "unique."[24]

Delbecq went slightly beyond Simon and Drucker with his three-point classification of decisions as follows:

1. *Routine decisions.* The organization or group agrees upon the desired goal, and technologies exist to achieve the goal.
2. *Creative decisions.* There is a lack of an agreed-upon method of dealing with the problem; this lack of certitude may relate to incomplete knowledge of causation, or lack of an appropriate solution strategy.
3. *Negotiated decisions.* Because of differences in norms, values, or vested interests, opposing factions confront each other concerning either ends or means, or both.[25]

Gore also proposed a triadic classification, composed of routine, adaptive, and innovative decisions. The basic distinctions in this classification scheme are that adaptive decisions deal with problems rather than with the recurring tasks of routine decisions, while innovative decisions are concerned with major changes in activities and operations that lead to changes in goals, purposes, or policies.[26] Even within this scheme, however, there is a high degree of interdependence among the decisions. In Gore's words,

Routine decisions activate, channel, and terminate hundreds of units of behavior in such a way that broad goals are implemented through the same activities that meet immediate objects. Since both the conditions under which the goals can be realized and the goals themselves are constantly changing, routinized activities must continually be adapted to maintain a satisfactory rate of goal achievement. But, since on a broader field, the objects embodied in goals are changed from time to time, the innovative decision exists. The essential rhythm of organizational adjust-

---

[24] Peter F. Drucker, *The Effective Executive* (New York: Harper and Row, 1967), pp. 122–125.

[25] Andre L. Delbecq, "The Management of Decision-Making Within the Firm: Three Strategies for Three Types of Decision-Making," *Academy of Management Journal* (December 1967): 329–339.

[26] William J. Gore, "Decision-Making Research: Some Prospects and Limitations," in *Concepts and Issues in Administrative Behavior*, ed. Sidney Mailick and Edward H. Van Ness (Englewood Cliffs, N.J.: Prentice-Hall, 1962), pp. 49–65.

ment is from routine to adaptive to routine; or from routine to adaptive to innovative and back to adaptive and eventually to routine again.[27]

Thompson imparted a dynamic quality to the foregoing classifications of decisions with his two-dimensional scheme for decision-making strategies. In this scheme, there are the following four basic strategies:

1. *Computational strategy.* There is considerable certainty regarding cause/effect relationships, and there are strong preferences regarding possible outcomes.
2. *Judgmental strategy.* Preferences regarding possible outcomes are strong, but cause/effect relationships are highly uncertain.
3. *Compromise strategy.* There is a good deal of certainty regarding cause/effect relationships, but preferences for possible outcomes are not strong.
4. *Inspirational strategy.* Preferences for possible outcomes are not strong, and there is considerable uncertainty regarding cause/effect relationships.[28]

Upon close analysis, it is not too difficult to detect a high degree of commonality among these several classification schemes for decisions and decision-making strategies. Essentially, each scheme can be reduced into two basic categories involving the matched pairs of (1) routine and nonroutine, (2) recurring and nonrecurring, and (3) certainty and uncertainty. To be sure, there are variables other than these three sets. However, they provide a single thread through the several classifications. Table 1.1 shows all the classes divided into two categories according to their structures and strategies. Category I includes the routine, recurring decisions that are handled with a high degree of certainty. Category II comprises the nonroutine, nonrecurring decisions characterized by considerable uncertainty as to the outcome.

The significance of differentiating between these two basic categories of decisions becomes apparent when one realizes that:

[27] Ibid., p. 58.
[28] James D. Thompson, *Organizations in Action* (New York: McGraw-Hill, 1967), pp. 134–135.

Table 1.1 A Categorization of Decision Characteristics

	Category I Decisions	Category II Decisions
Classifi-cations	Programmable, routine, generic, computational, negotiated, and compromise	Nonprogrammable, unique, judgmental, creative, adaptive, innovative, and inspirational
Structure	Proceduralized; predictable; certainty regarding cause/effect relationships; recurring; within existing technologies; well-defined information channels; definite decision criteria; outcome preferences may be certain or uncertain	Novel, unstructured, consequential, elusive, and complex; uncertain cause/effect relationships; nonrecurring; information channels undefined; incomplete knowledge; decision criteria may be unknown; outcome preferences may be certain or uncertain
Strategy	Reliance upon rules and principles; habitual reactions; prefabricated response; uniform processing; computational techniques; accepted methods for handling	Reliance on judgment, intuition, and creativity; individual processing; heuristic problem-solving techniques; rules of thumb; general problem-solving processes

The management of most companies' daily operations abounds with highly programmed decisions: Consider merely the highly routinized rules that normally guide the everyday management of inventories, production schedules, machine and manpower allocations, cost estimation, mark-up pricing, etc.[29]

Management should not treat routine decisions as if they were nonroutine. If a decision is indeed generic, it should be handled as such without expending valuable time and money on it as if it were unique. Moreover, it is essential that management not only differentiate the routine from the nonroutine decision but that it also gain greater understanding regarding the structure and strategy of the latter type. The rewards from such understanding are set forth in the following statement:

[29] Peer Soelberg, "Unprogrammed Decision Making," in *Studies in Managerial Process and Organizational Behavior*, ed. John H. Turner, Allan C. Filley, and Robert J. House (Glenview, Ill.: Scott, Foresman, 1972), p. 135.

It is precisely this type of nonprogrammed decision making that forms the basis for allocating billions of dollars worth of resources in the economy every year. And, ironically, until we better understand the nature of such unprogrammed human decision processes, our sophisticated computer technology will be of slight aid for making this type of decision more effectively. . . . The potential payoff to management of scientific understanding of the economic, psychological, sociological, and political "laws" of nonprogrammed human judgment can be enormous.[30]

The Locus of Choice

In terms of the organizational hierarchy, category I decisions, as reflected in Table 1.1, are normally made at the level of operating management. This is where the technology of the organization is applied in transforming raw inputs into finished outputs. Choices made at this level are usually routine and recurring, with a high degree of certainty associated with the outcome. Category I decisions may also be made at middle-management levels in the normal administrative processes of the organization. Again, the structure of the decision in terms of its nature, frequency, and degree of certainty will determine the strategy, which in turn will indicate the appropriate level of management at which the choice should be made.

Moreover, in this context, it seems obvious that in organizations of any appreciable size, category I decisions should not be made by top management, that is, at the vice-presidential or chief executive level. Managers at these levels are expected to conserve their time and energies for choices requiring the exercise of judgment and creativity, with a view toward adapting the organization to cope with inevitable change and preparing it to accept the innovations of a dynamic technology. Such managers should therefore concentrate primarily on category II decisions, which, by definition, are nonroutine and nonrecurring and which contain a good deal of uncertainty related to the outcome. In organizations

[30] Ibid., p. 136.

where top managers are preoccupied with category I choices, there is usually a lack of delegation to lower levels of management, with all of the attendant adverse effects on motivation, efficiency, and effectiveness. Further, in concerning themselves with category I decisions, top managers would tend to neglect long-range objectives and strategies, which would result in a kind of organizational myopia. In such situations, there is a general disregard for long-range planning and undue emphasis on short-range control. The ultimate consequences for the organization can only be unfavorable because, after all, in the absence of planning there is nothing to control; and operations tend to be conducted in a highly reactive mode with problematical consequences resulting from unplanned choices. Clearly, then, the proper concern of top management is category II choices, with category I decisions left to operating management. Middle management should, for the most part, also be concerned with category I choices, although in many situations this level of management will participate in category II decisions.

With regard to decision making at the levels of the individual and of the group within the context of a formal organization, the locus of choice seems evident. For example, individuals are more likely to make category I decisions because, as stated previously, such choices are routine and recurring and have a good deal of certainty associated with the outcome. Therefore, there is no need to convene a group to make such decisions. Yet it is interesting to note the number of organizations in which committees, task forces, and fact-finding groups spend countless man-hours making choices that have highly programmed outcomes. This is a classic example of treating generic decisions as if they were unique in the name of participative management. Participation through group membership in a category I choice, where the outcome of the decision is highly certain, represents a tremendous waste of human resources. It also embodies a misconception regarding one of the basic purposes of group decision making, which is to reduce unilateral choices that might work to the disadvantage of those affected by the choice. But the choice of principal concern here is one that involves the exercise of judgment, intuition, and creativity—in short, a category II decision. Such choices are the proper concern of group decision makers, at the middle-management or, more appropriately, top-management level in the formal organization.

Individuals are less likely to make category II decisions than are groups. Because of the relative complexity of such decisions, they usually require a broader range of expertise than is possessed by most individuals. To be sure, an individual chief executive or top administrator may formally ratify a category II decision made by one or more groups in the organization. But it is becoming less and less common for these nonrecurring and consequential choices to be made unilaterally.

In essence, then, and with specific reference to Table 1.1, category I decisions are most likely to be made by individual managers at the operating levels of the organization; although, depending upon the situation, such choices are also made by middle managers either individually or, with reduced effectiveness, in groups. For their part, top managers normally concentrate on category II decisions, which may be made in one or more groups, including middle managers, and formally ratified by the chief executive, or which, to a lesser extent, may be made unilaterally by him.

Supplemental References

Bross, Irwin D. J. *Design for Decision*. New York: Free Press, 1953.

Churchman, C. West. *Prediction and Optimal Decision*. Englewood Cliffs, N.J.: Prentice-Hall, 1961.

Costello, Timothy W., and Sheldon Zalkind (eds.). *Psychology in Administration*. Englewood Cliffs, N.J.: Prentice-Hall, 1963.

Cyert, R. M., Herbert A. Simon, and Donald B. Trow. "Observation of a Business Decision," *Readings Toward a General Theory*, ed. William B. Wolf. Belmont, Calif.: Wadsworth, 1964. pp. 175–188.

Elbing, Alvar O. *Behavioral Decisions in Organizations*. Glenview, Ill.: Scott, Foresman, 1970.

Greenwood, William T. (ed.). *Decision Theory and Information Systems*. Cincinnati: South-Western, 1969.

————. *Management and Organizational Behavior Theories: An Interdisciplinary Approach*. Cincinnati: South-Western, 1965.

Hodge, Billy J., and Herbert J. Johnson. *Management and Organizational Behavior*. New York: Wiley, 1970.

Jones, Manley Howe. *Executive Decision Making*. Homewood, Ill.: Richard D. Irwin, 1962.

Kast, Fremont E., and James E. Rosenzweig. *Organization and Management: A Systems Approach.* New York: McGraw-Hill, 1970.

Knudson, Harry R., Robert T. Woodworth, and Cecil H. Bell. *Management: An Experiential Approach.* New York: McGraw-Hill, 1973.

Koontz, Harold, and Cyril O'Donnell (eds.). *Management: A Book of Readings.* 3d ed. New York: McGraw-Hill, 1972.

LeBreton, Preston P. (ed.). *Comparative Administration Theory.* Seattle: University of Washington Press, 1968.

Litterer, Joseph A. *The Analysis of Organizations.* New York: Wiley, 1965.

March, James G., and Herbert A. Simon. *Organizations.* New York: Wiley, 1958.

Miller, David W., and Martin K. Starr. *The Structure of Human Decisions.* Englewood Cliffs, N. J.: Prentice-Hall, 1967.

Mockler, Robert J. *Management Decision Making and Action in Behavioral Situations.* Austin, Tex.: Austin Press, 1973.

Newman, William H., Charles E. Summer, and E. Kirby Warren. *The Process of Management: Concepts, Behavior, and Practice.* 2d ed. Englewood Cliffs, N. J.: Prentice-Hall, 1969.

Odiorne, George S. *Management Decisions by Objectives.* Englewood Cliffs, N.J.: Prentice-Hall, 1969.

Scott, William G. *Organization Theory: A Behavioral Analysis for Management.* Homewood, Ill.: Richard D. Irwin, 1967.

Sharkansky, Ira. *Public Administration: Policy Making in Government Agencies.* 2d ed. Chicago: Markham, 1972.

Simon, Herbert A. *Administrative Behavior.* 2d ed. New York: Free Press, 1957.

Steiner, George A. *Top Management Planning.* New York: Macmillan, 1969.

Weber, C. Edward, and Gerald Peters. *Management Action: Models of Administrative Decisions.* Scranton, Pa.: International Textbook, 1969.

Wortman, Max S., and Fred Luthans (eds.). *Emerging Concepts in Management.* New York: Macmillan, 1969.

Young, Stanley. *Management: A Decision-Making Approach.* Belmont, Calif.: Dickenson, 1968.

Library Administration & New Management Systems
By Richard De Gennaro

"The real danger with . . . management systems is that they offer mechanistic formulas for dealing with complex realities and keep us from thinking about and solving our management problems in practical, realistic, and common sense ways"

MONSIEUR JOURDAIN, Molière's *Bourgeois Gentilhomme*, was surprised and pleased to learn that he had been speaking prose all his life without knowing it. I felt the same way when I finally learned that I had been a manager for 20 years without knowing it. Well, I always knew that I was a library *administrator*, but somehow I never thought of myself as a *manager* because that term connoted a kind of modern professionalism that the more familiar term *administrator* lacked.

Ten years ago I attended the University of Maryland's excellent two-week development program for library administrators and was deeply impressed by the introductory courses and readings which covered the full range of subjects like McGregor's Theories X and Y, Management by Objectives (MBO), Program Budgeting (PPBS), Decision Theory, Cost-Benefit Analysis, Mathematical Modelling, Management Information Systems, etc. I came away thinking, somewhat naively, that business and other managers had mastered and were routinely using that arsenal of sophisticated management systems and techniques in their daily work, and that it was only library and perhaps academic administrators that were struggling along with the traditional methods. It was clear that we librarians had a lot of catching-up to do.

It was with some hesitation that I accepted the directorship of a large library in 1970 because I believed that research libraries were becoming increasingly costly and complex organizations and that I lacked the formal management training and skills that the job required. Determined to remedy my lack of formal training, I enrolled in the Harvard Business

---

Reprinted from *Library Journal*, December 15, 1978. Published by R. R. Bowker Co. (a Xerox Company). Copyright © 1978 by Xerox Corporation.

School's Advanced Management Program, a prestigious and expensive three-month program especially designed for high-level business, government, and military executives. I thought the "B-School" would work its magic and convert me from a self-taught library administrator into a certified modern manager, but I was disappointed.

Early in its history, the Harvard Business School developed the case method of instruction and it has used it almost exclusively in its teaching ever since. The case method can be very effective, but it was overused in the executive development program. In three months, we never read anything but cases, and since the cases were all efficiently reproduced and distributed in convenient packets, we never had the need or the occasion to use the rich resources of the Baker Library. In fact, we seldom had to read from a real book or journal. The classics of management science were rarely mentioned, and with the exception of a few sessions on decision theory and computer simulation, almost no mention was made of any of the new management systems that had been developed and were presumably being used routinely everywhere but in libraries. The Harvard program was useful, but it did not give me the management knowledge and skills that I needed and wanted; so I continued to read about management and to attend management institutes and workshops. (Among the best and most useful are the short programs offered by ARL's Office of Management Studies.) This reading and supplementary training helped me to develop and sharpen my management skills over the years. At the same time, I was gaining confidence and maturity and getting a lot of practical on-the-job experience.

I was also called upon to serve on a number of boards, commissions, and committees; this gave me the opportunity to work closely with and observe a peer group of top managers and executives, not only in libraries, but in universities, business firms, and government offices. I found that most of them, like me, had no special management training or education and were struggling, each in his or her own unscientific way, to do the management jobs to which they had been appointed. Some were more competent and effective than others, but previous formal management training seemed not to make any significant difference. Indeed, it was hard to tell who had training and who didn't. I noticed that there were few trained management experts in top level management positions. Instead, they were working as specialists in staff positions or as teachers, researchers, or consultants.

I could not see any real difference in what I was doing as a library director and what my peers in other fields were doing. After a while, I began to suspect that the reality of what we managers were experiencing in our day-to-day activities had more validity than the theoretical world of management that was being described in books and articles written by management professors and social scientists.

I was confirmed in that view when I read Henry

Mintzberg's *The Nature of Managerial Work*.[1,2] Mintzberg, a McGill University management professor, had a much different view of management and the way managers worked than the conventional authors; that view checked with my own experience as a library administrator. In order to find out and describe what managers actually did, he conducted a number of studies and also scanned the literature to integrate and synthesize the findings of other studies with his own.

How do managers manage?

The studies by Mintzberg and other researchers showed that from street gang leaders to the President of the United States, managers do not spend their time planning, organizing, coordinating, and controlling as the French industrialist, Henri Fayol said they did in 1916 and as most writers on management have continued to repeat ever since. They are not like the orchestra leader who directs the component parts of his organization with ease and precision. Instead, they spend their time reacting to crises, seizing special opportunities, attending meetings, negotiating, talking on the telephone, cultivating interpersonal and political relationships, gathering and disseminating information, and fulfilling a variety of ceremonial functions. Mintzberg says:

> I was struck during my study by the fact that the executives I was observing—all very competent by any standard—are fundamentally indistinguishable from their counterparts of a hundred years ago (or a thousand years ago, for that matter). The information they need differs, but they seek it in the same way—by word of mouth. Their decisions concern modern technology, but the procedures they use to make them are the same as the procedures of the 19th Century manager. Even the computer, so important for the specialized work of the organization, has apparently had no influence on the work procedures of general managers. In fact, the manager is in a kind of loop, with increasingly heavy work pressures but no aid forthcoming from management science.[3]

The Mintzberg view is by no means unique. There is a growing number of management scholars who are questioning the conventional view of management and what managers do. In a critical review of *On Management* (Harper, 1976), a book of articles selected from 25 years of the *Harvard Business Review*, Albert Shapero, a management professor at the University of Texas, strikes a similar note:

The term "management" conjures up images of control, rationality, systematics; but studies of what managers actually do depict behaviors and situations that are chaotic, unplanned, and charged with improvisation. The Managerial life at every level is reflexive—responding to calls, memos, personnel problems, fire drills, budget meetings, and personnel reviews. Occasionally, however, we find at managerial levels individuals who go 24 hours without being interrupted by meetings or phone calls. They are the long-range planners, the people in O.R., E.D.P., financial or market planning, or market research. Management is really for them. The bulk of the articles in *On Management* are concerned with ideas from the world of the staff functionary.[4]

Are management systems really used?

What about the claims of widespread use of new scientific management systems and techniques? Is it really true that managers in business, government, and other institutions are using them extensively while we library administrators are lagging far behind?

Let's first look at what a few of the management experts say about the use of these systems in general, and then we will look at their use in libraries.

William R. Dill, dean of the Graduate School of Business Administration at New York University, makes this sober assessment:

> For all the progress we have made in developing good approaches to planning, forecasting, budgeting, and control, and for all the enthusiasm we in schools of management have helped to build for these approaches, their use has been fitful and sporadic, even in the most analytically sophisticated and goal-oriented institutions. In corporations that are pointed out as models for what can be accomplished, the outputs of planning, budgeting, and modeling staffs are often quietly ignored by operating people when times are good; these outputs often seem irrelevant in times of sudden challenge or change. Analysis and planning are still far from foolproof ways to anticipate change and potential crises.[5]

Aaron Wildavsky, dean of the Graduate School of Public Policy at the University of California, Berkeley, has written a number of articles in which he argues convincingly, citing evidence and authorities, that the major modern information systems like PERT, MBO, PPBS, Social Indicators, and Zero Based Budgeting have not worked and cannot work. About PERT (Program Evaluation Review Technique), he says that "the few studies that exist suggest that outside of construction, where one activity tends to follow another, PERT is rarely successful."[6]

On MBO (Management by Objectives), he says: "The trouble with MBO is that the attempt to formalize procedures for choosing objectives without considering organizational dynamics leads to the opposite of what was intended—bad management, irrational choice, and ineffective decision-making."[7] "The main product of MBO, as experience in the United States federal government suggests, is, literally, a series of objectives. Aside from the unnecessary paper work, such exercises are self defeating because they become mechanisms for avoiding rather than making choices. Long lists of objectives are useless because rarely do resources remain beyond the first few."[8]

On PPBS, Wildavsky is equally harsh. He says that "Program budgeting does not work anywhere in the world it has been tried," and that "no one knows how to do program budgeting."[9] His assessments of Social Indicators and Zero Based Budgeting are in a similar vein.

These realistic assessments that we are getting from authorities like Mintzberg, Shapero, Dill, Wildavsky, and others should serve to remind us to maintain a healthy skepticism whenever we read about the effectiveness and widespread use of new management systems and techniques. We librarians should guard against the tendency we have to look for panaceas and to accept uncritically the claims and promises made on behalf of each new management theory or system that appears.

Consider the minimal impact on libraries as compared with the initial promise, for example, of PPBS, Operations Research, MBO, and even Participative Management.

To the best of my knowledge, PPBS has not been successfully implemented in a single library and I doubt that it ever will be.[10] Interest in it is rapidly waning.

The practical application of Operations Research in libraries has been extremely limited to date. One of the earliest and best known economic analyses of library decision making was done in the MIT Libraries in 1969. The report of that study came to this sobering conclusion: "Although helpful, an economic analysis of a university (or public) library is insufficient because libraries operate as political systems and thus improving libraries requires political analysis."[11] In an excellent article on library decision making, Jeffrey Raffel, an economist and co-author of the MIT study begins by saying that "in general, the more important the decision, the less beneficial a cost-benefit analysis is to library decision makers," and concludes by saying that "it is time that we all recognized the politics of libraries and acted accordingly."[12]

In a classic paper on Management by Objectives in academic libraries, James Michalko, after a thorough, critical review of the literature, recommends against the use of MBO in libraries on the grounds that it is a limited approach which is costly and difficult to implement and which yields uncertain results.[13]

Participative management is another "new" management technique that has been particularly oversold in the last decade. In fact, it is considered by many librarians to be the perfect management system. Good management has always included consultation and participation, it is just the name, the faddishness, and some of the formal structures that are new. When used properly and honestly, participative management is a useful process at all levels, and not just by top managers on major decisions as is sometimes assumed. It is essential that there be appropriate consultation and participation of interested and competent staff members on important decisions affecting them. But participative management will not bring on the management millenium in libraries.

Participative management is not decision making by committee or by staff plebiscite. Good management requires that when all the facts have been gathered and analyzed and all the advice is in, the appropriate administrator has to make the decision and take responsibility for it. Knowing when and how to seek and take advantage of consultative advice and prior approval of decisions where appropriate is one of the most important managerial skills. Decisions should be made at the lowest competent level. The library's critical strategy decisions involve a world outside the library and must usually be made by the director and his chief associates. Staff committees can give good advice on such matters, but they simply do not have the information, the knowledge, or the perspective required to make those decisions—and they cannot take responsibility for the results.

One extreme form of participative management, the collegial or faculty system of governance, was developed for academic departments; it works badly there and worse or not at all in libraries. Where it appears to work, it is because those involved have tacitly made concessions to traditional hierarchical systems and the demands of the environment while preserving the collegial form. A library is not an academic department, it is a service organization and should be so administered. A librarian by any other name is still a librarian and it is time for mature acceptance of that fact.

Perhaps the reason that participative management has been embraced so enthusiastically and uncritically by librarians in recent years is not because of its management benefits, but because it appears to be the model that best justifies faculty status. It is assumed that because faculty members participate in a collegial academic decision-making process, that model is the appropriate one to use in libraries—if librarians are to achieve faculty status. Much of the library-based management literature since 1970 is self-serving and reflects a direct or indirect preoccupation with matters of staff status and benefits frequently hidden behind arguments for participative management. It is time that we recognized this natural bias and took steps to overcome it by giving more attention and weight to the more objective management literature from outside the library field.

Two recent articles on participative management in libraries, one by James Govan and the other by Dennis Dickenson, give encouraging evidence that the library profession is beginning to take a more realistic and balanced view of the advantages and limitations of participative management and collegial governance. Govan reminds us that:

> Librarians cannot afford to degrade services nor alienate their users in an effort, however enlightened or well-intentioned, to make their jobs more challenging and satisfying. Participation and consultation cost time and money and often, like faculty deliberations, produce rather conservative results. In this connection, it is useful to remember Maslow's belief that Theory Y is possible only in periods of affluence. It is also healthy to recall Drucker's statement that service institutions do not operate for the people who work in them.[14]

In his perceptive article, Dickenson tries to provide "an antidote for some of the more extreme and sometimes naive interpretations of participative management that appear from time to time in library literature."[15]

Peter Drucker summed up an important truth about management when he said in response to an interviewer's question about the efficacy of new management techniques: "The young people today expect to see business run by theory, knowlege, concepts, and planning. But then they find it is run like the rest of the world—by experience and expediency, by who you know, and by the hydrostatic pressure in your bladder."[16]

This is not just the way business is run, it is the way libraries are run as well. And it is the way they will continue to be run despite the current rhetoric about the managerial revolution that is being ushered in by the use of new quantitative and psychological management systems and theories.

Why? Because a library operates in a political environment and nearly all the really important decisions that are made at the highest levels have an overriding political component. They are rarely the product of cost-benefit analysis or Operations Research where the various factors are weighed and compared and the "best" or most cost-effective course is chosen. These management techniques can be useful sometimes to implement a program or a project in the most effective manner *after* the political decision to proceed has been made. They can also be useful in providing a rationale to support some essentially political decision that is being proposed or advocated, or to impress higher authorities or constituents with the competence of the managers and the rationality of their decision making process. Management systems, particularly PPBS, ZBB, and PERT are used in government and military bureacracies largely because they are mandated by law or regulation.

In the library world, as in education, business, and government, few major program decisions are made solely or even largely on the basis of careful studies of needs and costs. Consider, for example, decisions to build a new library building, to open a new departmental or branch library, to achieve excellence in some special subject discipline, or to embark on a major automation program. These program decisions are usually the result of an initiative or vision by an imaginative and powerful person, perhaps a library director, a dean, a president, a mayor, or other official. They are political, emotional, or even personal decisions—justified, rationalized, and perhaps implemented with the assistance of various kinds of analyses and studies, but seldom derived from them.

It is important that librarians understand how and why these really critical decisions are made so that they will not be disillusioned or discouraged when they discover that the "best," the most efficient, or the least expensive solution frequently loses out to the one that is the most politically expedient or attractive.

The quantitative approach

I think it is important to make a distinction between the claims made on behalf of complex quantitative management systems such as Operations Research and Cost-Benefit Analysis, and the collection and analysis of quantitative data in libraries to assist in rational decision making. I am questioning the validity and usefulness of these complex systems, but I am not questioning the need for and use of quantitative studies for measuring and evaluating library services. Quite the contrary, we need to know more about libraries, their resources, and how they are actually used. We have relied historically upon input data, e.g., the number of books acquired, the number of serials subscribed to, the number of books circulated, the dollars spent, etc. The qualitative characteristics of these data are dubious; we desperately need reliable measures of library effectiveness.

Following the pioneering work by Fremont Rider[17] in 1940 on the growth of research libraries, there has been an increasing number of extremely valuable quantitative studies like those by Fussler,[18] Lancaster,[19] Buckland,[20] and other works of solid quality. The findings of such studies provide the the theoretical foundations and practical knowledge that working library managers need to draw on to help them think clearly and creatively about library management and to make sound decisions based on valid data. This is especially true in this time of transition when the conventional wisdom of our profession will not suffice to see us through.

As one of the library managers for whose benefit and use such studies are presumably made, I thank the authors and urge them on to greater productivity and precision. I also urge them to try to keep their studies as simple as possible and to summarize their findings in readable English.

Unfortunately, a good deal of the quantitative research that is done in the library field is unintelligible, irrelevant, or too complicated and theoretical for any practical use in libraries. Much of it is written in the language of higher mathematics which is incomprehensible to most managers. This is particularly true of studies that are made by academicans outside the library field such as statisticians, economists, psychologists, Operations Research people, etc. Their goal is not necessarily to do studies that are useful, but to demonstrate their mathematical prowess, to test theories and methodologies, to get published, and to award doctoral degrees to deserving graduate students. They select the library as their laboratory because it is convenient and because they think it is virgin territory ready for easy exploitation. They are more interested in the process than in the results.

The most useful library research is done by librarians or others with a serious long-term interest and involvement in libraries who work with librarians in a spirit of genuine collaboration. They are trying to make an impact. It is the difference between a class assignment and the real thing, between war games and war.

A notable exception to this criticism of academics is the landmark work by William J. Baumol and Matityahu Marcus, *Economics of Academic Libraries* (American Council on Education, Washington, D.C., 1973). These two economists went to unusual lengths to explain their statistical methods and to summarize their conclusions with refreshing brevity and clarity.

As a consequence, their work is widely read and frequently cited.

Management scientists and other quantitatively oriented researchers frequently wonder why the results of quantitative research studies are not used more by practicing library managers in the decision making process.[21] One reason is that the mathematics and the methodologies required are far too complex and difficult for operating managers to learn and apply in their busy work environments. Few senior library administrators have the kind of staff support needed to successfully carry out complex analyses. Another and equally important reason is that the quantitative approach does not and cannot take into sufficient account the complex of political, organizational, and psychological factors that characterize the real work where people are more potent than numbers or logic.

The quality of many decisions could be significantly improved if we had more and better data, but many of the more important decisions have a relatively small quantitative component. As a library director, I seldom have a critical need for more quantitative data than are available from regularly kept statistics or by having someone make a special and usually simple survey and analysis of the problem. When the data are simply not available or too difficult to assemble, I can usually find a satisfactory way to manage without them. My real problem has nearly always been to correctly assess the political rather than the economic or quantitative factors. It is fairly easy to determine the most cost-effective course of action with or without detailed data. It is much harder to map out and implement a successful strategy for achieving it, to assess how the various persons and groups affected will perceive the manager's intentions, and how they will react to the decision. Someone said that quantification is not synonymous with management. Finding the best or most cost-effective course of action is not the same as getting it accepted. Sometimes the quality of a decision is critical, other times, it is acceptance.

Effective decision making processes in large academic and public libraries involve complex sets of policies, procedures, and problems which require a variety of different kinds of information and approaches. Some decisions will be authoritarian, some will be collegial, some will be made by committees, and some will be made by combinations of the above. Library directors are not all-knowing, nor are the collective judgments of library faculties and committees infallible. Different situations call for different approaches. There are no simple formulas and no easy answers.

The new management systems that I have been discussing in this article divide into two general categories. There are *quantitative systems* such as Operations Research, PPBS, and ZBB, and *psychological* or *behavioral* systems such as Theory Y (and its variants) and MBO. In each system, there are a number of concepts, ideas, tools, and techniques that have validity and can be used to advantage by library managers, but as comprehensive systems they are all far too theoretical, complex, and simplistic to be applied successfully by ordinary managers in the day-to-day work environment. Few managers have the time or the specialized knowledge and skills required to make these systems work, and those that do are probably astute enough to manage as well or better without them.

In the hands of amateurs—and this is most of us—the quantitative systems frequently produce misleading and wrong solutions, while the psychological or behavioral systems can lead to the manipulation and misuse of people. The real danger with both kinds of management systems is that they offer mechanistic formulas for dealing with complex realities and keep us from thinking about and solving our management problems in practical, realistic, and common sense ways.

Despite the many claims to the contrary, management is not yet a science. It is still an art, but is very much an art that can and should be mastered and practiced by librarians.

References

1. Henry Mintzberg, *The Nature of Managerial Work*, Harper, 1973.
2. A very readable summary of Mintzberg's findings and views appeared in a much cited and reprinted article by him entitled "The Manager's Job: Folklore and Fact," *Harvard Business Review*, July-August 1975, p. 49-61.
3. Mintzberg. "The Manager's Job . . ." p. 54.
4. Albert Shapero, "What Management Says and What Managers Do," *Fortune*, May 1975, p. 275.
5. William R. Dill, "When Auld Acquaintance Be Forgot . . . From Cyert and March to Cyert vs. March," in: Richard M. Cyert. *The Management of Nonprofit Organizaitons*, Heath, 1975, p. 67.
6. Aaron Wildavksy, "Policy Analysis Is What Information Systems Are Not." Working Paper #53, July 1976. copy of a typescript of a paper delivered at the ASIS Conference, October 1976, p. 3.
7. Wildavsky, "Policy Analysis . . ." p. 5.
8. Wildavsky. "Policy Analysis . . ." p. 6.
9. Aaron Wildavsky. "Rescuing Policy Analysis from PPBS." *Public Administration Review*, March/April 1969, p. 193.
10. The reasons can be found in an authoritative study by Guy Joseph De Genaro, "A Planning-Programming-Budgeting System (PPBS) in Academic Libraries: Development of Objectives and Effectiveness Measures." Ph.D. dissertation, University of Florida, 1971.
11. Jeffrey A. Raffel. "From Economic to Political Analysis of Library Decision Making" *College & Research Libraries*, November 1974, p. 412.
12. Raffel. "From Economic to Political Analysis . . . ," p. 412, 421.
13. James Michalko, "Management by Objectives and the Academic Library: a Critical Overview," *Library Quarterly*, Vol. 45, No. 3, 1975, p. 235-52.
14. James F. Govan, "The Better Mousetrap: External Accountability and Staff Participation," *Library Trends*, Fall 1977, p. 264.
15. Dennis W. Dickenson, "Some Reflections on Participative Management in Libraries," *College & Research Libraries*, July 1978, p. 261.
16. Thomas J. Murray, "Peter Drucker Attacks: Our Top-heavy Corporations," *Dun's*, April 1974, p. 40.
17. Fremont Rider. *The Scholar and the Future of the Research Library*, Hadham Pr., 1944.
18. Herman H. Fussler & J. L. Simon. *Patterns in the Use of Books in Large Research Libraries*, Univ. of Chicago, Pr., 1969.
19. F. W. Lancaster. *The Measurement and Evaluation of Library Services*, Washington, D.C., Information Resources Press, 1977.
20. Michael K. Buckland. *Book Availability and the Library User*, Pergamon, 1975.
21. See for example: A. Graham McKenzie, "Whither Our Academic Libraries?" *Journal of Documentation*, June 1976, p. 129.

Leader Behavior in Changing Libraries
By Andrea C. Dragon

Theoretical foundations of modern leadership study and the methods and strategies used to empirically validate the theories are discussed. Data from a study of leadership in public libraries are presented and compared with similar data obtained for leadership in both economic and not-for-profit organizations. The results of the study are presented as evidence that a revision of traditional theories of leadership as it is manifested in libraries is needed. The new model of library leadership draws upon both the situational and behavioral models of leadership but also incorporates subordinate description of leader behavior. The model states that subordinate description of library leader behavior is influenced by the rate of environmental change affecting the library.

INTRODUCTION

While it may be possible to identify many factors influencing a library's goal achievement, some being outside the direct control of supervisors and administrators, the behavior of those in leadership positions is generally felt to be of critical importance. The repertory of behaviors exhibited by administrators and supervisors in their daily encounters with subordinates has an impact on the way subordinates feel about their relationship with their supervisor and their job. Even though leader behavior affects subordinate perceptions about their organization as a place to work, the precise determination of its *modus operandi* and its effects on such organizational outcomes as performance and job satisfaction has yet to be discovered. Research into the nature of the relationship between leader behavior and effectiveness as demonstrated by desirable outcome achievement is progressing but conclusive evidence is lacking. On the whole, research attempting to correlate specific leader behaviors with such outcomes as performance and satisfaction has not been as successful as research which attempts to describe leader behavior in situational terms and then attacks the problem of

---

Reprinted from *Library Research*, 1, pp. 53-66. Norwood, NJ: Ablex Publishing Corporation, 1979.

outcome correlation (Filley et al., 1976). This paper will briefly discuss theoretical and methodological foundations of several recent developments in leadership study and present the results of a study intended to validate and extend one of the models to leader behavior in libraries.

THE STUDY OF LEADERSHIP: TRAITS, SITUATIONS AND BEHAVIORS

Although leadership is generally considered an important factor in the management process,[1] management theorists and researchers have found it difficult to isolate and systematically study. Referring to this problem, Bennis (1959, pp. 259–260) has said:

> Probably more has been written and less is known about leadership than about any other topic in the behavioral sciences. Always it seems, the concept of leadership eludes us or turns up in another form to taunt us again with its slipperiness and complexity.

Perhaps Bennis was a bit more pessimistic than necessary. Leadership continues to be a favorite topic of behavioral scientists and because of their interest more is learned with the publication of each research report.[2] Empirical study of leadership is a relatively new phenomona, however. Before the advent of disciplined behavioral leadership research in the 1940s, most investigators focused their scholastic efforts on producing lists of traits possessed by those in powerful positions.

According to this theory, leadership equals certain traits. Leaders are born with these traits or they are acquired through some unknown process. A trait is defined as any distinctive physical or psychological characteristic of the individual to which the individual's behavior can be attributed. Traits are inferred from an individual's behavior and are offered as explanations as to why a particular behavior occurs. An example of this line of reasoning is the notion that if a supervisor often inquires after the health of a subordinate's ailing parent and offers assistance, then that supervisor possesses the trait of compassion.

Early writers on library administration echoed prevailing opinions concerning leadership as indicated by this quotation from John Adams Lowe (1928, pp. 17–18) in which he describes the qualities needed by a library's chief executive:

> The librarian must be orderly, both in person and in mind, he must be temperate, in speech and in act; he must be honest and square. He must have a good sense of time, that he may transact his business with dispatch, and have a good sense of propor-

---

[1] The management process consists of planning, organizing, leadership, controlling, and staffing or human resource administration. For a lucid account of the development of the concept of management as a process see Wren (1972).

[2] From 1968 to 1976 there were 1,368 references to leadership cited in *Psychological Abstracts*. That is a rate of 170 published items each year.

tion . . . He must resist the lure of the limelight . . . He must be prepared to accept success without vainglory and defeat without embitterment.

The belief that leadership is equal to a finite number of identifiable traits has persisted in library service. Thirty years after Lowe published his list Mumford and Rogers (1959, p. 366) also approached leadership through trait listing:

> A supervisor must have qualities other than the ability to do work, important though this is. Common sense, fairness, humanity, loyalty, courage and forcefulness (but short of the point of driving others) are some of the leadership qualities to look for. Since there is no oversupply of people with these virtues, a training program to develop supervisors is greatly desired.

The authors have illustrated the major difficulty with accepting the leadership trait concept as a viable means of studying and evaluating leadership. It is quite difficult, if not impossible, to train people to be virtuous. What teaching methods would trainers use to teach people to be courageous? What does it mean to be humane? If indeed humanity (or compassion, from the earlier example) is required for leadership, how would a trainee reveal to the trainers that he or she had "learned" to be humane?

A second difficulty with the trait approach to leadership is that even though there has been considerable effort expended in attempts to discover a finite number of traits which would differentiate successful from unsuccessful leaders, these efforts have not produced consistent results. It may be statistically possible to correlate certain traits with organizational level, but evidence does not support the belief that among those occupying the same level that the individual having a higher degree of a certain trait (more loyalty, perhaps) will be a more successful leader. The literature relating to leadership traits has been reviewed a number of times (Stogdill, 1948; 1974), but no consistent support for the trait approach to leadership study has been found.

While it is relatively easy, upon reflection, to be critical of the trait approach, it is more challenging to offer alternatives. Currently there are two major alternatives to the trait approach: the situational and the behavioral. Each has adherents and detractors, and each group has presented empirical evidence from which it argues that it holds the correct view. Opposition between the two groups may be ending as there are indications that the two approaches are being combined to fashion a hybrid approach to leadership study (Kerr et al., 1974). However, that development is still in the formative stages, therefore the two approaches will be discussed separately in this paper.

The situational approach focuses on the interaction between leaders and certain situational variables. Researchers in this area view leadership as a set of behaviors interacting with organizational variables that change with the situation. They seek to discover which variables permit certain behaviors to be effective in some situations but dysfunctional in others. Leader behaviors appropriate for a military officer may or may not be appropriate for a director of a college library.

The best-known situational theory of leadership is Fiedler's Contingency

Model (1967). It is rather complex and space limitations do not permit complete discussion in this paper, but its essential elements can be condensed in a few sentences. Fiedler contends that an individual manager has a relatively fixed leadership style and that the nature of this style can be determined by asking the manager to describe his or her least preferred co-worker (LPC). Managers who describe this person in favorable terms are considered to be people or relationships oriented. Those who describe their least preferred co-worker in rejecting, negative terms are considered to be task-oriented. Fiedler then proposes that one leadership style is preferred over the other depending on the favorableness (to the manager) of the situation. A situation is favorable if there is a high degree of task structure, the manager is in a strong power position and is well-liked by subordinates. It is important to note that Fiedler does not suggest that the leader change his or her orientation toward people or task depending upon situational favorableness, but that to diagnose the situation and determine if *it* can be changed to match the leader's orientation.

Fiedler's theory is alternately supported and criticized in the literature. Although there have been at least fifty empirical testings of the model (Fiedler, 1973), several of Fiedler's colleagues (Filley et al., 1976) point out the lack of operational definitions in his model and question the validity of the least preferred co-worker instrument.

At the 1976 Leadership Symposium at Southern Illinois University, Fiedler's Contingency Theory was soundly criticized by Schriescheim and Kerr. They said "lack of meaningful explanatory power renders the conceptual underpinnings of the theory nonoperational, making it impossible for researchers to test the theory's underlying assumptions" (Schriescheim and Kerr, 1977, p. 12). These criticisms were echoed by Stinson in his concluding comments concerning the usefulness of the LPC as a leadership measure, "Thus we must conclude that after twenty-five years the LPC remains a measure in search of a meaning" (Stinson, 1977, p. 113). It is because of these significant theoretical and methodological shortcomings that Fiedler's Contingency Model has been rejected as a theoretical base for this research project.

Another situational model of leadership considered, but ultimately rejected, for the theoretical base of the project, is that proposed by House (1973). The Path-Goal Theory of leadership consists of two basic propositions. The first concerns the role of the leader in providing rewards to subordinates and removing obstacles from the path leading to the rewards. The second involves the impact on subordinate motivation of leader behavior given certain subordinate characteristics and organizational constraints.

The Path-Goal Theory has been tested and found to have some face validity, but much of the empirical research attempting to validate the theory has in turn served to spark revisions in the original concept in order to fit the research results. For this reason the support offered by these studies is considerably weakened. Perhaps the main reason why the Path-Goal Theory was rejected as a theoretical base for this research is that it lacks specific operational measures. In fact, the Ohio State leadership scales (see below) often have been used and cited by House to test his theory. Schriescheim and Kerr point out that while the theory may have some usefulness, "it may well be that the theory is not sufficiently operational to provide clear, testable propositions" (Schriescheim and Kerr, 1977, p. 17).

In contrast to the situational approach, the behavioral approach has focused only on leader behavior as the most important independent variable. Although recently the concept of leader behavior as the primary predictor of organizational criteria has fallen into disfavor (Filley et al., 1976), the methodology employed in the original research continues to be used in constructing modified behavioral theories of leadership (Kerr et al., 1974).

The early work of researchers[3] studying leader behavior had the ultimate objective of learning the effects of leadership upon organizational effectiveness, but much of the research was conducted for purely descriptive purposes only, i.e., no attempt was made to correlate behavior with outcomes. These researchers believed in the value of descriptive methodology as a necessary preliminary to research predicting relationships between leader behavior and organizational outcomes. This descripive approach, as it is called, appears to be a prudent course for library leadership research. At present there is little agreement among practitioners and researchers concerning appropriate criterion (or outcome) measures in libraries. Even if there were some agreement, measurement of criteria not easily quantified, using instruments appropriate to the field, would be difficult and subject to much criticism. Description of the leader behavior of library administrators and supervisors is needed before attempting to predict job satisfaction, performance, or other effectiveness measures from those behaviors. The leadership theory and methods developed at Ohio State University provide the theoretical and research framework upon which a descriptive model of library leadership can be built.

THE OHIO STATE LEADERSHIP MODEL

The Ohio State Leadership Model had its origins at Ohio State University under the initial guidance of Carrol T. Shartle. His research group, which began studying leadership under a grant from the Office of Naval Research, in 1950 began compiling descriptive statements of the behaviors exhibited by those in supervisory positions. In their first study they asked Air Force crews to describe the behavior of their commanding officer. After much factor analysis, two factors emerged to account for much of the behavior as described by the subordinates. The development of these two factors, now referred to as the Ohio State Leadership Dimensions, *consideration* and *initiating structure*, is discussed by Stogdill and Coons (1957).

[3]For a history of the development of the model see Fleishman (1973).

What exactly do these dimensions mean in terms of observable leader behavior? *Consideration* has been defined as strengthening the self-esteem of subordinates, expressing appreciation, and contributing to the well-being of the group. *Initiating structure* has been defined as letting group members know what is expected of them, defining roles and relationships, and initiating the organizational structure in which the group carries out its activities.

Although *consideration* and *initiating structure* represent separate leader behaviors, they are complimentary rather than antagonistic. While some people are described as very high in one and very low in the other, most people exhibit both behaviors in varying amounts. The Ohio State Model is graphically presented thus:

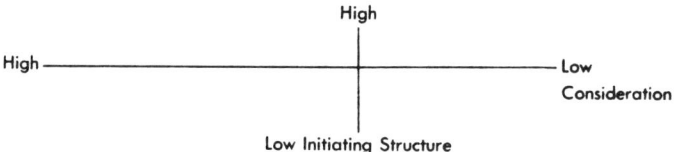

Translating these concepts into library experience is not difficult, it requires only a few minutes of informal discussion with library staff members. Complaints about supervisors generally fall into the two dimensions discussed above. First, one hears complaints about a supervisor's inconsiderate behavior, i.e., undue criticism, refusing to explain actions, not expressing appreciation, and a failure to regard the subordinate as a thinking, feeling human being. Second, there are the complaints that supervisors fail to make decisions, they are poor organizers, they fail to delegate authority, and they never tell subordinates what level of performance is expected of them; in short, complaints concerning supervisors' failure to initiate structure. Positive comments about supervisors also fall into the two dimensions of leader behavior. A boss is considered "good" if he or she behaves as if he or she is a co-worker and is sensitive to problems subordinates may have. A "good" boss also lets subordinates know where they stand and carefully explains procedures and rules.

Although subordinates in libraries as in other organizations have definite opinions about their supervisors' behavior, unless opinions and perceptions are standardized, they are of little use in empirical research. Feelings, opinions, and perceptions, however accurate, must be made part of a theoretical and methodological paradigm in order to be statistically manipulated and brought under the control of modern research methods.

THE LEADER BEHAVIOR DESCRIPTION QUESTIONNAIRE

The Ohio State research group met the problem of lack of standardization among subordinate descriptions of leader behavior by developing an instrument to measure behavior exhibited by supervisors as described by subordinates. This instrument, the Leader Behavior Description Questionnaire (LBDQ)—Form XII, measures *consideration* and *initiating structure* on scales scored from 0 to 50 (Stogdill, 1963). It is possible for the most considerate of supervisors to receive a score of 50 on the *consideration* scale. Likewise it is possible for the least structured of supervisors to receive a score of 0 from his or her subordinates on the *initiating structure* scale.

Some examples of items from each of the scales follow. (In the test booklet the items are interspersed with items representing other dimensions and, of course, are not labeled.)

Consideration					
1. He treats all group members as his equals	A	B	C	D	E
2. He gives advance notice of changes	A	B	C	D	C
*3. He keeps to himself	A	B	C	D	E
4. He puts suggestions made by the group into operation	A	B	C	D	E
5. He does little things to make it pleasant to be a member of the group	A	B	C	D	E
Initiating Structure					
1. He encourages the use of uniform procedures	A	B	C	D	E
2. He tries out his ideas in the group	A	B	C	D	E
3. He decides what shall be done	A	B	C	D	E
4. He assigns group members to do particular tasks	A	B	C	D	E
5. He makes his attitudes clear to the group	A	B	C	D	E

A—always; B—often; C—occasionally; D—seldom; E—never.
A = 5; B = 4; C = 3; D = 1; E = 0

*scored in reverse

The LBDQ is not without methodological shortcomings. Some studies of its validity and reliability yield disturbingly low correlations (Stinson, 1977). However, the LBDQ remains the most widely used leadership measure in the world, simply because, in the opinion of this researcher, it is better than the available alternatives. As evidence of its continued use in leadership study, the 1978 *Proceedings of the Academy of Management* includes a variety of papers using the LBDQ to measure leader behavior. One paper (Johns, 1978) used the LBDQ in a study of absence from work, another (Buterfield et al., 1978) used it in a study of leadership behavior related to performance of subordinate groups, a third (Petty and Bruning, 1978) used an alternate form of the LBDQ to measure leader behavior in a Public Welfare agency, and a fourth (Hollingsworth and Mobley, 1978) used the LBDQ to measure leader behavior in hospitals. Despite its psychometric difficulties, of which this researcher is aware, the LBDQ was chosen as the leadership measure in this study, because, first, until something better comes along it is the best available, and, second, it was necessary to use a standard measure so that comparisons between library leader behavior and leader behavior in other organizations would be possible.

USING THE OHIO STATE MODEL TO DESCRIBE LEADERS IN LIBRARIES

As part of a larger project (Dragon, 1976) the Leader Behavior Description Questionnaire—(LBDQ) Form XII was administered on site to twenty-eight subordinate groups consisting of 166 individual members in three large public libraries. The subordinate members were asked to use the LBDQ to describe the behavior of their supervisor, who might be the director of the library, the head of a department, or a clerical supervisor. Individual and group responses were averaged to obtain an index for the entire sample (Table A):

TABLE A
Mean Descriptions of 28 Library Supervisors
in Three Large Public Libraries

Scaled Dimension	Mean (N=166)
Consideration	37.4
Initiating structure	39.7

Library supervisors were described by their subordinates as higher in behaviors associated with *initiating structure* than in behaviors associated with *consideration*. When compared to other groups for which data is available (Stogdill, 1963), the high score on *initiating structure* is emphasized; librarians were described as high or higher on this dimension than several other groups of supervisors. The librarians were also described as lower in *consideration* than supervisors from the other groups.

TABLE B
Mean Subordinate Descriptions of Various
Groups of Supervisors

Supervisors	Consideration	Initiating Structure
1. Corporation Presidents	41.5	38.5
2. Labor Union Presidents	42.3	38.3
3. College Presidents	41.3	37.7
4. U.S. Senators	41.1	38.8
5. Highway Patrol Officers	36.9	39.7
6. Aircraft Engineers	37.1	36.6
7. Community Leaders	41.1	37.2

When the data were analyzed by professional status (Table C) a disparity between the two groups became apparent. Professional and nonprofessional subordinates described their supervisors' *consideration* behavior similarly, but there was a statistically significant difference between the two groups in their descriptions of *initiating structure*.

TABLE C
Mean Descriptions of Supervisors as Described by
Professional and Nonprofessional Subordinates

Subordinate Group	Consideration	Initiating Structure
Professional (N = 50)	37.2	38.4
Nonprofessional (N = 116)	37.6	40.3**

**Significant at the .05 level (two-tailed test).

These data indicate that professional subordinates perceive their supervisors as behaving in supportive ways, i.e., showing appreciation, consideration for feelings, etc., just about as often as nonprofessionals perceive their supervisors as behaving in these ways. However, nonprofessionals perceived such behaviors as giving orders and deciding how the work shall be done and who shall do it more strongly in their supervisors than did professionals.

The data were further analyzed by the sex of the supervisor (Table D), but there were no significant differences between descriptions made by subordinates of women and subordinates of men.

TABLE D
Women Supervisors and Men Supervisors
as Described by Subordinates

Group Described	Consideration	Initiating Structure
Women Supervisors (N = 15)	37.1	39.8
Men Supervisors (N = 13)	37.9	39.6

Although women supervisors were described as lower in *consideration* and higher in *initiating structure* than the men, the differences are not significant. In fact, the similarity between the two sets of scores is somewhat remarkable although similar results have been reported elsewhere. For example, Lee and Alvares (1977) found no differences in subordinate descriptions of male and female supervisors, except in the case of high *consideration* high *structure*. Male supervisors were described as lower in *initiating structure* than females. Earlier, Bartol and Wortman (1975) reported that they found no difference in the way in which the leader behavior of male vs. female supervisors is described by subordinates. They, too, found in their study that male supervisors were described lower than female supervisors in *initiating structure*.

These data appear to lend support to the belief that men and women respond similarly to the demands of leadership situations and are so perceived by subordinates. Incidentally, libraries are unique institutions, in that men and women supervise subordinate groups of both sexes. In other organizations, in which large numbers of women are supervisors, such as hospitals, the subordinate group is dominantly the same sex as the supervisor. The data examined here indicate that although the sex of the supervisor may vary, the behavior varies little.

RESEARCH IMPLICATIONS

The findings from this study indicate methodological directions for future research. This particular study indicates that it is certainly possible to utilize behavioral science methodology in libraries and obtain results not in contradiction with the behavioral science literature. In the study described above, no attempts were made to tailor the LBDQ to the library situation. The respondents answered a questionnaire identical to that administered to thousands of other subordinates in military, economic, and public organizations. Progress in library research has been impeded to a certain extent because of a failure to utilize methods that have been the stock-in-trade of other social science disciplines. Until it is recognized that libraries as formal organizations are really quite similar to other kinds of formal organizations and that scholarly efforts should be directed toward studying library variables as behavioral scientists study organizational variables, we greatly limit the scope and usefulness of our research endeavors, as well as our ability to interact with and learn from cognate disciplines.

In addition to these methodological considerations, this study has added to our knowledge of supervisory leadership in libraries by providing some empirical evidence upon which to begin the process theoretical model building. Although no behavioral perscriptions can be presented, because of the limited nature of the evidence, the subordinate descriptions of this particular group of library leaders naturally invites theoretical speculation. Do the high scores on *initiating structure* indicate that this group of librarians, as supervisors, are more highly structured individuals than corporation presidents, aircraft engineers, or community leaders? Perhaps. All that can be legitimately said is that the scores indicate subordinates in this study *perceived* their supervisors as behaving in ways more likely to initiate structure and bring order to their work groups than in ways which would increase the sense of group well-being. Nonprofessional library workers perceived more strongly the structuring behavior of their leaders than professionals.

TOWARD A DESCRIPTIVE BEHAVIORAL MODEL OF LIBRARY LEADERSHIP

Instead of attempting to explain the research data in terms of subordinate psychological motivation, it may be more useful to view the data as indicators of situational or environmental phenomena in libraries. While it is generally agreed that the relationship between leader behavior and organizational outcomes, such as performance, has not been discovered, there is some evidence to suggest that situational factors do predict leader behavior (Filley et al., 1976).

This seems particularly true when the relationship between rules and library service is considered. Ours is a field permeated with rules. There are cataloging rules, filing rules, standard practice manuals, and shelf-listing rules. Although the rules change from time to time, they are always an integral and necessary part of any library's operation. As libraries mechanize, a whole new set of rules for computerized data entry are superimposed upon the rules for manual processing. Rules and procedures are necessary because accuracy and consistency are vital to a system whose primary function is speedy retrieval of information. The high scores on the *structure* scale perhaps reflect the leaders' ability to insure consistency in library service.

In addition to internal pressures for accuracy and consistency library leaders must also respond to pressures placed upon the organization from the environment.

If it is assumed that part of the leader's task is to adjust the organization's structure and processes to meet demands placed on the organization by changes in the environment, then it also can be assumed that an increase in the rate of change in the environment requires corresponding increases in the rate of structural adjustment. Libraries are undergoing unprecedented changes during this last quarter of the century. In the past libraries could respond to change without changing basic organizational structures because the environmental change was primarily one of volume. Such change could be met by adding or subtracting resources. If circulation went up, the library added more staff or, perhaps, automated the system. If the periodical budget was cut, subscriptions were allowed to lapse. Now, however, libraries are confronted with change to which the library and its leaders can only respond by fundamental changes in the organization's objectives, structures, and processes. The on-line cataloging revolution and other technological developments cannot be adequately met by doing more or less of the same old thing. Specialized service demands from ethnic, aged, or handicapped citizens cannot be met by merely hiring another reference librarian. Libraries are undergoing unprecedented change, demanding equally unprecedented adjustments to traditional structures and processes.

It is the rapidly changing environment in which libraries find themselves that requires library leaders to respond by initiating structural changes within their subordinate groups. Leaders cannot respond to complex environmental change without changing task emphasis, task structure, roles, and relationships. Because the supervisor is occupied with responding to change by changing procedures, the subordinate perceives the supervisor as engaging in structuring behaviors more often than in consideration behaviors. When environmental and technological change is stable, there is supervisory time for counseling, coaching, and praise. When change forces library leaders to alter plans, objectives, and organizational structures, more supervisory time must be given over to instructing staff in new tasks, in planning and policy making, and in developing new approaches to task accomplishment.

A hybrid model of leadership description based on these findings follows:

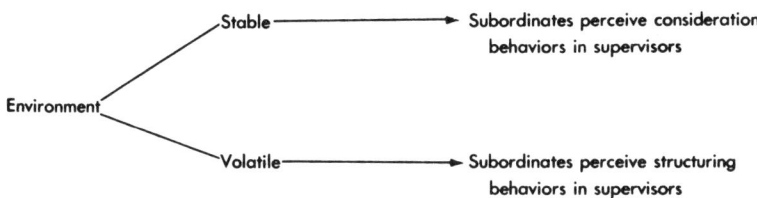

This discussion began with a quotation from Bennis. In it he despairs the fact that so much has been written about leadership, yet so little is known. In librarianship, little is written and less is known about supervisory leadership. It is important that research into libraries as organizations continue using behavioral science methodology to assure comparability with results obtained from other organizational research. Unless this kind of research is encouraged and supported, twenty years from now Bennis' statement, applied to library leadership, will still be true. Librarians need to recognize and test the universality of modern theories of leadership. It is possible that some may not survive the scalpel of empirical scrutiny, but their relevance to libraries must be presumed until proven otherwise.

It is hoped that this discussion has not only increased knowledge of the nature of library leadership but also has provided encouragement to those who would utilize behavioral science research techniques in their investigation of the library as a formal organization. The fact that libraries are unique social institutions with staff characteristics, clientele, and mission quite unlike any other is not in question. But, the library's leaders must plan, organize, control, and lead their organization in much the same way as leaders in hospitals, banks, insurance companies, or universities. If libraries are to continue being responsive to the needs of their clientele, then we need to learn as much as possible about how to effectively lead libraries toward desired goals. To do that it is first necessary to investigate the nature of leadership as it exists without evaluation. This is as good a time as any to begin.

REFERENCES

Bartol, K. M., and Wortman, M. S. (1975). Male versus female leaders—effects on perceived leader behavior and satisfaction in a hospital. *Personnel Psychology 28*, 533–554.

Bennis, W. G. (1959). Leadership theory and administrative behavior; the problems of authority. *Administrative Science Quarterly 4*, 259–301.

Buterfield, D. A., Powell, G. N., and Mainiero, L. A. (1978). Group performance effects on evaluations and descriptions of leadership behavior. *Proceedings of the Annual Meeting of the Academy of Management*, 50–54.

Dragon, A.C. (1976). "Self-Descriptions and Subordinate Descriptions of the Leader Behavior of Library Administrators." Unpublished dissertation, University of Minnesota.

Fiedler, F. E. (1967). "A Theory of Leadership Effectiveness." McGraw-Hill, New York.

Fiedler, F. E. (1973). Validation and extension of the contingency model of leadership effectiveness: A review of empirical findings. *In* "Readings in Organizational Behavior and Human Performance" (W. E. Scott and L. L. Cummings, eds.), pp. 468–485. Richard D. Irwin, Homewood, Illinois.

Filley, A. C., House, R. J., and Kerr, S. (1976). "Managerial Process and Organizational Behavior." Scott, Foresman and Company, Glenview, Illinois.

Fleishman, E. A. (1973). Twenty years of consideration and structure. *In* "Current Developments in the Study of Leadership" (E. A. Fleishman and J. G. Hunt, eds.), pp. 1–40. Southern Illinois University Press, Carbondale, Illinois.

Hollingsworth, T. A., and Mobley, W. H. (1978). Relationships among individual variables, organizational variables, performance and attrition in hospitals. *Proceedings of the Annual Meeting of the Academy of Management* 346–350.

House, R. J. (1973). A path—goal theory of leader effectiveness. *In* "Current Developments in the Study of Leadership" (E. A. Fleishman and J. G. Hunt, eds.), pp. 141–177. Southern Illinois University Press, Carbondale, Illinois.

Johns, G. (1978). A multivariate study of the absence from work. *Proceedings of the Annual Meeting of the Academy of Management*, 69–73.

Kerr, S., Schriescheim, C., Murphy, C. J., and Stogdill, R. M. (1974). Toward a contingency theory of leadership based on the consideration and initiating structure literature. *Organizational Behavior and Human Performance 12*, 62–82.

Lee, D. M., and Alvares, K. M. (1977). Effects of sex on descriptions and evaluations of supervisory behavior in a simulated industrial setting. *Journal of Applied Psychology 62*, 405–410.

Lowe, J. A. (1928). "Public Library Administration." American Library Association, Chicago, Illinois.

Mumford, L. Q., and Rogers, R. (1959). Library administration in its current development. *Library Trends 7*, 357–367.

Petty, M. M., and Bruning, N. S. (1978). Leader behavior and subordinate attitudes as predictors of leader effectiveness and agency ineffeciency in public welfare agencies. *Proceedings of the Annual Meeting of the Academy of Management*, 357–360.

Schriescheim, C. A., and Kerr, S. (1977). Theories and measures of leadership: A critical appraisal of current and future directions. *In* "Leadership: The Cutting Edge" (J. G. Hunt and L. L. Larson, eds.), pp. 9–45. Southern Illinois University Press, Carbondale, Illinois.

Stinson, J. E. (1977). The measurement of leadership. *In* "Leadership: The Cutting Edge" (J. G. Hunt and L. L. Larson, eds.), pp. 111–116. Southern Illinois University Press, Carbondale, Illinois.

Stogdill, R. M. (1948). Personal factors associated with leadership—a survey of the literature. *Journal of Psychology 25*, 35–71.

Stogdill, R. M. (1963). "Manual for the Leader Behavior Description Questionnaire—Form XII." Bureau of Business Research, Ohio State University, Columbus, Ohio.

Stogdill, R. M. (1974). "Handbook of Leadership." McGraw-Hill, New York.
Stogdill, R. M., and Coons, A. E., eds. (1957). "Leader Behavior: Its Description and Measurement." Bureau of Business Research, Ohio State University, Columbus, Ohio.
Wren, D. A. (1972). "The Evolution of Management Thought." Ronald Press, New York.

Part IV
PARTICIPATION

Introduction

The idea that shared decision making is essential to ensure organizational productivity has been, until very recently, one of the more enduring characteristics of management theory. Librarians particularly have been attracted to this form of management. As professionals, librarians believe they have much to contribute to whatever important policy decisions are to be made.

As the writers in this section point out, there are many ways for an organization to engage in shared decision making. While not willing to accept the whole package of participatory management (under which "shared decision making" can be subsumed), library administrators have found limited use of this form of management. Some degree of participation in decision making, however small, is employed by every administrator. However, it is the emphasis placed on participation by both administrators and staff that determines its ultimate success in helping or hindering an organization's achievement of its goals.

The potential success of shared decision making in various library contexts has not been subjected to much investigation; as Louis Kaplan's article clearly indicates. While there have been numerous exhortations on the subject by librarians, little is known about how library decision making is actually carried out. Kaplan's desire to see some theoretical justification for the employment of shared decision making is a point well taken, although understanding how decision making works in all types of libraries (not just academic libraries) is equally important.

Interestingly enough, one of the most acceptable forms of shared decision making, among librarians is MBO or Management By Objectives. There appear to be several reasons for this. MBO does not necessarily require substantial group involvement in decision making: it can often be exercised on a one-to-one basis between supervisor and supervised. In addition, its reliance on formal methods of procedure may be appealing to some librarians, although MBO need not be quite as formal as usually exists in non-library organizations. However, as James Michalko's classic article points out, successful implementation of MBO in a library may be more complex than first imagined. While MBO can indeed be reduced to a one-to-one negotiation process, its real usefulness can only be assessed after careful analysis of the existing managerial style in the library, although one may disagree with Michalko's assertion that MBO is more a managerial style than a set of techniques. An important question to be asked, and one not frequently asked, is whether the library employees really want to participate in decision making through MBO or any other similar mode of management. Difficult questions must be asked in a library before wholesale adoption of any "one best way" of decision making can take place, and Michalko suggests the form these questions might take.

The most common way in which shared decision making is implemented in libraries is committee management. Yet, what makes a committee effective? Sociologists and managerial theorists have long showed an interest in this subject. A. C. Filley, the non-librarian author in this section, describes typical characteristics of a committee in terms of size, influence relationships, and the various roles played by committee members. He then suggests guidelines, based on this research to improve committee effectiveness. His article reflects a new direction for library researchers, which can substantially contribute to more effective library management.

The use of shared decision-making administrative techniques cannot be viewed in a vacuum. Many other organizational variables will impact on the success or failure of such techniques. The idea of shared decision making and participation as panaceas to organizational problems has been replaced by a more objective view that such strategies are only tools. And, as with all tools, they must be used in the right situations and applied correctly if they are to be effective.

On Decision Sharing in Libraries: How Much Do We Know?

By Louis Kaplan

In recent years empirical studies have begun to appear on the decision sharing practices of executives in health and welfare agencies and managers in industrial firms. Two tentative conclusions can be drawn: (1) The typical high-level manager who has been studied does not employ a single decision making style but permits the circumstances to dictate whether a decision shall be one-sided, consultative, or delegative; (2) a considerable amount of decision sharing is permitted with subordinates. Similar and more extensively conceived research is needed on decision sharing in libraries; to this end a number of research problems are indicated. Additionally, several hypotheses are offered to provide the beginnings of a conceptual foundation for future research.

IN HIS BOOK ON THE LIFE OF THE AMERICAN SLAVE Genovese writes that the "Mammies" in the "Big House" acted the part of a "surrogate mistress," barking out orders, settling disputes among the servants in the mansion, and serving as "confidante to the children, the mistress and even the master." Among her other duties she taught the "courtesies to the white children as well as to those black children destined to work in the 'Big House!'"[1]

Power sharing, which Genovese is describing, takes various forms: delegation of authority is one; making decisions jointly between superior and subordinate is another; still a third kind takes place when a subordinate, permitted to give advice, exerts a decisive influence on a decision. In this essay answers to two important questions will be sought: How frequently is each of the decision-sharing styles employed, and what determines the choice of style?

In recent years empirical studies have begun to appear on the decision-sharing practices of executives as well as on their attitudes toward sharing. Two major conclusions can be drawn from this literature. First, an executive does not employ a single style; depending on the circumstances, some of the decisions may be one-sided, while others may be delegated. Still others might be made

---

Reprinted by permission of the American Library Association from "On Decision Sharing in Libraries: How Much Do We Know?," Louis Kaplan, *College and Research Libraries*, 38, pp. 25-31, copyright © 1977 by the American Library Association.

jointly. As one scholar has written, "It makes more sense to talk about participative and autocratic situations than it does to talk about participative and autocratic managers."[2]

The second conclusion (more tentative than the first) is that despite popular belief in the unbreakable chain of command in hierarchically structured organizations, superiors permit a considerable amount of influence to their subordinates. These conclusions will surprise those who still think of administrators in monolithic terms, yet much research has been published that is destructive of the monolithic image. Some executives, for example, are "people" oriented, while others are "task" oriented.[3] Higher-level managers, we are informed, have a stronger desire for "power and authority in their position than do lower-level managers."[4] Among managers in differentiated positions all showed a strong desire to lead and to direct, but these desires were strongest among those in charge of sales and weakest among the presidents of the manufacturing companies studied.[5] Even more noteworthy is the report that "inner-directed" persons (those whose conduct is not dominated by the desires of others) have been promoted to high positions in organizations.[6]

A Note on Terminology

In order to avoid the monotonous use of the term "decision sharing," two alternatives are employed, namely, "influence sharing" and "power sharing." Though not synonymous, the interchangeable use of these three terms within the meaning of this essay should not cause confusion. The terms, "executive," "administrator," and "manager," have taken on separate meanings, but the differences have little significance for this essay; for this reason these three terms, along with the word "leader," will be used as the context dictates.

STUDIES ON THE EXTENT OF POWER SHARING

Two major studies have been published describing the power sharing practices of high-level American managers. One, by Heller, deals with 260 "senior" managers in fifteen large "successful" manufacturing firms.[7] Though holding top-level positions, the subjects in this study were not presidents of their firms. The decisions of the subjects (as reported by themselves) related to their own work and to the work of their immediate managerial subordinates. The other publication, by Vroom and Yetton, tells of the decisions recalled by 268 managers "from a number of different firms."[8] As might be expected, the authors of these studies each employed a distinctive continuum of decision styles; nevertheless, a meaningful comparison of the two is possible.

Heller's continuum includes five styles, two of which encompass one-sided decisions made without prior consultation. These two are clearly outside the scope of influence sharing. His third style is also one-sided, but this kind of decision is not made until after consultation. The fourth is dyadic, that is, both managers have approximately equal influence. Delegation is the fifth style in this continuum.

In the continuum constructed by Vroom and Yetton there are also five styles. The fifth, different from any found in Heller, is described below. In two of these styles, one-sided decisions are made without prior consultation. In the remaining two the decision is not made until after consultation: In one of these the subordinates are consulted individually; in the other they are consulted in a group.

Heller indicates that of the decisions made by the "senior" managers, 73 percent were one-sided, but of these 37 percent were preceded by consultation. The remaining 27 percent were either dyadic or delegated. In the interpretation of these statistics much depends on whether prior consultation is regarded as a kind of power sharing. In part, the answer rests on how often the subordinate managers "steered" the ultimate decision. On this point (as shown later), Heller can offer only an educated guess.[9]

In one respect, the executives studied by Vroom were much like those reported on by Heller: About three-fourths of their decisions were one-sided. However, of these, about 51 percent were made only after consultation (compared to 37 percent in the Heller study). The remaining 28 percent fell within Vroom's fifth style of decision making. In this style the superior sits with the subordinates, but does not try (at least openly) to steer the decision. In this setting the leader may define the problem or even indicate alternative solutions. When this happens, the decision cannot be said to have been delegated. More properly, when the superior participates to that extent, the decision is better described as dyadic. Actually, Vroom's fifth style is much like Heller's fourth and fifth in combination, and interestingly these were used with equal frequency.[10]

In his oft-cited book on management, Likert decried all one-sided decisions, including those that were delegated.[11] Because he favored the dyadic, Likert would have approved of Vroom's fifth style only if the superior openly and fully shared in the making of decisions.

When and Why Do Superiors Permit Decision Sharing?

On the question as to when and why leaders permit influence sharing, Heller's work opens new vistas. His findings are best understood when classified as organizational or personal.[12] With regard to the organizational factors, Heller presented the following:

1. If the decision is perceived to be of great importance to the organization, the superior is likely to use a one-sided style.
2. If the decision is perceived to be important to the subordinate, the senior will likely use one of the three less autocratic styles.
3. If the decision is believed to be of greater significance to the senior than to the subordinate, a one-sided decision is likely to be made.
4. The greater the senior's "span" of control, the more likely will a time-saving style be employed, that is, autocratic or delegative.

Heller's findings are in part confirmed by Blau, who investigated fifty-three employment agencies in the United States.[13] The greater the risk, said Blau, the more reluctant would management be to delegate decision making. What is more, there is a tendency to decentralize authority when the "large size of an organization expands the volume of managerial decisions beyond the capacity of the top executive and his deputy."[14] Blau saw risk and size as the source of conflicting forces, size promoting decentralization of authority while risk worked in the opposite direction.[15]

According to Vroom, the most significant determinant of power sharing is the information needed to make a decision. If the senior believes no additional information is needed, a one-sided style is likely to be employed. If, however, the senior believes that the subordinate has information necessary to the decision, a participative style is likely to be permitted.[16]

As to personal factors that shape the making of decisions, Heller reported:

1. When the senior perceives the skills of the subordinate to be inadequate, an authoritative style is likely to be used.
2. The greater the experience of the senior, the more likely will a power-sharing style be employed.
3. The older the senior, the more likely will a decision sharing style be employed.[17]

Additional Studies Bearing on Power Sharing

In a study of the "authoritarian" personality in organizations, Vroom noted that in a parcel-delivery company supervisors who were submissive had the least interest in sharing power.[18]

In their attitude towards participation American managers were found to be little different from those in England, but the Americans revealed less confidence in the skills of their subordinates.[19] As already indicated, the perception of skills in subordinates, according to Heller, is an important factor in power sharing.

Students of organizational behavior have noted that the expectations of subordinates sometimes result in a larger degree of influence.[20] Professional employees present a good example. Professors, according to Blau, exert much influence on educational policy in some universities.[21] Those in the "semi-professions" (such as nurses and librarians), according to Hall, could expect to wield less influence than those in the more highly regarded professions. Furthermore, according to Hall, professionals in autonomous organizations (as opposed to those in organizations whose chief reports to a higher authority) perceive a greater amount of autonomy.[22]

Hage and Aiken, who studied sixteen health and welfare agencies, wrote that power sharing is more likely found in those organizations with a larger number of occupational specialties and where the employees have received more extensive professional training.[23] Blankenship and Miles investigated power sharing and autonomy among 190 managers in eight organizations (mainly in the electronics industry). On the question of their opportunities to influence decisions, 67 percent of those in the upper levels of management replied in the affirmative, compared to 51 percent of those in the middle range, and to 29 percent of those in the lower levels. Eighty percent of the upper-level managers compared to 40 percent of the middle and lower managers reported freedom to make "ultimate" decisions.[24]

In still another study, Mechanic affirmed that subordinates can win power by possession of expert knowledge or through propinquity to those in command.[25] An example of this is the administrative assistant to a chief librarian.

RESEARCH NEEDS

Two styles in the continuum used by Heller require further explication. These are "prior consultation" and "delegation." As Sherman has noted, it is important to identify the specific kind of delegation in question: Is it authority granted without accountability?[26] Heller has more recently come to see the need to identify delegation more precisely; he would distinguish between delegation that calls for immediate or delayed accountability.[27] On occasion, superiors delegate to subordinates the task of gathering information: Is this to be construed as a form of prior consultation? As for "prior consultation," is it possible clearly to differentiate between this style and decisions made jointly?

Heller writes that senior and subordinate managers had different perceptions of the styles of decisions being employed even though they were both reporting on the same decisions. Sometimes, for example, if the senior reported a one-sided decision preceded by consultation, the subordinate might report that decision to have been made jointly, or even delegated. Heller hypothesized that subordinates yearn for more influence than is permitted, which would account for the differences in perception.[28] But an additional explanation is possible, namely, that there was no clear understanding of the different styles.

In a study of managerial attitudes in a number of countries, Haire showed that American and English managers were favorably disposed toward participation; Haire then went on to claim, without evidence, that there was a gap between the stated attitudes of the Americans and their actual behavior, which, according to Haire, was generally authoritative. Haire explained the gap by pointing to the American democratic creed that effectively shut off public expression of undemocratic opinions.[29] But despite Haire, Heller found that the Americans and the English used his various decision styles with approximately the same frequency.[30] To this evidence Haire could reply that neither, on the record, is particularly democratic, considering that of the decisions made, little more than 25 percent were indisputably nonautocratic.

One of the weaknesses of the investigations by Heller and Vroom is that the managers were relied upon to recall the decision styles actually used. What is needed is studies in which decisions are recorded as they are made; unfortunately, gaining permission to do so is no simple matter. Heller's study, it is true, does lend partial credence to the accuracy of the reporting by the senior managers. Although he found other discrepancies between the reporting of the seniors and the subordinates, the two were in agreement with respect to the two autocratic styles (which were least likely to be misconstrued).[31]

Studies are needed on the subject of sharing decisions with groups as contrasted with individuals. Vroom distinguished between sharing a problem with subordinates separately or in a group, and he found that conferring with a group was preferred.[32] Within the process of consulting with a group is it possible to recognize a decision made jointly? If the superior clearly reveals a preference, can the outcome be regarded as dyadic? Based on a laboratory-type experiment, when the leader reveals a solution, the opinions of those in the group "coalesce."[33]

Heller studied only high-level executives. How different are those lower in the hierarchy? Do supervisors in libraries at lower levels experience little autonomy and few opportunities to give advice? And if so, what is the explanation? Is it true that top-level administrators are too busy coordinating and planning to monopolize the making of decisions? Is it possible that supervisors at the lower levels, less occupied, have more time for decisions?

In a study of library departments, Lynch attempted (without success) to find a meaningful relationship between degree of "routinization" and the amount of discretion given to workers.[34] Lynch attempted to measure discretion through worker responses. Perhaps a study such as Heller conducted, that is, based on supervisory decisions, might yield more positive results.

Heller has shown that managers in industry responsible for personnel work are less willing to share power than are those in production.[35] From this point of view a study of catalog departments might be especially revealing: Here is found a high degree of routinization and workers engaged in production.

Tannenbaum claims with respect to industrial workers in the U.S. that though they lack control of broad policy issues, "they do have informal influence through superiors concerning aspects of their daily work life."[36] Can the same be said of librarians? If not, is it unionization that accounts for the difference?

In a continuum conceived prior to Heller's, there were included those decisions that executives make tentatively, subject to discussion.[37] On a related point, Heller wrote that on the basis of an educated guess, "it is likely that up to half the decisions following consultation reflect the subordinate's influence."[38] On this point empirical evidence would be welcome, as would knowledge of how frequently decisions made tentatively are revised following consultation.

Span of control has a special significance to librarians, given the large number of branch libraries that have been established. Where there is a large number of these do the branch librarians enjoy a considerable amount of autonomy? Is the situation different when the number is not large?

In profit-making firms, decisions involving risk must be frequently made. Does "risk" in the library setting play an important role in the choice of decision styles?

Currently, librarians are trying to promote participation. Is it possible to identify those models of participation (UCLA? Columbia? Cornell? Miami?) that are productive of the largest amount of decision sharing?

CONCLUSION

Two points of view are possible (given the present indeterminate state of knowledge) with respect to libraries as a type of organization: either libraries are greatly different, or else they have much in common with other organizations.

My view is that libraries have fewer differences than similarities: among the significant similarities are a complex and hierarchical structure, a variety of professional specialties, and a mixture of professionals, subprofessionals, and nonprofessionals. Obviously, if these similarities are indeed significant, then libraries have much in common not only with hospitals and social work agencies, but with many industrial firms as well.

The question of differences and similarities has significance only because some persons argue that decision making in libraries bears no relationship or resemblance to most other organizations, and especially not to industrial firms. This is a matter that can be settled only through research, but it is not merely to settle this debate that research is needed.

Much of the library literature on participation, for example, could be explicated through a study of decision making styles among librarians. Still another example is the problem of autonomy for professionals (such as librarians) who work in heteronomous organizations. Is a lesser degree of autonomy inevitable for librarians? Is it possible, for example, that a democratic type of university administration will tend to produce the same kind of administration in that university's library? And still another: given the importance of supervisors at the lower levels of management, do we not need to know their decision styles?

Finally, to answer the question found in the title of this essay: how much do we know about decision sharing in libraries? Empirically, we know very little, but before empirical research is pursued a theory of decision making in libraries is needed. To the ultimate development of such a theory the propositions that follow may constitute a contribution. As is required of the component parts of a theory, each can be tested:

1. For several reasons (such as lesser risk), high-level library administrators will be found to use autocratic decision styles proportionately less frequently than do their counterparts in industry.
2. Investigators will find that proportionately fewer autocratic decisions are made in the less "routinized" library departments and in those units where the nonprofessionals are not overwhelmingly greater in number than the professionals.
3. In libraries where regulations are largely codified, departmental chiefs will be found to delegate a large proportion of those decisions that relate to the implementation of policies previously established. This proposition is based on Blau's study of the positive relationship of written regulations to nonautocratic styles.[39]
4. The greater the number of branch libraries and the greater the distances involved, the more frequently will the heads of branch libraries find decision making delegated to them.
5. Investigators will verify that there is no necessary clash between decision sharing and hierarchical structure. Tannenbaum, on the basis of empirical evidence, states that participation has a "mitigating effect" on authority in hierarchies and that in "effective participative" organizations superiors and subordinates are both influential even though there is a high total amount of control.[40]

REFERENCES

1. Eugene D. Genovese, *Roll, Jordan, Roll* (New York: Pantheon Books, 1972), p.355–56.
2. Victor H. Vroom, "A New Look at Managerial Decision Making," *Organizational Dynamics* 1:77 (1973).
3. Cyril Sofer, *Men in Mid-Career* (Cambridge: Cambridge University Press, 1970), p.36. See also R. Blake and Jane Mouton, *The Managerial Grid* (Houston: Gulf, 1964).
4. Victor H. Vroom, *Motivation in Management* (New York: American Foundation for Management Research, 1965), p.28.
5. Vroom, *Motivation in Management*, p.23–24.
6. Edward E. Lawler and Lyman W. Porter, "Antecedent Attitudes of Effective Managerial Performance," *Organizational Behavior and Human Performance* 2:141 (1967).
7. Frank A. Heller, *Managerial Decision-Making* (London: Tavistock, 1971).
8. Victor H. Vroom and Philip W. Yetton, *Leadership and Decision-Making* (Pittsburgh: Univ. of Pittsburgh Pr., 1973), p.74–78.
9. Heller, *Managerial Decision-Making*, p.xvi, 106.
10. Vroom and Yetton, *Leadership and Decision-Making*, p.13, 139.
11. Rensis Likert, *New Patterns of Management* (New York: McGraw-Hill, 1961), p.229.
12. Heller, *Managerial Decision-Making*, p.xvi–xx, 83–84, 105–8.
13. Peter M. Blau, "Decentralization in Bureaucracies," in Mayer N. Zald, ed., *Power in Organizations* (Nashville: Vanderbilt Univ. Pr., 1970), p.150–76.
14. Ibid., p. 168–69.
15. Ibid., p. 171.
16. Vroom and Yetton, *Leadership and Decision-Making*, p.83–84.
17. Heller, *Managerial Decision-Making*, p.xix.
18. Victor H. Vroom, "Some Personality Determinants of the Effects of Participation," *Journal of Abnormal and Social Psychology* 59:322–27 (1959).
19. Heller, *Managerial Decision-Making*, p.56.
20. Bruce R. Crowe, "The Effects of Subordinates' Behaviour on Managerial Style," *Human Relations* 25:215–37 (1972).
21. Peter M. Blau, *The Organization of Academic Work* (New York: John Wiley, 1973), p.184–88.
22. Richard H. Hall, "Some Organizational Considerations in the Professional-Organizational Relationship," *Administrative Science Quarterly* 12:461–78 (1967).
23. Jerald Hage and Michael Aiken, "Relationship of Centralization to Other Structural Properties," *Administrative Science Quarterly* 12:72–92 (1967).
24. L. Vaughn Blankenship and Raymond E. Miles, "Organizational Structure and Managerial Decision Behavior," *Administrative Science Quarterly* 13:106–20 (1968).
25. David Mechanic, "Sources of Power of Lower Participants in Complex Organizations," *Administrative Science Quarterly* 7:249–64 (1962).
26. Harvey Sherman, *It All Depends* (University, Alabama: Univ. of Alabama Pr., 1966), p.82–87.
27. Frank A. Heller, "Leadership, Decision-Making, and Contingency Theory," *Industrial Relations* 12:189 (1973).
28. Heller, *Managerial Decision-Making*, p.xvii, 73.
29. Mason Haire, and others, *Management Thinking: An International Study* (New York: John Wiley, 1966), p.22, 172.
30. Heller, *Managerial Decision-Making*, p.84. For the comparison with the English managers, see Heller, "Leadership, Decision Making and Contingency Theory," p.196.
31. Heller, *Managerial Decision-Making*, p.73, 106.
32. Vroom and Yetton, *Leadership and Decision-Making*, p.139.
33. Bernard M. Bass, "Some Effects on a Group of Whether and When the Head Reveals His Opinion," *Occupational Behavior and Human Performance* 2:375–81 (1967).
34. Beverly P. Lynch, "A Framework for a Comparative Analysis of Library Work," *College & Research Libraries* 35:432–43 (1974).
35. Heller, "Leadership, Decision Making and Contingency Theory," p.197.
36. Arnold S. Tannenbaum, and others, *Hierarchy in Organizations* (San Francisco: Jossey-Bass, 1974), p.61.
37. Robert Tannenbaum, "How to Choose a Leadership Pattern," *Harvard Business Review* 36:95–101 (March/April, 1958).
38. Heller, *Managerial Decision-Making*, p.xvi.
39. Peter M. Blau, *The Structure of Organizations* (New York: Basic Books, 1971), p.115–19.
40. Tannenbaum, *Hierarchy in Organizations*, p.195, 205.

Management By Objectives and the Academic Library: A Critical Overview
By James Michalko

Large organizations have developed a variety of techniques to deal with the areas of planning, control, and evaluation. One method that has received much attention is management by objectives (MBO). This paper explores the concept of MBO and the system that follows from it. A general criticism of the MBO approach is given, and the relevant research on MBO is detailed. Finally, the possibilities for MBO in the academic library are explored with particular attention to the nature of library objectives and participative decision making in the library setting.

The MBO Concept

Management by objectives (MBO) has taken its place beside grid training, sensitivity training, operations research, game theory, systems analysis, computer simulation, and organization development as just one of the many techniques that have been suggested to improve the management of organizational activities. These techniques are supposed to move the organization toward greater operating efficiency and ultimate performance improvement by improving planning, control, or evaluation. MBO is an all-embracing concept for approaching these areas.

MBO has achieved general acceptance as a management approach. This acceptance is evidenced by the disconcerting number of definitions connected with it and the frequency with which it is mentioned in the library literature. Unfortunately, library-related references to MBO often carry with them from the management literature an uncritical enthusiasm or an unwarrantably narrow scope. The MBO concept properly refers to a way of managing, a style of managing. It is a way of practicing the basic management functions of planning, organizing, directing, and controlling [1].

The distinguishing characteristics of the concept are a results orienta-

---

Reprinted by permission of the University of Chicago Press from *Library Quarterly*, vol. 45, no. 3, pp. 235-52. © 1975 by the University of Chicago. All rights reserved.

tion and a particular view of human behavior. Peter Drucker, writing in 1954, first propounded this combination as the foundation of a philosophy of management [2, pp. 128–32]. The ability of this philosophy to improve performance was said to be a result of MBO's conversion of corporate needs into personal goals. His formulation is still the essential statement of the concept; others have added to the reasoning and logic of its foundations and expanded it into a formalized system. Behavioral principles and a results orientation remain the foundations of MBO. The importance of focusing on results has become so much a part of the management ethos that it is often taken as given. MBO, however, makes the objective-setting process overt. By facing the process squarely, MBO tries to resolve inconsistencies and misunderstandings before they are rooted in the organizational structure.

The specific concept of human behavior and motivation in MBO is derived from certain widely held theories. The underlying theories are Maslow's now-familiar hierarchy of needs [3, pp. 35–46] and Herzberg's identification of motivators and hygiene factors in the work environment [4]. The motivators, such as achievement and responsibility, are identified with Maslow's higher-level needs, while hygiene factors such as salary and working conditions are related to the lower levels of the need hierarchy.

MBO also draws on McGregor's theory of management styles and Likert's views on participation. McGregor's Theory Y holds that work is natural and that employees, if properly motivated, become achievement oriented [5, pp. 47–48]. In this theory, "properly motivated" is translated "committed." Likert's participative style of leadership [6, pp. 3–11] is adopted as the method of fostering commitment to objectives. The MBO concept actively supports these theories in its implementation. It assumes the desire of workers to satisfy their higher-level needs on the job, and takes the position that they have the desire to get results. Moreover, they will assume responsibility and satisfactorily control their own performance if given the opportunity. The practice of MBO involves employees in the planning and control of their jobs. The MBO assumption is that such involvement fosters commitment, and that commitment motivates employees to channel their efforts in a way that will effectively contribute to the achievement of organizational objectives.

The MBO System and Its Benefits

The implementation of the MBO concept is a process by which all members of the organization set its goals. Each member in conjunction with his superior sets his goals in his area of responsibility. The results expected are stated in these objectives, and appropriate performance measures are agreed on. These measures permit the guidance of his work unit and act as standards against which his contribution to the total organization can be evaluated. Thus there are "four basic components of any MBO system: setting objectives, developing action plans, conducting periodic reviews and appraising annual performance" [1, p. 26]. Each of these basic components can be exploded into a variety of steps, techniques, and methods. Forms, diagrams, and handbooks can formalize the individual interpretation. The particulars of each component need not be examined in order to discuss the major organizational benefits that the MBO system claims.

Proponents of MBO commonly claim seven benefits. These are improvements in management performance, planning, coordination, control, flexibility, superior-subordinate relationships, and personal development [1, pp. 29–30; 7, pp. 54–68]. Of course, the exact area and the degree of improvement will vary from organization to organization because of the wide latitude permitted varying styles in the MBO concept. Yet such benefits as are claimed are viewed by proponents to follow quite logically from a well-conceived and determined effort to implement MBO. Recognizing the dangers of generalizing about a system that permits such variation, I will examine the logic and assumptions that underlie the range of proposed benefits.

The major benefit of improved management performance stems from increased managerial efficiency. MBO increases managers' commitment to organizational objectives by having the people responsible for the achievement of objectives set them individually. Once the manager and his superior agree on the goals and their means of attainment, the subordinate receives fast and accurate feedback about his progress in order to take corrective action. Thus, performance improvement comes from increased commitment through participation in goal setting, communication with superiors, accurate feedback, and a sense of direct responsibility.

Improvement in planning results because attention to the entire range of organizational objectives is demanded by the MBO process. Individual manager's goals are made consistent with one another and with organizational objectives as they are discussed with superiors. This mutual discussion includes agreement on the resources and assistance necessary to achieve objectives and thus can provide the basis for more effective coordination of the entire organization. Similarly, improved flexibility results from the manager's knowledge of his objectives and their priority for him and the organization. Feedback on progress can mean quicker attention to deviations, and the development of action plans will necessarily include anticipation of problem areas. Because objectives that depend on performance in other areas are outlined in the goal-setting process, contingency objectives can be created to improve the flexibility of the organization's responses.

Improvements in superior-subordinate relationships are expected because of the increased communication and participation during the objective-setting process and the more frequent feedback concerning progress that comes from the periodic performance appraisals. Because the appraisal focuses on demonstrable progress toward objectives, the superior can devote his energy to supporting his subordinates' progress and disassociate himself from subjective appraisals of personality and attitude. Such open communication and support, in satisfying his needs, moves the manager to commit his best efforts to the requirements of the organization. Similarly, MBO can encourage personal development through its fostering of personal responsibility. The will to perform more effectively can lead managers to acquire skills or knowledge that they lack. Personal-development objectives can even become part of the manager's formulation of his job.

Thus the organizational benefits of MBO reside partially in the process itself; the setting of objectives and the discussion with superiors, by eliminating duplication and inconsistencies, lead rather directly to better planning, control, coordination, and flexibility. The actual implementation of the process determines the extent of improvements in performance, superior-subordinate relations, and personal development. The style of the performance appraisal, the superior's sensitivity and concern, and the participation of the individual will affect the success of MBO in these areas. We should recognize that the type and extent of improvement depend not only on the basic steps in the MBO system but on the daily workings of the system. Despite these qualifications, the claims of MBO rest primarily on the combination in the MBO concept of a results orientation with specific theories of human behavior and motivation.

Criticism of MBO Foundations

The concept of management by objectives draws on the motivational theories of Maslow and Herzberg for its view of human behavior. Maslow's hierarchy of needs was not originally intended to apply to work motivation. It was Herzberg's two-factor theory of motivation that identified the higher-level needs of Maslow with motivators such as responsibility, achievement, and recognition. This theory changed the emphasis in efforts to motivate workers. Previously, when faced with a morale problem, employers responded with better pay, fringe benefits, or improved working conditions. According to Herzberg, this manipulation of "hygiene" factors could prevent dissatisfaction but would not lead to satisfaction. Real motivation of personnel was now thought to come only from a challenging job with opportunities for achievement, recognition, responsibility, and growth.

Herzberg's theory, while widely accepted, has also been severely criticized, especially in the work of Victor Vroom [8]. The results Herzberg obtained are thought to depend on the critical-incident methodology he used, and a recent study, using his own methodology, obtained results different from that predicted by his theory [9]. Although Herzberg's theory has substantially contributed to the understanding of work motivation, it is really a theory of job satisfaction and not a comprehensive theory of work motivation. The complex human motivational process is oversimplified by Herzberg's model, and the unwarranted equation of job satisfaction with improved performance is often drawn from it.

Although tempting, it is misleading to view job satisfaction and job performance in a cause-effect relationship. Locke, in a review paper, concludes that "satisfaction should be regarded primarily as a product of performance ... and only very indirectly as a determinant of performance" [10, p. 498]. Herzberg's, and consequently MBO's, view of human behavior is seriously disputed. The major danger in relying on this theory to explain motivation is the unconscious neglect of numerous other variables that affect the degree of motivation and ultimate performance.

Recent theories of motivation are much more complex and explanatory than Herzberg's model. None of these theories views job satisfaction as the determinant of job performance. Only three of the more prominent theories will be mentioned here, not to explain worker motivation but to suggest the range of variables that affect performance.

Vroom, one of Herzberg's serious challengers, offered an alternative model that has been called the valence model [8]. This model is built on the concepts of valence, expectancy, and force. Valence means the strength of an individual's preference for a certain outcome; it can be thought of as incentive or attitude. A positive valence means that the individual prefers attaining the outcome to not attaining it. The other input into valence is the instrumentality of a first-level outcome in obtaining a desired second-level outcome. If an individual desires advancement and feels that good performance is a large factor in achieving it, then his first-level outcomes are degrees of performance and the second-level outcome is advancement. The valance of performance is positive because it is viewed as instrumental in obtaining the second-level outcome of promotion. The concept of expectancy relates an individual's efforts to the first-level outcome. It is the probability that an action or effort will lead to a first-level outcome.

Vroom's theory stresses the individual differences in work motivation, since each individual has a unique combination of valences and expectancies. Unlike Maslow and Herzberg, it does not describe these differences. It does, however, indicate the conceptual determinants of motivation.

Another theory of motivation is the complex model of Porter and Lawler [11, p. 165]. They propose a multivariable model to explain the relationship between job attitudes and job performance. Like Vroom's, their model is based on an expectancy theory of motivation. The key variables are effort, performance, reward, and satisfaction. For our purposes, the most important implications of the model have to do with the satisfaction-performance relationship. Their model recognizes that satisfaction is determined by the rewards received and by the individual's perception of what reward *should* be received for a given performance level. Most important, the model makes satisfaction more dependent on performance than performance on satisfaction.

In contrast to Porter and Lawler's model, there is the relatively simple relational model of Smith and Cranny [12, p. 469]. They propose a three-way relationship between effort, satisfaction, and reward. Performance is at the center of this triangle and is affected only by effort. The feedback from performance can influence rewards and satisfaction, but only effort influences the level of performance. Smith and Cranny's model is a conceptual one that emphasizes the relations and dependencies of the major variables; it is not a comprehensive theory of motivation but a summary of the relations implied by the basic research of others.

Consideration of these theories of motivation highlights the undue simplicity of the Maslow and Herzberg formulation. Their theory is one of job satisfaction, not motivation and performance. Current thinking seriously challenges the cause-effect relationship between satisfaction and performance that the theory of Maslow and Herzberg implies. As a result, MBO's basic concept of human behavior and motivation must be considered overly simple and misleading.

MBO's Claim to Improve Performance

Although Maslow and Herzberg provide MBO with its basic concept of human work behavior, we have seen that MBO also draws on the Theory Y view of McGregor and the participative management style suggested by Likert. Thus the major claim of MBO to improve performance does not rest entirely on the efficacy of the Maslow and Herzberg theories but on a unique combination of factors based on all these theories. The relation that MBO makes explicit in practice is that improved performance comes from increased commitment to objectives. In the MBO system individual commitment is increased by two factors. The first is participation in goal setting and decision making. The second is the MBO appraisal method that is supposed to lead to better superior-subordinate communication; accurate, repeated feedback; and clarity of goals. We will consider these two factors separately.

The value of participation in decision making is an extremely complex issue. Whether participation is justified for its own sake on philosophical or moral grounds is not of interest to us. The simple hypothesis on which MBO operates is that participation affects the level of performance positively through the mediating attitude of commitment. This hypothesis has not been empirically proved. Lowin, in a review paper, says, "It is abundantly clear that any simplistic PDM [participative decision making] hypothesis is too gross to be proven or disproven" [13, p. 99]. His review of the literature demonstrates that research into the benefits of participation, in organizational and nonorganizational settings, has yielded only mixed results. The reason for these results, according to Lowin, is the myriad of intervening actor and environmental variables. Among the variables he mentions are the ego and financial motives of workers, the relevance and importance of participation, and the amount of information available to the subordinate [13, pp. 80–81].

The MBO appraisal method also represents a complex phenomenon. Under an MBO system, personality is supposed to be removed from the process by using mutually agreed upon goals as the critical measure. The communication, feedback, and clarity of goals generated in this process are presumed to increase the subordinate's acceptance of the appraisal and thus his use of it as an incentive to improve his performance. The simple assertion of the cause-effect does not, however, mean that an MBO appraisal creates these results. Again there are many intervening or underlying variables that could cause deviations from this ideal result.

There is a large body of relevant literature in psychology and personnel-management journals dealing with the performance-appraisal interview. Some of this research can help illuminate the conditions under which the MBO appraisal might have the desired effects. The research of French, Kay, and Meyer suggests that removing the feelings of threat from the appraisal can contribute to satisfaction and increased openness [14]. Lyons found that when the interview increases role clarity it reduces job tension [15]. Basset and Meyer found that a subordinate-prepared self-appraisal resulted in less defensive behavior and great perceived performance improvement [16]. And French, Kay, and Meyer found that when the interview turned criticism into specific future goals, there was a substantial effect on improved performance. In the same study, high normal levels of participation and high needs for independence were found to be significant variables in determining superior-subordinate relations and the acceptance of job goals [17, p. 18].

This research does not exhaust all the variables that are at work in the appraisal process, but it does suggest that the ultimate validity of MBO's appraisal rests in the complex interaction of the individual superior and subordinate. The MBO system of participative goal setting and an appraisal based on these goals are hardly enough to guarantee the increased commitment to objectives. This increased commitment could be fostered by a particular supervisor's understanding and subsequent handling of the interview process, but results will vary widely. Beyond the tenuous relation of the MBO appraisal to increased commitment, there is the danger of creating dysfunctional groups in the organization. If any particular supervisor uniformly mishandles his subordinates' appraisals, he can inadvertently create an atmosphere of tension and frustration in which a group could coalesce. In this case, the group of subordinates might bond together to commiserate and perhaps retaliate in some subtle way. The supervisor would have created, in the language of a famous study of group productivity, a group with high cohesiveness and negative induction [18]. The creation of groups and the variety of effects they might have on the organization are not explicitly considered in the MBO concept. Thus, while MBO appraisal might work under certain conditions, it could also have damaging effects on the organization under other conditions.

One critic of MBO has gone beyond these criticisms and suggested that the MBO performance-appraisal process is self-defeating over the long run [19, p. 126]. The inherent flaw in the process is the reward-punishment psychology that underlies the system and increases pressure on the individual while giving him only a limited choice of objectives. Improvement of the process would demand new attention to group processes and goal setting in the MBO system as well as appraisal of superiors by subordinates [19, pp. 131–32].

The preceding discussion reveals that management by objectives has its roots in a seriously challenged view of the path to improved performance. MBO's concept of motivation is disputable, its reliance on participation demands qualification, and its method of performance appraisal depends on variables not explicitly considered in the MBO concept. Moreover, the appraisal puts a burden of extreme sensitivity on the individual supervisor as well as ignoring the possibility of damaging group formation.

Although MBO is not often justified in terms of motivational theories other than that of Maslow and Herzberg, it is not necessarily incompatible with different motivation models. Raia explains how MBO, by clarifying the relation between first- and second-level outcomes and explicitly linking rewards and performance, can be consistent with the valence model of Vroom [20, pp. 95–96]. The important conclusion to be drawn from the criticism of MBO's foundations is that the MBO process is not as direct or as simply applied as it is often presented. One cannot conclude that MBO has no promise as a management style. It does, however, exist in the midst of conflicting research claims, and this puts a heavy burden of proof on empirical MBO research.

MBO Research

Existing MBO research is not prepared to shoulder the burden of proof that has been thrust upon it. Although articles about MBO are numerous, they are largely concerned with describing the process or imparting how-to hints. There are a number of anecdotal reports that describe the institution of MBO in an organization and relate the results. Humble offers a number of such company experiences [21]. For example, at the John Player and Sons tobacco division an MBO system was introduced with more than satisfactory results. Managers were said to be more aware of training needs and more appreciative of the need to monitor performance. Among the measurable improvements reported were higher machine output, reduction in rejected output, and a reduction in the time needed to fill orders [21, p. 59]. At the Colt Heating and

Ventilation Company, MBO was deemed responsible for better delegation, less interference by the boss, and new attention to long-range objectives [21, p. 45]. Moreover, suggestions elicited during the MBO process were said to be directly responsible for cost savings of £60,000 in a single year [21, p. 46].

Such accounts are, of course, suspect. Failures are not often detailed, and a single individual's account of a company-wide change, such as MBO, is bound to be biased, incomplete, and consequently inconclusive. The lack of hard research has not affected the number of corporations and government agencies that have tried or continue to use MBO. Among those who have used MBO or some variation of it are Rockwell Corporation, General Electric, Texas Instruments, the Royal Naval Supply and Transport Service (Great Britain), and the Department of Health, Education, and Welfare. Brady has effectively summarized the HEW experience [22].

Despite the variety of organizations that have used the MBO approach, very few rigorous organizational studies have been done. Raia's study of the Purex Corporation is the only identifiable study that has considered the question of performance improvement directly [23]. In this case there were significant improvements in production. Moreover, MBO worked well as perceived by plant and department managers. They felt there was better use of resources, better pinpointing of problem areas, a more objective measurement of performance, and improved communication [23, pp. 46–48].

Other studies have focused on critical procedural variables in the MBO system. Ivancevich, Donnelly, and Herbert found that need satisfaction increased among middle- and low-level managers when top management was responsible for starting MBO and when performance appraisals were done quarterly [24, pp. 148–49]. However, a follow-up study found that satisfaction later fell and attributed this to a lack of adequate reinforcement [25, pp. 132–35]. Carroll and Tosi confirmed that frequency of feedback, the amount of positive feedback, and the level of threat were key variables in the MBO appraisal method [26].

The results of the few available studies are mixed. Part of the cause may be the complex interactions that exist in organizational settings and the consequent inability to isolate effects. Although research has begun to explore the relationships among the many variables at work, it does not really focus on improved management performance. This lack of focus may be due to the underlying model in the MBO concept that equates improved satisfaction with improved performance. Sloan and Schreiber detail the inadequacies of available research and outline a variety of studies that would contribute to a rigorous evaluation of MBO. Among their suggestions are long-term, follow-up studies, a test of MBO against a "control" system that also critically examines and measures an organization's inputs and outputs, and using a control group of nonparticipants to isolate MBO effects [27].

Although research has not proved or disproved MBO claims, it has managed to discover a number of problem areas in the MBO system. In the Purex Corporation experience, Raia isolated five significant problems. They were (1) distortion of management philosophy, (2) uneven participation, (3) increased paperwork, (4) a slight decrease in goals, and (5) an emphasis on measurable areas [23, pp. 48–50]. In a later reexamination of the Purex program, Raia discovered that these problems still existed. His suggestion of the cause is not any particular element of the system, but a failure by individual managers to embrace and practice a philosophy of individual growth. These problems do not outweigh the many benefits that have accrued, but they keep the program from reaching its full potential [28, pp. 57–58].

Beyond the procedural problems that may arise in an MBO system, there might be structural factors blocking a successful implementation. Tosi and Carroll feel that successful subordinate-superior goal setting can occur only where influence can be and is significantly redistributed [29, p. 45]. In some cases management can manipulate organizational units and levels only slightly, thus making a redistribution impossible. Where influence is not shifted or cannot be shifted, MBO can cause great employee dissatisfaction. Thus MBO introduction demands either an understanding of structural constraints or the will to eliminate them. Detailed analysis or reorganization of this sort can be costly in both time and money.

The Academic Library and MBO

With the understanding that MBO is a complex process and that its impact on performance has limitations, we will explore the possibilities of MBO in the academic library. The first consideration is to determine if the library as an organization presents any absolute barriers to the use of MBO. Since the MBO approach does not depend on any specific type of enterprise, the only real barrier would be the inability to formulate appropriate objectives.

Discussing library objectives means involvement in the voluminous research on this subject as well as the subject of library performance measures. The literature on general library objectives is vast; Crum has outlined the literature and demonstrated its wide boundaries [30]. One of the most recent summaries indicates that progress is being made in formulating broad outlines of library objectives [31]. Such outlines are at the upper level of the hierarchy of objectives, are quite general, and really represent statements of grand design. It is in the refinement of broad objectives into key-result areas and performance measures that the library has difficulty.

The research in this area is ongoing and continually being rethought. DeProspo provides a good outline of the work on library performance measures [32, pp. 6–17]. Detailed, critical reviews of these efforts are beyond the scope of this paper. However, an examination of some portions of it is necessary to detail the central issues in creating a theoretical base of library performance measures. Before doing this, two general observations are in order.

The first concerns the role of systems analysis, operations research, cost/benefit analysis, and cost/effectiveness analysis in analyzing library operations. These techniques are such that they constitute a never-ending process. Refinement of objectives and new formulations of ultimate performance measures can continue outward from internal library operations to include wider and wider arenas of investigation. Such analysis is almost always a continuous process; its practical end corresponds to the limits on time and money rather than the theoretical resolution of the investigation. It is not clear that the search for library measures in terms of ultimate impact in the larger environment is profitable or even necessary. Lynch suggests that the library as a service organization responds to the larger environment and changes as it does [33]. This implies that, as the external environment changes, the nature of the library's impact on it will also change. Thus, even where analytic techniques could model performance measures based on the ultimate societal impact, they might not be generalizable from year to year or library to library.

The second observation concerns the restriction of analysis to internal operations. In this type of investigation, many processes can be modeled, performance measures derived, and satisfactory objectives arrived at. However, there remains a large portion of library operations consisting of personal interaction and service that can be modeled only tentatively. Even if certain portions of such personal services could be modeled, there would still remain a large portion whose ultimate impact would be unknown.

Turning to examples of library performance-measures research, consider the work of Morse [34] and that of Hamburg, Ramist, and Bommer [35] (especially Bommer's management system [36]). Morse's work clearly demonstrates that it is possible to model various library processes and derive objectives and performance measures. This successful modeling also demonstrates that certain other processes are difficult to model or evaluate adequately. His circulation model, for instance, uses as its performance measure the unsatisfied demand [34, pp. 67-68]. To improve the measure, one can manipulate the length of the loan period, the number of copies, or the reserve status of the book. This is, however, only one possible measure of effectiveness of a portion of the larger book-use problem. In addition, this represents a high-use situation that is more suited to statistical modeling. Morse says that ultimate book use is a "labyrinth of arguments" [34, p. 177]. He also acknowledges that many library processes have not been considered, especially those that are not hard quantifiable areas [34, p. 6]. Among these are browsing, reference, book purchase, research use, and research value. These represent more difficult areas to model, since they demand investigation beyond the library environment to determine their ultimate impact. Morse wisely chooses to concentrate on internal library operations.

Hamburg, Ramist, and Bommer, on the other hand, begin their analysis outside the library environment [35, pp. 109-11]. From this wide arena they argue back to a single, ultimate library objective and performance measure. The objective they arrive at is "to maximize the expected future exposure . . . to documents" [36, p. 262]. The performance measure based on this objective is one of item-use days. The thrust of their investigation is reasonable and seeks to satisfy the desire for a single overall measure of library effectiveness. However, it is not clear that actions based on this measure would be any different from those based on gross circulation statistics. A further problem is that this effectiveness measure cannot be used for comparisons between libraries, and only under special circumstances can it be used for year-to-year comparisons in any one library [36, pp. 51-52].

Such research efforts as these help reveal the interrelationships among various library activities and functions. They do not constitute an elegant model of library processes. They may even demonstrate the impossibility or undesirability of such a model. The difficulty in arriving at satisfactory, theoretically sound performance measures is not unique to the library or to nonprofit organizations. The private business sector is full of ongoing controversies over the best theoretical base for progress evaluation. In the area of financial management, for instance, there is a variety of opinion as to the appropriate mix of debt and equity capital for a firm in a particular business, and a similar controversy surrounds the capital-investment decision.

This difficulty aside, the library can and has outlined its essential services. It seems that the library is frustrated in attempts to quantify performance measures at the very broadest levels and at the very specific level. Certain intermediate processes have performance measures—for example, circulation. This state of affairs does not constitute a barrier to MBO. It may be a frustration in some instances and a blessing in others when using an MBO approach. For an MBO system, the important attributes of goals are that they be (1) mutually agreed upon and (2) verifiable. Bommer's program outline or Cornell's long-range action plans represent perfectly adequate starting points for objectives with these attributes [36, pp. 276-81; 37, pp. 143-55]. In addition, since one of the major MBO problems is an undue emphasis on quantifiable areas, the lack of such areas might prevent an MBO system from distorting library services.

Although the library has not considered MBO in its explicit formulation as an approach to planning, control, evaluation, and development [38], the attitudes toward participative decision making in the library may have direct implications for MBO possibilities in the library. Our purpose here is not to examine all aspects of participation in the library setting but to explore the impact it might have on MBO. The recent library literature reflects a special concern for this topic as well as certain assumptions about the value of participation. Marchant, for example, relates staff satisfaction to participation in decision making [39]. Goodman implies that satisfaction leads to improved performance [40]. A survey by Flener reports that staff liked and were interested in participation but does not explain why or how the staff should participate [41]. Kaser also suggests that the participation of professional staff is desirable, and explains that a peer group, faculty-like structure is the most promising method of participation [42].

All of these authors have explicit or implicit theories of motivation. These theories are, naturally, central to one's final evaluation of participation. Marchant is a follower of Likert, while Goodman accepts the self-actualization concept. Although the assessment of participation as good or bad is important, the method of participation is the real product that should be judged. Articles by DeProspo and Dutton suggest particular ways of involving the staff in decision making. DeProspo accepts McGregor's Theory Y and suggests a goals-methods performance appraisal (a type of MBO approach) [43]. Dutton explicitly suggests an MBO approach based on the traditional Maslow and Herzberg justification [44].

It is fairly clear that the library literature contains a great deal of enthusiasm for participative decision making. This enthusiasm is rarely tempered by an examination of the conflicts that exist over the value of participation and the limits of its effectiveness. Also, the collegial framework for participation that is suggested is naive in its assumptions about the library as an organization and the ultimate impact of participation structured in this way. The library is not, after all, involved directly in the faculty processes; it is a service organization whose effectiveness depends on the coordination of its members, not their independence. In the final analysis, an assessment of the value of participation depends on the ultimate goal desired, whether it is staff satisfaction or organizational effectiveness. As we have seen, the two are not necessarily related, although each may be a desirable goal in itself.

The stance the library should take in regard to participation is not a topic for this paper; what is important is to recognize that many discussions of participation in the library setting do not fully account for the complexity of the process or relate it to the mission of the library. The Lynch-Marchant exchange is an illuminating illustration of the issues [45, 46]. Marchant attempted to relate participation to library effectiveness but found an insignificant correlation. There was, though, a positive correlation with staff satisfaction. Lynch argued for alternatives to the Likert model used by Marchant and suggested the complexities of the relationship between satisfaction, participation, and performance.

The relation of MBO to the discussion of participation in the library is direct. We have seen that MBO can have a positive impact on staff satisfaction and that, where its complexities are recognized, it may lead to improved performance. Thus MBO might be a way to meet staff desires for participation and to meet the need for organizational effectiveness. MBO is based on participation, and it tries to make that participation particularly relevant by involving the employees in structuring their jobs—especially the tasks upon which they have immediate impact. A collegial approach would mean drastic changes in the library organizational structure as well as unknown effects on the organization's effectiveness. MBO would also change the organizational structure of the library, primarily by redistributing the influence over individual jobs, but its impact would likely be the improvements in planning, coordination, control, and flexibility that we noted earlier. This kind of participation would avoid staff involvement in policy setting, an area in which libraries have difficulty [47, pp. 31–32], without compromising the individual's role in determining the components of his job. This structuring of the immediate job can attain a broader relevance to the efforts of the entire library through attempts to make goals consistent with one another and to avoid duplication of effort. Thus, MBO provides a structure for participation in all relevant tasks as well as encouraging a broad, overall perspective on the library's services. Such a bridging of departmental boundaries could streamline the organization and provide a new perspective that emphasizes the importance of individual jobs. MBO, while far from the panacea for the participative dilemma, provides certain advantages that other schemes do not possess. Kaplan, in discussing participation, makes certain observations that are similar to the points we have made: participation in goal setting represents the best first step for the library moving toward participative management, the academic model for participation ignores the realities of organizational drives toward hierarchy, and any participative approach demands skill in implementation [48]. MBO seems to satisfy these demands well. It is a highly developed approach to participative goal setting, and it redistributes influence while maintaining a hierarchy of authority.

MBO's Utility for the Library

Having seen that the nature of library objectives does not bar the use of MBO, can this approach be recommended for the library? We think such a blanket recommendation is unwise. Our examination of MBO's foundations and of research into MBO has not yielded a clear-cut decision about the validity of MBO claims. The claim of improved performance has not been proved or disproved. Performance can improve as a result of MBO (if anecdotal reports or the Purex study are accepted), but the relationship is a complex one demanding appreciation for subtle interactions among individual personalities, attitudes, and the task at hand. Similarly, improvements in superior-subordinate relations are possible with an MBO system, but the major responsibility for success lies with the individual supervisor. The other MBO claims of improved planning, coordination, control, and flexibility seem more directly traceable to the use of MBO. These improvements occur as part of the self-examination of the organization's inputs and outputs and the detailed critical outlining of the various organizational processes. Here, perhaps, is the major reason that MBO has retained an attraction despite the conflicting theories and research surrounding it.

In the library setting, we have suggested that these benefits would represent a needed results orientation and a bridging of departmental concerns. Beyond these benefits, MBO could provide a sensible framework to meet the demands for a participative system that are so persistent in libraries. This last benefit is important only insofar as one judges participative decision making essential, necessary, or valuable in a given situation.

These benefits are admittedly attractive, but they would be limited in the library by structural constraints and existing procedural constraints. Structural considerations would restrict MBO to certain organizational levels and functional areas of the library. Functional areas would be limited to those where the attempt at quantification (of objectives and performance measures) would not distort service. Thus technical processes, plant operations, and circulation services would be good MBO candidates. Some parts of acquisition efforts might be managed by objectives—for example, book ordering. The area of reference services is a doubtful MBO possibility in any of its phases. Functional areas for MBO should be restricted to those where quantifiable, agreed-upon, verifiable objectives can be arrived at without serious distortion of services.

In terms of organizational levels, MBO will be restricted to middle management (section and department heads) of the library. MBO depends for its success on the individual's self-control of his job and performance evaluation based on final results. This level seems to be the lowest at which adequate responsibility for the management of final performance exists. The organizational levels that are managed by objectives should be limited to those where responsibility for final performance directly exists or can be adequately increased. This would imply that those involved in MBO would have some management skills or could and would like to be trained in these skills.

Procedural constraints will depend on the ultimate effects desired from MBO. For instance, rigid pay scales, an emphasis on seniority, or tightly prescribed work rules could respectively rule out connecting MBO with compensation, advancement, or personal development. Where such existing constraints are beyond the immediate ability of library management to change, the transition period could be made unduly difficult. With these constraints in mind, the conception of an MBO approach would be significantly changed. What was thought of as the coordination of shared responsibility throughout the organization would become in the library a way of managing managers.

Conclusion

Management by objectives in the library is a limited approach. Improved performance is related to the system only in an uncertain, tortuous way. The improvements in planning, control, and flexibility that accrue directly to the formal MBO process may be attainable through less formal examination of the organization's activities. As a participatory system, its level of applicability would be limited in the library and its consequent worth dependent on an individual assessment of formal participation as a management style.

Top management should be aware of these considerations when evaluating a formal MBO system. They should expect large expenditures of time, money, and planning effort as well as a difficult transition period. Only individual research by a library's management can assess these costs and weight them against the benefits that would result from their present combination of staff, services, and organizational efficiency. Such investigation, whether it resulted in the introduction of MBO or not, would certainly reveal some of the strengths and weaknesses of the current management style. MBO is, after all, a style and not a set of techniques. As a style, some of its central concepts may be profitably integrated with existing practices. One hopes such a conscientious examination would allow some of MBO's rigorous focus without risking the costs and pitfalls of the formal system.

REFERENCES

1. Reif, William E., and Bassford, Gerald. "What MBO Really Is." *Business Horizons* 16 (June 1973): 23–30.
2. Drucker, Peter F. *The Practice of Management.* New York: Harper & Bros., 1954.
3. Maslow, Abraham H. *Motivation and Personality.* New York: Harper & Bros., 1954.
4. Herzberg, Frederick; Mausner, Bernard; and Snyderman, Barbara Bloch. *The Motivation to Work.* New York: John Wiley & Sons, 1959.
5. McGregor, Douglas. *The Human Side of Enterprise.* New York: McGraw-Hill Book Co., 1960.
6. Likert, Rensis. *The Human Organization.* New York: McGraw-Hill Book Co., 1967.
7. Odiorne, George S. *Management by Objectives: A System of Managerial Leadership.* New York: Pitman Publishing Corp., 1965.
8. Vroom, Victor H. *Work and Motivation.* New York: John Wiley & Sons, 1964.
9. Schwab, Donald; Devitt, H. William; and Cummings, Larry L. "A Test of the Adequacy of the Two-Factor Theory as a Predictor of Self-Report Performance Effects." *Personnel Psychology* (Summer 1971), pp. 293–303.
10. Locke, Edwin A. "Job Satisfaction and Job Performance: A Theoretical Analysis." *Organizational Behavior and Human Performance* 5 (September 1970): 484–500.

11. Porter, Lyman W., and Lawler, Edward E., III. *Managerial Attitudes and Performance.* Homewood, Ill.: Richard D. Irwin, Inc., 1968.
12. Smith, Patricia Cain, and Cranny, C. J. "Psychology of Men at Work." *Annual Review of Psychology* 19 (1968): 467–96.
13. Lowin, Aaron. "Participative Decision Making: A Model, Literature Critique, and Prescriptions for Research." *Organizational Behavior and Human Performance* 3 (February 1968): 68–106.
14. French J. R. P., Jr.; Kay, E.; and Meyer, H. H. "Effects of Threat in a Performance Appraisal Interview." *Journal of Applied Psychology* 49 (October 1965): 311–17.
15. Lyons, T. F. "Role Clarity, Satisfaction, Tension and Withdrawal." *Organizational Behavior and Human Performance* 6 (January 1971): 99–110.
16. Basset, G. A., and Meyer, H. H. "Performance Appraisal Based on Self-Review." *Personel Psychology* 21 (Winter 1968): 421–30.
17. French, J. R. P., Jr.; Kay, E.; and Meyer, H. H. "Participation and the Appraisal System." *Human Relations* 19 (February 1966): 3–19.
18. Schachter, Stanley; Ellerston, Norris; McBride, Dorothy; and Gregory, Doris. "An Experimental Study of Cohesiveness and Productivity." *Human Relations* 4 (1951): 229–39.
19. Levinson, Harry. "Management by Whose Objectives." *Harvard Business Review* 48 (July–August 1970): 125–34.
20. Raia, Anthony P. *Managing by Objectives.* Glenview, Ill.: Scott, Foresman & Co., 1974.
21. Humble, John W., ed. *Management by Objectives in Action.* New York: McGraw-Hill Book Co., 1970.
22. Brady, Rodney H. "MBO Goes to Work in the Public Sector." *Harvard Business Review* 42 (March–April 1973): 65–74.
23. Raia, Anthony P. "Goal-Setting and Self-Control." *Journal of Management Studies* 2 (February 1965): 34–53.
24. Ivancevich, John M.; Donnelley, James H.; and Lyon, Herbert L. "A Study of the Impact of Management by Objectives on Perceived Need Satisfaction." *Personnel Psychology* 23 (Summer 1970): 139–51.
25. Ivancevich, John M. "A Longitudinal Assessment of Management by Objectives." *Administrative Science Quarterly* 17 (March 1972): 126–38.
26. Carroll, Stephen J., Jr., and Tosi, Henry L. "The Relationship of Characteristics of the Review Process to the Success of the 'Management by Objectives' Approach." *Journal of Business* 4 (July 1971): 299–305.
27. Sloan, Stanley, and Schreiber, David E. "What We Need to Know about Management by Objectives." *Personnel Journal* 49 (March 1970): 206–8.
28. Raia, Anthony P. "A Second Look at Goals and Controls." *California Management Review* 8 (Summer 1966): 49–58.
29. Tosi, Henry L., and Carroll, Stephen J., Jr. "Some Structural Factors Related to Goal Influence in the Management by Objectives Process." *MSU Business Topics* 17 (Spring 1969): 45–50.
30. Crum, Norman J. "Library Goals and Objectives: A Literature Review." ERIC 082 794. Washington, D.C.: Department of Health, Education, and Welfare, 1972.
31. Dionne, Richard J. "Review of the Formulation and Use of Objectives in Academic and Research Libraries." *ARL Management Supplement* 2 (January 1974): 1–4.
32. DeProspo, Ernest R. *Performance Measures for Public Libraries.* Chicago: Public Library Association, 1973.
33. Lynch, Beverly P. "The Academic Library and Its Environment." *College and Research Libraries* 35 (March 1974): 126–32.
34. Morse, Philip M. *Library Effectiveness: A Systems Approach.* Cambridge, Mass.: M.I.T. Press, 1968.
35. Hamburg, Morris; Ramist, Leonard E.; and Bommer, Michael R. W. "Library Objectives and Performance Measures and Their Use in Decision Making." In *Operations*

Research: Implications for Libraries, edited by Abraham Bookstein and Don R. Swanson. Chicago: University of Chicago Press, 1972.
36. Bommer, Michael R. W. "The Development of a Management System for Effective Decision Making and Planning in a University Library." Ph.D. dissertation, Wharton School, University of Pennsylvania, 1972.
37. McGrath, William E. "Development of a Long-Range Strategic Plan for a University Library: The Cornell Experience." ERIC 077 511. Ithaca, N.Y.: Cornell University Libraries, 1973.
38. Johnson, Edward R. "Applying Management by Objectives to the University Library." *College and Research Libraries* 34 (November 1973): 436-39.
39. Marchant, Maurice P. "Participative Management as Related to Personnel Development." *Library Trends* 20 (July 1971): 48-59.
40. Goodman, C. H. "Employee Motivation." *Library Trends* 20 (July 1971): 39-47.
41. Flener, J. G. "Staff Participation in Management in Large University Libraries." *College and Research Libraries* 34 (July 1973): 275-79.
42. Kaser, D. E. "Modernizing the University Library Structure." *College and Research Libraries* 31 (July 1970): 227-31.
43. DeProspo, Ernest R. "Personnel Evaluation as an Impetus to Growth." *Library Trends* 20 (July 1971): 60-70.
44. Dutton, B. G. "Staff Management and Staff Participation." *ASLIB Proceedings* 25 (March 1973): 111-25.
45. Lynch, Beverly P. "Participative Management in Relation to Library Effectiveness." *College and Research Libraries* 33 (September 1972): 382-90.
46. Marchant, Maurice P. "And a Response." *College and Research Libraries* 33 (September 1972): 391-97.
47. Holley, Edward. "Library Governance in Higher Education: What Is Evolving?" *ARL Minutes*, 80th meeting (May 1972), pp. 28-33.
48. Kaplan, Louis. "Participation: Some Basic Considerations on the Theme of Academe." *College and Research Libraries* 34 (September 1973): 235-41.

Committee Management: Guidelines from Social Science Research

By A. C. Filley

THE COMMITTEE is one of the most maligned, yet most frequently employed forms of organization structure. Yet despite the criticisms, committees are a fact of organization life. For example, a recent survey of 1,200 respondents revealed that 94 percent of firms with more than 10,000 employees and 64 percent with less than 250 employees reported having formal committees.[1] And, a survey of organization practices in 620 Ohio manufacturing firms showed a similar positive relationship between committee use and plant size.[2] These studies clearly indicate that committees are one of management's important organizational tools.

My thesis is that committee effectiveness can be increased by applying social science findings to answer such questions as:

- What functions do committees serve?
- What size should committees be?
- What is the appropriate style of leadership for committee chairmen?
- What mix of member characteristics makes for effective committee performance?

Committee Purposes and Functions

Committees are set up to pursue economy and efficiency within the enterprise. They do not create direct salable value, nor do they supervise operative employees who create such value.

The functions of the committee have been described by business executives as the exchange of views and information, recommending action, generating ideas, and making major decisions,[3] of which the first may well be the most common. After observing seventy-five conferences (which were also referred to as "committees"), Kriesberg concluded that most were concerned either with communicating information or with aiding an executive's decision process.[4] Executives said they called conferences to "sell" ideas rather than for group decision-making itself. As long as the executive does not manipulate the group covertly, but benefits by its ideas and screening processes, this activity is probably quite legitimate, for members are allowed to influence and to participate, to some extent, in executive decision-making.

Some committees also make specific operating decisions which commit individuals and organization units to prescribed goals and policies. Such is often the province of the general management committee composed of major executive officers. According to one survey, 30.3 percent of the respondents reported that their firms had such a committee and that the committees averaged 8.6 members and met 27 times per year.[5]

Several of the characteristics of committee organization have been the subject of authoritative opinion, or surveys of current practice, and lend themselves to evaluation through inferences from small-group research. Current practice and authoritative opinion are reviewed here, followed by more rigorous studies in which criteria of effectiveness are present. The specific focus is on committee size, membership, and chairmen.

Committee Size

Current Practice and Opinion

The typical committee should be, and is, relatively small. Recommended sizes range from three

---

© 1970 by the Regents of the University of California. Reprinted from *California Management Review*, volume XIII, number 1, pp. 13 to 21 by permission of the Regents.

to nine members, and surveys of actual practice seldom miss these prescriptions by much. Of the 1,658 committees recorded in the Harvard Business Review survey, the average membership was eight. When asked for their preference, the 79 percent who answered suggested an ideal committee size that averaged 4.6 members. Similarly, Kriesberg reported that, for the 75 conferences analyzed, there were typically five or six conferees in the meetings studied.[6]

Committees in the federal government tend to be larger than those in business. In the House of Representatives, Appropriations is the largest standing committee, with fifty members, and the Committee on Un-American Activities is smallest, with nine. Senate committees average thirteen members; the largest, also Appropriations, has twenty-three.[7] The problem of large committee size is overcome by the use of subcommittees and closed executive committee meetings. The larger committees seem to be more collections of subgroups than truly integrated operating units. In such cases, it would be interesting to know the size of the subcommittees.

Inferences from Small-Group Research

The extent to which a number is "ideal" may be measured in part in terms of the effects that size has on socio-emotional relations among group members and thus the extent to which the group operates as an integrated whole, rather than as fragmented subunits. Another criterion is how size affects the quality of the group's decision and the time required to reach it. Several small experimental group studies have evaluated the effect of size on group process.

Variables related to changes in group size include the individual's capacity to "attend" to differing numbers of objects, the effect of group size on interpersonal relations and communication, its impact on problem-solving functions, and the "feelings" that group members have about proper group size and the nature of group performance. To be sure, the effects of these variables are interrelated.

Attention to the Group.—Each member in a committee attends both to the group as a whole and to each individual as a member of the group. There seem to be limits on a person's ability to perform both of these processes—limits which vary with the size of the group and the time available. For example, summarizing a study by Taves,[8] Hare[9] reports that "Experiments on estimating the number of dots in a visual field with very short-time exposures indicate individual subjects can report the exact number up to and including seven with great confidence and practically no error, but above that number confidence and accuracy drop."

Perhaps for similar reasons, when two observers assessed leadership characteristics in problem-solving groups of college students, the raters reached maximum agreement in groups of six, rather than in two, four, eight, or twelve.[10]

The apparent limits on one's ability to attend both to the group and the individuals within it led Hare to conclude:

> The coincidence of these findings suggests that the ability of the observing individual to perceive, keep track of, and judge each member separately in a social interaction situation may not extend much beyond the size of six or seven. If this is true, one would expect members of groups larger than that size to tend to think of other members in terms of subgroups, or "classes" of some kind, and to deal with members of subgroups other than their own by more stereotyped methods of response.[11]

Interpersonal Relations and Communication.—Given a meeting lasting a fixed length of time, the opportunity for each individual to communicate is reduced, and the type of communication becomes differential among group members. Bales et al.[12] have shown that in groups of from three to eight members the proportion of infrequent contributors increases at a greater rate than that theoretically predicted from decreased opportunity to communicate. Similarly, in groups of from four to twelve, as reported by Stephen and Mishler,[13] size was related positively to the difference between participation initiated by the most active and the next most active person.

Increasing the group size seems to limit the extent to which individuals want to communicate, as well. For example, Gibb[14] studied idea productivity in forty-eight groups in eight size categories from 1 to 96. His results indicated that as group size increases a steadily increasing proportion of group members report feelings of threat and less willingness to initiate contributions. Similarly, Slater's[15] study of 24 groups of from two to seven men each working on a human relations problem indicated that members of the larger groups felt them to be disorderly and time-consuming, and complained that other members became too pushy, aggressive, and competitive.

Functions and Conflict.—An increase in group size seems to distort the pattern of communication and create stress in some group members, yet a decrease in group size also has dysfunctional effects. In the Slater study check-list responses by members rating smaller groups of 2, 3, or 4 were complimentary, rather than critical, as they had been for larger groups. Yet observer impressions were that small groups engaged in superficial discussion and avoided controversial subjects. Inferences from post hoc analysis suggested that small group members are too tense, passive, tactful, and constrained to work together in a satisfying manner. They are afraid of alienating others. Similar results have been reported in other studies regarding the inhibitions created by small group size, particularly in groups of two.[16]

Groups of three have the problem of an overpowerful majority, since two members can form a coalition against the unsupported third member. Four-member groups provide mutual support when two members oppose the other two, but such groups have higher rates of disagreement and antagonism than odd-numbered groups.[17]

The data reported above are not altogether consistent regarding the reasons for dysfunctional consequences of small groups. The "trying-too-hard-for-agreement" of the Slater study seems at odds with the conflict situations posed in the groups of three and four, yet both agree that for some reason tension is present.

Groups of Five.—While it is always dangerous to generalize about "ideal" numbers (or types, for that matter), there does appear to be logical and empirical support for groups of five members as a suitable size, if the necessary skills are possessed by the five members. In the Slater study, for example, none of the subjects felt that a group of five was too small or too large to carry out the assigned task, though they objected to the other sizes (two, three, four, six, and seven). Slater concluded:

> Size five emerged clearly . . . as the size group which from the subjects' viewpoint was most effective in dealing with an intellectual task involving the collection and exchange of information about a situation, the coordination analysis, and evaluation of this information, and a group decision regarding the appropriate administrative action to be taken in the situation. . . .

These findings suggest that maximal group satisfaction is achieved when the group is large enough so that the members feel able to express positive and negative feelings freely, and to make aggressive efforts toward problem solving even at the risk of antagonizing each other, yet small enough so that some regard will be shown for the feelings and needs of others; large enough so that the loss of a member could be tolerated, but small enough so that such a loss could not be altogether ignored.[18]

From this and other studies,[19] it appears that, excluding productivity measures, generally the optimum size of problem-solving groups is five. Considering group performance in terms of quality, speed, efficiency and productivity, the effect of size is less clear. Where problems are complex, relatively larger groups have been shown to produce better quality decisions. For example, in one study, groups of 12 or 13 produced higher quality decisions than groups of 6, 7, or 8.[20] Others have shown no differences among groups in the smaller size categories (2 to 7). Relatively smaller groups are often faster and more productive. For example, Hare found that groups of five take less time to make decisions than groups of 12.[21]

Several studies have also shown that larger groups are able to solve a greater variety of problems because of the variety of skills likely to increase with group size.[22] However, there is a point beyond which committee size should not increase because of diminishing returns. As group size increases coordination of the group tends to become difficult, and thus it becomes harder for members to reach consensus and to develop a spirit of teamwork and cohesiveness.

In general, it would appear that with respect to performance, a task which requires interaction, consensus and modification of opinion requires a relatively small group. On the other hand, where the task is one with clear criteria of correct performance, the addition of more members may increase group performance.

The Chairman

Current Practice and Opinion.—Most people probably serve on some type of committee in the process of participating in church, school, political, or social organizations and while in that capacity have observed the effect of the chairman on group progress. Where the chairman starts the meeting, for example, by saying, "Well, we all know each other here, so we'll dispense with any formality," the group flounders, until someone else takes a forceful, directive role.

If the committee is to be successful, it must have a chairman who understands group process. He must know the objectives of the committee and understand the problem at hand. He should be able to vary decision strategies according to the nature of the task and the feelings of the group members. He needs the acceptance of the group members and their confidence in his personal integrity. And he needs the skill to resist needless debate and to defer discussion upon issues which are not pertinent or where the committee lacks the facts upon which to act.

Surveys of executive opinion support these impressions of the chairman's role. The Harvard Business Review survey stated that "The great majority [of the suggestions from survey respondents] lead to this conclusion: the problem is not so much committees in management as it is the management of committees." This comment by a partner in a large management consulting firm was cited as typical:

Properly used, committees can be most helpful to a company. Most of the criticism I have run into, while probably justified, deals with the way in which committees are run (or committee meetings are run) and not with the principle of working with committees.[23]

A chairman too loose in his control of committee processes is by no means the only difficulty encountered. Indeed, the chronic problem in the federal government has been the domination of committee processes by the chairman. This results from the way in which the chairman is typically selected: he is traditionally the member of the majority party having the longest uninterrupted service on the committee. The dangers in such domination have been described as follows:

If there is a piece of legislation that he does not like, he kills it by declining to schedule a hearing on it. He usually appoints no standing subcommittees and he arranges the special subcommittees in such a way that his personal preferences are taken into account. Often there is no regular agenda at the meetings of his committee—when and if it meets . . . they proceed with an atmosphere of apathy, with junior members, especially, feeling frustrated and left out, like first graders at a seventh grade party.[24]

Inferences from Small Group Research.—The exact nature of the chairman's role is further clarified when we turn to more rigorous studies on group leadership.

We shall confine our discussion here to leader roles and functions, using three approaches. First, we shall discuss the nature of task leadership in the group and the apparent reasons for this role. Then we shall view more specifically the different role which the leader or leaders of the group may play. Finally, we shall consider the extent to which these more specific roles may be combined in a single individual.

Leader Control.—Studies of leadership in task-oriented, decision-making groups show a functional need for and, indeed, a member preference for directive influence by the chairman. The nature of this direction is illustrated in a study by Schlesinger, Jackson, and Butman.[25] The problem was to examine the influence process among leaders and members of small problem-solving groups when the designated leaders varied on the rated degree of control exerted. One hundred six members of twenty-three management committees participated in the study. As part of an initial investigation, committee members described in a questionnaire the amount of control and regulation which each member exercised when in the role of chairman. Each committee was then given a simulated but realistic problem for 1.5 hours, under controlled conditions and in the presence of three observers.

The questionnaire data showed that individuals seen as high in control were rated as more skillful chairmen and as more valuable contributors to the committee's work.

The study also demonstrated that leadership derives from group acceptance rather than from the unique acts of the chairman. "When the participants do not perceive the designated leader as satisfactorily performing the controlling functions, the participants increase their own attempts to influence their fellow members."[26] The acceptance of the leader was based upon task (good ideas) and chairmanship skills and had little to do with his personal popularity as a group member.

The importance of chairman control in committee action has been similarly demonstrated in several other studies.[27] In his study of 72 management conferences, for example, Berkowitz[28] found that a high degree of "leadership sharing" was related inversely to participant satisfaction and to a measure of output. The norms of these groups sanctioned a "take-charge" chairman. When the chairman failed to meet these expectations, he was rejected and both group satisfaction and group output suffered. These studies do not necessarily suggest that committees less concerned with task goals also prefer a directive chairman. Where the committees are composed of more socially oriented members, the preference for leader control may be less strong.[29]

Leadership Roles.—A second approach to understanding the leadership of committees is to investigate leadership roles in small groups. Pervading the research literature is a basic distinction between group activities directed to one or the other of two types of roles performed by leaders. They are defined by Benne and Sheats[30] as task roles, and as group-building and maintenance roles. Task roles are related to the direct accomplishment of group purpose, such as seeking information, initiating, evaluating, and seeking or giving opinion. The latter roles are concerned with group integration and solidarity through encouraging, harmonizing, compromising, and reducing conflict.

Several empirical investigations of leadership have demonstrated that both roles are usually performed within effective groups.[31] However, these roles are not always performed by the same person. Frequently one member is seen as the "task leader" and another as the "social leader" of the group.

Combined task and social roles.—Can or should these roles be combined in a single leader? The prototypes of the formal and the informal leader which we inherit from classical management lore tend to lead to the conclusion that such a combination is somehow impossible or perhaps undesirable. The research literature occasionally supports this point of view as well.

There is much to be said for a combination of roles. Several studies have shown that outstanding leaders are those who possess both task and social orientations.[32] The study by Borgotta, Couch, and Bales illustrates the point. These researchers assigned leaders high on both characteristics to problem-solving groups. The eleven leaders whom they called "great men" were selected from 126 in an experiment on the basis of high task ability, individual assertiveness, and social acceptability. These men also retained their ratings as "great men" throughout a series of different problem-solving sessions. When led by "great men" the groups achieved a higher rate of suggestion and agreement, a lower rate of "showing tension," and higher rates of showing solidarity and tension release than comparable groups without "great men."

When viewed collectively two conclusions emerge from the above studies. Consistent with existing opinion, the leader who is somewhat assertive and who takes charge and controls group proceedings is performing a valid and necessary role. However, such task leadership is a necessary but not a sufficient condition for effective committee performance. Someone in the group must perform the role of group-builder and maintainer of social relations among the members. Ideally both roles should probably be performed by the designated chairman. When he does not have the necessary skills to perform both roles, he should be the task leader and someone else should perform the social leadership role. Effective committee performance requires both roles to be performed, by a single person or by complementary performance of two or more members.

Committee Membership

The atmosphere of committee operations described in the classic literature is one where all members seem to be cooperating in the achievement of committee purpose. It is unclear, however, if cooperation is necessarily the best method of solving problems, or if competition among members or groups of members might not achieve more satisfactory results. Cooperation also seems to imply a sharing or homogeneity of values. To answer the question we must consider two related problems: the effects of cooperation or competition on committee effectiveness, and the effects of homogeneous or heterogeneous values on committee effectiveness.

Cooperation or Competition.—A number of studies have contrasted the impact of competition and cooperation on group satisfaction and productivity. In some cases the group is given a cooperative or competitive "treatment" through direction or incentive when it is established. In others, competition and cooperation are inferred from measures of groups in which members are operating primarily for personal interest, in contrast with groups in which members are more concerned with group needs. These studies show rather consistently that "group members who have been motivated to cooperate show more positive responses to each other, are more favorable in their perceptions, are more involved in the task, and have greater satisfaction with the task."[33]

The best known study regarding the effects of cooperation and competition was conducted by Deutsch[34] in ten experimental groups of college students, each containing five persons. Each group met for one three-hour period a week for six weeks, working on puzzles and human relations problems. Subjects completed a weekly and post-experimental questionnaire. Observers also recorded interactions and completed over-all rating scales at the end of each problem.

In some groups, a cooperative atmosphere was established by instructing members that the group as a whole would be evaluated in comparison with four similar groups, and that each person's course grade would depend upon the performance of the group itself. In others, a competitive relationship was established by telling the members that each would receive a different grade, depending upon his relative contribution to the group's problem solutions.

The results, as summarized by Hare, show that:

Compared with the competitively organized groups, the cooperative groups had the following characteristics: (1) Stronger individual motivation to complete the group task and stronger feelings of obligation toward other members.
(2) Greater division of labor both in content and frequency of interaction among members and greater coordination of effort.
(3) More effective inter-member communication. More ideas were verbalized, members were more attentive to one another, and more accepting of and affected by each other's ideas. Members also rated themselves as having fewer difficulties in communicating and understanding others.
(4) More friendliness was expressed in the discussion and members rated themselves higher on strength of desire to win the respect of one another. Members were also more satisfied with the group and its products.
(5) More group productivity. Puzzles were solved faster and the recommendations produced for the human-relations problems were longer and qualitatively better. However, there were no significant differences in the average individual productivity as a result of the two types of group experience nor were there any clear differences in the amounts of individual learning which occurred during the discussions.[35]

Similar evidence was found in the study of 72 decision-making conferences by Fouriezos, Hutt, and Guetzkow.[36] Based on observer ratings of self-oriented need behavior, correlational evidence showed that such self-centered behavior was positively related to participant ratings of high group conflict and negatively related to participant satisfaction, group solidarity, and task productivity.

In general, the findings of these and other studies suggest that groups in which members share in goal attainment, rather than compete privately or otherwise seek personal needs, will be more satisfied and productive.[37]

Homogeneity or Heterogeneity. -The effects of member composition in the committee should also be considered from the standpoint of the homogeneity or heterogeneity of its membership. Homogeneous groups are those in which members are similar in personality, value orientation, attitudes to supervision, or predisposition to accept or reject fellow members. Heterogeneity is induced in the group by creating negative expectations regarding potential contributions by fellow members, by introducing differing personality types into the group, or by creating subgroups which differ in their basis of attraction to the group.

Here the evidence is much less clear. Some homogeneous groups become satisfied and quite unproductive, while others become satisfied and quite productive. Similarly, heterogeneity may be shown to lead to both productive and unproductive conditions. While the answer to this paradox may be related to the different definitions of homogeneity or heterogeneity in the studies, it appears to have greater relevance to the task and interpersonal requirements of the group task.

In some studies, homogeneity clearly leads to more effective group performance. The work of Schutz[38] is illustrative. In his earlier writing, Schutz distinguished between two types of interpersonal relationships: power orientation and personal orientation. The first emphasizes authority symbols. The power-oriented person follows rules and adjusts to external systems of authority. People with personal orientations emphasize interpersonal considerations. They assume that the way a person achieves his goal is by working within a framework of close personal relations, that is, by being a "good guy," by liking others, by getting people to like him. In his later work, Schutz[39] distinguished among three types of needs: *inclusion,* or the need to establish and maintain a satisfactory relation with people with respect to interaction and association; *control,* or the need to establish and maintain a satisfactory relation with people with respect to control and power; and *affection,* or the need to establish and maintain a satisfactory relation with others with respect to love and affection.

Using attitude scales, Schutz established four groups in which people were compatible with respect to high needs for personal relations with others, four whose members were compatible with respect to low personal orientation, and four which contained subgroups differing in these needs. Each of the twelve groups met twelve times over a period of six weeks and participated in a series of different tasks.

The results showed that groups which are compatible, either on a basis of personalness or counterpersonalness, were significantly more productive than groups which had incompatible subgroups. There was no significant difference between the productivity of the two types of compatible groups. As might be expected, the difference in productivity between compatible and incompatible groups was greatest for tasks which required the most interaction and agreement under conditions of high-time pressure.

A similar positive relationship between homogeneity and productivity is reported for groups in which compatibility is established on the basis of prejudice or degree of conservatism, managerial personality traits, congeniality induced by directions from the researcher, or status congruence.[40] In Adams' study, technical performance first increased, then decreased, as status congruence became greater. Group social performance increased continuously with greater homogeneity, however.

The relationship posited above does not always hold, however. In some studies, heterogeneous groups were more productive than homogeneous. For example, Hoffman[41] constructed heterogeneous and homogeneous groups, based on personality profiles, and had them work on two different types of problems. On the first, which required consideration of a wide range of alternatives of a rather specific nature, heterogeneous groups produced significantly superior solutions. On the second problem, which required primarily group consensus and had no objectively "good" solution, the difference between group types was not significant. Ziller[12] also found heterogeneity to be associated with the ability of Air Force crews to judge the number of dots on a card.

Collins and Guetzkow[43] explain these contradictory findings by suggesting that increasing heterogeneity has at least two effects on group interaction: it increases the difficulty of building interpersonal relations, and it increases the problem-solving potential of the group, since errors are eliminated, more alternatives are generated, and wider criticism is possible. Thus, heterogeneity would seem to be valuable where the needs for task facilitation are greater than the need for strong interpersonal relations.

Considering our original question, it appears that, from the standpoint of cooperation versus competition in committees, the cooperative committee is to be preferred. If we look at the effects of homogeneous or heterogeneous committee membership, the deciding factor seems to be the nature of the task and the degree of interpersonal conflict which the committee can tolerate.

Summary and Conclusions

Research findings regarding committee size, leadership, and membership have been reviewed. Evidence has been cited showing that the ideal size is five, when the five members possess the necessary skills to solve the problems facing the committee. Viewed from the standpoint of the committee members' ability to attend to both the group and its members, or from the standpoint of balanced interpersonal needs, it seems safe to suggest that this number has normative value in planning committee operations. For technical problems additional members may be added to ensure the provision of necessary skills.

A second area of investigation concerned the functional separation of the leadership role and the influence of the role on other members. The research reviewed supports the notion that the committee chairman should be directive in his leadership, but a more specific definition of leadership roles makes questionable whether the chairman can or should perform as both the task and the social leader of the group. The evidence regarding the latter indicates that combined task and social leadership is an ideal which is seldom attained, but should be sought.

The final question concerned whether committee membership would be most effective when cooperative or competitive. When evaluated from the standpoint of research on cooperative versus competitive groups, it is clear that cooperative membership is more desirable. Committee operation can probably be enhanced by selecting members whose self-centered needs are of a less intense variety and by directions to the group which strengthen motivations of a cooperative nature. When the proposition is evaluated from the standpoint of heterogeneity or homogeneity of group membership, the conclusion is less clear. Apparently, heterogeneity in a group can produce both ideas and a screening process for evaluating their quality, but the advantage of this process depends upon the negative effects of heterogeneous attitudes upon interpersonal cooperation.

REFERENCES

Based on A. C. Filley and J. Robert House, *Managerial Process and Organizational Behavior* (Glenview, Ill.: Scott-Foresman, 1969).

1. Rollie Tillman, Jr., "Problems in Review: Committees on Trial," *Harvard Business Review*, 38 (May-June 1960), 6–12; 162–172. Firms with 1,001 to 10,000 reported 93 percent use; 250 to 1,000 reported 82 percent use.
2. J. H. Healey, *Executive Coordination and Control*, Monograph No. 78 (Columbus: Bureau of Business Research, The Ohio State University, 1956), p. 185.
3. "Committees," *Management Review*, 46 (October 1957), 4–10; 75–78.
4. M. Kriesberg, "Executives Evaluate Administrative Conferences," *Advanced Management*, 15 (March 1950), 15–17.
5. Tillman, *op. cit.*, p. 12.
6. Kriesberg, *op. cit.*, p. 15
7. "The Committee System—Congress at Work," *Congressional Digest*, 34 (February 1955), 47–49; 64.
8. E. H. Taves, "Two Mechanisms for the Perception of Visual Numerousness," *Archives of Psychology*, 37 (1941), 265.
9. A. Paul Hare, *Handbook of Small Group Research*, (New York: The Free Press of Glencoe, 1962), p. 227.
10. B. M. Bass, and F. M. Norton, "Group Size and Leaderless Discussions," *Journal of Applied Psychology*, 35 (1951), 397–400.
11. Hare, *op. cit.*, p. 228.
12. R. F. Bales, F. L. Strodtbeck, T. M. Mills, and M. E. Roseborough, "Channels of Communication in Small Groups," *American Sociological Review*, 16, (1951), 461–468.
13. F. F. Stephen and E. G. Mishler, "The Distribution of Participation in Small Groups: An Exponential Approximation," *American Sociological Review*, 17 (1952), 598–608.
14. J. R. Gibb, "The Effects of Group Size and of Threat Reduction Upon Creativity in a Problem-Solving Situation," *American Psychologist*, 6 (1951), 324. (Abstract)
15. P. Slater, "Contrasting Correlates of Group Size," *Sociometry*, 21 (1958), 129–139.
16. R. F. Bales, and E. F. Borgatta, "Size of Group as a Factor in the Interaction Profile," in *Small Groups: Studies in Social Interaction*, A. P. Hare, E. F. Borgatta, and R. F. Bales, eds (New York: Knopf, 1965, rev. ed.), pp. 495–512.
17. *Ibid.*, p. 512.
18. Slater, *op. cit.*, 137–138.
19. R. F. Bales, "In Conference," *Harvard Business Review*, 32 (March-April 1954), 44–50; also A. P. Hare, "A Study of Interaction and Consensus in Different Sized Groups," *American Sociological Review*, 17 (1952), 261–267.
20. D. Fox, I. Lorge, P. Weltz, and K. Herrold, "Comparison of Decisions Written by Large and Small Groups," *American Psychologist*, 8 (1953), 351. (Abstract)
21. A. Paul Hare, "Interaction and Consensus in Different Sized Groups," *American Sociological Review*, 17 (1952), 261–267.
22. G. B. Watson, "Do Groups Think More Efficiently Than Individuals?" *Journal of Abnormal and Social Psychology*, 23, (1928), 328–336; Also D. J. Taylor and W. L. Faust, "Twenty Questions: Efficiency in Problem Solving as a Function of Size of Group," *Journal of Experimental Psychology*, 44 (1952), 360–368.
23. Tillman, *op. cit.*, p. 168.
24. S. L. Udall, "Defense of the Seniority System," *New York Times Magazine* (January 13, 1957), 17.
25. L. Schlesinger, J. M. Jackson, and J. Butman, "Leader-Member Interaction in Management Committees," *Journal of Abnormal and Social Psychology*, 61, No. 3 (1960) 360–364.
26. *Ibid.*, p. 363.
27. L. Berkowitz, "Sharing Leadership in Small Decision-Making Groups," *Journal of Abnormal and Social Psychology*, 48 (1953), 231–238; also N. T. Fouriezos, M. L. Hutt, and H. Guetzkow, "Measurement of Self-Oriented Needs in Discussion Groups," *Journal of Abnormal and Social Psychology*, 45 (1950), 682–690; also H. P. Shelley, "Status Consensus, Leadership, and Satisfaction with the Group," *Journal of Social Psychology*, 51 (1960), 157–164.
28. Berkowitz, *Ibid.*, p. 237.
29. R. C. Anderson, "Learning in Discussions: A Resume of the Authoritarian-Democratic Studies," *Harvard Education Review*, 29 (1959), 201–214.
30. K. D. Benne, and P. Sheats, "Functional Roles of Group Members," *Journal of Social Issues*, 4 (Spring 1948), 41–49.
31. R. F. Bales, *Interaction Process Analysis* (Cambridge: Addison-Wesley, 1951); Also R. M. Stogdill and A. E. Coons (eds.), *Leader Behavior: Its Description and Measurement*, Monograph No. 88 (Columbus: Bureau of Business Research, The Ohio State University, 1957); Also A. W. Halpin, "The Leadership Behavior and Combat Performance of Airplane Commanders," *Journal of Abnormal and Social Psychology*, 49 (1954), 19–22.
32. E. G. Borgotta, A. S. Couch, and R. F. Bales, "Some Findings Relevant to the Great Man Theory of Leadership," *American Sociological Review*, 19 (1954), 755–759); Also E. A. Fleishman, and E. G. Harris, "Patterns of Leadership Behavior Related to Employee Grievances and Turnover," *Personnel Psychology*, 15, No. 1 (1962), 43–56; Also Stogdill and Coons, *Ibid.*; Also H. Oaklander and E. A. Fleishman, "Patterns of Leadership Related to Organizational Stress in Hospital Settings," *Administrative Science Quarterly*, 8 (March 1964), 520–532.
33. Hare, *Handbook of Small Group Research, op. cit.*, p. 254.
34. M. Deutsch, "The Effects of Cooperation and Competition Upon Group Process," in *Group Dynamics, Research and Theory*, D. Cartwright and A. Zander, eds., (New York: Harper and Row, 1953).

35. Hare, *Handbook of Small Group Research, op. cit.*, p. 263.

36. Fouriezos, Hutt, and Guetzkow, *op. cit.*

37. C. Stendler, D. Damrin and A. Haines, "Studies in Cooperation and Competition: I. The Effects of Working for Group and Individual Rewards on the Social Climate of Children's Groups," *Journal of Genetic Psychology*, 79 (1951), 173–197; Also A. Mintz, "Nonadaptive Group Behavior," *Journal of Abnormal and Social Psychology*, 46 (1951), 150–159; Also M. M. Grossack, "Some Effects of Cooperation and Competition Upon Small Group Behavior," *Journal of Abnormal and Social Psychology*, 49 (1954), 341–348; Also E. Gottheil, "Changes in Social Perceptions Contingent Upon Competing or Cooperating," *Sociometry*, 18 (1955), 132–137; Also A. Zander and D. Wolfe, "Administrative Rewards and Coordination Among Committee Members," *Administrative Science Quarterly*, 9 (June 1964), 50–69.

38. W. C. Schutz, "What Makes Groups Productive?" *Human Relations*, 8 (1955), 429–465.

39. W. C. Schutz, *FIRO: A Three-Dimensional Theory of Interpersonal Behavior*, (New York: Holt, Rinehart and Winston, 1958).

40. I. Altman and E. McGinnies, "Interpersonal Perception and Communication in Discussion Groups of Varied Attitudinal Composition," *Journal of Abnormal and Social Psychology*, 60 (May 1960), 390–393; Also W. A. Havthorn, E. H. Couch, D. Haefner, P. Langham and L. Carter, "The Behavior of Authoritarian and Equalitarian Personalities in Groups," *Human Relations*, 9 (1956), 57–74; Also E. E. Ghiselli and T. M. Lodahl, "Patterns of Managerial Traits and Group Effectiveness," *Journal of Abnormal and Social Psychology*, 57 (1958), 61–66; Also R. V. Exline, "Group Climate as a Factor in the Relevance and Accuracy of Social Perception," *Journal of Abnormal and Social Psychology*, 55 (1957), 382–388; Also S. Adams, "Status Congruency as a Variable in Small Group Performance," *Social Forces*, 32 (1953), 16–22.

41. L. R. Hoffman, "Homogeneity of Member Personality and Its Effect on Group Problem-Solving, *Journal of Abnormal and Social Psychology*, 58 (1959), 27–32.

42. R. C. Ziller, "Scales of Judgment: A Determinant of Accuracy of Group Decisions," *Human Relations*, 8 (1955), 153–164.

43. B. E. Collins and H. Guetzkow, *A Social Psychology of Group Process for Decision-Making*, (New York: John Wiley and Sons, 1965), p. 101.

Part V
COMMUNICATION AND INFORMATION MANAGEMENT

Introduction

Of all those elements that are thematic in management and administration, communication and information are closest to traditional areas of librarianship. However, library administrators are less familiar with the potential of communication and information management for promoting organizational success than one might expect. Both are vital elements of any management program, whether in a library or other organization. Their importance cannot be overstressed: organizations in which communication channels are blocked or severely limited, or where information required to conduct one's job is withheld or censored, cannot achieve goals and objectives. A central theme of selections in this chapter is that communication and information are interrelated and manipulable. Further, the notion that little attention to these variables is given by library administrators—who are often immersed in other administrative problems—also is presented.

The study of communication can, but need not, be complicated and highly abstract. Richard Emery's approach to the subject is highly pragmatic. After discussing the essential elements of the communication process itself, the author launches into a realistic appraisal of how communication can function within a library setting. His constant reiteration of communication as a *process* is vital to an understanding of how communication functions within an organization. As a process, communication is multidirectional, subject to the application of perceptual filters leading to failures in mutual understanding of what is desired, what is expected, and what can be accomplished. Mechanisms have been developed for reducing communication gaps and failures, mechanisms which Emery discusses in some depth.

However, communication that transmits what is usually called "noise" is neither useful nor desirable. To be efficient and effective, the communication process must transmit information that is easily recognizable by those for whom it is intended. Because accurate communication of relevant information is important, whatever is necessary in an organization to improve organizational information processing ought to be done—but how?

Charles R. McClure suggests that one way to improve the use of information for organizational decision making is to engage in "information management." The term "engage" is used deliberately: information management does not just happen. Without developing clear strategies to ensure that the right information reaches the right people at the right time, informal communication channels develop, grow, and can quickly replace the weaker, less effective, formal channels. From an administrative point of view, McClure notes that information management is a prerequisite to implement any of the more formal management systems, such as Management By Objectives or shared decision making. This is in keeping with the reasonable belief that if people know what is going on, they are more likely to accept it and be able to work more effectively toward the accomplishment of organizational goals.

McClure suggests that information management is so important that a separate branch of the organization should be established to oversee the way in which information is, and should be, communicated within a specific library organization, similar to what is already done in some businesses. The role of such an "information manager" would be threefold: first; that individual would reduce the administrator's dependence on just a few sources of information for decision making ("information nepotism"), second; the individual would study the number of programmed decisions so common in libraries and try to reduce them and, in so doing, reduce dependence on a severely limited number of sources as guides to action; and finally, the information manager would ensure that individuals have access to a variety of information sources beyond those ordinarily used for decision making. The use made of these sources would be studied and evaluated, with corrective action taken wherever necessary.

These two selections suggest the importance of information flow within the organization as an integrative and coordinating process that must be effective if the library/information center is to be able to make decisions on the broad range of topics facing the organization. Indeed, the underlying message appears to be that, before the library/information center can expect to be an effective service organization, librarians must learn how to exploit information resources for improved decision making.

The Process of Communication
By Richard Emery

COMMUNICATION IS NOT successful unless the person from whom it issues achieves his expected purpose or results. Information or ideas do not themselves constitute communication. They can be issued by one person in isolation without ever reaching or affecting others and in such circumstances do not constitute communication, which is an activity conducted between people, not merely by individuals in isolation. 'He has a mania for written memos' is a description applied to senior librarians in administrative positions which is quite often encountered. The inference is usually that many such memos are disregarded by receivers, due to their superficial contents or the sheer volume of their number.

The mere sending of a memorandum or giving an oral command only forms communication if it evokes a discriminatory response. Mere response to a stimulus does not justify the description 'communication'; response must be related to the intentions of the sender, providing intended results (successful communication) or disagreement. Thus E C Cherry defines communication not in terms of the response itself but the relationship set up by the transmission of stimuli and the evocation of response (Cherry 7).

Process
The notion of communication as a process, mentioned in chapter one, can be illustrated and appreciated from a consideration of the effects of communication. Simple models depicting the communicative act have figured in the literature of communication since the time of Shannon (Shannon & Weaver) and other writers concerned with the electrical transmission of information. Such models usually contain the following elements:

Reprinted from Richard Emery, *Staff Communication in Libraries* by Richard Emery, © 1975 (Linnet Books, Hamden, Connecticut).

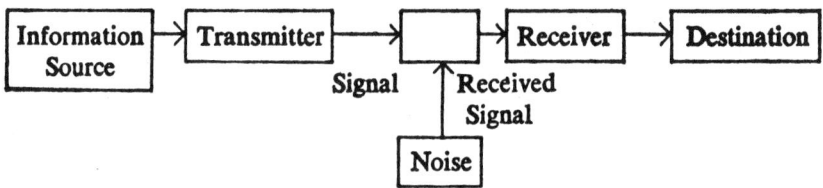

The process represented by the model involves a source selecting a message that is encoded into signals by a transmitter; a receiver decodes the signal so that the destination can recover the original message. The element of 'noise', interference or unwanted information, figured prominently in such models since the authors were concerned with the efficiency of transmission methods. The process is a linear one because it has a beginning and an end, a source and a destination. The messages that are received, however, also affect the messages that are sent in a communicative process. Subsequent writers therefore added further concepts to the basic model (*eg* that of feedback, introduced by Norbert Wiener) to create a circular process. An elaborated model can include the following elements and operations:

1	2	3	4	5	6
Sender's purpose	Sender's information	Encode	Transmit	Receive	Decode

7	8	9	10	11
Received message	Perceived intention	Receiver's reaction	Receiver's actions	Evaluation and feedback (return to 1)

Having established in his own mind his purposes for transmitting information, the sender must encode this or put it into the form of a message and transmit it via a channel (*ie* a means of communication, say, a written memo). Not all steps will necessarily appear in every communication attempt. There may, for example, be no provision for step 11 evaluation and feedback, although in such a case communication may prove to be ineffective in obtaining desired results.

'Feedback' is a term borrowed from electronics and information theory and describes the process which occurs when data regarding the performance of a system (*eg* a computer) is fed back into the system to permit correction and adjustment. The sender of a message is influenced, or should be so influenced, by the reactions his communication stimulates in the receiver, although reaction may not always be as explicit as in a speech dialogue. He may well modify future acts of communication on the basis of such experience or, in a situation of continuous communication involving the transmission of more than one piece of information (say in a conversation), adapt and modify his communication according to the response he is actually perceiving whilst so communicating. The communication model can therefore be drawn as a circle, or loop, with operation 11 leading on to 1, just as on a clock face the number 12 precedes that of 1. Acts of communication relevant to this model can hence be said to form a continuous process of reaction and adjustment.

The purpose and functions of communication have been discussed in chapter one. In everyday communication a person's purpose in initiating a communicative act or series of such acts will normally relate to more specific considerations than organisational goals. In initiating a regular series of staff meetings in his library a librarian may well be aiming at increased perception of, and progress towards, library goals as well as contributing factors such as staff morale. At a lower level of consideration, however, such as one item on a meeting's agenda or one order given orally in the course of a day's work, the librarian will be aiming at regulating behaviour according to some desired effect. In simplest terms, such regulation of behaviour can be viewed as the performance of a task (*eg* answering the telephone; relieving the reference librarian for his lunch break). More generally, the sender's purpose will be to: 1 modify an existing activity, 2 stop an activity, 3 start a new activity or 4 a combination of certain of these aims, such as stopping one activity and starting a new one (*eg* ceasing to issue books by the Browne method and starting to issue them by photocharging).

As well as having in mind certain actions resultant from the impact of his communication, the sender obviously also considers particular persons who are to perform these actions. Yet communication often produces response from persons to whom the communication was not directed. The sender may not have deliberately sought to exclude additional persons from the range of his communication for any such purpose as secrecy or discretion; it may simply be that he did not consider the content of the communication relevant to their work or interests. He can, however, often be mistaken in such assumptions and the receipt of part of a particular message by additional persons can lead to rumours, which in themselves may have a damaging effect on staff morale.

As will be seen in the chapter on informal communication, no librarian can foresee all the unintended consequences of his communicative actions but one possible safeguard, which will help minimise such disruptive consequences, is the open transmission and discussion of as much material as possible to all members of staff. If a library is particularly prone to unofficial group circulation or discussion of information, rumours or ill-informed resentment, the communication and morale positions may be improved almost at once by the introduction of certain minimum forms of regular communication such as a staff news sheet and staff meetings.

The actual effect of communication upon the receiver will depend upon: 1 his understanding of the message, 2 his perception of it—how he views it in relation to his own experiences, motivations, etc, and 3 his intention—what he intends to do about the message.

Understanding

A person may fail to understand a message because it contains inadequate information necessary for the performance of a particular task; the receiver cannot correct this deficiency merely by reinforcing his attention to the sender of the message, as he may well be unaware that the message is deficient. Thus a new junior member of a library staff, instructed to shelve books in the history sequence and to put all books on the shelves in order, could group books together by specific class numbers but ignore sub-arrangement by author within each grouping, unless the task was fully explained to the junior down to that level of detail. Inadequate performance of this duty could easily occur where symbols representing the authors' surnames did not form part of the classification notation and hence did not appear on the spines of books.

Alternatively, failure to understand a message may be due to simple lack of understanding of the message taken as a whole or certain words used in that message. Thus a library assistant instructed to put the fiction shelves in order may be given the following information: books are shelved alphabetically by author's surname; if the library has books by authors with the same surnames the alphabetical sequence of their first christian names is taken into account; if the library possesses more than one title by a particular author the works are sub-arranged alphabetically by the first words of the titles, omitting definite or indefinite articles; special forms by name, hyphenated surnames—arrange under the second part of the name, surnames with a prefix such as 'de' or 'van'—count the prefix as part of the surname; treat all forms of 'Mac' as one. The person so instructed could, however, arrange all books by authors whose names have the prefix 'Mac' in a sequence before those with the prefix 'Mc', not because the instructions have necessarily been inadequate, but simply because the task and problems involved are new to his experience, are unfamiliar and hence partly misunderstood. In a similar manner an assistant in a reference library, instructed by a more senior member of staff to answer an enquiry by looking in BUCOP or BHI, might be unfamiliar with these terms and the works the initials stand for. Hence the message could be incomprehensible.

In either of the above instances, where the whole message or certain words used as part of the message were not fully understood, resolution of the difficulty would necessitate further explanation on the part of the sender of the message. In the BUCOP example such explanation would be automatic upon the perception of the puzzled response to the first message (assuming it was not given in written form and opportunity for feedback was slight). In the case of the shelving of the 'Mac' books, however, the task could be performed incorrectly (albeit correctly according to the junior's perception of the case) and explanation would follow only if the sender checked the junior's work, *ie* checked that his message had had its intended consequences. In either case it will be evident that adequate and effective communication is closely related to understanding by the sender of the possible defects in his message and sensible supervision of work.

Admittedly, it is easy for the senior librarian giving instructions to overestimate his listener's fund of knowledge and background information. Being familiar with a subject himself it is sometimes difficult for the supervisor to be accurately aware of how much information he needs to impart or to realise that he has omitted certain vital details. The receiver may not always help in such situations. Many listeners hate to admit that they lack information, due to reasons of pride or fear of appearing ignorant or stupid. Hence care and thought are required in issuing instructions on matters which are familiar to the sender but not the receiver.

Perception

A consideration of 'perception' helps to indicate that meaning is not inherent in words or language but is related to the physical world and human attitudes and associations. Ogden and Richards in their 'triangle' of meaning define 'meaning' as a relational term, that is a complex term made up of three elements: the symbol, the reference (thought) and the referent (thing out there in the world which is referred to; this term was coined by Ogden and Richards to designate the object in the physical environment to which the symbols referred, but always indirectly through the reference) (Ogden & Richards 11).

Dictionary definitions present merely crude approximations to the word meanings shared by individuals who communicate with each other about 'things'. If words, whose basic meaning is imprecise, are not reinforced by relations of action, quality and so on, relating to mutual experience of sender and receiver of messages, understanding may be lacking. Meaning cannot be transmitted as readily as mere words, since meaning or connotative meaning is a relationship between a sign, an object and a person, and is concerned with social as well as physical or formal reality.

Many difficulties encountered in industrial relations relate to imprecise definitions (*eg* 'cooling-off period') or the lack of reinforcement and explanation of such terms through the common experience of management and labour. In libraries, where all staff (save perhaps manual staff) share more of a common background and education than is the case in industry, such difficulties should be less but must still be borne in mind by the communicator.

A person's attitude towards messages, how he views and interprets them, is not a topic which can easily be explained or described. Likert has indicated that 'an individual's reaction to any situation is always a function not of the absolute character of the interaction but of his perception of it. It is how he sees things that count, not objective reality' (Likert, 1959 161). Perception in this context is, in fact, a function of a person's experience, needs and motivations. Shared background experience, mentioned above, aids the receiver to get the message as it is meant to be received and understood by the sender. It is unrealistic always to expect the sender to anticipate difficulties of understanding encountered by the receiver. The receiver also has to make an effort to take into account not only the bare informational content of the sender's message but also what he perceives to be the sender's intention (or lack of it), the situation and so on.

Perception encompasses considerations of the degree to which a person actually notices a message and how he views and interprets that message—his attitudes toward it. A message is often of greater importance or significance to the sender than it is to the receiver. At the time of communicating it is likely that the message is uppermost in the sender's thoughts. Furthermore, he may well have given a problem involved in the communication, and also his means of communicating (choice of words, written or spoken), considerable thought. Yet the message may strike no established thought pattern or basis of experience in the receiver. F C Bartlett has suggested that one of the chief functions of the mind, when it is active, is ' filling up gaps ', that is constantly trying to link new material into the pattern of older material, in order to make it meaningful (Bartlett 121-4). Such a process is slow and often difficult, since our minds prefer the simple, regular and familiar to the complex, irregular or unfamiliar. Hence the value of attempting to assess the response to communication by supervision and observation of resulting actions and the reinforcement of messages by further additional or supportive communication. The reinforcement of orders or information initially conveyed orally by a written elaboration is an obvious example here.

Henry Heaney, Librarian of Queen's University, Belfast, has introduced a particularly useful method of recording and reinforcing decisions made by himself in oral consultation with his staff. Should any member of his staff (usually a senior member) consult him with the intention of eliciting a decision from him (*eg* on the type of library statistical records to be kept) the member of staff concerned is required later to submit a written version of his request and his interpretation of the decision arrived at orally. Such a record enables the receiver (in this case the librarian) to match the sender's advantage of prior thought and study of the problem, as well as affording him the opportunity of giving the case further thought when studying the sender's written version of request and decision.

An investigation by Ross A Webber leads to the conclusion that although any initiator tends to perceive more while the receiver perceives less, there are consistent differences in the perceptions of superiors and subordinates. The absolute discrepancy between the subordinate's and superior's perception of the superior's downward initiation is greater than the discrepancy between perceptions of the subordinate's upward initiation (Webber 239). Hence reinforcement of communication is particularly important in so far as downward communication is concerned (*ie* as opposed to upward communication of which Queen's University, Belfast, is an instance).

In any day-to-day work situation many communications are likely to lose their intended impact, thus not strictly speaking forming part of the 'communication' process, while many other completed circuits of the continuing process are likely to be soon forgotten, especially by the receiver. In an investigation into perceived interactions (*ie* communication which was perceived and hence subsequently remembered by the sender and receiver), T D Weinshall revealed that only in less than one half of all mutually perceived interactions did the 'recipient' of the communication understand the spirit in which it was meant to be delivered by the 'transmitter' of the communication. The communication did not 'pass' ('go through') in the spirit it was intended to go in 53 percent of the recorded mutually perceived interactions (Weinshall 625-6). Testings conducted by R G Nichols and L A Stevens into response and powers of assimilation indicate that two months after listening to a talk the average employee will remember only about 25 percent of what was said. Furthermore, after a person has barely learned something ' he tends to forget from one half to one third of it within eight hours ' (Nichols & Stevens 86). These considerations apply to intelligent as well as unintelligent persons.

It is obvious from the results of such research that the communicator needs to take active care in disseminating messages lest they are to be neglected in as casual a manner as that in which they are sent. Communication is related to habit and if it is desired to produce learning or changed attitudes in a receiver the sender must break some existing habit patterns and establish new ones. Undue repetition can, of course, lead to boredom and inattention, thus negating the sender's aims but certainly some repetition and reinforcement is necessary, especially when communicating new information or directions.

Besides tending to perceive what is expected or familiar more readily than what is unexpected or unfamiliar, individuals' perception of communication will vary according to their need for such communication. Thus an assistant librarian may well take more note of advice on how to reply to a request or complaint from a member of the public than, say, a memo instructing him to keep his desk tidy. In the former case he is seeking response to his own communication (*ie* his request for advice) in order to conclude an action (replying to a letter). In the latter case, besides arousing feelings of unbelief or hostility, the message was not sought by the receiver and may well be disregarded.

Closely related to considerations of need are those of volume of communication and relevance. A person receiving a great deal of communication will vary his response according to what he perceives to be the importance of individual messages and hence what may be an important communication in a sender's view may provoke little or no attention, let alone response, from a harassed receiver. Even interesting information tends to fade in a receiver's mind if it is unused by that person. Correspondingly, if a person has relatively limited communication with other members of staff (*eg* a branch librarian geographically separated from library staff other than his own branch staff), interaction with other staff (*eg* chief librarian or branch supervisor on the occasion of their visits to the branch) will appear more vivid to such a person. Hence such communication may have greater and more lasting impact on him than upon someone who communicates a great deal with many other staff (*eg* the chief librarian or branch supervisor in the present example).

It is difficult for a sender of messages to motivate an intended response since the receiver's response will in part depend on the latter's attitude to the sender and his previous communications, plus his attitude to the library and its purpose in general. A person's relationship with an object, event, idea or other person will play some part in determining the attention which he gives to it or to the other person. Thus people will tend to pay more attention to the unexpected or unusual than the familiar and will be differently ' tuned in ' to persons of different status. An assistant librarian will, for example, be receptive in different ways to his chief and fellow staff of comparable status. He may well pay more attention to the communications of his chief because they are more important, carry more authority, are less frequent and more unusual, than those of his fellow staff.

The mixture of a person's powers of reasoning and emotions,

all internal factors and senses which shape his views and actions, are termed a 'conceptual/evaluative system' by L O Thayer, indicating that an individual both conceives (*ie* comprehends) and evaluates an event, thing, idea, relationship, feeling and so on. Thayer indicates that this system is 'an extremely complex and intricately organised multidimensional hierarchy of concepts, values, beliefs, etc, and of clusters of concepts, values, beliefs, etc' (Thayer, 1968 43).

Such a statement adequately indicates the complex nervous system which determines a person's motivations. It may be possible to alter the relationship between an individual and his perceived environment (*eg* by counselling to make a member of staff more aware of the need to cooperate with his immediate superior). To motivate a person directly into adopting an orientation to himself or his work that is not at least latently understood and acceptable to him is, however, a much more complex task, possibly an impossible one. At a practical level, the most that the communicator can perhaps attempt is to try to provoke a rational response by a full and logical presentation of information; further than this a chief librarian or senior in an administrative or supervisory position can attempt to motivate intended response to individual acts of communication by maintaining general and consistent good staff relations and communication.

Intention
Even if a person receives a message that is structurally perfect and a perfect semantic accord (meaning) between sender and receiver is evident, the receiver may still take no action to enact the requirements specified by the sender (*ie* assuming the message is not simply 'to take no action' on a particular matter). In such a situation we can still speak of 'communication' as having taken place. The message has been received and understood, although no action ensues; hence the term 'negative communication' is appropriate in such an instance. This fact will, however, be of slight satisfaction to the sender whose underlying purpose in the use of information has been thwarted.

As seen above, we tend to select sources of information with which we already agree. This is not necessarily a deliberate conscious choice to avoid seeing the other side of a question or to reinforce one's prejudices. Rather it is because the information from these sources tends to be understood more easily. Occasionally, however, an individual's attitudes can be deliberately obstructive. The decision of a receiver to take no action in such an instance may be due to his opinion that: 1 the course of action required by the sender is unnecessary, unjustified or misguided, 2 to simple lethargy and inertia, 3 positive decisions not to take action to annoy the sender or thwart his intentions or 4 lack of time or ability to pursue the course of action. In the latter case some fault can be attached to the sender for not perceiving such facts. In the first instance, that the action would be unnecessary, unjustified or misguided, the receiver's opinion may well have some logical or correct basis and feedback or response should stimulate the continuing process of further communication to resolve the difference of opinion. In the second instance the receiver is clearly at fault. With routine communication (*eg* a memo on staff punctuality) his obstruction may not be evident to the sender of the message. Should the communication be of a more important and individual nature (*eg* a direction from the chief librarian to the head of a department to commence a series of staff training exercises in his department) the obstruction will obviously come to light more easily and quickly and must be resolved by the sender.

A further cause of inaction may relate to a person's dissatisfaction with his position in a library and attempts to emphasise his own self-importance. Thus J M Jackson refers to a study of senior staff in a British engineering plant which led to the discovery of a process of 'status protection'. When these men received instructions from their superiors they often treated the items as merely information or advice. In this manner they, in effect, achieved a relative improvement in their own position in the authority structure by acting as if no one had the right to direct their activity (Jackson 166).

Improving Efficiency
In the above examples of obstruction it is obvious that communication is closely related to decision making and the other elements of organisational administration outlined in chapter one. The present chapter attempts to show how communication, as well as being closely related to the whole organisation and its administrative processes, is also closely connected to the whole person, his experience and knowledge, his attitudes and motivations. This may

be reassuring to someone seeking clues as to the importance of communication but it also increases the complications attached to the communicative process, the difficulties of transmitting meaningful and worthwhile messages, and hence the care and attention which should be paid to communication. Unfortunately such care and attention is often taken for granted by librarians as a self-generating and easy accomplishment, not requiring constant conscious and detailed thought and study.

The communicator, be he senior or junior, be he communicating in a downward, horizontal or upward direction, can take certain steps to improve the efficiency of his communicative processes. Besides preparing himself for communication, in the sense of collecting all the facts necessary for his messages and choosing the most appropriate medium (spoken—to an individual or group at a staff meeting; written—by memo, or via the staff news sheet, etc), the communicator must obviously make his message relevant to its recipient and to his own purpose in sending the message.

'Metacommunication' is a term used to describe any clue or evidence a person may use in slanting his message so as to ensure adequate reception. Such clues or evidence may relate to what other people are saying, how a particular situation is developing and so on. Hence it is evident that a communicator takes, or should take, into account more than the mere content of what is being said or written. The receiver of a message similarly takes into account more than the content of a message. As indicated above, he is affected by who is transmitting the message, that person's attitudes, expressions and so on. Thus metacommunication refers to the perception and actions of the receiver as well as sender, although in this section of chapter two it is the efficiency of the sender or initiating communicator which is under consideration.

Expectations are an important consideration in any communicative process. Expectations about each other's behaviour accompany any interaction between one person and another. In interpersonal behaviour we interpret our own behaviour in the context of what we assume to be the other person's interests, orientations, expectations, values and beliefs. In a communication situation the sender will adapt his messages and form of presentation to what he thinks will be the receiver's possible reaction and should hence always give due thought to the reception of his messages and the receiver's expectations regarding himself (*ie* the sender). Due thought and attention is needed to this aspect of communication since communication is usually an automatic process in the sense that the individual is not generally aware of considerations relating to source of motivation and expectation. Empathy, identifying with the other person, being able to see his point of view, understanding his needs, desires, feelings and expectations, is necessary for effective communication. Since all communication is persuasive, such understanding outlined above can readily facilitate the communication process.

'Noise', in the theoretical or electrical engineering sense, is often viewed as being a hindrance to communication. However, as E Berne has written 'In interpersonal communication "noise" is of more value than "information", since in such cases it is of more value to the communicants to know about each other's states than to give "information" to each other. "Noise" carries latent communications from the communicant' (Berne 197). Hence noise can be regarded as feedback and also metacommunication, particularly from the sender's point of view. Such noise will not reduce intelligibly, as it would in a telephone system, but will form part of the communication process, will help shape content and facilitate understanding and rational reaction.

The human comprehending system (Thayer's comprehension/ evaluation system) has the advantage of being an adaptive one, responding to its environment, being influenced by it and influencing it in turn. In terms of staff the environment will consist partly of an administrative atmosphere or complex, containing decisions, orders and so on. Hence senior administrators, as communicators, have certain advantages on their side. A member of staff subjected to a particular administrative pattern or tone will usually become responsive and adaptive to it, hence aiding the process of communication. The proviso which needs to be stressed, of course, and has been indicated in this chapter, is that communicators should give due weight to the importance of form and means of communication, plus metacommunication, such as individual complexities, and feedback (or the individual's efforts at shaping his administrative environment).

The communicator who is aware of such factors affecting his efficiency is at least in the position of being able to attempt implementation of his theories in an effort to facilitate organisational efficiency and the provision of library services. Efficiency, of course, is not necessarily evidence of effectiveness. The efficiency of an action or process (immediate communication encounters) may be accepted as evidence of its effectiveness, whereas in fact it may be to the long range disadvantage of the staff and the library. Thus the imposition or restructuring of a system of library fines may be accomplished with great efficiency by counter, or circulation, staff. The results, however, may be to the disadvantage of senior staff morale in so far as the staff is particularly concerned with library service to the community and tends to oppose such charges and also to general library service in so far as it affects public attitudes to and use of the library. The resolution of such dilemmas can only be attempted by senior librarians viewing communication as a vital part of the administrative process and fully considering its function as contributing to the fulfilment of library goals. Some errors are bound to occur in communication but a recognition of the importance of communication in a library can help to reduce its deficiencies.

Strategies for Organizational Information Management
By Charles R. McClure

THE NEED

Our administrative ability to operate effectively a service-oriented organization, such as an academic library, will depend in no small part upon our ability to marshal various information sources to resolve complex decision situations. Organizational information management, that is, the production, collection, organization, and dissemination of information related to the accomplishment of the organization's goals, should be encouraged. Organizational information management attempts to utilize the information resources of organizational members to full potential. Such an administrative stance is likely to improve the organization's access to both quantitative and qualitative information as well as improve the organization's ability to interact effectively with its environment.

The need for increased attention to organizational information handling is evidenced by recent societal changes. Office overhead is 30 to 50 percent of total costs in many business organizations; however, office productivity has increased only about 70 percent during the last century while factory productivity has increased by 1000 percent.[1] These figures are better understood when one considers that the average blue collar worker is supported by $30,000 worth of equipment, the farm worker by $55,000 worth of equipment, and the office worker by only $2,000 worth of equipment.[2] The librarian, as a typical office worker, simply has not been supported to increase his or her information-handling ability. Although better utilization of new technology is clearly needed in many libraries, the central problem is one of recognizing the importance of organizational information management.

Strategies can be developed in the organization to better manage, acquire, and utilize information for decision making. However, a number of assumptions must be recognized by the organization before specific strategies can be developed and implemented. A first crucial assumption that must be met is that the organization is willing to change. Clearly, some of the strategies will rely on changing existing attitudes, administrative structures, and other existing techniques in the organization.

A second key assumption has to do with the administrative structure of the organization. Effective strategies for improved information handling will depend, in large part, on the managerial techniques and organizational climate in the library. As previously pointed out, effective utilization of information in the organization is based on the ideas that (1) every employee is a decision maker, and (2) the most important resource of the organization is the individual. Appropriate administrative strategies may have to be developed first to integrate these concepts into the library *before* strategies for organizational information handling can be successfully developed.

Article reprinted from *Information for Academic Library Decision Making* by Charles R. McClure and used with the permission of the publisher, Greenwood Press, a division of Congressional Information Service, Inc., Westport, Connecticut.

CONTINGENCY MANAGEMENT STYLES

A primary need that can be identified for successful information management is the development of management styles and organizational climates that respond individually to unique situations to maximize goal attainment. Such styles must provide input and feedback from the library's environment, recognize the importance of rational decision making, and facilitate the contact, selection, and dissemination of information to all organizational members. Furthermore, these contingency styles of management must provide clear evidence of administrative accountability by decentralizing the control over organizational sources of information.

Typically, such contingency views recognize the potential for various shared decision-making styles. These management styles assume that employees are both willing and able to contribute to the decision-making process if they are adequately informed by administration and if they assume responsibility for contacting adequate information sources and selecting accurate and relevant information sources for decision making. All organizational members assume the responsibility for developing organizational structures to encourage shared decision making as well as the decentralization of information sources.

The term "shared decision making" is used to indicate more of a concept of management than a specific technique such as MBO. Shared decision making implies a process of power equalization in the organization, with administration encouraging informational input into the decision-making process and sharing responsibility for the consequences resulting from the decision with those who were involved in making the decision. Participation is a type of shared decision making and involves all members of the organization or all stakeholders in a given decision situation who provide informational input but who do not necessarily assume responsibility for the consequences of the decision.[3]

Librarians wishing to move their organization toward shared decision-making managerial styles must first recognize the importance of key information-related variables such as (1) the individual's access to organizational information sources, (2) the individual's contact with organizational information sources, (3) the individual's selection of sources as input for decision making, and (4) the informal dissemination of information within the organization. Further, it may be suggested that ignorance of the importance of these key variables largely explains the failure of many shared decision-making management styles in a number of library organizations.

Effective organizational information management appears to be a prerequisite for the various shared decision-making styles. Furthermore, a period of preparation in which information-related variables are modified also appears to be a prerequisite for shared decision-making styles. Superimposing management styles on library environments where information contact, flow, and availability are minimal often may result in a self-fulfilling prophecy of doom for the new style. Organizational information management has not been recognized as an important determinant of the introduction and change of management styles.

Furthermore, the question of responsibility must be raised. Does the administrator have a responsibility to encourage professional librarians to come into contact with information sources? The answer appears to be yes if he or she is trying to move the organization to a more shared decision-making style of management. Do professional librarians have a responsibility to come into contact with more information sources and facilitate the flow of information within the organization? The answer appears to be yes if they wish to become involved in decision making and make participatory styles of management more effective.

REDUCE PROGRAMMED DECISION SITUATIONS

A specific strategy that can be employed to encourage contact with information sources is to reduce the degree to which "programmed" decisions are determining employee activity. Job satisfaction and increased productivity appear to be likely when professionals have new challenges to address—challenges for which increased contact with information sources provides a basis for the individuals to develop their potential as decision makers. Administrators as well as other individuals must strive to include "non-programmed" decision situations in their environment. From such situations comes the need for unique or new information that may provide the basis for innovation and change.

One method to reduce the degree to which librarians deal only with programmed decisions is to encourage their contact with decision situations outside their immediate department. Because employees in an organization receive more information related to their immediate work environment than information related to the organization as a whole,[4] strategies should be employed to provide the employee with a broader view of the organization. Such a strategy not only increases the employee's contact with nonprogrammed decision situations but also encourages the employee to relate the needs and objectives of various organizational parts to each other.

For the most part, the research suggests that librarians are not educated consumers of information; a need exists for librarians to learn how to evaluate information as potential input to decision making. A strategy that can be employed to respond to this need is reeducation. Specifically, the central points to be addressed are (1) explanation of the importance of information input in the decision-making process, (2) accepting as a professional responsibility to be informed and current vis-à-vis matters affecting the organization, (3) learning how to achieve access effectively to the broad array of information sources that have potential input to organizational decision making, and (4) developing the ability to critically evaluate the information one contacts or selects as to its "value" for decision making. Reeducation is necessary if programmed decision making is to be reduced.

EDUCATION ABOUT INFORMATION HANDLING

Reeducation of librarians about information management can be addressed at two levels. The first level is that of students currently obtaining their professional training in library/information science. Traditional library science management courses of an historical nature which begin with scientific management and conclude with systems management cannot be the student's only contact with organizational information management. The process of information handling in the organizational setting must be presented along with the various strategies of organizational information management.

Indeed, the usefulness of organizational information management is not limited to library/information science students. Conversations with various professionals in other disciplines suggest that most professional graduates from institutions of higher education are unprepared to effectively utilize the various information sources in their fields, to contribute information to the organizational decision-making process, or to organize and control their personal information-related activities in an organizational setting. Producing professionals of any type who are unable to cope with the realities of the information society is a disservice both to the individuals and to society at large.

There is some evidence that educators are recognizing the need for such informational training. A recent publication, *Evaluating Information: A Guide for Users of Social Science Research*, attempts to educate students, regardless of discipline, to be consumers of information.[5] The assumption of the work is that all professionals must be able to assess the accuracy and appropriateness of the mass of research findings currently being produced. This is an excellent strategy to integrate into various courses at both the graduate and the undergraduate level. Students exposed to this strategy are more likely to have increased information potential in the organization where they ultimately work, regardless of their specific job responsibilities.

A second level of educating must be accomplished for those professionals already in the field. The amount of work that must be done here is staggering. The data in this study suggest that many librarians are inadequately prepared to contact and select information sources for decision making. Currently, there is growing pressure for professionals to improve their information-handling techniques. However, future demands for accountability and justification of decisions will force the librarian to be better informed, more selective, and more aware of organizational information management techniques.

Three strategies are possible at this level. First, library educators must assume responsibility for reeducating professionals in the field, and the profession at large must accept the need for some type of an ongoing certification program to *insure* that librarians improve their capacity for current developments and better information management. Such strategies are already accepted in the professions of medicine, education, law, and dentistry. Paradoxically, the professionals of library/information science do not *require* their professional members to attend a designated number of instructional programs after compltion of the initial degree.

Second, library administrators must assume responsibility for information management training programs. This strategy would contribute to the decentralization of information control as well as provide a laboratory environment for the development of organizational information managerial skills. Specific techniques for improving the organization's contact with information, production of information, and dissemination of information can be fostered in this manner. Library administrators must provide the opportunity for in-house training sessions; they must encourage staff participation in the sessions; and they must assume responsibility for providing leaders for those sessions who are knowledgeable about organizational information management.

Third, the development of training manuals, procedures, and other guides is an excellent first step toward improved information resource management. Such guides can be developed to fit the specific needs of an organization and can aid in the transition from manual information handling to automated information handling. Such a strategy helps to insure appropriate information flows within the organization and can encourage decentralization of information. A number of these guides have been produced by organizations in government and the business world and provide useful models for the library environment.[6] Furthermore, there are a number of recent books that provide an excellent basis for analyzing and developing information resources in the organization. Examination of such books can be a positive first step in readying the organization for procedures, changes, and new strategies vis-à-vis improved information handling.

THE INFORMATION MANAGER

Throughout the research there is evidence that no one has overall responsibility for organizational information management in the library environment. This need can be addressed by establishing authority and responsibilities to improve organizational information handling. Although there is no lack of "administrators," the appreciation of information contact, information dissemination, and information selection for decision making is not recognized as a responsibility either for administrators or for librarians in general.

The job title "information manager" is becoming much more common in a number of businesses as well as in government sectors. Specific responsibilities for the information manager include the following:[7]

1. Direct the overall development of information resources for improved organizational decision making.
2. Coordinate the organization's access to and dissemination of information related to the accomplishment of goals and objectives.
3. Facilitate the exchange of organizational information among organizational members.
4. Organize the production of analytical information related to the organization's interaction with the environment for purposes of planning.
5. Provide a storage and retrieval system for information resources related to the organization's operations and services.
6. Evaluate existing mechanisms of information access and dissemination and propose alternative methods by which organizational members will have access to information resources for decision making.

These responsibilities must be clearly assigned to one individual in the organization, preferably an administrator.

The designated individual must have broad skills and knowledge of information sciences, information technology in all its various formats, personnel and social psychology, contingency management techniques, systems analysis and program planning, and at least basic statistical skills for summary and analysis of information. Such an individual is a broker or counselor who acts as a facilitator between information resources and organizational decision making. "Perhaps above all else the information manager is a resource manager ... to enhance, and conserve information resources to help the organization achieve its lawful goals and objectives."[8]

Specific strategies that can be utilized by the information manager to accomplish the responsibilities of the position are many and are limited only by one's imagination. Indeed, many of the strategies that have been successfully utilized in the business world such as (1) project management, (2) brainstorming sessions, (3) selective dissemination of information for company professionals, (4) creation of an information resource center, and (5) training sessions on how to improve one's information potential are most appropriate for the service sector such as academic libraries.[9] Until such strategies are implemented we will continue to lose the full potential of our professionals as decision makers.

The information manager may also serve as a means to respond to another need clearly identified in this study—the nonproduction of information in the form of reports, studies, and statistical analyses. Libraries must initiate responsibility for institutional research—research that deals with both the internal operations and services of the library and the library's impact on and relationship with its environment. The production of unique information that addresses specific aspects of the library and its environment is crucial for improved organizational decision making.

However, the purpose of the position is not to centralize further the control of information in the organization. Because all professionals are decision makers, special emphasis should be placed on extending access to information resources throughout the organization. As such, the individual also serves as an advisor to the staff on how to utilize information sources for daily decision making. The assumption that only top administration needs adequate access to and control of information resources must be challenged. The decentralization of information resources encourages all staff members to develop their full potential as organizational decision makers, a potential which appears to be largely untapped in many academic libraries today.

DECENTRALIZATION OF INFORMATION

In a general sense, decentralization of information can be encouraged by restructuring various task responsibilities. As shown in this study, many typical positions in the library environment have little uncertainty associated with their performance. Yet, recent research suggests that tasks perceived as more uncertain will be associated with more frequent use of information sources.[10] Thus a strategy of restructuring various librarian positions to include responsibility for nonprogrammed decisions (ones in which there is some uncertainty) will tend to encourage information acquisition and organizational decentralization of information.

The concept of organizational power is closely related to control of information and, thus, the centralization of information. When administrators maintain tight controls over the organization and dissemination of information, they also create a power base because the information can be used to reduce organizational uncertainties.[11] Although an advantage is maintained by administrators in terms of organizational control, the disadvantage of not utilizing the full potential of organizational employees is severe.

Nonetheless, given the magnitude of the information environment in which the typical librarian finds himself, administrators only can control *internally*-generated information. As pointed out previously in this study, the typical academic library studied produced very little such information. Thus, the librarian can clearly increase/improve the quality of his or her contacts with externally generated information. Furthermore, one should note that it is the externally generated information that tends to be "reality-bound," to provide greater validity than much internally generated information.[12]

Access to externally generated information provides a basis for a validity check, or perhaps a discrepancy check, between activities in the organization and its environment with the decision process within the organization. Therefore, one broad approach to limiting administrative control of information is consciously to acquire and disseminate externally generated information into the organization. Such an approach is especially useful when the discrepancy between internal activities and decisions do not match the evidence or information from the environment at-large.

Decentralization of information can be accomplished by a number of strategies. One approach is to maintain an open file system whereby all organizational memos, correspondence, reports, and so on are organized for employee availability. Another approach is to circulate summary data in the form of annual or quarterly reports from the various department heads throughout the organization. Furthermore, individuals in the organization can be assigned to a project group to study and make a report on certain decision situations, the results of which are circulated. Informal "group think" sessions and designated periods of time when administrators must report and be questioned on "current happenings" also can be set up. And, finally, librarians must learn to exchange information outside their specific departmental area; informal meetings can be established to do this.

Decentralization of information dissemination must also occur at the departmental level. As this research has shown, librarians tend to seek information from the immediate department supervisor. Such communication networks should be modified to encourage cross-departmental communication as well as integrating communication isolates into various communication networks in the library. Manipulation of membership in these communication networks may tend to significantly increase accuracy of information flow, creativity and problem-solving ability, as well as increase the coordination among the various departments. Inclusion of certain opinion leaders or information rich in specific network situations also may contribute to greater effectiveness of organizational information resource management.

However, the response of "forming a committee" may not always be a viable approach. The proliferation of committees does not necessarily equal decentralization of information. Committee structure is most effective *after* decentralization of information. Individuals must have access to organizational information before a meeting takes place so that meaningful analysis is possible. Agendas, provision of information related to the agenda items, and position papers encourage a dynamic environment of information exchange as a basis for committee effectiveness.[13]

REDUCING INFORMATION NEPOTISM

The disturbing aspect of nonproduction of information and its resulting information nepotism is that it does not encourage, but in fact generally precludes, the selection of information sources that have specific relevance and applicability to the specific decision under consideration. Thus, the very sources that are unique to the decision affecting the organization generally are ignored. If it is true, as it appears to be, that decision makers select and utilize a few fondly remembered information sources regardless of the problem at hand, the efficacy of the decisions is, at least, questionable.

Administrators can reduce information nepotism by encouraging the production of internal studies, reports, and statistical summaries. They should attempt to train, retrain, and promote basic writing and research skills. They should insist on empirical evidence as a basis for decisions whenever possible. They must expand their contact with and selection of information sources to those approximating the unique conditions in their library. They must encourage others in the organization to analyze the nature of the decision in terms of clearly defined objectives, establish alternatives, and evaluate alternatives based on clearly identified criteria. Finally, they must recognize the need for cross-departmental communication patterns and develop strategies to increase nonprogrammed decision situations for individual librarians.

Other decision makers (librarians) in the organization must critically examine the process by which they make decisions. What specific information resources (if any) were considered as input to the decision situation? How valuable were the information sources that were selected to resolve the decision situation? What patterns of informal information seeking were pursued? Did you *produce* information as a means of resolving the decision situation? How did you obtain critical feedback on the reliability and validity of the information contacted? How will you diversify your access to a broad range of information sources and increase your contact with those sources especially appropriate for your decision-making responsibilities?

Although these suggestions may be appropriate for administrators as well as librarians, the overall problem of information nepotism and the limited production of information resources must be addressed by all organizational members. Librarians might be organized into project teams to produce certain documents related to organizational activities and decisions. Such a strategy improves cross-departmental communication, increases the likelihood of creativity and innovation, and allows for the project team to be dissolved once the task is accomplished. Throughout this process, administration must encourage an organizational climate that supports access to information, production of information, and decentralization of information.

At present, individuals have not examined the information acquisition, processing, and dissemination characteristics of the people in the organization and, therefore, do not know who tends to be information rich, who tends to rely on other organization members who are information rich, or who relies on organization members with very low information potential as measured in that organization. The actual involvement of employees who might be termed organizational information rich within the decision-making process is little appreciated; indeed, self and organizational analysis of information processing is virtually nonexistent.

Those individuals who can be identified as information rich should be encouraged by the information manager to facilitate information handling in the organization. Perhaps special consideration should be shown to such organizational information rich employees in terms of allocation of information-related resources. External contacts with other professionals at conferences, meetings, and other occasions could be encouraged. Physical arrangements could be made to take advantage of the organizational information rich's expertise by placing them in easily accessible situations or where they could have more accessibility to prime information sources. Furthermore, communication networks in the organization could be studied to determine sources of information, exchange sequences, and relationships with other organizational employees.

Indeed, the whole question of resource allocation vis-à-vis information resources should be reexamined. Because information must be utilized *in conjunction with other resources* to be effective, administrators must examine the resources available to organizational members that encourage information exploitation. A long-distance call that costs $12.00 may in fact save the organization hundreds of dollars in other resources! Availability of time to examine and produce information also is a prerequisite, as well as information-handling equipment such as text editors, computers, and even telephones. Once the staff member has more self-determination regarding resources such as time, space, status, money, and equipment, he or she can better exploit information resources through other traditional resources and ultimately increase their information potential to the organization.

EVALUATING FOR INFORMATION POTENTIAL

Because a number of librarians (including administrators) appear not to appreciate the importance of information-related variables, performance evaluation of individuals based on their information potential may provide a useful stimulus for improved organizational information management. Evidence in the area of information performance evaluation is limited, but a recent study of interpersonal communication in a formal organization by Roberts and O'Reilly concluded that "both the quantity and quality of information [contacted by the employee] appear to be important correlates of individual performance *across a variety of tasks and functions*" (author's emphasis).[14] In another paper these two authors write that "the ability to obtain information is directly related to individual and group performance."[15] Information resources clearly are critical determinants for overall organizational effectiveness.

Managers in research and development organizations are being urged to evaluate employees on such criteria as "information potential," that is, the individual's ability to possess more and better information and to make the information more accessible to his or her colleagues. Winfred Holland suggests that "potential employees should be evaluated on their IP [information potential] as well as their personal productivity," to achieve maximum information transfer into the organization.[16] Allen's concern that management must recognize the importance of an individual's "information potential" is being acknowledged for research and development organizations, but the concept appears to have made little advancement in literature related to the management of public service institutions, such as libraries.

The notion of evaluation and performance measures of employees' information activity—contacts with factual information sources, interpersonal contacts, and dissemination of information to other organizational members—clearly deserves more attention in the organization. Traditional evaluation methods either of personality characteristics or ability to accomplish predetermined goals may be ignoring important determinants of organizational effectiveness when information activity is not considered. Additional attention to the individual's information potential through performance evaluation may be a most effective strategy to improve organizational information management.

THE ADMINISTRATIVE CHALLENGE

If one believes, as do many reputable scientists, that information is the ultimate frontier,[17] professionals in many organizational settings such as an academic library can look forward to an administrative challenge of significant magnitude. Paradoxically, librarians, who are information specialists, exhibit limited skills in organizational information management. The advent of microtechnology in computers, imagery, and other information-handling techniques for administrative purposes is but an image on the horizon for many public service institutions. Indeed, the vast armada of new information technologies has caused one information scientist to ask, "Whither libraries, or, wither libraries?"[18] Currently, our administrative use of information to make effective decisions appears to be tied into the "withering" process.

The realizations coming from a post-industrial society engaged in a true information revolution have raised considerable interest for improved information management and organizational decision making. And in the face of needed information support systems for administrative purposes, little significant progress has been made in libraries. Man's limited information-handling ability must be supported by new technologies including the computer. However, a prerequisite for such support systems is administration's awareness of the importance of information-related variables for improved organizational decision making.

Increased demands have been placed on administrators to justify their operations and increase the effectiveness of their organization. Academic libraries, as other types of public institutions, have not been excluded from such demands. It may be suggested that future strategies for improved organizational effectiveness will rely largely on process, or managerial solutions, rather than input, or increased levels of funding, staffing, and other resources. The marshalling of information-related resources will increase the administrator's responses as well as his or her ability to cope with rapid change. As this volume has suggested, the administrative challenge will be centered on the effectiveness of organizational information management and the administrator's ability to increase the information potential of individuals within the organization. Better utilization and integration of information and human resources may be our single best strategy for improved overall library effectiveness.

NOTES

[1] Frank Greenwood, "Your New Job in Information Management Resource," *Journal of Systems Management*, 30 (April 1979): 24.

[2] Milton Rutherbusch, "Information Management in the Modern Automated Office," *Information & Records Management* (April 1979): 28.

[3] Charles R. McClure, "Academic Librarians, Information Sources, and Shared Decision Making," *Journal of Academic Librarianship* 6 (March 1980): 9-15.

[4] Gerald M. Goldhaber et al., "Organizational Communication: 1978," *Human Communication Research*, 5 (Fall 1978): 90-91.

[5] Jeffrey Katzer, Kenneth H. Cook, and Wayne W. Crouch, *Evaluating Information: A Guide for Users of Social Science Research* (Reading, Mass.: Addison-Wesley, 1978).

[6] U. S., Federal Paperwork Commission, *Reference Manual for Program and Information Officials*, 2 vols. (Washington, D.C.: U. S. Government Printing Office, 1978).

[7] Forest W. Horton, Jr., *How to Harness Information Resources: A Systems Approach* (Cleveland, Ohio: Association for Systems Management, 1974).

[8] Forest Woody Horton, Jr., "A Government Occupational Standard for Information Manager," *Information Manager*, 1 (March-April 1979): 34-36.

[9] Monroe S. Kuttner, *Managing the Paperwork Pipeline* (New York: John Wiley & Sons, 1978).

[10] Charles A. O'Reilly, III, "Variations in Decision Makers' Use of Information Sources: The Impact of Quality and Accessibility of Information" (mimeograph available from the author, Berkeley: University of California, School of Business Administration, February 1979).

[11] Jeffrey Pfeffer, *Organizational Design* (Arlington Heights, Illinois: AHM Publishing Co., 1978), pp. 82-83.

[12] Gerald M. Goldhaber, Harry S. Dennis, Gary M. Richetto, and Osmo A. Wiio, *Information Strategies: New Pathways to Corporate Power* (Englewood Cliffs, N.J.: Prentice-Hall, Inc., 1979), pp. 35-36.

[13] A. C. Filley, "Committee Management: Guidelines from Social Science Research," *California Management Review*, 13, no. 1 (1970): 13-21.

[14] Karlene H. Roberts and Charles A. O'Reilly, III, *Interpersonal Communication, Personnel Ratings, and Systematic Performance Characteristics in Organizations* (Berkeley: University of California, Institute of Industrial Relations, 1975), NTIS Document no. AD A013874/7GA.

[15] Karlene H. Roberts and Charles A. O'Reilly, III, "Some Correlations of Communication Roles in Organizations," *Academy of Management Journal*, 22 (March 1979): 46.

[16] Winford E. Holland, "The Special Communicator and His Behavior in Research Organizations: A Key to the Management of Informal Technical Information Flow," *IEEE Transactions on Professional Communication*, Vol. PC-17 (September-December 1974): 48-53.

[17] Lewis M. Branscomb, "Information: The Ultimate Frontier," *Science*, 23 (January 12, 1979): 54-57.

[18] F. Wilfrid Lancaster, "Whither Libraries? Or, Wither Libraries?" *College & Research Libraries*, 39 (September 1978): 345-57.

Part VI
FINANCIAL BASIS OF THE LIBRARY

Introduction

Putting the library on a sound financial basis is a prerequisite to providing information services. Without money, the library cannot do very much no matter how good the intentions. Unfortunately, most librarians have only a limited comprehension of what decisions need to be made in allocating resources, where the money is going to come from, and what constraints are likely to exist in using this money. Knowing this sort of information is crucial to managing any organization, not just a library.

The question "just what is a budget anyway" is discussed in some detail in this section by Ann E. Prentice, whose analysis of the financial basis of the public library is not only one of the most recent treatments of the subject, but also one easily understood by librarians not intensively involved in daily resource allocation decisions. Prentice defines terms, describes budgeting systems, and provides a useful breakdown of what categories need to be considered in constructing the library budget. Prentice is service-oriented in her perspective, viewing the budget as a means of exploring alternative ways of accomplishing library goals and objectives. Thus, the process of budgeting becomes far more than merely a monetary distribution system. It assumes the role of directing all library activities to achieve maximum success. Perhaps more importantly, budgeting forces librarians to consider carefully what it is that they really want to do—and whether it is worth doing in the first place.

Anne G. Sarndal's paper is limited to a discussion of one budgeting strategy, zero-based budgeting (ZBB). The use of the word "strategy" is important in understanding Sarndal's perspective. As does Prentice, Sarndal views ZBB as an all-encompassing series of events leading to the accomplishment of library goals. In the process, she dispells certain persistent myths about ZBB and replaces them with more realistic and factual information. Sarndal neither minimizes the difficulties of implementing ZBB nor overemphasizes its potential benefits. ZBB is presented in a frank and balanced manner, easily understood by librarians who may be faced with the necessity of implementing mandated budgeting systems they do not understand.

The benefits of ZBB, as with most programming budgeting systems, do not lie necessarily in increasing the efficiency of resource allocation, but also in the increased comprehension and understanding of whatever services and operations are ultimately decided upon by the library. As Sarndal views it, the higher degree of "understanding, and communication, better planning, and increased creative efforts to find better ways of doing things" may more than outweigh the initial difficulty of implementing a ZBB system in a library.

Finally, Jacob Cohen and Kenneth W. Leeson provide an introduction to how funds are actually used in an academic library setting. While Cohen and Leeson's treatment of resource allocation is more technical than that of either Prentice or Sarndal, it presents operational level data and shows precisely what allocation decisions were made among a limited set of academic libraries, and how these decisions affect library operations in general. The numerical breakdowns of allocation decisions are of particular interest and are worth studying by any librarian concerned with effective and efficient distribution of resources. Clearly, budgetary decisions should be based on a data base of information describing existing allocations and the effectiveness of those allocations.

The allocation of limited resources to different library operations and services is an administrative duty that wins few friends among library staff or patrons. Nearly everyone wants more than can be allocated. But available funds often depend on non-library related events, events that are often little understood. Unlike some other types of organizations, libraries are not necessarily viewed as an essential service by many and are therefore more subject to budgetary restrictions. Understanding the nature of library resource allocation, the sources of resources to be allocated, and the way in which sound allocation procedures can contribute to, or detract from, good library service is important for all librarians, whether administrators directly responsible for fiscal control or librarians who must live under whatever restrictions are made necessary by such control.

Budgeting
By Ann E. Prentice

The budget is a financial plan by which the library outlines its priorities and programs in monetary terms. The library's budget, in turn, is part of a larger budget that outlines the priorities and programs of the local government of which it is a unit. As a planning document, the budget is a presentation of the library's objectives in terms of specific programs to be carried out within a specified period of time. As a political document, the budget, when stated and approved in terms of full funding for "visible" programs, is a statement of the importance of library service relative to other local services, such as fire protection, police protection, and sanitation. It is also a negotiated agreement between the local government and the library, stating that the library will provide specified services at an agreed upon price. Internally, to the trustees and the library staff, the budget is a primary planning document. In its preparation the objectives and priorities of the library are reevaluated to determine future directions. In its implementation the budget is an aid to effective management and control of the library. These roles of the budget state the ideal. In fact, however, budgets often do not identify objectives and programs but are cut-and-patch results of political maneuvering.

Historically, the word budget comes from *bouget*, a large leather bag that was carried by the treasurer to the king of England. In the bag were documents explaining to Parliament the needs of king and country, plus petty cash for payment of immediate expenses. As time passed, the word budget shifted from the bag to the documents themselves, and from this inauspicious beginning government budgeting developed in England. The basic budgeting principles of taxation—only by common

---

Reprinted by permission of the American Library Association from *Public Library Finance*, by Ann E. Prentice, copyright © 1977 by the American Library Association.

consent of the taxed, the recording of all revenue and expenditure, and an annual public statement of public finances—which are currently followed by local governments in the United States and Canada, derive directly from the English model.

In nineteenth-century America, public budgeting was at best inefficient, with little or no standardization or control. To improve upon this situation, the National Municipal League in 1899 developed a model municipal corporation act, placing responsibility for budgeting with the mayor. Despite this improvement, budgets tended to be a collection of needs or requests by city departments rather than an overall plan indicating a direction or priorities for the city. In 1907 the New York Bureau of Municipal Research issued a detailed analysis of the city department of health, whose findings and recommendations resulted in adoption of a budgetary system with standardized budget information and systematized accounting. During the decade 1910 to 1920, reform of city government was widespread, and an important factor in the reform movement was the development of systematized budgeting under the direction of the mayor and city council.

During the depression of the 1930s, many businessmen expressed concern over their tax burdens and the continuing laxity in public budget reform, particularly in accounting. Pressure by the business community resulted in a more professional approach to the budget process. The need for very careful budgeting by cities, to balance their budgets in the face of reduced revenues, accelerated the process, as did expanded state supervision of local financing. Gradually it became apparent to city officials that budgeting is more than bookkeeping. It is also planning: planning the use of future income in relation to specific objectives of benefit to the community. The Hoover Commission report in 1949 reemphasized the planning role of the budget and recommendations were made for "performance" budgeting. With the gradual professionalization of finance through the education of specialists in local-government administration, the budgeting process in recent decades has become a strong factor in the operation of government and government agencies.

The budget is a political as well as a legal document and must be responsive to its political environment. In some communities the environment is nonpartisan while in others it is not. The library's budget makers must be responsive to the environment and aware of who the political leaders are, who holds power, and who may gain power and the difference it may make. Political parties and party leaders may hold differing views about libraries, and although the library itself remains nonpartisan, library leaders must know what these attitudes are. The budget makers also need to be aware of the potential power of third-party groups, taxpayers' reform groups, and pressure and interest groups representing education, labor, religion, business, etc. Their interests and concerns are important in that they can sway opinion, and therefore votes, in support of or against funding library services. The individual who is a community leader and whose opinion is respected may also contribute to the environment of budgeting. One does not necessarily respond to each of these interests, but they must each be considered. Responding to its political environment, the Cleveland (Ohio) Public Library 1975 Levy Campaign Committee prepared a brochure indicating the need to vote for Issue 12 on the November ballot to raise additional funds for the library's program of service. Supporting a positive vote on Issue 12 and listed in the brochure were twenty-five organizations, from the AFL-CIO and senior citizens groups to ethnic associations and community groups.

Part of the political environment is the chief executive of the municipality, who is responsive to the needs and wishes of the community and to members of the party in power. He is also responsible for the organization of the budget for all city departments and for its presentation to the legislative body, which is even more responsive to the groups that comprise the political climate. Local legislators are experienced in politics and government. Many are long-term officeholders and authorities in various areas of government, often in budget making and, more specifically, in certain areas of budgeting.

Also of prime importance is the economic environment of budget preparation. Because a community's resources are limited, it has a finite ability to pay for services and therefore decisions must be made to determine priorities and levels of service it is possible to support. "A profound knowledge of the economic base of the community by the budget officer becomes at once one of his greatest sources of strength and the prudent use of that knowledge becomes his greatest responsibility."[1]

The budget officer must know the prevailing economic conditions, economic level of the community, and the level of library service it can realistically be expected to support. As with other aspects of budget making, this knowledge comes as the result of continuous observation and not annual testing of the economic climate.

The historical context within which budget makers work is also a factor. A pattern for budget requests from the library, indicating a general level of support, will have developed over time. With the preparation of a new budget, certain expectations and measures are held by political interests, based upon past performance, and change tends to be slow. Wildavesky suggests that, for this reason, new ideas should be mentioned in a budget repeatedly so that legislators will come to accept and eventually fund some of them.[2] Historical expectations modify budget requests by keeping next year's levels in general conformity with those of the previous year.

A further historical factor in a library's budget in most communities is a board of trustees who is responsible to the governing agency for the library and who may place it at a distance from direct executive control. The budget officer may need to go not directly to the library director or library budget officer for clarification or modification of items but to the board of trustees and its treasurer. This places the budget officer in the position of dealing with a citizens' group rather than with a professional counterpart in the library. Lines of communication between budget officer and library director and to or through the board should be determined, either formally or informally, so that the board members are kept aware of discussions and negotiations without slowing the process of budget preparation and review.

There are various budgeting methods, but most fall into one of three categories: the line item budget, the program budget, and the performance budget. Each of these is supported by a theoretical base and operational experience. In practice, most budgets are some combination of the three rather than a pure expression of one format. The line item budget, or as it is often called, the object of expenditure budget, is the traditional format and is still the most widely used (see figure 1).

As the library budget is part of the larger local-government budget, items are often mandated and codes for each item are provided so that the library budget will be in the same format as other departmental budgets. Cost figures for each item in the line item budget are determined by the financial officer and budget committee through a review of the previous year's budget. What items were overspent? Were some items underspent? What are the increased costs in materials, in services? Have salaries increased and at what rate? Has new legislation affecting salaries and benefits, such as an increase in the minimum wage or additional disability requirements, been passed? Are building repairs (not a capital expense) required by the insurance agency? Each item in the previous year's budget is reviewed and a decision is made to increase, decrease, or maintain the same expenditure figure. Inflation and its effect on the cost of goods and services is also taken into account.

This approach to budgeting is relatively simple and can be carried out by relatively inexperienced individuals, but the major difficulty with this format is that it emphasizes the tools of a library rather than what the tools are to do. Personnel costs are listed in terms of salaries and benefits rather than by what the personnel *do* to carry out the library's objectives. In a sense, the line item budget is a first step in data collecting and presents undigested figures. Because it is simple and is not program related, it is easy for legislators to cut without considering the effects of these cuts on programs.

```
                        SYSTEM_____
                        NAME OF LIBRARY_____
                        LOCATION OF LIBRARY_____
===============================================================

OPERATING DISBURSEMENTS

PERSONAL SERVICES
  Library Staff                       $_____
  Custodial Staff                      _____
  Employee Benefits                    _____
TOTAL PERSONAL SERVICES                                $_____

LIBRARY MATERIALS
  Books                                _____
  Serials                              _____
  Nonbook
    Audiovisual Materials
      Films, Filmstrips, Slides        _____
      Recordings [Discs and Tapes]     _____
      Audiovisual Aid Rental           _____
        Total Audiovisual              _____
    Other Nonbook
      Materials for the Blind          _____
      Itemized Nonbook                 _____
        Total Other Nonbook            _____
  Bookbinding                          _____
TOTAL LIBRARY MATERIALS                                _____

OTHER OPERATING DISBURSEMENTS
  Library Supplies                     _____
  Insurance                            _____
  Fuels and Utilities                  _____
  Rental of Quarters                   _____
  Miscellaneous
    Rental, Repair, and Maintenance of
      Office Machines              A   _____
    Automotive Expenses             B  _____
    Travel                          C  _____
    Membership Dues                 D  _____
      Total A through D                _____
  Contracts with Libraries and Firms   _____
  Other Miscellaneous                  _____
TOTAL OTHER OPERATING                                  _____

TOTAL OPERATING                                        ==========
```

Fig. 1. Operating Budget, 1978, Line Item Format

The program budget is a planning-oriented budget that groups expenditures around an objective, an output, a program, or a function that is output oriented, and that covers a span of one or more years (see figure 2). Some authorities recommend development of a five-year plan or program which is then broken down into annual budgets which will conform more directly to immediate budget needs. In this format the cost of each program, such as children's services or outreach programs, or of such functions as technical services or reference are calculated. Costs of each item in the program are stated but emphasis is on program rather than individual items.

```
                                        Name of Library _____
                                        Location of Library _____




Administration

    Personal Services
        Salaries
        Personal Benefits
        Training and Conferences

    Interdepartmental Services
        Auditing
        Insurance
        Automobile Expenses
        Building and Grounds Maintenance
        Printing and Duplicating

    Contractual Services
        Rental of Space
        Telephone
        Utilities
        Equipment Rental
        Maintenance Service
        Membership and Dues

    Supplies and Materials
        Office Supplies
        Postage
        Maintenance Supplies
        Janitorial Supplies

    TOTAL ADMINISTRATION                    _____
```

Fig. 2. Operating Budget, Program Format (continues to next page)

Circulation Services (Sample Narrative)

Description: Record all loan transactions; maintain circulation and registration records; generate required statistics; keep collection, card catalog, and other collection access tools in order.

Anticipated Accomplishments: Convert charging system to a new automated format.

Workload Indicators: Annual circulation statistics for three prior years, and a projection for budget year based on the past year's experience.

    Positions
        Professional
        Nonprofessional
        Clerical
        Benefits

    Equipment
        Charging Equipment
        Card Catalog Unit
        Book Truck

    Supplies
        Listing of all paper, forms, record-keeping supplies necessary to circulation service

    Contractual
        Rental of Copy Machine
        Printing
        Binding
        Collection Rentals

    Reference Services

    Childrens Services

    Audiovisual Services

    Bookmobile

    Outreach

    Branches

    Special Services (e.g., federal grant to be administered which would be recorded here with grant funding to be reported under income)

TOTAL   _____

Fig. 2(cont.). Operating Budget, Program Format

In designing the program budget certain factors must be kept in mind and certain steps must be taken. Program budgeting as a planning activity requires involvement by trustees, library administrators and, where possible, library staff, and the success of the planning is dependent upon the accuracy of the data used in planning and the insight into operations which results.[3] Initial planning requires a view of the total system called "library." What are the objectives of the library as seen by its staff? What are its objectives as seen by members of the community? How closely do they mesh? What are the mutually agreed upon objectives? What are the interrelationships between the library and other agencies in the community? What are the limits of library service? What services does the library perform? What services does the library specifically *not* perform? Once library objectives and services are identified and agreed upon, it is necessary to determine the resources available for carrying them out. The final planning step is investigation of the management of the library—how resources are allocated and used by the library and how efficiently they are used. A survey or study may be undertaken to answer these questions. Once objectives have been established, resources identified, and a means for carrying them out has been outlined and labeled "program," the next step is collection of data to support the program.

As an example of the way in which a library's financial data are collected and organized into budgeting format, consider the following. Assume that reference services to the municipal government are a number-one priority for your library. The needs of this subgroup of your total clientele have grown and it would be desirable to add a librarian to the reference staff so that this service may be conducted without further taxing the overworked reference staff. Exactly what will be the costs of adding this specialized service to your library and how do you determine them?

The first cost to calculate is that of personnel, which includes the salary of the proposed librarian and the salaries of any necessary support staff, such as a part-time assistant, clerk, or other individuals needed to staff this expanded service. Benefits such as vacations, sick days, insurance, and the like must be included, as well as administrative costs relating to the time needed to maintain employee records.

The next figure to be determined is the exact amount of time spent by each staff member on the program. For a proposed program, estimate the time needed to carry out the program. For an ongoing program, the best technique is to conduct a personnel survey to see how much time is spent by various-level staff members on each activity.

Often classed as overhead or fixed overhead are the administrative and supervisory costs of the operation. Here the costs of full-time supervisory and administrative staff and the percentage of time those in a part-time supervisory and administrative position spend on these activities are calculated and pro-rated. In some instances separate costs are calculated for supervision and administration.

Floor-space costs are determined by calculating the average square-foot cost of general maintenance, such as heat, light, security, cleaning, and the average square-foot repayment costs (the latter are averaged over the mortgage period and consist of capital costs per square foot plus interest). If the mortgage has been paid, a depreciation rate per square foot is figured in. Supplies must be figured into overall costs and they include all materials, down to file folders, pens, and rubber bands. Equipment, including typewriters, calculators, furniture, and similar long-term investments, is pro-rated over the useful life of each item.

All of these figures (with the exception of the time study) are available in the library's records. They may be difficult to assemble initially, but once you have them they can readily be updated for later use. In this manner you can "cost out" a program to determine its dollar requirements; you can also cost out alternative methods of service to see which would be less expensive. You can also determine unit costs. For library services broadly conceived (e.g., reference, circulation), there are no alternatives. When specific processes within these services and their alternatives are "costed," it is possible to make choices.

An often cited example deals with the relative value of microfilming a book or storing it in its original form. To determine the more economical alternative you calculate the cost of storing the book and the cost of microfilming it and storing the microfilm. Storage costs for microfilm are less than for hard copy but the initial costs of microfilming are higher. If you pro-rate the cost of microfilm over its expected useful life, how much would it cost per year? Would this be offset by cheaper storage costs? Also, you would add the cost of microfilm "readers," which includes pro-rated equipment costs, storage costs, and instruction of patrons in use of the equipment. With all the costs of microfilm considered, then you are in a position to make a decision.

In a similar manner, you can cost out and reach dollar answers to such questions as "Is it cheaper to buy certain titles or borrow them through interlibrary loan?" and "Which is cheaper, leasing office equipment or buying it outright?" Different processing alternatives in technical services can be costed out to determine which is more economical. In most cases, quantifiable activities can be analyzed and dollar figures applied.

Dollar figures, however, are only one type of input that is relevant to library decisions. Through cost analysis, it may prove to be economical to "double up" on staff office space and assign three staff members in an office intended for two—but the staff reaction may be sufficiently negative to compromise the expedient. You may find that rearranging library hours results in a more efficient use of staff, but this may not be acceptable to patrons. Dollar input is essential, but also essential are the human inputs, and they must be taken into consideration. When you evaluate the cost-benefit relationships of a program, it is necessary to go back and ask exactly what are the program objectives within the program and its priorities—those relating to the library or to the user? Finally, the impact of a program on the institutions of which it is part should be taken into consideration. If there is a conflict in priorities between library and user, the user comes first, and if community or institutional pressures affect programs, they must be acknowledged.

The final step in the planning process is to determine which programs the library wishes to pursue, in accord with its goals and objectives and the cost analysis procedure as it is modified by cost-benefit factors. Individual programs, assessed in this fashion, are combined to form the planning program budget. Because the planning program budget is presented in terms of services and objectives, it is a better forecasting of needs than the traditional line by line budget which emphasizes activities. Each of the services listed would be expanded in the same fashion as the circulation service program (see figure 2) with a brief description of the service, the anticipated accomplishments, and a breakdown of all costs. Reported under the Administration program are costs of administrative staff plus costs of activities which are spread over all library programs such as building maintenance, insurance, and staff training and conferences. In a program format adhering closely to the definition, administrative costs would be divided among each of the services on the basis of amount of staff training, floor space occupied, and so on, but the modification shown in figure 2 is quite appropriate to a library budget and less time-consuming to develop. A workload indicator is included as well. This provides past data on workload and a projection for the budget year. It is one figure against which actual workload can be measured.

The Planning Program Budgeting System (PPBS) carries the program budget an additional step. As in the program budget, its initial step is to state the objective: why the library is in business. Next it identifies basic programs or functions and subdivides them so that each activity in the total operation is visible. Each subprogram is to be justified by a statement of why you do what you are doing and where you plan to do it. Another statement, of how you plan to carry out the task and how much it will cost, is also necessary. The PPBS like the program budget, built upon cost accounting and work measurement statistics, is more difficult to prepare initially than the line by line budget. In small libraries, where resources and staff serve in several capacities, it is often difficult to determine the cost of one program. There is also the problem of obtaining accurate work-measurement statistics when one deals with public services because it is difficult to develop valid standards for such services as reference or reader services. In addition, there is the problem that most statistics measure input and output rather than the quality of response.

The final step in PPBS, which separates it from program budgeting, is the plan for feedback and evaluation, a form of management-by-objective as applied to budget figures. The system is an analysis of library operations, a summary statement of the cost of a program, the preferred course of action, considered through cost analysis as the best way to allocate funds, which programs to stress, and the best combination of resources to achieve results. It then provides for periodic reviews to see if costs are within the guidelines and to determine output results.

```
Administration

    Personal Services
       Salaries
       Personal Benefits
       Training and Conferences

    Interdepartmental Services
       Auditing
       Insurance
       Automobile Expenses
       Building and Grounds Maintenance
       Printing and Duplicating

    Contractual Services
       Rental of Space
       Telephone
       Utilities
       Equipment Rental
       Maintenance Service
       Membership and Dues

    Supplies and Materials
       Office Supplies
       Postage
       Maintenance Supplies
       Janitorial Supplies

    TOTAL ADMINISTRATION                    _____
```

Fig. 3. Operating Budget, Performance Budget Format

Input Cost	Service	Program Objective	Output Totals	Cost per Output
$84,430	General Service	Provide library materials and equipment	187,650 persons	$ .45
63,570	Circulation Service	Lend materials to public	298,460 items	.21
35,280	Reference Service	Provide readers advisory and reference service	33,601 persons	1.05
36,000	Bookmobile Service	Provide circulation and services to patrons in Greene and Stone counties	4 bookmobiles	9,000.00
6,960	Outreach Service	Provide materials for physically handicapped and institutionalized	12 stations	580.00
14,640	Records Service	Maintain records of use and users for statistical reports and planning input, overdues sent, etc.	11,340 persons	1.29
15,860	Special Services	SDI, special research projects to individuals or groups	463 services	34.26
1,300	Public Relations Service	Publicize library resources and programs	104 programs	12.50

Fig. 3(cont.). Operating Budget

The ability to determine if output totals are correctly estimated and if cost per output falls within acceptable limits allows for closer check than other formats. This presupposes a long-term planning program upon which the annual budget rests, an ability to identify with accuracy the parameters of a program, and the ability to measure output. In format PPBS can be similar to the program budget with the added feature of a plan for evaluating performance during as well as at the end of the budget years. Output quantities are given as the objectives to be met. The degree of success in attaining objectives will be taken into account when budgeting for the next year (see figure 3).

Like the sample program format, figure 3 does not show a pure format because administrative overhead is separated from the programs, but it could be connected to a total PPBS by dividing those costs among the programs. Input cost represents the total cost of the program or service, output total represents the estimated number of clientele, of items circulated, and so forth, while cost per output represents the unit cost of the activity. In a total PPBS, input cost and cost per output would reflect administrative overhead as well as the service itself.

PPBS tries to measure the success with which objectives are reached. Measuring library output for PBS or PPBS in terms of circulation, number of questions answered, books processed, and the like is unsatisfactory as these measures do not address themselves directly to the objectives of the library in providing an information service, and output units provided by the library do not measure benefit to users. Librarians who follow PPBS format, however, are forced to use these and similar measures for lack of better ones. An evaluation methodology that identifies the real, quantifiable measure of library service may be impossible, but the need to justify a program and a budget and the increasing demand by higher levels of government to measure output make it essential that we try. It would appear that surveys devoted to satisfaction of needs are a useful way to measure library effectiveness. Attitude surveys do exist but they have not been designed for the purpose of evaluating particular programs. Whatever measures are devised they must take into account the qualitative as well as the quantitative aspects of library service.

Public libraries have been slow to adopt program budgeting or PPBS, perhaps because they are unaware of their use as effective planning tools, or perhaps because of reluctance to convert to this system from the traditional line item format, a process which is admittedly time consuming in the initial year or two. Budget development continues to be an important facet of local government, and as local government grows in sophistication, demands for corresponding sophistication will be made of library budget makers.

In academic libraries there is a trend toward formula budgeting—a line item technique that sets numerical guidelines for fund allocation related to preestablished standards of adequacy and accepted levels of attainment. It is an attempt to mathematically balance the distribution of available resources among the organizations within one's jurisdiction.[4] Formula budgeting is mechanical and therefore easy to prepare, but it does not consider differences in service modes or qualitative ingredients of service. It has not been generally suggested that formula budgeting be applied to public libraries, but the possibility should be explored by public librarians, preferably in advance of study by the municipal budget office so that alternatives will be available.

Local-government budgeting formats are modified by the overall governmental structure and the controls imposed by that structure. States can require a line item format (New Jersey), can issue guidelines for budget preparation (Ohio), or require other specific format procedures. As states have control over all levels of government below them, they control the ways in which budgets are developed and presented; however, budgets can be by local option so long as that option does not contradict state law. The state's constitution and statutes, local ordinances, administrative decisions, library charters, and court decisions form the legal base for the budget. The underlying purpose is to ensure that each unit of local government prepares and presents its budget in a uniform, systematized format. The library budget, as part of a larger budget, must be constructed in conformity to that budget. Additional legal requirements require a balanced budget, a budget calendar determining the beginning of the fiscal year and due dates for various budget formats, hearing dates, and the like, as well as the form accountability should take, be it a published annual report, audit, or the like. Legal controls vary from state to state and from locality to locality, depending upon the historical and economic climates in which they were enacted.

Composition of the budget-making library committee may vary but it usually is headed by the library director or an individual designated by the director, such as the assistant director or the financial officer. Other members of the budget committee are usually department heads and/or program directors, each of whom is responsible for data collection and budget development from his or her department or program. This committee is responsible for budget development in accord with all external and internal requirements. The budget committee submits the prepared budget to the board of trustees for its review and approval and then to the local-governmental authority.

The initial step in budget preparation is development of a year-long budget calendar that covers each phase of budget preparation, from review of objectives and requests for information, through hearings, to final approval and adoption. In some areas the budget cycle is specified by law while in others it is determined on a more informal basis. In either case, budgeting is a year-round process, and guidelines as well as deadlines should be set. The first step, to be taken early in the budget year, is to project the next year in general terms of the economic situation and to estimate how this will affect library funding requests. The current year's programs should be considered in terms of objectives and priorities. Some libraries operate on a zero-base approach—each program or function must be justified on the basis of whether it should exist in the next year's budget, rather than justifying an increase or decrease of the program's support.

From early projections of the overall economic climate and review of library objectives the library budget makers and the board of trustees determine what the budget policy will be—whether priorities for spending will change, whether cutbacks in service may be required and how they will be determined. This is done with as much input as possible from local-government officials. At the same time, each department should review its functions to assure that it is working to the limit of its responsibilities—but not beyond. Department heads are also consulted on projected workload needs. More staff? Why? In what capacity? Is the present staff working to capacity? Estimates of all materials and expenses, in addition to staff, are made and are justified on the basis of standard sources for price guidelines.

At the same time that the operating budget is considered, the long-term capital program is reviewed in terms of the library's objectives. The capital budget and the operating budget are based on the same objectives and, to a large degree, are interdependent. The capital budget covers major long-term expenses such as a new building or major renovation and requires accommodation in the operating budget, as capital expenses will be reflected in staff size, cost of utilities, insurance, and the like.

The process of budget construction begins once the objectives are reviewed and some consideration has been made of the level of support that can be anticipated for the next fiscal year. The first step, estimating budget needs, can be done in several ways, such as estimating the cost of providing the optimum program.

Each item in the budget should be checked to see if it is needed and the extent to which it will be needed in the next year. Should items be increased or decreased? What effect will each action have on the overall program? To the greatest degree possible, work measurement and unit-cost figures should be developed and expenditures should be expressed in these terms. It is very helpful, though time consuming, to construct alternative budgets that indicate the effect of a 5 percent increase or decrease in funding. If this is done, based on a line item format, specific line items (such as personnel, books, utilities, etc.) would be increased or decreased, while in a program format, programs such as outreach or senior citizen programs could be added or cut. Within the programs, items could be varied. Politically, a program format is more useful as eliminated programs have greater impact than reduced line items. This indicates to the library and its staff what specific effects changes in requested amounts would have. Alternative budgets have both a planning and a political purpose.

A ceiling may be placed by the municipal government on the amount each department can budget, and then, within the library, spending limits will be placed on each department. This technique of limiting expenditures is a means of enforcing savings within a department, and in times of economic difficulty can actually be a cut. Departments may be asked not only to estimate the cost of programs but to list them in priority order —those most essential and those least essential. This not only further defines the library's objectives but identifies programs that will be sacrificed if necessary.

The most important single element of the budget to be reviewed is staff. Libraries are high-labor-input departments and the major portion of the budget is for staff. The size and cost of current staffing patterns require a thorough annual review. Libraries may conduct management studies to determine the amount of work to be done, the qualifications for each type of work, and the most efficient means of completing tasks. The need for each professional and nonprofessional employee should be reviewed in terms of the job that is done. Does new equipment (such as introduction of OCLC) affect staffing patterns and needs? What are the staffing needs if a new building is opened or a new program begun? These possibilities need review and recommendations for future staffing needs and costs.

Also to be reviewed are the costs of contractual services such as architect or legal fees. The costs of workshops conducted by outside personnel, computer time, cleaning services, and rental of equipment and buildings should be reviewed, as should supply items, in terms of their continued need and price increase. Equipment should be inventoried and its replacement dates predicted so that there is a steady replacement program rather than crisis replacement situations. With these figures, a preliminary budget is developed and it should be in line with whatever requirements have been set by the board and the municipal authority (e.g., only a 5 percent increase).

To support the preliminary budget, descriptive material should be developed, such as workload data and trend charts that indicate growth in services or increase in prices. The need is to select those key statistics which best support your budget requests. Has circulation increased in relation to circulation staff so that a need for additional personnel in that department is obvious? Have reference questions increased to the extent that the need for additional reference librarians is obvious? Is circulation up 10 percent but the budget only 5 percent? The need to justify current staff allocation or addition to the collection at a certain rate is important. Here again the budget is more than figures; it is a management tool and a public relations tool as well.

After this review, the budget is organized according to local requirements so that it conforms to the local format. Figures are then checked for accuracy and to ensure that anticipated expenditures and income match. The board reviews and, after careful study, approves the budget, which is to be submitted to the municipal government for analysis. It is to be hoped that the budget is reviewed by someone who is familiar with the library and its needs and, even more, that this person has been available to the library budget officer throughout the budget's development. In reviewing the budget, salaries are checked to assure that pay rates are in line with those of other agencies and that supply, equipment, and contractual service costs are also in line. Substantial new programs are reviewed in terms of objectives as well as costs. The budget examiner will check all costs and suggest changes or cuts.

At a private hearing, library representatives have an opportunity to discuss problem areas and indicate the effects of cuts. Typically, no decisions are made at a closed hearing, but the information serves as input for the final budget figures, which are formulated and sent to the municipal executive officer who evaluates the library budget as part of the overall budget.

The first decisions made by the chief executive are usually policy decisions—personal preference, political preference, community preference for certain programs over others. The final review of the budget is conducted by the chief executive with input from department heads and open hearings. The budget advisors then prepare the final budget, which is submitted to the legislature and the public. The budget calendar allows ample time for the legislature to review the budget and for civic groups, employee groups, and the public to respond. From this final reaction and review the legislature can modify and act upon the revised budget. Once approved by the legislature, the budget is a legal document. The library revises its budget to conform with the official budget. Thus the current budget is completed and planning for the following year's budget can begin.

To determine for this study how public libraries deal with the budgeting process, particularly in terms of format and reporting, 127 medium and large public libraries were asked for copies of their operating budgets so that various approaches and formats and other information could be sampled. The libraries, representing thirty-seven states, range in population served from 70,000 to 2.5 million and, in budget, from $100,000 to $12 million. Little or no relationship between population and budget format or between budget size and format was evident.

Of the libraries in the sample, ninety-five (75 percent) use a line item budget. The number of line item entries, category headings, and specificity differed, but basically they followed the traditional format. The budgets also differed in their explanatory material—the extent of justification and program narrative followed by line item entries, for example. In most line item presentations the figures and breakdowns referred largely to personnel costs. Supplies, informational materials, and equipment were often lump-sum entries under single lines. In some instances the library budget was a separate unit within the city budget, while in others all municipal expenditures were united within a single budget. The difficulties a library planner has following the latter format (imposed by higher levels of government) are evident when books are listed in the city budget under "miscellaneous" or "capital outlay" and when there is no place other than "gifts" to list state or system support of the local library.

Other libraries follow a modified program format. Some prepare external line item formats to satisfy legal requirements and then prepare a program format for internal use. The McLennan County Library in Waco, Texas, prepares a line item budget for the city and a program budget as the basis for internal planning. The Wilmington (Delaware) Public Library must declare its functions and programs annually in a brief summary statement, before it prepares a line item budget. The Hartford (Connecticut) Public Library prepares a program and a line item format and uses both in public hearings, as the librarian found that some people understand one format better than the other.

Of the thirty-two libraries (25 percent) which have adopted a program or performance budget or variation thereof, sixteen (approximately half) are in California. These budgets are part of a larger budget which labels 'the library" as a municipal program and views library programs as subprograms. In some cases the library's responsibilities and objectives have been outlined by the local government and the library budget, after a brief restatement of goals, consists of program costs. Other library budgets, such as that of Long Beach, California, provide a detailed commentary stating the library's goals, programs, and subprograms. This budget includes performance elements in that indicators of performance, such as patrons in the library and circulation statistics, are included. The San Diego Public Library's program budget includes a description of programs, the authority or responsibility for implementation, objectives, and a list of outputs—circulation statistics, attendance, and reference questions. San Jose and Oakland have similar approaches, as does Los Angeles, which provides the description, objective, and workload for every program.

Examples of two operational budgeting formats which are excellent in approach and clarity are those of the District of Columbia Public Library (Martin Luther King Memorial Library) in Washington, D.C., and the Seattle Public Library. Both have performance formats and are designed to serve the many purposes of the budget. The District of Columbia Public Library budget is prefaced by a statement of goals, as supported by the philosophy of the library, and a review of past performance (in line with these goals) and the next steps necessary for their implementation. The budget defines four categories: administration, technical services, public services, and building and grounds. For each category and subprogram a narrative statement of work expectations, cost, and measures is presented, so that justification is by program and within the stated goals (see figure 4).

Seattle's performance budget was developed for 1975 as a product of an extensive analysis of library operations in 1974. "Through a series of discussions about policy alternatives with the consultant and library staff, the Board established a set of policy directions. These were subsequently communicated to the library staff and were to form the basis of their budget development efforts."[5] In its planning mode, the budget indicated reorganization of the library into three divisions and recommended internal allocations and changes. Programs and subprograms were identified and changes and directions were stated, along with criteria for evaluation. This example of a PPBS budgeting system, growing out of a management study, indicates the intertwining of planning, organizing, and budgeting for libraries.

Many libraries are rethinking their priorities in the light of changing economic conditions. Many are constrained by state and local regulations pertaining to library activities and reporting mechanisms and are restrained by lack of expertise in conducting a sophisticated review of library operations. As library administrators must increasingly be accountable for the way they spend their funds, and as it is not enough just to spend them carefully, a careful look at budgeting procedures in terms of planning and accountability is essential.

For most libraries, a modified program format as shown in figure 2 would provide sufficient program costing figures for planning. For those libraries required by law to submit a line item budget, it would be possible to develop the line item format to meet that responsibility and a modified program budget for planning and public relations purposes. A gradual move toward program budgeting would seem to be a positive direction for the library.

DISTRICT OF COLUMBIA GOVERNMENT	$ THOUSANDS **FY 75**	JUSTIFICATION AGENCY Public Library CATEGORY Technical Services								SCHEDULE **5**	Congressional SUBMISSION
			Obligations (FY 73)		Allotment (FY 74)		Adjusted Base (FY 75)		Increases (FY 75)		Request (FY 75)
Code		Category Total & Sub Category	Positions	Amount	Positions	Amount	Positions	Amount	Positions	Amount	Positions	Amount
CE-200		Technical Services............	73	763.9	73	822.4	70	768.8	...	...	70	768.8
		Total	73	763.9	73	822.4	70	768.8	...	...	70	768.8

Annual Work Program	Indicator/Source	FY 73	FY 74	FY 76
		(Thousands)	(Thousands)	(Thousands)
	Books purchased	98.0	98.0	155.2
	Total additions to collection	168.5	170.0	225.2
	New titles cataloged	15.4	15.4	16.0
	Bound volumes in collection	2,133.1	2,134.0	2,205.2

To order, classify and catalog, as well as physically prepare for public use an estimated 100,000 new books to be purchased for Library collections in FY 1974; to maintain a collection totalling above 2,000,000 volumes in a physical condition encouraging public use; to maintain a system of catalogs and shelflists providing bibliographic access to all Library collections, and to order, physically prepare for use and maintain periodicals, pamphlets, newspapers, government documents, phonograph records, educational films, microfilms and other microtexts, music scores, framed pictures, prints, etc.

The library is redirecting $30,378 from binding to the book fund because of the urgent need for funds for books.

PAGE CE-21 Rev.

Fig. 4. Sample Page, District of Columbia Library Budget. (SOURCE: *District of Columbia Public Library, 1975 Budget Submission* [Washington, D.C.: The Library, 1974], p. CE-21 Rev.)

REFERENCES

1. Lennox L. Moak and Kathryn W. Killian, *A Manual of Techniques for the Preparation, Consideration, Adoption and Administration of Operating Budgets* (Chicago: Municipal Finance Officers' Assn. of the U.S. and Canada, 1963), p.46.
2. Aaron Wildavesky, *The Politics of the Budgetary Process* (Boston: Little, 1964).
3. Reginald L. Jones and H. George Trenton, *Budgeting: Key to Planning and Control* (rev. ed.; New York: American Management Assn., 1971).
4. *Review of Budgeting Techniques in Academic and Research Libraries* (Washington, D.C.: Office of University Library Management Studies, 1973), p.3.
5. Seattle Public Library, *Library* (Seattle: The Library, 1975), p.379.

Zero Base Budgeting
By Anne G. Sarndal

■ Zero base budgeting, which is considered to be as much a management technique as a method of budgeting, is discussed. Traditional budgeting starts with the previous year's budget, but zero base budgeting operates with the premise that each activity must be justified from "scratch," and establishes a number of increments for each unit, in order of priority. Given the set of increments and the dollars available, management can determine the activities that warrant financing and the increments of these activities that will have to be given up. If additional funds become available it will be clear which additional increments have highest priority.

CONCEPTUALLY, zero base budgeting (ZBB) is one of the most simple budgeting approaches possible. It can be explained in about five minutes or less; in practice, however, it is more difficult and time consuming. On the whole, however, it is probably worthwhile if it is done seriously, not because it guarantees great savings, but because it fosters a better understanding of the organization, its objectives, and how these objectives can be best achieved, given the resources. Two ideas must be noted at this point. First, the phrase "given the resources" means that even if the budget may be increased, ZBB is still useful in making sure that the increased funds go where the greatest benefit would result.

Second, "understanding the organization, its objectives and how those objectives can be best achieved" emphasizes that ZBB stresses management and planning, not just the dollars of the budget.

Peter Pyhrr defines zero-base budgeting as "a planning and budgeting process which requires each manager to justify his entire budget request in detail from scratch (hence zero base) and shifts the burden of proof to each manager to justify why he should spend any money at all. The approach requires that all activities be analyzed in 'decision packages' which are evaluated by systematic analysis and ranked in order of importance" (1).

In traditional budgeting exercises,

Reprinted from *Special Libraries*, Vol. no. 70 (no. 12): 527-532 (December 1979). © copyright by Special Libraries Association.

the previous year's budget is taken as the base; only increases or new projects have to be defended. If cuts must be made, they are often across the board, or new programs are deferred while existing programs are continued that may actually have lower priority. This often induces managers to pad their requests, since they expect cuts; they might also spend recklessly at the end of the budget year, fearing that if anything is left unspent, the next year's budget may be decreased. ZBB starts from scratch and examines all activities.

Furthermore, traditional budgeting does not require managers to look at their operations to try to find new ways of operating, nor to give anything other than a final figure for the budget request. ZBB begins by examining the objectives and goals, specifically looking at and analyzing alternatives, and setting out several levels of operation for management to consider. By having clear priorities, management can determine where cuts can be made most efficiently or where funds can be spent most efficiently if more money is available.

Some resistance to ZBB is based on the false premise that it necessarily will put people out of jobs. While it is true that it has gained popularity during a period of tight budgets, it is just as useful when funds are plentiful. Furthermore, while positions may be reduced it is often possible, through attrition, transfer, and retraining, to minimize the number of people who lose jobs. For example, in the case of Georgia, the state Department of Agriculture found that there were ten positions of beekeeper buried in ongoing expense (1, p. 41). These were put at low priority; however, it was the policy of the then Governor Carter not to fire anyone. The positions were put into a special category so that they could not be refilled. Within a month, two of the beekeepers quit and the positions were then eliminated, although within a week local politicians had handed in names for replacements—under a normal budget, replacements would have been made. Who knows how many cases of low priority jobs continue because no one actually examines each part of the operation.

ZBB is not a new concept, and similar methods have been used before. In 1962, the Department of Agriculture tried it for one year, and the PPB (Planning–Programming–Budgeting) system developed during Robert McNamara's term in the Department of Defense is a type of comprehensive budget that requires analysis of all budget expenses. ZBB goes further, however, in its demand for analysis.

In 1969 Texas Instrument, which had been using traditional incremental approach, began using the ZBB approach developed by Peter Pyhrr. An article in a 1970 issue of *Harvard Business Review* (2) written by Pyhrr was read by Governor Carter who got Pyhrr to help install ZBB for the State of Georgia. Since that time it has been adopted by many government bodies and companies.

Planning and Budgeting are developed in four basic stages (1, p. 37):

- Long-term planning stage where the organization's goals and strategies are defined and developed.
- The stage where the operating plan and budget for the upcoming year are developed.
- The operating plan and budget must be presented to top management for appraisal.
- The final detailed budget is set out.

The second step is the primary place

where zero base budgeting fits; however, unless the first stage is done properly and the decisions are communicated, ZBB starts off with problems.

The basic framework is as follows (3): (each step will be discussed in detail). Note that in practice the steps will be adjusted for each organization, so there will be slight variations on the format. Also note that, unless the process is carefully adjusted, the exercise will not be as helpful as it could be.

1. Develop planning assumptions: basic objectives of the organization, environmental factors that enter, i.e., inflation rate, salary increases, and so on.

2. Identify "decision units," that is, the basic activities to be considered. The decision units may be cost centers, people, projects, services, capital expenditures, and so on.

3. Analyze each decision unit, setting out objectives, current operations, workload and performance measures, alternatives and incremental analysis.

4. Rank the various activities and increments according to priority.

5. Prepare a budget at various levels of effort.

6. Evaluate performance.

The ZBB Framework in Detail

Looking at each step in more detail, its operation can be understood, and possible problems can be considered.

1. *Develop planning assumptions:* Many organizations fail to show the implications of the overall plan for individual decision units. For example, the demand for circulation services is unlikely to be less just because funds have been cut. Across-the-board cuts will not be effective. External factors such as increased cost of books, increased salaries, reduced revenues, and so on, must be examined carefully to determine the implications for each unit, as well as for the entire organization. This plan usually comes from the top, but it needs to be comprehensive and to be communicated to the individual units.

2. *Identify decision units:* A decision unit is the unit around which the analysis centers. It may be a person, such as the cataloger; a service, such as reference services; a department, such as acquisitions; a capital expenditure, such as a new computer terminal for automating circulation; or some combination of these. The decision units should cover all activities in one way or another. The decision units should be roughly the same size if possible, otherwise ranking is more difficult. If they are too small it is difficult to make increments. For example, if one person is the unit, what is an increment? What can be done with half a person? It is possible to use one person but it can lead to difficulties.

Choosing decision units becomes more difficult if the organization is large and decentralized. For example, suppose the library system has a number of branches. Should a service, such as circulation, be taken as one unit and the services of all the branches be made part of that, or should each branch be used as a different unit? If each branch is a different unit, then each branch must have subunits, if the analysis is going to be complete.

3. *Analyze decision units:* This is the heart of the approach and therefore will be examined in more detail.

First, the purposes and objectives of the decision unit should be carefully set out. This might include some historical or perhaps legal reason for the unit's existence, and a careful statement of what the unit is expected to achieve. If the unit is doing many things—for example the library may be one decision unit as far as the total company is concerned—it will be useful to break it down into minicomponents for further analysis. In this stage, however, set out the basic objective of the library as a whole.

This step is important because upper management may not realize just how important the library is, how much it is being used and what services are being given. This is the place to point out the objectives of the unit.

Second, the minicomponents must be set up. These include reference service, acquisitions, cataloging, and so on. Describe the current operation in each, what services are being provided, and what resources are used to provide these services.

Next, set out performance and workload measurements. This is often difficult because standards may never have been established before and very little quantitative data may be available. It is important to keep statistics about circulation, reference questions handled, and so on, in order to make such statements as, for example, the loss of one person will result in 20% less time for reference services. These measures need to be stressed as it is difficult to evaluate the work otherwise.

At this point the consequences of eliminating the decision unit must also be determined and noted. It may appear at first blush that the cost of the unit could be saved; however, if the work is simply shifted to another department the cost of that unit will increase and this should be quantified as well as possible.

Then, alternative methods should be presented, with the costs and benefits sketched out. This is one of the most important steps and causes much difficulty. People are often prone to think that the way they are doing things is the only way. This is the chance to be creative and imaginative. Most ideas may be tossed aside before reaching paper, but a few alternatives should be devised.

One of the alternatives might be to do away with the unit, or at least to curtail the services drastically. Carefully point out the effects on the organization of the loss in service, and if the cut will increase workloads elsewhere, be sure to point that out.

One should not think only of a change in the amount or quantity of service given, but the type. In other words, try to come up with completely different ways of doing things.

After the alternatives have been set out, choose two or so and subject them to further, more detailed analysis. Then, choose the operation method you want to recommend. Many might choose the current method; if one of the alternatives is chosen, the present method would be put into the section of alternatives not recommended but presented for upper level managers to consider.

Next, a detailed incremental analysis is performed. Note that any new programs proposed should also be analyzed. This is the key and perhaps the most difficult part of the job. First, one must present the minimum level of service. Note that this does not mean "how can we give the same service with fewer resources" unless, of course, the library is overstaffed or resources can be reallocated in such a way as to provide the same level of service. In this proposal, a completely different *level* of service has to be considered, one that will be in keeping with the objectives, to be sure, but the very minimum. Then start adding. With an extra increment of resources, what extra increment of service can be provided. This analysis should give several different levels, in order of priority for meeting objectives.

The question, of course, is how minimal is minimum? A rough rule of thumb is 50-70% of present level, but it varies. One is often tempted to say "We cannot go any lower," but part of the test of a good manager is to be able to delineate different levels of service and the resources needed to provide them. In any case, one or two levels lower than the current level should be given, then the current level and one or two levels above.

Finally, once the various levels have been set out, detailed costs should be developed for each increment to show costs attached to the benefits or services provided by each level.

4. *Rank activities and increments:* After all the activities and increments have been set out, ranking must take place at the next highest level or in the department if minicomponents have been set up. Suppose there are five minicomponents and three increments for each, then there are fifteen increments for which priorities must be shown. If all minicomponents are essential then the first level of each would be given. It may not be possible to rank those in order. For example, cataloging and acquisitions: without books, cataloging may not be needed and without cataloguing the library cannot keep up with its books. Usually it is not necessary to distinguish between first and third priority, but there must be a difference between third and eighth, for example.

Once the decision unit manager has ranked his increments, they go to the next level manager, together with those of other decision unit managers in his area for further ranking. This continues until top management receives ranking from all areas.

5. *Prepare a budget:* Having completed the ranking it is possible to prepare detailed budgets. Note here that not one budget is prepared but a series of budgets. Suppose, for example, that after all ranking of increments, there were one hundred increments. It would be possible to show the budget for, say, seventy-five of these increments, with incremental budget estimates for the next twenty-five. Once top management knows what funds are available, it knows the cut-off point. If less funds are available, it knows what will be sacrificed—those with lower priority. If additional funds are available, it knows where they can best be used.

6. *Evaluate performance:* After the budget has gone into effect, periodic reviews should be undertaken to see if actual expenses are in keeping with budget—and if actual services are being provided.

Zero based budgeting, for all its supporters, is not without problems. Any method that seems to be used for cutting jobs is going to cause negative reaction. Furthermore, it requires a great commitment of time and effort, which means a great deal of planning, organization, and preparation. First, the people involved must be assured that everyone is going through the same ordeal, or at least everyone at the same level, to keep the unit from feeling that it is being singled out. The program should be designed carefully to fit the needs of the organization; sufficient time should be devoted to explaining how the system operates and what is to be accomplished. Communication is always important but here it is most critical.

Some of the specific problems that have been found are as follows:

- Planning results have not been linked to individual units to show implications.
- Difficulties arise in identifying decision units. This especially applies to problems of size and function.
- Decision unit analysis causes problems because it may be difficult to get managers to give serious thought to alternatives and increments of service. They may have difficulty in setting priorities. Another problem deals with workload and performance measures.
- Ranking also causes problems, particularly if presentations are not consistent. Here it is important to have managers sit down together to discuss issues since it may be difficult to get ideas across on paper, particularly if there are time constraints.

Conclusions

Studies that have been done indicate both advantages and disadvantages of the system. Some of the disadvantages are that it is very time consuming and generates a great deal of paper, that there may be resistance to change, or that it may get bogged down in bureaucracy; it may even be sabotaged by people with vested interests. Its effectiveness can be destroyed completely if people use it for political ends or covering up weak spots. If carefully done, however, there are many advantages.

Among the top advantages that may be claimed, particularly in these times of tight budgets, is the ability to help allocate resources more efficiently. Another great advantage that may be undervalued, however, is the increased understanding on the part of managers for what their units are doing, and on the part of top management for what the entire organization is doing. Even if ZBB does not cut cost at all, it will often be worthwhile in terms of increased understanding and communication, better planning, and increased creative efforts to find better ways of doing things.

Literature Cited

1. Pyhrr, Peter/ZBB. *Across the Board* (Nov., 1977) p. 34-41. See also *Zero-Base Budgeting: A Practical Tool for Evaluating Expenses*, John Wiley & Sons, Inc., 1973.
2. Pyhrr, Peter/Zero-Base Budgeting. When Budgeting for Next Year, Most Companies Use the Current Budget as Starting Point; But One Company Prefers to Start from Scratch. *Harvard Business Review*, 48:111-121 (Nov/Dec, 1970).
3. Stonich, Paul J./*Zero-Base Planning and Budgeting*, New York, Dow Jones-Irwin, 1977, p. 20-31.

Sources and Uses of Funds of Academic Libraries

By Jacob Cohen and Kenneth W. Leeson

WHERE DO UNIVERSITY LIBRARIES get their money and how do they spend it?[1] While the expenditures of academic libraries are relatively well documented, this is not true of the sources of funding. For example, much more is known about how expenditures are divided between salary and materials than about the relative importance of foundation support versus gifts in kind. In this paper, the analysis of the uses of funds relies heavily on the Machlup and Leeson study of the dissemination of information.[2] The portion on sources of funds is drawn from the results of a questionnaire sent to members of the Association of Research Libraries.

SOURCES OF FUNDS

To provide an initial perspective on the magnitudes involved, Table 1 shows total operating expenditures (excluding capital outlays) for all college and university libraries. These figures represent funds from all sources (excluding those for capital expenditures).

With no adjustments for inflation, total funds in current dollars are seen to have steadily increased, in fact, tripling over the 11-year period studied. By 1975, academic libraries had become a "billion-dollar industry." In real terms, however, the increase is a less impressive 66 percent — from $528 million to $877 million. On a per student basis (with allowances made for growth in the student population), the overall increase is 80 percent in nominal dollars. In real dollars, funds per student are vir-

---

Reprinted from *Library Trends*, vol. 28, no. 1, Summer 1979, by permission of the publisher. © 1979 Board of Trustees of the University of Illinois.

TABLE 1. Aggregate Sources of Funds of Academic Libraries, 1967-77

	1967	1968	1969	1970	1971	1972	1973	1974	1975	1976	1977
1. Total funds in current dollars (millions)	$416	510	585	650	737	796	867	960	1,092	1,180	1,250
2. GNP deflator for printing and publishing (1972 = 100)	79	83	87	93	97	100	104	113	129	133	143
3. Funds in real dollars (1 ÷ 2)	$528	613	674	698	757	796	838	850	849	887	877
4. Annual percentage change in 3		16.1	9.9	3.7	8.5	5.1	5.2	1.4	−.12	4.5	−1.1
5. Funds per student in current dollars (millions)	$ 59	70	75	81	90	95	89	93	97.5	102.6	107
6. Funds per student in real dollars (5 ÷ 2)	$ 75	84	86	87	92	95	86	83	76	77	75
7. Annual percentage change in 6		11.6	2.8	1.1	5.8	2.6	−8.9	−4.4	−8.2	1.7	−2.8
8. Expenditures as percentage of total educational and general expenditures*	3.7	3.7	4.3*	4.2*	4.2*	4.8	4.8	4.7	3.9	3.9	3.9

* The method of computing the library expenditures index was changed significantly in 1968. In that year, an institution's educational and general expenditure figure was redefined in accordance with recommendations of the National Association of College and University Business Officers. Of the changes made, the one of most importance was the deletion of federally sponsored organized research from the educational and general expenditures category. Hence, the mean library expenditure index was higher than usual for a few years.

Source: Lines 1, 5 and 8, Glick, Nada B., and Simora, Filomena, eds., comps. *The Bowker Annual of Library & Book Trade Information.* 23d ed. New York, Bowker, 1978, pp. 246-47; line 2, U.S. Dept. of Commerce, Bureau of Economic Analysis. Workfile.

tually unchanged. The annual percentage increase in funds per student was positive until 1973, and negative thereafter (except for 1976). This suggests rising revenues during the first half of the period under study, followed by a decline. Without an allowance for student growth, percentage increases in real dollars do not become negative until 1977. The decline in per capita support after 1972 roughly coincides with a decline in library expenditures in proportion to total university expenditures. Library support from the university budget (by far the library's major source of funds, as later discussion will show) declined from a high of 4.8 percent in the years 1972-73, to 3.9 percent for 1975-77.

THE OVERALL OPERATING BUDGET

The thirty university libraries responding to the questionnaire were divided into three categories — north public, north private and south public, with the bulk of the respondents falling into the second category (see Table 2). Clearly, the sample is not adequate for all these categories.

The change in budget size for the years covered in the questionnaire responses indicates a larger percentage increase in southern public universities due primarily to the library budget increases of universities 29 and 30. University support of the library is analyzed in the last two columns of Table 2. That "financial effort" is not a determinant of budget size is evidenced by the weak relation between library budgets and percentages of support from the total university budget (the rank correlation is −.01). The responses indicate a weakening in university support; the weighted average change in this area was a −.66 percent for north public universities. Nevertheless, budgetary growth is correlated with a change in the percent of university support (the rank correlation is a significant 44 percent).[3] While the size of library budgets is apparently more a function of the size of the institution's overall budget than of the degree of support, growth of the budget has depended on an increased percentage of support.

Many of the libraries exceed the 5 percent level of support (expressed as a percentage of university budget) suggested by the Committee on Standards of the Association of College and Research Libraries in its 1959 statement.[4] On the average, however, they fall short, even the north public universities. The revision of this statement calls for 6 percent outlays.[5] These percentages of support can be compared with data compiled by the Association of Research Libraries. The results of their 1975 questionnaire show the median percentage of support for eighty-eight libraries to be 3.5 percent; the maximum, 8.3 percent; and the minimum, 1.1 percent.[6]

TABLE 2. Overall Library Budgets

University Number	Library Budget (latest complete year figures)	Change in % over Years Covered	Years Covered	Funds from University as % of Univ. Budget	Change in % of Univ. Budget
North Private					
1	$ 5,773,339	109.5	1970–77	3.51	.16
2	12,083,000	57.5	1970–77	4.10	.80
3	3,016,407	79.1	1970–77	4.72	.25
4	3,494,000	46.9	1974–77	1.51	−.28
5	3,951,140	58.3	1970–77	3.60	−.53
6	6,189,466	41.7	1972–77		
7	5,945,000	44.9	1973–77	2.00	.10
8	2,575,920	48.1	1973–77	5.00	0.00
Average	5,378,534	60.6		3.48	.24
North Public					
9	6,404,000	89.4	1970–77	2.43	−1.51
10	11,654,873	77.8	1969–77	4.31	−3.04
11	3,726,188	9.4	1974–77		
12	2,258,869	83.4	1970–77		
13	4,627,619	24.6	1972–77	5.20	−.30
14	3,254,762	18.7	1973–76	2.13	−.26
15	7,406,990	82.1	1969–77	4.84	.54 (1970–77)
16	4,417,475	35.4	1970–77	3.00	−1.70
17	2,469,198	29.3	1970–77	6.48	1.37 (1974–77)
18	2,264,074	26.9	1970–77	1.90	−.50
19	2,985,264	28.3	1970–77	6.60	−.50
20	8,026,280	106.9	1970–77	3.30	−.10
21	5,052,000	60.7	1970–77	7.00	−1.00 (1971–77)
22	5,508,000	83.3	1970–77	7.20	−2.70
23	3,623,988	23.6	1974–77	4.70	−.40
24	11,865,876	92.8	1970–77	4.80	1.00
25	2,707,566	121.5	1970–77	4.20	1.10
26	8,960,000	49.6	1970–77	4.54	−0.36
Average	5,406,279	64.4		4.55	−.66
South Public					
27	4,814,800	18.8	1974–77	3.00	−.30
28	978,555	−20.8	1973–77	2.53	−3.47
29	6,245,000	116.4	1971–77		
30	3,266,565	106.4	1970–77	4.92	1.87
Average	3,826,230	74.8		3.64	.14

Source: Replies to questionnaire sent to ARL members.

BREAKDOWN OF THE LIBRARY BUDGET

Table 3 shows a breakdown of the library budget. Respondents were asked to provide historical data for the years 1970-77, and earlier if available, on sources of funds from the university; from federal, state and local grants; gifts in kind; endowment income (including consumption of capital); and fees and fines. In a number of libraries, fees and fines revert to the university budget. Nevertheless, when these data were supplied, they were included. The most recent year's figures were used for each library consistent with the comprehensiveness of the data supplied. Initially, averages were used for the years covered in the responses, but this seemed to have had a distorting effect due to frequent data omissions.

The problems of comparing these libraries are, of course, enormous due to the uniqueness of each responding institution. More campus libraries may have been included in one response than in another. Some special revenues received may have been reported under different headings. Data indicated as not available had to be treated as a zero value for averaging purposes. The notes accompanying the table partially indicate the diversity of budgetary practices.

Several generalizations emerge from analysis of Table 3. The dominance of university funds is overwhelming. Southern public universities show the highest dependence (97 percent), followed by northern public universities (92 percent). Those least dependent on such funding are northern private universities (83 percent). The obverse aspect is the significance of gifts and endowment income for private universities. The weighted average (probably understated because "not available" amounts are treated as zero) for northern private universities is 13 percent, compared with 3 percent and 1 percent for northern and southern public university libraries, respectively. The 27 percent figure for a leading eastern private university (no. 2) is particularly noteworthy.

Cash gifts include foundation support. Table 4 provides a statistical view of the uses to which this support is put. Books and other materials rank relatively low; the bulk of foundation funds is used for construction, special studies, faculty research grants and other purposes. Some prominent support foundations are Ahmanson, Kresge, Danforth, Lilly, Mellon, Rockefeller, and the Council on Library Resources.[7]

Most public grants are state funded. The figures for two Illinois academic libraries that are members of ILLINET reflect state reimbursement for their interlibrary loan activities. The four research and reference centers, specified in Illinois law, and three special resource centers, both of which categories include academic libraries, earned a total of $678,440

TABLE 3. Individual Sources of Funds as a Percentage of Total Library Budget

University Number	University Funds	GRANTS			GIFTS		Endow. Income	Fees & Fines	Total Budget
		Federal	State	Local	In Kind	In Cash			
North Private									
1	81.2	0.3	0.3	11.2	0.2		5.9	0.9	100
2	70.8	1.9				11.0	16.4		100
3	85.8	0.1	0.1			1.3	12.1	0.6	100
4	95.6						4.3	0.1	100
5	92.5	0.1	0.2		0.1	3.9	1.5	1.7	100
6	81.6	3.4	0.3		0.6	12.2	1.0		100
7	93.3					2.8	2.0	1.9	100
8	95.7	0.2	0.6				3.5		100
Weighted Average	83.4		2.7			13.3			100
North Public									
9	93.0	1.5			3.3	0.3	1.6	0.3	100
10	95.5				1.8		1.2	1.5	100
11	96.7	0.3			1.5		0.8	0.7	100
12	93.1	1.2				1.0		4.6	100
13	97.8	1.5				0.4	0.3		100
14	96.2	0.7				0.1	0.1	2.9	100
15	86.8	0.1	2.3			0.5		10.8	100
16	91.5	6.5	0.1	0.1		0.1		1.8	100
17	95.0	0.2	4.7		0.01	0.2			100
18	99.6	0.2				0.3			100
19	99.9	0.1							100
20	83.7	2.0	6.1			4.1	0.3	3.8	100
21	97.0	1.3	0.6		0.6	0.5			100
22	90.8	4.8	2.5			0.1	1.2	0.6	100
23	92.5	0.1				5.0		2.5	100
24	85.4	2.7	1.7	0.3		1.2	8.4	0.3	100
25	93.0	1.4				0.3	5.3		100
26	97.2	0.1	0.4			0.2	1.3	0.7	100
Weighted Average	92.4		2.7			3.0			100
South Public									
27	99.2	0.1					0.6	0.2	100
28	95.7	0.4	3.7			0.3			100
29	94.6	0.1					2.2	3.0	100
30	98.9	0.2				0.8		0.1	100
Weighted Average	97.0		0.3			1.3			100

Notes to Table 3:
No. 1 — Local Grant comes from Venezuela, for only one year
No. 2 — Fees and Fines included under Gifts in Cash

TABLE 3. — Continued

No. 4 — Endowment Income includes small grant from U.S. DHEW
No. 5 — One major group of libraries is excluded
No. 11 — Gifts in Kind were indicated as "gifts"
No. 12 — Fees and Fines are really "fees and cost recovery"
No. 15 — The 10.8 percent shown under Fees and Fines reflects largely "institutional funds" and, to a lesser extent, "auxiliary enterprises." Institutional funds are an allocation to the library of a portion of total indirect cost funds coming to the university from outside grants and contracts. "Auxiliary enterprises" represents profits from copying machines in the library.
No. 17 — State Grants refers to money earned through ILLINET for state interlibrary loan
No. 22 — Fees and Fines includes sales and services
No. 24 — Fees and Fines includes book replacements, publication programs and self-supporting programs
No. 25 — Federal Grants includes state and local grants
No. 27 — Gifts in Cash included in Endowment Income
No. 29 — Endowment Income includes miscellaneous trust funds and cash gifts

TABLE 4. FOUNDATION GRANTS TO ACADEMIC LIBRARIES FOR 1976-77

	1976	1977
Total number of colleges and universities	111	102
Uses of Funds		
Construction	$ 4,200,000	$ 2,619,489
Books	1,210,000	801,652
Other materials	817,400	641,424
Special studies	942,731	4,141,526
Faculty research grants	5,751,418	1,710,276
Other purposes	4,215,359	2,674,407
Total	$17,149,408	$12,588,774

Source: The Foundation Center. *Comsearch for Libraries.* 1976, 1977.

in FY 1978.[8] The New York State Interlibrary Loan Program (NYSILL) has contracts with twelve libraries, including academic libraries. Each referral library receives an annual participation grant plus a unit fee for each request that is searched and/or filled.[9]

The importance of federal grants to academic libraries is probably understated in Table 3. The Higher Education Act of Nov. 1965 has provided financial support for materials purchases (Title II-A), library training and research (Title II-B), and resource-sharing (Title II-C).[10] The grants under Title II-A are relatively trivial from the standpoint of the large research library. Three to four thousand flat grants of between $3500 and $4000 are made annually to every eligible academic library in the country. The distribution of funds for fiscal years 1968-75 is shown in Table 5.

Title II-B funds cover two programs. The first, funded at $1 million annually, provides grants for research and demonstration projects, some of which may have gone to academic libraries. The other program finances fellowships for library school students, and supports workshops and institutes to update the skills of practicing librarians. Neither of these programs adds to the unrestricted revenues of academic libraries since they are earmarked for these specific purposes. Data on library education programs are given in Table 6.

Title II-C was first funded in FY 1978, and provides grants to research libraries to stimulate resource-sharing. Twenty major grants, chiefly to large university libraries, were made that year; federal legislation has authorized 150 grants per year.

When allowance is made for federal library expenditures, federal support is enormously increased. It has been estimated that federal "use" expenditures for 1977 totaled $2.3 billion.[11] This includes expenditures of $193 million for scientific and technical libraries; $82 million in direct federal subsidies, such as the Library Services and Construction Act of 1964 (LSCA)[12] and the Higher Education General Information Survey (HEGIS); an estimated $45 million for abstracting and indexing services; $768 million for federally supported search services; and $120 million for other library services.[13]

THE CAPITAL BUDGET

A record of construction expenditures for 1966-76 indicates a total cost of $1.9 billion, two-thirds of which applies to the first half of this period. From 1966 to 1971, library projects were principally funded by federal grants and loans. In the second five years, financing was largely through local public or private funds.[14] The average cost of projects after 1966 suggests the increasing involvement of larger institutions, with smaller ones dropping out.

USES OF FUNDS

CHOICES AMONG ALTERNATIVE USES

Several choices have to be made by librarians when they plan how to make the most efficient use of the funds available to them. They must decide how to divide disbursements among broad categories of expense, including salaries and wages, equipment and supplies, binding, building

TABLE 5. Distribution of Funds Under Title II-A

FY	Authorization	Cumulative Authorization (in millions)	Appropriation	Obligations	NUMBER OF GRANTS Basic	Supplemental	Special
1966	$50	$ 50	$10	$ 8,400,000	1,830		
1967	50	100	25	24,500,000	1,989	1,266	132
1968	50	150	25	24,900,000	2,111	1,524	60
1969	25	175	25	24,900,000	2,224	1,747	77
1970	75	250	12.5	9,816,000	2,201	1,783	
1971	90	340	9.9	9,900,000	548	531	115
1972	18	358	11	10,993,000	504	494	21
1973	52.5	410.5	12.5	12,500,000	2,061		65
1974	59.5	470	9.985	9,960,200	2,377		
1975	70	540	9.75				
Totals			$150.635	$135,869,200	15,845	7,345	470

Source: Figures on appropriations, obligations, and numbers of grants from: Stevens, Frank A., and Carl, Herbert A. "Higher Education Act, Title II A." In *Bowker Annual . . . 1975.* New York, Bowker, 1975, p. 139, "Table 2, Number of Grants Issued."

TABLE 6. Library Education Programs

| Academic Year | Institutions | FELLOWSHIPS/TRAINEESHIPS | | | | | INSTITUTES | | Appropriations |
		Doctoral	Post Master's	Master's	Associate	Total	Institutions	Participants	
1966/67	24	52	25	62		139			$ 1,000,000
1967/68	38	116	58	327		501	66	2,084	3,750,000
1968/69	51	168	47	494		709	91	3,101	8,250,000
1969/70	56	193	30	379		602	46	1,347	8,250,000
1970/71	48	171	15	200[a]		386	38	1,557	4,000,000
1971/72	19	116	6	([a])		122	39	981	3,900,000
1972/73	14	39	3	([a])		42	24	654	2,000,000
1973/74	39	21	4	159[b]	17	201	29	1,346[c]	3,572,000
1974/75	50	21	3	171[d]	5	200	30	1,339	2,850,000
1975/76									2,000,000
Total	339	897	191	1,792	22	2,902	363	12,409	$39,572,000

[a] Twenty traineeships were awarded in each of these years in an experimental program at SUNY-Albany.
[b] Includes 14 traineeships.
[c] Includes 45 traineeships.
[d] Includes 3 traineeships.

Source: Reed, Sarah R. "Federally Funded Training for Librarianship," *Library Trends* 24:90, July 1975.

operation and maintenance, and library materials. With regard to their collections, they have to decide how the funds set aside for materials will be divided between purchases of books and purchases of serial publications, including newspapers, magazines, newsletters, research journals, and so on. They have to decide how much money to spend on newly published book titles and current subscriptions to serials, and how much to spend for the purchase of backlist titles of books and for old issues of serial publications that are needed to fill gaps in the collection. They must decide how many of their publications shall be purchased in the conventional hard copy form and how many in microform. They must also decide how much to spend on books and serials in physics, philosophy, economics, urban studies, art and all of the other subject areas in which they maintain collections. Though not as a result of deliberate choices, some material will come from university presses, some from commercial publishers, and some from professional societies and associations; some will come from foreign publishers, and some from publishers located in the United States.

This is only a partial list of the choices facing librarians in their decisions regarding use of funds, but it has already raised more questions than could be dealt with adequately here. Attention shall be focused on the following four questions:

1. Over the period 1970-76, how did a sample of academic libraries distribute available funds among three major expenditure categories — materials, wages and salaries, and all other expenses?
2. Over the same period, how did the librarians divide their expenditures on materials between books and serials, and how much of each were they able to buy in "real" terms (number of book titles, number of serial subscriptions)?
3. In 1976 how did these libraries divide their total expenditures on materials between current and backlist books and serials?
4. How did they divide their total expenditures on materials between imported and domestically produced books and serials?

In formulating answers to these questions, we sall rely most heavily on the findings of a recent study of library operations that included a survey of collection development in academic libraries.[15]

A RECENT SURVEY OF LIBRARIES

The Machlup and Leeson survey of collection development in libraries relied on an elaborate random-sampling plan to try to obtain various kinds of information from a "representative" sample of academic, public, special, and federal libraries in the United States. Here we shall discuss only the findings pertaining to academic libraries.

Altogether 329 academic libraries (out of a total of nearly 3000 in the United States at the time) were selected and sent questionnaires. Of these, 131 returned at least partially filled out forms for a rate of response just under 40 percent. Considering the length of the questionnaire — 5 major parts in 26 pages containing over 400 questions — and the great detail in which data were sought, this can be considered a rather gratifying rate of response. Nevertheless, because some 60 percent of the chosen sample did not respond, the extent of "representativeness" of the responding sample may be questioned and there may be biases present in the results, some known, but most unknown. One known bias can be mentioned at once. The responding group of 131 libraries contains a disproportionate number of *large* academic libraries. This is due primarily to an extremely high response rate from member-libraries of the Association of Research Libraries. Thanks to the endorsement and cooperation of that association, 75 of the 105 members completed the questionnaires they had been sent.

Although 131 academic libraries returned usable questionnaires, many failed to answer some of the questions posed or to provide annual data for some of the years for which they had been requested, 1970 through 1976. Hence, in order to have, for the presentation of annual data, a consistent sample containing the same libraries from year to year, only those that were able to provide data for all seven years requested are included in the statistical tables. There were seventy-five such libraries.

Providing definitive answers, that is, conclusive findings, to all four questions posed would require a good deal more quantitative data than are at present available. By drawing on the findings of the Machlup and Leeson study, however, partial or tentative answers can be provided. They will be based in some instances on more or less dependable "measured" magnitudes of dollar outlay, and in other instances on less dependable rough estimations and "impressions" obtained from the librarians.

MAJOR EXPENSE CATEGORIES

In order to see on a nationwide scale how librarians at academic institutions have been allocating their total funds among the three major expense categories — materials (books, serials, and other materials), salaries and wages, and all other (plant operation and maintenance, supplies and equipment) — data compiled by the National Center for Education Statistics (NCES) and reported for benchmark years in *Library Statistics of Colleges and Universities* may be examined. The left side of Table 7

TABLE 7. EXPENDITURES BY ALL U.S. ACADEMIC LIBRARIES

Year	Number of Libraries	Total Expenditures (excluding capital outlays, in thousands)	Materials (in thousands)	% Total	Wages & Salaries (in thousands)	% Total	All Other (in thousands)	% Total
1960	1,951	$ 137,200	$ 40,700	29.7	$ 84,100	61.3	$12,400	9.0
1964	2,140	246,000	79,000	32.1	145,000	59.0	22,000	8.9
1968	2,370	509,800	187,900	36.9	274,100	53.8	47,800	9.3
1969	2,431	584,800	212,900	36.4	317,400	54.3	54,500	9.3
1971	2,535	737,500	247,700	33.6	417,300	56.6	72,500	9.8
1973	2,887	866,800	282,200	32.6	496,500	57.3	88,100	10.1
1975	2,972	1,058,800	327,900	31.0	654,100	61.8	76,800	7.2
Percent change	52.3	81.1	54.0		106.1		40.9	

Source: National Center for Education Statistics. *Library Statistics of Colleges and Universities, Fall 1969: Analytical Report.* Washington, D.C., USGPO, 1969, p. 4; _____. *Library Statistics of Colleges and Universities, Fall 1971: Analytical Report.* Washington, D.C., USGPO, 1971, p. 3; _____. *Library Statistics of Colleges and Universities, Fall 1973: Summary Data.* Washington, D.C., USGPO, 1973, p. 9; and _____. *Library Statistics of Colleges and Universities, Fall 1975: Analytical Report.* Washington, D.C., USGPO, 1975.

shows NCES data on total expenditures and expenditures in each of the three subcategories for all academic libraries in the United States for the years 1960, 1964, 1968, 1969, 1971, 1973 and 1975. The number of academic libraries grew by 1021 institutions over the period, from 1951 in 1960 to 2972 in 1975, an increase of 52.3 percent. Over the same period total expenditures, excluding capital outlays, increased by 81.1 percent, from $137.2 million in 1960 to $1058.8 million in 1975. This increase reflects the combined effects of a growing population and a growth in expenditures by individual libraries that had occurred over the period. We can obtain some idea of how the expenditures of individual libraries had grown by calculating the average expenditures per library for 1960 and 1975. Thus the "average" academic library spent $70,300 in 1960, and $356,300 in 1975, an increase of over 400 percent.

The increase would be far less than this if the expenditure figures were adjusted to account for price inflation in the goods and services purchased by the libraries over the period in question. Thus, if we express both figures in terms of 1977 dollars by using the GNP implicit price deflator applying to the industrial category "printing and publishing," we find that the average library in 1960 had, in constant 1977 dollars, total expenditures of $139,400; in 1975 the average library had, in 1977 dollars, total expenditures of $394,600, an increase of 183 percent. Since we are primarily interested in the *distribution* of funds among the three categories rather than the absolute amounts, we shall not bother to correct the remaining figures for inflation, an adjustment that would have no effect on the percent distributions of expenses among the three subcategories.

Table 7 shows that the percentage of total expenditures going for materials, primarily books and serials, was 29.7 percent in 1960 and 31.0 percent in 1975; salaries and wages accounted for 61.3 percent of total expenditures in 1960 and 61.8 percent in 1975; and all other categories accounted for 9.0 percent in the earlier year and 7.2 percent in 1975. Comparisons of the observed distribution of funds for the first and last years shown on the table would by themselves suggest a remarkable stability in spending patterns over the period. This was not the case in actual fact. There was a gradual increase in the proportion of funds spent on materials between 1960 and the end of the decade, and a corresponding decline in the proportion spent on salaries and wages. By 1968, expenditures on books, serials and other materials had reached 36.9 percent of the total, and expenditures on salaries and wages had fallen to 53.8 percent. By 1969 the gradual redistribution of funds from salaries and wages to materials had ended and a shift in the opposite direction had begun. The figures for the years 1969, 1971, 1973 and 1975 show clearly that the reversal that began in 1968 continued and remained uninterrupted through 1975, bringing the relative amounts spent on the two categories very near to the distribution observed for 1960. The "all other" category seemed to remain relatively stable in the 1960s, accounting for some 9 percent of total expenditures. The percentage rose to 10.1 percent in 1973, and then fell by 1975 to its lowest point, 7.2 percent, for any of the years shown. This category is a residual, and accounts for a relatively small proportion of expenditures. Our main interest lies with the other two categories discussed.

Although we cannot offer hard data or conclusive evidence, we are prepared to venture a few guesses as to what caused the observed shifts in the distribution of expenditures between the two major categories. Government support for colleges and universities is known to have increased in the 1960s, particularly in the second half of the decade. As beneficiaries of a portion of the new funds flowing into educational institutions, librarians were able to spend more on all categories of expense. It is likely, however, that their immediate reaction was to use the funds to purchase more books and serials, rather than to increase significantly the size of their staffs. The former alternative would quickly help accommodate a growing student population and would involve no long-term obligations. Spending on materials could easily be reduced in subsequent years. The latter alternative, however, would require some fundamental adjustments. The decision to increase staff is one that may take a good amount of time to make, and even more time to put into action.

By the late sixties and into the early seventies, however, these adjustments would have had time to work themselves out. Moreover, reduced funding, tighter budgets, rapid price inflation and falling college enrollments were probably felt by that time, causing a more immediate cutback in expenditures on materials than on staff and explaining the reversal in the trends observed for the earlier years.

The trends observed for the data in Table 8 will help in the interpretation of the data in Table 7. The annual expenditure figures shown in Table 8 are for a sample composed of seventy-five libraries, the same seventy-five each year, and span the period 1970-76. Although on the average, the sample contains larger libraries than does the population as a whole — in 1975 total expenditures for the average library in the sample was $2.3 million compared with only $356,000 for the whole population of libraries — the distribution of total expenditures among the three major categories is strikingly similar and exhibits the same trend over the period — a decline in the percentage of funds spent on materials, from 32.8 percent in 1970 to 29.2 percent in 1976, and an increase in the

TABLE 8. Expenditures by a Sample of Seventy-five Academic Libraries

Year	Total Expenditures (excluding capital outlays, in thousands)	Materials (in thousands)	% Total	Wages & Salaries (in thousands)	% Total	All Other (in thousands)	% Total
1970	$117,800	$38,600	32.8	$66,200	56.2	$13,000	11.0
1971	124,400	38,400	30.9	73,000	58.6	13,000	10.5
1972	130,600	38,700	29.6	78,100	59.9	13,800	10.5
1973	139,900	41,100	29.4	83,400	59.6	15,400	11.0
1974	154,600	45,000	29.1	92,500	59.8	17,100	11.1
1975	169,400	48,100	28.4	102,100	60.3	19,200	11.3
1976	181,400	53,000	29.2	109,300	60.3	19,100	10.5
Percent change	54.0	37.3		65.1		46.9	

Source: Machlup, Fritz, and Leeson, Kenneth. *Information Through the Printed Word.* New York, Praeger, 1978, vol. 3, Table 6.5.4.

percentage spent on salaries and wages, from 56.2 percent in 1970 to 60.3 percent in 1976. Without the benefit of the longer time series, we might be tempted to infer that the observed decline signified a departure from earlier spending patterns, rather than a return to earlier patterns. Of course, a look at even longer time series might suggest yet another interpretation.

The question of whether these spending patterns are returning to, or departing from, historical norms may be put aside, and trends of the recent past shall be considered by themselves. For all academic libraries, expenditures on materials rose by 54.0 percent from 1969 to 1975, while expenditures on wages and salaries rose by 106.1 percent. For the sample of 75 academic libraries, expenditures on materials rose by 37.3 percent from 1970 to 1976, while expenditures on wages and salaries rose by 65.1 percent. Thus, funds spent on wages and salaries grew at a rate nearly double that of funds spent on materials, during a period when the prices of books and serials rose rapidly. What effect did this comparatively lethargic growth in the materials budgets have on the way librarians apportioned their funds among the various types of materials, and what did it mean in terms of the physical quantities of materials they were able to acquire? We shall consider these questions in turn.

CHOOSING BETWEEN BOOKS AND SERIALS

The data presented in Tables 7 and 8 suggest that librarians have been compelled to spend an ever-increasing proportion of their total budgets on wages and salaries over the first half of the current decade, and consequently a decreasing proportion on materials. With the prices of published materials increasing rapidly over the same period, some difficult choices had to be made about how to allocate funds available for acquisitions among the various kinds of material — principally between books and serials. The figures pertaining to the seventy-five academic libraries reveal a startling picture of the choices that were made (see Table 9).

Total expenditures on materials for the seventy-five libraries are reproduced in Column 1 of Table 9. Columns 2, 3, and 4 of the table show, respectively, how much of the total went for the purchase of books, how much for the purchase of serials, and how much for the purchase of other materials. Even in terms of current dollars (that is, dollars not adjusted for changes in prices), the amounts spent by the sample on books actually fell

TABLE 9. EXPENDITURES ON MATERIALS BY SEVENTY-FIVE ACADEMIC LIBRARIES, AVERAGE PRICES OF BOOKS AND SERIALS, AND NUMBER OF BOOKS AND SERIAL SUBSCRIPTIONS THAT COULD HAVE BEEN PURCHASED WITH AVAILABLE FUNDS, 1970-76

Year	Total	EXPENDITURES (in millions)							Average Price of Hardbound Books	No. of Books that could have been bought with available funds (in millions)	Average Price of Serial Subscriptions	No. of Serials that could have been bought with available funds (in millions)
		Books	% Total	Serials	% Total	Other	% Total					
1970	$38.6	$23.8	62	$13.2	34	$1.6	4		$11.66	2.0	$10.41	1.3
1971	38.4	21.8	57	14.8	39	1.8	5		13.25	1.6	11.66	1.3
1972	38.7	21.0	54	16.3	42	1.4	4		12.99	1.6	13.23	1.2
1973	41.1	21.6	53	17.3	42	2.2	5		12.20	1.8	16.20	1.1
1974	45.0	22.1	49	20.6	46	2.3	5		14.09	1.6	17.71	1.2
1975	48.1	22.1	46	23.0	48	3.0	6		16.19	1.4	19.94	1.2
1976	53.0	23.5	44	26.4	50	3.1	6		17.39	1.4	22.52	1.2
Percent change	37.3	-1.3		100		93.8			49.1	-30.0	116.3	-7.6

Sources: "U.S. Hardcover Trade-Technical Books: Average Prices and Price Indexes." In *Bowker Annual of Library & Book Trade Information, 1971.* New York, Bowker, 1971, p. 90; *Bowker Annual . . . 1975.* New York, Bowker, 1975, p. 180; *Bowker Annual . . . 1976.* New York, Bowker, 1976, pp. 183, 206; *Bowker Annual . . . 1978.* New York, Bowker, 1978, p. 320; Tuttle, Helen W. "Price Indexes for 1970: U.S. Periodicals and Serial Service," *Library Journal* 95:2427, July 1970; ———. "Price Indexes for 1971: U.S. Periodicals and Serial Service," *Library Journal* 96:2271, July 1971; Brown, Norman B. "Price Indexes for 1972: U.S. Periodicals and Serial Service," *Library Journal* 97:2355, July 1972; ———. "Price Indexes for 1973: U.S. Periodicals and Serial Service," *Library Journal* 98:2052, July 1973; ———. "Price Indexes for 1974," *Library Journal* 99:1775, July 1974; ———. "Price Indexes for 1975," *Library Journal* 100:1291, July 1975; ———. "Price Indexes for '76," *Library Journal* 101:1600, Aug. 1976; and Machlup, Fritz, and Leeson, Kenneth. *Information Through the Printed Word.* New York, Praeger, 1978, vol. 3, Table 6.5.5.

by 1.3 percent, over the period, from $23.8 million in 1970 to $23.5 million in 1976. The figures for the intervening years are all lower than either of those at the end points. Over the same period, expenditures on serials *increased* by 100 percent, from $13.2 million in 1970 to $26.4 million in 1976. Expenditures on other materials increased by over 90 percent as well, but they account for a comparatively small proportion of total expenditures.

These figures constitute significant, almost incredible, shifts in the buying patterns of the libraries. Over the period shown, the proportion of total expenditures on materials going for books fell from 62 percent to 44 percent, while the proportion going for serials rose from 34 percent to 50 percent, demonstrating that when confronted by an economic pinch, the librarians opted to maintain their serials collection at the expense of books.

This point is made more vividly by the figures shown in Columns 5 through 8 of Table 9. Column 5 contains the average prices of hardbound books for the years 1970-76 and Column 7 contains the average prices for serial subscriptions. The former increased by 49.1 percent over the period, the latter by 116.3 percent. If we divide the dollars spent on books and serials by the average price of each, we obtain a measure of the *number* of books and the *number* of serial subscriptions that could be purchased with the money.[16] From Column 6 of the table we see that the number of books purchased annually dropped drastically by 30.0 percent, from 2.0 million in 1970 to 1.4 million in 1976. Column 8 shows that for serial subscriptions, the prices of which had risen much faster than the prices of books, the number of subscriptions dropped by only 7.6 percent, from 1.3 million for the 75 libraries in 1970 to 1.2 million in 1976.

Why the librarains demonstrated such a strong preference in favor of maintaining their serials collections even if it means making severe cutbacks on book purchases is not revealed by the data. We can speculate, however, that books may have been considered more expendable than journals, chiefly because the latter are generally thought to contain the "newest" knowledge, and hence to be indispensable for maintaining an up-to-date, comprehensive collection. There may also have been a reluctance to discontinue subscriptions to journals that had been held for years and years. Perhaps the librarians believed that they could, at some time in the future when budget pressures eased up, replenish their book collections by buying from the publishers' backlists some of the book titles that were not purchased when first published. Judging from the apparent backlog of such postponed purchases, however, it seems that a great deal of "catching up" would be required.

BACKLIST PURCHASES AND IMPORTS

There are two final aspects of the use of funds we should like to consider: the amounts spent on backlist material and the amounts spent on imported material. Unlike the preceding discussions, however, we are unable to provide annual figures of dollars spent, chiefly because librarians do not usually record their purchases of materials by year of publication or country of origin.

To try to obtain some idea of how much backlist and imported materials the librarians *believe* they are purchasing, Machlup and Leeson posed the following questions separately for books and for serials: "Indicate what percent of your 1976 book (serial) expenditures was for books (serials) published prior to 1970 (to 1976)," and "Of your library's total book (serial) expenditures for 1976, ... please estimate the percent that went for the purchase of volumes published outside the United States." In Table 10 the responses are shown for the various samples of libraries that responded broken down into four ranges of their total expenditures in 1976.

On the question of purchases of backlist books, the seventy-five responding libraries indicated that approximately 11 percent of their expenditures on books in 1976 were for books published prior to 1970. There seems to be a tendency for the largest and smallest libraries in the sample, in terms of total expenditures, to purchase slightly higher proportions of backlist books than the libraries falling in between. For a sample of seventy-eight libraries, containing most of the members of the sample of seventy-five plus a few more, the proportion of expenditures in 1976 on issues of serials published prior to 1976 is 4.6 percent. Again, there is nothing particularly striking about the practices of libraries of different size. What these results for books and for serials seem to suggest is consistent with the speculations advanced earlier when reasons were being sought to explain the shifting of funds from book purchases to serial purchases. Apparently, a good deal more purchasing of backlist books is necessary than of back issues of serials. This would be the case if librarians tended to sacrifice the purchase of new books each year in order to maintain the serial subscriptions they wanted.

On the question of imported books and serials, the respondents indicated that some 29.8 percent of their total expenditures on books in 1976

TABLE 10. PURCHASES OF BOOKS AND SERIALS THAT ARE BACKLIST OR BACK ISSUES AND IMPORTED, SHOWN BY SIZE OF TOTAL EXPENDITURES FOR 1976

Total Expenditures	No. Reporting	% Expenditure for Books Published Before 1970	No. Reporting	% Expenditure for Serials Published Before 1976	No. Reporting	% Expenditure for Imported Books	No. Reporting	% Expenditure for Imported Serials
$4,000,000+	13	12.4	13	4.8	20	38.9	17	39.8
2,000,000–3,999,999	21	9.6	25	4.3	25	23.7	20	30.6
1,000,000–1,999,999	14	8.2	15	4.9	16	18.1	13	25.3
Less than $1,000,000	27	12.8	25	5.5	26	6.5	21	16.7
All expenditure brackets	75	10.8	78	4.6	87	29.8	71	34.0

Note: Reported average percentage figures weighted by each library's expenditures on books or serials.

Source: Machlup, Fritz, and Leeson, Kenneth. *Information Through the Printed Word*. New York, Praeger, 1978, vol. 3, Tables 6.6.2, 6.6.3, 6.6.4, and 6.6.6.

went for purchases of imported books and 34.0 percent of their total expenditures on serials went for serials published abroad. Here we see a clear relationship between the size of the libraries and the proportion of total material expenditures going for imports. The largest libraries, those with total expenditures of $4.0 million or more in 1976, devoted the largest percentage of their funds to imports, 38.9 percent and 39.8 percent for books and for serials, respectively. As we move from the largest libraries to the smallest, the percentages shown become smaller as well.

These results seem to be consistent with what might be expected. The libraries with the largest expenditures are simply able to purchase more material and hence can both satisfy their appetites for "homegrown" materials and acquire some of the usually more expensive overseas products. Libraries with smaller budgets cannot.

REMAINING ISSUES

We have been able to present some information on a few of the questions raised in an earlier section on the way librarians use their funds. Several other interesting issues, however, have not been covered in this paper. Among these is how librarians have been purchasing materials in the various subject areas. On this topic we shall offer nothing at this time, partly because an adequate discussion would require a separate article, and partly because of the weakness of the available data on purchases by field. The interested reader can, however, refer to the Machlup and Leeson study for a discussion of the problems involved in research in this area, and even for some interesting, though rather soft, data regarding the libraries' acquisitions broken down by field.

CONCLUSIONS

The generalization from a study of sources of funds based on questionnaire responses is that academic libraries, particularly public ones, depend on their universities for the bulk of their financial support. Library budgets seem to be more of a function of size of institutional budgets than high percentage allocations to the library, although budgetary growth in recent years seems to reflect increased financial effort. Decline in real support on a per student basis since 1972 is also evident from a study of aggregative data.

On a direct basis at least, federal grants to academic libraries are minuscule compared to the feleral government's total level of transfer payments. In 1976, for example, the amount transferred to individuals and state and local governments was well over $150 billion.[17] Tables 4 and 5 reveal total appropriations under the Higher Education Act over a 10-year period of less than $200 million. On the other hand, the picture changes drastically if credit is given to the federal sector for its total library expenditures and subventions for library construction.

On the uses side, two main generalizations are suggested by the Machlup and Leeson sample data and by "population" data for academic libraries. The latter data indicate that between 1960 and 1969, rising dollar expenditures were redistributed from salaries and wages to materials (primarily books and serials), and thereafter a shift began in the opposite direction. The sample results covering the 1970-75 period confirm the latter shift.

A possible linkage between sources and uses may explain these successive shifts. An increase in government support in the second half of the 1960s encouraged relatively more spending on materials since this adjustment could be achieved faster than staff expansion. Moreover, an increasing student population encouraged building up the materials collection.

The second major trend in uses, based on the sample survey, is the redistribution of the materials budget in favor of serials acquisitions, 1970-76. The figures reveal a drastic drop (in physical units) in books purchased annually, with only a relatively slight drop in subscriptions.

From the standpoint of rational decision-making, do these historical choices make sense? Similarly, was (and is) the degree of university library support the optimal one? Hopefully, the other chapters in this volume will suggest some approaches to evaluation.

References

1. Jacob Cohen is largely responsible for the discussion on sources of funds, and Kenneth Leeson for the discussion on uses of funds. Thanks are owed to Fritz Machlup for his helpful comments on the material pertaining to uses of funds. Research assistance was provided by Wim Vijverberg, Ms. C. Chen, Michael Bardos, Richard Weiss, Trude Kronwinkler and Sharon Spellman. We are indebted to those members of the Association of Research Libraries who responded to our questionnaire on sources of funds. Special thanks are due Dean Thomas J. Galvin, University of Pittsburgh, for saving us from many errors. The remaining errors are those of the authors.

2. Machlup, Fritz, and Leeson, Kenneth. *Information Through the Printed Word*. 3 vols. New York, Praeger, 1978.

3. Twenty-six usable observations underlie the first rank correlation and 23 the second.

4. ACRL Committee on Standards. "Standards for College Libraries," *College & Research Libraries* 20:275, July 1959.

5. ACRL Ad Hoc Committee to Revise the 1959 Standards. "Draft: Standards for College Libraries; 1975 Revision," *College & Research Libraries News* 35:304-05, Dec. 1974. We are indebted to Thomas J. Galvin, University of Pittsburgh, for these references on library standards.

6. Association of Research Libraries. *ARL Statistics 1975-1976*. Washington, D.C., ARL, 1976, p. 22.

7. For information on the activities of the Council on Library Resources and other foundations, *see* Gwinn, Nancy E. "Foundation Grants." *In* Nada B. Glick and Filomena Simora, eds., comps. *The Bowker Annual of Library & Book Trade Information*. 23d ed. New York, Bowker, 1978, pp. 168-78. Further discussion of foundation funding of libraries can be found *in* Patricia S. Breivik. "Foundation Funding," *Library Journal* 100:2298-302, Dec. 15, 1975.

8. Kathryn J. Gesterfield, Director, Illinois State Library, Springfield, Illinois, to Cohen, Sept. 29, 1978.

9. Jane G. Rollins, Associate in Library Services, New York State Library, Albany, New York, to Cohen, Sept. 11, 1978.

10. Smith, Alan Carter. "The Higher Education Act, Title II-A: Its Impact on the Academic Library," *Library Trends* 24:63-84, July 1975; Reed, Sarah R. "Federally Funded Training for Librarianship," *Library Trends* 24:85-100, July 1975; and Janaske, Paul C. "Federally Funded Research in Librarianship," *Library Trends* 24:101-14, July 1975. For information regarding recent II-A programs, *see* Fisher, Sheldon Z., and Stevens, Frank A. "Higher Education Act, Title II-A, College Library Resources." *In* Glick and Simora, op. cit., pp. 142-44.

11. King, Donald W., et al. "The Journal System of Scientific and Technical Communication in the United States." Rockville, Md., King Research, Inc., 1978, p. 308. (NSF Contract DSI75-06942)

12. LSCA money goes almost entirely to public libraries except where states elect to use these funds to support multiple networks. The Illinois and New York network programs discussed earlier probably receive support from a combination of LSCA and state funds.

13. King, op. cit.

14. Orne, Jerrold, and Gosling, Jean O. "Academic Library Building in 1976." *In* Nada B. Glick and Sarah L. Prakken, eds., comps. *The Bowker Annual of Library & Book Trade Information*. 22d ed. New York, Bowker, 1977, p. 299.

15. Machlup and Leeson, op. cit., vol. 3, pp. 37-155.

16. Using unweighted averages list prices, that is, averages calculated without weighting the components by the sales volume of books of each list price, to calculate "real" purchases is a somewhat questionable practice. Unfortunately, unweighted averages are all that is available. Even though the results in terms of numbers purchased calculated with unweighted prices are not very accurate measurements, they will be of a reasonable order of magnitude.

17. Dornbusch, Rudiger, and Fischer, Stanley. *Macroeconomics*. New York, McGraw-Hill, 1978, pp. 9, 446.

Part VII
PLANNING AND EVALUATION OF LIBRARY SERVICES

Introduction

Recently there has been a substantial growth of interest among librarians in the development of better methods of predicting the organization's future through careful and meaningful planning. The American Library Association's interest in this area has resulted in a number of publications on planning for public libraries as well as the formation of discussion groups that continually study the problems associated with library planning. As long as librarians are willing to view the entire planning process in perspective, not just as a series of disjointed events, this increased emphasis will prove fruitful. However, librarians must know precisely what planning is, what it can accomplish, and what its limitations are. In addition, librarians who want to implement a program of effective planning must be prepared to engage in substantial organizational activity that may not necessarily lead to immediate results.

The joining of "planning" with "evaluation" is far more than just a convenient marriage of two similar terms. The concepts inherent in both terms are vital to any planning process. Just as there are various types of planning for different types of libraries, so are there different types of evaluation techniques. Finding a proper mix between the two conceptual areas is an important responsibility of the planner before, not after, planning activity is begun.

Planning theorists generally present rather complex models of what they perceive to be essential elements in planning and evaluation. In this section, Charles R. McClure's discussion of planning, while based on theory, is an example of a more practical approach, one that not only defines the terminology of planning but also places planning within an academic library context which might easily be transferred to other types of libraries. Viewing planning and evaluation as highly interrelated, McClure suggests that the planning process, while difficult, is by no means beyond the reach of even the smallest library. What *is* important, however, is the development of a desire to plan, a wish to engage in future thinking rather than to remain mired in the highly present-oriented and often repetitious activities which too often pass for "library planning." Read in conjunction with other sections of this volume, McClure's article provides an integrated view of planning which places the subject in perspective.

Carol Weiss, on the other hand, is less concerned with an overall view of the planning process than she is with the details of evaluation, itself an essential part of planning. In addition to providing basic definitions of evaluation (e.g. "what is formative evaluation, what is summative evaluation"), Weiss places particular emphasis on the pitfalls of evaluation and the conditions under which it is likely to succeed, as well as those which can cause failure. Viewing evaluation as a process-oriented activity, Weiss provides some very practical suggestions for those organizations that wish to evaluate their activities and improve their products—not merely to satisfy some outside-imposed requirement. Of particular interest is Weiss's discussion of *who* is responsible for *what* and her answer to the question, "Why evaluate?"

Taken together, the articles in this section provide a brief overview of basic considerations related to library planning and evaluation. However, McClure and Weiss do not, nor can they, provide answers to the myriad of complex problems pervading both activities. The ideas, suggestions, models, and points of view presented in both articles should be supplemented by careful review and understanding of an organization's readiness and willingness to plan. It is only in the context of the individual organizational environment that planning and evaluation can be carried through to a successful conclusion.

The Planning Process: Strategies for Action
By Charles R. McClure

Planning is the process of identifying organizational goals and objectives, developing programs or services to accomplish those objectives, and evaluating the success of those programs vis-à-vis the stated objectives. The importance and purposes of planning as a means to increase organizational effectiveness are stressed. A model of the planning process is presented, and the various components of the model are described in terms of implementation. The paper concludes with the author suggesting some pragmatic strategies and considerations that may facilitate the implementation of organizational planning in an academic library.

"PLANNING? Naw, we don't have enough time for planning. We don't even have enough staff or support to perform the basic services. How can we plan?" This sentiment is frequently encountered in many library organizations regarding the planning process. Indeed, a current state of crisis management is likely to be a direct result of *not* developing an organizational planning process. Continuous efforts to solve yesterday's problems make planning for tomorrow even more difficult. Development of goals and objectives as part of an organizational planning process is absolutely necessary if the library is to respond effectively to the information needs of its environment.

Planning is a process of identifying organizational goals and objectives, developing programs or services to accomplish those objectives, and evaluating the success of those programs vis-à-vis the stated objectives.[1] A plan is a written document formalizing the planning process. It determines which objectives and which services will be allocated various resources. Plans and the planning process recognize the fact that organizations cannot do everything; therefore, they must allocate resources on a priority basis to do those activities that lead to the effective accomplishment of goals and objectives.

The word *effectiveness* must be stressed, as it implies the ability of the organization to accomplish stated goals and objectives. Effectiveness asks the question, "What is the organization doing?" Efficiency, on the other hand, implies the ability of the organization to accomplish a task in the least amount of time with less cost. Efficiency asks the question, "How well are we doing it?" Organizations may be doing things well (efficiently) that need not be done (ineffec-

---

Reprinted from *College and Research Libraries*, November 1978, pp. 456-66.

tive) or vice-versa. Planning addresses both the effectiveness and efficiency questions but places primary importance on effectiveness: What is the organization doing?[2]

For too long a time planning has been seen as a responsibility only of top administration. If administrators chose not to develop formalized mechanisms for planning or failed to develop formalized planning documents, such was their prerogative. However, planning is much too important to be left to the discretion of library administrators. All organizational members—especially other professional librarians—have a responsibility to develop a planning process as well as formalized plans for their given areas of responsibility.

The purpose of planning is to facilitate the accomplishment of organizational objectives. Planning has primacy in terms of organizational effectiveness; without goals, without plans, no rational indicator of effectiveness can be determined. Planning is pervasive; it can and should be done at all organizational levels; it can and should be done with all organizational members; and it is an ongoing, continuous process.[3]

In these times of economic difficulties for many academic libraries, the need for a planning process takes on significant importance in six general areas.

First, planning provides for a rational response to uncertainty and change. Although the organization cannot control its environment, it may be able to manipulate it—assuming there is an objective to be accomplished.

Second, planning focuses attention on goals and objectives. Does your organization have a written set of goals and objectives? If not, dysfunctions, departmental competition, and ineffective resource allocation are likely.

Third, planning is important as an aid to resource allocation by establishing priorities for funding. Which services can be provided at the least cost and for the most benefit?

Fourth, planning also serves as a basis for determining individual, departmental, organizational, or program accountability.

Fifth, planning facilitates control of organizational operations by collecting information to evaluate the various programs or services.

Finally, planning orients the organization to a futuristic stance. Instead of always *reacting* to problem situations, the organization attempts to foresee and mitigate against future problems *before* they become crises.

Some academic librarians already may have witnessed the results when the planning process is ignored and formalized plans are not developed. Typical management styles in such situations may be described as laissez-faire—organizational members basically "do their own thing." Laissez-faire management styles can digress into crisis management—the problems from yesterday are never solved, only elongated. Without planning, snap decisions replace deliberate decisions in terms of organizational activity. And lastly, no planning will be evidenced by uncoordinated, piecemeal activities encouraging internal organization competition for scarce resources.

The purpose of this paper is to present the reader with a general overview of the planning process in an academic library setting. A model of planning will be suggested and explained in such a way that organizational members in an academic library can use the model as a means of improving the planning process in their organization.

The three components of planning, i.e., the mission statement, program development, and evaluation, will be discussed, followed by some strategic considerations for successful organizational planning. No attempt is made to provide a comprehensive review of the literature although relevant sources will be referred to as needed. The author is less concerned with the voluminous writings on the subject and prefers a pragmatic approach: developing strategies for planning to be implemented and formalized in the academic library.

OVERVIEW OF PLANNING

Systems thinking has been used as a basis for developing the planning process in organizations by a number of management scientists.[4] Such a view is also used by this writer as a basis for developing the planning process. Additionally, it is based on the writings and research of Ernest R. DeProspo, who has been instrumental in the formulation of a planning process for the library environment.[5] Although much of his work has been done in the public library setting, many of his concepts can be extended to the academic library.

An overview of the planning process is provided in figure 1. This overview suggests specific activities that can be part of the planning process in the academic library organization. It is intended to provide both a conceptual description of planning and practical procedures for developing written plans as a basis for organizational, departmental, or specific program activities.

Within the paradigm of systems thinking, it must be recognized that planning takes place within a context or environment. That environment includes the social, political, and economic milieu in which an organiza-

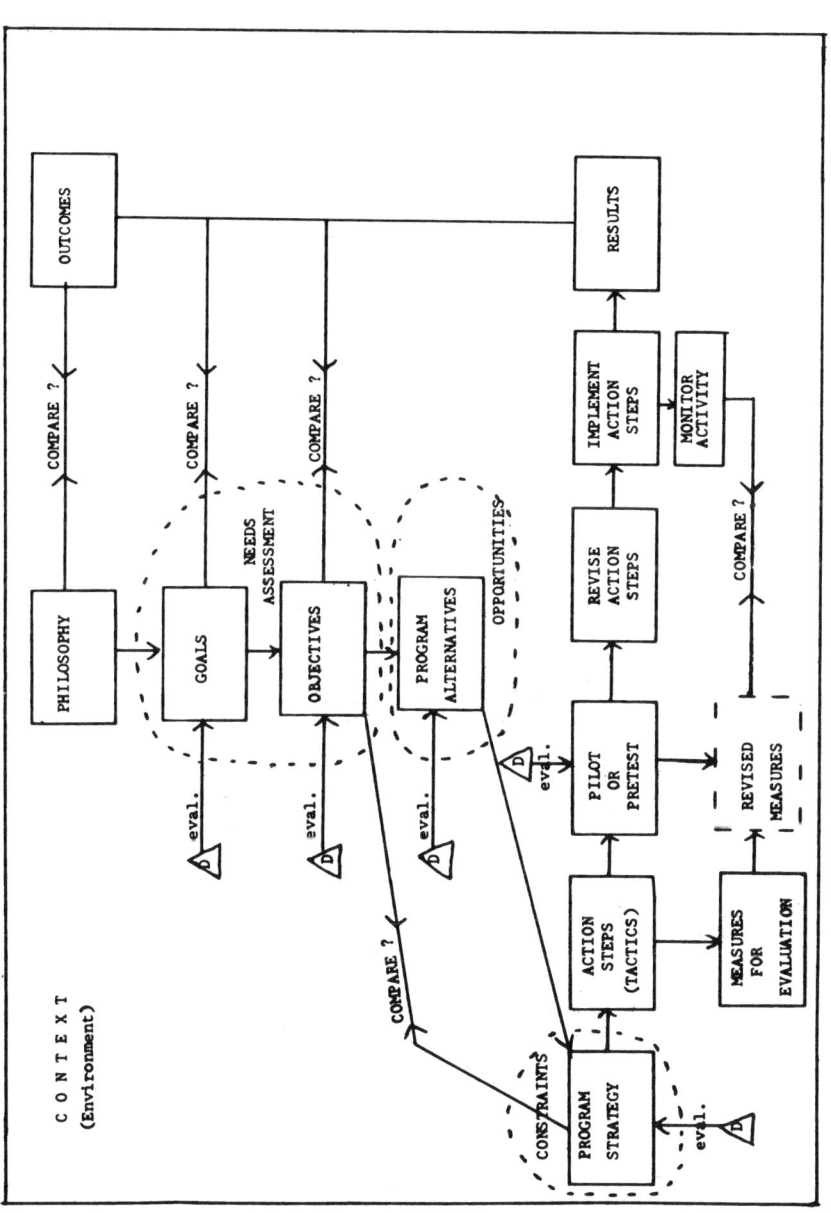

Fig. 1
Generalized Model for Program Planning

tion struggles for survival and effectiveness. Open systems thinking stresses the flow of resources (information) between the organization and the environment in which it operates. Recognition of this relationship is critical to the development of both input and feedback throughout the planning process.

Mission Statement

The first component of the planning process is the development of a mission statement. A mission statement is a formal written document developed by the members of the library under the leadership of the organization's administration. Typically, the document begins with a brief statement of the historical background of the library as well as its current activities; significant dates and developments in the history should be included. The purpose of this section is to recognize the origins of the library, draw upon its historical strengths, and identify critical experiences in its development.

A typical mistake made by the organization when beginning the planning process is to begin immediately with statements of goals and objectives. In such instances the philosophical assumptions held by the organizational members regarding "appropriate" roles of the organization in its environmental context and "appropriate" values to determine organizational activities are not made explicit.[6] A statement of organizational philosophy must be developed to form a basis or agreement among organizational members *from which* goals and objectives logically can follow.

The assumptions within the organizational philosophy usually are of two varieties. The first includes assumptions regarding the role of the institution in the environment and recognition of the factors that appear to have significant implications regarding future operations of the organization. This first set of assumptions may deal with topics such as technology, intellectual freedom, societal responsibility of the library, or information/knowledge production.

The second set of assumptions are value decisions as to "appropriate" responses to the first set of assumptions for services to be provided by the organization. Issues regarding the type of "appropriate" library services as well as their degree of implementation should be raised here. Topics included in the second set of assumptions include the role of the librarian during library decision making and program development, identification of "appropriate" user groups to be served, and "adequate" services to be provided. Both types of assumptions must be made explicit. Key terms and concepts should be defined to ensure that all organizational members agree upon various aspects of value-laden words such as *service, information, reference,* etc.

The development of goals and objectives takes place in an atmosphere of needs assessment. This term may be defined as the difference between where we are (what we're doing now) and where we want to be (what we want to be doing). The needs assessment process is input for the development of goals and objectives. Many methods can be used for needs assessment: previous surveys, organizational reports, or other written documents; community analysis; or other means of gathering empirical data. The point is that needs assessment provides environmental input into the process of goal and objective identification. Based on the needs assessment, organizational members agree upon goals and objectives through discussion and compromise or a more formalized method such as the Delphi technique.[7]

One must recognize the difference between goals and objectives—they are not the same. Goals provide long-range guidelines (five years or more) for organizational activity; they might never be accomplished, and they are not measured. In contrast, objectives are measurable, short-range, and time-limited; specific responsibility is given to individuals for accomplishment of an objective. Figure 2 suggests some criteria for judging the validity of an objective.[8]

Differentiating between goals and objectives is especially important because many academic libraries include sizable numbers of branch libraries scattered about campus. Each branch may operate in an environment somewhat different from the main library and may need goals and objectives to accommodate such differences. Therefore, each branch may have different goals and

> 1. Is it, generally speaking, a guide to action?
> 2. Does it suggest alternative courses of action?
> 3. Is it explicit enough to suggest certain types of action?
> 4. Can it be measured?
> 5. Is it time-limited?
> 6. Is it ambitious enough to be challenging?
> 7. Does it support both the goals and the institutional philosophy?

Fig. 2
Criteria for Judging the Validity of an Objective

objectives, but they all will stem from the same organizational philosophy. The primary consideration to be recognized is that all parts of the organization must develop goals that are mutually supportive. Such an occurrence is more likely when there is agreement as to organizational philosophy.

The combination of the historical background, philosophy, definitions, goals, and objectives forms a document which may be described as a mission statement. The development of such a document is the initial, and perhaps most important, step in the planning process. An excellent example of a mission statement for a public library recently appeared in *American Libraries*.[9] Whether one agrees or disagrees with the substance of this document, it contains a straightforward explication of historical development and assumptions (philosophy), followed by definitions, goals, and objectives.

Thus the statements of organizational philosophy, goals, and objectives should be developed as a written document that may be called the mission statement. It is this document that forms the basis for identifying and selecting programs to accomplish the objectives. Additionally, it is on the basis of this document that organizational units develop strategies to accomplish goals, cooperate in resource allocation, and take *action*.

Programs for Action

Organizational goals and objectives in themselves are of little value until they are translated into a program (or service) that will accomplish the stated objectives. It is in this translation of objectives into actions that the library responds to the wants of its patrons as well as addresses the information needs of its environment. Here a stance of *action*, of formulating plans to accomplish the objective, is developed.

Program development for academic libraries must consider (1) information constituencies and (2) information services. An examination of these two concepts in a matrix format (see figure 3) suggests four specific strategies that may be used as a basis for program development.[10] This procedure is one method of examining the environment for opportunities. Opportunities are a favorable set of circumstances that can be exploited to help accomplish a given objective. A technique that can be used to identify opportunities is forecasting—the process of identifying critical changes and developments in the environment that may affect organizational goals and objectives.[11]

Forecasting assumes that mere mortals can indeed foresee *some* of the future changes and factors that may affect the organization. Both empirical information and subjective information are used in the process. A typical forecast for the next three to five years may include possible trends or changes in terms of technology, economy, politics, and society. Although it is recognized that *all* trends or changes cannot be foreseen, some can be identified. Development of programs that anticipate *some* trends or changes has a greater likelihood of success than programs developed in an environmental vacuum.

Once the objective is agreed upon, an attempt should be made to develop alternative programs that may accomplish the objective. Developing alternatives encourages the creative and innovative aspect of program development. One finds more possible alternatives than originally expected if alternatives are explicitly and consciously sought. Development of alternative programs forces us, then, to choose or rank the programs on some kind of rational basis.

Figure 4 presents a typical library objective and includes three alternative programs which may all help to accomplish that goal. Once alternatives are suggested, they can be compared and contrasted based on a set of criteria that include organizational constraints. Although criteria and constraints will vary among organizations and programs selected, such a comparison is a rational basis to evaluate the various alternatives and

		INFORMATION SERVICES	
		Present Information Services	New Information Services
INFORMATION CONSTITUENCIES	Present Users	1. Market Penetration	2. Information Services Development
	New User Groups	3. User Group Expansion	4. Diversification

1. *Market Penetration:* The Organization Seeks Change through Increasing Its Share of Present User Groups from Its Present Services
2. *Information Services Development:* The Organization Seeks Change by Developing Improved or New Services for Its Present User Groups
3. *User Group Expansion:* The Organization Seeks Change by Taking Its Present Services into Different Types of User Groups
4. *Diversification:* The Organization Seeks Change by Taking New Information Services into Different Types of User Groups

Fig. 3
Strategies for Program Development*

*Adapted from Phillip Kotler, *Marketing for Nonprofit Organizations* (Englewood Cliffs, N.J.: Prentice-Hall, 1975), p.166–67.

	ALTERNATIVE PROGRAMS		
CRITERIA	1. Provide Evening and Weekend Reference Service	2. Provide Document Delivery Service to Faculty	3. Provide Instruction on the Use of the Library
1. Target Audience Description			
2. Target Audience Size			
3. Potential Number of Contact Hours			
4. Staff Hours for Planning			
5. Staff Hours for Program Operation			
6. Facilities Needed and Est. Cost			
7. Promotion and Public Relations			
8. Impact (Social, Political, or Economic)			
9. Program Evaluation Measures			
10. Risk of Failure			
11. Other			
Program Rank			

Fig. 4
Evaluating Alternatives
(Objective: To Increase Contact Hours between the Librarians and the Patrons)

determine which programs will be implemented.

The process of identifying opportunities and alternative programs and then selecting the "best" programs for action assumes: Program strategies are more likely to succeed when alternatives are compared and contrasted; for every objective there are at least two (and probably many) alternatives; identification of opportunities and alternative programs fosters creativity and innovation; and the better the decision maker can recognize and anticipate constraints critical to attaining an objective, the more clearly and accurately can the best program alternatives be selected.

Once the programs have been selected, action steps should be developed for activating the program. Action steps simply are a set of procedures which, when followed, will accomplish a given objective. One should be able to describe every program by a set of action steps; if this is not possible the nature of the program should be reconsidered. Furthermore, adequate publicity, advertisements, and program announcements should be distributed to appropriate media to ensure that potential users are aware of the program.

Each program also must contain a tentative budget. At a minimum level, the budget contains cost categories such as (1) personnel, (2) equipment, (3) contracted services, and (4) supplies and support material. Depending on the complexity and length of the program, the budget may be more or less detailed and subdivided within the above (or other) cost categories.[12]

One method to determine the viability of the program is to conduct a pilot study or pretest. A pilot is a scaled-down version of the actual program—a trial of its procedures to determine their usefulness and accuracy. The purpose of the pilot is to determine which parts of the program can be improved before the program is actually implemented. Potential problems identified at this stage are easier to correct than during full-scale implementation. Based on such a pilot, the program can be revised and modified.[13]

Finally, the program is implemented and put into action. At this stage, it is essential that all participants know what they are supposed to do, how it is to be done, and when it is to be done. Additionally, specific responsibilities for completion of specific action steps by specific individuals must be clearly delineated. Written task and scheduling charts such as a Gantt chart or flow process chart will be useful at this point.[14]

As figure 1 suggests, the program is selected from a list of possible alternatives and judged in light of opportunities and constraints affecting the organization. The program is revised as a result of a pilot project or pretest, and action steps are specified. Task responsibilities are clearly delineated before implementation of the program. All of these decisions must be set forth in a written document for the sake of clarity as well as for evaluation.

Evaluation

As suggested earlier, a possible mistake an organization can make when developing a planning process is to begin with goals and objectives without first examining organizational philosophy. A second typical mistake is for the organization to consider the planning process complete upon implementation of the program. At this point, the planning process is still incomplete. The last and significant portion of organizational planning is the evaluation of the planning process and the success of the selected programs.

Evaluation is the accountability aspect of planning and represents a measurement of effectiveness in reaching some predetermined goal.[15] Failure to include evaluation as part of the library planning process may result in the creation of a self-serving bureaucracy, increased distance between information and users, ineffective allocation of resources, poor credibility with governing bodies, reinforcement of status quo, and, most important, the continuance of programs that should have been ended because they no longer contribute to the accomplishment of organizational goals and objectives.

It is useful to suggest that evaluation may be one of two kinds. The first is generally referred to as *formative* evaluation. Formative evaluation is an ongoing and continuous process and generates information that can be used to modify a system while it is in operation. *Summative* evaluation occurs at the end of an operation and is product oriented. The difference between the two can be summed up by saying the purpose of summative evaluation is to *prove;* the purpose of formative evaluation is to *improve.* Both types of evaluation have a role in the planning process, and one is not intrinsically better than the other.[16]

Referring again to figure 1, one finds that there are two key areas for evaluation to take place. The first is during the development of the program itself. During this development, planners are most interested in formative evaluation as they strive to improve the program strategy. Methods for such formative evaluation are stressed as a result of comparing alternative programs and developing a pilot or pretest of the program. Based on these techniques, the program may be revised or improved before it is actually implemented.

In a more limited sense, formative evaluation also takes place in examining the goals and objectives. The needs assessment can be seen as a technique of formative evaluation during the development of goals and objectives. These more limited, but not less important, formative evaluations are represented in figure 1 with a "D" for *decision* inside a triangle connected to that planning component where formative evaluation takes place.

The evaluation during program development is *process* oriented; it examines the program in terms of how it can be improved on an ongoing, continuous basis. In order for this function to be performed, information must be collected and analyzed about the process. Three steps must be considered to accomplish this. First, one delineates or determines what pieces of information are needed to evaluate the process; second, one obtains that information via a data collection technique; and third, one provides the information to the decision makers in order for the evaluation decision to be made.[17]

The second key area for evaluation is product oriented and takes place in two basic areas of the planning process. Returning to the program development, it is critical to know if, in fact, the program is a success or a failure. Thus, during program development, measures for summative evaluation are devised. These measures, perhaps increasing librarian-patron contact hours by 25 percent, are then used as a basis to determine the success or failure of the program. It should be stressed that multiple evaluation measures for each component as well as the total success of the program should be developed.[18]

Similar to the formative evaluation aspect of planning, the summative evaluation also depends on delineating, obtaining, and providing information to make the evaluation decision. This information collection is usually done as part of the monitoring function (see figure 1). By comparing the information from the monitoring activity of the program to the predetermined measures for program success, summative evaluation of the program is accomplished.

The second aspect of summative evaluation is accomplished when the results or output from the program are compared to the organizational goals. The question being asked is, "To what degree did this program achieve the stated organizational goals and objectives?" This summative evaluation is effectiveness oriented—"Did we achieve what we wanted to accomplish?" If yes, the program may be judged a success. If no, the program may be judged a failure and either dropped from further use or modified to better accomplish the objective.

Finally, the planner must consider the outcomes from the program. Outcomes may be differentiated from outputs (results) in that outcomes are the impact of the outputs on the environment. If the reference librarians initiate extensive instructional programs about the use of the library, the *output* may be better-educated users who have substantial competence about the services of the library. However, the *outcome* of the instructional programs may be a marked increase in the use of the library's materials and services. If there are not enough materials or staff to accommodate the additional demand, the outcome may be dysfunctional to library goals and objectives. Typically, the library as an organization fails to consider the outcomes, or impacts, of its programs on the environment.

Admittedly, identification—to say nothing of measurement—of outputs and outcomes is difficult. But until we recognize their existence, we cannot identify them; and until we identify them, they cannot be measured. Such measures must be user oriented—determined only in the context of the information environment of the users of the program.[19] It is likely that measures such as awareness can be identified and measured. Identifying and measuring the outputs and outcomes are the challenge of tomorrow for academic library planning.[20] At present there are researchers, such as Douglas Zweizig, who stress the importance of measures of output or services and suggest possible indexes by which such measurement can be made.[21]

The evaluation process—both summative and formative—is an integral part of organizational planning. Planning without evaluation is like taking a test and never knowing how well or poorly you did. The evaluation component in organizational planning provides organizational members with important feedback to improve the total effectiveness of the organization as a service agency responding to the needs and wants of its patrons.

STRATEGIES FOR SUCCESS

The overview of planning in an academic library that has been presented in this discussion is intended to serve as a general conceptual guide to the planning process as well as a set of suggestions for procedural implementation. Because various library environments are different, readers are urged to develop specific procedures for their library situation. There is no specific set of instructions for the prospective planner to follow that will take into consideration all the various contingencies inherent to a specific library situation. In short, this overview is a tool by which organizational members can build a planning process whose use will facilitate the effectiveness of academic library organizations and their responsiveness to the information environments they serve.

However, before members utilize a total approach to organizational planning, some questions need first be asked. Are organizational members willing to accept the responsibilities of the planning process? Are they willing to grow and develop on both a professional and a personal basis? Are they willing to take risks and to implement strategies for change? Are they willing to step outside the library in an attempt to determine user and nonuser needs and wants?

Academic library administrators may wish to consider some questions as well. Do you have confidence in your staff to learn how to participate in the planning process? Have you established effective and open channels of communication for information dissemination among all organizational members? Are you willing to experiment with the delegation of authority to organizational members? Are you willing to take a personal role of leadership in developing an organizational planning system?

Furthermore, library staff members should be aware of their responsibilities during the planning process. Planning assumes that organizational members can agree on "appropriate" goals, objectives, programs, and evaluation measures; planning assumes that the staff can direct the activities of the organization to respond to environmental needs; planning assumes that the staff is willing to experiment with organizational change; and, finally, planning assumes that librarians can measure the degree to which change takes place, the degree to which objectives are accomplished, and the impact of various programs on the environment. The experiences of this writer suggest that the vast majority of academic librarians would welcome such responsibility.

Superimposing an organizational planning system on a library organization unwilling to work under these assumptions or unwilling to accept the responsibilities inherent in the planning process will end in frustration, false expectations, and, ultimately, failure. Such failure is not an indication of the value of planning; rather it is an indicator of the degree to which the organizational members were prepared and committed to implementing a planning process.

For organizations where ongoing planning has not been the rule, a wise strategy might be to spend some months discussing at an organizational level of analysis the importance and framework of planning in that academic library. It is essential that organizational information which is to be used in the planning process be readily available to all organizational members. Furthermore, administrators must develop a leadership stance in terms of preparing organizational members to take on the various skills and responsibilities needed for successful planning.

To facilitate this preparation, an organizational member (preferably an administrator) who is knowledgeable about planning can be appointed or elected as planning officer. This person then would serve as a catalyst for preparing the organizational members for new responsibilities as well as serving as the person responsible for organizational planning once the planning process is implemented. This strategy would demonstrate management's seriousness with the planning process as well as providing a person for organizational members to contact should questions arise during the planning process.

The planning officer's first task is preparing the organization for the planning process. A second task for this officer is to lead the organization through the process of developing a mission statement. After the mission statement has been completed, task forces can be created to deal with specific concerns facing the organization by developing programs to accomplish specific objectives and evaluating the results.

Excuses for not planning abound: too few staff, not enough time, too little money, dispersed geographical locations, too many projects already, too busy solving yesterday's crises, etc. These conditions are continuous facts of life for typical library operations and are likely to be with us for some time to come. Changing these conditions begins with *making time available* for the development of an organizational planning system.

The development of organizational planning in a systematic and ongoing fashion is crucial for the effectiveness of the library both on an internal and external basis. Internally, planning encompasses the entire span of organizational activities, identifies program priorities, encourages rational resource allocation, and provides a framework of challenge and responsibility for all organizational members. Externally, planning provides a means to respond to environmental changes and suggests specific actions to satisfy the needs of various user groups. Perhaps even more important, planning provides proof positive to the library's governing bodies of rational decision making and organizational purpose.

The suggestions in this paper can serve as one possible approach to implement organizational planning. Those academic libraries interested in new techniques to meet the current and future challenges of providing information services in a complex environment are likely to be more effective with a specific approach to organizational planning than libraries making decisions on a day-to-day basis. Ultimately, the planning process provides a means for the library to take a leadership role as an integral and dynamic force in accomplishing the educational goals of the college or university.

REFERENCES

1. Fremont E. Kast and James E. Rosenzweig, *Organization and Management: A Systems Approach* (2d ed.; New York: McGraw-Hill, 1974), p.437-40.
2. Ernest R. DeProspo and James W. Liesener, "Media Program Evaluation: A Working Framework," *School Media Quarterly* 3:290 (Summer 1975).
3. Harold Koontz and Cyril O'Donnel, *Management: A Systems and Contingency Analysis of Managerial Functions* (6th ed.; New York: McGraw-Hill, 1976), p.130-33.
4. Fremont E. Kast and James E. Rosenzweig, "General Systems Theory: Applications for Organization and Management," *Academy of Management Journal* 15:447-68 (Dec. 1972).
5. Ernest R. DeProspo and Alan R. Samuels, *A Program Planning and Evaluation Self-Instructional Manual* (New York: College Entrance Examination Board, 1977).

6. Archie Donald, "On the Starting of Goals," *Journal of Systems Engineering* 4:89–95 (Jan. 1976).
7. Kevin D. Reilly, "The Delphi Technique: Fundamentals and Applications," in Harold Borko, ed., *Targets for Research in Library Education* (Chicago: American Library Assn., 1973), p.187–99.
8. Charles H. Granger, "The Hierarchy of Objectives," *Harvard Business Review* 42:64–65 (May–June 1964).
9. American Library Association, Public Library Association Goals, Guidelines, and Standards Committee, "A Mission Statement for Public Libraries: Guidelines for Public Library Service, Part I," *American Libraries* 8:615–20 (Dec. 1977).
10. Adapted from Phillip Kotler, *Marketing for Nonprofit Organizations* (Englewood Cliffs, N.J.: Prentice-Hall, 1975) p.166–67.
11. Koontz and O'Donnel, *Management*, p.180–86.
12. For additional information on developing a program budget, see Stephen J. Knezevich, *Program Budgeting* (Berkeley: McCutchan Publishing Corp., 1973).
13. Nan Lin, *Foundations of Social Research* (New York: McGraw-Hill, 1976), p.199–200.
14. A brief explanation of a Gantt (for Henry L. Gantt) and PERT (Program Evaluation and Review Technique) chart may be found in G. Edward Evans, *Management Techniques for Librarians* (New York: Academic Press, 1976), p.254–59.
15. Edward A. Suchman, "Action for What? A Critique of Evaluation Research," in Carol H. Weiss, *Evaluating Action Programs* (Boston: Allyn & Bacon, 1972), p.53.
16. Carol H. Weiss, *Evaluation Research: Methods of Assessing Program Effectiveness* (Englewood Cliffs, N.J.: Prentice-Hall, 1972), p.16–17.
17. Daniel L. Stufflebeam, "The CIPP Model of Evaluation," in David D. Thomson, ed., *Planning and Evaluation for Statewide Library Development: New Directions* (Columbus: Ohio State Univ. Evaluation Center, 1972), p.34–42.
18. An excellent handbook here is Irwin Epstein and Tony Tripodi, *Research Techniques for Program Planning, Monitoring, and Evaluation* (New York: Columbia Univ. Pr., 1977), p.35–110.
19. Douglas L. Zweizig, "With Our Eye on the User: Needed Research for Information and Referral in the Public Library," *Drexel Library Quarterly* 12:55 (Jan.–April 1976).
20. DeProspo and Samuels, *A Program Planning and Evaluation Self-Instructional Manual*.
21. Douglas L. Zweizig, "Measuring Library Use," *Drexel Library Quarterly* 13:3–15 (July 1977).

Purposes of Evaluation
By Carol H. Weiss

In this chapter, we will discuss the purposes, acknowledged and unacknowledged, for which people decide to undertake program evaluation. We suggest that the evaluator find out what decision makers really seek from the study and how they expect to use the results. With this knowledge, he can most effectively tailor the study to provide information for decision making. The location of the evaluation unit—where it fits into the organizational structure—can make a difference in whether the study has sufficient latitude to be useful.

Before we get on with these matters, let us raise a prior question. Is evaluation always warranted? Should all programs if they are good little programs go out and get themselves evaluated? The answer, heretical as it may seem, is No. Evaluation as an applied research is committed to the principle of utility. If it is not going to have any effect on decisions, it is an exercise in futility. Evaluation is probably not worth doing in four kinds of circumstances:

1. When there are no questions about the program. It goes on, and decisions about its future either do not come up or have already been made.

2. When the program has no clear orientation. Program staff improvise activities from day to day, based on little thought and less principle, and the program shifts and changes, wanders around and seeks direction. There is little here to call "a program."

Carol H. Weiss, *Evaluation Research: Methods for Assessing Program Effectiveness,* © 1972, pp. 10-23. Reprinted by permission of Prentice-Hall, Inc., Englewood Cliffs, New Jersey.

3. When people who should know cannot agree on what the program is trying to achieve. If there are vast discrepancies in perceived goals, evaluation has no ground to stand on.
4. When there is not enough money or no staff sufficiently qualified to conduct the evaluation. Evaluation is a demanding business, calling for time, money, imagination, tenacity, and skill.

There are those who argue that even in such dismal circumstances, evaluation research can produce something of value, some glimmering of insight that will light a candle for the future. This is a fetching notion, and from time to time in this volume, we succumb to it. But experience suggests that even good evaluation studies of well-defined programs, directed to clear decisional purposes, often wind up as litter in the bureaucratic mill. It will be a rare study indeed that provides illumination under unfavorable conditions.

Overt and Covert Purposes

People decide to have a program evaluated for many different reasons, from the eminently rational to the patently political. Ideally, an administrator is seeking answers to pressing questions about the program's future: Should it be continued? Should it be expanded? Should changes be made in its operation? But there are occasions when he turns to evaluation for less legitimate reasons.

Postponement. The decision maker may be looking for ways to delay a decision. Instead of resorting to the usual ploy of appointing a committee and waiting for its report, he can commission an evaluation study, which takes even longer.

Ducking responsibility. Sometimes one faction in the program organization is espousing one course of action and another faction is opposing it. The administrators look to evaluation to get them off the hook by producing dispassionate evidence that will make the decision for them. There are cases in which administrators know what the decision will be even before they call in the evaluators, but want to cloak it in the legitimate trappings of research.

Public relations. Occasionally, evaluation is seen as a way of self-glorification. The administrator believes that he has a highly successful program and looks for a way to make it visible. A good study will fill the bill. Copies of the report, favorable of course, can be sent to boards of trustees, members of legislative committees, executives of philanthropic foundations who give large sums to successful programs, and other influential people. Suchman [1] suggests two related purposes: eyewash and whitewash. In an eyewash evaluation, an attempt is made to justify a weak program by selecting for evaluation only those aspects that look good on the surface. A whitewash attempts to cover up program failure by avoiding any objective appraisal.

The program administrator's motives are not, of course, necessarily crooked or selfish. Often, there is a need to justify the program to the people who pay the bills, and he is seeking support for a concept and a project in which he believes. Generating support for existing programs is a common motive for embarking on evaluation.

Fulfilling grant requirements. Increasingly, the decision to evaluate stems from sources outside the program. Many federal grants for demonstration projects and innovative programs are tagged with an evaluation requirement; for example, all projects for disadvantaged pupils funded under Title I of the Elementary and Secondary Education Act are required to be evaluated.

From the point of view of the funders, who are taking a chance on an untried project, it is reasonable to require that there be some evidence on the extent to which the project is working. To the operators of a project, the demands of starting up and running the new program take priority. Plagued as they often are by immediate problems of staffing, budgets, logistics, community relations, and all the other trials of pioneers, they tend to neglect the evaluation. They see it mainly as a ritual designed to placate the funding bodies, without any real usefulness to them.

Evaluation, then, is a rational enterprise often undertaken for nonrational, or at least noninformational, reasons. We could continue the catalog of the varieties of covert purposes (justifying a program to Congress, "getting" the program director, increasing the prestige of the agency), but the important point is that such motives have consequences for the evaluation that can be serious and bleak.[2]

---

[1] Edward A. Suchman, "Action for What? A Critique of Evaluative Research," in *The Organization, Management, and Tactics of Social Research,* ed. Richard O'Toole (Cambridge, Mass.: Schenkman Publishing Co., Inc., 1970).

[2] See Sar Levitan, "Facts, Fancies, and Freeloaders in Evaluating Antipoverty Programs," *Poverty and Human Resources Abstracts,* IV, No. 6 (1969), 13–16; Richard H. Hall, "The Applied Sociologist and Organizational Sociology," in *So-*

An evaluator who is asked to study a particular program usually assumes that he is there because people want answers about what the program is doing well and poorly. When this is not the case, he may in his naïveté become a pawn in intraorganizational power struggles, a means of delaying action, or the rallying point for one ideology or another. Some evaluators have found only after their study was done that they had unwittingly played a role in a larger political game. They found that nobody was particularly interested in applying their results to the decisions at hand, but only in using them (or any quotable piece of them) as ammunition to destroy or to justify.

Lesson No. 1 for the evaluator newly arrived on the scene is: Find out who initiated the idea of having an evaluation of the program and for what purposes. Were there other groups in the organization who questioned or objected to the evaluation? What were their motives? Is there real commitment among practitioners, administrators, and/or funders to using the results of the evaluation to improve future decision making? If the real purposes for the evaluation are not oriented to better decision making and there is little commitment to applying results, the project is probably a poor candidate for evaluation. The evaluator might well ponder whether he wishes to get involved in the situation or whether he can find more productive uses for his talents elsewhere.

Intended Uses

Even when evaluation is undertaken for bona fide purposes (that is, to learn how well the program is reaching its goals), people can have widely differing expectations of the kinds of answers that will be produced. If the evaluator is not to be caught unawares, it behooves him to know from the outset what kinds of answers are expected from his study.[3]

---

ciology in Action, ed. Arthur B. Shostak (Homewood, Ill.: Dorsey Press, Inc., 1966), pp. 33–38; Joseph W. Eaton, "Symbolic and Substantive Evaluative Research," *Administrative Science Quarterly*, VI, No. 4 (1962), 421–42; Lewis A. Dexter, "Impressions About Utility and Wastefulness in Applied Social Science Studies," *American Behavioral Scientist*, IX, No. 6 (1966), 9–10.

[3] Downs makes the point that the extent of applied research should be economically justified by the value of the information it produces for decision making. Evaluators, like other researchers, can become fascinated with the problem and do more research than the program needs. But he also stresses the point that clients frequently need redefinition of the problem and the suggestion of alternative approaches. Anthony Downs, "Some Thoughts on Giving People Economic Advice," *American Behavioral Scientist*, IX, No. 1 (1965), 30–32. Of course, far more common than spending too much money is trying to conduct evaluation with funds grossly inadequate for the extent and precision of the results expected.

Who expects what?

Expectations for the evaluation generally vary with a person's position in the system.[4] Top policy makers need the kind of information that will help them address the broad issues: Should the program be continued or dropped, institutionalized throughout the system or limited to a pilot program, continued with the same procedures and techniques or modified? Should more money be allocated to this program or to others? They want information on the overall effectiveness of the program.

The directors of the program face other issues. They want to know not only how well their program is achieving the desired ends, but also which general strategies are more or less successful, which are achieving results most efficiently and economically, which features of the program are essential and which can be changed or dropped.

Direct-service staff deal with individuals and small groups. They have practical day-to-day concerns about techniques. Should they spend more time on developing good work habits and less time on teaching subject matter? Put more emphasis on group discussions or films or lectures? Should they accept more younger people (who are not already set in their ways) or more older people (who have greater responsibilities and more need)? Practitioners, who are accustomed to relying on their own experience and intuitive judgment, often challenge evaluation to come up with something practical on topics such as these.

Nor do these three sets of actors—policy makers, program directors, and practitioners—exhaust the list of those with a possible oar in the evaluation. The funders of evaluation research, particularly when they are outside the direct line of operations, may have an interest in adding to the pool of knowledge in the field. They may want answers less to operating questions than to questions of theory and method. Can social group work help improve the parental performance of young couples? Does increasing the available career opportunities for low-income youth result in less juvenile deliquency? If coordination among community health services is increased, will people receive better health care? Here is another purpose for evaluation—to test propositions about the utility of concepts or models of service. The public too has a stake, as taxpayers, as parents of schoolchildren, as contributors to voluntary organizations.[5] They are concerned that their money is wisely and efficiently spent.

[4] A useful discussion appears in Louis Ferman, "Some Perspectives on Evaluating Social Welfare Programs," *Annals of the American Academy of Political and Social Science,* Vol. 385 (September 1969), 143–56.

[5] Edward Wynne, in "Evaluating Educational Programs: A Symposium," *Urban Review,* III, No. 4 (1969), 19–20.

Recently, another actor has entered the decision-making arena—the consumer of services. He may see a use for evaluation in asking "client-eye" questions about the program under study. Is the program serving the goals that the intended beneficiaries of service value?[6] Recently, there has been rising opposition, particularly in some black communities, to traditional formulations of program goals.[7] Activists are concerned not only with how well programs work to improve school achievement or health care, but also with their political legitimacy. They are interested in community participation or community control of programs and institutions. When such issues are paramount, evaluative questions derive from a radically different perspective.

Compatibility of purposes

With all the possible uses for evaluation to serve, the evaluator has to make choices. The all-purpose evaluation is a myth. Although a number of different types of questions can be considered within the bounds of a single study, this takes meticulous planning and design. Inevitably not even the best-planned study will provide information on all the questions that people will think of. In fact, some purposes for evaluation are incompatible with others. Let us consider the evaluation of a particular educational program for slow learners.

The teaching staff wants to use the results to improve the presentations and teaching methods of the course, session by session, in order to maximize student learning. The state college of education wants to know whether the instructional program, based on a particular theory of learning, will improve pupil performance. In the first case, the evaluator will have to examine immediate short-term effects (learnings after the morning drill). He need not be concerned about generalizing the results to other populations, and needs neither control groups nor sophisticated statistics. He will want to maximize feedback of results to the teachers so that they can modify their techniques as they go along.

On the other hand, when evaluation is testing the proposition that a program developed from certain theories of learning will be successful with slow learners, it is concerned with long-range effects. It requires rigorous design so that observed results can be attributed to the stimulus of the

---

[6] Philip H. Taylor, "The Role and Function of Educational Research," *Educational Research,* IX, No. 1 (1966), 11–15; Edmund deS. Brunner, "Evaluation Research in Adult Education," *International Review of Community Development,* No. 17–18 (1967), 97–102.

[7] David K. Cohen, "Politics and Research: Evaluation of Social Action Programs in Education," *Review of Educational Research,* XL, No. 2 (1970), 232.

program and not to extraneous events. The results have to be generalizable beyond the specific group of students. The instructional program should be insulated from alterations during its course in order to preserve the clarity of the program that led to the effects observed.

In theory, it is possible to achieve both an assessment of overall program effectiveness and a test of the effectiveness of component strategies. Textbooks on the design of experiments [8] present methods of factorial design that allow the experimenter to discover both total effect and the effects of each "experimental treatment." In practice, evaluation can seldom go about the business so systematically. The constraints of the field situation hobble the evalution—too few clients, demand for quick feedback of information, inadequate funds, "contamination" of the special-treatment groups by receipt of other services, drop-outs from the program, lack of access to records and data, changes in program, and so on.

Some researchers say that to try to satisfy a multiplicity of demands and uses under usual field conditions invites frustration. The evaluator who identifies the key decision pending and gears his study to supplying information relevant to that issue is on firmer ground. Others believe that there are ways—not necessarily formal and elegant—to study a range of issues concurrently.[9] Some of these methods will be discussed in Chapters 3 and 4. Nevertheless, it remains important for the evaluator to know the priority among the purposes. If the crunch comes, he can jettison the extra baggage and fight for the essentials.

Formative and summative evaluation

We have identified several types of uses for evaluation. Evaluation can be asked to investigate the extent of program success so that decisions such as these can be made:

1. To continue or discontinue the program
2. To improve its practices and procedures
3. To add or drop specific program strategies and techniques
4. To institute similar programs elsewhere

[8] A good example is B. J. Winer, *Statistical Principles in Experimental Design* (New York: McGraw-Hill Book Company, 1962). F. Stuart Chapin, W. G. Cochran and G. M. Cox, D. R. Cox, A. L. Edwards, R. A. Fisher, R. E. Kirk and E. F. Lindquist, among others, have also written useful texts on experimental design. Some of these are listed in the third section of the bibliography.

[9] See Robert E. Stake, "Generalizability of Program Evaluation: The Need for Limits," and James L. Wardrop, "Generalizability of Program Evaluation: The Dangers of Limits," *Educational Product Report*, II, No. 5 (1969), 38–40, 41–42.

5. To allocate resources among competing programs
6. To accept or reject a program approach or theory

A useful distinction has been introduced into the discussion of purpose by Scriven.[10] In discussing the evaluation of educational curriculums, he distinguishes between *formative* and *summative* evaluation. Formative evaluation produces information that is fed back during the development of a curriculum to help improve it. It serves the needs of developers. Summative evaluation is done after the curriculum is finished. It provides information about effectiveness to school decision makers who are considering adopting it.[11]

This distinction can be applied to other types of programs as well, with obvious advantages for the clarification of purpose. Many programs, however, are never "finished" in the sense that a curriculum is finished, and continued modification and adaptation will be necessary both at the original site and in other locations that use the program. The evaluator still has some hard thinking to do.

In practice, evaluation is most often called on to help with decisions about improving programs. Go/no-go, live-or-die decisions are relatively rare. Even when evaluation results show the program to be a failure, the usual reaction is to patch it up and try again. Rare, too, is the use of evaluation in theory-oriented tests of program approaches and models. These are more readily studied under controlled laboratory conditions. It is the search for improvements in strategies and techniques that supports much evaluation activity at present.

Even when decision makers start out with global questions (Is the program worth continuing?), they often end up receiving qualified results ("There are these good effects, but . . .") that lead them to look for ways to modify present practice. They become interested in the likelihood of improved results with different components, a different mix of services, different client groups, different staffing patterns, different organizational structure, different procedures and mechanics. One of the ironies of evaluation practice is that it has performed well at assessment of overall impact, suited to the uncommon go/no-go decision; it is relatively undeveloped in designs that produce information on the effectiveness of comparative strategies. We shall return to this point in Chapter 4.

[10] Michael Scriven, "The Methodology of Evaluation," in *Perspectives of Curriculum Evaluation,* ed. Ralph W. Tyler, Robert M. Gagné, and Michael Scriven, AERA Monograph Series on Curriculum Evaluation, No. 1 (Chicago: Rand McNally & Co., 1967), pp. 39–83.

[11] See also Thomas J. Hastings, "Curriculum Evaluation: The Why of Outcomes," *Journal of Educational Measurement,* III, No. 3 (1966), 27–32.

Whose Use Shall Be Served?

Some possible users of the evaluation have been mentioned:

1. A funding organization (government, private, foundation)
2. A national agency (governmental, private)
3. A local agency
4. The directors of the specific project
5. Direct-service staff
6. Clients of the program
7. Scholars in the disciplines and professions

Which purposes shall the evaluation serve and for whom? In some cases, the question is academic. The evaluator is on the staff of some organization—national organization, pilot program—and he does the job assigned to him. But more often, the evaluator has a number of options open. If he is on the staff of an outside research organization that is being asked to undertake the evaluation, he may have the opportunity to negotiate the purpose and focus of the study. Even if he is more closely attached to the project, there is commonly such an amazing lack of clarity among the other parties that he has wide room to maneuver.

If he can help shape the basic focus of the study, the evaluator will consider a number of things. First is probably his own set of values. A summer program for ghetto youth can be evaluated for city officialdom to see if it cools out the kids and prevents riots and looting. The evaluator may want to view the program from the youths' perspective as well and see if it has improved their job prospects, work skills, and enjoyment. The data such a study produces can give a wider frame of reference to the decision of whether or not to continue the summer programs. It is important that the evaluator be able to live with the study, its uses, and his conscience at the same time.

Beyond this point, the paramount consideration in what use the study should be designed to serve is: What decision has to be made? The pending question may be one of extending a small pilot program in one hospital ward to other wards in the same hospital. It may be allocating money to one project or to another. There may have to be a decision on the adoption of one technique (reduced case loads, nonprofessional aides) throughout the system. Perhaps the upcoming decisions have to do with staffing, structure, or target populations. Once the evaluator finds out what key decisions are pending and when they will come up, he can gear his study to provide the maximum payoff.

Often there is no critical decision pending, at least that anyone can identify at the moment. There are, however, "users" who are interested in learning from the study and applying the results and others who are not. When the local program managers are conscientiously seeking better ways to serve their clients while the policy makers at higher levels are looking primarily for "program vindicators," the local managers' questions may deserve more attention. On the other hand, if the locals want a whitewash and the higher levels want to know where to put further appropriations, the evaluator should place more emphasis on comparative assessment of overall outcome.

The next task, then, is designing the evaluation to provide the answers that are needed. Finding out what answers are needed is not always an easy job. As we shall see in Chapter 3, it is the rare program that is articulate about goals, objectives, criteria, and bases for decision. Nevertheless, based on his best estimate of intended use, the evaluator has to make decisions on the measures to be used (see Chapter 3), sources of information (Chapter 3), and research design (Chapter 4). He will be abetted or hindered by the location of the evaluation within the organizational structure. It is to this issue that we now turn.

Structure of the Evaluation

An evaluation study can be staffed and structured in different ways. A research unit or department within the program agency can do the evaluation, or special evaluators can be hired and attached to the program. (This is often the way federally funded demonstration projects handle their evaluation requirement.) Outsiders, usually university faculty members, are sometimes paid to serve as consultants, and either advise the evaluators on staff or carry out some of the evaluation tasks themselves in close cooperation with staff. These kinds of arrangements can be lumped together as "in-house."

Another approach is for the agency to contract with an outside research organization to do the study. The research organization, whether it is an academic group, a nonprofit organization, or a commercial firm, is responsible to the persons (and the level in the program agency) who commission it. Still another kind of arrangement is for a national agency (such as the U.S. Office of Education or the national YMCA) to employ a research organization to study a number of the local programs it supports or oversees.

Inside vs. outside evaluation

There is a long tradition of controversy, mainly oral, about whether in-house or outside evaluations are preferable.[12] The answer seems to be that neither has a monopoly on the advantages. Some of the factors to be considered are administrative confidence, objectivity, understanding of the program, potential for utilization, and autonomy.

Administrative confidence. Administrators must have confidence in the professional skills of the evaluation staff. Sometimes agency personnel are impressed only by the credentials and reputations of academic researchers and assume that the research people it has on staff or can hire are second-raters. Conversely, it may view outside evaluators as too remote from the realities, too ivory-tower and abstract, to produce information of practical value. Occasionally, it is important to ensure public confidence by engaging evaluators who have no stake in the program to be studied. Competence, of course, is a big factor in ensuring confidence and deserves priority consideration.

Objectivity. Objectivity requires that evaluators be insulated from any possibility of biasing their data or its interpretation by a desire to make things look good. Points usually go to outsiders on this score, although fine evaluation has been done by staff evaluators of scrupulous integrity. It even happens that an outside research firm will sweeten the interpretation of program results (by choice of respondents, by types of statistical tests applied) in order to ingratiate itself with a program and get further contracts. In any event, safeguarding the study against even unintentional bias is important.

Understanding of the program. Knowledge of what is going on in the program is vital for an evaluation staff. They need to know both the real issues facing the agency and the real events that are taking place in the program if their evaluation is to be relevant. It is here that in-house staffs chalk up points, although outsiders too can find out about program proc-

---

[12] See Elmer Luchterhand, "Research and the Dilemmas in Developing Social Programs," in *The Uses of Sociology*, ed. P. F. Lazarsfeld, W. H. Sewell, and H. L. Wilensky (New York: Basic Books, Inc., Publishers, 1967), pp. 513–17; Rensis Likert and Ronald Lippitt, "The Utilization of Social Science," in *Research Methods in the Behavioral Sciences,* ed. Leon Festinger and Daniel Katz (New York: Holt, Rinehart & Winston, Inc., 1953), pp. 581–646; Martin Weinberger, "Evaluating Educational Programs: Observations by a Market Researcher," *Urban Review,* III, No. 4 (1969), 23–26.

esses if they make the effort and are given access to sources of information.

Potential for utilization. Utilization of results often requires that evaluators take an active role in moving from research data to interpretation of the results in a policy context. In-house staff, who are willing to make recommendations on the basis of results and advocate them in agency meetings and conferences, may be better able to secure them a hearing. But sometimes it is outsiders, with their prestige and authority, who are able to induce the agency to pay attention to the evaluation.

Autonomy. Insiders generally take the program's basic assumptions and organizational arrangements as given and conduct their evaluation within the existing framework. The outsider may be able to exercise more autonomy and take a wider perspective. While respecting the formulation of issues set by the program, he may be able to introduce alternatives that are a marked departure from the status quo. The implications he draws from evaluation data may be oriented less to tinkering and more to fundamental restructuring of the program.[13] However, such a broader approach is neither common among outsiders nor unknown among insiders.

All these considerations have to be balanced against each other. There is no one "best site" for evaluation. The agency must weigh the factors afresh in each case and make an estimate of the way which the benefits pile up.

Level in the structure

Whoever actually does the evaluation, the evaluation staff fits somewhere in the organizational bureaucracy. The evaluator reports to a person at some level of authority in the program organization or its supervisory or funding body, and he is responsible to that person and that position for the work he does. If the evaluator is an insider, he reports on a regular basis. The outsider researcher also receives his assignment and reports his results to (and may get intermediate advice from) the holder of a particular organizational position.

The important distinction in organizational location for our discussion is the difference between the policy maker and the program manager. To abridge our earlier catalog of users of evaluation and the decisions they have to make, the key points are these:

[13] Robert K. Merton, "Role of the Intellectual in Public Bureaucracy," in *Social Theory and Social Structure* (New York: The Free Press, 1964), pp. 207–24.

User	Decision
Policy maker	Whether to expand, contract, or change the program
Program manager	Which methods, structures, techniques, or staff patterns to use

The evaluation should be placed within the organizational structure at a level consonant with its mission. If it is directed at answering the policy questions (How good is the program overall?), evaluators should report to policy makers. If the basic shape of the program is unquestioned and the evaluation issue centers on variations in specific features, the evaluator should probably be responsible to the program managers.[14]

Real problems arise when the evaluation is inappropriately located in the structure. An evaluation that is initiated by and responsible to program managers is under all kinds of pressure not to come up with findings that disparage the effectiveness of the whole program. If it does, the managers are likely to stall the report at the program level and it will never receive consideration in higher councils.[15] On the other other hand, when top policy makers initiate and oversee the evaluation, their questions are paramount, and questions about operations may get the short end of the budget. Nor do the evaluators have the easy, informal contact with program managers and practitioners that allows them to hear and understand the problems and options they face. It sometimes becomes difficult to study the effectiveness of different program components because staff see the evaluators as "inspectors" checking up on them and become vary of divulging information that might reflect poorly on their performance. Nor are they always cooperative in maintaining the conditions necessary for evaluation research, particularly if there is competition among program levels and the evaluation is viewed as an effort to assert the priorities of the higher level.

The problem of structural location becomes more complex when the evaluation is serving both masters. By and large, it appears best to report in at the higher level. In that way, the evaluator maintains greater autonomy. But then he has to make special efforts to learn enough about critical issues in day-to-day program operations to incorporate them into the study and to maintain the support of local program managers for appropriate research conditions.

---

[14] This rule of thumb applies whether the evaluation is performed by an in-house evaluation unit or by an outside research organization. Either one should report in at the level of decision to which its work is addressed. The outsiders probably have greater latitude in going around the organizational chain of command and finding access to an appropriate ear, but even they will be circumscribed by improper location.

[15] This point is discussed in Likert and Lippitt, *op. cit.*

Good placement in the structure is important. A recent report by Wholey et al. on federal evaluation practice [16] discusses this issue in terms of federal agencies' responsibilities. It recommends that a central evaluation staff in each agency should have responsibility for planning and coordinating all evaluation work in the department, but that staff at different levels should be responsible for direct supervision of evaluation studies depending on their scope and purpose.

> Policy makers are most often called upon to make choices among national programs; program managers are most often called upon to make choices of emphasis or decisions on the future of individual projects *within* national programs. To the extent possible, program impact evaluations, designed to discover the worth of an entire national program, should be directed by persons not immediately involved in management of the program and operation. Program strategy evaluation should be directed by persons close enough to the program to introduce variations into the program.[17]

Wherever the evaluation project sits in the structure, it should have the autonomy that all research requires to report objectively on the evidence and to pursue issues, criteria, and analysis beyond the limits set by the program in order to better understand and interpret the phenomena under study.

[16] Joseph S. Wholey et al., *Federal Evaluation Policy* (Washington, D.C.: The Urban Institute, 1970), pp. 54–71.

[17] *Ibid.*, p. 65.

Part VIII
MOTIVATION AND JOB SATISFACTION

Introduction

Motivation is one of those words used in the library/information center that everyone apparently "understands." However, separating fact from fiction regarding motivation is more difficult than first imagined. In organizations where conditions are not likely to be optimum for high productivity (service organizations such as libraries), knowing what motivation is, how to motivate employees positively, and the impact of motivation on other administrative activities becomes critical and something that cannot be done by instinct.

The lack of agreement among managerial theorists as to what constitutes "good" motivation makes prescriptive admonitions difficult at best and disastrous at worst. What can be done, however, is to present a number of views regarding motivation, and summarize recent research related to the topic as it applies to libraries. Only then can the library administrator make an intelligent and rational decision as to how best to select an appropriate motivational strategy from the wide variety of theoretical perspectives available.

Fundamental to the understanding of what constitutes motivation is a realization that "to motivate" implies movement. It is the direction in which this movement takes place that can either hurt or help the organization. Additionally, whether or not such movement is generated by a series of conditions outside the worker's control or internally through events under the power of the individual forms the basis of much motivational theory. The traditional view of individuals as essentially rational and economic in nature, able to be controlled solely through incentives such as wages or working conditions, needs to be tempered by more modern views of individuals as psychological beings, subject to behaviors which seem not to be rational. The secret to effective worker motivation seems to lie somewhere between the rational and irrational. People *are* motivated by economic conditions, but only in combination with other, more transient, less physical, aspects of the workplace.

Donald J. Morton's view is that humanistic management does indeed have a place in the labor intensive, relatively mechanistic world of library operations. Humanistic management does not necessarily and invariably imply participative management, something which may not be entirely desired by librarians anyway. Understanding the assumptions underlying both "Theory X" and "Theory Y" ought to enable administrators to act in ways that facilitate use of each point of view, depending upon local library conditions. The utility of Morton's approach is that it specifies these conditions and sets forth guidelines that can prevent incorrect application of what is usually assumed to be theory but is in reality a continuum of assumptions held by administrators about their employees.

Maurice P. Marchant is already well-known in library administrative circles for his research on applying Likert's participative management theory to library situations. Although emphasizing the application of Likert's theory in academic libraries, Marchant has enlarged the definition of participatory management to encompass more than just one library type. His article reviews work conducted in libraries by librarians and provides an integrated view of how job satisfaction can affect motivation. Of particular interest is Marchant's suggestions for using the committee structure of many libraries to promote worker satisfaction, a satisfaction that is internally generated by the worker rather than externally imposed by a management convinced its approach is, by definition, the right approach.

Throughout these and other writings, "the right approach" to motivation rests minimally on 1) the rewards available, 2) the rewards desired, 3) degree of commitment to organizational goals, 4) the ability of the organization to meet worker's expectations, and 5) the myriad factors related to personality, attitude, and innate characteristics. Arriving at an appropriate understanding of the interaction of these and other variables, is indeed a challenge.

Applying Theory Y to Library Management
By Donald J. Morton

Theory Y is described as a desirable and widely accepted philosophy of personnel management. A review of library literature shows that its acceptance by librarians is relatively slight and that it is invariably considered to be the equivalent of participative management. The author disagrees with this comparison and believes that participative management has little effect upon the motivations associated with Theory Y. Instead, the author discusses several measures which he feels from experience can provide Theory Y benefits in library operations.

THEORY Y IS A TERM often used in personnel management to denote a liberalized type of administrative philosophy based upon a belief that employees are responsible workers more likely to be influenced by their own internal motivations than by the external threats and inducements of management. Because of its importance, library administrators need to be aware of this theory and of its possible adaptation to library operations. Therefore, this paper is intended to review the principles of the Theory Y approach, report upon its coverage in library literature, distinguish between the concepts of Theory Y and participative management, and, finally, discuss how Theory Y's application in a small academic library recommends its use for library operations in general.

McGREGOR AND THEORY Y

In the late 1950s, McGregor revolutionized management theory by incorporating into it Maslow's view that man is subject to a range of motivations that can affect his behavior.[1] These desires extend from the lowest-level or physiological needs through the safety, social, and esteem wants to the highest-level motivators, which Maslow termed "self-actualization" to represent man's need to be what he feels he must be.[2] McGregor believed traditional carrot-stick methods of stimulating production are effective only when man's lower-level needs (food, shelter, clothing, security, etc.) are inadequately met and, as an illustration, noted that man normally has ample air to breathe and thus would not be expected to work harder merely to

---

Reprinted by permission of the American Library Association from "Applying Theory Y to Library Management," Donald J. Morton, *College and Research Libraries*, vol. 36 (July 1975), pp. 302-307, copyright © 1975 by the American Library Association.

obtain more air. Once the basic needs are satisfied, people become motivated primarily by their desire for esteem (self-respect and reputation) and self-actualization. McGregor called the conventional managerial philosophy Theory X and his new interpretation Theory Y, thereby polarizing the science of management into two easy-to-grasp reference points. The significance of these ideas has so influenced the field of administration that much of its subsequent literature has dealt with the ramifications of McGregor's simplified approach. Reider recently typified this attitude by stating that McGregor's "insights regarding managerial assumptions about people are timeless" and must be considered the starting point for conducting a performance review.[3] Drucker credits McGregor's *The Human Side of Enterprise* with being "the most widely read and quoted" of books about modern personnel management.[4]

A brief description of a Theory Y environment is that, consistent with maintaining the objectives of an organization, an employee is given the maximum opportunity for self-determination and is subjected to the minimum amount of obvious authority, which means, in current terminology, that he should feel he's doing his thing. His innate desires to be creative, useful, respected, and superior should be encouraged rather than thwarted.

A common misconception with respect to Theory Y is that it represents a permissive, lax type of administration which coddles employees in the hope that they will respond by wanting to work. On the contrary, it requires the same ultimate authority needed with Theory X except that such authority should be kept sufficiently remote to preclude intruding upon an employee's pursuit of higher-level goals. Thus Theory Y's administration is more subtle than Theory X's and necessitates careful planning in order to attain the optimum balance between authority and freedom. Similarly, employees under Theory Y have a more, rather than a less, demanding task than do those under Theory X because, as Maslow noted, they must replace the comforting security of order and direction with the burden of responsibility and self-discipline.[5]

Drucker used the term "knowledge worker" to describe an employee who, in contrast to a "manual worker," needs the benefits of a formal education to perform his services, adding that the knowledge worker does not produce well if managed under Theory X.[6] Thus a good example of Theory Y in practice may be found in the management of knowledge workers, as typified by a research laboratory where the employer's objective is to discover profitable techniques and products. The highly educated employees may not share these corporate goals but, instead, are motivated to create research which can be published to enhance their professional reputations. Consequently, the objectives of the employer and those of the employees are different but require the same output on the part of the employees. The result is that progress toward increasing the employer's profits is favored by a climate which allows the employees to freely follow their own drives for esteem.

THEORY Y IN LIBRARY LITERATURE

Because Theory Y has had such an impact upon the current concepts of management, the author decided to determine whether this approach has been implemented by library administrators and, if so, whether results have been favorable. Therefore, the literature of library management was reviewed in order to establish what recognition has been given to Theory Y and what use has been made of this concept in the management of library employees.

A number of references to McGregor's Theory Y were found in library literature. Some were merely reprints or rehashes of papers by professional administrators which had previously appeared in managerial publications and, as they did not stress library operations, were not considered indicative of the thinking in library circles.[7] There were, however, several articles by librarians in which Theory Y was recognized and, to varying degrees, recommended for use.

Kipp, reviewing the literature of management, said that McGregor's philosophy "probably provides the most useable concepts in management literature by librarians." He suggested librarians might benefit from this approach but didn't apply it to specific library procedures.[8]

Betty Jo Mitchell developed a training program for library assistants who supervised clerical personnel or student assistants. She patterned her program after McGregor by having her trainees read his discussions along with other recent books on administration. The students concluded that Theory Y in its pure form was not satisfactory but should be modified, as suggested by Morse and Lorsch, to fit the tasks and people involved. This modification was based upon Drucker's opinion that Theory Y works with knowledge workers but Theory X often is more effective with manual workers.[9]

Robert and Charlene Lee, referring to Theory Y as "management by participation," said it is "a tough-minded management style—and it works." They encouraged the idea that personnel planning should be concerned with an individual's aspirations and should provide him or her with opportunities for participation and growth.[10]

Dickinson cited McGregor and stated that "Libraries . . . need to be aware of certain world-wide trends in work theory, according to which meaningful and significant work (attained through participative management) replaces economic rewards as the central institutional incentive." She proposed a sequence of steps which could be followed for changing from a hierarchical to a participative type of management and recommended such an arrangement for activizing the professional staff.[11]

DeProspo thought that Theory Y requires a move away from "management by control" to one of "management by objectives." He favored a model in which the active participation of staff and line employees is encouraged and felt that evaluations of personnel should stress goals rather than traits.[12]

Marchant noted that "new theories direct attention towards other sources of motivation besides the economic," basing this opinion upon Maslow's hierarchy of motivations. He believed that participative management is an important means of enabling employees to operate with higher-level motivations, but reported that a literature search found no studies of library staff participation in decision making. After evaluating library situations, he concluded that "active staff development programs and participative management in libraries appear well suited for each other; they ought to be getting together."[13]

The preceding references show that some libraries recognize Theory Y and, furthermore, believe it is typified by participative management. In addition, several other papers were found which did not mention Theory Y as such but stressed the value of participative management for libraries.[14] McGregor said that when participative management "grows out of the assumptions of Theory Y," it can provide "ego satisfaction for the subordinate" and "thus affect motivation towards organizational objectives." He believed this satisfaction results from the tackling and solving of problems, the feeling of greater independence and influence, and the increased recognition received from peers and superiors for making worthwhile contributions.[15] Consequently, participative management is related to Theory Y in that its use helps establish an environment in which ego needs may be fulfilled.

Despite its intrinsic merits, however, it is questionable whether participative management illustrates Theory Y's basic tenet that an employee's self-motivation to pursue his own goals can help satisfy his employer's organizational objectives. Any such effect would be remote at best and would be limited to those decisions where an employee's responsibilities and relationships would be so altered as to affect his higher-level motivations.

THE USE OF THEORY Y IN A LIBRARY

Consequently, the way to induce Theory Y management in libraries is to focus not upon participatory management, which, though desirable in its own right, can give only random Theory Y benefits, but, instead, upon the characteristics of each employee's position. In this regard, the author has worked with a variety of personnel during the development of a new library and, based upon these experiences, suggests that some of the more effective policies for eliciting Theory Y motivations include providing employees with (1) definite and unique responsibilities; (2) a short administrative chain of command; (3) adequate means to exhibit productivity to others; (4) freedom from fear of failure; and (5) opportunities to merge self-actualization with normal responsibilities.

Probably the most important of these policies is the assigning to each employee of a clear set of responsibilities which do not overlap those of anyone else because, without this basic arrangement, there can be little hope of having Theory Y conditions. Unless a person can unmistakably identify with the fruits of his labor, there is little chance that any of his higher-level needs will directly motivate his productivity. Any sharing of responsibilities between employees dulls this motivation and increases the opportunities for dissatisfaction. In practice, this means dividing responsibilities between available personnel rather than assigning more than one person to an area. For example, if two catalogers are employed, they should not both routinely share all of the responsibilities but, rather, should each be given a discrete and approximately equal portion of the load according to some criterion such as subject or type of material. Within a designated area of responsibility, an employee should be free to determine how to manage his own operations as long as his output conforms with organizational goals and his procedures don't conflict with operations in other areas.

In addition, the lines of authority should be kept as short as possible in order to maximize the sole responsibility of each employee. Using the above example of two catalogers, it would be preferable to have each one answering directly to the highest feasible level of administration rather than having one cataloger answering to the other because, in the latter case, both catalogers would be responsible for the duties of the subordinate one. Besides this direct Theory Y benefit, shorter organizational lines have the indirect value of increasing lateral communication between employees and the practical merit of reducing misunderstandings by decreasing the number of times an idea must be relayed. According to Townsend, each extra "level of management lowers communication effectiveness within the organization by about 25 percent."[16]

Another characteristic of a Theory Y position is that each person's performance must be visible enough to be capable of earning respect from others. Hence, to stimulate the esteem needs for respect and admiration, each employee's productivity should be subject to the scrutiny of other employees. An acquisitions librarian might be judged by the quality of new books, a cataloger by the arrangement and accessibility of the collection, and a public services librarian by the reactions of the library users to the available services. Then, each person's output would be self-regulated by the motivation to be respected, and the administration could watch from a nonintrusive distance for signs that adjustments were needed.

A self-regulating operation, however, must be free to alter its procedures or else an employee may not accept responsibility for his output. This means that management should exhibit confidence in an employee to the extent that failures will not be used as a basis for embarrassment or punishment but, instead, will be evaluated as demonstrating an employee's willingness to improve operations by taking calculated risks. Similarly, any criticisms made should avoid placing an employee on the defensive, as Gibb pointed out in his excellent discussion on the subject. Penalizing errors and inciting defensiveness not only will discourage initiative but also will promote the concealment of mistakes, thereby hindering communication and providing a distorted view of operations.[17]

Finally, the ultimate expression of Theory Y management may be realized if there are opportunities for an employee to identify his responsibilities with his desire for self-actualization, Maslow's highest level of motivation. In Townsend's words, this means having the employee "enjoy his work so much he comes in on Saturday instead of playing golf or cutting grass,"[18] which, in a librarian's terms, might signify an employee who experiments with his procedures and presents papers on the results to professional colleagues. Measures which arouse these tendencies include the previously mentioned freedom to make mistakes plus the encouragement and financial support of the administration to join organizations and attend meetings. In this type of atmosphere, employees may become so absorbed in their career interests that their tendencies toward self-actualization will be expressed within the framework of normal occupational duties.

A distinction should be made between the factors described above which directly affect employee higher-level motivations and indirect factors which act instead to create a Theory Y environment. Such indirect factors are important because, although they do not affect productivity in an obvious manner, their presence encourages employees to feel trusted, appreciated, and responsible, and thus to be more receptive to the stimuli of Theory Y motivators. Examples of these environmental influences include (1) favoring intercommunication between all employees; (2) delegating the maximum feasible amount of the organization's decision making process, as in participative management; (3) cultivating feelings of fair play; and (4) showing appreciation and sensitivity for employee efforts, achievements, and problems.

CONCLUSION

In conclusion, the author believes that libraries are suitable institutions for the application of Theory Y because of several reasons. First, librarians are by nature knowledge workers who have professional interests and thus are especially susceptible to motivations based upon desires for esteem and self-actualization. Next, the attitudes and duties of librarians are usually oriented toward providing information desired by patrons rather than toward obtaining financial returns; as a result, higher-level motivations may often be satisfied through the idealistic performance of services. Finally, libraries can usually be organized so that each worker has a rewarding, interesting, and unique area of responsibility, thereby stimulating the fulfillment of ego motivators. Consequently, it is recommended that library administrators seriously consider adopting measures that favor Theory Y management in order to promote employee satisfaction while simultaneously improving employee performance levels.

References

1. Douglas M. McGregor, "The Human Side of Enterprise," in his *Leadership and Motivation* (Cambridge, Mass.: MIT Press, 1966), p.3–20, first published in *Adventures in Thought and Action, Proceedings of the Fifth Anniversary Convocation of the School of Industrial Management, Massachusetts Institute of Technology, Cambridge, April 9, 1957* (Cambridge, Mass.: MIT School of Industrial Management, 1957); Douglas M. McGregor, *The Human Side of Enterprise* (New York: McGraw-Hill, 1960).
2. Abraham H. Maslow, *Motivation and Personality* (2d ed.; New York: Harper, 1970), p.35–58.
3. George A. Reider, "Performance Review—A Mixed Bag," *Harvard Business Review* 51:61–67 (July-Aug. 1973).
4. Peter Drucker, *Management* (New York: Harper, 1974), p.231.
5. Abraham H. Maslow, *Eupsychian Management* (Homewood, Ill.: Irwin, 1965), p.24–33.
6. Peter Drucker, *The Effective Executive* (New York: Harper, 1966), p.2–9, 172–74; Peter Drucker, *Management* (New York: Harper, 1974), p.241.
7. Charles H. Goodman, "Incentives and Motivations for Staff Development," in Elizabeth W. Stone, ed., *New Directions in Staff Development* (Chicago: American Library Assn., 1971), p.51–57; Charles H. Goodman, "Employee Motivation," *Library Trends* 20:39–47 (July 1971); Douglas M. McGregor, "The Human Side of Enterprise," in Paul Wasserman and Mary Lee Bundy, eds., *Reader in Library Administration* (Washington, D.C.; NCR, 1968), p.210–16; Charles Martell, "Which Way—Traditional Practice or Modern Theory?" *College & Research Libraries* 33:104–12 (March 1972).
8. Laurence Kipp, "Management Literature for Librarians," *Library Journal* 97:158–60 (Jan. 15, 1972).
9. Betty Jo Mitchell, "In-House Training of Supervisory Library Assistants in a Large Academic Library," *College & Research Libraries* 34:114–49 (March 1973); John J. Morse and Jay W. Lorsch, "Beyond Theory Y," *Harvard Business Review* 48:61–68 (May-June 1970); Peter Drucker, *Management* (New York: Harper, 1974), p.241.
10. Robert Lee and Charlene Swarthout Lee, "Personnel Planning for a Library Manpower System," *Library Trends* 20:19–38 (July 1971).
11. Fidelia Dickinson, "Participative Management: A Left Fielder's View," *California Librarian* 34:24–33 (April 1973).
12. Ernest D. DeProspo, "Management by Objectives: An Approach to Staff Development," in Elizabeth W. Stone, ed., *New Directions in Staff Development* (Chicago: American Library Assn., 1971), p.39–47; Ernest D. DeProspo, "Personnel Evaluation as an Impetus to Growth," *Library Trends* 20:60–70 (July 1971).
13. Maurice P. Marchant, "Participative Management in Libraries," in Elizabeth W. Stone, ed., *New Directions in Staff Development* (Chicago: American Library Assn., 1971), p.28–38; Maurice P. Marchant, "Participative Management as Related to Personnel Development," *Library Trends* 20:48–59 (July 1971).
14. David Kaser, "Modernizing the University Library Structure," *College & Research Libraries* 31:227–31 (July 1970); Donald J. Sayer, "Administrative Experiment Tried in Elyria, Ohio," *Library Journal* 95:1430 (April 15, 1970); Helen L. Norris, "How Far Should Staff Democracy Go?" *Library Journal* 84:1054–57 (April 1, 1959); Jane G. Flener, "Staff Participation in Management in Large University Libraries," *College & Research Libraries* 34:275–79 (July 1973); Richard DeGennaro, "Participative Management or Unionization?" *College & Research Libraries* 33:173–74 (May 1972).
15. McGregor, *The Human Side of Enterprise*, p.130–31.
16. Robert Townsend, *Up the Organization* (New York: Knopf, 1970), p.22.
17. J. R. Gibb, "Defensive Communication," *Journal of Communication* 11:141–48 (Sept. 1961).
18. Townsend, *Up the Organization*, p.142.

Managing Motivation and Job Satisfaction
By Maurice P. Marchant

What can we learn from research into job satisfaction and motivation that will help in the operation of libraries? The answers are not all in, but tentative answers are available that have great potential for improving libraries as work environments and as service organizations. The purpose of this paper is to provide a summary of the primary theories of job satisfaction and the research testing them, and of the interrelation between job satisfaction, its causes, and its effects, with special attention paid to research directed at libraries and librarians. Research from the behavioral sciences as well as librarianship will be reported.

Motivation has long been considered a primary factor affecting job performance and productivity, and job satisfaction is generally considered to be closely related to, though not synonymous with, motivation. Job satisfaction is an emotional outcome resulting from the congruence of one's job expectations and their fulfillment, whereas motivation is a stimulus to action. In systems terms, the first is an outcome, or dependent variable, whereas the second is an input, or independent variable. But outcomes in one system or in part of a system often become the input affecting other systems or other parts of the same system. The earliest motivational theory developed in modern times, coming from scientific management, declared that workers are motivated to high productivity by economic reward and that tying economic reward to productivity results in job satisfaction.[1] Later studies from the human relations school challenged the economic motivation theory and focused on noneconomic factors as motivators. Developing what might be called the "contented cow" theory, they declared that satisfied workers will work harder and better than dissatisfied ones.[2] Both of these approaches have been found to be inadequate. Job satisfaction's causal relationship to improved performance is unclear. Even its relationship to motivation needs clarification. Moreover, job satisfaction itself is a highly complex topic rather than the simple one it was once thought to be, and is still not well understood despite vigorous research. One study of the literature of job satisfaction estimated that at least 3,350 articles and dissertations had been written on it prior to 1972 and others were coming out at the rate of 111 per year.[3]

JOB SATISFACTION THEORIES

A few theories dominate most of the discussion of job satisfaction. For the purposes of this paper, those which have been tested and have specific relevance to libraries will be discussed.

The author would like to express appreciation to Fredrick Ray Brady for his assistance in gathering information for this study.

Likert's Theory of Participative Management

Rensis Likert synthesized his theory of participative management from observations regarding management style's relationship to productivity. He observed that high production organizations tend to treat employees with greater confidence and are more concerned for their welfare than low performance ones. This good feeling is expressed in many ways, including staff involvement in decision making, group decision making, more and better communication, more group interaction, and staff involvement in goal setting and evaluation.[4] His theory of participative management covers much more than job satisfaction and motivation, but they are included.

Likert emphasizes three categories of variables: causal, intervening, and end-result. Causal variables determine the course of developments within an organization and the results achieved. Only those independent variables which can be altered or changed by the organization and its management are considered to be causal. Management style is causal, and Likert provides an instrument, the Profile of Organizational Characteristics, to measure it on a continuum from highly authoritarian to participative. Intervening variables reflect the internal state and health of the organization, including such factors as loyalties, attitudes, motivations, and job satisfaction. The end result variables are the dependent variables that reflect organizational achievements, such as productivity. Causal variables affect intervening variables and, through them, end-result variables. Thus management style, which can be controlled by management, affects workers' job satisfaction and motivation, and, through them, productivity.[5]

Changes in the intervening variables predict later changes in the end results. But the intervening variables, not directly amenable to change, must be affected through manipulation of the causal variables. If an administrator recognized a decline in staff job satisfaction as a precursor of declining production, he might consider modifying his management style to improve job satisfaction and to bring production back up.

Likert does not provide an instrument for measuring intervening (or end-result) variables, but he suggests some common errors to avoid. He points out that people's explanations for their feelings, when asked directly, are often invalid, that people are not necessarily aware of the causes of their feelings. Moreover, the factors they place highest on a list will not necessarily be the most important in influencing how they feel about a job. The effect of specific job attitudes on overall job satisfaction is best determined by their correlation with overall satisfaction. Combining the scores of several specific factors, he points out, will not result in a good overall satisfaction measurement, as the various factors do not have equal weight.[6]

Marchant tested the Likert model on academic libraries.[7] He measured causal, intervening and end-result variables and tested for the interrelations predicted by the theory. The primary causal variable was management style, measured with the use of Likert's instrument. Other causal variables were also studied. The intervening variables that provided the best information were a set of specific and overall staff job satisfaction variables. The end-result variable was faculty evaluation of the library, measured by an instrument designed and validated by Covey.[8] Using somewhat sophisticated statistical procedures, a sequence of relationships was discovered between management style, library funding per student, job satisfaction, and the faculty's evaluation of the library.

Statistically, the relationships were reasonably strong and conformed to the Likert theoretical model. Even so, Lynch complained of data analysis faults and questioned the relationships claimed between job satisfaction and the causal and end-product variables.[9] D'Elia spoke of the simplicity of Marchant's study of job satisfaction.[10]

While D'Elia's appraisal is accurate, the Marchant study of job satisfaction provides insights useful to library administrators. He found that 85% of the variance in overall job satisfaction could be predicted by satisfaction in four areas: satisfaction with 1) currently assigned duties, 2) relations with supervisors, 3) opportunities for salary increases, and 4) relations with clientele. He also identified relations between the specific satisfaction variables and various causal variables. Thus, he supplied presumed causal models that administrators might use to make improvements in staff job satisfaction and in the quality of the library. Management style's influence flows through relations with supervisors and opportunity for salary increases, and funding affects relations with clientele and assigned duties.

Marchant interprets the data this way. High funding results in a larger staff and more books, allowing the library staff to give more attention to patrons from a better collection with which to satisfy their informational needs. Consequently, the librarian's sense of satisfaction with assigned duties and relations with patrons is high. When management style is participative, management expresses confidence in staff members and involves them in program planning, evaluation, personnel policy development, and so forth. As a result, staff satisfaction is high regarding their relations with supervisors and opportunities for salary increases. Job satisfaction thus derived reflects adequate resources, a good work environment, and the opportunity to turn them into quality library service as perceived by faculty members. Satisfaction does not create the motivation to serve well. The desire must already exist. If it does, the opportunity to express it results in high performance and in satisfaction.

Theory of Work Adjustment

The theory of work adjustment has been used largely in vocational counseling. It is based on the concept of correspondence, or agreement, between the individual and the work environment. Good correspondence implies harmony between the individual's needs and what the environment provides. (It belongs to the broader management concept known as contingency theory, which says that the best management style depends on the situation.) The individual brings defined requirements or needs to the job, expecting the work environment to provide opportunities, or reinforcement, adequate to satisfy them. The work environment brings its requirements to the relationship expecting the individual to provide abilities adequate to fulfill them. Correspondence is achieved when the individual fulfills at least the minimally acceptable requirements of the work environment and the work environment fulfills at least the minimally acceptable requirements of the individual.[11]

That each individual seeks to achieve and maintain correspondence with the environment is a basic assumption of the theory. Achieving and maintaining this correspondence are thought to be basic motives of human behavior. Finding it, one seeks to maintain it. Not finding it, one seeks to establish it or, failing, leaves the environment. Remaining on the job, termed job tenure, is a function of correspondence.

Satisfaction and satisfactoriness derive from correspondence. Satisfaction results when the individual's needs are fulfilled. Satisfactoriness means that the worker's performance is acceptable; it derives from fulfilling the needs of the work environment. By observing a large group of workers with continuing employment in an occupation, minimally acceptable levels of satisfaction and satisfactoriness can be determined. They can also be queried regarding the extent to which the work environment satisfies various needs. Generalizing such responses provides a profile of job characteristics. Job characteristics that allow satisfaction to occur are referred to as reinforcers.

The theory of work has been developed at the University of Minnesota, where the Work Adjustment Project of the Industrial Relations Center has used it in the area of vocational rehabilitation and adjustment to work. Four diagnostic instruments have been designed for the study of job satisfaction and satisfactoriness.[12] Accumulation of responses from many individuals with substantial tenure in a given occupation provides norms by which the occupation can be appraised and compared to other occupations. A vocational counselor can use the instruments in matching up a client's needs and abilities with the normative data characterizing many occupations, and can then recommend those occupations in which the client is likely to find correspondence.

D'Elia used the Minnesota Importance Questionnaire (MIQ), Minnesota Job Description Questionnaire (MJDQ), and Minnesota Satisfaction Questionnaire (MSQ) in studying librarians' job satisfaction. His study was limited to newly graduated librarians with 6 to 18 months of work experience. He studied satisfaction relationships to sex, type of library job environment, importance of vocational needs, and availability of job reinforcers. The needs, reinforcers, and satisfactions came from the MIQ, MJDQ, and MSQ. All three included the same 20 dimensions.[13] The MIQ measures the importance of each dimension to the employee, the MJDQ measured the degree to which an employee perceives the dimension is present in the job environment (its reinforcement), and the MSQ measures the degree of satisfaction experienced by the employee with each dimension. In addition, autonomy is included in the reinforcer and satisfaction instruments. General satisfaction is computed by summing up the individual satisfaction scores and is added to the MIQ.

D'Elia found the highest relationships between the reinforcers and their parallel satisfactions. The extent to which a library job included (or excluded) a given characteristic seemed to affect the librarian's satisfaction with that characteristic. Correlations between importance of the need dimensions and satisfaction regarding them were not as high.[14]

The relationships between reinforcers and satisfactions led D'Elia to try to predict overall satisfaction from the reinforcers. Two reinforcers constituted the optimal set of predictors: supervision-human relations and ability utilization. He came to the conclusion that the two predicting reinforcers represented two much broader factors: 1) the supervisory climate, including the human relations and technical aspects of supervision and the fairness with which policies are administered within the library, and 2) mastery of the job, including the extent to which abilities are utilized, opportunities to achieve and be creative exist, work is recognized, and responsibility is given.

The theory claims an interaction between felt needs, reinforcers, and satisfactions that D'Elia did not test. Satisfaction presumably derives from correspondence between felt need and the reinforcer system of the job. Librarians with a high felt need on a job providing comparably high reinforcement for that need would experience high satisfaction. High need and low reinforcement would yield low satisfaction. The second prediction was found true for the mastery of the job variables. While management needs were not high, they were so poorly met that satisfaction suffered. Respondents highly valued the opportunity to use their abilities, to achieve, and to be creative, and potential satisfaction from allowing them to was very high. It did not occur because the opportunities were inadequate.

The messages to library administrators are clear. High job satisfaction will require the adjustment of librarians' roles to allow greater use of their abilities and greater opportunities to achieve and be creative. Improved management would also improve job satisfaction. The suggested areas are fairly simplistic. They call for being fair in enforcing policies and procedures, providing adequate training for new employees, and supporting them by bringing their accomplishments to the attention of top management. That librarians are poorly satisfied with these basic management factors suggests that management generally needs improving in libraries. Marchant's research supports this conclusion and predicts improved job satisfaction and better performance as a result. D'Elia, however, does not claim any effect on production from improved satisfaction.

Whether job satisfaction varies by type of library or type of activity was also tested by D'Elia. He found only minor differences. School librarians were more satisfied with their creative opportunities than others. Technical services librarians seemed to be more satisfied with the independence available to them and less satisfied with their public service involvement.

Satisfaction differences between the sexes also came under scrutiny. Unlike Wahba, D'Elia reported no significant difference in job satisfaction between men and women, tested at the .01 level. (Wahba's study will be discussed later.[15]) Had he used the .05 level test, he would have identified three differences, regarding satisfaction with authority, creativity, and moral values. Women were more satisfied than men in each case. Satisfaction differences between the sexes were found not to be great. Only in the area of creativity is satisfaction likely to have any operational meaning.

Maslow's Need Hierarchy Theory

Abraham H. Maslow's need hierarchy theory claims that people are motivated to satisfy five basic categories of needs: 1) physiological needs, including food, water, and air; 2) safety needs, including freedom from physical threats and harm, and economic security; 3) belongingness and love needs; 4) esteem needs of two types: the need for mastery and achievement and the need for recognition and approval of others; and 5) the need for self-actualization, to become what one is capable of becoming. As one need is satisfied, it is replaced with the next higher one; and the satisfied need no longer motivates. Thus, as people's physiological and safety needs are fulfilled, they become complacent regarding them and turn to the need to acquire love and acceptance. Healthy people are viewed as motivated toward the actualization of potentials, capacities, talents, and self-improvement in ways that are also socially appropriate.[16]

Operating under this theory, a supervisor would want to deal with subordinates individually. A worker at the belongingness stage should be given much attention and group activity. Being allowed group involvement and attention should motivate toward performance that will merit praise. The supervisor would offer rewards for good performance appropriate to the employee's place on the hierarchy ladder.

Locke has noted inadequate proof for the theory and several weaknesses.[17] Maslow offers no proof. While the existence of the physiological needs is well established, the existence of the others is not. The meaning of self-actualization is fuzzy at best and self-contradictory. Maslow confuses needs and values, claiming a near-perfect corespondence between them that does not exist. Locke points out that thoughts and actions are dominated more by one's values than by needs, and those values can be self-destructive as well as healthy.

The theory's great popularity seems to rely on its intuitive appeal, its message of optimism, and its correspondence with personal experiences. Blackler and Williams note that interpreting situations by Maslow's model is easier than testing it out.[18] Its major thesis—a fixed hierarchy of needs automatically controls action—seems to have little empirical support.

One study using five categories similar to Maslow's has tested job satisfaction differences between male and female librarians.[19] Wahba based her study on a need-gratification model, using the Need Satisfaction Questionnaire (NSQ) to acquire data from New York City academic librarians.[20] The five need categories studied were security, social, esteem, autonomy, and self-actualization.

Wahba found the following. Women expressed lower need fulfillment than men regarding esteem and autonomy but not security, social, nor self-actualization needs.

Women's needs were more deficient than men's in all categories but social. Autonomy was judged less important by women. (Wahba stated that women regarded self-actualization as having lower importance also, but her data fail to support this.) The sexes seem not to disagree significantly on the importance of the other needs.

The need-gratification model was designed to provide an indirect measurement, with two advantages: 1) since the respondent is not asked directly about satisfaction, the tendency to manipulate the satisfaction measure is reduced; 2) it is designed to be a realistic and meaningful measure for comparing groups.[21] However, no reliability data were provided, and it was designed for use with managers and to test differences between management levels rather than between men and women, some of whom are not managers. The differences Wahba identified might be attributed to management level rather than sex differences, since men are known to dominate library top management positions and management level differences have been demonstrated.[22] Wahba's data suggest that the need deficiency differences for security and, to a lesser degree, self-actualization resulted from the relatively higher expectations of women. Since security and self-actualization are on the two ends of Maslow's hierarchy, the results are hardly what the theory would project.

Moreover, the results conflict with D'Elia's, who found little difference between the sexes regarding satisfaction. To the extent any existed, it favored women. But he was studying only newly graduated librarians, who were likely quite homogeneous regarding management level. D'Elia suggested that Wahba's differences were associated with cumulative random error resulting from score computation from two variables each contributing error variance. Also possible are differences resulting from management level that are related to sex. That the jobs of top management offer more opportunities for satisfying experiences of the esteem, autonomy, and self-actualizing categories seems fairly evident from observation and from Porter's research. Improvements in female librarians' job satisfaction might, therefore, be tied to improved opportunities for administrative promotion for women.

Herzberg's Motivation-Hygiene Theory

Somewhat related to Maslow's theory is Frederick Herzberg's dual-factor motivation-hygiene theory that dichotomizes job satisfaction into motivators producing high performance and non-motivators, which he calls hygiene factors. The motivators are intrinsic to the job and consist of achievement, recognition, responsibility, advancement, and growth in competence. Their availability brings job satisfaction, but lack of them does not bring dissatisfaction. Hygiene factors are extrinsic to the job and include interpersonal relations, supervision, company policies, pay, working conditions, status, security, and personal life. Hygiene factors tend to represent Maslow's lower level needs while motivators are the higher needs.[23]

Herzberg tied these concepts to a specific view of the nature of man as containing two separate and unrelated classes of human needs: physical needs we share with animals, and psychological needs rooted in man's reasoning mind. Psychological growth needs are satisfied by increasing one's knowledge and cognitive skills and appear closely related to Maslow's self-actualization category. Physical needs, according to Herzberg, motivate action according to a pain-avoidance principle directed at reducing discomfort but not providing pleasure. By contrast, psychological growth needs motivate only positively, bringing pleasure when successful but not displeasure in failure.[24]

Herzberg's theory has been widely discussed and challenged. Locke's critical appraisal cumulates seven complaints, including the following.[25] 1) Herzberg's incident classification system contains logical inconsistencies. For example, if an employee reports being given new responsibility, the event is classified with "responsibility." But if the supervisor refuses to delegate responsibility, the event is classified with "supervision." 2) Herzberg's minimizing of satisfaction and dissatisfaction is not defensible, particularly if human values are recognized as more directly affecting satisfaction and dissatisfaction than needs.

Despite these and the other criticisms, Herzberg has made a major contribution to our understanding of job satisfaction by stressing the importance of psychological growth coming from the work itself as a precondition of job satisfaction. This awareness has led to many improvements in job design.

Plate and Stone replicated Herzberg's research with librarians, and their results matched his general pattern.[26] Achievement was the highest cause of satisfaction followed by recognition and, to a lesser extent, the work itself. Responsibility, advancement, and growth made minor contributions to job satisfaction. These were the motivators.

The major dissatisfiers (hygiene factors) were, in order of frequency, institutional policy and administration, supervision, and interpersonal relationships. Working conditions, status, security, and salary made minor contributions. Hygiene factors infrequently provided satisfaction, but 19% of the dissatisfactory incidents were classified under motivators.

D'Elia and Marchant both found satisfaction with supervision relatively low, supporting the Plate and Stone data. But Marchant also found relations with supervisors highly related to professional growth and promotion. The Plate and Stone article provides several instances in which recognition and achievement involve supervisors and administrators. Good supervisory relations bring about recognition, growth, advancement, and accomplishment. But poor supervisory relationships are expressed as unsatisfactory supervision.

An important test of Herzberg's theory by Hackman and Lawler found evidence that the extent to which employees are interested in higher order need satisfaction was related to high motivation, high job satisfaction, low absence from work, and high quality of job performance when their jobs contained higher order needs.[27] Availability of higher order needs increased with administrative level. The effect of differences in people's values places a restriction on Herzberg's theory. Combining the defensible aspects of Maslow's and Herzberg's theories suggests, in Locke's words, that

> job satisfaction results from the appraisal of one's job as attaining or allowing the attainment of one's important job values, providing these values are congruent with or help fulfill one's basic needs. These needs are of two separable but interdependent types: bodily or physical needs and psychological needs, especially the need for growth. Growth is made possible mainly by the nature of the work itself.[28]

Expectancy/Valence Theory

Known also as instrumentality theory, the expectancy/valence theory of motivation draws heavily on the work of Victor Vroom.[29] Basically, the theory consists of three components: 1) the individual's perception of the probability that increased effort will result in good job performance, 2) the individual's perception that good performance will lead to certain outcomes or rewards, and 3) valence, or the value or attractiveness, of the outcomes or rewards. For an individual to be motivated, he or she must believe that increasing effort will improve performance, which in turn, will bring valuable rewards or outcomes. Motivational failure can occur because of any of the three components. A manager concerned for inadequate staff motivation might check the components against the situation to identify the reason and then take the proper corrective action.

One way to apply the theory is to compare one group of workers to another. Hulin used the concept to test female clerical workers' job dissatisfaction to predict job termination.[30] Since each replacement was costing the company about $1,000, reducing turnover by increasing satisfaction could save a great deal of money.

Hulin used the Job Description Index (JDI) to measure job satisfaction.[31] It covers five aspects of a worker's satisfaction: Satisfaction with work done, with the pay, with promotional opportunities and policies, with co-workers, and with the supervisor. Hulin modified it to include also a scale for atmosphere. JDI is a cumulative-point, adjective checklist type of scale. It has been subjected to an extensive validation program and has a reputation of being among the best instruments available for measuring job satisfaction. It also has two obvious weaknesses. 1) It explicitly measures job content rather than satisfaction. But the two are highly related, as the D'Elia study demonstrated. When asking clerks working for the same company to respond to it, variability can be expected to be largely a measure of varying job satisfaction. 2) It emphasizes lower order satisfaction factors. This weakness would be more serious in a study of librarians than of clerks.

The JDI was also used in a comparative analysis of job satisfaction in six university libraries in Texas by Vaughn and Dunn.[32] No conclusions regarding job satisfaction in libraries in general were provided, nor did the authors demonstrate any relationships of satisfaction to causal or end-result variables. The authors' contribution was limited to an explanation of the use of the instrument in comparative analysis. The report provides no standards or norms against which to compare another library's scores except those of the five libraries studied.

CONCLUSIONS AND RECOMMENDATIONS

Much still remains to be learned about job satisfaction and motivation. No theory has emerged that lacks significant criticism, and no measuring device has been developed that lacks weaknesses. Still, important results have emerged from the research that can contribute to the improvement of the library as a place to work and to the effective operation of libraries. Of particular relevance are the following conclusions.

1. Libraries tend not to be designed to encourage high performance. The work environment often frustrates librarians who want to be creative and high achievers. Yet librarians as a group want to achieve, be creative, and use their skills and abilities. One approach to reducing the frustration would be to select employees who do not value higher order needs. However, doing so would assure mediocre or inferior performance. The option is to restructure librarians' roles so they can use their competencies and feel a sense of accomplishment from their work. In part, this might call for turning some of the routine duties now performed by librarians over to technicians.

2. Improved administration of libraries offers substantial opportunities for an improved work environment. Library administrators need to learn and practice modern administrative skills and attitudes recommended by Likert and others. They ought to cultivate a greater sense of confidence in their staffs and assign them a larger role in goal setting, planning, and evaluation. They should provide opportunities for staff development and growth. They also need to provide reliable personnel evaluation systems based on objective standards of competence and expectation. If current administrators will not or cannot make these changes, they should be replaced with managers who can. This exchange is already occurring, and we are experiencing a new breed of competent administrators in important administrative positions.

3. Inadequate opportunities for promotion are hindering librarians' satisfaction because higher levels of administration carry with them greater autonomy, esteem, and more challenging work. While improved opportunities for promotion may not be possible, restructuring librarian jobs might offer those same improvements.

4. Libraries experiencing high absenteeism and/or turnover can reduce them by a selective approach to job satisfaction. Higher pay may help, but other factors are important, too, particularly supervision. Reducing dissatisfaction is the major key to reducing absences and resignations.

5. High performance results from a) selecting people who value high achievement and have the skills to achieve, b) respecting them and showing it by involving them in managing their own jobs, c) providing them with the human, informational, and material resources necessary to achieve, d) setting high performance goals and operating under plans consistent with those goals, and e) supplying adequate feedback regarding their performance. Any library wanting to achieve high staff job satisfaction, high morale, and high quality library service is advised to follow these five recommendations.

A Strategy for Improving the Motivational Environment

The research previously discussed provides appropriate cues for developing a strategy for improving library staff job satisfaction and motivation. The strategy should focus on two factors: improved management and enriched job content. Happily, they are not in conflict, and management reform can be used as a vehicle for job enrichment.

Administrators who want these improvements must start with themselves. They must have generally positive attitudes toward their staffs, and must express these attitudes so that staff members feel trusted. Trust and confidence are not necessarily expressed in the same proportions in which they are felt, and their expressions may not be interpreted the way they are intended. Improvements in staff satisfaction and motivation are affected by the staff's perception of being trusted. The manager must express a sense of trust in ways that are recognized by the staff. Moreover, the staff must feel deserving of it and approve of the forms of recognition being used.

The change in management should not be so radical that the staff does not approve. They must accept the new patterns as legitimate. Often, middle managers are the most resistant to change and constitute a special problem. If changes are made too fast for them, the library runs the risk of harming their credibility with their subordinates and their ability to supervise. They constitute a valuable human resource investment for their professional and technical competency, and every effort should be made to retain that investment while upgrading supervisory skills. Middle management especially must be competent both in librarian and supervisory skills. Expertise in one area does not make up for failure in the other.

The change might well begin by sending proposals for policy or procedure revisions to the staff for comments while modifications can still be made, then paying attention to the advice received. All advice will not be useful, but some of it will. It all deserves recognition and response, and the staff must know that their concerns are being taken seriously.

The establishment of committees can provide a means of staff involvement. Start with single-issue committees that are dissolved upon completion of their assignments. Later, standing committees might be established. Committees that have been successful are concerned with policy and planning rather than judging individual cases. Standing committees might be used to deal with collection development, public services, technical processing, personnel administration, and staff development. But guard against the improper use of committee assignments by some individuals to develop bases of personal power. Give everyone the chance of involvement. At the same time, recognize that the quality of committee achievement is affected by the quality of the committee's composition.

The need for staff development in group interaction may require special training, which might be accomplished by attending workshops or classes or by setting up training sessions or retreats, perhaps involving consultants. Training in planning procedures would be especially useful.

Work units should be encouraged to hold periodic meetings to evaluate their work and make adjustments. Supervisors must take precautions against dominating these meetings and are responsible for assuring broad staff involvement.

Role adjustments resulting in greater creativity and use of staff abilities ought to come naturally from staff involvement in evaluation and decision processes, since librarians aspire to greater such involvement. Staff involvement in management decisions is a major role adjustment, but it allows even greater changes in public and technical service activities. Beyond that, the administration should provide opportunities for creative research and development activities.

The extent to which the resultant increase in staff satisfaction and motivation improves the library's performance will be affected by the direction management provides. Creativity and research can go in many directions. They should be directed toward improvement in the library, since the library is paying for them. Managers owe their libraries well-thought-out goals and objectives that can give direction to activities and provide a firm basis for evaluation and determination of rewards. And they should not only allow but require quality planning of major programs and services.

Libraries are adjusting so rapidly today as a result of social and technological changes that they need the use of all the knowledge, skill, and creativity their staffs can offer. No good excuse exists for managerial ineptness in organizing and using human resources. Nor is low staff satisfaction resulting from poor management justifiable. The major problem is not unrealistic demands by staff but enlightened management that recognizes the opportunities inherent in better use of currently available personnel.

REFERENCES

[1] Frederick Winslow Taylor, *The Principles of Scientific Management* (New York: Harper, 1911).

[2] Amitai Etzioni, *Modern Organizations* (Englewood Cliffs, NJ: Prentice-Hall, 1964), pp. 39-40.

[3] Edwin A. Locke, "The Nature and Causes of Job Satisfaction," in *Handbook of Industrial and Organizational Psychology*, ed. Marvin D. Dunnette (Chicago: Rand McNally, 1976), pp. 1297-349.

[4] An explanation of his theory and the instrument he has designed to study organizational dynamics will be found in the following two books: Rensis Likert, *New Patterns of Management* (New York: McGraw-Hill, 1961); and Rensis Likert, *The Human Organization: Its Management and Value* (New York: McGraw-Hill, 1967).

[5] Likert, *The Human Organization*, pp. 75-77.

[6] Likert, *New Patterns of Management*, pp. 195-96.

[7] The major report on this research is Maurice P. Marchant, *Participative Management in Academic Libraries* (Westport, CT: Greenwood Press, 1976).

[8] Alan Dale Covey, *Evaluation of College Libraries for Accreditation Purposes*, Ed.D. dissertation, Stanford University, 1955.

[9] Beverly Lynch, review of *Participative Management in Academic Libraries*, by Maurice P. Marchant, in *Library Quarterly*, 48 (January 1978), 77-78. Beverly Lynch, "Participative Management in Relation to Library Effectiveness," *College and Research Libraries*, 33 (September 1972), 382-90. See also the response, Maurice P. Marchant, "And a Response," *College and Research Libraries*, 33 (September 1972), 391-97.

[10] George D'Elia, "Determinants of Job Satisfaction Among Beginning Librarians," *Library Quarterly*, 49 (July 1979), 284-85.

[11] Rene V. Darvis, Lloyd H. Lofquist, David J. Weiss, *A Theory of Work Adjustment (a Revision)*, Minnesota Studies in Vocational Rehabilitation no. 23 (Minneapolis: Industrial Relations Center, University of Minnesota, April 1968).

[12] The Minnesota Importance Questionnaire (MIQ) measures an individual's needs. The Minnesota Job Description Questionnaire (MJDQ) measures the availability on the job of reinforcers. The Minnesota Satisfaction Questionnaire (MSQ) measures a worker's satisfaction. The Minnesota Satisfactoriness Scales (MSS) measure workers' satisfactoriness. The manuals written to explain these instruments are: Evan G. Gay and others, *Manual for the Minnesota Importance Questionnaire*, Minnesota Studies in Vocational Rehabilitation no. 28 (Minneapolis: Industrial Relations Center, University of Minnesota, June 1971); Stuart D. Rosen and others, *Occupational Reinforcer Patterns (second volume)*, Minnesota Studies in Vocational Rehabilitation no. 29 (Minneapolis: Industrial Relations Center, University of Minnesota, April 1972); David J. Weiss and others, *Manual for the Minnesota Satisfaction Questionnaire*, Minnesota Studies in Vocational Rehabilitation no. 22 (Minneapolis: Industrial Relations Center, University of

Minnesota, October 1967); Dennis L. Gibson and others, *Manual for the Minnesota Satisfaction Scales*, Minnesota Studies in Vocational Rehabilitation no. 27 (Minneapolis: Industrial Relations Center, University of Minnesota, December 1970).

[13]The dimensions are 1) ability utilization (utilization of abilities), 2) achievement (accomplishment), 3) activity (being busy all the time), 4) advancement, 5) authority (telling others what to do), 6) company policies and practices (fairly administered policies), 7) compensation (pay comparable to other workers), 8) co-workers (ease in making friends), 9) creativity (trying own ideas), 10) independence (working alone), 11) moral values (work not morally wrong), 12) recognition, 13) responsibility (make own decisions), 14) security (steady employment), 15) social service (do things for others), 16) social status (community recognition), 17) supervision-human relations (boss backs employees with top management), 18) supervision-technical (boss trains employees well), 19) variety (do different things), and 20) working conditions.

[14]D'Elia, p. 295.

[15]Suzanne Patterson Wahba, "Job Satisfaction in Librarians: A Comparison Between Men and Women," *College and Research Libraries*, 36 (January 1975), 45-51.

[16]An early explanation of the hierarchical structure is in A. H. Maslow, "A Theory of Human Motivation," *Psychological Review*, 50 (July 1943), 370-96. Both Maslow and others have discussed his theory in many publications as it has developed since then. Two of Maslow's books are *Motivation and Personality* (New York: Harper, 1954) and *Toward a Psychology of Being*, 2nd ed. (New York: Van Nostrand Reinhold, 1968).

[17]Locke, pp. 1308-1309.

[18]F. Blackler and R. Williams, "People's Motives at Work," in *Psychology at Work*, ed. Peter B. Warr (Baltimore, MD: Penguin, 1971), p. 291.

[19]Wahba, pp. 45-51.

[20]John P. Robinson, Robert Athanasiou, and Kendra B. Head, *Measures of Occupational Attitudes and Occupational Characteristics* (Appendix A to *Measures of Political Attitudes*) (Ann Arbor, MI: Survey Research Center, Institute for Social Research, February 1969), pp. 148-51.

[21]Lyman W. Porter, "Job Attitudes in Management: Perceived Deficiencies in Need Fulfillment as a Function of Job Level," *Journal of Applied Psychology*, 46 (December 1962), 378.

[22]Porter, pp. 378-84.

[23]Frederick Herzberg, "One More Time: How Do You Motivate Employees?," *Harvard Business Review*, 46 (January-February 1968), 53-62.

[24]Frederick Herzberg, *Work and the Nature of Man* (Cleveland, OH: World Publishing, 1966).

[25]Locke, pp. 1310-19.

[26]Kenneth H. Plate and Elizabeth W. Stone, "Factors Affecting Librarians' Job Satisfaction: A Report of Two Studies," *Library Quarterly*, 44 (April 1974), 97-110.

[27]J. Richard Hackman and Edward E. Lawler, III, "Employee Reactions to Job Characteristics," *Journal of Applied Psychology*, 55 (June 1971), 259-86.

[28]Locke, p. 1319.

[29]For an early explanation of the theory, see Victor H. Vroom, *Work and Motivation* (New York: Wiley, 1964).

[30]Charles L. Hulin, "Job Satisfaction and Turnover in a Female Clerical Population," *Journal of Applied Psychology*, 50 (August 1966), 280-85.

[31]Robinson, pp. 105-109.

[32]William J. Vaughn and J. D. Dunn, "A Study of Job Satisfaction in Six University Libraries," *College and Research Libraries*, 35 (May 1974), 163-77.

Part IX
PERSONNEL

Introduction

The term "personnel" conjures up various pictures. It can refer to a specific department in a large organization which has the responsibility to screen applicants for jobs, develop job descriptions and specifications, care for employee benefits, develop in-service training programs, and a host of other organization-related activities and duties. All of these functions of a personnel department are legitimate. Yet the conceptual basis of personnel work is often overlooked. Personnel is, after all, the study of the human element in any organization, how it functions, what makes it tick, and how seemingly illogical behavior can seem entirely logical to employees. In actuality, the study of people from a psychological perspective, not necessarily an economic one, is the business of personnel. In a labor intensive organization such as a library, so dependent on its human resources, this study becomes even more critical. It is *people* who communicate much of the information contained in the materials that are so carefully stored in libraries.

Few libraries have formal personnel departments. Yet every librarian is intimately involved in personnel work. To say that every librarian is a manager is, in a very real sense, merely stating the facts of library work. A librarian deals with patrons, colleagues, subordinates, and supervisors. This interaction between library staff members is the stuff of personnel work in its very widest sense.

The selections in this chapter focus on personnel work from a variety of perspectives. James S. Healey provides the most general overview of personnel work in his discussion of how administrators view their employees—and why such views often create the very situations administrators seek to avoid. His approach is essentially theoretical, but with very practical implications. After dealing with the theoretical underpinnings of modern personnel work, Healey sets out certain strategies that administrators might use to meet the psychological needs of their employees. What is it that employees really want? That there is no definite or final answer to this question reflects the complexity of the individual psyche. It is, as Healey puts it, a matter of "chemistry." As Healey points out, the administrator must adopt a contingency view of how to deal with employees based on a mutual understanding of what is expected by the organization and what can be accomplished by an individual worker. This is not an easy process, nor is it a short one. It is, however, a rewarding one, which is liable to have lasting positive effects on the organization.

But personnel work deals with more than generalities. There are very concrete duties that must be accomplished by any administrator involved in such activity. Not least of these is enumerating the requirements of a job, clearly indicating what is to be done, and developing logical, consistent, and fair methods of evaluating a worker's performance on the job. Several librarians have suggested methods of doing this sort of job analysis. For the most part, however, library job descriptions are either couched in generalities or broken down into so many minute particles that freedom of activity is denied to the worker. This may be due in part to a lack of knowledge by administrators on precisely what a job description and analysis ought to accomplish. But this knowledge does exist, and can be acquired. B. G. Dutton, for example, suggests a variety of job factors which need to be taken into account in analyzing a job and, consequently, analyzing an individual's ability to perform that job. Only after knowing what a job is really all about can one go about restructuring it to make it more meaningful and rewarding to the worker, or evaluating one's performance on the job. There is little sense in rewarding or punishing performance without such knowledge.

Dimity S. Berkner's approach to personnel work is similar to that of Dutton. It is, however, more specific in its description of performance appraisal, certainly one of the core elements of personnel administration. After reviewing a variety of methods currently in use for improving worker performance, Berkner suggests that Management By Objectives is more likely to satisfy the need to participate in managerial activities held by many employees. It is this mutual objective setting that creates the climate of fairness of which Healey writes. People are likely to become committed to that which they have helped to develop rather than that which has been imposed upon them from outside. Ensuring such commitment is a very definite administrative responsibility, and Berkner provides guidelines for accomplishing this.

In the final analysis, personnel administration is more than developing procedures for annual review, fringe benefits, equal opportunity, and a host of other activities. The human, and psychological "chemistry" of personnel management stresses an ability to deal with staff in such a way that they are productive, satisfied, and given an opportunity to develop both their personal and professional competencies. With 60-70% of the budget typically allocated in support of personnel, successful administration of human resources is critical for overall organizational effectiveness.

Developing Human Resources: An Administrative View
By James S. Healey

INTRODUCTION

Every library administrator regardless of staff size has to be concerned with personnel management. The school librarian with a single clerical assistant, the head of a major division in a large public library, and the director of an ARL library, all share the problems and opportunities of dealing with human beings. The recognition of the importance of that activity in libraries has been obscured by a belief that worker productivity is not of great importance. Thus, effective personnel management has been ignored by many library managers. Book and serial collections, new cataloging regulations and their effect on in-use systems, and a myriad of other "professional" matters usually take precedence over the effective use of the organization's human resources.

Much of the "How-to-Do-It" management literature of librarianship describes problems with which every worker is familiar. The solutions proposed are mostly ad hoc, e.g., moving the surly worker away from the front desk, assigning individuals less than peak hours, and the like. The solutions generally fail because they attack symptoms, not causes, and in fact, are likely to cause more problems than they are supposed to solve. Use of that approach often produces an image of a "Boss" who is too busy or uninterested in effective problem solving, in short, a manager who really doesn't care about the staff. One of the reactions against such managerial styles has been the unionization of library employees. Despite the long-term disadvantages of such a move, in too many instances the employees have been left with no other viable alternative for improving their treatment.

There are ways out of this morass, and this essay will attempt to point out some of them. First, effective personnel management from the administrator's view is defined. With that in hand, the paper will move to a discussion of the social fabric in which worker and administrator currently co-exist. That will be followed by a discussion of the concerns of the contemporary employee. The next section will deal with some major theories of personnel administration, followed by a brief discussion of contingency-situational management and its role in setting appropriate administrative environments. The essay concludes with a description of some of the techniques that can be used in dealing with people, and the effects those techniques may have.

Author's note: This paper was written using the male pronoun for purposes of style. The female pronoun could have been used without changing the meaning of the piece.

As noted above, people are a resource, much as are funds, quarters, equipment. But there is a significant difference. While the administrator is charged with getting maximum utilization of his employees, he must remember that people are not chips to be pushed around, nor resources to be used up and discarded. People are a self-renewing resource, and the more self-renewing they are, the greater their effectiveness. Thus the operative principle underlying effective personnel management is simply stated: to use human resources to gain the organization's objective at the least cost, with greatest productivity, while at the time providing the human resources the opportunities for continued professional and personal development.

SOCIAL FABRIC

As institutions spring from the unique social fabric of a nation, the theories of operating those institutions also emerge from the same fabric. One example can be cited in the following way. The work of Frederick Taylor, the father of scientific management, was indeed a product of his time and social milieu. Writing shortly after the turn of the century, one of Taylor's famous pieces describes "ditch digging."[1] To the modern reader, Taylor's exhortations on how to dig a ditch seem quaint, particularly when watching a front-end loader lift hundreds of shovelsful at once. But, Taylor's work evolved in a time when there were no front-end loaders, for his world was one of modest technology.

Taylor and his disciples would be surprised by today's world. Since the end of World War II, the world, and particularly the United States, has experienced a constant revolution in technological and social change. Rapid movement of people from one place to another, instant worldwide video communication, and the computer come quickly to mind as but three of the ways change has occurred.

Whereas during World War II, ferrying B-17 bombers to England was a 20-24 hour task, today, the London to New York run is made by most people in six hours, and by some in four, and international travel has indeed made the world smaller. While it was a privilege to hear Edward R. Murrow broadcasting from London during the Blitz, it was a narrow experience when viewed in terms of the satellite communication systems that brought the Kennedy funeral and live coverage of bleeding bodies in Vietnam to the world. And while the first computers were being used to improve the accuracy of long-distance weapons in 1944, in 1980 the myriad future uses of computers can only be conjectured.

Technological change brought social change. Reisman was one of the first both to see what was ahead and to carefully predict results:

> If the other-directed people should discover how much needless work they do, discover that their own thoughts and their own lives are quite as interesting as other people's, that, indeed they no more assuage their loneliness in a crowd of peers than one can assuage one's thirst by drinking salt water, then we might expect them to become more attentive to their own feelings and emotions.[2]

Reisman's accuracy was uncanny. Many of those who had been "outer directed," changed to a life of "inner direction." Later, their children pushed the boundaries of inner direction to unheard of lengths. Two examples will suffice. While parents may have had an occasional sexual "fling," their children experimented with "open marriage," or simply "relationships." And while in the past, people saved for a "rainy day," contemporary mores express little disapproval of the credit-card society. What had taken place was a revolution in how individuals saw themselves in a variety of frameworks. From this revolution came the "self-awareness movement." One was to learn to "be in touch with oneself and one's needs." This increased emphasis on inner direction has had its effect on those who work.

THE CONTEMPORARY EMPLOYEE

Due to these changes, Howe and Mindell could list the ways in which contemporary employees differ from traditional (older) employees. Summing up the list, the authors state that contemporary employees:

1) Are more concerned with organizational recognition than with compensation.

2) Are more concerned with short- rather than long-term organizational goals.

3) Are more apt to place their priorities on leisure and family than on loyalty and commitment to the organization.

4) Are more concerned with communication and information, particularly in the decision-making process in which they wish to be involved.

5) Want their jobs to be interesting, worthwhile, challenging, creative, and ultimately developmental.[3]

Whereas in the past, an individual was very concerned with job security, long-term commitments and pay, the new employee is less so. It is not hard to understand why. Those who lived through the Depression saw the vagaries of fate intervene disastrously at all levels. To have a job was to eat, in a time when 25% of the labor force went hungry or worse. To those who came after World War II, the nation, with the exception of a few "down-turns" or recessions, has scarcely seen more than 7-8% of the work force idled. The children of these families are now in the work force themselves, and know that getting a job in order to eat is "no big deal."

For these individuals, organizational recognition is far more important. They want to be viewed as good workers, more for the psychological compensation than for what appears in the pay check. Contemporary employees generally do tend to want a say in the decisions that affect their lives. In many cases, reared in homes where the child was given autonomy and opportunities for inner or self-direction, the contemporary employee often resists being told what to do. Part of that is the general distrust of authority—parental, work, political. Yet, more of it has to do with the personal refinement of needs and wants, and the increasing concern with self-fulfillment.

These individuals also want greater access to information. The information desired covers a wide range of data—about the organization as a whole, information that affects the individual directly, and most certainly the information that will affect the decisions one is to make. The words "interesting," "worthwhile," "challenging," and "creative," and ultimately "developmental" have been heard often, both in this context and in others. They have become the great concern of millions of workers even in nations where capitalism is viewed as work of the devil.

The authors were speaking in general terms when they discussed the contemporary employee. But if one looks specifically at a contemporary professional employee, the words take on a deeper hue. The professional, by virtue of his educational experience, has ostensibly been more deeply immersed in the value systems described above. For example, not only does he want more information, he believes he can use it effectively. And, not only does he want a part in decisions, he believes he is capable of making accurate ones, and can carry out those decisions effectively. The library worker, of course, is one of these professionals. It would be a highly useful experiment for the reader to test Howe & Mindell's hypothesis on himself.

PERSONNEL THEORIES

Theories dealing with personnel administration, the psychology of work, and organizational development have all been affected by the changes above. Etzioni's work, *Modern Organizations*, is perhaps the classic in the last of the above named areas, and should be read by every administrator.[4] He quickly sketches the changes in organizational theory from the Scientific Management School of the 1910-1920 period, to what he calls the "Structuralist School" of current times. Etzioni's work is cited because of its seminal importance to the framework of personnel administration, because people work in organizations.

Three individuals, spanning two decades, have been most influential in the areas of the psychology of work and personnel administration. The ideas are experiential with substantial testing in research situations. The first of the trio was Douglas McGregor,[5] and his "Theory X and Theory Y" management styles. Theory X people were viewed as poorly self-motivated, responding better to threat of punishment (the stick) than possible rewards (the carrot). And, since his Theory X people did not effectively motivate themselves, it was left to the Theory X administrator to do it for them, usually in a dictatorial manner.

But McGregor saw an opposite pole—Theory Y people. They were highly motivated and responded well to "adult" leadership. Because these people were so well motivated, they needed little direction and, thus, needed a Theory Y administrator. This type of laissez-faire individual was to interfere as little as possible in the direction of the staff's activities.

Reality, of course, lay somewhere between the poles. That middle ground was sought by Abraham Maslow.[6] He identified the fact that people (workers) respond to even more basic motivations than being fired or getting a raise. Maslow attempted to deal with the individual as a human being who happens to find himself, from time to time, in a work situation. Maslow claimed that the individual's response in that situation is far more dependent on his psychological well-being than the Boss' stick and/or carrot.

Maslow pointed out that as the individual satisfied a basic need, he would then seek to satisfy the next need level, and those levels stretched from such basics as eating to the most esoteric one of finding, as Maslow put it, one's place in the universe. It is important to recognize that Maslow saw this not necessarily as a function of the job or profession only, but as an integral part of the *total* activity of *well* human beings. However, Maslow did point out that the workplace could provide a framework and locus in which these need satisfactions could, in fact should, be found.

Drucker,[7] writing a decade later, refined the theory still further. He agreed with Maslow's idea of a need hierarchy, but disagreed as to whether a need, once satisfied, stays that way. He states that needs change and the word "basic" is itself continuously redefined. For example, the hungry man can only think of earning money to buy bread. Once he eats his fill, he can begin to satisfy other needs. But as he does, and moves up the hierarchy, a curious occurrence takes place. The man now redefines the basic need, in terms of his perceptions of his worth, status, and a number of variables. Having done so, the basic need of satisfying hunger is transmuted into *how* to satisfy hunger. Whereas previously it was a simple matter of bread, at a later time, it may be how many times a week one has steak, and even later, how often in the period of a month can one afford to eat at a fine restaurant. Thus, needs, and the means of satisfying them, are constantly being redefined and new challenges established.

Summing up, we have seen the theories of personnel development that have grown out of the social milieu of the post-World War II "post-technological society." These theories are closely attuned to the way in which society wants "psychic" as well as real income. How then to deal with this new employee; how then to implement the operative principle noted above? It is the manager (administrator) that must set the stage and find the strategies to provide the means.

THE CONTINGENCY-SITUATIONAL APPROACH TO MANAGEMENT

One of the more important contemporary theories of management that works effectively in this area is contingency management. Luthans states the hypothesis thusly, "A contingent relationship ... can be simply thought of as an if-then functional relationship. The *if* is the independent variable (where one has free choice) and the *then* is the dependent variable (where one has little choice) in this functional relationship."[8] (Emphasis the author's.) Results are contingent on means. Thus, the "if" statement could represent "means to an objective" and the "then" statement could represent the likely outcome. Since results are the end of some activity, the two are related by function. Using the example above, an independent variable might be a book budget, the spending of which is controlled by one's free choice (how many copies, which titles, and the like). The dependent variable would be the results of the spending of the budget. Further, it is the use of the independent variable where one exercises judgment and control. If one freely chooses to buy books, one cannot expect to buy pencils with the same money.

Contingency management is particularly important in the matter of personnel. First, most of any organization's budget is spent on personnel. Thus, such choices as "If I spend here ..." are of supreme financial concern. Further, it is the personnel that will accomplish the organization's tasks. Once again, "If I hire this person ..." has profound meaning for the organization's services. Still further, when developing a management approach or style, the "If I use this approach ..." choice is crucial to the results desired. Consequently, contingency planning is paramount to any hoped for success in dealing with people. The careful framing of and application of choices is vital.

Situational management presents a similar view. While one must maintain a careful attitude toward choices and results, situations continually change, thus affecting the results desired. And it is in this area wherein the administrator can himself cause variables to change. For example, a university administrator put it thusly:

> You go along making plans, and in some cases do not involve a particular department in these plans. But, then, along comes a department chair who wants to see the department improve and prosper. In one situation, a chair literally forced his way into our planning and forced us to rethink our planning process.[9]

The statement points up the fact that the administrator can create new environments. Depending on one's vision and ingenuity, the organizational environment can be changed in a variety of ways, as can the environment of one's personnel. In each case, as the administrator changes the environment, his response to the newly created environment must change as well. The *if-then* of contingency management comes together most profoundly in the process of personnel management. For it rests within the administrator's power to ask the important "if" questions, which eventually bring forth the results one intends.

THE PROCESS OF PERSONNEL MANAGEMENT

The basic strategy for organizational development is to build a process of growth, of innovation, of challenge. The word "process" is used precisely because the task of motivating and challenging employees is never-ending. As Drucker notes, the needs, because they are constantly being redefined, constantly demand new satisfactions which generally come from new as well as different challenges.[10] Thus, the process is open-ended, and always unfinished. One can strive for improvement or refinement in the process but never its conclusion.

A second matter is the administrator's own system of values, and his view of human beings. Golembiewski for example, speaks of the "Judaeo-Christian Administrative Ethic,"[11] which, simply stated, is "Do unto others as you would have them do unto you." Employing that ethic, one is less likely to be guilty of paternalism, authoritarianism, or disdain for the individual and the individual's well-being. Thus, a personal and consciously developed belief in the worth of the individual is crucial to the process, for one's basic beliefs in human beings, positive or negative, quickly show through any facade. Attitudes set the stage for assembling the parts of the process.

Still another building block in the process is organizational structure, which is a great deal more than boxes and lines on a chart. Each employee needs to know what is expected of him, when it is expected, where it is expected and why, as well as how his work fits into the overall organization. The employee must know to whom he reports and for what, who his subordinates are, and for what they are responsible. He needs to know the lines of communication—upwards, downwards, and laterally.

This structure provides not only organizational order, but personal security. Regardless of how highly motivated one may be, one needs a base to which one can return when there is a space between challenges. The individual must know where that place is for him, so that when a space is needed in which to catch one's breath, he can, if you will, pull in his antennae and breathe. The structure provides minimums of performance, activities beyond which the individual does not have to reach each day. While it is also important to indicate clearly to the employee that performance beyond the minimum will be rewarded, it is equally important to allow the employee more freedom to decide how and when those minimums will be exceeded and when it is proper to meet only the minimum. For who has not had a day or a week in which it was simply not possible to motivate oneself to reach above one's minimum level? It is a human attribute, and the employee must be granted the right to say, "I just can't take on anything more right now." Structure provides a resting place, a re-charging place so that the employee can, when he decides, emerge refreshed. Obviously, if an employee rests too long in such a place, it is incumbent on the administrator to find out why and to try to remedy the dysfunctional behavior.

Communication plays a vital role in the process. Without effective communication, the process collapses. The organization can be viewed as an information network, taking in external messages, transmitting, filtering, diminishing, or increasing the volume both laterally and horizontally within the organization and sending internal messages out. The information activity includes information gathering, dissemination, and use. External information comes from a variety of sources—written, spoken, overheard and so on. Employees must be encouraged to listen and read so that they become what McClure calls "Information Rich."[12] To be "information rich" is to have a great deal of information about what is happening both inside and outside of the organization. Here one returns to the contingency aspect. *If* I, as an administrator, see to it that my employees have as much information as I can move to them, *then* they will be better able to deal with the problems and situations that arise. And again, *if* the employees can deal more effectively with those problems and situations, *then* the library will be equally effective in accomplishing its mission.

The "how" of developing information-rich employees is very simple, yet, at the same time, very threatening to many. The simple part is encompassed in the administrator's own approach. If he is open and willing to share what information he has, then his employees will have the information they need. But in that simplicity lies what many consider a threat. They view information as power—which is true—and resolve that they will retain and not share information so they will not have to share power. Power need not be a matter of awesomeness. It can be as simple a thing as "who knows when vacation times will be assigned," for each individual views the idea of power in different ways. Thus, the administrator is the key to information dissemination.

The administrator who is willing to share his information with his subordinates, and insists that his subordinates share their information with their subordinates, will eventually build an information process. That process will improve communication down the hierarchy, as well as up. Gibb's model of a High Trust/Low Fear organization clearly demonstrates the benefits to be accrued from such an open communication environment.[13]

Briefly summarized, Gibb states that information, good news and bad, must be disseminated quickly, without filtering, unvarnished as it were. Employees quickly learn that the administrator sees to it that everyone knows what's going on. Employees will test the assumption that the administrator is being honest, and if they find he is, and, that information will not be used as a weapon, they learn to trust him. They in turn will learn to share information. This further cements trust and confidence. As trust is built, the organization becomes more open and receptive to improved communication at all levels. Thus, it is not only what is done with information but how it is done that is important.

Another component, and perhaps the most difficult to master, is that of employee motivation. It is also the most important. Motivation is seen by some as "button-pushing" as in, "If I push this button, Jones reacts in such and such a way." It has been used that way, and if one's view of the world is Pavlovian or Skinnerian, that is how one will expect people to react. One usually gets from people what one expects to get from them. (Look at McGregor's Theory X people to know that the theory becomes a self-fulfilling prophecy.) Motivation is a highly personal activity that rests completely on the administrator's view of the world and the people in it. But holding a positive view is not enough. The various techniques of human motivation must be brought into play. And one must ask, in a sense, "What makes Sammy run?" Motivational strategies are different for each employee, and once again, the administrator must at once carefully develop his choices, as well as comprehend situations. Below, in no particular order, are some of the strategies that can be employed to encourage worker improvement.

The Need To Be Challenged

Some employees need constant challenge. They need to feel that they are being pitted against great odds and that the problems they face are major. This can be communicated to the employee in various ways—but *never dishonestly*. It should be noted that only some employees react well to this strategy. Some find the idea of great odds very uncomfortable, too pressure filled, and for them such a strategy is counter-productive. But for those who thrive on pressure filled situations, this strategy is extremely effective and will bring the organization excellent results.

The Need to Excel

Some employees react most affirmatively to a situation in which they are given the opportunity to exceed even their own personal expectations. It can be as simple a thing as saying, "Here you'll have the chance to see how good you can be." The employees that react to this approach are generally the most productive, in terms of quantity and quality. Of course, such an approach brings problems too, one of which is providing the employee with the needed resources. Finding the money, the personnel, the equipment that the employee may need is not easy, and may be impossible.

The Need for Responsibility

Some employees react well to assignments that place major responsibility in their hands. They want to believe that the administrator has sufficient confidence in their ability to allow them the freedom to act. Thus, with such people, the administrator can begin by assigning non-major responsibilities. As these are handled effectively, the administrator can delegate larger and more important tasks. With each succeeding task, employee and administrator gain greater confidence, and the employee learns that his efforts are important to the organization.

Tangible Rewards

Tangible rewards should not be ignored as a motivating factor. A substantial raise, a promotion, or chance for a better job cannot be discounted as a means of motivating some individuals.

The Need To Be Directed

Lest the reader think that all employees react only to positive stimuli, it must be recognized that some never respond to any positive motivation. There will always be some, in every organization (hopefully fewer rather than more), that will only react to direct orders. They volunteer as little as possible; communication and trust are foreign to them. For the administrator, these individuals provide a high level of frustration because nothing seems to work. Nevertheless, they are part of the organization, they are paid by the organization, and the maximum contribution must be sought from them. It is indeed a challenge.

It is the administrator's task to determine what will work with each of his people. This takes time, and is also a constant source of tension, since mistakes *are* made. But, in a learning process, and particularly when that process is aimed at learning more about people, mistakes are to be expected.

This brings up the matter of failure and how to deal with it, for everyone fails from time to time. If the administrator is supportive, and attempts to use the situation as a learning experience, then the experience will be productive and the administrator will gain more trust. "The Boss believes in me," will likely be the mental response, and the psychological response will be one of increased loyalty and trust and even heightened motivation. Again, the learning will be affected by the attitudes expressed, verbally or non-verbally.

Another element in the process is personnel involvement in decision-making. There has been a movement that claims everyone should be involved in the decision-making process, and library literature is replete with this kind of nonsense. There are good and sufficient reasons why everyone should *not* be involved in every decision. First of all, it takes enormous amounts of time, and often, the product is not worth the time spent. There is no substitute for hard-headed, clear thinking. And problem analysis by a small group of persons is usually eminently more successful.

Furthermore, a decision may have nothing to do with a particular individual, and his involvement is a waste of his time and the organization's. In another instance, the employee may neither care nor want to participate. That is the employee's choice to make and must be honored. But, an employee should be involved with those decisions that may affect his life. There is a dynamic activity involved in such involvement. The employee comes to feel more of a part of the organization. He feels more intimately attuned to the organization's goals and objectives. He feels good about his involvement because the administrator has demonstrated faith in the employee, and the belief that what the employee may have to add may be important.

Once the decision that encompasses the solutions and ideas of an employee is made, the dynamic expands. The individual feels compelled to work harder to achieve success. He does so because his idea is on the line, and he responds to that impetus. He responds as well to the trust being placed in him. Thus, the organization reaps enormous benefits, as does the employee.

Yet, even with the best of intentions, it is important to recognize that no administrator succeeds with all employees. The why's of this reality are:

1) Administrative Inexperience
   It may well be that the new administrator (a factor of days on the job, and years of age) is simply too new to know how to employ the various strategies. Thus, the first time around has to be viewed as a learning experience, and the learner (the administrator) should be ready to admit his mistakes, noting what *if* and *then* questions he did not pose, and try again.

2) Situational Constraints
   The organization itself can stifle the effectiveness of the techniques. If one is in an organization where such concerns are considered unimportant, the middle level manager's efforts will likely meet only moderate success. Using trust-oriented strategies in an atmosphere that is full of distrust hardly guarantees success.

3) Chemical Constraints
   While it can be documented only with difficulty, it is evident from most people's experience that what is commonly known as "personal chemistry" does make a difference. At times, it provides the basis for great success. But, more often, it is apparent that chemistry works the other way. It can prevent, or at the least, inhibit effective communication.

4) Human Constraints
   It has been noted above that Maslow posits his thesis on the concept of the psychologically "well" employee. That does not mean that the psychologically "unwell" human being is certifiable for mental rehabilitation. Rather, if the individual is closed, secretive, ungiving, then most of the techniques noted above will simply not work. Those techniques are posited on the ideal that all are ready to be free and open. When one finds those who are not, then responses must be changed.

The final element in the process is to create an environment in which debate and exchange of views can take place. This is a difficult task, because so often people's psyches are involved. Yet the organization's good health depends on the willingness of its members to discuss sensitive issues freely and without rancor. Thus, it devolves upon the administrator to set the tone. If his ideas can be attacked, and even mauled in a general discussion without reprisal, then anyone's can be. That is not to say that the administrator should be forced to sit by and take unkind words, in order to prove he's a "regular guy." But, it is the administrator's task to provide an open forum, governed by certain rules of decorum. No one should be attacked, and matters should not be discussed in personal terms.

CONCLUSION

What, then, are the major parts of building a process for personnel development? Briefly, they are as follows:

1) Establish a basic understanding of how human beings behave in work situations.

2) Establish a basic philosophical approach to dealing with people, tempered with a recognition that people are different, and work at different speeds and levels of commitment.

3) Understand the values that underlie the organization's employees, and the need to develop different responses to deal with different value structures.

4) Develop a structure in which all know their proper role and function; a structure that people can use as the base for improved productivity and to which they may return when a rest is needed.

5) Develop effective information gathering, dissemination, and use.

6) Build a climate of trust and openness, as opposed to one of fear and distrust.

7) Motivate the employee:
   a. provide the employee with a climate in which to develop to his fullest potential.
   b. Provide the employee with the resources and information necessary to achieve the potential.
   c. Reward the employee when he meets with success, and supportive understanding when the result is a failed task.

8) Offer an employee the opportunity to take part in the decisions affecting himself as well as the organization, recognizing that not all will actually take part but that all must be granted the opportunity.

9) Manipulate the environment and resource availability to encourage desired behaviors.

At the end of all of this, one has the right to ask, "Will it work?" The answer—yes and no. Contingency management assumes that the "right" questions will be asked. When dealing with people, it is very difficult to know what the "right" questions are. Further, it is equally difficult to know whether the environment has been established in which growth, innovation, and challenge can occur.

The development of the "right" questions is difficult and takes time—in some cases years. It requires an even greater understanding of oneself. The author advises anyone who plans a career in administration, at whatever level, to undergo some basic group therapy. This is not to say that one should probe the Freudian depths but only should try to gain some perspectives on one's own approach to the world. It is you, the administrator, who will be asking the *If* and *Then* questions; you who will be attempting to put the process into place. It would be well then, before you ask the questions, to know where you stand.

For success (asking the right questions) often appears to elude the administrator. There are times when one may well wonder if the effort is worth it. Mistakes will occur, and hoped for plans will go awry. Yet, the major factor in delivering the message to a staff is that the administrator is at least attempting to do the "right" thing. Most, although not all, adults will recognize when a valid attempt is being made, and, in many cases, those adults will be gentle in criticizing someone who is at least trying.

And, perhaps to sum up the essence of the process, the underlying factor which permeates all the rest and that which brings the most affirmative responses from others is one supplied by the title of a work by the Father of Cybernetics, Norbert Weiner. Written three decades ago, as computers were beginning to make their intrusive way into all of human endeavor, Weiner wanted to make certain that the human element would remain uppermost. His title? Very simply, "The Human Use of Human Beings." There is no more acute guideline for the administrator to remember.

REFERENCES

[1] Frederick W. Taylor, *Scientific Management* (New York: Harper, 1911).

[2] David Reisman, Nathan Glazer, and Denney Revel, *The Lonely Crowd* (New Haven, CT: Yale University Press, 1950), p. 349.

[3] Roger J. Howe and Mark G. Mindell, "Motivating the Contemporary Employee," *Management Review* LXVII, No. 9 (September 1979), 51-55.

[4] Amatai Etzioni, *Modern Organizations* (Englewood Cliffs, NJ: Prentice-Hall, 1964).

[5] Douglas McGregor, *The Human Side of Enterprise* (New York: McGraw-Hill, 1960).

[6] Abraham Maslow, *Motivation and Personality* (New York: Harper and Row, 1954).

[7] Peter Drucker, *Management: Tasks, Responsibilities, Practices* (New York: Harper and Row, 1974), p. 195.

[8] Fred Luthans, *Introduction to Management: A Contingency Approach* (New York: McGraw-Hill, 1976), p. 29.

[9] J. R. Morris, Provost of the University of Oklahoma, Personal Interview, March 15, 1980.

[10] Drucker, p. 195.

[11] Robert T. Golembiewski, *Men, Management and Morality* (New York: McGraw-Hill, 1965).

[12] Charles R. McClure, *Information for Academic Library Decision Making* (Westport, CT: Greenwood Press, 1980).

[13] Jack R. Gibb. Gibb has expressed this concept in a number of his works. Perhaps the most succinct exposition is in the film, *Emergent Management*, available from University Extension of the University of California, Berkeley, 94720.

Job Assessment and Job Evaluation
By B. G. Dutton

Paper presented at an Aslib Evening Meeting held in London on 21st May 1975

JOB EVALUATION IN a Library and Information (L&I) environment is not the easiest of subjects to write about. It is not well documented; it is a subject which does not interest most people *per se* but only (like the Budget speech) if its application leads to a change in material conditions; and there are very real constraints on trying to go it alone—the unit will normally have to keep broadly in step with the parent organization. Nevertheless, an understanding of the principles can help considerably in ensuring adequate treatment for L&I jobs, and an internal job evaluation study can serve other useful purposes that I will come to later.

Before discussing what job evaluation is or how it works it may be helpful to examine briefly a major problem to which it is one solution, and that is the problem of arriving at a fair salary structure, for this not only makes salaries more easily controllable but also is an essential prerequisite for job motivation. If we look at the history of UK salary movements over the past half century, three distinct phases can be distinguished:

—through the inter-war years, movements of pay—which could go down as well as up—depended very much on the level of activity in a particular industry

—during the first two post-war decades, movements of pay were upward only and changes were bigger and more frequent, but the main distinguishing feature from pre-war years was that the rises were very general with the size in any year being governed by the state of the economy as a whole rather than by that in particular industries

—finally, from about 1968, the links with economic conditions seem to have been broken, and unemployment and the rate of rise of pay have gone up together, to levels unprecedented for both since the war.

Use of economic arguments to judge pay claims has been replaced by claimants' opinion of what they are morally entitled to and this approach is moving up through professional levels of job grades.

Reproduced by permission from *Aslib Proceedings*, vol. 28, no. 4 (April 1976), pp. 144-60. B. G. Dutton is Division Information Unit Manager, Imperial Chemical Industries Limited, Runcorn, Cheshire, England.

There are three grounds on which such opinion is based:

—the seemingly inevitable rise in the cost of living, since the last settlement seems to rob the employee of any rise in his standard of living
—successive governments have encouraged employees to expect a steady rise in the standard of living as a result of economic growth
—fair comparison—and its close relationship with the question of differentials.

It has been said that there are no pay disputes, only disputes about differentials. This is not just a question of 'I'm not going to be left behind' although if one particular group gets large rises, other groups will try hard to keep up. Just as important is the feeling that relativities in pay are proportional to differences in job requirements: hence a slip in the league table means not only that one is getting less than just price for one's work, but also that one's status has been impaired—that there has been a loss of the respect due to one from one's neighbours for the work one does. A workman's differential is a badge that he displays with the same pride that the professional man displays qualification abbreviations after his name.

Clearly then from the point of view of controlling inflation, differentials are a critical factor. Government attempts to lessen the significance attached to comparisons between trends of income in different employments have met with no great success, but an alternative approach is to ensure that differentials are based on real justice. Baroness Wootton is quoted as saying 'that which has lasted 15 years is readily believed to be part of the eternal order of nature' and job evaluation is an attempt to replace tradition by a detailed and up-to-date evaluation of the requirements of particular jobs.

What then is job evaluation? It may be defined as 'the process of analysis and assessment of the relative content of jobs, to place them in an acceptable rank order which can be used as a basis for a pay structure'. It is based on the idea that a job can be broken down into a number of unit tasks which can be treated as common units where jobs cannot. The concept is not new. Shaw in one of his plays muses on how one might fix a just wage between poets laureate and sausage makers and some of the earliest practical schemes date back as far as 1909, but development has followed the same approximate time law that seems to apply to technological innovation, and job evaluation on a significant scale did not begin until some two decades later in the USA, with a third decade elapsing before significant penetration into other countries became evident. The US position at the end of the '60s is usefully illustrated in a survey carried out on 239 randomly selected corporations with 250 or more employees.[1] Figure 1 shows the intensity of activity moving towards increasingly professional sectors of employment between 1940 and 1968. One reason for this derived from the experience of organizations with the introduction by governments of salary freezes, during which organizations with no plans for the systematic evaluation of management positions lacked any sound bases for justifying salary increases to correct inequities or to reward merit. Their executives often became 'forgotten men' at such times.

Figure 2 shows that by 1968 the degree of professional activity in a job made little difference on whether job evaluation schemes had been planned, installed, changed or abandoned. Growth of interest can be attributed to the lack of alternative satisfactory ways of relating large numbers of different jobs in times of constant change.

I should like next to consider the methodology of job evaluation. Whilst there are a number of standard methods,[2] little has been written on their practical application to L&I jobs. There is much in common in principles between them and I propose only to outline aspects of approach common to most methods, and then to describe in some detail one system which is used in my own organization (ICI) in the UK for evaluating jobs in the range which encompasses almost all L&I jobs.

Job evaluation methods in common use can be divided broadly into two groups—non-analytical, qualitative and analytical, quantitative. There are two qualitative methods which are the converse of each other:

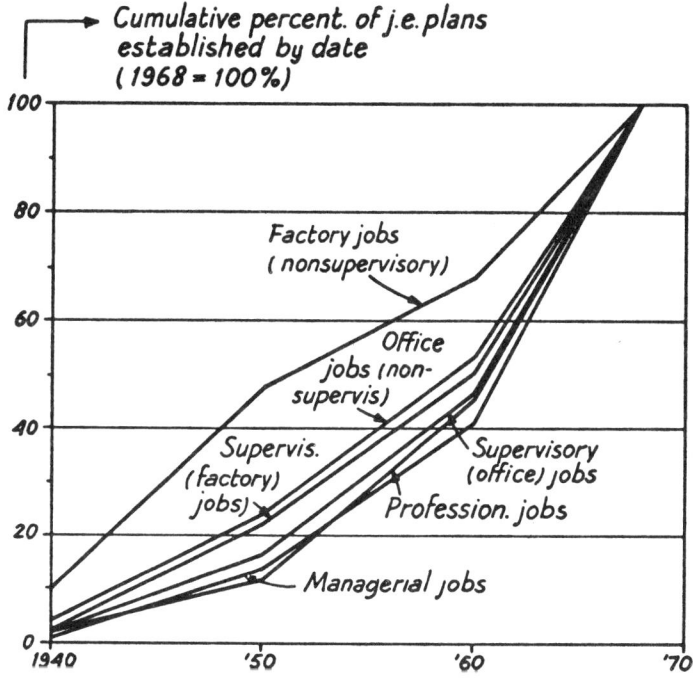

Source of data: Survey by Akalin and Hassan, 1971

FIG. 1: *Date of establishment of job evaluation plans in the USA (1968)*

FIGURES 1 AND 2 REPRODUCED BY KIND PERMISSION OF THE PUBLISHERS FROM 'SOME APPROACHES TO NATIONAL JOB EVALUATION', FOUNDATION FOR BUSINESS RESPONSIBILITY, 1972 (REF. 1)

—Job Ranking, in which jobs are compared against each other and arranged or valued in the order of their importance, difficulty or value to the firm.
—Job Grading (or Classification), which recognizes that there are differences in the levels of duties, responsibilities and skills required for the performance of different jobs. These differences are identified and expressed as grades. The grades are then defined and jobs classified by the selection of a particular grade for each job to correspond to its worth.

The principal quantitative methods are based on the identification of job factors such as mental, physical, responsibility, skill requirements, and working conditions, the determination of the relative roles which each factor plays in a given job, and also the relative significance of a given factor between jobs.

For example, in the Factor Comparison method, key jobs are selected for which the existing absolute pay and also the relative pay one to another are acceptable (therein lies a difficulty) and for each job, the percentage pay attributable to each factor is decided. A table of actual hourly pay rate against

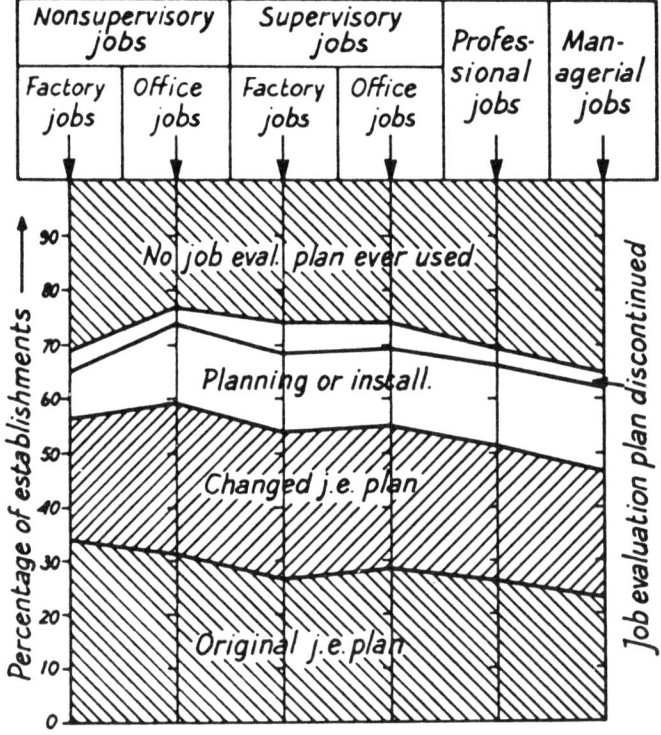

Source of data: Survey by Akalin and Hassan, 1971

FIG. 2: *The use of formal job evaluation plans in the USA (1968)*

factor is then drawn up with each job inserted at the correct pay level for each factor; other jobs are then slotted in. To check the ranking, a second matrix is drawn up independently in which each job is ranked against the others, factor by factor.

The scheme is complicated to work because it requires many committee decisions and is not easy to explain to participants. In the Points Comparison method, a range of points is allocated to each factor according to relative difficulty by a six-stage procedure. This consists of listing all the separate tasks which form the job and finding the percentage time which each task occupies. Next a series of factors, such as know-how, accountability, etc, which are considered to define the overall requirements of the job, must be drawn up, and graded definitions, from most elementary to most advanced, allocated for each factor. A points rating system is needed and since job differences usually widen at higher levels, percentage increases are often considered better to reflect successive increases in difficulty and to keep these in the same relationship. Finally, a formula must be drawn up linking job content with grading and this will subsequently need to be related to a remuneration scale.

It must be remembered that most information units are small compared to the size of the organization they serve and, since they do not contribute to profit in any obvious way, their importance is not self-evident. In order to gain a fair assessment of their jobs therefore, it is essential that these jobs be understandable, measurable and comparable with other jobs in the organization. To do this, the special jargon and detailed mystique of the actual library and information tasks must be cut out and the job content exposed in terms which are meaningful in relation to the running of the organization as a whole.

I give this advice with a certain humility because, about six years ago, a small working party was set up within ICI at the instigation of its professional information managers to investigate job descriptions and grading of staffs within the company's library and information units. The qualitative Job Grading approach was chosen and a system drawn up which did spell out job levels in terms of L&I tasks and nomenclature. The system was described[3] at an Aslib symposium in 1970 and the speaker in concluding remarked that 'no man is an island and no unit of an organization can be considered in isolation'. These words proved prophetic and although the proposals were noted by the Company's central personnel department they were not implemented.

Before commencing an exercise—and this is more likely to be an attempt to ensure that your existing job evaluation system is felt to be fair in relation to the assessment of L&I jobs, rather than the introduction of a completely new system—a most important first step is to involve a sufficiently senior person in the same part of the organization. Superficially it might seem most appropriate to talk to the personnel function but, in fact, personnel actions often reflect corporate policies rather than establish them. Remembering that the main object of job evaluation is to produce a salary level which is felt to be fair by the job holder, then the more understanding and participation that the job holder and his supervisors have in the evaluation procedure, the more is the evaluation likely to convince. The head of the information unit should make every effort to ensure that he understands fully the factors considered to be important in job ratings in his own organization and, equally, should endeavour to be consulted over the composition of the assessment panel. This should include someone familiar with the type of job to be assessed.

The person whose job is to be assessed must be told why (sometimes he may have taken the initiative in asking for an assessment) and he should be asked to write out a job description, preferably with guidance. This can be on a special form designed to assist the assessors to rate the relative importance of the various job factors but questions should nevertheless be couched in a style and sequence which will draw out the elements of the job in a fairly natural way. An organization chart showing the job in relation to the holder's department is always useful since job titles can be misleading. A look at job title versus job level in L&I jobs in ICI in 1975 showed that four job titles were particularly favoured. In each case there was an incumbent somewhere at one or other of eight levels of job, each level having a 10 per cent difference of responsibility from its neighbours.

Provision of the job description should be followed by an interview which is neither a trial by jury nor a school-type examination, but provides an opportunity for the assessors to meet the job-holder and to discuss the job in detail to ensure that all important aspects are appreciated. To help this, the job-holder should be asked to be prepared during the discussion to give examples of incidents to support his answers. He should also be encouraged to bring along any documentation which he considers may help to illustrate his work and, at the end of formal discussion, he should be invited to raise any aspects of his work which he feels may not have been adequately covered. Subsequently, the Panel may, if it is felt appropriate, visit the site of the job.

Immediately after the interview, the assessors should clarify any doubts or obscurities remaining with the assessee's supervisor and, if necessary, with his supervisor. Our experience shows that a main source of doubt involves the overlap of responsibilities between the assessee and his colleagues.

Having familiarized themselves with the job, the assessors have the task of relating its content to that of other jobs in the organization at large. In my organization we consider that this can be done successfully by relating job content to as few as three principal factors, it being felt that as the number of factors increases, the proportion of them which relates to personal characteristics rather than the job requirements becomes higher. The three factors are:

—management content of the job, in relation to both people and work
—relationships content, both as regards range and depth
—decisions content, both direct and advisory

and whilst in no way wishing to imply that this approach is better than that of other variations, the fact that it has survived substantially unchanged, in a very large-scale application, for over a decade, must be a certain testimony to its practical utility, and I propose to develop the aspects contained in these factors to show how they can provide a framework against which the tasks of a library or information job can be put into a general organizational context. Too much stress cannot be placed on the accuracy with which job level definitions are written. Endless discussions can result from definitions that are not clear, concise, objective and positive and in which simple language and correct nomenclature are not used. Definitions should consist of easily understood phrases which mean what they say, so that the rating panel will have the same concept as to what each degree means with regard to job context.

Description of the job factors and how they are considered

1 MANAGEMENT

Under this factor are grouped the job's requirements in terms of organizing, using and controlling the resources available to the job holder. It is examined under the two broad aspects of 'man management' and 'work management'.

Man-management
Under this heading the panel considers the number of staff supervised and whether their work is similar or varied in such a way that it places greater demands on the job holder. It considers also the type of leadership required by the job and the responsibility for rewarding and developing staff.

Supervision: Are the group supervised large or small, dispersed or concentrated, and are they engaged in similar tasks or diverse activities? Do they respond directly to a supervisor or is supervision indirect? How far have task methods and practices to be defined? What is the nature and frequency of control and redirection? Does man-management involve ensuring that subordinates adhere to a defined plan provided —or does it involve frequent change of direction and pace to meet fluctuating and unpredictable demands?

Motivation: Are subordinates' targets and objectives self-evident or prescribed or do they require that subordinates need explanation or involvement to understand their part in the work-team's objectives? To what extent do they need leadership and support, rather than direction or instruction, in identifying and removing obstacles to their own effectiveness?

What is the responsibility for recruitment, performance appraisal, salary revision and promotion? What involvement does the individual have with the identification of training needs and the design and implementation of training programmes and career development plans?

Work management
Here, the panel considers the working system of which the job is part to determine if it is well defined, demanding only prompt reaction to external events and circumstances, or whether the job holder has consciously to manage a work plan to achieve the job objectives.

Planning: How far does the job form part of a well-defined working system, demanding only prompt reaction to external events and circumstances—or how far is the job holder consciously required to plan his activities in advance to achieve his job objectives? Does his work plan involve the integration of separate tasks carried out by his subordinates? Does he produce long-term work programmes involving the integration of separate jobs? Does he need to take into account contributory or related activities in other work groups external to his own? Does his plan encompass activities of others outside his own work group but directed to a common objective? How much is prescribed or limited by budgetary or other resource constraints?

Co-ordination: Does the job involve responsibility for the co-ordination of separate tasks or jobs within the job holder's direct control—or is it concerned with the integration of activities across group boundaries—how wide and significant are these boundaries; do they stretch beyond the job holder's own function or organizational unit? Are priorities largely self-evident or prescribed—or are they difficult to agree in the face of competing demands from a number of external functional streams?

Monitoring and control: Is there a requirement to monitor progress against a plan or policy or is there a requirement simply to note and report deviations? What authority and responsibility does the job carry to alter plans as necessary and to re-allocate resources to ensure adherence to the plan? What impact does his freedom from control have on work groups other than his own?

2 RELATIONSHIPS

Under this heading, the assessment is concerned with the contacts generated by the job inside and outside the organization. Consideration is given to the demands the contacts make on the job holder and the social skills which have to be employed to obtain the co-operation, commitment and goodwill from others in order to achieve the job objectives. Two aspects are considered: the range of contacts and their depth.

Range: The number and type of persons contacted; are these concerned with just a few colleagues within a small group or is there a wide range of contacts inside and outside the organization? Are the contacts at an equivalent level or are some at a much senior level? Do these contacts involve simply passing or receiving information in a restricted field of activity or do they involve a reporting, advising or influencing situation covering a wide range of activity? Does the frequency and duration of the contacts cause disruption or harassment?

Depth: Does the nature of the job and its environment demand more than common courtesy in dealing with others—does it call for skills of persuasion and tact to secure agreement for action, *e.g.* on priorities? Do contacts have to be initiated by the job holder—and at what level—inside or outside the organization? Is there a requirement to promote group participation or involvement—demanding what level of skills in the management of interpersonal and inter-group conflict? Is the sensitivity and risk in the relationships—from a personal or business viewpoint—such as to demand an awareness of the need for appropriate behavioural response and the exercise of diplomacy and advocacy?

3 DECISIONS/PROBLEM SOLVING

The first two factors, Management and Relationships, are concerned with some of the important skills and other qualities which are needed to carry out the job. Clearly decisions are made and problem solving situations arise in managing a job and in dealing with other people.

The Decisions/Problem solving factor, however, is concerned with the end results of the job—the job objective; it concentrates therefore on 'operational' decisions and problems. It is the most important of the three assessment factors.

Under this factor, the assessors consider the decisions to be made in a job in terms of their contribution to the business, which includes such considerations as the importance of the basic subject matter, the complexity of the information required and available to work on, the knowledge, judgment and degree of originality needed, and the time pressures.

The main divisions of this factor are 'direct' decisions and 'problem solving and advisory' decisions. A 'direct' decision is one a job holder takes, an 'advisory' decision is one a job holder helps others to take.

Decisions ('direct' decisions)
  Discretion: Are decisions taken within a closely prescribed working system—or within more loosely defined but standardized working practices—or do they involve the prior interpretation of broad guide lines or policy? What sort of check or control is exercised at a higher level?
  Complexity: Does the job require frequent decisions under time pressure? Do decisions involve a choice between known alternatives? Do they involve consideration of a number of inter-relating factors? Is the information on which decisions are based readily to hand or does it have to be selected, sought out and interpreted? Do the decisions require an understanding of the responsibilities of other functional streams?
  Impact: Do the decisions commit other people to action—and to what level—work team, department or organization? Do they affect others' priorities or work targets? What could be the consequences of errors of omission of judgment? How long before the impact becomes evident—immediately or in the distant future?

Problem solving and advisory decisions
The solution of problems is involved to some degree in all decisions. This section of the assessment scheme is concerned primarily with jobs where the ultimate authority for action is divorced from the job or where the implementation may be remote in time. The expert 'advisor' is frequently in a position where he may carry no executive authority—but where his 'advice' or conclusions can only be ignored at peril. In other cases solutions to present problems may result in decisions determining future action which cannot be checked until after the action has been taken.
  Diagnostic skill: Are the problems self-evident or difficult to isolate and define? What intensity of analysis is required before key aspects can be identified? Is there need to separate symptoms from causes before problems can be defined in precise terms? To what extent do problems arise from known and predictable circumstances? To what extent do they arise in environments of high uncertainty and concerned with unprecedented situations?
  Complexity of solution: Is there an obvious answer to the problem—does it necessitate a choice from known possible solutions—is there need to test a number of alternatives and reach a solution by a process of repetitive testing and improvement? What is the degree of certainty or confidence in the solution to the problem?
  Skills and knowledge required: What level of technical or vocational skills, knowledge and experience is demanded by problems posed in the job? What intensity of reasoning is involved—ranging from selecting tested and proven alternatives to the highly creative?

As the assessment proceeds, each assessor will individually allot grade markings to each factor in turn and subsequently the panel will resolve any differences between individual markings by discussion, and then record a panel mark. Although, as I indicated earlier, the assessment panel should preferably include someone familiar with the type of job being assessed, in cases of conflict, averaged judgment is to be preferred to expert individual judgment because the situation is largely one of checkable fact rather than of something unmeasurable. The final step is then to read off the job grade from the formula converting marks to job grades.

One important point with regard to the practical working of the ICI scheme that I would draw attention to, is that the panel of assessors is not told the existing level for a job which is being re-examined, hence in theory the assessment might lower the job level. In practice, the consistency of marking between panels is such that this hardly ever occurs because of variations in judgment, but it can occur when a long-established job is looked at for the first time.

Such cases may have arisen from the job having drifted gradually upwards as the result of a supervisor confusing reward for the job holder's individual performance with actual level of job difficulty—a situation which the job evaluation scheme, once established, should prevent from recurring. It is important, therefore, that this fact be recognized. Remedies include moving the holder to a more responsible job or, in cases where the holder is judged to have reached his maximum potential, simply protecting actual salary level.

As I examined the factors in detail, you may well have queried the degree to which some of the aspects were relevant to situations prevailing in a formal information unit. Indeed, some are not, although I suspect that when adequate allowance is made for differences in terminology, there is greater relevance than may appear at first sight. I would suggest that, in any event, they comprise a framework against which we can expect to be measured, and in the light of which, therefore, we would be wise to measure up our jobs.

No matter how well a job evaluation scheme devised in-house may function, it has one disadvantage which becomes progressively more serious as the jobs under consideration become more responsible—it is not easily possible to make inter-firm comparisons to see how the remuneration which you apply to a particular level of job difficulty compares with that offered by other organizations. A commercially available variant of the points assessment method which has become popular because it can do just that is the 'Hay–MSL' method (sometimes called the Guide-Chart Profile Method).

In outline the scheme is not too different from the one I have just described.[4] A job description is first drawn up as in most schemes, but this is done jointly by the incumbent and by a Hay consultant, who may be internal or external, to ensure that all relevant aspects of the job are brought out in a standard way. The description is then evaluated by a panel of very senior executives guided by the consultant against three factors—Know-how, Problem-solving and Accountability—allocating points as appropriate. The complexity and inter-relationship of certain factors such as breadth/depth of knowledge is brought out by use of two- or three-dimensional grid arrangements as exemplified by Figure 3. A plot of individual salaries against scores is then constructed and can serve both to show the general pattern of remuneration within the organization (Figure 4) and also to effect inter-firm comparisons (Figure 5). Although the system has been most used to evaluate higher-level jobs it is generally applicable to L&I jobs.

I would stress that job evaluation schemes must not be regarded as scientific and objective because they are not. They are codified systems of value judgments in which the subjective element is even a strength in that it calls for a high

		BREADTH OF MANAGERIAL KNOW-HOW										
		Minimal			Partial			Substantial			Total		
		1	2	3	1	2	3	1	2	3	1	2	3
SKILLS	Primary												
	Secondary plus work indoctrination												
	Determinative special technical mastery												
	Exceptional professional mastery												

FIG. 3: *Know-how in the Hay–M.S.L. system. There are three dimensions to this factor: skills, which includes experience and technical expertise; breadth of managerial know-how and human relation skills. The numbers refer to the human relations skills: (1) marginal, (2) important and (3) crucial. This chart is shown merely to illustrate the Hay method; it is not a copy of an actual chart used by Hay–M.S.L., only a simplified example*

FIGURES 3, 4 AND 5 ARE REPRODUCED BY KIND PERMISSION OF THE PUBLISHERS FROM *Management development*, BUSINESS BOOKS, 1968 (REF. 4)

degree of staff involvement in formulation and introduction and hence of commitment to the product because the schemes are, or should be, both systematic and logical. In addition to constituting a potential control mechanism against inflation, a fair and equitable salary structure (we are taught by the behavioural scientists) is also an essential pre-requisite to establishing a high level of job motivation among staff. The relationship is not however quite as simple as might appear at first sight. An Indian, Lakhanpal, recently wrote on job evaluation 'if the Library Administration wants that the employees should

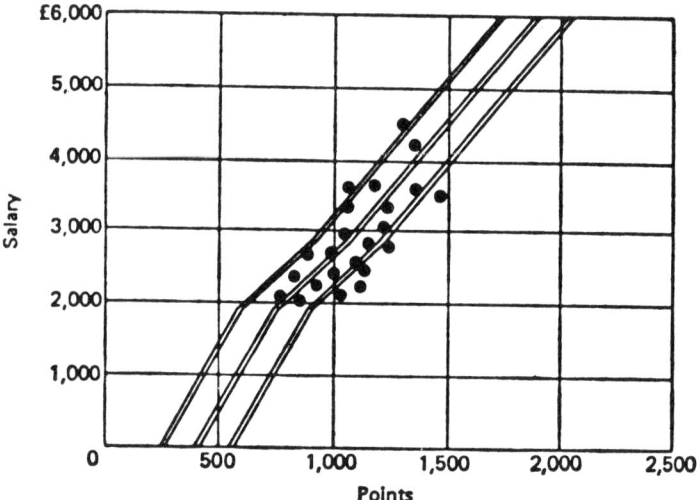

FIG. 4: *The general pattern of remuneration within a firm, shown on a scattergram. This chart is shown merely to illustrate the Hay method; it is not a copy of an actual chart used by Hay–M.S.L., only a simplified example*

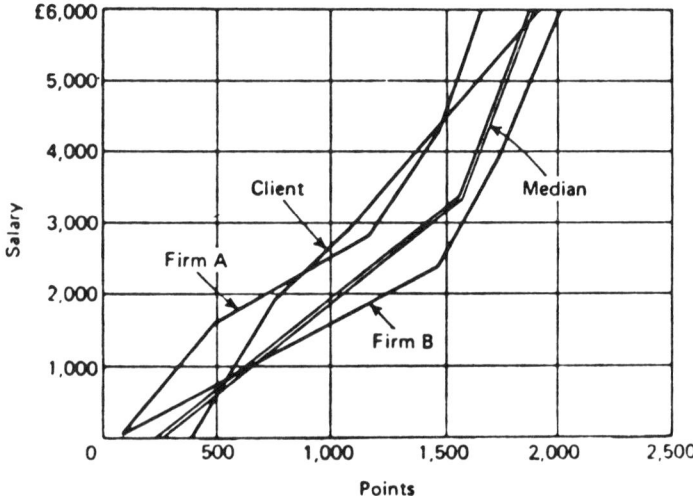

FIG. 5: *The market rating of jobs, charted to provide an inter-firm comparison. The median is the average of firms A and B; the actual diagrams plot the salary structures of more than twenty companies. This chart is shown merely to illustrate the Hay method; it is not a copy of an actual chart used by Hay–M.S.L., only a simplified example*

consider their work to be enjoyable and interesting, it must bring their salaries to an equitable level. A sound salary structure evolved after a careful job classification will increase job satisfaction'.[5] I would suggest that whilst a sound salary structure can increase satisfaction with a job, it does not increase satisfaction in the job. In fact the majority of evidence points towards such a structure as only making the recipient receptive to true job motivation, and suggests that a given individual is motivated by two classes of need—basic needs, and those that are socially determined, and that both of these must be satisfied to allow emotional maturity. These various needs have been helpfully portrayed[6] by an American psychologist, Maslow, as a five-level pyramid hierarchy of human needs, and he suggested that as one type becomes satisfied, and only at that point, the next higher type of need begins to exercise a subconscious motivation on the individual.

At the base of the pyramid are the primary physiological needs for food, clothing, shelter etc, which are optimally satisfied by adequate remuneration applied by a fair method. Job evaluation provides one such method. The individual then becomes receptive by similar stages of satisfaction to considerations of belonging, esteem and finally, of true job motivation. Herzberg, a further American worker, has extended this theory of needs in a way which has important practical applications for both job evaluation and staff motivation. Herzberg made an extensive examination of claimed job satisfactions and dissatisfactions among various classes of professional and non-professional staff in developed industrial countries and found[7] that the causes of satisfaction at work were not the same as the causes of dissatisfaction. If factors providing satisfaction in a job-situation were absent, and Herzberg called these motivating factors, the result was not dissatisfaction but simply indifference. Likewise, if causes of dissatisfaction were absent, and Herzberg called these hygiene factors, the result was not satisfaction but, again, indifference.

Two features are particularly significant relevant to the structuring of the job. The nature of the work itself is a motivating factor—give someone a poorly made-up job and he will complain, but only little and ephemerally, but provide a well-constructed job and the motivation will be widespread and long term.

Secondly, whereas one might expect salary and working conditions to be important, they are only so in a negative sense—when poor they cause dissatisfaction, but when good, they are not consciously noted. There is, in fact, strong correlation between the factors which give active satisfaction when present and those in the highest levels of Maslow's hierarchy, whilst those which cause most dissatisfaction when poor relate to the lower levels. Although Herzberg obtained supportive evidence for his theory from a very wide range of work groups he does not make reference to L&I staff.

Subsequent work has been reported[8] which attempts to fill this gap using data on North American librarians. Some caution is necessary in accepting the results since all those concerned provided the data as part of job motivation courses. Figures 6 and 7 summarize the responses. These show the same typical histogram of response found for the other groups, with motivators making up 99 per cent of all factors contributing to job satisfaction but to only 19 per cent of job

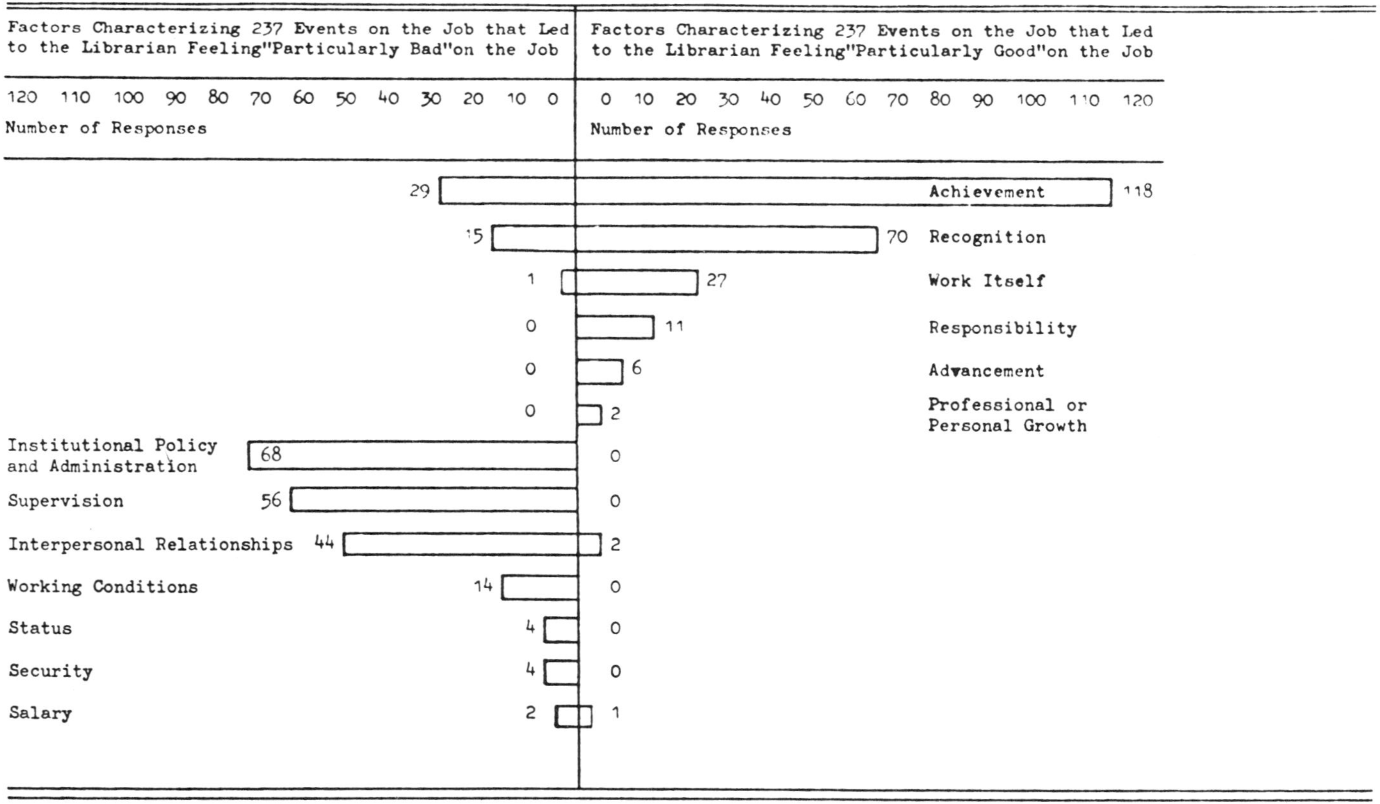

FIG. 6: *Factors affecting job responses as reported in two studies of librarians*

FIGURES 6 AND 7 REPRODUCED BY KIND PERMISSION OF THE PUBLISHERS, UNIVERSITY OF CHICAGO PRESS, FROM K. H. PLATE AND E. W. STONE IN *The Library Quarterly* APRIL 1974 (REF. 8) dissatisfiers whereas hygiene factors contributed 81 per cent of job dissatisfiers and only 1 per cent of satisfiers. However, in these studies, salary concerns seems to have played only a minor role.

Thus we can see that the role of job evaluation in motivating performance is that of pre-conditioner, in that it can ensure the adequate hygiene satisfaction that is necessary before staff become receptive to positively motivating factors, of which achievement, recognition, responsibility, and the nature of the work itself—all factors divorced from remuneration considerations—are the most

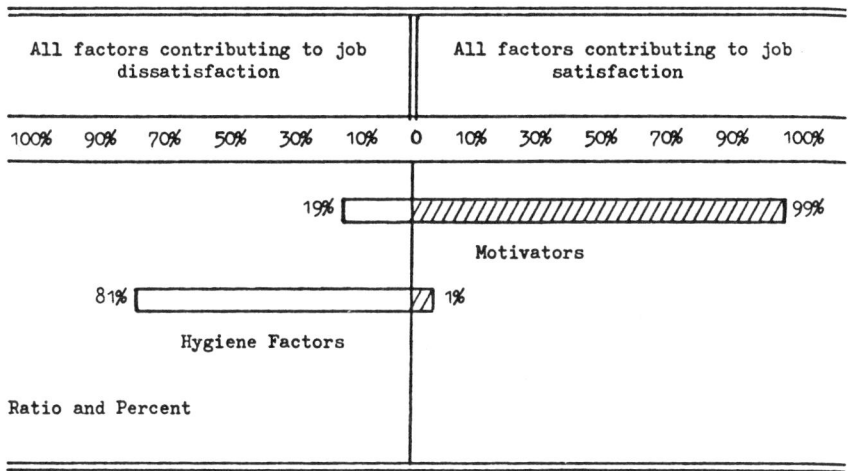

FIG. 7: *Relationship between sources of dissatisfaction and sources of satisfaction in the job situation*

important. In a sense, therefore, you might say that pre-conditioning a worker towards job motivation was a spin-off from a successful job evaluation. A great deal of effort is needed to obtain the information necessary to carry out job evaluation and the final part of my paper draws attention to other benefits which can be derived more directly from use of this information (Figure 8).

One such is the contribution which can be made to organizational analysis and change—task elements, functions and responsibilities can be reallocated into new work mixes which can lead to more efficient working and more meaningful jobs. Mutual discussion of job content leads to improved communications and shared information.

Clearly defined and evaluated jobs also aid in selection and recruitment of staff as well as in training and development. Well-defined career ladders can be constructed. Staff can be transferred to other parts of the organization without resulting salary disarray.

However, the most important spin-off, in my opinion, is that job evaluation provides a valuable reference framework for periodically appraising the performance of an individual. An organization clearly does not necessarily have to practise job evaluation of its L&I jobs in order to appraise performance but in the absence of a clearly defined and related network of jobs it is easy to fall into the trap of criticizing the personality of your staff instead of concentrating on the job. Even positive criticism in the abstract, whilst it may flatter, cannot lead to increased effectiveness. The human personality is a complex and highly abstract concept and attempts to judge the individual in terms of his personality are likely to induce long-term hostility and block fruitful communication. When the level of the individual's job performance has been appraised, he can be rewarded by applying positive or negative increments to the basic salary as determined through job evaluation.[9]

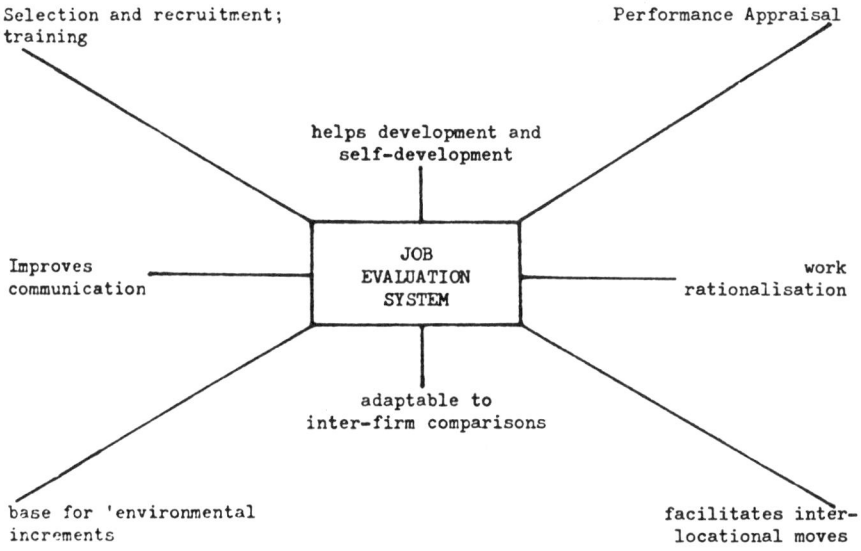

FIG. 8: *Spin-off from job evaluation*

But from whatever point of view you may be considering job evaluation, do remember that it is a slow-moving beast with high inertia. I was contacted recently by the systems development manager of a well-known organization. He told me that a man to whom he had recently allocated the job of creating a new library now wished to become its librarian, but that he, the supervisor, was unable to convince the firm's job evaluators that the new job was worth more than the minimum level in his own section. Having had his attention drawn to my paper he telephoned me, implicitly in the hope of an instant solution. However, if the job was indeed undervalued, then a re-presentation would be necessary, more aligned to the terms of reference against which jobs in that particular organization were judged and this could not be accomplished in isolation overnight. In this field, patience is indeed a virtue.

REFERENCES

1 DE JONG, J. R. Job evaluation: history and trends, in *Some approaches to national job evaluation*. London, Foundation for Business Responsibility, 1972.

2 BRITISH INSTITUTE OF MANAGEMENT, Management Reading List, 'Job Evaluation and Job Grading' is a useful guide to basic reading.
3 BOODSON, K. The significance of staff structure and promotion policy. *Aslib Proceedings*, 22 (6) June 1970, p. 267-75.
4 BERNSTEIN, L. *Management development*. London, Business Books, 1968.
5 LAKHANPAL, S. K. Job classification and evaluation—the basis for equitable salary administration in libraries. *Indian Librarian*, 24 (1) June 1969, p. 5.
6 MASLOW, A. H. A theory of human motivation. *Psychological Review*, 50, July 1943, p. 370-96.
7 HERZBERG, F. *Work and the nature of man*. Cleveland, USA, World Publishing Co., 1966.
8 PLATE, K. H. *and* STONE, E. W. Factors affecting librarians' job satisfaction: a report of two studies. *The Library Quarterly*, 44 (2) April 1974, p. 97.
9 For a fuller discussion of job motivation and performance appraisal *see* DUTTON, B. G. Staff management and staff participation. *Aslib Proceedings*, 25 (3) March 1973, p. 111-25.

The views expressed here are those of the author and not necessarily those of ICI Ltd. Nevertheless he is most grateful for information received from various colleagues in the company.

Library Staff Development through Performance Appraisal

By Dimity S. Berkner

The use of performance evaluation is suggested as a means of improving staff motivation and expertise and of providing a higher level of library service. A summary of the types and uses of performance appraisal and the arguments for and against its effectiveness are followed by a proposal for including this tool in a total program of management communication, goal-setting, and evaluation as they can impact on professional development and job satisfaction rather than directly on promotions and salary increases.

IN AN EFFECTIVE academic library the professional staff can be the most valuable resource—more important than any other one component: books, card catalog, documents, etc. A good professional staff is the key to all the rest, providing access to information whether through selection, cataloging, reference, interlibrary loan, or administration of others. Giving the level of service that offers total access to information requires a staff that is well trained, highly motivated, and cooperative; and the encouragement of such a staff has been a continuing goal of administrators.

One method of encouraging higher standards of performance that has been popular for about the last twenty years in business is the use of performance evaluation. A variety of appraisal techniques have been used, ranging from essays to absolute rating scales, forced comparisons, or ranking of employees. (An excellent short summary of standard methods and their applicability was provided by Winston Oberg in 1972.)[1]

Performance appraisal is applied for a variety of goals:

1. To improve performance in the present job.
2. To provide a basis for recommending promotion, salary increases, or dismissal.
3. To give the employee a chance to "know where he or she stands" in the supervisor's estimation.
4. To develop an inventory of human resources for the use of management—a record of the available talents and potential among the present staff.
5. To provide a method of counseling and encouraging staff members to grow and to plan for future development.

As early as 1957, however, Douglas McGregor pointed out the dangers of using the same technique to try to accomplish such diverse goals.[2] The evaluation of a subordinate can force the supervisor into "playing God," judging performance on personality rather than on results, employing subjective standards, demanding that one employee be measured against another in a win-lose situation, and requiring an uncomfortable face-to-face interview in which

---

Reprinted by permission of the American Library Association from "Library Staff Development through Performance Appraisal," Dimity S. Beckner, *College and Research Libraries*, Vol. 40, No. 4 (July 1979), pp. 335-44, copyright © 1979 by the American Library Association.

neither manager nor subordinate is prepared to give or receive criticism.

The problems inherent in traditional appraisal systems are summarized in Marjorie Johnson's 1972 academic library survey,[3] and specific psychological errors to avoid when evaluating an employee are described in the Pennsylvania State University Libraries "Management Guide to Performance Evaluation."[4]

These errors include the "halo effect" (an overall or early impression of the employee that affects the rating of the individual work factors); the "central tendency" error (rating most people toward the middle of any scale); unconscious prejudice or partiality based on race, politics, friendship, etc.; "contrast" error (rating an employee on his or her potential, rather than on actual performance); inappropriate upgrading of all ratings (to compete with what the supervisor thinks that other department heads are doing, to prevent unfavorable reflections on the supervisor's managerial ability, or to avoid any direct confrontation with the employee); as well as many others.

Pizam discussed still another intrinsic error, "social differentiation."[5] It has been found that some appraisers have difficulty in evaluating subordinates objectively simply because they never recognize wide differentiations in behavior and do not use most of the scale in rating their employees. "It appears therefore that the act of appraisal . . . merely expresses the appraiser's differentiating ability or style of rating behavior. . . . Low differentiators tend to ignore or suppress differences, perceiving the universe as more uniform than it really is."[6]

The credibility of traditional performance evaluation programs was further undermined by studies done at the General Electric Company, which concluded:

Criticism has a negative effect on achievement of goals.

Praise [relating to general performance characteristics] has little effect one way or another.

Performance improves most when specific goals are established.

Defensiveness resulting from critical appraisal produces inferior performance.

Coaching should be a day-to-day, not a once-a-year, activity.

Mutual goal setting, not criticism, improves performance.

Interviews designed primarily to improve a man's [sic] performance should not at the same time weigh his salary or promotion in the balance.

Participation by the employee in the goal-setting procedure helps produce favorable results.[7]

As one of the few carefully documented, methodologically acceptable management studies on the effect of criticism and mutual goal setting, the study has provided the rationale for many recent performance appraisal programs—including the one proposed in this paper. The conclusions reached at General Electric support current psychological findings about the use of behavior modification to encourage and reinforce positive behavior while extinguishing negative behavior by, to put it simply, ignoring it.

MANAGEMENT-BY-OBJECTIVES (MBO)

An important part of the General Electric study was to confirm what Peter Drucker had presented and McGregor had recommended years earlier: the use of management-by-objectives (MBO) as the basis for professional performance evaluation.[8,9] This system involves the supervisor and employee in the establishment of priorities and goals, with specific objectives to be accomplished (by a certain date) to further these goals. The evaluative process then becomes an analysis with an emphasis on the future and on the strengths and potential of the employee. It should blunt some of the judgmental aspects of appraisal and promote a better relationship between superior and subordinate.

An article by Thompson and Dalton provides a good defense of the management-by-objectives approach because it is future-oriented rather than focusing on mistakes of the past. It is an open system in which employees are compared with their own objectives rather than on a scale where some must be ranked lower than others, and it is a flexible system that can be tailored to promote the strengths of each individual.[10]

The pendulum has now swung away from the old judgmental ranking scales with their emphasis on "traits" (aspects of personality, which are supposed to have a bearing on job performance, such as "dependability," "initiative," etc.) toward management-by-objectives and/or a discussion of observable behavior only (number of books cataloged, reference questions answered). Sometimes this is supported by the use of techniques such as "critical incidents," where the supervisor records actual occurrences that exemplify positive or negative behavior.

We are beginning to recognize the use of performance appraisal as a tool that can be appropriate for counseling, career planning, and staff development. A summary of recent research into the use of performance appraisal, with suggestions for affecting motivation, is found in Belcher's excellent text *Compensation Administration*.[11,12]

PERFORMANCE APPRAISAL FOR STAFF DEVELOPMENT

In 1971 Ernest deProspo[13] applied Kindall and Gatza's five-step program[14] to libraries in an effort to focus on employee growth through appraisal. This program includes discussions by the individual and the supervisor on job content, setting of performance targets by the employee, review of these with the supervisor, establishment of evaluative checkpoints, and appraisal of results at the end of the time period.

At about the same time Harry Levinson sounded a warning against unqualified use of MBO. Levinson called MBO "one of the greatest management illusions" and recommended that an MBO program include consideration of an individual's motivation and personal goals, avoidance of the static job description, which is so often a basis for the objectives, and the recognition that the way in which an individual goes about achieving these goals can be as important as the goals themselves.[15,16] He makes a point that is particularly applicable to libraries, since supportive working relationships can do so much to improve service and increase motivation.

Every organization is a social system, a network of interpersonal relationships. A man may do an excellent job by objective standards of measurement, but may fail miserably as a partner, subordinate, superior or colleague.[17]

In the library these interpersonal relationships can be even more important because so many areas of professional librarianship cannot be appropriately measured by objective standards. How does one cope with the colleague in the selection department who refuses to buy interdisciplinary material out of his or her departmental book budget, thus keeping carefully within set financial limits and building a narrow, specialized collection in depth, but ignoring new fields of interest to the students and cross-disciplinary faculty? A straight MBO approach to evaluation is unlikely to reveal or discourage this inadequacy.

Current practice in academic libraries, according to Yarbrough's *ARL Management Supplement*,[18] includes much use of mutual goal setting and evaluation by librarian and supervisor (and often library director), along with or as a substitute for other procedures such as traditional appraisals (in checklist or essay form), peer evaluations (mainly to recommend for or against promotion, tenure, or salary increases), and even appraisal of supervisors by their subordinates.

One of the most innovative and detailed approaches to performance evaluation was developed at McGill University Libraries in cooperation with the ARL Office of University Library Management Studies in 1975.[19] The key to its uniqueness is the focus on supervisory training in motivation, evaluation, and counseling that appear to be essential in developing such a program. It then recommends the setting of unit and individual work goals, followed by semiannual performance reviews. Salary decisions are treated as a separate procedure, although a formal, annual evaluation does go into the employee's file.

The bases for the McGill program are excellent, but there seems to be a heavy emphasis upon improving the *library's* performance with too little regard for the individual's motivation and for the General Electric findings that "criticism has a negative effect on achievement of goals" and that *general* praise (which is treated almost as an aside in the McGill program) has little effect either way. While the McGill program does recognize that an individual's performance may be helped or hindered by that of some other unit, it does not deal with a solution to this dependency or with the idea of teamwork.

THE "CRITICAL INCIDENT" TECHNIQUE

Current performance appraisal, as exemplified by MBO, by statements of accomplishments on typical faculty (library) evaluation forms, and by the McGill program, focuses not on behavior but on the results of behavior. This stems from the aversion to judging personality when one should be measuring performance. It is certainly true that goals can be legitimately attained by many means, but there is a danger in considering only quantifiable or objective achievements in a service-oriented field like librarianship.

In other words, the *way in which* one reaches specified objectives is as important as actually reaching them. However, the process of identifying appropriate behavior in specific instances is a difficult, time-consuming one—but one that can lead to genuine staff growth and to the development of future managers and/or specialists. One useful technique in describing specific behavior (such as how to handle the reference interview) is the "critical incident" process.

Let us suppose that the head librarian of the reference department has two librarians who need to be developed into reference specialists. In observing the behavior of the first librarian, the department head might note that individual failed to probe sufficiently when a student inquired about articles on air pollution. The librarian pointed out *Public Affairs Information Service*; the student wandered away, and the librarian returned to a project of selecting books from *Choice*.

The second librarian received a query on behavior modification and, not stopping to find out that the student was a freshman with a two-page summary to prepare, totally overwhelmed the student with a half-hour explanation on the use of *Psychological Abstracts*, on-line access to the ERIC data base, and a tremendous amount of material in the card catalog. During the process, however, the librarian forgot to explain to the freshman how to get from a bibliographic journal citation to the actual printed article.

Now these descriptions are exaggerated, but they illustrate that the "critical incident" records actual, specific behaviors, which can then form the basis for a future learning discussion. It is also quite important that positive incidents be recorded so that the employee can recognize and receive reinforcement for appropriate behaviors.

PERFORMANCE PROFILES

Critical incidents can also form the basis for a general list of important behavior aspects in each department or in general interaction in the library. In order to analyze *how* something was accomplished or the *quality* of performance, it is necessary to identify the important behaviors expected of employees and how those can be recognized in specific situations, for example, in open meetings, in patron contact, in telephone answering, etc. The actual process of identifying these is most helpful if everyone participates.

In another example from business of the use of critical incidents, the Corning Glass Company developed a fascinating "performance profile" that isolated behaviors which managers could specifically identify, recognize, and discuss with subordinates to give them concrete ideas on how to improve performance and strengthen managerial abilities.[20] A sample of the behaviors that were isolated by identifying approximately 300 critical incidents and translating these into 150 general behavioral descriptions included:

a. Objects to ideas before they are explained.
b. Takes the initiative in group meetings.
c. Has difficulty in meeting project deadlines.
d. Sees his problems in light of the problems of others (that is, does not limit his thinking to his own position or organizational unit.)[21]

Appropriate behavioral descriptions for each individual, depending on his or her position and goals, can be selected from such a general list, to be used as a personal performance profile to reflect strengths, weaknesses, and planned areas of improvement.

DEVELOPING MANAGERIAL ABILITIES

At the beginning of this paper I said that the professional staff of an academic library can be its most important resource. I now suggest that positive, constructive performance appraisal can contribute to the development of that resource both for the good of the library and for the personal and professional growth of the individual librarian; and that in the long run these goals are more relevant to the library than concern about using evaluation for salary and promotion purposes per se.

A typical university library has a percentage of librarians who, having served for a few years, have tenure in fact if not in theory. Operating at a level of membership motivation (wishing to continue to belong to the organization) but not sufficiently motivated to perform,[22] they often develop attitudes that tend to encourage mediocrity, until they are working at a decreased level of output, service, morale, and personal satisfaction.[23] This atmosphere can discourage new employees and cause the loss of valuable talent to the library.

A staff development program has the potential to expand both specific service skills and general managerial abilities. By managerial abilities I am not necessarily referring only to the ability to supervise but to organizational and leadership qualities, generally accepted as desirable managerial traits in any organizational setting. Charles Gibbons called them the "marks of a mature manager"[24] and stated that the individual should:

1. Possess well-defined goals.
2. Be able to allocate resources according to priorities.
3. Be able to make decisions, act upon them, and accept responsibility for them.
4. Be willing to compromise.
5. Be able to delegate and to depend on subordinates.
6. Be self-motivated and self-controlled.
7. Be able to organize, plan, and communicate for effective use of resources.
8. Maintain good relationships with others.
9. Possess emotional maturity and the internal resources to cope with frustration, disappointment, and stress.
10. Be able to appraise oneself and one's performance objectively, to admit to being wrong.
11. Expect that one will keep on growing, improve one's performance, and continue to develop.

I would add to this list two qualities that Harlan Cleveland stresses in his excellent book *The Future Executive*.[26] These are a tolerance for ambiguity and an openness to change. A performance appraisal program that is aimed at professional growth should contribute to the development of these characteristics in the professional staff.[27]

THE LIBRARY AS AN INTERACTIVE SYSTEM

If libraries are to participate actively in technological developments and cope positively with the information explosion while faced with the pressures of decreasing staff and collection funds, then the best talents of that staff must be recognized, cultivated, and used. An emphasis on teamwork rather than competition, an acknowledgment that each department is part of a cooperative system, is essential.

Discussions and negotiations for participation in national and regional library networks and academic consortia have become commonplace; yet in my experience, true day-to-day cooperation among departments within one organization is less usual.

The need for accountability and performance measures is recognized when dealing with large library projects, and these serve as motivating factors for the project directors. In a similar way, performance appraisal can be used as feedback within a library to keep the system functioning on the highest level and as one organization rather than as fragmented pieces with conflicting goals.

In the establishment of a performance appraisal program for an individual library, the organization and its employees can be considered as an interactive system involved with mutual goals for the library, the department, the unit, and the librarian, including for each a feedback loop where goal setting is one input, performance is an output, and evaluation is used to correct the system and keep it on course. The action of departments and users upon each other should be kept in mind at every stage of the program.

For example, the interdependence of the acquisitions, collection development, and catalog departments in providing access to a book is usually recognized and talked about—like the weather—but little is done to contribute to meaningful cooperation. Goals can be set for such things as the quantity of orders placed in a given time, the length of time for receipt of the book, and optimum use of bibliographic searchers in handling the book before and during cataloging. But much of this is based on the quantity and cyclical flow of orders from the selection librarians into the acquisitions department or the percentage of receipts through standing orders and approval programs, which the cataloging department can then handle. The development of such quantitative goals, therefore, might best be done jointly with an open acknowledgment of the interdependence of these departments rather than with a fruitless competition between them.

A Program Proposal

Let us consider the use of performance evaluation in an interactive system that includes supervisory training, mutual goal setting, peer discussions, and teamwork, with an emphasis on behavior as well as results, as a means of developing future leaders and promoting better library service while providing satisfaction for the individual.

The program outlined below is an attempt to use performance appraisal as a library management development tool. It can be modified to meet individual needs and library situations, and whether it should be implemented formally or informally depends to a great extent on the resources of manpower and time available. It does require the support of the library administration, but the procedures themselves could easily be guided by members of a professional development committee if there is no specific personnel librarian at the institution. In any case, its focus should remain the same: communication training for supervisors, goal setting as part of an interactive system, positive motivation, and the highest utilization of and response to individual needs, skills, and strengths.

Step 1: Training of Library Supervisors

The goal setting and analysis, both individually and collectively, that this program requires will call for supervisors to act as facilitators, to listen carefully and accurately, to spot nonverbal messages, to keep a discussion on track, and to avert the gameplaying that often develops out of self-defense when one's ego is threatened. To prepare them for this, the first step is a workshop for supervisors. This ought best be led by an outside consultant or an internal specialist in communication skills (perhaps from the psychology, public administration, or business department in a college or university) to cover active listening, group discussion leadership, how to reach a consensus, how to motivate positively, etc. An interesting approach might be to make use of *The OK Boss* by Muriel James[27] as background reading to introduce the concept of transactional analysis and then to use this tool as a basis for the communication skills to be developed in the workshop.

Step 2: Goal Setting

This involves group meetings for all staff units of the library, to discuss the purposes and responsibilities of the library, the department, and the individual. These discussions ought to begin at the level of the library director and associate directors meeting with their department heads. It is easy enough to say that a library provides information, but what are its priorities?

In a specific academic setting, who comes first—faculty, students (graduate, undergraduate, transfer), community, alumni, university staff, library staff, who? Each has different needs, and the priorities that are established will ultimately have an impact on the type and scope of reference service, the emphasis in book selection, the key hours for staffing public desks or keeping the library open, etc.

What are the priorities in terms of time versus money, expenditures for staff salaries versus books, for automated systems, for cooperative projects? (If any part of the staff is unionized, the union will have to be brought into the discussions at some point too.)

This kind of discussion and planning is so often lost in the day-to-day, crisis management that harried administrators are forced into. I realize that the examples above are issues for which there is no one right answer, but some consideration and thought given to these priorities at the beginning of the project is the best basis for rational and consistent goal setting in each department down the line.

As supervisors next participate in sessions of goal setting for their departments, it will be quickly recognized by the group that each department member has certain strengths that can be most effectively used in particular projects. This does not deny the need for job descriptions and the use of these in setting objectives (as has been generally recommended). However, job descriptions are static and based on past experience and needs. Goal setting, which looks toward the future, optimal utilization of available resources, and an open feeling of cooperation among peers to achieve similar objectives can result in a whole new use of skills.

A traditional reference department, which assigns each librarian to three hours of desk duty a day, might find that the optimal use of manpower would call for a division on the basis of subject expertise (depending on the question asked), with a student assistant to respond to those general queries that are routine (Where's the drinking fountain? What are the hours of the reserve reading room? Where's the latest issue of *Readers' Guide?*) At the same time the reference librarians may realize that their work of interpreting the card catalog to users might be enhanced by a short orientation or refresher course run by the catalog department for the rest of the staff. They might wish to be brought up to date on such questions as, What's the best way to locate government documents? How are branch library holdings handled in the main catalog?

These thoughts lead us directly into step 3.

Step 3: System Interaction

As each department has a chance to discuss its responsibilities, priorities, and goals internally, the staff members will recognize their interdependence with other departments. The supervisor can keep track of these relationships and the particular points of congruency, to be used as a basis for discussions between departments. The usual procedure, when conflicts of interest arise, has been for the two department heads to meet privately and try to work it out. More often than not, however, a win-lose situation develops in which neither can compromise without losing face. A general meeting between the acquisitions and the catalog departments to discuss bibliographic searching, with the head of technical services as facilitator, can do much to clear the air, promote cooperation, and develop a workable compromise—or at least foster an understanding of the other point of view.

Step 4: Refresher

At this point, if not before, it is time for a one-day refresher workshop for the supervisors. They will have participated in goal-setting discussions with their own superiors, with their own departments, and with related departments (all group sessions) and will now have all kinds of situations to discuss: where their group got off the track, when the expected consensus was not reached, where face-saving or game-playing took the place of constructive negotiations. Role-playing and further guidance in transactional analysis and facilitation are appropriate here.

Step 5: Individual Goal Setting

Each librarian should now be prepared to list his or her goals—professional, departmental, and personal career or life goals—relating them to the operation of the department and the library, building on strengths in order to best utilize one's talents. Each goal should be accompanied by specific, recognizable means to attain this. For instance, the librarian whose goal is to head the acquisitions department might plan to prepare for this responsibility by:

1. Gaining knowledge of publishers and vendors through regular reading of *Publishers Weekly*, scanning catalogs, and visiting exhibitors' displays at conventions;

2. Attending acquisitions discussion groups and applicable committee meetings at professional conferences;

3. Taking a continuing education course in out-of-print acquisitions;

4. Assisting with budget and book fund allocations (with the support of the present department head).

The supervisor will then take this list of goals and the specific means to achieve them and discuss these with the staff member, offering guidance, suggestions, and support. The more positive the response that can be given, the better. At the same time, however, the manager has an obligation to see that the goals and tactics are realistic—within the librarian's abilities but requiring a consistent effort.

Specific target dates must be set wherever possible, and if the goal or project is a long-term one, then benchmarks should be established to measure interim achievement. If the librarian's goal is to become a specialist in rare books, this may require courses, conferences, contacts, reading, an internship or exchange, etc. To begin with, a tentative curriculum can be listed, the most relevant conferences targeted, a special collections bibliography prepared in an area that will benefit the library users. Out of this may come an application for a grant, travel funds, or professional leave time, and a structured program to achieve this expertise.

The supervisor must also be realistic with the employee, even encouraging him or her to seek other opportunities if the librarian's goals are not compatible with the library situation at all, or when the librarian is really ready for additional responsibilities but no openings are expected to exist for some time. In all areas, once agreement is reached, the supervisor has an obligation to assist in the achievement of the goals.

By listing individual goals and strategies and then discussing these with the supervisor, the librarian will also begin formulating a performance profile that shows strengths and developmental needs.[28] These are relative to the individual, not on a scale that compares one person with another. As this profile is developed, it can form the basis for future appraisals and then future goals. Figure 1 gives an example of the form that might be used for this purpose.

Step 6: Critical Incidents

Another component in building a performance profile is the use of critical incidents, as described earlier. This technique should be used informally to record observable, applicable occurrences, rather than depending upon memory, judgment, and impressions. Emphasis should be placed on specific, positive contributions made by the employee and on noting occasions when the librarian does demonstrate improvement in an area of the performance profile as this is developed. The critical incidents will form the basis of private discussions between the supervisor and the librarian, both to specifically praise good performance and to determine individual strengths and weaknesses that both parties recognize are pertinent to goal achievement.

For the library with sufficient time or interest, an extrapolation of performance needs from critical incidents can form the basis for preparing general performance profile characteristics against which each staff member may wish to measure himself or herself.[29]

Step 7: Review and Analysis

An essential part of performance evaluation is to establish feedback loops through frequent, supportive, scheduled, and unscheduled work review and analysis sessions, again building on strengths and future potential rather than on past performance failures. The first informal checkpoint should be in three months, with a midyear goal reevaluation after six months. This is the time to redefine goals that no longer seem realistic or where financial or technological developments in the library require new responsibilities or new directions.

	Strength	Weakness	Improving
ability to set priorities			
organizational perspective			
ability to complete a project			
decisiveness			
accuracy			
willingness to delegate			
ability to follow up			

Name _____ Date Set _____ Interim Follow-Up _____ Review Date _____

Fig. 1
Performance Appraisal Form

At each step—the first unit meetings, the interdepartmental discussions, the individual goal setting and reviews—it is up to the supervisor to keep the conversations focused on the relevant topics (without stifling productive discussions), to come to decisions, and to record progress.

Preliminary preparation by all parties will contribute to productive meetings, but it is easy for busy staff members to forget to prepare lists or goals before the meeting is scheduled to start. To avoid this, it is helpful to allow fifteen minutes at the start of the unit meetings particularly for each person to consider the subject of the meeting and his or her views on it and to make a list of goals and priorities for discussion with the group.

Step 9: Evaluation of the Evaluation

Since this is an experimental program, which should be designed and adapted to respond to staff and service needs, an evaluation of its effectiveness is necessary. This can be done in two parts:

1. An attitude questionnaire for staff, management, and client groups (faculty and students, library users and nonusers). The same questionnaire should be administered before the program begins, after one year of activity, and after two.

2. An examination of actual goals achieved after two years—on each level and through interaction and cooperation among the parts of the library system. All examples of cooperation, improvement of service, or professional development that were not originally specified goals should be noted as well, with an attempt to discover whether these arose in part or in whole out of the performance evaluation program.

CONCLUSION

The entire process of defining responsibilities, establishing goals and the means to achieve them, developing performance profiles, and then evaluating achievement should all follow a regular cycle. The process should begin again annually with goal setting by the library administration, and a refresher course in communication for the supervisors or the entire staff would also not be amiss.

The proposed program is, indeed, a time-consuming one. The underlying principles of MBO and participatory management, however, have been applied in academic libraries around the country through the Management Review and Analysis Program[30] and its more recent small-library counterpart, the Academic Library Development Program.[31] In contrast, this proposal presents an opportunity to improve communication, performance, and morale through a limited area of library management, which can, however, have broad-reaching effects. With support from the library administration (mandatory for the success of any of these projects), the old concept of performance evaluation will make a positive impact on librarians and library service.

REFERENCES

1. Winston Oberg, "Make Performance Appraisal Relevant," *Harvard Business Review* 50:61–67 (Jan.–Feb. 1972).
2. Douglas McGregor, "An Uneasy Look at Performance Appraisal," *Harvard Business Review* 35:89–94 (May–June 1957).
3. Marjorie Johnson, "Performance Appraisal for Librarians—A Survey," *College & Research Libraries* 33:359–67 (Sept. 1972).
4. Pennsylvania State University Libraries, "Management Guide to Performance Evaluation," February 15, 1972. In Association of Research Libraries, Office of University Library Management Studies, Systems and Procedures Exchange Center, *SPEC Kit: Performance Review* (Washington, D.C.: Association of Research Libraries, Office of University Library Management Studies, 1974).
5. Abraham Pizam, "Social Differentiation—A New Psychological Barrier to Performance Appraisal," *Public Personnel Management* 4:244–47 (July 1975).
6. Ibid., p.245.
7. Herbert H. Meyer, Emanuel Kay, and John R. P. French, Jr., "Split Roles in Performance Appraisal," *Harvard Business Review* 43:124 (Jan.–Feb. 1965).
8. Peter Drucker, *The Practice of Management* (New York: Harper & Bros., 1954).
9. McGregor, "An Uneasy Look at Performance Appraisal," p.91.
10. Paul H. Thompson and Gene W. Dalton,

"Performance Appraisal: Managers Beware," *Harvard Business Review* 48:149–57 (Jan.–Feb. 1970).
11. David W. Belcher, *Compensation Administration* (Englewood Cliffs: Prentice-Hall, 1974), esp., p.199–215.
12. An opposing point of view is presented by E. C. Keil, *Performance Appraisal and the Manager* (New York: Lebhar-Friedman Books, 1977). This is an excellent practical summary of performance review, with emphasis on the interview itself, but Keil concludes that a manager is not qualified to become involved in long-range career development; this is better left to an outside consultant. Believing that most libraries cannot afford this luxury, I have proposed an alternative approach in the second half of this article.
13. Ernest DeProspo, "Personnel Evaluation as an Impetus to Growth," *Library Trends* 20:60–70 (July 1971).
14. Alva F. Kindall and James Gatza, "Positive Program for Performance Appraisal," *Harvard Business Review* 41:153–66 (Nov.–Dec. 1963).
15. Harry Levinson, "Management by *Whose* Objectives?" *Harvard Business Review* 48:125–34 (July–Aug. 1970).
16. Harry Levinson, "Appraisal of *What* Performance?" *Harvard Business Review* 54:30–36 (July–Aug. 1976).
17. Levinson, "Management by *Whose* Objectives?" p.127.
18. Larry N. Yarbrough, "Performance Appraisal in Academic and Research Libraries," *ARL Management Supplement* 3 (May 1975).
19. Association of Research Libraries, Office of University Library Management Studies and McGill University Libraries, *Staff Performance Evaluation Program at the McGill University Libraries: A Program Description of a Goals-Based Performance Evaluation Process with Accompanying Supervisor's Manual* (Washington, D.C.: ARL Office of University Library Management Studies, 1976).
20. Michael Beer and Robert A. Ruh, "Employee Growth through Performance Management," *Harvard Business Review* 54:59–66 (July–Aug. 1976).
21. Ibid., p.62.
22. For further comments and citations, see the discussion of equity theory and expectancy theory in Belcher, *Compensation Administration*, p.50–68.
23. An expansion of these ideas can be found in Edward Roseman, *Confronting Nonpromotability: How to Manage a Stalled Career* (New York: AMACOM, 1977). Part one, "Concerns of the Manager" (p.1–148), gives advice on appraising, counseling, and motivating employees.
24. Charles C. Gibbons, "Marks of a Mature Manager," *Business Horizons* 18:54–56 (Oct. 1975).
25. Harlan Cleveland, *The Future Executive: A Guide for Tomorrow's Managers* (New York: Harper & Row, 1972).
26. Practical aspects of the appraisal interview in developing mature behavior (which he calls Q4 attitudes) are detailed in Robert E. Lefton and others, *Effective Motivation Through Performance Appraisal* (New York: Wiley, 1977), esp., p.282–90.
27. Muriel James, *The OK Boss* (Reading, Mass.: Addison-Wesley, 1975).
28. This is discussed in detail in Beer and Ruh, "Employee Growth," p.63. However, they suggest that the supervisors use an already developed performance profile and rate each employee. I believe a similar device can be developed by the librarian and supervisor together, even where there is no personnel specialist available for regular assistance.
29. As done at the Corning Glass Company (discussed above) and described by Beer and Ruh, "Employee Growth."
30. Michael K. Buckland, ed., "The Management Review and Analysis Program: A Symposium," *Journal of Academic Librarianship* 1:4–14 (Jan. 1976).
31. Grady Morein and others, "The Academic Library Development Program," *College & Research Libraries* 38:37–45 (Jan. 1977).

Part X
UNIONIZATION

Introduction

Unionization of librarians is a relatively new phenomenon. Traditionally, librarians have tended to view joining any sort of union or participating in union activities as inconsistent with professionalism. The results of this point of view have been, in part, the development of immense professional associations (such as the American Library Association) whose interests are oriented toward issues rather than working conditions. Nevertheless, as library salaries and working conditions continue to remain relatively stagnant, strong pressures develop among library staff to initiate some sort of collective action to secure those things with which unions have been generally concerned—salaries, benefits, and good working conditions.

In the past, these pressures have taken many forms. On college and university campuses, quasi-union organizations such as A.A.U.P. have been quick to enlist librarians in their quest for greater faculty benefits. Municipalities, especially the larger ones with already well-established public service employee unions, found themselves faced with a new breed of militant librarian, one quite willing to join with other civil servants in seeking redress for actual or imagined wrongs. These librarians, far different from the stereotype often promoted by those unfamiliar with the profession, not only were willing to take action leading to strikes and work stoppages, but also refused to view such activities as inconsistent with their professional status. Librarians who were comfortable in their jobs, who participated in decision making, who had clearly recognized rights and responsibilities embodied in written contracts, were more ready and able to perform their duties than those who did not have such benefits.

The first article in this section, written by George Viele, a public library director, suggests that one way to avoid the pitfalls caused by lack of knowledge is communication. Librarians must be made aware of what factors govern library operation beyond those of immediate interest to the job. In the final analysis, it is the administrator who is responsible for the actions of his or her staff. If an administrator assumes an adversary position to staff, unionization may be inevitable. But whether unionization is, or is not, in and of itself desirable ignores the wider issues revolving around library management. Viele's point of view stresses that good management requires consistency and adherence to what has often been called the "doctrine of equity." In earlier, less complicated times, this doctrine might be rephrased as a "fair day's pay for a fair day's work." But in today's complex managerial world, the reduction of management to basic economic facts of life is inadequate. Careful attention to all aspects of management, those concerned with economic conditions and those more psychological in nature, may avoid the more dysfunctional aspects of unionization, though not necessarily unionization itself.

If unions are not quite consistent with professionalism, what then? Are there viable alternatives to unions, alternatives which will accomplish much the same things as do unions, but without the stigmata often attached to doing what is "not professional?" Without necessarily answering the question, Dora Biblarz and her colleagues provide some valuable insights into the nature of library professional organizations. Precisely what are they and what do they do? Unfortunately, Biblarz et al. assert, both unions and professional associations try to do too much. In the process, their activities overlap and duplicate each other, a situation entirely inconsistent with the avowed purpose of either type of organization. As the authors point out, it is not particularly useful to dichotomize between management and labor in libraries because every librarian is a manager, whether of information or of people. The issue unionization versus professionalism then becomes irrelevant. Unions and professional associations have separate duties, to consolidate, rather than dissipate, the energies of either in pursuit of goals with which they ought not be concerned.

But what if the union is already in the library? How do librarians behave then? In the final selection, Carol Moss sets out definitions, responsibilities, and activities in which unions engage. Basic questions are answered, such as "what is collective bargaining and what does it entail?" In the process of answering these questions, Moss presents a broad overview and analysis of employee-management relationships. Her recommendation that both library administrators and staff need greater expertise, knowledge, and training regarding collective bargaining and union-labor relations must be emphasized.

While no recent comprehensive study has been done on the reactions librarians today have toward unions, it is reasonable to assume that resistance to library unions, or to joining other union-like organizations, is still strong. However, as library workers become more sophisticated, more knowledgeable, more responsible for a variety of complicated technical processes, this resistance is likely to decrease, to be replaced by a more favorable view of unionization than might have hitherto existed. Therefore, it is most important that library administrators rather quickly develop an awareness and understanding of what factors cause the urge to unionize among librarians.

It is simplistic for librarians to take an "us or them" attitude to unions: they are part of library life. However, unionization is the end product of a series of management-related events: how an administrator deals with staff, that administrator's set of assumptions which govern managerial style, and to what extent that administrator understands the complex legal and moral restrictions under which he or she must operate. All of these factors affect the extent to which unionization can either be prevented or utilized for the good of the library.

Problems and Strategies for Collective Bargaining in Public Libraries
By George B. Viele

Today's public library administrators face a multitude of serious and dire problems which, if not properly understood, managed, and resolved, could result in the demise of the public library as we know it today. The public library's illustrious past in no way reflects what it needs to be today or to become tomorrow in this ever-changing world. The public library is an agency that is like every other enterprise or organization in that it lives and grows or withers and dies directly in relationship to its ability to satisfy human needs and the demands of the market place.

The market place for non-profit organizations consists of the budgetary limitations within which the agency or enterprise must operate.[1] It is within this framework of budgetary limitations that the dynamic process of collective bargaining becomes the meeting place for library workers, management, and governmental officials to resolve mutual problems evolving out of the effort to provide public library service, all too often without adequate material resources or financial support.

Because each and every public library system is unique, the internal and external forces acting upon it can create situations from which problems can and do arise. Because few library science administration textbooks discuss collective bargaining in public libraries and the curriculum of few library schools prepare their students with essential information and knowledge[2] of the collective bargaining process, I have endeavored to identify the difficulties of resolving public library problems through the collective bargaining process and to identify viable strategies for management that can preclude the advent of unionization in a public library, or that can mitigate library "differences" between management and workers where unions are already vying for a greater share of power.

THE LIBRARY ENVIRONMENT AND UNIONIZATION/COLLECTIVE BARGAINING

Today public library administrators face a rapidly changing world—a world wrought with strife, diminishing non-replaceable resources, double-digit inflation, and eroding tax bases. Concurrent with the latter is the tax revolt through which citizens have clearly told their elected representatives that the latter need to put a brake on wasteful and unneeded governmental programs, whether they be federal, state, or local.

The Goals, Guidelines, and Standards Committee (GGSC) of the Public Library Association states that the nation's public libraries are in serious trouble in a rapidly changing world[3] and that individuals and institutions suffer "a sense of alienation from the world and from themselves, a sense of powerlessness in controlling or even coping with the direction of life."[4]

The GGSC has also stated that this is a time for rethinking and re-examining national, institutional, and individual priorities.[5] It is in this context that library workers, unionized or non-unionized, and library management must accept the fact that institutions usually grow or die. The question of the size and the speed of growth of public libraries is related to the balance of power that exists between management and the workers. S. D. Spero perhaps said it best when he stated that "The life of a free society depends upon the maintenance of freedom and authority in delicate balance. The preservation of this balance depends in turn upon mutual restraint on the part of both government and its employees."[6]

In essence, the survival of the public library is dependent upon balance between management and employees—a delicate balance. An important question at this point is "How does collective bargaining impart balance and how does management counterbalance the workers' demands?" However, before answering this question, discussion of specific internal and external factors effecting collective bargaining is necessary.

INTERNAL FORCES EFFECTING COLLECTIVE BARGAINING

Internal forces such as 1) collection growth, 2) staff growth, 3) plant or facility growth, and 4) growth of use in technology are vital aspects effecting collective bargaining. These diverse forces have a direct bearing on issues which underlie the working conditions and the job satisfaction of employees.

Working conditions are almost always a topic for discussion sometime during the process of collective bargaining. And as much as working conditions are part of collective bargaining, collection growth is an essential part of public libraries. Collection growth usually occurs in two or three areas; books, periodicals, and films. Recent double-digit inflation has meant that the average public library has had to increase its materials budget substantially in order to stay even with present purchasing power.

Implications for collective bargaining by this factor alone are quite obvious if the library board and the director decide that the materials dollar is going to be maintained at the present purchasing power level and that wages will not. Immediately an issue arises if the staff is unionized. If the staff is non-union, it certainly might consider the value and strength of collectively requesting the powers-that-be to reconsider their position on a wage freeze.

Wages play an important role in the determination of sound relationships between management and staff. Directly related to wages is size of staff and the growth or decline of that size. Most public libraries have adequate staff to provide a satisfactory level of service. Sometimes misplaced priorities or poor management prohibits the best utilization of existing staff. This is one area where collective bargaining may play a strategic role in creating better use of staff time.

The efficiency of staff is determined in part by supervision and in part by working space needed to do a specific task. Staff size is directly related to the number of services provided the public and the back-up tasks supporting those providing service. The number of people and their tasks determine and are determined by the space assigned them by management.

Several factors have to be considered by management in evaluating the space requirements of a given library. These factors include essential services, frills or unnecessary services, and the size of the population being served. By eliminating the "frills," administrators can come down to the basics of deciding the amount of space necessary for providing good library services to a given population.

According to population forecasts the number of school age children will either decrease or remain at the present level until the mid 1990s. Then there will be a slight increase in this age group with another leveling off around the year 2000. This is important as school children constitute the largest user group of public libraries. This demographic factor is important also when external factors, to be discussed later, are taken into consideration.

The foregoing statements should not be interpreted to mean that all public libraries have more space than they can utilize or justify. These observations are intended to emphasize that library administrators must start planning, planning which could well result in their providing better and even expanded services without increased staff or physical plant size. Most important, though, is that the matter of adequate space or adequate-sized staff is one that needs to be *bilaterally* decided and *not* handed down from the administrator without employee input.

Future staff size and available space will be determined by technology. The technological growth in some public libraries is inevitable, especially those in which size of staff is frozen and physical space limited. Many public libraries located in cities and counties which want to hedge on personnel costs and also avoid future building costs will have to go the route of automation.

Circulation, cataloging, and acquisition are of concern to employees because the tasks within these areas lend themselves to being automated. Workers or staff are bound to be concerned about job security, reassignments to other duties, and productivity. These concerns are uppermost in the minds of employees, especially when they hear that some aspect of their job is going to be automated.

In essence, internal forces raise potential problems between management and workers, and, consequently, collective bargaining and/or other strategies will have to be implemented to resolve problems stemming from these forces. Underlying nearly all problems, regardless of their cause, is the basic problem of who is going to rule or where the power in public libraries is going to reside. Currently, management in public libraries has nearly all the power, unless the workers are unionized.

Internal forces create issues on their own. These issues are often intensified by outside forces, which neither library management nor staff has control over but which seriously impinges on their accomplishing their goals and objectives.

EXTERNAL FORCES EFFECTING COLLECTIVE BARGAINING

External forces such as inflation, energy costs, and the tax revolt of citizens adversely affect the funding, purchasing power, and operating costs of public libraries. They also have a direct bearing on relationships between library employees and their administrators.

Inflation has been increasing at a faster rate than any institution or individual can afford and faster than taxpayers would be willing to be taxed to keep a library at the same level of operation. Thus, salaries and fringe benefits of library employees are being squeezed. It is specifically in the areas of pay and remuneration that unions in both the public and the private sector concentrate their bargaining efforts. Salaries, fringe benefits, and working conditions are or are becoming open avenues for the process of collective bargaining.

The side of finite resources is often overlooked, not only by library people but by government officials and citizens alike. The pertinent question is where the energy is going to come from to meet the growth many libraries need in terms of their physical plants, which in some places are woefully inadequate to meet community needs. The fact remains that new construction or adding-on to a present facility will cost additional energy — energy for producing the building materials, energy for transporting the building materials to the building site, and energy to operate the building.

Library administrators are not oblivious to the high costs of heating or air conditioning their buildings at comfortable levels for staff and the public. Conservation of existing energy must be a consideration of management, too. Energy costs will force them to consider conservation even if they are inclined to be wasteful.

Library administrators must also take into consideration the plight of the taxpayer—the third external force. The taxpayer gets hit in many different ways—but especially so when he or she is pushed into a higher income bracket because of a wage adjustment that is lower than the rate of inflation. Necessities like food, medical care, operating costs of the family automobile, and local property taxes are included in the inflation spiral. It adds up to total frustration and anger for the taxpayer which is often directed toward the one category citizens can generally do something about—property taxes. When property taxes are reduced, or the rate remains the same with the advent of inflation, library services may be impaired, impaired because the property tax is the biggest source of public library support.

Inflation, the energy problem, and the ongoing tax rebellions are three vital concerns of importance to all public library employees. External forces combining with internal forces present conditions or problems related to salaries, fringe benefits, and working conditions. The delicate balancing of internal and external forces with public library activities is a formidable task challenging library administrators and employees during the process of collective bargaining.

COMPARISON OF LIBRARY COLLECTIVE BARGAINING TO OTHER FORMS OF INSTITUTIONAL COLLECTIVE BARGAINING

Collective bargaining for government workers will not be a process without great difficulty. According to George H. Hildebrand there are four main elements that distinguish collective bargaining for government workers from that of workers in the private sector. These elements are that 1) government workers are generally forbidden to strike; 2) most government services are free in that there generally is no direct charge for a service; 3) management in the public sector at the local level may not have final authority; and 4) legislative bodies do not easily give up any of their sovereignty of power.[7]

The first two of Hildebrand's elements are not significant for employees as they attempt to gain some of the power from their management. For example, the strike can be or is a powerful tool for public employees if they are large in number and their services are of vital necessity for the safety and welfare of the public. But this is just not true for public library employees. They are few in number in most communities and their services, while important and essential to the quality of life in a community, are not absolutely vital.

Hildebrand's second element—free government services—is of little importance to library employees in the collective bargaining process because most library services are supported by and provided through local property taxes. The percent of local taxes used to support public libraries is frighteningly low because public libraries are not generally very high on the priority list of the local power structure—be it city council or county commissioners.

While the percent of local taxes used to support public libraries is only a very, very small part of any community's total revenues from all taxes, local appropriations usually constitute about 75-80% of a public library's budget. The remainder of the library's budget comes from gifts, state government, and federal grants.

Hildebrand's last two elements are where public library employees will encounter their greatest problems in the collective bargaining process. The governance of libraries varies from one city to another, one county to another, one region to another, and from state to state. Thus it is difficult to determine who has the final authority at the local level to reach an agreement with library employees during the bargaining process. Final authority does not always rest with the library board of trustees. In some cases public library boards serve in an advisory capacity to the director, who in turn is responsible to either a city or a county manager.

Library governance starts at the state level through the legislative process when state laws are made saying that either city or county officials may establish public libraries in their political areas. But that is not always the case. Often citizens have voluntarily established public libraries and sought operating funds from local authorities who could appropriate non-tax funds received by them to support a library. In some states citizens have requested that their state legislatures pass a special act establishing a public library. Sometimes these special acts create a library without specifying from where the source of funds will come to support the library the legislators have created by law.

In some cases two or more counties have decided on forming a regional library according to provisions of their state law with the board of trustees composed of representatives from each of the counties making up the region. In some large counties with many small, incorporated towns, independent public libraries within the towns will contract for supporting services from a library established by the county commissioners. In the latter case it is not unusual for each town to have its own library board, which may or may not be self-appointing and self-perpetuating as a result. Frequently, the local library provides monies for personnel, operating costs, and capital. The county library board through support at the county government level provides professional advice, books, and other library materials.

At the regional level a library board may operate on funds received from each of the counties in the region and from state aid. The regional library board sometimes operates only on funds from the state. In either case state aid funds are usually distributed by the state library according to a specific formula established in rules and regulations governing state aid distribution. When regional library boards do not receive any funds except from the state, it is because each of the counties constituting the region maintains its own financial accounts and library fund for its local library which is part of a regional system.

In many cases, libraries that are part of a region in name have their own library board and retain their autonomy. The library director of the regional library in the situation just described does not have any control of the library personnel within a given county library. Nor in similar situations does the director have responsibility to negotiate in bargaining with the library employees of the county. In short there is no paradigm for public library governance, and therein lies one of the biggest problems for library workers endeavoring to use the process of collective bargaining to resolve their labor disputes.

Sovereignty of legislative bodies—Hildebrand's fourth element—includes 1) their position of power from which to create cities and counties, 2) regulating how local governments may levy taxes and at what levels, and 3) how they may spend their monies. Henry W. Maier, former mayor of Milwaukee, says that cities are creatures of the state and that cities are limited or restricted as to what they can do by state law.[8] More specifically, state governments reserve powers or prescribe specific limitations which limit cities and counties in terms of what they can negotiate with union officials or representatives. States through wide control of the various tax sources do not get into difficulty in establishing positions during collective bargaining procedures.

In private employment collective bargaining is a bilateral process—usually just between the employer and the union representing the employees. Collective bargaining is a multi-lateral process in the public sector.⁹ The multi-lateral aspect relates not only to library management, the city or county manager, and the city council or county commissioners with whom union officials have to bargain or negotiate; it also involves citizens' views and various interest or power groups found in local communities.

City and county officials are elected through the political process and are responsible to and sensitive of citizens' concerns. The political process often is an integral part of collective bargaining between the union representatives and local governments.

HOW LIBRARY MANAGEMENT AND LIBRARY EMPLOYEES VIEW COLLECTIVE BARGAINING

A recent survey in industry revealed that one of the major concerns of employees today is communication with their supervisors. Workers admitted that the way "managers communicated—or failed to—had a major influence on their performance."[10] The same situation is true in libraries. One of the biggest problems from the employees' point of view is that whatever they are told they are told too late.

Library employees complain frequently about the lack of promotional opportunities existing in their given libraries. They voice their concerns especially when they are bypassed by management which sometimes hires an outsider. Of course, these are serious matters, but they are not the primary causes of workers' organizing a union or joining an existing one.

Salaries, fringe benefits, and working conditions lie at the leart of unionization. Workers know that management will listen to their collective voice. They also know that management will not bend to the winds of discontent or dissatisfaction of the individual employee acting alone. Through collective bargaining workers see higher wages, better fringe benefits, and improved working conditions.

Management, from their perspective, sees another picture entirely. It is impossible to explain the entire spectrum of managerial views. However, several points stand out in all philosophies of good management. Good managers view their staff members as individuals whom they depend upon to carry out the philosophy of service held by the management. Good managers realize that everything in an organization is done by people. They also recognize that the problems of the library are not really the problems of the library but of the employees in the library.

Therefore, good management can keep problems resolved or mitigated and thus preclude the unionization of the staff. If the latter is already unionized, good managerial practices will enhance the process of collective bargaining, keeping negotiations to short sessions in duration and achieving mutually beneficial conclusions for management and workers.

Management readily acknowledges that unions arise out of the desires of the workers rather than as a decision of management. The managers concede that they should work out the best means for people to work together individually and collectively to produce the best library service at minimum cost.

One major aspect of collective bargaining and unions is, of course, the egalitarian views of the employees. Managers admit that moderate egalitarianism has produced essential measures such as minimum wage laws.[11] They argue and rightly claim that egalitarianism of the kind that "ignores differences in native capacity, means rule by committee, subordinates the individual to the group, and rules out the striving for excellence"[12] is diametrically opposite democratic management. Democratic management stresses the performance of the individual as the basis for merit raises and promotion to higher classifications. The egalitarian views prevalent among library workers are almost a guarantee of workers' needing to bargain with management when the latter insists on rewarding individuals for excellent work, good attendance, and healthy cooperative attitudes which all add up to a high quality of library service.

Management views unionization and collective bargaining not only as an essential part of trying to provide library service to the public, but also as a threat to their effectiveness as managers and supervisors. Unions are definitely perceived as a threat to the power that emanates from managements' position. Consequently, most library managers will yield begrudgingly on each point in negotiations and will strive to retain as much power as possible.

For the most part, library administrators would rather deal with non-union employees in informal settings. Therefore, the administrator will usually strive to establish and maintain a library atmosphere that promotes worker harmony and satisfaction.

MANAGERIAL STRATEGIES

Managerial strategies in a non-unionized library must include the development and establishment of sound, practical personnel rules and regulations which cover areas of base salaries, promotions, disciplinary measures, fringe benefits, grievance procedures, and any other matters relevant to the needs and interests of the library and its staff.

Generally, if the local library is part of either a city or county government, the local government's personnel rules wil apply to library personnel. But if the library is an independent agency with its own policy-making library board, a well-developed personnel policy will probably not exist or be inadequate if there already is one.

Personnel rules provide the avenues to assure fairness, consistency, and a unanimity of understanding between the employer and the employee. But the existing rules do not cover all aspects of a work situation. There are essentially only two kinds of employees in a library—professional and non-professional. It is necessary for management to realize this and to create a climate in which the professionals are treated accordingly and in which they have an opportunity to function as professionals. One of the better ways to accomplish this is by adopting "Management by Objectives" for the professional staff.

The MBO approach should engender better salaries, fringe benefits, and working conditions for the professional librarian—who often has the same education as the director or other library managers. By using MBO techniques, the professional librarian has an opportunity to discuss with the supervisor his or her specific objectives and goals for a given time frame—usually six months or a year. At the same time, management has an opportunity to evaluate the worker's goals and objectives in light of the overall goals and objectives of the library. Once the parties have agreed upon the specific goals and objectives, the latter becomes a vehicle for determining both the quality and quantity of work produced. This in turn would serve as the basis for determining a salary increase for the individual. The professional employee through MBO has the opportunity to have some input and some degree of freedom to perform in a professional way.

Management by Objectives is a system that produces benefits to both managers and employees. Specific benefits include 1) increased motivation of and commitment by employees as a result of their participation in goal setting; 2) better planning because MBO is built into budget planning, performance appraisal, and merit salary increases; and 3) improved relations between the supervisor and the supervised, based upon their mutually deciding what has to be done and how well it was done, allowing for the freedom to operate as independently as possible.

The non-professional employee has to be treated equally and fairly by management if the latter wishes to avoid antagonizing that employee. While MBO procedures are not applicable to most non-professional jobs in a library, there are things managers and administrators can do that will encourage worker input and job satisfaction. One of the best ways is the establishment of work performance standards for each non-professional job in the library. These standards have to be developed and agreed upon by the worker *and* the supervisor. The performance standards serve as a basis for determining salary increases and promotions.

A technique or tool recently making a comeback in the area of public libraries is the community analysis. This procedure offers to management and employees alike improved understanding of the ability of a community to meet the demands of both. A community analysis would be beneficial and worthwhile for both non-unionized and unionized libraries. In either case, the library staff and management would have a greater knowledge of the library needs of the community in relation to other needs, and of the community's ability to support the library and the demands of its workers. Perhaps equally important, both parties would have the opportunity to work as equals in establishing realistic goals and objectives for the library relevant to the needs of the community and its ability to maintain and operate a good public library.

It is almost impossible to state specifically or to outline in depth the strategies library management should deploy in dealing with union workers or their representatives for the simple reason that every community, jurisdiction, or state has its own unique characteristics and no single idea or opinion would make any sense in them all.

CONCLUSIONS

Collective bargaining amounts to determining in the long run where the balance of power is in the library. Is management going to be all-powerful? Are the workers? Or is the power going to be equitably divided so that the outcome is also beneficial to the public interest, which has to be paramount in any discussion between workers and their bosses.

The balance of power or the struggle for power can be either beneficial or deleterious to service given the public. If the bargaining climate is one of doubt, distrust, and animosity, ill will and unhappiness may be carried over into the area of public service by the workers. On the other hand, efforts by both sides to bargain honestly and openly should result in an overall gain in which both parties insist and agree on outcomes that enhance the opportunity for better public library service. Failure to do so by either side may result in someone winning the battle but losing the war.

Throughout this article the author has emphasized 1) that public libraries face a multitude of problems caused by external and internal forces which threaten their survival and 2) that, through good management, using accepted managerial strategies, and the process of collective bargaining, public library problems can be mitigated if not actually overcome. The author has stressed that collective bargaining is a process—a process that involves the struggle for power between management and the worker. Power is dependent upon many things. It is determined to some extent by the bargaining skill of the individuals negotiating and the resources each side may call upon.[13] It is the recommendation of this author that management and employees alike need 1) to familiarize themselves with the state and local laws governing them as public employees; 2) know their rights and respective responsibilities; and 3) accept the fact that their united and combined efforts will in no small way affect the ultimate future of the public library. Their mutual cooperation is part of the missing element in the equation of institutional survival.

REFERENCES

[1] Edwin F. Beal and Edward D. Wickersham, *The Practice of Collective Bargaining* (Homewood, IL: Richard D. Irwin, 1963), p. 11.

[2] Michael J. Simonds, "Work Attitudes and Union Membership," *College & Research Libraries*, 36:136 (March 1975).

[3] Public Library Association. Goals, Guidelines, and Standards Committee, *The Public Library Mission Statement and Its Imperatives for Service* (Chicago: American Library Association, 1979), p. iii.

[4] Public Library Association, *Mission Statement*, p. iii.

[5] Public Library Association, *Mission Statement*, p. iii.

[6] Sterling Denhard Spero, *Government as Employer* (New York: Remsen Press, 1948), p. 487.

[7] George H. Hildebrand, "The Public Sector," in *Frontiers of Collective Bargaining*, John T. Dunlop and Neil W. Chamberlain, eds. (New York: Harper & Row, 1967), pp. 126-27.

[8] Henry W. Maier, "Collective Bargaining and the Municipal Employer," in *Public Workers and Public Unions*, Sam Zagoria, ed. (Englewood Cliffs, NJ: Prentice-Hall, 1972), p. 58.

[9] Kenneth McLennan and Michael H. Moskow, "Multi-lateral Bargaining in the Public Sector," in *Twenty-First Annual Proceedings* (Madison, WI: Industrial Relations Research Association, 1969), pp. 31-40.

[10] Ted Pollack, "What Employees Want," *Industrial Supervisor*, 44:3 (Feb. 1980).

[11] John W. Gardner, *Excellence* (New York: Harper & Row, 1961), p. 15.

[12] Gardner, *Excellence*, p. 15.

[13] Hildebrand, "The Public Sector," p. 148.

BIBLIOGRAPHY

American Assembly. *Challenges to Collective Bargaining*. Englewood Cliffs, NJ: Prentice-Hall, 1967.

Beal, Edwin F., and Edward D. Wickersham. *The Practice of Collective Bargaining*. Homewood, IL: Richard D. Irwin, 1963.

Chicago. University. Graduate School of Business. *The Structure of Collective Bargaining: Problems and Perspectives*. New York: The Free Press of Glencoe, 1961.

College and Research Libraries. vol. 36, no. 2 (March 1975).

Dunlop, John T., and Neil W. Chamberlain, eds. *Frontiers of Collective Bargaining*. New York: Harper and Row, 1967.

"Employee Organizations and Collective Bargaining in Libraries," *Library Trends*, vol. 25, no. 2 (October 1976).

Gardner, John W. *Excellence*. New York: Harper & Row, 1961.

Healey, James J., ed. *Creative Collective Bargaining: Meeting Today's Challenges to Labor-Management Relations*. Englewood Cliffs, NJ: Prentice-Hall, 1965.

Hildebrand, George H. "The Public Sector," *Frontiers of Collective Bargaining*. New York: Harper and Row, 1967.

Maier, Henry W. "Collective Bargaining and the Municipal Employer," *Public Workers and Public Unions*. Englewood Cliffs, NJ: Prentice-Hall, 1972.

McLennan, Kenneth, and Michael H. Moskow. "Multi-lateral Bargaining in the Public Sector," *Twenty-First Annual Proceedings*. Madison, WI: Industrial Relations Research Association, 1969.

Moskow, Michael H., and others. *Collective Bargaining in Public Employment*. New York: Random House, 1970.

Murphy, Edward F. *Management Vs. the Unions: How to Win*. New York: Stein and Day, 1971.

Pollack, Ted. "What Employees Want," *Industrial Supervisor*, vol. 44, no. 3 (February 1980).

Public Library Association. Goals, Guidelines and Standards Committee. *The Public Library Mission Statement and Its Imperatives for Service*. Chicago: American Library Association, 1979.

Richardson, Reed C. *Collective Bargaining by Objectives: A Positive Approach*. Englewood Cliffs, NJ: Prentice-Hall, 1977.

Rukeyser, Merryle Stanley. *Collective Bargaining: The Power to Destroy*. New York: Delacorte Press, 1968.

Spero, Sterling Denhard. *Government as Employer*. New York: Remsen Press, 1948.

Stueart, Robert D., and John Taylor Eastlick. *Library Management*, 2nd ed. Littleton, CO: Libraries Unlimited, 1981.

Vignone, Joseph A. *Collective Bargaining Procedures for Public Library Employees: An Inquiry into the Opinions and Attitudes of Public Librarians, Directors and Board Members*. Metuchen, NJ: Scarecrow Press, 1971.

Zagoria, Sam, ed. *Public Workers and Public Unions*. Englewood Cliffs, NJ: Prentice-Hall, 1972.

Professional Associations and Unions: Future Impact of Today's Decisions
By Dora Biblarz, Margaret Capron, Linda Kennedy, Johanna Ross, and David Weinerth

The experiences of one librarians' association are the springboard for a discussion of the impact of professional associations and unions on the individual, professional, and organizational goals of librarians. Both associations are seen as necessary forms of organization. Their objectives only occasionally overlap; each has its own mode of operation and experiential opportunities. In spite of the temptation to try to solve immediate problems by turning completely to union representation, librarians are urged not to desert the professional association, which among its other functions, can be seen to have an important role for the future development of librarians.

INTRODUCTION

THE WRITERS OF THIS ARTICLE began their work as an *ad hoc* committee of the Librarians' Association of the University of California at Davis (LAUC-D), charged with the preparation of a consensus statement on a controversial report transmitted by a committee of the statewide University of California Librarians' Association (LAUC), of which LAUC-D is an autonomous unit. While the specifics of the case are unique to the University of California (UC), the issues raised are crucial to all academic librarians facing a changing structure of librarianship within their institutions, especially with regard to the possibility of collective bargaining. Professional associations in particular are in a quandary over the labor issue: Will they become the collective bargaining agents, or is this role precluded by their very nature? Will professional associations even survive if collective bargaining legislation becomes the order of the day?

The statewide LAUC committee report urged the affiliation of the Librarians' Association with other employee associations, specifically unions, such as the American Federation of Teachers (AFT), the California State Employees' Association (CSEA), and the American Association of University Professors (AAUP).[1] In examining the nature and

---

Reprinted by permission of the American Library Association from "Professional Associations and Unions' Future Impact of Today's Decisions," Dora Biblarz, Margaret Capron, Linda Kennedy, Johanna Ross, and David Weinerth, *College and Research Libraries*, vol. 36 (March 1975), pp. 121-28, copyright © 1975 by the American Library Association.

background of LAUC in relation to the other organizations mentioned, the writers discerned irreconcilable differences which made affiliation between them impossible and ultimately destructive to LAUC.[2] We also came to a sense of some important changes taking place in librarianship, a result of both the role of librarians' associations in library administration and of factors such as library networks, increasing automation, and the offering of computerized information retrieval services. We also regretfully came to the conclusion that librarians were letting important opportunities pass them by in not being aware of the implications of these changes and their resulting need for new kinds of librarians and new kinds of services.

THE UNIVERSITY OF CALIFORNIA EXPERIENCE

The problem of conflicting roles of unions and professional associations inevitably arises when discussions of matters of vital concern to both groups take place. Frequently these are the areas of salary and personnel actions. The UC controversy began when the librarian series of the University of California was restructured to three ranks: Assistant Librarian, Associate Librarian, and Librarian. At the same time, new criteria for promotion and merit increases were initiated, criteria that paralleled some of those of the faculty: the requirement of professional competence, professional activity outside the library, university and public service, and research. There were no alterations in work scheduling, however, to allow the development necessary to meet the new criteria. Also, it was not to be assumed that everyone would reach the rank of Librarian: "There is no obligation on the part of the University to promote an Associate Librarian to the rank of Librarian solely on the basis of years of service."[3]

Librarians recommended these changes through the newly formed statewide and local campus Librarians' Association of the University of California, but had also recommended a work year that matched the faculty work year and provisions for released time for research. The administration had adopted the more stringent requirements, but had rejected the means to meet the requirements for a majority of librarians. This caused concern in the library community, voiced through the professional association and the union as well.

LAUC had been officially organized statewide in 1968, to "create a forum where matters of concern to librarians in the University of California may be discussed and an appropriate course of action determined."[4] The genesis of this association is found in the dissatisfaction of librarians in the University of California with established national and state associations. These were deemed insufficient to fill the needs for discussion of local problems or to satisfy the desire for a voice in university affairs.

The privileges granted LAUC—use of the university name and university facilities, released time to conduct association business—may or may not be shared by similar professional associations which have relations with a parent organization. LAUC is one example of the type of professional association which unifies librarians of similar interests and acts *internally* within a larger parent organization, rather than a detached association working on a state or national level and including librarians of diverse interests. The opportunities for librarian development offered by the workings of an association such as LAUC derive from these structural characteristics.

The university is expected to make LAUC's *de facto* status *de jure* in the very near future. Assigned duties may include advising the chancellors and the library administrators on matters of concern to librarians and the university in the operation of libraries, including matters of collections, personnel, and service. Ambiguities between the role of the union and the professional association has led LAUC to request this official status.

As LAUC progressed from infancy to adolescence, library administration increasingly asked and relied upon the membership for advice both at the local and statewide level. Each campus association became involved in the peer review process for promotion, merit increase, and appointment. LAUC, in relieving the administration of such burdens, achieved its greatest gains in credibility and influence through its efficient work. By virtue of its special relationship to the administration, it assumed that it would be consulted in the planned restructuring of salaries, an issue that had been pursued with increasing intensity from the time LAUC was formed. A LAUC-appointed study committee was subsequently superseded by an administration-appointed advisory committee. The committee documented a wide salary discrepancy between UC librarians and librarians at other California academic institutions, and within UC between librarians and other employees with similar education and experience. University salary recommendations were blue penciled from the state budget by the governor. When a special bill for librarian inequity increases was passed by the legislature, it in turn was vetoed by the governor on the grounds that the proper place for salary actions was in the budget. This and similar actions frustrated the library community. Many librarians joined unions for the first time, seeing a new and perhaps stronger avenue for action.

Unions and Professional Associations

Many of the actions that unions were requesting had also been suggested by LAUC. With the American Federation of Teachers, the California State Employees' Association, and the American Association of University Professors working for many of the things important to librarians, it was suggested that LAUC investigate the legal and organizational problems of cooperating with these associations on matters of concern to both. LAUC appointed a committee to study the relationship between LAUC and voluntary employee associations. This was done, and a report was issued to the membership.

The statewide committee was not unanimous in its conclusions and issued both a majority and a minority opinion. Four of the members advocated close cooperation with voluntary employee associations. Cooperation was to be effected by the formation of a committee composed of one member from each association which chose to participate and one member representing statewide LAUC. This group would then determine when LAUC should combine forces with voluntary employee associations in order to more effectively influence events in favor of librarians. The minority opinion, given by one member, stated that such a course of action violated the spirit and purpose for which LAUC was established. The general LAUC membership was unclear as to the best course of action, so each campus was instructed to study the report and be ready to vote on it at the next statewide meeting.

The Davis division of LAUC appointed a committee to study the statewide report and to prepare a consensus statement and recommendations for this division's voice at the statewide meeting. The authors of this article comprised that committee. We found that, at first glance, clear-cut distinctions between professional and employee associations are difficult to make, for the goals and objectives of both overlap in many respects.

The internal professional association, if we can use the objectives of LAUC as representative, seeks to create a forum for discussion of issues of common concern. It investigates professional standards and attempts to make recommendations for their establishment and enforcement. It may participate in peer review. In addition, it seeks the full utilization of the professional skills of its members and the improvement of library service. All this is accomplished through the advisory role it has established with the organization, allowing librarians a voice in the formal structure of decision making.

Unions and other employee associations work towards many short-term goals such as inequity increases, better working conditions, a collective bargaining agreement with the administration —the "personal" aspects of the job. Unlike professional associations, they most often become active when an employee with a grievance requests their assistance after an administrative decision has been made. When collective bargaining agreements exist, they negotiate with the organization in matters of salary and working conditions. If we accept the premise that a mass statement carries more weight than a single voice when issues of personal relevance are being discussed, then we can recognize the value of such an association. Unions have the "clout" that no single person can wield, both in the fact that they work collectively and in that they have the support of affiliated employee associations. Unlike the professional association, which is limited to an advisory role, it has the freedom to take an adversary position and the power to challenge the organization.

Typical among the concerns of the union or employee association, in addition to the ones mentioned, are the maintenance and promotion of high standards of education and the latter's availability to the general public; encouragement of true equality of opportunity for all the employees it serves, regardless of membership. The accomplishment of these is sought through lobbying in the legislature, concerted action by all local chapters, and even joint action with similar interest groups whenever appropriate.

The long-range concerns shared by the professional and employee associations are the maintenance of high standards, encouragement of equality of opportunity, and general promotion of the welfare of the members. It is in working towards the short-term goals that the tactics of the employee association conflict with the sanctioned activities of the professional ones; these include lobbying for legislation, assisting members with grievances, and negotiating for salaries and benefits at the bargaining table. The first of these would be impossible for a professional association such as LAUC to pursue, since university employees are forbidden to lobby as a group, or even to communicate with government officials on university letterhead without permission. Political communication at the employee level is thus channeled into the role of the ordinary citizen: librarians at UC may communicate with their elected representatives as individuals. Any attempt at collective action as an official group not only carries the risk of official censure, but also the risk of alteration of the nature of the professional association itself. Having aligned itself with library administration through participation in peer review and advisory committees on all aspects of library policy and operation, a group can hardly then challenge the library's higher administration by lobbying action at the state level without severely jeopardizing the privileges it has attained.

THE INDIVIDUAL
AND THE ORGANIZATION

To understand better how librarians' associations work within the institution, it would be useful at this point to take a broader perspective of ourselves, not just as librarians, but as human beings practicing a profession in a large organization that must apportion its resources to perform a variety of services. It may be a college, a business firm, a local, state, or federal government, or even a school district. A library system, often complex in itself, usually exists within one or more of these organizations, which in turn provide the capital resources and operating funds while representing the constituency of the library and its services. Though we can imagine a situation in which librarians operate as architects or lawyers do, contracting their services on a one-to-one basis with their clientele, the opportunities for this are rare in librarianship (or at least unevenly distributed), given the present state of information technology.

It is fair, then, to assume that the common experience of librarians is fielded within a library *system* and includes financial dependence upon an organization that speaks for the constituency of that system. As a group, we have specialized knowledge and skills that we consider unique to us by virtue of training and inclination. We regard our professional schools and associations as depositories and spokesmen for our values. Most of us look to each other for mutual support in an on-going concern for appropriate recognition and compensation for our services.

Yet, and Patricia Knapp has phrased this well, "Whenever professionals work in the context of an organization, there is inevitable tension between the authority inherent in the formal structure and procedures (*i.e.*, the 'rationality') of the organization and the authority of specialized knowledge and training (the expertise) inherent in the professional role. This tension has potential for creative as well as harmful effects."[5] Appropriately, the professional association might be regarded as an effort on the part of its members to pursue creative interaction.

But prior to this we are all human beings with singular experiences and situations. Firmly committed though we may be to service, we also have personal obligations and values which we find sometimes place us in an antagonistic position with regard to our professional or organizational roles. Adjustments must be made between group and individual interests—interests that further provide for creative as well as harmful interaction.

There emerges for our consideration not two, but three complex entities interacting in a framework that extends beyond the merely sociological: the individual, the profession, the organization. Each has needs and goals for self-fulfillment that, pursued simultaneously, produce a situation fraught with conflict. While we as individuals feel these conflicts within ourselves, we may sometimes find it difficult to identify the sources of these tensions. They are often perceived as dichotomous, and we may seek relief by directing our energies to the weaker side in order to restore balance. The point here is that there are not two sides to the question, but three; and a resolution is not easily found.

Another way to approach this is to acknowledge that of the three complex entities defined above, we as individuals are the *most* complex. We can identify varying degrees of our vested interests not only in our own lives but in librarianship and the organization as well. We may wish to influence decisions from within, challenge them from without; all with the intent of modifying the organization, the profession, or other individuals. It would follow that no single institution that we might devise could address all our needs even in the limited areas of our professional lives.

The need for different modes of action should be kept in mind when considering the frequently asked question: Do we need professional associations in this age of collective bargaining? Some union leaders are advocating they be disbanded in order that librarians not "dissipate their energies." Since unions have power by right of their collective bargaining role to handle questions of salary and working conditions, this call for concerted action is all too inviting. Yet by channeling all our energies into union activities, we run the risk of neglecting the role we play regarding our professional contributions to the management of the organization. When the requirements of the union, the individual, and the organization get out of balance, the end result may spell catastrophe to the clientele the organization is designed to serve, and ultimately the individuals and the professional association. As the phenomenon of collective bargaining spreads throughout the country, the need for rational judgments becomes more critical. A recent *Library Journal* editorial illustrates this point all too well.[6]

Perhaps an effective way to derive constructive benefits from our institutions is to recognize their limitations and to allow them to pursue the relatively simple goals they are designed to handle; while we, as individuals, exercise our right to analyze our needs and to associate ourselves with whichever combination of groups best responds to them. With wider personal encounters in divergent settings, we are in a better position to recognize opportunities for creative interaction between these forces.

What does this suggest for professional associations? We should recognize that they are instruments for enhancing our professional roles within the organization. Although individual considerations are important, their furtherance cannot be the primary goal of the professional association if it is to be effective. Unions are better equipped to handle such considerations. Making decisions as to the most effective distribution of one's affiliations demands courage and wisdom. We feel that this should be a personal decision about personal activities.

New Roles and Directions

It is important that we take another look at the role professional associations play in our professional lives, particularly in relation to what we perceive to be two separate crises in the development of librarianship.

The first crisis is the immediate one: the failure of our salaries to keep up with the rising costs of living and our own sense of what we are worth in terms of education, experience, and community contribution. As much as we are aware that other occupational groups are caught in similar situations, we are equally aware that, for some of these groups, action is getting results. A sense of urgency pervades the issue of salaries. Calls for alignment and collective action between the unions and the internal professional association have a convincing ring, but actions must be channeled into the association best suited to accomplish the desired goals. Few options are better than none; we still have an opportunity to think before we cast the ballot.

We urge our colleagues to view the immediate crisis alongside of another, more subtle, but ultimately more devastating one. We refer to the growing sophistication and usage of information-handling techniques and the accompanying changes in the structure of decision making on the peripheries of librarianship. That it was left to the information scientist and computer programmer to apply the computer to the "information problem" is now history; an opportunity for us was overlooked and it is gone. But that managers in outside and related professions are fast developing information-handling sophistication and are starting to offer what resemble qualifications for the administration of libraries is a present reality about which too many of us demonstrate a naive unconcern.

We invoke this observation as a cause for alarm but not panic. It is an invitation to reconstruct our perceptions of our working-day activities and their potential for change. Librarianship has always been much more than the manipulation of information, yet today we are overloaded with the routine; our energies are being drained with the just plain monotonous. Application of programming techniques to our information-handling activities is a viable solution, and we are already moving in that direction. Although we have not yet achieved a consensual definition of what it is we will be free to *do* with our de-encumbered energies, of one thing we can be certain: While library networks, automatic data processing, and the like vastly accelerate the rate of "clerical operations," they also increase the number of decisions that must be made *about* the operations. The incipient stages of this situation might be recognized in libraries relying on little or no programmed activities. By necessity they are dependent upon other libraries in the system that have introduced more sophisticated automated techniques.

This should indicate a new working mode for the majority of librarians. Presently only a portion of us fill what are termed managerial positions; and while this did reflect the proportion of guiding decisions to routine operations in the past, and may be merely inadequate today, it assuredly will not reflect the demands of the new technology. Too many choices will have to be made at too rapid a pace and affecting too many people.

Librarians, we think, should regard themselves as evolving into a management profession specializing in libraries. If we do not, we may discover that when the future becomes now, we will have nothing to inherit. Not only would our specialized knowledge be for naught if we have not developed the abilities in each of us to make good choices in applying it, but the economics of failure would turn a spotlight on the experienced managers on the periphery of our profession, and the protective borders of librarianship could come tumbling down.

We believe that managerial roles will proliferate in the new library systems whether librarians are prepared to fill them or not. This seems apparent without venturing to project the changes that may be in store for the structure of managerial relationships. We suggest only that the widespread necessity of managerial roles will be a condition of any such structure.

The realization of librarianship as a specialized management profession is not, we admit, a universally shared objective. We urge, however, that it be universally considered. For, viewed from within this present-to-future context, the professional association's role in our professional lives gains a new dimension when it is seen that all librarians have an opportunity to develop decision-making abilities in a real context and they can do it *now*. Such an organization emerges as a managerial workshop, a keystone in our strategy for achieving true professional status.

We are left facing the possibility that the experiential level of many librarians may be seriously challenged in their own field by strong competition from without if proper thought is not directed to this matter in advance. Again, this suggests that we be especially cautious when considering the prompting of some of our colleagues that the professional association align itself as an internal professional group with external groups in common defiance of the administration. While this may appear to be a good tactic for alleviating the present distress, it has hazardous implications. In one fell swoop we will have achieved, as professionals, permanent self-identification as an employee group-*contra*-management and regained our forty-hour work week with business (you can be sure) as usual. We could succeed in closing the door on our own future, having forfeited our potential status and our very means for attaining it.

CONCLUSION

Professional associations, particularly those closely related to academic multicampus universities, or associations bound to a common class of clientele, must retain the objectives for which they were formed. If associations neglect their professional commitment by close cooperation with unions on immediate issues such as salaries, important though they may be, we run the risk of forfeiting our professional development by ignoring the growing requirements for managerial talents at all levels.

A judicious redirecting of our energies can have implications we can but dimly foresee today. Although contributions of participatory management as effected through professional associations are too distant to be brought into focus, it is still clear that the librarian of the future will have to make more decisions and make them at what is now a lower level if the system is to function effectively.

Those who feel the professional association can fill all our needs may be satisfied with the *status quo* of salaries, but they are dwindling in number. Those who expect unions to satisfy all the professional needs would do well to examine all the issues and to assess them in the light of the future requirements of the profession. For a viable choice to exist, *both* associations are necessary.

REFERENCES

1. "Report of the Ad Hoc Committee to Study the Relationship of LAUC and Voluntary Employee Organizations," by P. Coyle, E. Eaton, P. Hoehn, M. Sassé, D. Schippers, chairperson. April 10, 1973. Unpublished.
2. "Report of the LAUC-D Committee to Prepare a Consensus Statement on the Statewide Report of the Committee to Study the Relationship of LAUC and Voluntary Employee Organizations," by D. Biblarz, M. Capron, L. Kennedy, D. Weinerth, J. Ross, chairperson. April 1974. Unpublished.
3. University of California, *Academic Personnel Manual*, Section 82-17b (3). 7-1-72.
4. Librarians' Association of the University of California, *By-laws* (November 1972).
5. Patricia B. Knapp, "The Library as a Complex Organization: Implications for Library Education," in *Toward a Theory of Librarianship*, ed. Conrad Rawski (Metuchen, N.J.: Scarecrow, 1973), p.473.
6. "UFT and/or ALA," *Library Journal* 99: 1503 (June 1, 1974).

Bargaining's Effect on Library Management and Operation
By Carol E. Moss

PUBLIC EMPLOYEE unionization has grown so rapidly in the past decade that a greater proportion of public employees, as opposed to private sector employees, now belong to unions and associations. Membership in unions by public employees in the United States is rapidly approaching 5 million.[1] State and local governments alone account for 2½ million union members. The federal government has more than 1 million employees who are union members, and public education has another 1 million unionized employees. All data indicates a continuing increase in public employee organizing.

GROWTH OF UNIONISM IN THE PUBLIC SECTOR

A few employee groups such as postal employees, teachers and law enforcement workers have had organizations with deep historical roots dating back to the 1930s, but their early development was very slow. The recent spread of unionism among government civil employees and teachers, however, is a partial answer to the old question of whether substantial numbers of white-collar employees can be unionized. While it is true that much of the growth of public sector unionism has been among blue-collar employees, some important footholds have been gained among white-collar workers and professionals. This is due primarily to the fact that teachers comprise the largest unionized group because they represent 25 percent of all public employees at the local and state level.[2] Teachers are proving that they have power and are capable of using it to advantage.

Nurses and social workers, particularly in the big cities, are now making demands and extending their unionism. In spite of legislation encouraging employees in public employment to establish collective

---

Reprinted from *Library Trends* vol. 25, October 1976, by permission of the publisher. © 1976 Board of Trustees of the University of Illinois.

bargaining relationships, many groups of workers still remain outside the area of protected collective bargaining activity. The rapid growth of unionization among teachers, nurses, and social workers has all but hidden the union organizing attempts in the quasi-public employment field. A quasi-public institution is one which is associated with a public endeavor but is a private corporate institution supported in part by public funds. The cultural institutions in New York, including the zoological societies, botanical gardens, museums, and libraries, come under this definition. One of the early efforts in New York to organize library employees and, in particular, the professional librarian classification merits comment.

The American Federation of State, County and Municipal Employees (AFSCME) started an organizing campaign at the Brooklyn Public Library in early 1966.[3] In autumn of that year, an election was conducted among two separate units of employees. The first unit was composed of all professional librarians except the major administrative officers of the library. The second unit was composed mainly of the clerical and maintenance staffs. While the union did not achieve the resounding results it had hoped for, it did obtain the required majority in each election unit.

Immediately following the election the union asked for a procedure to be instituted which would facilitate dues collection among the employees and for a formalized grievance procedure. In January 1967, a preliminary set of demands was submitted to the administration in addition to requests for the dues and grievance procedures. These included the benefits which had been enjoyed by the long-established Brooklyn Public Library Staff Association: (1) use of library bulletin boards to publicize union activity; (2) use of the internal branch mail system to distribute union material; (3) distribution by the library of union literature and an application for membership to all new employees; and (4) use of working time and library facilities to conduct union business.

The library resisted these requests because of the obvious encroachment that their granting would have on service to the public. Of equal importance was the fact that the granting of these privileges would, in effect, make the library administration an agent of the union in conducting union affairs, communication with members, and recruiting new members. During the negotiations it was particularly difficult to convince the union representatives that the union was not the staff association, but was instead a new entity which had a separate and distinct legal relationship to the library and its employees.

The Los Angeles County Public Library System became unionized in 1970. Both AFSCME and the Los Angeles County Employees Association (LACEA) competed for membership. LACEA won the right to be on the "Librarian" election ballot in a hearing before the County Employee Relations Commission (CERCOM).

There were two classes of voters in the election: librarians and library assistants (library assistants were considered nonprofessional according to the County Employee Relations Ordinance definition). The three issues on the ballot were: (1) Should LACEA be designated as the library's negotiating representative? (2) Should library assistants be included in the librarians' unit? (Only librarians could vote on this issue.) (3) Should "no" organization be designated as the certified unit?

There was an estimated turnout of over 70 percent of those eligible to vote—60 percent was necessary for the election to be valid. A strictly supervised secret ballot election was held under the auspices of the County Registrar of Voters. The unit chose LACEA as their certified "bargaining" representative by a vote of 234 to 33. The professional librarians voted 110 to 37 to include the class of library assistant in the librarians' unit.

Early in 1970 the work of hammering out the first union agreement with the Los Angeles County Librarians Unit began in earnest. The major point of contention during the long months of negotiations was premium pay for overtime. Finally, in November 1970, the first Memorandum of Understanding (MOU) was signed. It was ratified by the Board of Supervisors on November 17, 1970, with the stipulation that the subject of overtime be submitted to factfinding. This issue was resolved, at least for the 1970/71 fiscal year, in February 1971 with the signed understanding, following the factfinder's recommendations, that:

Not withstanding the provisions of Article IX of the Memorandum of Understanding for the Librarians Unit, employees on the payroll as of November 17, 1970 will not be required to work on Sunday, except where such Sunday work exceeds their regular 40-hour week, and on such occasions the employees shall be paid the premium rate for such Sunday work. Employees who may volunteer to work Sunday as a part of their 40-hour week will not receive such premium pay. Any person who has sincere religious conviction will not be compelled to work hours prohibited by his religious belief.[4]

Former County Librarian, William S. Geller, in recounting the development of the union, said, "California librarians could take a perverse pride, in that formation of the County Library bargaining unit was probably the most intransigent, bitter and longest 'argument' of all 50 units in Los Angeles County."[5] It was the last of all the units to reach agreement, a posture which caused county management to develop a new image of librarians as assertive and agressive—much to their surprise.

LEGISLATION

FEDERAL

President Kennedy signed two Executive Orders on January 17, 1962 in response to recommendations by the Task Force on Employee-Management Relations in the Federal Service. As Ann Holland states: "Executive Order 10988, 'Employee-Management Cooperation in the Federal Service,' and its sister order Executive Order 10987, 'Agency Systems for Appeals from Adverse Actions,' have ushered in a new era in employee-management relations in the Federal service as the first major policy change in fifty years."[6]

Executive Order 10987 recognizes that it is in the public interest to provide safeguards which protect employees against unjust adverse actions, and that prompt reconsideration of protested decisions will improve employee-management relations and promote the efficiency of the service.

Executive Order 10988 proclaims that "participation of employees in the formulation and implementation of personnel policies affecting them contributes to effective conduct of public business," and that "the efficient administration of the Government and the well-being of employees require that orderly and constructive relationships be maintained between employee organizations and management officials." The order further proclaims the right of federal employees to organize.

After several years of implementation under Executive Order 10988, dissatisfaction with the order and its interpretations by federal agencies increased as collective bargaining units and agreements spread among federal employees.[7] In September 1967, President

Johnson appointed a panel to study the operations of Executive Order 10988. The panel was to review what the program had accomplished and in what ways it was deficient.

The report of the review panel, although never released officially by President Johnson, was issued in draft form as part of the 1968 annual report of the U.S. Department of Labor. The report contained nineteen recommendations designed to respond to complaints raised during the public hearings and to influence the course of the federal labor relations program.

Most of the recommendations of the review panel were accepted by a cabinet-level group established by President Nixon and were eventually incorporated into Executive Order 11491, effective October 29, 1969. The main changes in Executive Order 11491 were: (1) the removal of authority from the agency head, (2) an attempt to standardize the federal labor-management relations system, and (3) a closer conformity of the system to that in the private sector.

STATE

Executive Order 10988 was issued in 1962 and had a noticeable impact on state and local government. By the mid-1960s,

> several states began to enact laws that showed the distinctive influence of the federal model provided by Kennedy's order. The overwhelming majority of state statutes pertaining to public employee relations have been enacted since 1965, and each year brings additional states into the picture, either through amendments or enactment of new laws.[8]

The need for determination of state policy with regard to public employee labor relations is clear. The rise in union membership and in union militancy and strikes suggest that the need for policy response exists in all of the states. State policy is needed, preferably before the problems become more acute. In the absence of legislative guidelines, some administrators have entered into bargaining arrangements which most experts would consider unwise.[9] Because of their naïveté, they have permitted an unusually broad scope of bargaining, which may interfere with their abilities to manage. Most authorities agree that the preferred solution would be a set of guidelines developed after careful study by each state legislature for its specific situation.

There are currently forty-two states which have enacted some sort of law requiring or permitting either negotiations or consultation between governmental authorities and public employee unions.[10] There are basically two policy responses that a state legislature may consider: (1) to adopt legislation for recognition without bargaining, generally known as "meet and confer" legislation; (2) to adopt legislation authorizing and regulating collective bargaining.

The California public employees relations law is the Meyers-Milias-Brown Act, first effective in January 1968. The stated purpose of this legislation is as follows:

> . . . to promote full communication between public employers and their employees by providing a reasonable method of resolving disputes regarding wages, hours, and other terms and conditions of employment between public employers and public employee organizations. It is also the purpose of this chapter to promote the improvement of personnel management and employer-employee relations within the various public agencies in the State of California by providing a uniform basis for recognizing the right of public employees to join organizations of their own choice and be represented by such organizations in their employment relationships with public agencies. Nothing contained herein shall be deemed to supersede the provisions of existing state law and the charters, ordinances, and rules of local public agencies which establish and regulate a merit or civil service system or which provide for other methods of administering employer-employee relations nor is it intended that this chapter be binding upon those public agencies which provide procedures for the administration of employer-employee relations in accordance with the provision of this chapter. This chapter is intended, instead, to strengthen merit, civil service and other methods of administering employer-employee relations through the establishment of uniform and orderly methods of communication between employees and the public agencies by which they are employed.[11]

The Meyers-Milias-Brown Act is a "meet and confer" law; California is the largest state with it and operates without a labor board. Other provisions of the Meyers-Milias-Brown Act are that it does not contain a strike prohibition and it requires a sharing of costs between the parties for mediation.

"MEET AND CONFER" v. COLLECTIVE BARGAINING

Although most states, when determining positive policies in public employee labor relations, have opted for a full collective bargaining approach, some solid support exists for the "meet and confer" relationship. "Meet and confer" refers to a formalized relationship between organized employees and public management whereby the employee organization is guaranteed the right to present viewpoints to public management, and management in turn has the duty to listen. Decisions in the area of terms and conditions of employment cannot be made legally without prior consultation with labor organizations. The final decision is unilateral on the part of management, however, and is not an agreement between the parties.

As indicated previously, California is a "meet and confer" state. Legislation establishes procedures under which the employee representatives are determined. Once chosen, the representative has certain rights. The public employer is forbidden by law to change wages, benefits or working conditions without first consulting with the employee representative. If agreement is reached during this process of consultation, the two parties can put their agreement in writing. The agreement or Memorandum of Understanding is not effective, however, until the legislative body acts by statute, ordinance, or resolution on subjects requiring legislative action.

"Meet and confer" can give employees an effective voice in the determination of conditions of employment, particularly if they have an effective political voice that assures them of legislative consideration. "Meet and confer" also satisfies those who believe that collective bargaining undermines the prerogatives of management.

Unions normally dislike this approach, believing that when they sit down across the table from management, they should have powers equal to those of management. The right of petition is not the same as the right to bargain. It takes two to bargain, but only one—management—to make decisions following consultation. The unions therefore reason that as long as employees are supplicants they are in a second-class relationship. Because of union dissatisfaction with "meet and confer," it can be anticipated that unions will continue to press for full bargaining status. It is therefore advisable to give some thought to the possible temporary nature of the "meet and confer" relationship. It might be considered as an initial stage in union-management relations.[12] In this case, it is advisable to avoid setting up conditions which might have to be undone if the relationship were to change to collective bargaining.

Collective bargaining implies bilateral decision-making. Union and management discuss terms and conditions of employment, and they must agree to the same conditions. The union voice in bargaining is as strong as that of management. A union refusal is just as final as a management refusal; either party has the power of veto over any proposal.

Management is typically more comfortable in a unilateral decision-making posture. It is much easier to direct someone what to do than to sell him on the merits of the case. It is comfortable to know that once a decision has been made, one has the authority to implement it. With the advent of the unions and collective bargaining, however, management can no longer follow the typical textbook approach to decision-making about the determination of terms and conditions of employment. The union wants to assist with decisions even though no assistance has been sought.

Although it is often difficult for management to adjust to sharing the decision-making process, it is possible and it must be done. After all, management engages in bilateralism in many other decision-making areas. For example, buying property, equipment, or books are typically negotiated decisions: bargaining takes place between buyer and seller before a decision to purchase is final. Other examples are the increasing community involvement in the decision-making authority in the urban areas, and the student involvement in the academic sector. The problem then, is management's understandable unwillingness to surrender historical rights and to bargain bilaterally.

Management rights clauses are present in both private and public employment. Executive Order 11491 provides that all agreements shall state that the responsibility of management officials for a government activity requires them to retain the right, in accordance with applicable laws and regulations, to: (1) direct its employees; (2) hire, promote, transfer, assign and retain employees in positions within the agency, and to suspend, demote, discharge, or take other disciplinary action against employees; (3) relieve employees from duties because of lack of work or for other legitimate reasons; (4) maintain the efficiency of the government operations entrusted to them; (5) determine the methods, means and personnel for conducting such operations; and (6) take any necessary action to carry out the mission of the agency in situations of emergency.[13] In a bargaining situation, management must be prepared to present its demands; the union always presents its demands. Management may wish to have work practices changed or policies implemented that may be subject to bargaining. John A. Hanson has said that "collective bargaining is a two-way street, with management having as much right to make demands as the union."[14] Management should take a positive position in asserting its demands. Regardless of management's feeling about the collective bargaining process, it is essential that management prepare for and deal with it in a way which recognizes the right of employees to organize and bargain collectively, and which represents management effectively and retains its right to manage.

DETERMINING THE BARGAINING UNIT

Collective bargaining and "meet and confer" statutes provide for determination of bargaining units. A bargaining unit is a group of workers in a public agency who are represented by one union or eligible to be represented by that union. Unit determination is among the most difficult tasks in public employee labor relations.[15] Decisions about the inclusiveness of a bargaining unit—the group of employees to be represented by one union under one contract—can be crucial.

Essentially, a bargaining unit should be limited to those groups which have a community of interest in decisions concerning their employment.[16] For example, many laws, including the National Labor Relations Act, forbid the grouping of professionals with nonprofessionals unless the professionals vote for inclusion. It is most difficult to determine the scope of a bargaining unit in a typical government agency because of the wide variety of employment classifications, the many diverse services and functions, and geographically dispersed operations. By contrast, the decision is comparatively easy in private industry since the typical factory usually produces one or a limited number of products.

There are some categories of employees which are restricted from union membership because of the confidential or other special nature of the duties. Examples of these employees who are excluded from a bargaining unit are personnel or industrial relations employees, confidential secretaries and assistants, administrative employees, and supervisory employees.

Determination of the appropriate level of supervision that should be excluded from the bargaining unit is extremely important to management. It is generally accepted that, if supervisors are loyal to the organization, their loyalty to the employee is compromised. Supervisors who are excluded from the bargaining unit which includes their subordinates are those whose duties differ from the duties of subordinates and include the rights to recommend hiring and firing and to handle grievances.

A clear conflict of interest exists, posing many problems for management, between the supervisor's responsibility to perform the management function with regard to the employees and the maintenance of discipline, and membership in a union. If the supervisor is the president of the local union, with whom does the employee file a grievance against the supervisor? Can the supervisor maintain an effective supervisory relationship with a fellow union member?

RIGHT TO STRIKE

Historically, the union's role: "in the private sector has been one of protest—against low wages, long hours, oppressive working conditions. The traditional instrument for protest has been the strike."[17] As unions have become better established (often as a result of strike actions), collective bargaining has prevailed and the use of the strike has become more selective, for times when bargaining failed or when agreement could not be reached on the terms of a new contract.

In the public sector, strikes have almost universally been held to be contrary to either specific statute, government policy, or the common law. Various penalties, including mandatory dismissal, fines, and occasionally prison sentences, have been imposed with increasing frequency since 1960.

Despite the sometimes severe nature of the sanctions against striking, strike bans have not been effective. Serious strikes have occurred in states with laws prohibiting strikes and providing for sanctions against strikers and their leaders.[18] A number of factors have provoked this disregard of law. In some instances, bargaining agents and leaders have found it in their interest to suffer the consequences of the strike, exploiting the short imprisonment or payment of fines to make themselves "martyrs to the cause." In other instances, there has been no disposition on the part of administrative officers to enforce the sanctions permitted by law. The major factor, however, has been the basic shortcoming in most of the existing legislation: its failure to provide effective legal machinery for the resolution of impasses.

Public employee strikes have occurred and will continue to occur with increasing frequency. A table entitled "Summary of State and Local Government Work Stoppages, by State: 12 Month Periods Ended October 1972 and October 1974" shows an increase of total work stoppages in the United States from 382 in 1972 to 471 in 1974. The total number of employees involved was 130,935 in 1972 and 162,115 in 1974; the total number of days of idleness was 1,127,911 in 1972 and 1,404,768 in 1974, representing a 24.5 percent increase.[19]

There are clearly two opposing views with respect to public employee strikes. Those who oppose a blanket prohibition on strikes in government argue that there cannot be genuine collective bargaining without the right to strike. Without the strike threat, public and private employers alike will realize that they have the upper hand and will not engage in real collective bargaining. Others consider it illogical and inequitable to deny the right to strike to government employees when it is not denied to employees in private industry doing the same work, such as hospital workers, transit workers, printing plant workers, etc.[20]

Those who support the prohibition against all government strikes do so primarily on three grounds: (1) the fear that the principle of sovereignty will be imperiled by legalizing any strikes in government, (2) the difficulty in differentiating between essential and nonessential activities, and (3) the belief that the strike is an economic weapon which, in government, is not matched by countervailing power normally available in private industry.

Regardless of which view is more correct or appropriate, public employee strikes are extremely costly and inconvenient. They affect the delivery of services provided through a public agency and create a distortion of the political process, a major long-run social cost. The distortion results when the union obtains too much power (relative to other interest groups) in decisions affecting the level of taxes and the allocation of tax dollars.[21]

In the event of a strike or work stoppage, public managers should attempt to reduce the vulnerability of the public employer. The strike should not be feared, but should be dealt with as positively as possible, with management analyzing the most effective ways of maintaining services while employees are away from work.

The first things management should consider are the various ways in which the effect of strikes by public employees can be mitigated. Careful contingency planning must be done. While there are limits to what can be accomplished through planning, certain things can be done, such as determination of emergency traffic patterns and parking facilities to offset some of the consequences of a transit strike. Contingency plans to use neighboring hospitals may prevent disasters during a hospital strike. Automating the most critical functions before a dispute occurs can reduce the impact of a strike enormously. For example, many utility strikes today are hardly noticed by the public because automation permits continued service. Another approach to lessening the impact of strikes deserves consideration. It seems evident that emergencies, and most severe inconveniences caused by strikes, can be avoided by partial operation of the struck facility. The goal of any partial operation scheme is to ensure performance of those functions essential to health and safety and the avoidance of severe inconveniences.[22] This condition of limited services would also apply pressure to both the government and the union to settle.

Many library directors have had the experience of developing a contingency plan or a plan of operation in the event of a work stoppage. These plans are usually based upon certain management and supervisory personnel carrying out only very limited public service functions. All other library functions would cease for the duration of the work stoppage.

PRODUCTIVITY

The concept of work productivity is still an unpopular one to most people. A Harris poll conducted for the National Commission on Productivity "shows that 70% of the public believe that productivity gains benefit stockholders 'a lot,' but only 20% believe it benefits employees."[23] Actually, the word *productivity*, with its emphasis on products, is probably a misnomer today. More than two-thirds of the nation's work force is engaged in performing services rather than in producing goods, and the percentage of workers employed on the production assembly line is less than 2 percent of the total work force. In government, the percentage of those employed in services is certainly higher than the national average. Perhaps a more apt definition would include the concepts of improved managerial and employee performance and more effective delivery of service.

As dramatically shown by the New York City fiscal crisis, this is a period of escalating costs, increased taxes, steady wage increases; there are a broadening of benefits and creation of new ones, and a trend toward public employees retiring earlier and living longer (with consequent strain on pension funds). At the same time there is "taxpayer revolt" over the impact of these trends on their pocketbooks. There are growing complaints about the services rendered, and widespread feelings that government at all levels is doing too many things poorly and at too high a price.[24]

How can these attitudes and conditions be changed while coping with shrinking budgets? It can be accomplished through an analytical approach to productivity with emphasis on reorganization, computerization, procurement of new and improved equipment, scheduling changes, project management, budget reform, assignment of productivity targets and posting of periodic progress reports. Massive efforts are being undertaken throughout the country; if these are to be truly effective, however, they must involve organized labor-management relationships.

Improving employee performance will not be easy. As government units grow larger, the distance between the public employer and the individual employee increases. This contributes to alienation, frustration, and a feeling of being ignored and unappreciated. Since all change is unsettling and usually resisted, a successful productivity program requires the involvement of employees and their acceptance of the soundness and fairness of the approach.

A spokesman for the AFL-CIO has charged that "the most fundamental obstacle to real advances in public sector productivity gains has been the resistance of public employers to accept true collective bargaining."[25] Public management has held that it has an inviolate prerogative in directing the work force and in establishing conditions of employment. Proponents maintain that true collective bargaining brings about an understanding and cooperative attitude between employers and employees. Such an attitude establishes the appropriate climate for discussions on productivity.

Productivity bargaining is an element in bargaining dealing with methods for improving productivity. This may involve changes in traditional occupations, work jurisdictions, job rights or established customs. These become very sensitive areas since work patterns develop a certain tradition and become institutionalized as established practice. In Los Angeles County, after a five-year battle in the courts, the Joint Council of LACEA and Eligibility Workers Local 535 have made a significant breakthrough on the "past practice" issue. The 1975/76 Memoranda of Understanding with the Child Welfare Workers and the Eligibility Workers units contain, for the first time, clauses relating to caseloads. These clauses limit management's ability to assign caseloads and adjust workload.[26]

Another major difficulty to overcome if productivity bargaining is to be effective is the basic difference in approach to productivity held by management and by labor unions. Management typically views increased productivity as an alternative to service cutbacks and higher taxes. In a recent report to the Los Angeles County Board of Supervisors,[27] Harry L. Hufford, Chief Administrative Officer, cites a policy statement, in which the Committee for Economic Development called upon politicians, public managers, unions and citizen groups to make better performance a political issue and driving force behind the operations of these government organizations. In view of prevailing financial situations,[28] which can be characterized by an excess of program requirements in competition for limited dollar resources, the mandate to government managers to accelerate and expand productivity efforts is clear.

Conversely, the union position is strongly opposed to productivity bargaining as a budget reduction device. They feel that any gains resulting from productivity improvement must be shared. Unions believe that the worker should be in a position to recommend productivity improvements and that the motivation to do so would result from the knowledge that he or she will share in the savings. Unions do not advocate pay incentive systems, however, but rather seek to establish programs attuned to the needs and aspirations of the workers. Such proposals would include job enrichment programs aimed toward making the job more interesting, challenging, rewarding, or convenient. Frequently where job enrichment programs have been emphasized, increased productivity results even if productivity had not been one of the stated goals of the program.

How, then, can these two viewpoints be reconciled? Unfortunately, not all points at issue may be totally resolved and it is realistic to anticipate that new problems will replace old ones. Nevertheless, it appears that improved management skills and training in work simplification and measurement can provide substantial relief to the problem.

Hufford's report to the Board of Supervisors, mentioned earlier, recommends a productivity enhancement program in three areas: (1) productivity measurement,* (2) productivity awareness and train-

---

*Appendix 2 of the report graphically displayed labor productivity index of the Los Angeles County Library System. It showed that library productivity increased an average of 3.7 percent/year for the three-year period from 1972 to 1975. By comparison, productivity increases in U.S. private industry have averaged 3 percent/year since World War II. The library productivity index shows an uptrend, which demonstrates improvement and it establishes a basis for future evaluation.

ing at the supervisory and managerial level, and (3) work simplification and system improvement.[29] The program is to be carried out by productivity review teams, which will employ survey techniques, specialized training and workshops, and employee and customer attitudinal surveys to accomplish the following:

—Improve basic management skills, with particular reference to productivity improvement and work simplification. Performance evaluation skills will be strengthened to define levels of expectation, improve standards of evaluation, and handle productivity-related disciplinary problems, such as absenteeism and tardiness.
—Identify targets of opportunity, that is, bottlenecks, methods problems, or opportunities for cost reduction, and assist the department in correcting them during the survey.
—Establish or refine productivity indexes and quality indexes.
—Establish measure of program effectiveness and customer satisfaction.[30]

The program is designed to improve productivity in the departments being studied and (ideally) to save money.

IMPACT ON PERSONNEL FUNCTION

The foregoing discussions on strikes and work stoppages and productivity have suggested the negative impacts on budgets and on service to users which can result from collective bargaining. The financial impact is obvious. The increase in wages and fringe benefits caused by aggressive union activity through the years has had a strong impact on city and county treasuries across the nation. The negotiations process is also extremely costly in terms of time spent in consultation, preparation, negotiation and the grievance procedure. A union attempting to gain popularity, for example, will defend everyone in a grievance action no matter how illogical or unjustified the grievance may be. Disciplinary problems will be carefully watched by unions, and members will be defended by union attorneys. Union membership will be considered by the individual employee in certain classifications as more important and more protective than civil service status.

Various institutional procedures related to the personnel function are being challenged. Chief among these are the historic civil service system and "merit" pay increases.[31] Merit increases are believed by the unions to be based on subjective standards. This accusation is difficult to deny, and the result is that merit increases are frequently replaced with across-the-board increases in each bargaining unit. The union philosophy is that promotion should be based upon seniority rather than on merit or performance.

Recruitment and selection techniques are carefully scrutinized by the unions. If these techniques and procedures are not of the best quality, union activity can be a healthy force for change, requiring local governments to undertake some basic reexamination of elementary, but neglected, matters.

Performance evaluations or efficiency ratings and position classification are also controversial matters which are of concern to the unions. Civil service has come to be identified with the employer, even though its original purpose was to protect employees from the employer. Thus, the many challenges by employee organizations of personnel practices typically the responsibility of the civil service system tend to erode and curtail the authority of civil service. The adversary relationship between the union and management in libraries with sound adequate personnel policies will be less strained than in those libraries having outmoded, sloppy personnel practices.

SCOPE OF PROFESSIONAL NEGOTIATIONS

Professional negotiations sometimes present a problem unique to the public service. Frequently, professionals such as teachers, nurses, social workers and librarians seek to extend the scope of bargaining beyond a point recognized in industry.[32] School teacher organizations often attempt to negotiate what boards of education consider to be policy matters. The teachers argue that many so-called policy decisions affect their conditions of work, and that as professionals they have a significant contribution to make in determining policy issues. It can be predicted that librarians, as professionals, will use the collective bargaining process to determine institutional policies at the bargaining table jointly with administrators, and that after the contract has been signed, both sides will carry out their part of the provisions under the contract.[33]

FUTURE TRENDS

This article has described many facets, conflicts and problems surrounding the union-management relationship among public employees, with particular emphasis on library employees. In researching the article, certain trends have become apparent; some discussion of the future direction of public employee labor relations is therefore warranted at this point.

Public employee unions will continue to increase in membership. The extent of future organizing gains in the public sector will vary according to occupation.[34] For example, because of the demand for health services and the number of persons employed in these occupations, many unions will concentrate on the health service occupations. Conversely, only limited increases will occur in public education because of the already high degree of organization by professional associations.

The scope of bargaining in the public sector will continue to widen in future years. As the parties get accustomed to each other and become more sophisticated in the techniques of the bargaining process, more topics will be negotiated. Decisions affecting professional employees pose new problems for unions and public employers alike. Some formal procedure may be developed to allow professional employees a voice in important decisions. Collective bargaining will continue to expand among unorganized public employees. Where collective bargaining has already been instituted, the pace will intensify.

The need for more expertise and training in employee relations must be stressed. Management must develop skills in labor relations if other leadership efforts are going to be effective in daily operating situations. If reasonable union-management harmony is to prevail, means of reducing the effects of the adversary relationship must be found. It is not possible to generalize on how this can be accomplished. The key is in the attitude of the parties toward each other—a condition which varies from one agency to another. This condition can be as simple or as complex as good interpersonal relations.

References

1. U.S. Labor-Management Services Administration. Division of Public Employee Labor Relations. *Summary of State Policy Regulations for Public Sector Labor Relations.* Washington, D.C., U.S.G.P.O., 1975, p. i.

2. Kassalow, Everett M. "Trade Unionism Goes Public," *Public Interest* 14:118-22, Winter 1969.

3. Lewis, Robert. "A New Dimension in Library Administration—Negotiating a Union Contract," *A.L.A. Bulletin* 63:455-64, April 1969.

4. County of Los Angeles and LACEA. Stipulation of Agreement, Feb. 5, 1971.

5. Geller, William S. "Working with the Library Union—An Administrator's Experience," *California Librarian* 33:57, Jan. 1972.

6. Holland, Ann. "Unions are Here to Stay" (Pamphlet No. 17). Society for Personnel Administration, 1962.

7. Moskow, Michael H. *Collective Bargaining in Public Employment.* New York, Random House, 1970.

8. Murphy, Richard J. "The State and Local Experience in Employee Relations," *In* Richard J. Murphy and Morris Sackman, eds. *The Crisis in Public Employee Relations in the Decade of the Seventies.* Washington, D.C., The Bureau of National Affairs, Inc., 1970, p. 16.

9. Council of State Governments. *State-Local Employee Labor Relations* (R.R. No. 18). Lexington, Ky., Council of State Governments, 1970, p. 4.

10. U.S. Bureau of the Census. *Labor-Management Relations in State and Local Governments: 1974* (State and Local Government Special Studies No. 75). Washington D.C., U.S.G.P.O., Feb. 1976, p. 33.

11. State of California. Dept. of General Services. Documents and Publications Section. *Government Code of the State of California.* Sacramento, State of California, 1975, chap. 10, § 3500.

12. Council of State Governments, *op. cit.*, p. 29.

13. Holland, *op. cit.*, pp. 22, 23.

14. Hanson, John A. "How to Bargain in the Public Sector," *Public Management* 57:17, Feb. 1975.

15. Council of State Governments, *op. cit.*, p. 15.

16. Heisel, W. Donald. *New Questions and Answers on Public Employee Negotiation.* Chicago, International Personnel Management Association, 1973, p. 13.

17. Henle, Peter. "Some Reflections on Organized Labor and the New Militants," *Monthly Labor Review* 92:23, July 1969.

18. Ackerly, Robert L., and Johnson, W. Stanfield. "Critical Issues in Negotiations Legislation" (Professional Negotiations No. 3). Washington, D.C., National Assocation of Secondary School Principals, 1969.

19. U.S. Bureau of the Census, *op. cit.*, p. 73.

20. Walsh, Robert E. *Sorry—No Government Today: Unions v. City Hall.* Boston, Beacon Press, 1969, p. 245.

21. Wellington, Harry H., and Winter, Ralph K., Jr. *The Unions and the Cities.* Washington, D.C., Brookings Institution, 1971, p. 167.

22. *Ibid.*, p. 197.

23. Zagoria, Sam. "Productivity Bargaining," *Public Management* 55:14, July 1973.

24. *Ibid.*, p. 15.

25. Oswald, Rudy. "Public Productivity Tied to Bargaining," *AFL-CIO American Federationist* 83:20, March 1976.

26. County of Los Angeles. Memoranda of Understanding regarding the Child Welfare Workers and the Social Service Investigators employee representation units, May 1975.

27. Hufford, Harry L. "Report on County Productivity Activities." Report presented to the Los Angeles County Board of Supervisors, April 1976.

28. *Ibid.*

29. *Ibid.*

30. *Ibid.*
31. Weiford, Douglas G. "Organizing Management for Employee Relations." *In* Kenneth O. Warner, ed. *Developments in Public Employee Relations.* Chicago, Public Personnel Association, 1965, pp. 92-94.
32. Heisel, *op. cit.*, p. 48.
33. Brose, Friedrich K. "Collective Bargaining: Can We Adjust to It?" *California Librarian* 36:37-47, April 1975.
34. Moskow, *op. cit.*, p. 288.

Part XI
SYSTEMS PERSPECTIVE AND TECHNOLOGY

Introduction

Administrators of libraries and information centers must consider new management concepts and approaches as means of improving the overall performance of the library. Three recent developments that have great potential for library and information center administration are applying general systems concepts to the organization, utilizing operations research techniques to analyze library activities, and implementing computerized information systems.

Systems thinking, i.e., the recognition that a system is composed of interdependent parts with common goals is not especially new. However, its application to organizations and administration is a recent phenomenon. As Fremont E. Kast and James E. Rosenzweig suggest, a number of basic system concepts, such as the input-transformation-output model, open systems view, dynamic equilibrium, equifinality, and negative entropy, can be useful conceptual tools to assist administrators in better understanding the "why" of administrative techniques.

Perhaps the most useful aspect of general systems thinking is that it provides a model, or paradigm by which we can analyze and better understand the flow of resources through the organization, how these resources are processed into services or products, and the ability of the organization to interact and respond effectively to environmental change. The importance of general systems thinking is its utility as a conceptual tool to understand the interrelationships among myriad administrative activities. Systems thinking forces administrators to consider the impacts and alternatives of decision making vis-à-vis other organizational activities and goals.

But Bommer would suggest that sometimes the application of interdisciplinary and non-library originated techniques, such as operations research in the library, can backfire. While everyone can agree upon the importance of critically assessing the operations of the organization by way of empirical research, developing models to describe those activities, and using sophisticated analytic/statistical techniques, Michael Bommer points out in his article that the "sobering reality is that few libraries are currently employing any analytical models."

This indictment of library and information center management is significant because it suggests that library decision making is not based on empirical evidence. However, Bommer notes that the failure to apply operations research in libraries is due in part to operations researchers themselves, who tend to develop mathematical models too complex to be understood by practitioners, which thus cannot be implemented. His suggestions as to how operations research techniques *can* become a useful tool for library administration deserve careful consideration by library and information center administrators.

In a related area, the impact of computer technology on the library has brought both benefits and problems to administrators. Theodore D. Sterling suggests that inadequate consideration of the impact of computerized information systems on humans may be a primary reason for the failure of these systems in formal organizations. Further, he recognizes the fact that computer system costs in terms of dignity, self-respect, and other uniquely "human" characteristics to the organization may be significant if not considered before implementation.

Sterling's comments are especially useful for library and information center administrators because his analysis includes the impact of computerized systems on users or clients, as well as the organization itself. This perspective is important for library administration because we are developing both types of systems, often without adequate consideration of the different requirements and purposes of systems for users versus systems for internal library activities. Indeed, more thought is needed to develop systems that can serve both constituencies and still be "humanized" adequately to ensure their effective use.

These three topics, systems thinking, operations research, and humanizing computerized information systems all reflect the need for library administrators to be able to identify concepts and develop innovative approaches to resolve problems related to analysis and technology in the library. Systems thinking can provide a base by which techniques such as operations research and information systems can be better understood and applied to improve productivity and effectiveness. Clearly, increasing pressures will be placed on the library to cut costs yet increase their services and overall effectiveness. General systems thinking, operations research techniques, and humanizing computerized information systems may assist us to think more clearly about library decision areas and apply more effectively the potential of the computer and other technologies for improved library services.

General Systems Theory: Applications for Organization and Management
By Fremont E. Kast and James E. Rosenzweig

General systems theory has been proposed as a basis for the unification of science. The open systems model has stimulated many new conceptualizations in organization theory and management practice. However, experience in utilizing these concepts suggests many unresolved dilemmas. Contingency views represent a step toward less abstraction, more explicit patterns of relationships, and more applicable theory. Sophistication will come when we have a more complete understanding of organizations as total systems (configurations of subsystems) so that we can prescribe more appropriate organizational designs and managerial systems. Ultimately, organization theory should serve as the foundation for more effective management practice.

Biological and social scientists generally have embraced systems concepts. Many organization and management theorists seem anxious to identify with this movement and to contribute to the development of an approach which purports to offer the ultimate—the unification of all science into one grand conceptual model. Who possibly could resist? General

---

Reprinted by permission from *Academy of Management Journal*, vol. 15 (December 1972), pp. 447-65.

systems theory seems to provide a relief from the limitations of more mechanistic approaches and a rationale for rejecting "principles" based on relatively "closed-system" thinking. This theory provides the paradigm for organization and management theorists to "crank into their systems model" all of the diverse knowledge from relevant underlying disciplines. It has become almost mandatory to have the word "system" in the title of recent articles and books (many of us have compromised and placed it only in the subtitle).[1]

But where did it all start? This question takes us back into history and brings to mind the long-standing philosophical arguments between mechanistic and organismic models of the 19th and early 20th centuries. As Deutsch says:

> Both mechanistic and organismic models were based substantially on experiences and operations known before 1850. Since then, the experience of almost a century of scientific and technological progress has so far not been utilized for any significant new model for the study of organization and in particular of human thought [12, p. 389].

General systems theory even revives the specter of the "vitalists" and their views on "life force" and most certainly brings forth renewed questions of teleological or purposeful behavior of both living and nonliving systems. Phillips and others have suggested that the philosophical roots of general systems theory go back even further, at least to the German philosopher Hegel (1770-1831) [29, p. 56]. Thus, we should recognize that in the adoption of the systems approach for the study of organizations we are not dealing with newly discovered ideas—they have a rich genealogy.

Even in the field of organization and management theory, systems views are not new. Chester Barnard used a basic systems framework.

> A cooperative system is a complex of physical, biological, personal, and social components which are in a specific systematic relationship by reason of the cooperation of two or more persons for at least one definite end. Such a system is evidently a subordinate unit of larger systems from one point of view; and itself embraces subsidiary systems—physical, biological, etc.—from another point of view. One of the systems comprised within a cooperative system, the one which is implicit in the phrase "cooperation of two or more persons," is called an "organization" [3, p. 65].

And Barnard was influenced by the "systems views" of Vilfredo Pareto and Talcott Parsons. Certainly this quote (dressed up a bit to give the term "system" more emphasis) could be the introduction to a 1972 book on organizations.

Miller points out that Alexander Bogdanov, the Russian philosopher, developed a theory of tektology or universal organization science in 1912 which foreshadowed general systems theory and used many of the same concepts as modern systems theorists [26, p. 249-250].

---

[1] An entire article could be devoted to a discussion of ingenious ways in which the term "systems approach" has been used in the literature pertinent to organization theory and management practice.

However, in spite of a long history of organismic and holistic thinking, the utilization of the systems approach did not become the accepted model for organization and management writers until relatively recently. It is difficult to specify the turning point exactly. The momentum of systems thinking was identified by Scott in 1961 when he described the relationship between general systems theory and organization theory.

> The distinctive qualities of modern organization theory are its conceptual-analytical base, its reliance on empirical research data, and above all, its integrating nature. These qualities are framed in a philosophy which accepts the premise that the only meaningful way to study organization is to study it as a system . . . Modern organization theory and general system theory are similar in that they look at organization as an integrated whole [33, pp. 15-21].

Scott said explicitly what many in our field had been thinking and/or implying—he helped us put into perspective the important writings of Herbert Simon, James March, Talcott Parsons, George Homans, E. Wight Bakke, Kenneth Boulding, and many others.

But how far have we really advanced over the past decade in applying general systems theory to organizations and their management? Is it still a "skeleton," or have we been able to "put some meat on the bones"? The systems approach has been touted because of its potential usefulness in understanding the complexities of "live" organizations. Has this approach really helped us in this endeavor or has it compounded confusion with chaos? Herbert Simon describes the challenge for the systems approach:

> In both science and engineering, the study of "systems" is an increasingly popular activity. Its popularity is more a response to a pressing need for synthesizing and analyzing complexity than it is to any large development of a body of knowledge and technique for dealing with complexity. If this popularity is to be more than a fad, necessity will have to mother invention and provide substance to go with the name [35, p. 114].

In this article we will explore the issue of whether we are providing substance for the term *systems approach* as it relates to the study of organizations and their management. There are many interesting historical and philosophical questions concerning the relationship between the mechanistic and organistic approaches and their applicability to the various fields of science, as well as other interesting digressions into the evolution of systems approaches. However, we will resist those temptations and plunge directly into a discussion of the key concepts of general systems theory, the way in which these ideas have been used by organization theorists, the limitations in their application, and some suggestions for the future.

KEY CONCEPTS OF GENERAL SYSTEMS THEORY

The key concepts of general systems theory have been set forth by many writers [6, 7, 13, 17, 25, 28, 39] and have been used by many organization and management theorists [10, 14, 18, 19, 22, 23, 24, 32]. It is not our purpose here to elaborate on them in great detail because we anticipate that most readers will have been exposed to them in some depth. Figure I provides a very brief review of those characteristics of systems which seem to have wide acceptance. The review is far from complete. It is diffi-

FIGURE I
Key Concepts of General Systems Theory

Subsystems or Components: A system by definition is composed of interrelated parts or elements. This is true for all systems—mechanical, biological, and social. Every system has at least two elements, and these elements are interconnected.

Holism, Synergism, Organicism, and Gestalt: The whole is not just the sum of the parts; the system itself can be explained only as a totality. Holism is the opposite of elementarism, which views the total as the sum of its individual parts.

Open Systems View: Systems can be considered in two ways: (1) closed or (2) open. Open systems exchange information, energy, or material with their environments. Biological and social systems are inherently open systems; mechanical systems may be open or closed. The concepts of open and closed systems are difficult to defend in the absolute. We prefer to think of open-closed as a dimension; that is, systems are relatively open or relatively closed.

Input-Transformation-Output Model: The open system can be viewed as a transformation model. In a dynamic relationship with its environment, it receives various inputs, transforms these inputs in some way, and exports outputs.

System Boundaries: It follows that systems have boundaries which separate them from their environments. The concept of boundaries helps us understand the distinction between open and closed systems. The relatively closed system has rigid, impenetrable boundaries; whereas the open system has permeable boundaries between itself and a broader suprasystem. Boundaries are relatively easily defined in physical and biological systems, but are very difficult to delineate in social systems, such as organizations.

Negative Entropy: Closed, physical systems are subject to the force of entropy which increases until eventually the entire system fails. The tendency toward maximum entropy is a movement to disorder, complete lack of resource transformation, and death. In a closed system, the change in entropy must always be positive; however, in open biological or social systems, entropy can be arrested and may even be transformed into negative entropy—a process of more complete organization and ability to transform resources—because the system imports resources from its environment.

Steady State, Dynamic Equilibrium, and Homeostasis: The concept of steady state is closely related to that of negative entropy. A closed system eventually must attain an equilibrium state with maximum entropy—death or disorganization. However, an open system may attain a state where the system remains in dynamic equilibrium through the continuous inflow of materials, energy, and information.

Feedback: The concept of feedback is important in understanding how a system maintains a steady state. Information concerning the outputs or the process of the system is fed back as an input into the system, perhaps leading to changes in the transformation process and/or future outputs. Feedback can be both positive and negative, although the field of cybernetics is based on negative feedback. Negative feedback is informational input which indicates that the system is deviating from a prescribed course and should readjust to a new steady state.

Hierarchy: A basic concept in systems thinking is that of hierarchical relationships between systems. A system is composed of subsystems of a lower order and is also part of a suprasystem. Thus, there is a hierarchy of the components of the system.

Internal Elaboration: Closed systems move toward entropy and disorganization. In contrast, open systems appear to move in the direction of greater differentiation, elaboration, and a higher level of organization.

Multiple Goal-Seeking: Biological and social systems appear to have multiple goals or purposes. Social organizations seek multiple goals, if for no other reason than that they are composed of individuals and subunits with different values and objectives.

Equifinality of Open Systems: In mechanistic systems there is a direct cause and effect relationship between the initial conditions and the final state. Biological and social systems operate differently. Equifinality suggests that certain results may be achieved with different initial conditions and in different ways. This view suggests that social organizations can accomplish their objectives with diverse inputs and with varying internal activities (conversion processes).

cult to identify a "complete" list of characteristics derived from general systems theory; moreover, it is merely a first-order classification. There are many derived second- and third-order characteristics which could be considered. For example, James G. Miller sets forth *165* hypotheses, stemming from open systems theory, which might be applicable to two or more levels of systems [25]. He suggests that they are *general* systems theoretical hypotheses and qualifies them by suggesting that they are propositions applicable to general systems *behavior* theory and would thus exclude non-living systems. He does not limit these propositions to individual organisms, but considers them appropriate for social systems as well. His hypotheses are related to such issues as structure, process, subsystems, information, growth, and integration. It is obviously impossible to discuss all of these hypotheses; we want only to indicate the extent to which many interesting propositions are being posed which might have relevance to many different types of systems. It will be a very long time (if ever) before most of these hypotheses are validated; however, we are surprised at how many of them can be agreed with intuitively, and we can see their possible verification in studies of social organizations.

We turn now to a closer look at how successful or unsuccessful we have been in utilizing these concepts in the development of "modern organization theory."

A BEGINNING: ENTHUSIASTIC BUT INCOMPLETE

We have embraced general systems theory but, really, how completely? We could review a vast literature in modern organization theory which has explicitly or implicitly adopted systems theory as a frame of reference, and we have investigated in detail a few representative examples of the literature in assessing the "state of the art" [18, 19, 22, 23, 31, 38]. It was found that most of these books professed to utilize general systems theory. Indeed, in the first few chapters, many of them did an excellent job of presenting basic systems concepts and showing their relationship to organizations; however, when they moved further into the discussion of more specific subject matter, they departed substantially from systems theory. The studies appear to use a "partial systems approach" and leave for the reader the problem of integrating the various ideas into a systemic whole. It also appears that many of the authors are unable, because of limitations of knowledge about subsystem relationships, to carry out the task of using general systems theory as a conceptual basis for organization theory.

Furthermore, it is evident that each author had many "good ideas" stemming from the existing body of knowledge or current research on organizations which did not fit neatly into a "systems model." For example, they might discuss leadership from a relatively closed-system point of view and not consider it in relation to organizational technology, structure, or other variables. Our review of the literature suggests that much remains to be done in applying general systems theory to organization theory and management practice.

SOME DILEMMAS IN APPLYING GST TO ORGANIZATIONS

Why have writers embracing general systems theory as a basis for studying organizations had so much difficulty in following through? Part of this difficulty may stem from the newness of the paradigm and our inability to operationalize "all we think we know" about this approach. Or it may be because we know too little about the systems under investigation. Both of these possibilities will be covered later, but first we need to look at some of the more specific conceptual problems.

Organizations as Organisms

One of the basic contributions of general systems theory was the rejection of the traditional closed-system or mechanistic view of social organizations. But, did general systems theory free us from this constraint only to impose another, less obvious one? General systems theory grew out of the organismic views of von Bertalanffy and other biologists; thus, many of the characteristics are relevant to the living organism. It is conceptually easy to draw the analogy between living organisms and social organizations. "There is, after all, an intuitive similarity between the organization of the human body and the kinds of organizations men create. And so, undaunted by the failures of the human-social analogy through time, new theorists try afresh in each epoch" [2, p. 660]. General systems theory would have us accept this analogy between organism and social organization. Yet, we have a hard time swallowing it whole. Katz and Kahn warn us of the danger:

> There has been no more pervasive, persistent, and futile fallacy handicapping the social sciences than the use of the physical model for the understanding of social structures. The biological metaphor, with its crude comparisons of the physical parts of the body to the parts of the social system, has been replaced by more subtle but equally misleading analogies between biological and social functioning. This figurative type of thinking ignores the essential difference between the socially contrived nature of social systems and the physical structure of the machine or the human organism. So long as writers are committed to a theoretical framework based upon the physical model, they will miss the essential social-psychological facts of the highly variable, loosely articulated character of social systems [19, p. 31].

In spite of this warning, Katz and Kahn do embrace much of the general systems theory concepts which are based on the biological metaphor. We must be very cautious about trying to make this analogy too literal. We agree with Silverman who says, "It may, therefore, be necessary to drop the analogy between an organization and an organism: organizations may be systems but not necessarily *natural* systems" [34, p. 31].

Distinction between Organization and an Organization

General systems theory emphasizes that systems are organized—they are composed of interdependent components in some relationship. The social organization would then follow logically as just another system. But, we are perhaps being caught in circular thinking. It is true that all systems (physical, biological, and social) are by definition organized, but are all systems organizations? Rapoport and Horvath distinguish "organization theory" and "the theory of organizations" as follows:

> We see organization theory as dealing with general and abstract organizational principles; it applies to any system exhibiting organized complexity. As such, organization theory is seen as an extension of mathematical physics or, even more generally, of mathematics designed to deal with organized systems. The theory of organizations, on the other hand, purports to be a social science. It puts real human organizations at the center of interest. It may study the social structure of organizations and so can be viewed as a branch of sociology; it can study the behavior of individuals or groups as members of organizations and can be viewed as a part of social psychology; it can study power relations and principles of control in organizations and so fits into political science [30, pp. 74-75].

Why make an issue of this distinction? It seems to us that there is a vital matter involved. All systems may be considered to be organized, and more advanced systems may display differentiation in the activities of component parts—such as the specialization of human organs. However, all systems *do not* have purposeful entities. Can the heart or lungs be considered as purposeful entities in themselves or are they only components of the larger purposeful system, the human body? By contrast, the social organization is composed of two or more purposeful elements. "An organization consists of elements that have and can exercise their own wills" [1, p. 669]. Organisms, the foundation stone of general systems theory, do not contain purposeful elements which exercise their own will. This distinction between the organism and the social organization is of importance. In much of general systems theory, the concern is primarily with the way in which the *organism* responds to environmentally generated inputs. Feedback concepts and the maintenance of a steady state are based on internal adaptations to environmental forces. (This is particularly true of cybernetic models.) But, what about those changes and adaptations which occur from *within* social organizations? Purposeful elements within the social organization may initiate activities and adaptations which are difficult to subsume under feedback and steady state concepts.

Opened and Closed Systems

Another dilemma stemming from general systems theory is the tendency to dichotomize all systems as opened or closed. We have been led to think of physical systems as closed, subject to the laws of entropy, and to think of biological systems as open to their environment and, possibly, becoming negentropic. But applying this strict polarization to social organizations creates many difficulties. In fact, most social organizations and their subsytems are "partially open" and "partially closed." Open and closed are a matter of degree. Unfortunately, there seems to be a widely held view (often more implicit than explicit) that *open-system thinking is good and closed-system thinking is bad.* We have not become sufficiently sophisticated to recognize that both are appropriate under certain conditions. For example, one of the most useful conceptualizations set forth by Thompson is that the social organization *must seek* to use closed-system concepts (particularly at the technical core) to reduce uncertainty and to create more effective performance at this level.

Still Subsystems Thinking

Even though we preach a general systems approach, we often practice subsystems thinking. Each of the academic disciplines and each of us personally have limited perspective of the system we are studying. While proclaiming a broad systems viewpoint, we often dismiss variables outside our interest or competence as being irrelevant, and we only open our system to those inputs which we can handle with our disciplinary bag of tools. We are hampered because each of the academic disciplines has taken a narrow "partial systems view" and find comfort in the relative certainty which this creates. Of course, this is not a problem unique to modern organization theory. Under the more traditional process approach to the study of management, we were able to do an admirable job of delineating and discussing planning, organizing, and controlling as separate activities. We were much less successful in discussing them as integrated and interrelated activities.

How Does Our Knowledge Fit?

One of the major problems in utilizing general systems theory is that we know (or think we know) more about certain relationships than we can fit into a general systems model. For example, we are beginning to understand the two-variable relationship between technology and structure. But, when we introduce another variable, say psychosocial relationships, our models become too complex. Consequently, in order to discuss all the things we know about organizations, we depart from a systems approach. Perhaps it is because we know a great deal more about the elements or subsystems of an organization than we do about the interrelationships and interactions between these subsystems. And, general systems theory forces us to consider those relationships about which we know the least—a true dilemma. So we continue to elaborate on those aspects of the organization which we know best—a partial systems view.

Failure to Delineate a Specific System

When the social sciences embraced general systems theory, the total system became the focus of attention and terminology tended toward vagueness. In the utilization of systems theory, we should be more precise in delineating the specific system under consideration. Failure to do this leads to much confusion. As Murray suggests:

> I am wary of the word "system" because social scientists use it very frequently without specifying which of several possible different denotations they have in mind; but more particularly because, today, "system" is a highly cathected term, loaded with prestige; hence, we are all strongly tempted to employ it even when we have nothing definite in mind and its only service is to indicate that we subscribe to the general premise respecting the interdependence of things—basic to organismic theory, holism, field theory, interactionism, transactionism, etc. . . . When definitions of the units of a system are lacking, the term stands for no more than an article of faith, and is misleading to boot, insofar as it suggests a condition of affairs that may not actually exist [27, pp. 50-51].

We need to be much more precise in delineating both the boundaries of the system under consideration and the level of our analysis. There is a tendency for current writers in organization theory to accept general systems theory and then to move indiscriminately across systems boundaries and between levels of systems without being very precise (and letting their readers in on what is occurring). James Miller suggests the need for clear delineation of levels in applying systems theory, "It is important to follow one procedural rule in systems theory in order to avoid confusion. Every discussion should begin with an identification of the level of reference, and the discourse should not change to another level without a specific statement that this is occurring" [25, p. 216]. Our field is replete with these confusions about systems levels. For example, when we use the term "organizational behavior" are we talking about the way the organization behaves as a system or are we talking about the behavior of the individual participants? By goals, do we mean the goals of the organization or the goals of the individuals within the organization? In using systems theory we must become more precise in our delineation of systems boundaries and systems levels if we are to prevent confusing conceptual ambiguity.

Recognition That Organizations Are "Contrived Systems"

We have a vague uneasiness that general systems theory truly does not recognize the "contrived" nature of social organizations. With its predominate emphasis on natural organisms, it may understate some characteristics which are vital for the social organization. Social organizations do not occur naturally in nature; they are contrived by man. They have structure; but it is the structure of events rather than of physical components, and it cannot be separated from the processes of the system. The fact that social organizations are contrived by human beings suggests that they can be established for an infinite variety of purposes and do not follow the same life-cycle patterns of birth, growth, maturity, and death as biological systems. As Katz and Kahn say:

> Social structures are essentially contrived systems. They are made of men and are imperfect systems. They can come apart at the seams overnight, but they can also outlast by centuries the biological organisms which originally created them. The cement which holds them together is essentially psychological rather than biological. Social systems are anchored in the attitudes, perceptions, beliefs, motivations, habits, and expectations of human beings [19, p. 33].

Recognizing that the social organization is contrived again cautions us against making an exact analogy between it and physical or biological systems.

Questions of Systems Effectiveness

General systems theory with its biological orientation would appear to have an evolutionary view of system effectiveness. That living system which best adapts to its environment prospers and survives. The primary measure of effectiveness is perpetuation of the organism's species. Teleological behavior is therefore directed toward survival. But, is survival the only criterion of effectiveness of the social system? It is probably an essential but not all-inclusive measure of effectiveness.

General systems theory emphasizes the organism's survival goal and does not fully relate to the question of the effectiveness of the system in its suprasystem—the environment. Parsonian functional-structural views provide a contrast. "The *raison d'etre* of complex organizations, according to this analysis, is mainly to benefit the society in which they belong, and that society is, therefore, the appropriate frame of reference for the evaluation of organizational effectiveness" [41, p. 896].

But, this view seems to go to the opposite extreme from the survival view of general systems theory—the organization exists to serve the society. It seems to us that the truth lies somewhere between these two viewpoints. And it is likely that a systems viewpoint (modified from the species survival view of general systems theory) will be most appropriate. Yuchtman and Seashore suggest:

> The organization's success over a period of time in this competition for resources —i.e., its bargaining position in a given environment—is regarded as an expression of its overall effctiveness. Since the resources are of various kinds, and the competitive relationships are multiple, and since there is interchangeability among classes of resources, the assessment of organizational effectiveness must be in terms not of any single criterion but of an open-ended multidimensional set of criteria [41, p. 891].

This viewpoint suggests that questions of organizational effectiveness must be concerned with at least three levels of analysis. The level of the environment, the level of the social organization as a system, and the level of the subsystems (human participants) within the organization. Perhaps much of our confusion and ambiguity concerning organizational effectiveness stems from our failure to clearly delineate the level of our analysis and, even more important, our failure really to understand the relationships among these levels.

Our discussion of some of the problems associated with the application of general systems theory to the study of social organizations might suggest that we completely reject the appropriateness of this model. On the contrary, we see the systems approach as the new paradigm for the study of organizations; but, like all new concepts in the sciences, one which has to be applied, modified, and elaborated to make it as useful as possible.

SYSTEMS THEORY PROVIDES THE NEW PARADIGM

We hope the discussion of GST and organizations provides a realistic appraisal. We do not want to promote the value of the systems approach as a matter of faith; however, we do see systems theory as vital to the study of social organizations and as providing the major new paradigm for our field of study.

Thomas Kuhn provides an interesting interpretation of the nature of scientific revolution [20]. He suggests that major changes in all fields of science occur with the development of new conceptual schemes or "paradigms." These new paradigms do not just represent a step-by-step advancement in "normal" science (the science generally accepted and practiced) but, rather, a revolutionary change in the way the scientific field is perceived by the practitioners. Kuhn says:

> The historian of science may be tempted to exclaim that when paradigms change, the world itself changes with them. Led by a new paradigm, scientists adopt new instruments and look in new places. Even more important, during revolutions scientists see new and different things when looking with familiar instruments in places they have looked before. It is rather as if the professional community has been suddenly transported to another planet where familiar objects are seen in a different light and are joined by unfamiliar ones as well. . . . Paradigm changes do cause scientists to see the world of their research-engagement differently. Insofar as their only recourse to that world is through what they see and do, we may want to say that after a revolution scientists are responding to a different world [20, p. 110].

New paradigms frequently are rejected by the scientific community. (At first they may seem crude and limited—offering very little more than older paradigms.) They frequently lack the apparent spohistication of the older paradigms which they ultimately replace. They do not display the clarity and certainty of older paradigms which have been refined through years of research and writing. But, a new paradigm does provide for a "new start" and opens up new directions which were not possible under the old. "We must recognize how very limited in both scope and precision a paradigm can be at the time of its first appearance. Paradigms gain their status because they are more successful than their competitors in solving a few problems that the group of practitioners has come to recognize as acute. To be more successful is not, however, to be either completely successful with a single problem or notably successful with any large number" [20, p. 23].

Systems theory does provide a new paradigm for the study of social organizations and their management. At this stage it is obviously crude and lacking in precision. In some ways it may not be much better than older paradigms which have been accepted and used for a long time (such as the management process approach). As in other fields of scientific endeavor, the new paradigm must be applied, clarified, elaborated, and made more precise. But, it does provide a fundamentally different view of the reality of social organizations and can serve as the basis for major advancements in our field.

We see many exciting examples of the utilization of the new systems paradigm in the field of organization and management. Several of these have been referred to earlier [7, 13, 19, 22, 23, 24, 31, 38], and there have been many others. Burns and Stalker made substantial use of systems views in setting forth their concepts of mechanistic and organic managerial systems [8]. Their studies of the characteristics of these two organization types lack precise definition of the variables and relationships, but their colleagues have used the systems approach to look at the relationship of organizations to their environment and also among the technical, structural, and behavioral characteristics within the organization [24]. Chamberlain used a system view in studying enterprises and their environment, which is substantially different from traditional microeconomics [9]. The emerging field of "environmental sciences" and "environmental administration" has found the systems paradigm vital.

Thus, the systems theory paradigm is being used extensively in the investigation of relationships between subsystems within organizations and in studying the environmental interfaces. But, it still has not advanced sufficiently to meet the needs. One of the major problems is that the practical need to deal with comprehensive systems of relationships is overrunning our ability to fully understand and predict these relationships. *We vitally need the systems paradigm but we are not sufficiently sophisticated to use it appropriately.* This is the dilemma. Do our current failures to fully utilize the systems paradigm suggest that we reject it and return to the older, more traditional, and time-tested paradigms? Or do we work with systems theory to make it more precise, to understand the relationships among subsystems, and to gather the informational inputs which are necessary to make the systems approach really work? We think the latter course offers the best opportunity.

Thus, we prefer to accept current limitations of systems theory, while working to reduce them and to develop more complete and sophisticated approaches for its application. We agree with Rapoport who says:

> The system approach to the study of man can be appreciated as an effort to restore meaning (in terms of intuitively grasped understanding of wholes) while adhering to the principles of *disciplined* generalizations and rigorous deduction. It is, in short, an attempt to make the study of man both scientific and meaningful [7, p. xxii].

We are sympathetic with the second part of Rapoport's comment, the need to apply the systems approach but to make disciplined generalizations and rigorous deductions. This is a vital necessity and yet a major current limitation. We do have some indication that progress (although very slow) is being made.

WHAT DO WE NEED NOW?

Everything is related to everything else—but how? General systems theory provides us with the macro paradigm for the study of social organizations. As Scott and others have pointed out, most sciences go through a macro-micro-macro cycle or sequence of emphasis [33]. Traditional bureaucratic theory provided the first major macro view of organizations. Administrative management theorists concentrated on the development of macro "principles of management" which were applicable to all organizations. When these macro views seemed incomplete (unable to explain important phenomena), attention turned to the micro level—more detailed analysis of components or parts of the organization, thus the interest in human relations, technology, or structural dimensions.

The systems approach returns us to the macro level with a new paradigm. General systems theory emphasizes a very high level of abstraction. Phillips classifies it as a third-order study [29] that attempts to develop macro concepts appropriate for all types of biological, physical, and social systems.

In our view, we are now ready to move down a level of abstraction to consider second-order systems studies or midrange concepts. These will be based on general systems theory but will be more concrete and will emphasize more specific characteristics and relationships in social organizations. They will operate within the broad paradigm of systems theory but at a less abstract level.

What should we call this new midrange level of analysis? Various authors have referred to it as a "contingency view," a study of "patterns of relationships," or a search for "configurations among subsystems." Lorsch and Lawrence reflect this view:

> During the past few years there has been evident a new trend in the study of organizational phenomena. Underlying this new approach is the idea that the internal functioning of organizations must be consistent with the demands of the organization task, technology, or external environment, and the needs of its members if the organization is to be effective. Rather than searching for the panacea of the one best way to organize under all conditions, investigators have more and more tended to examine the functioning of organizations in relation to the needs of their particular members and the external pressures facing them. Basically, this approach seems to be leading to the development of a "contingency" theory of organization with the appropriate internal states and processes of the organization contingent upon external requirements and member needs [21, p. 1].

Numerous others have stressed a similar viewpoint. Thompson suggests that the essence of administration lies in understanding basic configurations which exist between the various subsystems and with the environment. "The basic function of administration appears to be co-alignment, not merely of people (in coalitions) but of institutionalized action—of technology and task environment into a viable domain, and of organizational design and structure appropriate to it [38, p. 157].

Bringing these ideas together we can provide a more precise definition of the contingency view:

> The contingency view of organizations and their management suggests that an organization is a system composed of subsystems and delineated by identifiable boundaries from its environmental suprasystem. The contingency view seeks to understand the interrelationships within and among subsystems as well as between the organization and its environment and to define patterns of relationships or configurations of variables. It emphasizes the multivariate nature of organizations and attempts to understand how organizations operate under varying conditions and in specific circumstances. Contingency views are ultimately directed toward suggesting organizational designs and managerial systems most appropriate for specific situations.

But, it is not enough to suggest that a "contingency view" based on systems concepts of organizations and their management is more appropriate than the simplistic "principles approach." If organization theory is to advance and make contributions to managerial practice, it must define more explicitly certain patterns of relationships between organizational variables. This is the major challenge facing our field.

Just how do we go about using systems theory to develop these midrange or contingency views. We see no alternative but to engage in intensive comparative investigation of many organizations following the advice of Blau:

> A theory of organization, whatever its specific nature, and regardless of how subtle the organizational processes it takes into account, has as its central aim to establish the constellations of characteristics that develop in organizations of various kinds. Comparative studies of many organizations are necessary, not alone to test the hypotheses implied by such a theory, but also to provide a basis for initial exploration and refinement of the theory by indicating the conditions on which relationships, originally assumed to hold universally are contingent. . . . Systematic research on many organizations that provides the data needed to determine the interrelationships between several organizational features is, however, extremely rare [5, p. 332].

Various conceptual designs for the comparative study of organizations and their subsystems are emerging to help in the development of a contingency view. We do not want to impose our model as to what should be considered in looking for these patterns of relationships. However, the tentative matrix shown in Figure II suggests this approach. We have used as a starting point the two polar organization types which have been emphasized in the literature—closed/stable/mechanistic and open/adaptive/organic.

We will consider the environmental suprasystem and organizational subsystems (goals and values, technical, structural, psychosocial, and managerial) plus various dimensions or characteristics of each of these systems. By way of illustration we have indicated several specific subcategories under the Environmental Suprasystem as well as the Goals and Values subsystem. This process would have to be completed and extended to all of the subsystems. The next step would be the development of appropriate descriptive language (based on research and conceptualization) for each relevant characteristic across the continuum of organization types. For example, on the "stability" dimension for Goals and Values we would

FIGURE II
Matrix of Patterns of Relationships between Organization Types and Systems Variables

Organizational Supra- and Subsystems	Continuum of Organization Types	
	Closed/Stable/Mechanistic	Open/Adaptive/Organic
Environmental relationships		
General nature	Placid	Turbulent
Predictability	Certain, determinate	Uncertain, indeterminate
Boundary relationships	Relatively closed; limited to few participants (sales, purchasing, etc.); fixed and well-defined	Relatively open; many participants have external relationships; varied and not clearly defined
Goals and values		
Organizational goals in general	Efficient performance, stability, maintenance	Effective problem-solving, innovation, growth
Goal set	Single, clear-cut	Multiple, determined by necessity to satisfy a set of constraints
Stability	Stable	Unstable
Technical		
Structural		
Psychosocial		
Managerial		

have High, Medium, and Low at appropriate places on the continuum. If the entire matrix were filled in, it is likely that we would begin to see discernible patterns of relationships among subsystems.

We do not expect this matrix to provide *the* midrange model for everyone. It is highly doubtful that we will be able to follow through with the field work investigations necessary to fill in all the squares. Nevertheless, it does illustrate a possible approach for the translation of more abstract general systems theory into an appropriate midrange model which is relevant for organization theory and management practice. Frankly, we see this as a major long-term effort on the part of many researchers, investigating a wide variety of organizations. In spite of the difficulties involved in such research, the endeavor has practical significance. Sophistication in the study of organizations will come when we have a more complete understanding of organizations as total systems (configurations of subsystems) so that we can prescribe more appropriate organizational designs and managerial systems. Ultimately, organization theory should serve as the foundation for more effective management practice.

APPLICATION OF SYSTEMS CONCEPTS TO MANAGEMENT PRACTICE

The study of organizations is an applied science because the resulting knowledge is relevant to problem-solving in on-going institutions. Contributions to organization theory come from many sources. Deductive and inductive research in a variety of disciplines provide a theoretical base of propositions which are useful for understanding organizations and for managing them. Experience gained in management practice is also an important input to organization theory. In short, management is based on the body of knowledge generated by practical experience *and* eclectic scientific research concerning organizations. The body of knowledge developed through theory and research should be translatable into more effective organizational design and managerial practices.

Do systems concepts and contingency views provide a panacea for solving problems in organizations? The answer is an emphatic *no;* this approach does not provide "ten easy steps" to success in management. Such cookbook approaches, while seemingly applicable and easy to grasp, are usually shortsighted, narrow in perspective, and superficial—in short, unrealistic. Fundamental ideas, such as systems concepts and contingency views, are more difficult to comprehend. However, they facilitate more thorough understanding of complex situations and increase the likelihood of appropriate action.

It is important to recognize that many managers have used and will continue to use a systems approach and contingency views intuitively and implicitly. Without much knowledge of the underlying body of organization theory, they have an intuitive "sense of the situation," are flexible diagnosticians, and adjust their actions and decisions accordingly. Thus, systems concepts and contingency views are not new. However, if this approach to organization theory and management practice can be made more explicit, we can facilitate better management and more effective organizations.

Practicing managers in business firms, hospitals, and government agencies continue to function on a day-to-day basis. Therefore, they must use whatever theory is available, they cannot wait for the *ultimate* body of knowledge (there is none!). Practitioners should be included in the search for new knowledge because they control access to an essential ingredient—organizational data—and they are the ones who ultimately put the theory to the test. Mutual understanding among managers, teachers, and researchers will facilitate the development of a relevant body of knowledge.

Simultaneously with the refinement of the body of knowledge, a concerted effort should be directed toward applying what we do know. We need ways of making systems and contingency views more usable. Without oversimplification, we need some relevant guidelines for practicing managers.

The general tenor of the contingency view is somewhere between simplistic, specific principles and complex, vague notions. It is a midrange concept which recognizes the complexity involved in managing modern organizations but uses patterns of relationships and/or configurations of subsystems in order to facilitate improved practice. The art of management depends on a reasonable success rate for actions in a probabilistic environment. Our hope is that systems concepts and contingency views, while continually being refined by scientists/researchers/theorists, will also be made more applicable.

REFERENCES

1. Ackoff, Russell L., "Towards a System of Systems Concepts," *Management Science* (July 1971).
2. Back, Kurt W., "Biological Models of Social Change," *American Sociological Review* (August 1971).
3. Barnard, Chester I., *The Functions of the Executive* (Cambridge, Mass.: Harvard University Press, 1938).
4. Berrien, F. Kenneth, *General and Social Systems* (New Brunswick, N.J.: Rutgers University Press, 1968).
5. Blau, Peter M., "The Comparative Study of Organizations," *Industrial and Labor Relations Review* (April 1965).
6. Boulding, Kenneth E., "General Systems Theory: The Skeleton of Science," *Management Science* (April 1956).
7. Buckley, Walter, ed., *Modern Systems Research for the Behavioral Scientist* (Chicago: Aldine Publishing Company, 1968).
8. Burns, Tom and G. M. Stalker, *The Management of Innovation* (London: Tavistock Publications, 1961).
9. Chamberlain, Neil W., *Enterprise and Environment: The Firm in Time and Place* (New York: McGraw-Hill Book Company, 1968).

10. Churchman, C. West, *The Systems Approach* (New York: Dell Publishing Company, Inc., 1968).
11. DeGreene, Kenyon, ed., *Systems Psychology* (New York: Mc-Graw Hill Book Company, 1970).
12. Deutsch, Karl W., "Toward a Cybernetic Model of Man and Society," in Walter Buckley, ed., *Modern Systems Research for the Behavioral Scientist* (Chicago: Aldine Publishing Company, 1968).
13. Easton, David, *A Systems Analysis of Political Life* (New York: John Wiley & Sons, Inc., 1965).
14. Emery, F. E. and E. L. Trist, "Socio-technical Systems," in C. West Churchman and Michele Verhulst, eds., *Management Sciences: Models and Techniques* (New York: Pergamon Press, 1960).
15. Emshoff, James R., *Analysis of Behavioral Systems* (New York: The Macmillan Company, 1971).
16. Gross, Bertram M., "The Coming General Systems Models of Social Systems," *Human Relations* (November 1967).
17. Hall, A. D. and R. E. Eagen, "Definition of System," *General Systems, Yearbook for the Society for the Advancement of General Systems Theory,* Vol 1 (1956).
18. Kast, Fremont E. and James E. Rosenzweig, *Organization and Management Theory: A Systems Approach* (New York: McGraw-Hill Book Company, 1970).
19. Katz, Daniel and Robert L. Kahn, *The Social Psychology of Organizations* (New York: John Wiley & Sons, Inc., 1966).
20. Kuhn, Thomas S., *The Structure of Scientific Revolutions* (Chicago: University of Chicago Press, 1962).
21. Lorsch, Jay W. and Paul R. Lawrence, *Studies in Organizational Design* (Homewood, Illinois: Irwin-Dorsey, 1970).
22. Litterer, Joseph A., *Organizations: Structure and Behavior,* Vol 1 (New York: John Wiley & Sons, Inc., 1969).
23. ——————, *Organizations: Systems, Control and Adaptation,* Vol 2 (New York: John Wiley & Sons, Inc., 1969).
24. Miller, E. J. and A. K. Rice, *Systems of Organizations* (London: Tavistock Publications, 1967).
25. Miller, James G., "Living Systems: Basic Concepts," *Behavioral Science* (July 1965).
26. Miller, Robert F., "The New Science of Administration in the USSR," *Administrative Science Quarterly* (September 1971).
27. Murray, Henry A., "Preparation for the Scaffold of a Comprehensive System," in Sigmund Koch, ed., *Psychology: A Study of a Science,* Vol 3 (New York: McGraw-Hill Book Company, 1959).
28. Parsons, Talcott, *The Social System* (New York: The Free Press of Glencoe, 1951).
29. Phillips, D. C., "Systems Theory—A Discredited Philosophy," in Peter P. Schoderbek, *Management Systems* (New York: John Wiley & Sons, Inc., 1971).
30. Rapoport, Anatol and William J. Horvath, "Thoughts on Organization Theory," in Walter Buckley, ed., *Modern Systems Research for the Behavioral Scientist* (Chicago: Aldine Publishing Company, 1968).
31. Rice, A. K., *The Modern University* (London: Tavistock Publications, 1970).
32. Schein, Edgar, *Organizational Psychology,* rev. ed. (Englewood Cliffs, New Jersey: Prentice-Hall, Inc., 1970).
33. Scott, William G., "Organization Theory: An Overview and an Appraisal," *Academy of Management Journal* (April 1961).
34. Silverman, David, *The Theory of Organizations* (New York: Basic Books, Inc., 1971).
35. Simon, Herbert A., "The Architecture of Complexity," in Joseph A. Litterer, *Organizations: Systems, Control and Adaptation,* Vol 2 (New York: John Wiley & Sons, Inc., 1969).

36. Springer, Michael, "Social Indicators, Reports, and Accounts: Toward the Management of Society," *The Annals of the American Academy of Political and Social Science* (March 1970).
37. Terreberry, Shirley, "The Evolution of Organizational Environments," *Administrative Science Quarterly* (March 1968).
38. Thompson, James D., *Organizations in Action* (New York: McGraw-Hill Book Company, 1967).
39. von Bertalanffy, Ludwig, *General System Theory* (New York: George Braziller, 1968).
40. —————, The Theory of Open Systems in Physics and Biology," *Science* (January 13, 1950).
41. Yuchtman, Ephraim and Stanley E. Seashore, "A System Resource Approach to Organizational Effectiveness," *American Sociological Review* (December 1967).

Operations Research in Libraries: A Critical Assessment
By Michael Bommer

In the past decade a multitude of operations research models have appeared in the literature, each promising to help library managers in making better plans and decisions. To date, few of these models are being employed by libraries. The major reasons which seem to be preventing operations research from achieving its potential and fulfilling the expectations of its proponents in library management are explored. Finally, a prescription is formulated to guide library managers in working more effectively with operations researchers.

● Introduction

In the past decade, a multitude of operations research models have appeared in the literature, each promising to help library managers in making better plans and decisions. Models have been proposed for almost every aspect of library operations: e.g., locating libraries; selecting titles; determining multiple copy requirements; classifying and cataloging documents; selecting journals; storing documents; weeding documents, controlling documents; providing reference service; and establishing loan policies. Information systems and networks are other areas in which operations research studies have been developed (1). In many instances there are a multiplicity of models covering the same library operation.

One might get the impression that the library has become a playground for operations research model builders! With such a plethora of models developed, it would seem logical to conclude that most libraries are placing a heavy reliance on models in the decision-making and planning process. The sobering reality is that few libraries are currently employing any analytical models. Considering the discrepancy between the abundant supply of models on the one hand and the lack of demand for their use on the other, it is appropriate to critically assess the reasons for the failure of operations research to achieve the expectations of its proponents in the area of library management.

This article explores some of the more important factors which appear to restrain or impede operations research from attaining its potential in library management. Once these factors are identified, a prescription is formulated to guide library managers in their quest for developing more effective management systems.

● Too Much Mathematics

The first reason why operations research has failed to achieve its potential in library management is that *far too much attention has been devoted to the construction and solution of complex mathematical models*. For the most part, these models are comprehensible only to operations researchers. Herein lies the "achilles heel". Too often the primary motive of an operations researcher undertaking a library project is either to write a dissertation, or to publish an article in a professional journal, or to prove his/her mathematical prowess. There seems to exist an analytical snobbery which places in higher esteem those who build models which are more analytically abstract and complex, with little regard to their applicability. This snobbery influences operations researchers to devote an inordinate amount of attention to the construction and solution of highly complex, theoretically abstract, mathematical models.

The ramifications of this phenomenon are grave. First is that, too often, the degree of model sophistication exceeds the technical capability of the organization (2). The model is too demanding in terms of understanding, data requirements, computer time requirements, etc., to be successfully integrated into the library management system.

Second is that, again too often, crucial variables are "assumed away" or ignored in a quest to obtain an optimal solution to the model (3). The net result of this complex modelling process is the attainment of a *perfect* solution to a *hypothetical* problem. Meanwhile, the real problem facing the manager remains unsolved.

Finally, the exactness of a solution derived from a complex, analytical model conveys a sense of accuracy

---

Reprinted from *Journal of the American Society for Information Science*, vol. 26 (May-June 1975), pp. 137-39 by permission of John Wiley & Sons, Inc. © 1975 by John Wiley & Sons, Inc.

which is often misleading. Too often this precision tends to dominate and obscure the contribution of equally relevant and important non-quantifiable behavioral, organizational and political considerations.

● **Too Little Implementation**

The second major reason why operations research has not achieved its full potential in libraries is that *too little attention has been placed on the implementation aspect of an operations research model.* Successful implementation requires a climate of mutual understanding between the operations researcher and the library manager. This climate should be developed from the inception of the project. The operations researcher must understand the manager's perceptions, needs, expectations, pressures and limitations. The manager must understand the capabilities and demands of the operations research process. Each becomes a teacher, and each becomes a learner in the process of bridging the gap between their different worlds.

If this process is successful, the operations researcher will be less apt to propose a model which exceeds the resources and interest level of the manager—thus increasing the probability of eventual implementation. The manager, on the other hand, by understanding how the model contributes to the management system will have less cause for fear or resistance to change, an inherent human quality, again increasing the probability of eventual implementation.

Successful implementation also depends upon the identification and clarification of political, behavioral and organizational considerations relevant to the problem. Although these considerations are not always amenable to quantification for incorporation into a model, they can usually be structured and placed in proper perspective for the decision maker.

Finally, successful implementation requires a continuous surveillance over the direction of the study to assure that the focus will be on providing a workable solution to the library manager's problem. Too often the operations researcher working alone will develop a highly sophisticated model for a problem which is no longer real because of the model's limiting assumptions. This type of model will never be successfully implemented.

● **The Operations Research Process**

The third major reason why operations research has not achieved its expectations in libraries is that *too little emphasis has been focused upon the process of operations research.* Operations research is an organic process of inquiry aimed at understanding a managed system through research, and at designing better ways of controlling this system (4). Too often operations research is viewed as a *product* (e.g., a final model) rather than a *process* of successive understanding (e.g., an inquiry).

As Elton *et. al.* point out, the process of: "making objectives explicit, deriving suitable measures of the extent of meeting them, developing simple quantitative relations between input and output, and identifying constraints that one should pay to remove have proved considerably more valuable than the mere manipulation of complicated mathematical models (5)." This is not meant to imply that the importance of models should be discounted. They play an important role in the process. The precision and structure required to construct a model enhances critical, disciplined thinking, which results in greater clarity of the basic understandings. Models help to overcome problems of uncertainty and complexity, allowing the variables and interrelationships to be dealt with simultaneously. The consequences of a change in the system can be predicted when parameters of models are manipulated without having to disrupt the actual system. Models also provide a deeper understanding of the system by the transformation of data into information about the system. However, it should be recognized that the process of clarifying issues, identifying relationships, exploring barriers, investigating alternatives, examining values and assessing behavioral, organizational and political ramifications of a problem can yield invaluable benefits.

● **Strategic Library Management Problems**

The fourth and final major reason why operations research has failed to achieve its potential is that *too little attention has been placed on the pressing strategic problems of library managers.* Too often operations researchers have searched for a problem which is most conducive to analytical model building, irrespective of the manager's needs. Operations research must shift its emphasis from tackling the neat, simple tactical problems, or refining approaches to previously solved problems, and tackle the tougher, less structured, strategic problems (6). Little effort has been devoted, for example, to answering such vitally important questions as:

● How can a manager better justify resource inputs in terms of library outputs (7)?
● What is the value of a library's output to society in comparison with other competing programs such as law enforcement, public works, waste disposal, recreation, etc. for public libraries and programs such as instruction, athletics, maintenance, student affairs, etc. for the academic library?
● What effect do the available resources of the library exert upon the generation of demand for library service?
● How best can a problem-solving system be designed for libraries that identifies and solves present problems, prevents future problems and implements and maintains solutions under changing conditions (8)?
● What is a good marketing strategy for stimulating use of the library?
● How can library managers play a more active role in *shaping* the future rather than merely attempting to predict and adapt to future needs?

This is not to imply that research accomplished to date has been trivial. It is believed, however, that operations research *must* tackle some of the more pressing strategic problems of the manager.

● **Conclusion**

This concludes the exploration of what seems to be the major commissions and omissions which have barred operations research from achieving its potential effectiveness in library management.

In closing it would seem appropriate to impart some advice to library managers in dealing with operations researchers. *Close the playground.* Inform operations researchers that the building of highly sophisticated mathematical models for unrealistic problems will no longer be tolerated. Demand that the operations research studies be directed toward the development of workable solutions to pressing, real-world problems. Be open to learning and the possibility of changing established methods and behavior. Demand that *all* ramifications of the problem be considered, not just those that are quantifiable. From the inception, ask how the project might be implemented, including cost, time and data requirements. Do not settle for the role of consultant. Be prepared to invest a good deal of time as a member of the operations research team. As with most ventures, the more the library manager invests of his time and energies, the more he will get out. The potential benefits reaped when operations researchers work with library managers are great—but only if the process is steered back on the right course.

References

1. **Hamburg, M., R. Clelland, M. Bommer, L. Ramist** and **R. Whitfield**, *Library Planning and Decision-Making Systems*, Cambridge, MA: The MIT Press (1974).
2. **Leimkuhler, F.**, "Large Scale Library Systems," *Library Trends*, 21 (No. 4): 575-585 (1973).
3. **Grayson, J.C.**, "Management Science and Business Practice," *Harvard Business Review*, 51 (No. 4): 41-48 (1973).
4. **Ackoff, R.**, "Frontiers of Management Science," *The Bulletin of the Institute of Management Sciences*, 1 (No. 2): 19-24 (1971).
5. **Elton, M.** and **B. Vicker**, "The Scope for Operational Research in the Library and Information Field," *ASLIB Proceedings*, 25 (No. 8): 305-319 (1973).
6. **Grayson, J.C.**, *op. cit.*
7. **Hamburg, M., L. Ramist** and **M. Bommer**, 'Library Objectives and Performance Measures and their Use in Decision Making," *The Library Quarterly*, 42 (No. 1): 107-128 (January 1972).
8. **Ackoff, R.**, *op. cit.*

Humanizing Computerized Information Systems
By Theodore D. Sterling

The accumulation and control of information is a critical function for government and private, industrial and nonindustrial organizations. Yet the role of information as an organizational resource is not very well understood, especially as it is related to the organization's environment. What does appear is that computerized information systems have become a facilitating technology that interacts with organizational, historical, and environmental pressures and goals to shape not only the internal structure of an organization but also its interactions with society (1, 2). There is little doubt that the computerized or automated information system is revolutionizing the management of most, if not all, systems by which goods and services are produced or information is accumulated. This should be a source of great concern.

Weizenbaum (3) asked whether large computerized systems can be used by anybody except governments and really large corporations and whether such organizations will not use them mainly for antihuman purposes. The power of computerized information systems to control large enterprises answers the need to manage large systems and make them amenable to human control. By any criteria of management performance, computerization of a system permits its detailed control, and thus the computer is the ideal management tool. But the cost of the control is high.

Start-up costs to redesign and computerize large-scale enterprises are immense. In concentrating on feasibility and workability and simultaneously minimizing costs, few systems designers seem to have been concerned about whether their products will be used for antihuman purposes.

In many ways, it is immaterial whether control over the management network is exercised by manual means or by automation. As long as official procedures are detrimental to human dignity, nothing is changed in converting to automation except that individuals may shift the blame for their oppression from the human cog to the computer cog. It may be necessary, therefore, to clarify the dehumanizing components of a management system, which may be present whether or not the system has been automated, and to provide relief for any suffering they may have caused.

In a previous analysis (4) I pointed to two design strategies that account in large part for the presence of dehumanizing features in a management system. First, the efficiency of an enterprise is commonly increased by treating the recipients of the service and participants in the system as unpaid components whose time, effort, and intelligence do not appear in the cost accounting. Then, in order to maintain the efficiency of procedures once they have been established, the system is made exceedingly rigid, permitting freedom of ac-

---

Reprinted by permission from *Science*, vol. 190 (December 1975), pp. 1168-72.

tion at only a few, usually hidden, focal points of real control. Dehumanizing features are thus already ingrained in most systems of management, and automation of such systems simply transfers the dehumanizing practice from one means of exercising control to another, codifies it in computer programs, and expands its influence to a larger circle of recipients and participants. To provide for the smooth and efficient operation of a largely computerized management system, the automation process makes demands of its own on all participants which decrease the area of free action remaining to the individual. Rules of procedure are thus dictated by the growth of machines and not by the needs of man. As a consequence, it is possible for the machine to capture the prerogative to formulate questions important to man. If we take such developments as inevitable we are surrendering our humanity.

The point is that an intelligent understanding of a machine mode of control may be delayed until long after this control has been exercised. Wiener (5) argued that although procedures laid down to satisfy a process of automation are subject to human criticism and modification, such criticism may be ineffective because it may not surface until long after it is relevant. It may be too late then to correct the damage to the human condition. Systems are not detached from the people they interact with and the settings they create, and people strive for a sense of dignity, have needs that should be taken seriously, like to be treated with consideration and courtesy, and occasionally act as individuals — in short, they are entitled to be treated as human beings.

Despite the overriding importance of a person's dignity and humanity, little is known in terms of "scientific" specifics about the operational meaning of these concepts or the antecedent conditions that enhance or diminish them. Relatively few analyses have been devoted to systems features that may humanize organizations (6, 7). We know of only one attempt to incorporate humanizing features in a system and to evaluate their effects (8). Yet we cannot afford to wait for knowledge to accumulate about the procedures to be incorporated in information systems or information parts of systems to help avoid dehumanizing or add humanizing qualities to them. We live in a time of active proliferation of new and revised management procedures, and designers of information systems are organizational designers as well, who cannot avoid changing organizations (7, 9). This is especially true of the proliferation of management information systems, which are more than information systems in the technical sense, as they include all bureaucratic procedures and perhaps all systems components that enter into the production and distribution of goods and services and so dominate the economic, political, and social management of society. Organizational design should be taken on as an explicit activity and management information systems implemented in such a way that they create a more humane setting.

Gouldner (10) showed how rules and regulations respond to the self-interest of those who govern and are governed. But to influence the shaping of new bureaucracies and other management systems, it is first necessary to isolate the crucial categories of design features that may make manifest humanizing or dehumanizing qualities of information systems. The analysis presented here is based on the guidelines developed by the Stanley House workshop on humanizing computerized information systems (11, 12) in a serious attempt to isolate such design features. The guidelines are grouped into five broad categories, as shown in Table 1.

Many of the Stanley House criteria make sense as procedures for softening a bureaucracy as well as making an information system less rigid. There is no real distinction between manual and automated systems, and guidelines apply whether or not computers are used.

Table 1. Stanley House criteria for humanizing information systems.

A. Procedures for dealing with users
1. The language of a system should be easy to understand.
2. Transactions with a system should be courteous.
3. A system should be quick to react.
4. A system should respond quickly to users (if it is unable to resolve its intended procedure).
5. A system should relieve the users of unnecessary chores.
6. A system should provide for human information interface.
7. A system should include provisions for corrections.
8. Management should be held responsible for mismanagement.

B. Procedures for dealing with exceptions
1. A system should recognize as much as possible that it deals with different classes of individuals.
2. A system should recognize that special conditions might occur that could require special actions by it.
3. A system must allow for alternatives in input and processing.
4. A system should give individuals choices on how to deal with it.
5. A procedure must exist to override the system.

C. Action of the system with respect to information
1. There should be provisions to permit individuals to inspect information about themselves.
2. There should be provisions to correct errors.
3. There should be provisions for evaluating information stored in the system.
4. There should be provisions for individuals to add information that they consider important.
5. It should be made known in general what information is stored in systems and what use will be made of that information.

D. The problem of privacy
1. In the design of a system all procedures should be evaluated with respect to both privacy and humanization requirements.
2. The decision to merge information from different files and systems should never occur automatically. Whenever information from one file is made available to another file, it should be examined first for its implications for privacy and humanization.

E. Guidelines for system design having a bearing on ethics
1. A system should not trick or deceive.
2. A system should assist participants and users and not manipulate them.
3. A system should not eliminate opportunities for employment without a careful examination of consequences to other available jobs.
4. System designers should not participate in the creation or maintenance of secret data banks.
5. A system should treat with consideration all individuals who come in contact with it.

Discussion of Guidelines

By and large, the Stanley House guidelines are self-descriptive. This discussion is designed to illuminate their less obvious aspects and point to special problems that arise in connection with their implementation.

Criterion A2 is not a commonly encountered consideration in systems design. And, indeed, courtesy is not a substitute for real rewards, high quality of service, or other qualities. However, it is possible that courtesy is a prerequisite of humane society. In a rehabilitation hospital where courteous communications were part of a specially designed hospital information system, employees were pleased with that feature and regarded it highly (8). It is difficult to evaluate the importance of this courtesy criterion precisely because experience with courtesy in automated systems has been so rare.

Criterion A5 has far-reaching implications for a system's cost and efficiency. One of the favorite methods for optimizing the efficiency and minimizing the cost of a bureaucratic system is to require the individuals being served to supply the necessary information at each procedural component with which they are involved. Further, in order to ensure an uninterrupted flow of work, recipients of service are required to stand in queues at each point. Yet very often the required information can be made available to each procedural component at relatively small cost. It may be particularly important to do this at times when participating individuals are under additional pressures. One pernicious example is the queuing of hospital patients before special treatment or diagnostic centers (such as physical therapy or radiology). Appointments for individual patients made through the hospital information system could eliminate the queues of sick people in drafty corridors so typical of hospital operations. Similarly, a good system could eliminate unnecessary queues and travel by job seekers. On the other side of the coin, we find that the repetitive and unrelieved need to supply a service to queues of recipients is often dehumanizing to service personnel, and the constant demands of the queue prevent trained personnel from applying their skills in a selective manner (8).

Criteria A6 and A7 may be related. Large-scale systems tend to be converted onto computers as cheaply as possible. In order to do this a global method of design is often used in which all subprocedures are rigidly defined into a single large structure. The more flexible, albeit much more expensive, way is to build a basic system of linkages to which different procedural modules can be attached. Whenever modifications are required it is then only necessary to reprogram the one affected module. One of the side effects of the global method of design is that it is difficult to modify the system to deal with errors that had not been anticipated. Yet errors of every sort, especially those related to information input, are almost unavoidable in a system that handles a large number of transactions. There is a suspicion in the concerned data processing communities that many corporations leave some errors uncorrected because it is cheaper to lose an occasional customer than to correct for each mistake. The human interface would be a desirable component of a system, even when correction of error may not be the major need. Human contact may be needed for individuals in vulnerable positions, such as the unemployed or the sick, to answer questions about unavoidable delays in providing a service or replying to an application; or just to soften the impact of an impersonal bureaucracy.

The human interface is lacking in most systems we have examined so far, and it may well be that the interface will have to be provided from the outside. One extraorganizational scheme is to have a computer ombudsman serving a large community. Such an ombudsman service could be provided by a professional, consumer, or governmental body, or by a combination of organizations, and would be the mediating link between the perplexed citizen and the perplexing system (13).

Related to A6 and A7 is A8, the criterion that management ought to be held responsible for the situation where faulty design causes discomfort and frustration to individuals unable to get relief or attention from a system. Poorly designed systems are often not corrected because no one is really responsible for their actions. As a consequence, Kafkaesque nightmares may be created for users and participants.

In many ways, procedures for dealing with exceptions may be the most necessary components of a humanized system. The human condition is never so homogeneous that a set of rules can be devised to cover all exigencies. Once bureaucratic procedures are structured, they tend to become rigid even though they may contain provisions to deal with human needs. Exceptions are always difficult to manage. To provide for such flexibility, it is absolutely necessary to provide access to focal points of information or control in order to accommodate a departure from the "norm" where the users' needs require it.

I do not believe that there are technical obstacles to incorporating in working systems the kind of criteria that would permit the consideration of exceptions. My main concern is that obstacles will be generated by unavoidable conflict among humanizing criteria and between such criteria and the use of the system. Consider criterion B1, for example. Some employers of manual job bank programs rely on the face-to-face system to weed out those whom they regard as undesirable applicants. Here is an unstated trade-off between flexibility and equity. Also unstated may be the need to specify whom the system serves. What defines a class of individuals depends, in each case, on the kind of services the system provides or the demands it makes on participants. It is easy to say that a system should at least be aware that affected individuals differ in many personal characteristics and needs and should be accorded correspondingly different types of treatment. However, to achieve that may require an explicit definition of the purposes of a system. For instance, does a job bank serve the job seeker or the employer? It obviously serves the needs of both, and when a conflict exists between these needs it may not be feasible to make that conflict explicit.

In a similar sense conflicts may be created by criterion B4. There is a large variety of situations in which individuals may not wish to avail themselves of services or to provide a system with information touching on their private lives. The whole idea of "choice" is foreign to most large-scale systems, whether automated or manual. The provision of choices may very well mark the border between the dehumanizing and the humanizing system. However, it will add greatly to the complexity of systems, because permitting individual choices may set up conflicts with other criteria or services, including some through which the system seeks to become less dehumanizing. For example, in Canada, Provincial Health Services send an account of services rendered to the head of household. This would seem to fulfill the requirement of keeping the user or recipient of a service informed. Other members of the family, however, might object to finding their health needs reported to the head of household (without necessarily detracting from the affection they might feel for their spouse, parent, or provider). While this problem could be alleviated by addressing the report to the concerned individual, other situations may arise that cannot be easily resolved without providing a wide variety of choices. The spouse of the head of household or the adult children may not wish to inform the head that they have sought medical services. In fact, reporting such information may be harmful to a course of therapy or may needlessly disrupt family life, as when members of a family are seeking treatment for venereal disease or drug addiction, for example.

Opinions are divided about the extent to which information about individuals ought to be withheld from them and from others. Yet there is general agreement that provisions are needed for making access to and evaluation and correction of that information possible.

Criteria concerning actions of the system with respect to information have been widely discussed, so no additional comments may be necessary except in one case—criterion C4. This would make it possible for individuals to add to the system information which they think bears importantly on their background or needs, even if the information is not important for processing their files. This might not add anything to the efficiency of a system, but would add a great deal to the psychological comfort of affected individuals.

Requirements for safeguarding the privacy of individual records may seriously conflict with requirements for humanizing an automated system. In general, the more information a system has about individuals who are affected by it, the more likely it is that it can be humanized, but also the easier it becomes to misuse that information and to violate individual needs or desires for privacy and confidentiality. The extent to which individuals are entitled to privacy or even wish privacy is a matter of political or social decision, as is the extent to which individuals ought not to be dehumanized by a system. Privacy versus humanization is an issue that has not received sufficient attention, and our experience with these concepts is too limited for it to be possible to compare requirements for privacy with those for humanization or make judgments on which is more important. However, it is clear that a very private system with no humane provisions may be just as undesirable as a very humane system with no safeguards to protect the privacy of its participants.

What makes procedural features desirable or undesirable with respect to privacy or humanization can be determined only in the context of the purpose of the system and the safeguards possible. Some systems that list individuals and information about them are desirable and others are not. They may also be desirable and undesirable to different people. For instance, a detailed file on handicapped children in the community would be useful for providing individual services, allocating community resources, and directing planning for schools and recreational facilities. On the other hand, attempts have been made to keep on file the names and records of minors who have been convicted of criminal offenses and to merge such files with other record systems. This has met with opposition from thoughtful members of the community, including members of the police department, and would be very objectionable, at least until adequate safeguards against abuse of such systems have been firmly defined and can be implemented. In the final analysis, it is not only a file's existence but its use which determines its ethical value. Nevertheless, the social and political considerations underlying criterion D1 can be resolved within the context of a particular system. What we are saying is that society can decide whether and how a file of handicapped children or of juvenile offenders should be assembled, maintained, and used.

It may be much more difficult to deal with criterion D2. Central to the problem of privacy is the very much enlarged information base available to government agencies when it becomes possible to merge information from different files. Merging of information may also make many systems more efficient and might make their action more equitable or even more humane. But it may be more to the point that under the guise of humanizing systems or making them more equitable (not necessarily the same thing), the rights of individuals for privacy and freedom from government surveillance in a democratic society may be seriously compromised. For example, the new Insurance Corporation of British Columbia, which is regulated and run by the provincial government, provides compulsory insurance under the name Autoplan for all drivers and car owners and bases its rate structure on records of driver violations. It is disquieting to note the ease with which Autoplan has been able to merge court and police files with records of largely business activities of Canadians in British Columbia without a public examination of this important step. Nor has there been public opposition to the extension of Autoplan to other insurance areas. In a similar vein, Lauden (1) has shown for four U.S. police and welfare systems how easily information from many sources may be merged. These are perfect examples of the type of activities warned against by Wiener (5), who predicted that the needs of large-scale government systems would generate practices which would be discovered only after they were well established.

It is thus clear that the extent to which a system can or will incorporate humanizing or dehumanizing features depends on economic, social, and political decisions. There are limits to the power of managers, engineers, systems designers, and scientists to provide for the inclusion of many desirable features in systems. So we suggest a set of ethical principles—criteria E1 to E5—which, if followed, will ensure that within any set of constraints a system will tend to be humane rather than dehumanizing

Largely because many transactions of an automated system are difficult to inspect and by their very nature are less open to view than their manual predecessors, the requirement that systems should not deceive or trick, criterion E1, becomes of paramount importance. But even when a system is restrained from deception by law, it may still try to violate the spirit if not the letter of the law. (Common examples are billing practices whereby attempts are made to hide the amount of interest that is being collected from customers or that would be collected if the customer pays only part of what he owes.)

Computerized transactions make it possible for systems to assist participants without needlessly exploiting their labor (criterion E2). The idea that users must provide supportive services in order that a system may function is deeply ingrained not only in the designers of systems but also in the individuals they serve. Members of society are conditioned from birth to stand in line and fill out forms in order to register, to pay, or to receive. They have been habituated to supply information and contribute by their labor wherever they sought to receive a service, were ill, or provided a service for the government (such as paying taxes). It is grotesque but true that when the Nazis led millions of people into concentration camps and eventually into gas chambers, the victims had to stand in lines and deliver their possessions, provide information, and perform all the necessary services required to part them from their goods, their loved ones, and finally their lives. Manual systems burden recipients of a service with a great deal of effort to make the systems function smoothly. Computerized systems do not need to do so, or not really to the same extent. However, the temptation is always there to exploit the willing and conditioned cooperation of members of society. A contrary attitude, that the system should be burdened rather than the human component, needs to be fostered.

Similarly, an attitude should be cultivated by systems designers that all individuals, including employees, who come in contact with a system should be treated with the same consideration (criterion E5). It has been established that organizational structure produces characteristic patterns of alienation. For instance, Blauner (*14*)

has shown that workers may develop perceptions of "meaninglessness," "powerlessness," and "work estrangement," depending on how they are fitted into an industry's technology (*15*).

We have chosen to group criterion E3 with ethical rather than economic and social or political considerations. Within the area of information systems and systems control through computers, there are many types of employment that are relatively pleasant and interesting and offer opportunities to large numbers of individuals which are difficult to find elsewhere. The overall cost of eliminating such jobs may be high. This is true when computerization of technology affects jobs that rely heavily on human skills and qualities of perception, attention, and intelligence. There are severe costs when sources of employment that provide interesting, challenging, and above all human types of employment are eliminated. One example of an endangered group, victims of the computerization of communication networks, is telephone operators. It is questionable that replacement jobs for this large number of eliminated positions which offer equally acceptable work for humans are available. The cost of finding employment for the communication workers who ordinarily would have worked for the telephone system has to be borne by society and not by the telephone company, and there is no way to assess or repay the costs to individuals who are forced into less satisfactory employment because opportunities for interesting and humane jobs are eliminated. From an economic point of view, this example shows that a cost-benefit analysis of job elimination through automation should not be based on the effects on a particular industry alone, but should include society as a whole. While it is recognized that it may be difficult for the systems designer to resist the temptation to eliminate such desirable jobs, he should be the first to recognize when they are in danger of being eliminated, and it behooves him as a human being to sound the alarm.

A Final Word About Economics

Perhaps the most serious obstacle to the inclusion of humanizing modules is that they reduce the efficiency of most information systems. Their inclusion will increase overhead in terms of design effort, complexity of procedures, and execution time. It may even be necessary to add to the physical resources of central computers (to provide a larger memory, a greater ratio of input to output, and so on). Consequently, appreciable research along these lines is not expected to be initiated by systems designers and managers, whose primary commitment is to efficiency. While our discussion is not designed to come to grips with the concern of those who are highly cost-conscious, we are nevertheless suspicious of those who refer to humanistic features as negative externalities and who hope that some market mechanism will handle their underlying problem. There is also a "humanistic" side to the debate (12, 16).

Lauden (1) makes a convincing case that the arrival of the third-generation computer offered new hope for administrative reformers, and indeed many administrative reformers attempted to fulfill this hope almost immediately. The new computer technology promised more closely integrated (which meant centralized) elements of federal, state, and local bureaucracies. It promised better decision-making, better government, better production, better distribution, and better allocation technology. Another important factor, Lauden stressed, is that the value to society of changes in (computerized) information systems does not have to be tested through the electoral process. Similarly, technological changes in industry rarely depend on decisions by stockholders. There are thus factors that shape computerized information systems and restructure means of producing and allocating goods and services or collecting information that are determined solely by political or industrial management and are neither controlled by nor responsive to social pressures. In the case of information systems, political ends are often achieved by management under the guise of instituting cost-saving efficiencies.

The utility of humanizing procedures will not be revealed in ordinary cost-benefit calculations but in the quality of life. Should we burden ourselves and future generations with dehumanizing practices designed and implemented today? Must not the wish to keep systems humane and dignified take its place with the desire to keep the air and the water palatable as a necessary countermotive to the drive of government and industry to be as efficient and cost-conscious as possible?

Summary

Computerized management information systems increasingly determine all bureaucratic and management procedures that control the production and distribution of goods and services and the collection of information. Thus, they begin to dominate the economic, political, and social management of society. With this domination come procedural features that may dehumanize participants or users affected by the working of most public and private organizations. Yet, despite the overriding importance of a person's dignity and humanity, little is known in terms of scientific specifics about the operational meaning of these concepts or of the antecedent conditions that enhance or diminish them. It will be too late if we wait for knowledge to accumulate about procedures to be incorporated in information systems or information parts of systems to avoid dehumanizing or to add humanizing qualities to them. A set of guidelines has been developed in a series of workshops sponsored by the Canadian Information Processing Society, Canada Council, and Simon Fraser University. These guidelines may apply where organizational design needs may be met and management information systems implemented in such a way that they create a more humane setting.

References and Notes

1. The most recent analysis for computerized agencies is in K. Lauden, *Computers and Bureaucratic Reform* (Wiley, New York, 1974).
2. For an example of the impact of technology (but not computerization) on an organization see P. Blau, *The Dynamics of Bureaucracy* (Univ. of Chicago Press, Chicago, 1963).
3. J. Weizenbaum, *Science* 176, 609 (1972).
4. T. Sterling, *Humanist in Canada* 25, 2 (1973).
5. N. Wiener, *The Human Use of Human Beings* (Doubleday-Anchor, Garden City, N.Y., 1954); *Science* 131, 1355 (1960).
6. C. Argyris, *Integrating the Individual in the Organization* (Irwin-Dorsey, Georgetown, Ontario, 1965); *Public Admin. Rev.* 33, 253 (May-June 1973); R. Kling, in *Proceedings of the Association for Computing Machinery Computers in the Service of Man* (Association for Computing Machinery, New York, 1973), pp. 387-391.
7. R. Bougeslaw, *The New Utopians* (Prentice-Hall, Englewood Cliffs, N.J., 1965).
8. T. Sterling, S. Pollack, W. Spencer, *Int. J. Biomed Comput* 15, 51 (1974).
9. J. Galbraith, *Organizational Design* (Addison-Wesley, Reading, Mass., 1973), T. Whisler, *The Impact of Computer Orgnaizations* (Pergamon, New York, 1970).
10. A Gouldner, *Patterns of Industrial Bureaucracy* (Free Press, New York, 1954).
11. The guidelines were generated during a number of workshops held at Stanley House, a small estate in the Gaspé at which Canada Council schedules intensive seminars. Canada Council and the Canadian Information Processing Society sponsored one workshop each in 1973. Participating in various of these workshops and otherwise contributing to the formation of these guidelines were R. Ashenhurst, computer scientist (University of Chicago); M. Bockelman, police department (Kansas City); L. Brereton, editor, *Humanist in Canada*; C. Capstick, computer scientist (Guelph University); A. Close, barrister (Law Reform Commission); G. Cunningham, assistant commissioner (Royal Canadian Mounted Police); V. Douglas, psychologist (McGill University); C. Gotlieb, computer scientist (University of Toronto); H. Kalman, historian (University of British Columbia); R. Kling, computer scientist (University of California, Los Angeles); T. Kuch, philosopher (Department of Health, Education, and Welfare); P. Lykos, computer scientist (National Science Foundation); S. Pollack, computer scientist (Washington University); H. Schlaginweit, manager (British Columbia Telephone Co.); W. Rogers, provincial auditor (Alberta); D. Seely, computer scientist (Simon Fraser University); M. Shepherd, programmer (Toronto); T. Stelring, computer scientist (Simon Fraser University); and J. Weizenbaum, computer scientist (Massachusetts Institute of Technology). For a detailed description fo the guidelines see Sterling (*12*).
12. T. Sterling, *Commun. ACM* 17 (No. 11), 609 (1974).
13. The Canadian computer ombudsman scheme is developed around a joint effort of the Canadian Information Processing Society and the Consumer Association of Canada (see T. Stelring, *J. CIPS*, in press). The U.S. effort, spearheaded by the Association for Computing Machinery, has as its main concern eliminating an incorrect image of computerized systems and is thus different from the Canadian model.
14. R. Blauner, *Alienation and Freedom* (Univ. of Chicago Press, Chicago, 1964).
15. For confirming evidence of Blauner's findings, see F. C. Mann and L. R. Hoffman, *Automation and the Worker* (Holt, Rinehart & Winston, New York, 1960); C. R. Walker, *Toward the Automatic Factory* (Yale Univ. Press, New Haven, Conn., 1957); A. N. Turner and P. R. Lawrence, *Industrial Jobs and the Worker* (Harvard Univ. Press, Cambridge, Mass., 1965).
16. See, for instance, K. W. M. Kapp, *The Social Costs of Private Enterprise* (Schocken, New York, 1950); E. Richardson, *Work in America* (MIT Press, Cambridge, Mass., 1973).

Part XII
MARKETING THE LIBRARY

Introduction

Historically, the library has been looked upon as an institution much like the statue in the park, the art museum, or other similar objects which remain relatively unknown to the community. Whether that community is a corporation, a college or university, or a municipality, libraries tend to present a serene facade, apparently unmoved by changing environmental conditions. People feel comfortable knowing what to expect from a library, in spite of the library's attempts to impinge upon community life through promotion of innovative activities and services. The changes and innovations that take place within the library are frequently unknown to those who use that library.

Ignorance about the library, its responsibilities, and its services can be changed, but not unless librarians are willing to adopt a more aggressive stance toward its patrons, potential and actual, and to the community which it serves. Basic and fundamental questions must be asked about the applicability of current library services to that library's community. Libraries must carefully study what market exists for their services, and what these services should be. All of this, while relatively new to librarians, is certainly not new to other organizations. The recent interest in applying market research techniques to library operations is indicative of the need by librarians to remove the limitations on service which walls and procedures create. While some types of libraries, at least, have pursued this course through specialized services usually referred to as "outreach," Information and Referral, or some other similar term, or have adopted new programs such as adult independent learning services in an effort to win more adherents to libraries, the majority of libraries, particularly those which are non-public in nature, have remained relatively aloof from such activities, preferring to emphasize traditional services. The question, are these services relevant to the library's community,? is asked less often than it should.

A marketing strategy needs to be adopted, one that stresses direct responsibility by community members for the continued existence of its library. But to develop such a strategy, libraries must devote far more time to assessing community needs and *potential* information demands than has hitherto been the case. This does *not* mean that a library must abdicate its responsibility to continually develop innovative services in order to meet existing community needs. However, it *does* mean that libraries should not limit themselves to such services. Developing and promoting entirely different, not merely innovative, services, services for which there might not be an immediate demand, is as important to libraries as circulating books.

The articles in this chapter provide guidelines for adopting a marketing strategy to library services. Andrea C. Dragon's paper suggests that libraries are no different than other organizations in their need to use aggressive marketing techniques to ensure their survival in a world of constantly changing information needs. She points out that libraries must ask themselves fundamental questions, and must answer these questions truthfully rather than basing such answers upon traditional assumptions—which are likely to be incorrect. To answer these questions, however, requires accurate knowledge of who we should serve, how best might they be served, and, most importantly, with which other services does the library compete?

While Dragon calls for adoption of a general marketing strategy by libraries, Christine Oldman's article is more cautionary. Uncritical use of marketing techniques in library planning may not cause the desired results. In addition, concentrating solely on the library as a physical entity rather than as a transmitter of information may cause us to miss ways in which information can be coupled with other non-library elements (such as community values) in order to create what is usually referred to as the "marketing mix." As Oldman points out, "... marketing is more than a set of techniques, it is a perspective." As such, what is relevant for library marketing strategies need not be relevant for other, non-library, strategies. What is important, however, is that the attempt to identify relevant marketing variables be pursued vigorously and that, once found, these variables be integrated into a general marketing plan for library services that is both aggressive and potentially important to information consumers.

Marketing the Library
By Andrea C. Dragon

When Ojai (Calif.) learned that its library would be shut down due to lack of funds for staffing and supplies, a committee was quickly formed to save the people's library. Volunteers came forth to man it, donations pledged to supply it, and the library will remain—now, more than ever—the people's library. The community, which always took pride in its little library, will now have a greater pride because it will now feel *directly* responsible for its existence and maintenance.

—From an editorial in the *New York Times*, July 19, 1978, by Marsha K. Strong, a writer for the Ojai Valley News

Unlike the sanguine writer of this editorial, the library profession cannot help but cringe at the idea of losing jobs to well meaning but incompetent amateurs. One shudders at the thought of all the "donations" of cast-off books that will be thrust upon the shelves of the "people's" library. However distasteful the situation in Ojai appears to a profession dedicated to quality services, still the library will not be so fortunate.

The passage of Proposition 13 will have a severe impact on public libraries in California. If local officials there are forced to choose between reducing the funding for schools, for fire and police protection, for their own position—or for libraries, it will be the libraries and not the city clerk's office that feel the pinch. At this time it is difficult to determine if other states will pass similar tax-cutting measures, but library administrators throughout the country should prepare for the possibility. Reductions in library funding are not new, of course, but the magnitude of the cuts required by the severe property tax limits of Proposition 13 mandates that libraries adopt an altogether new orientation toward the public dollar. This new orientation is the old concept of marketing.

Just as Pepsi-Cola and Coca-Cola compete in the supermarket for the consumer dollar, the library must compete with schools, social welfare agencies, police and fire departments, parks, and street maintenance for the public dollar. In addition, the library is in a fierce battle with television, films, bookstores, and cultural organizations for patrons. Funding for libraries is often tied to increasing patronage, and this often can only be done by increasing resources. The library's administration is caught on a treadmill of trying to raise the level of public funding, which is dependent upon patronage, which is dependent upon funding.

The way off the treadmill is to adopt a marketing orientation that will increase both patronage and funding.

Marketing is a systematic approach to planning and achieving desired exchange relations with other groups. Marketing is concerned with developing, maintaining, and/or regulating exchange relations involving products, services, organizations, persons, or causes.[1]

A library becomes a marketer by exchanging the products it offers for "sale" for the public's tax dollars and patronage. Marketing differs from selling in that in the latter personal powers of persuasion are used to "sell" a product to a would-be customer. In marketing one relies less on personal persuasion than on a planned approach of bringing together the consumer and the product and facilitating the exchange between them. Marketing is primarily a strategy for educating the public as to the

---

Reprinted by permission from the March 1979 issue of the *Wilson Library Bulletin*. Copyright © 1979 by the H. W. Wilson Company.

value of the organization's products. Libraries have an advantage over some corporations, which must market products of little worth. The library's "products" are among the world's most valuable, and for this reason libraries need not feel hesitant about using aggressive marketing.

Playing the market

Tiffany's does not advertise its diamonds in the *Minneapolis Star*. Rolls Royce does not advertise its Bentley in *Hot Rod*. The Erotic Book Club does not mail its promotional materials to members of religious orders. Each of these concerns has *identified its market,* and each concentrates its activities where they will be most effective. Tiffany's market is wealthy New Yorkers, Rolls Royce's is the readers of *Country Life,* and the Erotic Book Club's is the readers of *Playboy*. A market is "a distinct group of people and/or organizations that have resources which they want to exchange, or might conceivably exchange, for distinct benefits."[2]

Businesses spend vast amounts for research identifying markets, analyzing needs and preferences, and determining what will be offered in exchange for the organization's products. For too long the library has assumed that its market was every living human being in the community. That view has led libraries to offer too many hastily produced products for too few patrons. Effective libraries identify their market and offer products that will satisfy its needs. For example, prison libraries supply recreational and educational materials suitable for poorly educated men and women. School libraries offer products and services to satisfy the informational and recreational needs of their primary market, children, and their secondary market, teachers. Public libraries offer products and services to reading adults, with secondary markets including children and the local business community.

As the library learns more about its market, its needs, demographics, and perceptions, the institution can tailor its tactics to maintain its position in the actual market (the steady customers) and penetrate the potential market (those who currently satisfy their informational and reading needs elsewhere). If the library is serious in its efforts to adopt a marketing orientation, obtaining the services of a market research organization can be a wise investment. The tools of the market analyst, although sophisticated and often expensive, have been finely honed, and most business organizations willingly assume the costs of this research and consumer analysis. A poorly designed, quickly duplicated questionnaire mailed to heads of households is hardly a sophisticated market research device. As businesses have known for a long time, it is sometimes necessary to spend money to get money.

The library's objective is to create a market in which it exchanges recreational reading, information services, and the like for public support in the form of tax dollars, patronage, and private contributions. It may have to stimulate the market by using the following traditional mechanisms: price, product, promotion, and place.

Price

Cultural organizations like symphonies, civic theaters, and art museums have at their disposal a pricing mechanism to attract patronage. By reducing their admission fees, having "free" days, or allowing large groups of school children to attend performances at a nominal cost, they attract large numbers of the public that might otherwise have never ventured inside. These new "patrons" boost attendance figures, which are then presented to funding authorities as evidence that the organiaztion is successfully penetrating the potential market and therefore deserves more money.

To most library administrators charging an entrance fee is out of the question. It flies in the face of all that is decent in this country. However, entrance fees or "donations" may become a necessity if public support does not keep pace with costs.

Product

Libraries, which have a quite diverse line of products to offer, have an advantage over their competitors for the public dollar. Some of the products are tangible, thus appealing to the patrons who insist on having something for their money (others are services appealing to patrons less concerned about obtaining a visible object for their tax money).

It must be remembered that any product has a definite life cycle in which it enjoys a healthy popularity followed by decline. Historically, it has been difficult for libraries to withdraw from the market products that have outlived their demand. Weeding is notoriously neglected. Urban public libraries maintain extensive children's services long after the child-producing couples have moved to the suburbs and school libraries have captured much of the city market. By fiercely maintaining a grip on a weak product, the library not only ties up scarce resources, but it delays aggressive search for replacement products. A sound marketing strategy would be to review periodically the vitality of each product in the entire line and withdraw those for which there is no demand. If demand cannot be stimulated, then hard decisions must be made to abandon products and services that have come to the end of their productive life.

Promotion

Historically, libraries have limited promotion to three categories: point-of-sale displays, publicity, and personal contact.

The first are of limited effectiveness because they can only increase "sales" to patrons who have already responded to the library's products by entering. However, despite their limitations point-of-sale displays can be used to create an atmosphere that encourages circulation. Department stores like Bloomingdale's in New York carefully create an in-store atmosphere so attractive that customers enter simply to enjoy the experience of shopping. Once inside, point-of-sale displays catch the customer's eye and make the decision *not* to buy more difficult. It should be possible to create an atmosphere in the library so appealing that patrons will enter to browse and exit with books.

If a library's market consists primarily of scholars and researchers, the interior might resemble an Edwardian study with long tables and incandescent lamps and padded armchairs. If a library is trying to penetrate the business and industry information service market, the atmosphere in that department should be one of clean, uncluttered efficiency with children not admitted. College and university libraries have different markets from public libraries and need to create atmospheres and displays directed to students and faculty; they should not resemble the suburban public library.

Bookstores rely heavily on point-of-sale displays, and librarians can learn a lot about promotion by regular visits to the local B. Dalton's or Marboro's. Not only do many people find browsing in a bookstore rather enjoyable, but most find it difficult to resist making a purchase. One reason for this is that bookstores, like other retail outlets, calculate their sales in terms of value of product sold per square foot of selling floor. This accounts for the density of merchandise seen on the selling floors of department stores. Many libraries have large amounts of floor space in public areas not utilized for marketing purposes—or any purpose at all. A marketing approach would utilize now empty spaces either to display or promote the library's products. Sears and Penney's manage to stock and restock their selling floors despite the density of merchandise—and so can libraries. Another even more simple marketing device bookstores use is the full-cover displays—books are laid flat on tables. There is no reason why libraries could not adopt this technique for selected titles.

Libraries promote their activities by planting "news" items in the local press. Rarely do they purchase media advertising as do such organizations as the March of Dimes, the military, symphonies, museums, and, more recently, colleges. Publicity is in fact free advertising, but often libraries underestimate the promotional skills required to write a good news release. Publicity is often the main promotional tool of financially crippled libraries, yet few bother to obtain the services of a good publicist. Schools of journalism are producing each year hundreds of gifted writers willing to write news releases on a free-lance basis. A news release is too important not to assign to a professional.

Personal contact is the least costly but often the most effective promotional device at the library's disposal. It costs nothing to insist that the telephone receptionist answer calls with a "smile" in his or her voice. It costs nothing to insist that public service librarians smile and greet patrons as valued customers. It costs nothing to insist that circulation staff cheerfully relax the regulations for valued patrons. It costs nothing to insist that reference personnel step out from behind the desk and inquire, "May I help you find something?" of patrons fumbling at the card catalog or wandering among the stacks. These no-cost promotional efforts will yield results equal to highly sophisticated and expensive advertising. I believe that surly or indifferent service has caused more patrons to withdraw support for libraries than any other factor. Perhaps if patrons were encouraged to complain about the service, it would improve.

Personal contact can lead to word-of-mouth advertising, which is probably the most effective promotional technique. One satisfied patron can easily bring to the library several new patrons who might not be responsive to publicity. For many years the Hershey Chocolate

Company relied solely on world-of-mouth advertising. A regular user of the library's products might continue to do so despite poor service, but that patron will hesitate to encourage less motivated friends to enter the library.

Lobbying is an extension of personal contact, but instead of the consumer market, efforts are aimed at the legislative (or other funding-authority) market. Lobbying should not be something that occurs once a year when the library director pleads with the local government for more money, but rather should be a continuing program of formal and informal communication between the library and those who hold the purse strings.

The funding authorities (library board, city council, mayor, county government, or state legislature) must be made aware of what the library has to offer *and* the demand for it so that they will allocate the funds necessary to purchase more of the products most in demand. The library staff should make periodic visits to funding authorities to inform them of activities and provide them with attractive, professionally photographed reports recording patron use. Funding authorities with small children should receive personal invitations to story hours and films. Those with ill or aged parents should receive personal notices of services to the house bound.

There is no reason why the library cannot organize elegant private parties for the authorities, in the library if local law permits alcoholic beverages, elsewhere if it does not, during which staff members and influential patrons familiar with library products can engage in informal lobbying. Staff members would probably make voluntary contributions to fund such gatherings because their future salaries and ability to provide service might be enhanced by doing so.

Place
The library has available to it a fourth marketing strategy—place. If the library is not conveniently located, patrons will decide the services offered do not outweigh the cost (in time and effort) of "making a trip to the library." As already shown, it is possible to enhance the library experience to such an extent that patons will eagerly anticipate visiting the library and even paying parking fees, but for most patrons convenience is the key. Communities deciding to build new libraries and branches need to look closely at locations adjacent to shopping malls or in downtown shopping areas. The ideal situation for the patron would be the ability to combine a shopping or business trip downtown with a visit to the library without having to repark the car or transfer to another bus or subway line. Communities with old buildings in deteriorating neighborhoods need to plan promotional activities and create products that will stimulate their market despite location and physical appearance.

Some concluding thoughts
Librarians can no longer assume that the public will continue to accept increases in taxation for the support of libraries. Whining about the situation and appealing to taxpayers' civic pride or sense of humanity will have little effect. Positive action, through marketing, must be taken to capture the library's share of the tax dollar. If such action is not taken, the library will lose the competition to city governments, licensing bureaus, high school marching bands, and public golf courses. Each of these organizations believes its products are worthy of the public's support through taxes, and each will be competing vigorously in California and elsewhere for its share. Libraries need to enter the competition with pride in their products and with a determination to win. 回

References
1. Philip Kotler. *Marketing for Nonprofit Organizations.* Prentice-Hall, 1975, p.13.
2. *Ibid.,* p.22.

Marketing Library and Information Services: The Strengths and Weaknesses of a Marketing Approach
By Christine Oldman

I wish to argue that marketing, as I understand it, can be of great help in the design and in the actual operation of library and information services. This comment must immediately be qualified. Library and information services have particular characteristics which, paradoxically, both suggest a strong alliance between marketing and information science and warn against an injudicious use of marketing principles and techniques. I should make clear the position from which I will argue in this paper. I regard myself as first and foremost an "information person" (I shall carefully avoid defining that phrase). My association with management education may be only a temporary one.

THE NATURE OF INFORMATION PROBLEMS

In order to explain the paradox which has just been suggested, it first seems necessary to provide both a definition of library and information services and a summary of the problems faced by those working in such organisations. Libraries have been part of civilisation almost since its beginning. Any developed or developing society has both formal and informal information systems. Libraries, as part of the formal system, play a part in the gathering, preservation and dissemination of recorded knowledge. The information professional is an intermediary between the producer of recorded knowledge and the consumer of recorded knowledge. The latter may or may not be *seeking* information. The title of this paper refers to library *and* information services. The choice of title reflects more the attitudes of the information professional world rather than my own views. It will become clearer that the distinction that the professional makes between something called a library and something called an information service is rather crucial to the theme of this seminar. It is doubtful whether the user of information makes such a distinction. It may be true to say that the existence of such a distinction, which is reflected in the training of the practitioner, is due to feelings of status, insecurity, etc. The information scientist would argue that his job is far more exciting, far more intellectually demanding, than that of the librarian.

However, we can now return to a more sober examination of what might constitute a library and what might constitute an information service. A library or information service is any collection of documents, people and capital equipment serving a "parent" organisation. The word organisation must be generously defined so as to include the public library situation. The public library's parent organisation is a community. Any service can be placed on a continuum. At one end is the highly active service anticipating every information need and at the other end there is the highly passive service responding to demands made on it. The emphasis is different. At the active end the concern may be with information, (I will dodge, for the moment, the problem of defining information) and at the passive end the concern may be with documents. Referring again to the three functions of gathering, preserving and disseminating recorded knowledge, the active end will place more emphasis on the later function and the passive end will place more emphasis on the first two functions.

Throughout the rest of this paper I shall use the term "information system". It includes both library and information services and is a more economical phrase. However, I will be excluding from my discussion certain entities such as data access systems and management information systems which are certainly regarded as being information systems. The definition I have given above is narrower than that provided in a review article on the evaluation of information systems. Debons and Montgomery[1] write: "Information systems are environments composed of people, equipment and procedures organised to achieve specific information objectives."

Certainly the word information system can have a variety of meanings. Writers such as Debons and Montgomery depict an information system as being almost metaphysical, a state of mind. I am concerned that my definition is more concrete. I refer to tangible phenomena, organisation structures subsidiary to other organisational structures, passive or active, with extensive or minimal "data bases".

Information is a word which defies definition. It is an elusive concept which has attracted the attention of all manner of people, economists, managers, computer scientists, psychologists and social psychologists and last but not least information professionals — librarians or information officers. Ironically, the information profession is an introspective one. It is only fairly recently, within the last twenty years or so that the practitioners began to communicate with each other. Their now extensive literature, though, is largely neglected by other information interests. It is very largely written and read by the information professional. The computer, however, as an information system, is a glamorous topic of research. The information professionals lack a developed theoretical backing for their activities. Some concepts and methodologies are "native", some are borrowed from other disciplines. A better theoretical framework would help with the understanding and solution of the two fundamental problems of today's information professional:

(1) The quantity/quality paradox, overabundance of information at the source (the overworked expression for this phenomenon is "information explosion") and scarcity of relevant information for the user at the destination[2];

(2) The necessity to justify a service in face of threats posed by inflation. Information systems may well be regarded by the larger organisation as a luxury.

The two problems are probably inversely related. The first is a perennial one, somewhat tempered by economic factors and the second is temporal. In other words there is evidence that the current economic recession is reducing the exponential rate of information growth. When there are no threats to the service in circumstances of economic expansion the first problem looms larger.

MARKETING AND INFORMATION SCIENCE

I would like to suggest that the discipline of marketing and the discipline of information science have very much in common. This is not a universally held view. Michael Brittain, a psychologist who has made a great contribution to the study of what the information profession calls "user needs" in a section titled "unconventional methodologies of a book"[3] on this subject feels that market research, although unconnected to information science, has some part to play. Brittain, like many other information writers, is seeing marketing only as a set of techniques. The appropriateness of particular marketing techniques to information systems will be subjected in this paper to discussion. However, marketing is more than a set of techniques, it is a perspective. It would seem to be concerned with the complex linkage between producers and consumers. In order to give *and* gather information about the exchange of goods and services it employs insights from better established disciplines such as economics, psychology and social psychology. The hybrid nature of marketing is therefore not dissimilar to the hybrid nature of information science. The information system intercedes, either explicitly or implicitly, between producers of information and consumers of information. The key concept that links marketing and information science is communication. However, too much can be made of this analogy. Marketing, of course, is identified with the *producer* of the goods or services. The information system is a third party. It is supposed to possess a neutrality. However, this is another issue subject to debate. There is plenty of evidence that the information professional can, wittingly or not, determine the behaviour of the information consumer.

Information practitioners talk about something called information science which they feel is the intellectual support for their operational activities. However, the point has already been made that information people, like marketing people, borrow from many other subject areas. I believe it is a little presumptuous and premature to talk too much about information science. There does not at the moment exist a body of knowledge about information which possesses enough cohesion to be an intellectual discipline. When that day does dawn, marketing could well be one of that discipline's components. Meanwhile marketing can probably do more for what might be better termed "informationship", (as opposed to librarianship) than the other way round. However, the latter can contribute something to the unknown areas in marketing. I shall be discussing the contribution that buyer behaviour models, particularly consumer decision models, can make to the understanding of the information consumer.

A central tenet of these decision models is that the consumer is an information processor. Decision making is an information processing activity. However, information people would probably like to stand that idea on its head. Information seeking, acquisition and processing is a decision making activity. The information component of the various consumer decision models is the least explored element of these models. Perhaps it is not being too optimistic to suggest that if *information* consumer models can be developed a little more they can assist the development of buyer behaviour models.

THE VALUE OF A MARKETING PERSPECTIVE

Having identified a conceptual similarity between the activity of marketing and the operation of information systems we can now turn to more concrete matters. How can those in marketing market themselves to information people? How can they communicate the idea that marketing's contribution to information management can be more profound than its public reputation for being over-zealous regarding market research and advertising suggests? If a charge is levelled against information professionals that they are product and not user orientated they will quite strongly resent the criticism. It is certainly very true there is a user orientation tradition in the information systems world. However, if that user orientation is examined carefully, those well-worn ideas of Levitt's about correctly defining what business you are in, do have a validity in the information context. I think there is evidence that information professionals are myopic and that if those who operate at the passive end of the "active-passive" continuum I sketched earlier on, saw themselves as being in the communication business and not in the book supply business, they would have a better chance of surviving or of, at least, not having their funds slashed dramatically.

My evidence comes from a research investigation which I am just completing at Cranfield School of Management. We were testing different methods of measuring the value of academic libraries. A minority, but a considerable minority, used a library service not only as a supplement to their course but as an educational alternative to it. We called these people maximisers. They were sometimes critical of the very structured style of education they were being offered and used the library as an alternative source of ideas. It seems important that library managers should have some appreciation of this sort of circumstance. Admittedly the consequence of such insights into how libraries are valued are wide reaching and could involve considerable argument. An injection of £X into the book fund rather than the appointment of one more marketing lecturer will produce more able students? There are people in the information world, particularly those at the active end of my continuum, who argue that defining one's role generously and seeking evidence of the information unit's impact on the organisation it serves rather than simply supplying evidence of use, is the correct approach. John Blagden of the GLC's Department of Architecture and Civil Design argues in this vein[4].

My assertion that information people are insufficiently user orientated derives from an overall research conclusion. There are many more specific examples. Microfiche, a relatively recent technological innovation which from a product-viewpoint had obvious cost and management advantages, has not been particularly accepted by users. They would seem to have "aesthetic" preferences for hard copy. Geoffrey Ford in an article[5] on user studies reports a nice example of product orientation. Some academic libraries pay meticulous attention to cataloguing rules. Ford reports users who were delighted that they had "cracked" their library's rule for dealing with the umlaut. It would be quite simple for libraries to be more user minded and deal with the umlaut in the way that most German dictionaries do. Returning to my own investigation one small part of it was quite illuminating. I reported to a librarian, that human biology students had complained of the physical scattering of their subject in the library. The answer was, that is how Dewey (the classification system) operates. Although I have cited some product-oriented examples, I am not advocating a policy of "the user rules OK". Indeed, the issue concerning what management decisions are made as a result of users' expressed preferences, is an exceedingly complex and controversial one which I will allude to later on.

I have mentioned that there is a long tradition of user orientation in the information world but it is not of the type that is going to help very much with the two main problems, referred to at the beginning of this paper, facing the profession today: (i) filtering the information wheat from the information chaff; (ii) saving one's job. The literature on user studies is voluminous, even the bibliographies are quite extensive. There have been broad brush approaches—a famous example is the Bath University Investigation[6], the INFROSS study (Information Requirements for Social Scientists). The respondents were asked to complete a lengthy questionnaire on all matters relating to their "information habits". One respondent volunteered the comment: "The importance of information can be overrated. More information does not always result in increased knowledge and probably seldom produces increased wisdom." His observations will be taken up later on. Other studies have looked at some very specific user populations. What is lacking about the majority of these studies is they *describe*, they do not *explain* the decision making processes behind any particular information strategy. So, as John Martyn[7] says in a recent review article, "Gee Whizz", so what. They are not designed as management tools which could lead to improved decision making. Philip Kuehl of Maryland University who has participated in an experimental seminar of marketers and information professionals funded by the US Department of Education and Welfare has written lucidly on the need for an *adequate* user orientation.

> "The 'new' marketing concept focuses on the full examination and assessment of user needs. It suggests that organisational resources must be focused on precisely identifying the utility, behavioural-psychological and end-use variables which encompass the needs of user groups.... To implement a need orientated perspective, all organisation functions in an information system (document collection, abstracting, processing etc.) must be integrated under the single objective and focuus of user need fulfilment."[8]

A user orientation leads to a policy of benefit segmentation. The notion that different user groups require different information products will be an unremarkable one to information people. However, they rarely pursue a conscious market segmentation policy when making management decisions.

STYLES OF INFORMATION MANAGEMENT RESEARCH

There has in the last ten years or so been a reaction in the information world against user studies. There has been justifiable criticism of the techniques and the results of user studies. The questions posed are often of the crude—"What are your information needs?" "Are you satisfied with your information service?"—variety. Herbert Menzel, one of the most authoritative writers in the "information science" field, is critical of what he would call information needs research. Valuable information may not be the information that users are aware of wanting, not even the information that would be good for them, but instead the information that would be good for the progress of scientific research[9]. Hansen[10], likewise questions the wisdom of designing an information system based on user preferences. Many writers believe that user research will provide information on how users value their information system but will not say anything about the *quality* of the library. "There is no valid quantitative relationship between user attitude and the quality of the library."[11]

It is this sort of thinking that is the dominant theme in information systems management today. There has been in some, by no means all, quarters a dramatic swing from the view that librarians are custodians of knowledge, themselves no mean scholars, to what I call by the catch phrase the "systems approach". In a concern to replace rule of thumb by a more scientific approach some information people became very management orientated. However, it is a poacher turned gamekeeper situation. Converts become the best preachers. A certain rather one sided view of management has been accepted hook, line and sinker. There is an aversion to what is seen as subjective, that is "user" approaches, to information system design. Stecher[11] reports an investigation at Purdue University. Students rated Purdue University library as inferior to other American college libraries. Stecher finds this a meaningless finding since Purdue was at the time "in the top dozen of American research libraries". However, consumers and providers of an information service will have different perceptions of value.

Operations research has provided much of the theoretical and practical input to the particular style of management favoured by information people. A variety of types of model have been applied to a variety of problems. The problems, however, could be classified under the general heading of "stock control". The focus of attention is on the product not on the user. Most of the operations research of this nature has been conducted on large systems, serving academic institutions. They are usually at the passive end of the continuum I have referred to. The assumption, often implicit, is that the library's basic function is that of a warehouse. Such studies include other assumptions. Libraries are not so very different from many other organisations which will be discussed during this seminar. They must allocate resources to non-financial goals. The measure of effectiveness employed in these studies is a surrogate for value. Utilisation measures are substituted for more direct measures of use. Use is presumed to equal usefulness. A valid performance objective is thought to be the maximisation of what is often called document exposure — eyeball to page contact. The user-information system point of contact is examined; the decision to seek, acquire information is not explored. In other words the system is explored in isolation from the organisation it serves. The concentration of effort is on manifest demand. However, users will only demand of an information system what they think it can deliver. These models are necessarily conservative since they are only monitoring how well the system is coping with explicit demand. (I am aware the systems analyst would disagree with me on this point.) The particular style of systems analysis which has dominated has contributed much to the management of libraries. However, the extent to which it has provided real answers to the two problems which fex the information practitioner is arguable. To recapitulate, these problems are (i) filtering the information wheat from the chaff and (ii) saving one's job. Since the emphasis is on the use of products, not the user and certainly not the non-user, the systems approach does not particularly assist problem (i). Similarly with problem (ii), sophisticated work has been done on the allocation of resources but in today's harsh climate some real effort must be made to establish the information system's impact on the organisation it serves. How much good is it doing as well as how good is it?

The reaction from some people when it is suggested that a marketing type approach can contribute something to these problems is, to say the least, cool. Like many other professionals these people have such a passionate belief in their activities that they forget the rest of the world may not feel quite the same. Selling is undignified. This sort of sentiment is easily dealt with by presenting the correct version of marketing. There is, however, a more subtle problem. Information specialists are no different from marketing people or anybody else. They are concerned that their service should be used. It has already been noted the OR tradition often bases its models on the *maximisation* of use premise. To advocate such an objective whether from a marketing or any other perspective could be unwise counsel. We are still, as I shall indicate, very ignorant about the behaviour of the information consumer. However, it is fairly apparent that overabundance can bring as many problems as insufficient information. As the social scientist already quoted in this paper said, more information does not always result in increased knowledge. More information does not always lead to a better degree, a better decision, etc. Information sources available to people are numerous. It simply may not be in the best interests of client groups to extract information from formal information systems. The marketing of information services must proceed with caution. Information does possess characteristics which make it different in some ways from other goods, services and utilities. Information is not an end in itself. It is a means to some other end.

The fundamental problem is that of defining information. When we talk about marketing information are we talking about marketing of a service, a product or a utility?

Wyckam argues that it can be unsound marketing strategy to make a distinction between products and services.

Information people would argue that what they deal in is very different from what anybody else deals in. I think in some ways they are right, and in other ways they are wrong. Information services are usually located in the non-market sector of the economy. Information is a free good, a fact, which, writers like Stecher[11] feel, causes people to have massive, unreasonable expectations. (Work that has been done at Cranfield has indicated that this is far from the case.) It follows that the objectives of an information system are difficult to measure. How are such benefits of information as creativity, avoidance of duplication of research, self confidence, to be measured? This problem is similar to that of, for example, a welfare service. One can measure output — the extent of the market for meals-on-wheels to old people. Establishing direct measures of the impact of this service, the effect on the health of old people is very much more difficult. These then are problems that are probably shared by the providers of all the services that are being discussed during this seminar. However, information would appear to possess idiosyncratic characteristics. If I supply a piece of information to a consumer I still have the information after the exchange. There is no obvious measure of a unit of information. The measure of the information theorists — the bit — is unhelpful for most purposes since it is not related to the importance or value of information. Information to communications engineers means that which reduces uncertainty. Boulding[13] argues that a unit is needed which he would call the "wit" for conveying the content of information. The most fundamental difficulty about information relates to uncertainty and ignorance about its value. Information is often acquired without knowledge of either its use or outcome. I have tried to indicate some of the obstacles which make the application of well tried marketing techniques either difficult or in appropriate.

INFORMATION NEEDS

My objective, so far, has been to set the scene for a discussion on the essence of any information system — information need. There are numerous definitions of information need. I shall use that of an experienced information system researcher, Maurice Line, as being reasonably representative. He defines "need" as what an individual ought to have; "want" as what an individual would like to have; "demand" as what an individual asks for and "use" as what an individual actually uses[14]. The consensus view is that since the user will not know what information he needs for a task in hand, user studies are not a reliable tool for information systems planning. Other approaches are believed to be more fruitful. Systems analysts construct, for example, predictive models based on the principle that future demand for services is influenced by past demand. The modellers also turn to "bibliometrics" for help. Bibliometrics is the study of the statistical regularities exhibited in the structure of recorded knowledge. It is possible to analyse the citation pattern of subject fields. A minority of journals will account for the majority of references. Literatures are subject to decay; the "life" can be measured. These two phenomena are called, respectively, scatter and obsolescence. Citation analysis can be used as a tool for selecting and relegating stock. It is particularly attractive to the hard headed information system researcher since contact with the user can be avoided.

I feel it is imperative to convince the information world that if information systems are both going to survive and assist the people they service, information needs research is necessary *in conjunction* with these other approaches. Many people do not need much convincing that the dominant trend in information systems management in concentrating on the logistics of the service serves only those users whose needs are specific — the known—item searchers. There is considerable evidence that users will only demand what they think can be delivered. For instance an OR investigation at Lancaster University Library found that satisfaction level (number of known specific items available) was 60 per cent. The system was improved by identifying the popular items and putting them on restricted loan. Satisfaction level rose to 80 per cent. Six months later it had returned to its previous level of 60 per cent. Users' expectations had increased. The "laws" of scatter and obsolescence are not immutable, natural laws, rather are they generalisations of a *social* nature. They are expressions of how information consumers have behaved in the past. These "laws" are in danger of becoming immutable if information system managers base all their decisions on them. Future generations of users can only use what their information systems require. Unwittingly or not, information specialists powerfully influence the information behaviour of their users by structuring the system in certain ways. It is a self reinforcing situation. The most cited journals are the most available journals and thus most likely to be cited again. However, information people do need persuading that the task of assisting people other than the known item user, the habitual user, is not as hopeless as they believe.

The first step in the task of encouraging those who are pessimistic about information need is to present a revised definition. When the information professional talks about information need he is consciously or unconsciously more often than not talking about information products, communication artefacts, books, journals, research reports, etc. Information needs and information products are not synonymous. An information need is the context in which information is sought. Information specialists can learn a lot from the recent work on Management Information Systems. Decisions are identified and only then the associated information inputs. Most university libraries now have what are called "user education" programmes. What perhaps is necessary is a programme of "librarian's education" which would enable the librarian to have some idea of his clients' intellectual problems. MIS designers have now recognised that the problems confronting them are largely behavioural not technological. It is not suggested that it is an easy task to set up a dialogue with users about their problem solving or decision making activities. Aguilar[15] in his discussion of the information requirements of top management warns of the problem. An executive questioned by Aguilar says of information:

"This is a difficult subject to talk about. It is so much a part of everyday goings on that one does not think about it. It is as if you were asking someone how he walks. He would probably tell you that he puts one foot in front of the other ... and find it difficult to say much more."

Nevertheless the interactions between information specialists and their clients can be successful. One such example is a project supported by the National Science Foundation at Hameline University in Minnesota[16]. The unit of analysis was an educational course. In other words the research thought processes were—what is information needed for? A task model was constructed for each course. This model generated data on the objectives of each course and the methods of achieving these objectives.

Having convinced critics that information needs and information products are not the same thing, the argument that information need is not a "hard" entity can be taken further. It is helpful to examine in a fairly discursive way why people do *not* use information systems. It is quicker, easier, more convenient for people to obtain information from sources other than from formal systems; individuals do not realise they have an information problem; they are not aware of the system's facilities; they have had no satisfaction from past or present experiences; talking to people is preferable to reading books. An American study[17] of the information needs of urban communities prior to its empirical work, unlike so many other studies, constructed a framework to assist an understanding of some of the barriers to information use. Their model has four component elements: individuals, needs, sources, and solutions. The linkages are: individuals to their needs, individuals to their information sources, individuals to solutions of their needs and problems and, lastly, sources to information needs and problems. In order to cope optimally with information need the individual must have access to information along five different dimensions — social, institutional, physical, psychological and intellectual. Incidentally this study confronts and finds no solution to the question which has been formulated at great length in this paper. What is information? An individual wants information on tomorrow's weather, he may also want to know how to patch up his marriage. When is the latter need satisfied? When the information specialist tells him where the marriage bureau is or when the advice is perceived to be satisfactorily delivered?

It is this sort of view of information need which may assist the information specialist more than the prevailing tight intellectual notion of need. We must attempt to understand views towards information far more than we do now. Why is there boredom, indifference towards information, why is an information service regarded as a luxury by management? The cliché that attack is the best form of defence, i.e., that the information specialist should argue that his information budget should be increased because of, not despite, an economic recession — information is a vital resource — only has validity if we have some idea of what the contrary attitudes are. In conclusion then, information specialists should be aware of an information cycle. The connection between an individual and information system can be seen as a series of states — a predisposition to use an information system (this is composed of two elements, an expectation and an inclination to use), contact with the system, use of system's products and effect of using the system's products.

THE INFORMATION CONSUMER

I have laboured the point that most user studies are fact gathering exercises which lack a framework. I have discussed the necessity to explore the context in which information is needed. More specifically, however, what does the information specialist need to understand in order to be both adaptive *and* formative. Kuehl[8] has identified five key questions:

(1) How and when do user groups recognize their need for information services and products?
(2) What circumstances and activities characterize user external search processes for information products and services?
(3) How are competing information sources evaluated by users?
(4) What behavioural factors characterise actual information source access?
(5) Do post-use variables affect the user's satisfaction with utilised sources?

I have indicated that many information system phenomena exhibit "Zipf" characteristics. The psychological idea behind Zipf's mathematics is the *principle of least effort*. It is the only principle which information science has to guide it in answering Kuehl's five questions. It is, however, too broad a concept to be helpful. It is a hold-all for any observation. For example, Rosenberg's[18] finding that for a sample of US government and industrial scientists ease of use was more important than amount of information, fits comfortable within its embrace. More help is perhaps forthcoming from consumer decision models particularly the most recent of these which see the consumer as an information processor. For example, Howard and Sheth's[19] taxonomy of problem solving behaviours—extensive, limited and routinised—seems an attractive categorisation to borrow. The point at issue is can Howard's categorisation of problem solving which was applied to the dynamics of the buying progress—a decision to buy an unfamiliar brand in an unfamiliar product class, or a routinised purchase of a familiar product—be happily extrapolated to the information system? It has a certain intuitive appeal. We have some evidence from the Cranfield study that information consumers will perceive their problems in this sort of way and will apply the appropriate information strategy. For example, a thorough information search will be mounted if a problem is perceived to be extensive. However, this is all a little trite and doesn't take us very far. It is not explanatory. Information strategy is a subsidiary to the Howard and Sheth model. The model sets out to *explain* in what situations the different sorts of problem solving occur. The accompanying information strategy is supplementary to the model. The information specialist needs an explanation of why problems are perceived differently by information consumers. Similarly the concept of perceived risk common to many consumer decision models fits but does not explain much. If a phenomenon is not understood we require more variables to understand it. We collect information to give us confidence. A tentative finding from the study conducted at Cranfield supports this idea. Those post graduate management students who were having difficulty with principles and techniques went beyond the information presented in case packs etc., and sought further ammunition from libraries and other places. We did confirm the notion that information is valued on two dimensions—information has both a predictive value and a confidence value.

It may be that translating from buyer behaviour models is not going to help answer Kuehl's five questions; to help answer what every information professional wants to know—how and in what situations is a formal information system used, how and in what situations is it by-passed? Perhaps I am back again at the problem of defining information. It is perhaps unwise to isolate "information activities" from any other activity. Perhaps we should not be trying to build models of information consumers but instead a series of decision models.

Marketing's broad view of economic utility extending beyond the form and tangibility notions of value provides not answers to Kuehl's point but some useful insights. Information will be valued not simply for its end-use consequences but for its possession of the right form, time, place and possession utilities. For example, if the language or format of an information product is not understood, or if the product is received before need is perceived, the value will diminish. Andrus[20] suggests actions that can be taken to enhance the value, for example, translate, revise or change the format, store against possible future need.

TWO EMPIRICAL STUDIES

I want to conclude by referring to two pieces of empirical work that have been influenced by marketing thinking. One of these was located in the public library and the other is the study that Gordon Wills and myself are currently conducting at Cranfield. Coleman and Yorke[21] attempted to identify the library needs of a community preparatory to the provision of a new branch library in the Manchester area. It is easy to quibble. Interviews were very short, the sampling techniques employed a little dubious. However, some fairly fundamental criticism can be made. The researchers were seeking collective views about what services the public would like to see provided in the future. Respondents were being asked to think seriously about services not previously provided which they would like included in the new services. The hypothetical nature of the survey made the respondent's task very difficult. The researchers did not make their assumptions explicit. Presumably they feel that public libraries respond to public requirements. Some acknowledgement at least should have been made to the great debate as to whether public libraries reflect or mould public requirements. This Manchester work, however, is quite interesting and could be further developed. It would be interesting, for example, to relate expressed preferences to existing borrowing habits.

Having been critical of others' research, I must now come clean about an investigation I have conducted over the last three years. The task was to study the costs and benefits of academic library services. The allocation of library resources has been a fairly arbitrary exercise. We became convinced that a cost-benefit analysis was not the best approach to the question of value. We concentrated on identifying the benefits of two technological academic institutions, Cranfield and Loughborough. The argument was that the library manager is able to be more effective in resource allocation arguments if he has some understanding of his information system's contribution to the organisation it serves. We attempted to identify, not simply the outputs of the services, but also the impact of the service. What good does it do a student to use an on-line information retrieval system? What harm is done if he waits six weeks for a thesis from the inter-library loan service?

As with many research projects there is a disappointing gap between the conceptual framework and the empirical work. The research design was influenced by the sort of thinking which has been discussed in the paper. More specifically it was based on the following assertions.

(1) The focus of attention should be on the *user*, not *uses* of information products.
(2) The library is part of an information system which consists of formal and informal elements.
(3) A user will have *expectations* of what a library can do for him and he will have experiences of contact with the system.

We wanted to identify the perceptual difference between expectations and experiences of contact (called perceptions of actuality). Expectations are a composite notion:

Individual elements — psychological characteristics, for example, individual's previous library background.

Inter personal — communication between all the actors in the environment; the teachers and the taught, researchers and librarians.

Organisational — Structure of knowledge in the subject (sole focus of most library research investigations). Educational philosophy and educational mechanisms which are the manifestation of this philosophy.

The use (behaviour) of a library is caused by something else. We summarised this something else by the word "expectations". What would be the relative strengths of the constituent elements and what is the effect of library behaviour? It is a complex dynamic situation. What effect does contact have on future expectations and what effect do these expectations have on contact? The value of a university library (labelled by us derived value) is the difference between expectations and perceived actuality. The implication of our expression of derived value is that a good service (good defined in terms of financial support) could deliver less derived value because of the high expectations it raises and *vice versa*. This situation unless exploited can be rather a dismal one. The receiving community is continually satisfied and there is no support for an injection of resources.

We employed a variety of techniques to identify benefit. I intend, as with my discussion on the research design, simply to introduce one or two points. At the very beginning of the academic year at Cranfield we administered a questionnaire to "freshman" post graduate management and engineering students. We called this the Initial Expectations Study. Our respondents were "uncontaminated" by the Cranfield system. Their expectations, therefore, would be unaffected by contact with that system. The questionnaire was constructed from a "model" of a structured course. A consistently high score (Likert scales were used) implied that the respondent valued a library stereo-type — a library serving a structured course. Each of the statements represented a "benefit", a belief about libraries servicing a structured course. These statements were derived from unstructured interviews conducted in the first year of the project. Respondents were asked to say (i) what their expectations were of the "mechanics" of their study and (ii) what their expectations were of libraries. The design of the questionnaire was influenced by Fishbein's work. We were convinced that the educational mechanisms, e.g., number of class contact hours, the importance of the spoken word, individual or group approach to projects, were influential on expectations. Throughout the year a further five questionnaires were administered in order to observe the extent expectations would change as a result of exposure to the educational and information system. The other major tool was an information panel. Students were asked to log, in diaries, their "educational" tasks and to say how they solved them. We were able to isolate the library's part in this process. Quantitative data (issue statistics) were collected at various stages to match with the self-reported data. It will be apparent this was a very ambitious methodological exercise. Any results have to be very carefully examined in the context of the two fieldwork locations.

CONCLUSION

I have tried to indicate that information management research has followed certain directions. As a consequence it has not been discovered that the use of an information system has an effect on anything else. Insights from marketing which is a similar activity to that of operating an information system may help to demonstrate that the system does have an effect on something else — thus enabling the system to survive. I think that information does present some very difficult problems and that the marketing of information services is different from marketing other services. Most of my exploration has concentrated on the consumer behaviour side of marketing. I have not thought at all of an information system being a distribution channel. It would be very exciting if someone could start thinking along those lines.

REFERENCES

[1] Debons, A., and Montgomery, K. L., "Design and evaluation of information systems", *Annual Review of Information Science and Technology*, Vol. 9, 1974, pp. 25-58.

[2] Saracevic, T., *et al.*, *An Information utility*, Case Western Reserve University, Eurim preprint, 1974, p. 2.

[3] Brittain, J. M., *Information and its users — a review with special references to the social sciences*, Oriel Press, 1970.

[4] Blagden, J., "Communication: a library management problem", *Aslib Proceedings*, Vol. 27, No. 8, 1975, pp. 319-26.

⁵Ford, G., "Research in user behaviour in university libraries", *Journal of Documentation*, Vol. 29, No. 1, 1973, pp. 85-106.

⁶Bath University, *Investigation into information requirements of researchers in the social sciences*, 2 vols., 1971.

⁷Martyn, J., "Information needs and users", *Annual Review of Information Science and Technology*, Vol. 9, 1974, pp. 3-21.

⁸Kuehl, P., *Marketing viewpoints for user need studies*, Syracuse University, Summer symposium on Economics of Information Dissemination, 1973.

⁹Menzel, H., "Can science information needs be ascertained empirically?", in Thayer, L. (ed.), *Communication, concepts and perspectives*, Spartan Books, 1967.

¹⁰Hansen, I. B., *The value of user studies in the planning of library and documentation services*, Eurim, 1974, pp. 3-21.

¹¹Stecher, G., "Library evaluation: a survey of studies in quantification", *Australian Academics and Research Libaries*, Vol. 6, 1975, pp. 1-19.

¹²Wyckam, R. G. et al., "Marketing of services: an evaluation of the theeory", *Journal of Marketing*, Vol. 9, No. 1, 1975, pp. 59-67.

¹³Boulding, K., "The economics of knowledge and the knowledge of economics", *American Economic Review*, Vol. 56, No. 2, 1965, pp. 1-13.

¹⁴Line, M., "Draft definitions", *Aslib Proceedings*, Vol. 26, No. 2, 1974, p. 87.

¹⁵Aguilar, F. J., *Scanning the business environment*, Macmillan, 1967.

¹⁶Mavor, A., and Vaughan, W. S., *Development and implementation of a curriculum-based information support system for Hameline University*, Hameline University, St. Paul, Minnesota, 1974, Grant GN 873.

¹⁷Warner, E. S. et al., *Information needs of urban residents*, US Department of Health, Education and Welfare, Office of Education, 1973.

¹⁸Rosenberg, V., *The application of psychometric techniques to determine the attitudes of individuals towards information seeking*, Lehigh University, 1966.

¹⁹Howard, J. A., and Sheth, J. N., *A theory of buying behaviour*, Wiley, 1969.

²⁰Andrus, R. R., "Approaches to information evaluation", *MSU Business Topics*, Summer 1971, pp. 40-5.

²¹Coleman, P., and Yorke, D., "A public library experiment with market research", *Library Association Record*, Vol. 77, No. 5, 1975, pp. 107-9.

Part XIII
CHANGE

Introduction

"Change" is a recurring theme in library administration. However, change can have a very mechanistic meaning. One speaks of "changing technologies" or "changing procedures" without really understanding what change is, or what it implies for the library organization. Also, we often confuse "change" with "innovation." They are not necessarily the same. "Innovation" can either be the cause of, or the result of, the organizational change process.

The change process usually results in a new set of circumstances, such as a reallocation of resources, which is liable to have marked effect on the way in which organizational members view their organization and on the way they view the products of that organization. The services which can result from this process may also be referred to as "innovative." In any case, a major characteristic of the change process is that it is continuous and evolving. Organizations are continually changing for better or worse. The results of this change process are not always beneficial to that organization. Unless the change process is carefully managed, serious dysfunctions to both the organization as a whole and to those who work within it can occur.

One important element running through the chapters in this part is that the *process* of change is of vital importance. Declaring that a particular innovation is desirable is insufficient to ensure its successful adoption. People must be convinced that change is desirable and will improve existing conditions. Above all, library administrators and staff desiring change must plan to change. Haphazard and unmanaged change has the potential to reduce severely whatever effectiveness an organization might have.

Miriam A. Drake's analysis of the change process in academic libraries reflects the complexity of forces which can impel a library to adopt innovative practices. These forces result from perceptions of environmental conditions which, while suggesting that change is necessary, are not necessarily accompanied by clear ideas of what direction change should take. If change is purposeful, as Drake and others suggest, then an understanding of that purpose is essential to provide information on the precise direction that the change process must take. Although no change is without risk, and some changes are very risky indeed, the chances of failure can be reduced by establishing a set of organizational conditions which encourages the change process and views it as an important part of organizational development.

Alan R. Samuels' article emphasizes the importance of creating a climate within which the change process can operate smoothly. Defining climate as the way in which people perceive the functioning of an organization, Samuels suggests that one way to facilitate the change process is to achieve agreement among organizational members that change is desirable. To do this, it is necessary to know what people really think, a task which cannot be accomplished through ad-hoc judgments by library administrators acting through intuition. Knowing whether or not an organization is ready to change, ready to engage in the often disruptive processes that change implies, requires knowing whether people who will be engaged in the process, and who will be affected by the process, have a clear understanding of the necessity and desirability of change. Samuels is suggesting that any planned change requires a pre-planning stage which, by creating a climate of change acceptance, can insure change success.

Each organization perceives needed changes differently. The direction change will take is contingent upon a variety of factors, not all of which are created by the nature of the change itself. An organization must examine its own capacity for development and develop a program of planned change which is suitable for itself but which may not work in other similar organizations. As J. A. Millar points out, this "contingency view" of change is not, and cannot be, prescriptive for all organizations. Millar's view of organizations as value-laden bodies implies that it is these values which form the true contingencies that change agents must address. Values may be changed, but ignoring them is dangerous.

Managing Innovation in Academic Libraries
By Miriam A. Drake

Innovation is an economic or social change resulting from a deliberate and purposeful process. Academic libraries could be substantially changed by the adoption of technological innovation in information service or made obsolete by competition from the private sector. This paper explores key issues related to innovation in academic libraries and concludes that innovation requires a conducive climate, capital investment, and a leadership that is enthusiastic and committed.

FUNDAMENTAL CHANGES in the economics and technology of academic library operations have stimulated librarians and administrators to seek ways of introducing and implementing innovation in libraries.

Zaltman has observed, "The impetus to innovation arises when organizational decision makers perceive that the organization's present course of action is unsatisfactory. When a discrepancy exists between what the organization is doing and what its decision makers believed it ought to be doing, there is a performance gap."[1]

Many academic library decision makers are feeling the frustration of this "performance gap." Several new ideas and innovations are serving to help close the gap, such as the proposed National Periodicals Center, shared cataloging through RLIN, WLN, and OCLC, and the interlibrary loan system of OCLC.

While these services are contributing to the efficiency of libraries, they are not sufficient, by themselves, to close the gap between current library and information service and the potential for service that could become a reality if existing technology were adapted to user information needs. These services are also not sufficient to close the gaps between user expectations and the library's ability to meet those expectations.

Lancaster has observed, "The profession seems to have its head in the sand. The paperless society is rapidly approaching. Ignoring this fact will not cause it to go away."[2] In a forecast of telecommunications in the year 2000, Martino has stated, "Rather than visiting a library, any individual might be able to search the library files electronically and receive a printout of specific information or a facsimile copy of a desired document."[3]

During the 1980s libraries could be reduced to archival repositories because people will be accessing bibliographic data bases and text through computers in their homes and offices. These predictions while extreme and painful are indicative of trends with which librarians must deal. There is little doubt that technology can make these predictions become a reality; however, they ignore the human service functions fulfilled by libraries.

Adoption of computer and telecommunications technologies to library and information service needs will require capital and innovative thinking in the library profession. How can libraries maintain their function of human service in a machine environment? How can libraries use this technology to

---

Reprinted by permission of the American Library Association from "Managing Innovation in Academic Libraries," *College and Research Libraries*, vol. 40, no. 6 (November 1979), pp. 503-510. copyright © 1979 by the American Library Association.

provide more responsive service? These questions are only two of the many that need to be addressed.

The purpose of this paper is to present issues related to the managerial aspects of innovation in academic libraries. The specific issues to be covered include performance gaps, incentives to innovate, nature of innovation, barriers and constraints, impact of innovation, and implementation of innovative strategies.

PERFORMANCE GAPS

Library directors, librarians, and support staff appear to agree that something is wrong in the library. In many cases, teaching faculties, students, and institutional administrators agree that the library is not performing as they would like. The performance gaps relate to the differences between services being provided and services that could be provided with the adoption of technology, relationships between library and teaching faculties, library and institutional administrations, and library administration and staff.

Perceptions of the service gap cannot be generalized. They vary from library to library and depend on faculty and student awareness of technology, budget situations, and user demands. Several library directors have expressed extreme frustration over the decreasing purchasing power of funds at a time when faculty demands for instant gratification in the form of more books are increasing. Other library directors, dealing with technologically aware faculty, are trying to find capital to provide improved information retrieval services and faster document delivery methods.

These pressures are exacerbated in some institutions by administrators who are trying to compensate for enrollment declines with greater sponsored research activity. More intense competition among faculty members for tenure and promotion causes them to place greater demands on libraries. These demands coupled with budget pressures and other barriers to innovation create a performance gap.

Growing and changing demands will place greater pressure on library administrators to enhance fuzzy mission statements with operational goals and objectives. McClure states, "One must recognize the difference between goals and objectives—they are not the same. Goals provide long-range guidelines (five years or more) for organizational activity; they might never be accomplished, and they are not measured. In contrast, objectives are measurable, short range, and time limited."[4] McAnally and Downs indicated that the libraries have rarely done a good job of planning.[5]

Without purpose, planning is an exercise in futility. Achievement of objectives may require the elimination as well as the addition of services and materials. In order to have operational objectives, the library, teaching faculty, and institutional administration will have to agree on specific services and materials to be provided by the library and adjust their expectations to fit the objectives. This task is particularly difficult in a large university where faculties are often in conflict with one another. Humanities faculties tend to equate good libraries with big libraries, while engineers and management people seek information rather than books. In the setting of goals and objectives, the library and academic administrators become negotiators between the warring factions.

The administration of the college or university will need to acquire a greater understanding and sensitivity to the economics of libraries in terms of costs and benefits as well as inputs and outputs. Since libraries are part of overhead costs and administrators are charged with keeping costs as low as possible, academic administrators are likely to look to the library as a place to cut costs.

Many library budget cuts are not purposeful cuts. The director is told to cut X percent from the budget and may not be given any guidance on what services or materials to cut. Academic administrators facing severe overhead cost problems engendered by a variety of federal regulations may not realize or be sensitive to the impact of undirected cuts in terms of the library's ability to serve the needs of its clientele.

Staff present a different set of problems to library administrators. McAnally and Downs observed in 1973 that library staff ranked second out of five in the growing pressures on library directors. They further observed, "It may seem strange that the director should be under attack from his own staff, or fail to receive badly needed support in relations with administration and faculty, but it is so in many cases. . . . They want and expect a share in policy decisions affecting themselves and the library."[6]

Library directors have tried and are trying a variety of schemes to involve staff in the decision-making process. Dickinson has pointed out that ". . . 'participative management' has been used indiscriminately to mean everything from a situation wherein the library management simply seeks information and/or advice from staff members to one wherein the library is governed by plebiscite."[7]

Despite the best efforts of many library directors to change managerial style, rely more heavily on committees, and generally involve staff in decision-making processes, staff remain dissatisfied. In recent years, staff discontent has been exacerbated by the failure of salaries to keep pace with the cost of living, changing student and faculty demands, and potential changes inherent in computer and telecommunications technologies. Some library staff members may feel that their jobs or work habits are threatened by technological innovation.

INCENTIVES TO INNOVATE

Despite the potential threat to the professional and psychological well-being of some library personnel, library administrators may have no choice but to adopt innovative strategies to meet objectives and goals in a different society. Lancaster and others have raised the question of whether libraries will be needed in an electronic world. He states that the library problem may not be lack of space or financial resources; "rather it is likely to be one of justification for existence and simple survival."[8]

Technology can and will bring information directly into the home and office of the future. The place of the library in society will depend on how rapidly it integrates technology into its operations and how rapidly the engineers and designers of information systems will recognize the library as an important link in the system. While technology appears to be the major driving force for innovation, there are other factors contributing to the need to innovate. As technology has developed more effective and cheaper electronic computing and telecommunications devices, the economics of library operations has changed dramatically.

The rate of increase in the cost of library inputs has been consistently higher than the general inflation rate. Library output costs consisting largely of labor have not risen as rapidly. Because input costs are generally fixed costs in a library, the average cost per unit of output is rising in libraries where output levels have remained relatively constant or decreased.

Labor productivity and user productivity have been declining as collections, catalogs, and files have increased in size. The amount of capital invested in laborsaving equipment and processes is minimal in most libraries. Teaching faculties and librarians may find the term *productivity* offensive as it is usually related to the output of factory workers and farmers. Productivity in a library context relates the value of results obtained by staff or users from a given amount of effort in searching for information or documents.

Changing patterns of demand also provide incentives to innovate. In addition to providing course-related reading material, libraries are being asked to provide substantive information when needed and in a form that is convenient for the user. The potential of technology to provide information when and where needed coupled with the need to reduce the labor intensity of library operations is a prime motivator in innovation.

THE NATURE OF INNOVATION

Innovation is not limited to science and technology. Drucker's broader definition is ". . . the task of endowing human and material resources with new and greater wealth producing capacity."[9] In Drucker's terms, innovation is economic and social change which does not create new knowledge but creates potential for action and added wealth. Sawyer defines *innovation* as a "useful new combination of resources."[10] Innovation is not a device or a scheme. Rather it is a concept or a change in human activity. The concept is "continually evolving as the uncertainties are made to disappear and the targets turn into outcome."[11] Innovation is a deliberate process rather than a chance happening or discovery. Motivating people to want to change and to implement new plans and ideas is at the heart of innovation. "Innovation is not R & D, though it begins with research and continues with the entirely different process of development."[12] While research may result in invention and development may refine an invention into a finished, marketable product or process, innovation results in a change in the way people live and accomplish specific tasks. Innovation may be adoption of a technological device or process or it may be a new managerial or social process. Whatever it is, it relies heavily on human perceptions of something better in the future.

This development usually is to achieve a specific purpose and is a directed effort. The development of the MARC record, shared cataloging, electronic message systems, and management by objectives represents innovations that were initiated, developed, and implemented to achieve specific outcomes.

The literature of innovation, for the most part, deals with the concept in profit-making corporations. Discussions of innovation in the public sector point out that service industries and state and local governments are consumers of innovation rather than producers. The federal government is both a consumer and producer of innovation.[13] Innovation in information retrieval and other areas of human activity was funded initially by the federal government.

BARRIERS TO INNOVATION

There are a variety of barriers to innovation in academic institutions and libraries. These barriers relate to psychology, organizational factors, perceptions of the future, and economic factors.

The psychological constraints to innovate stem from fear of change, especially planned change, and the unknown. Library staff and users accustomed to the present-day library are reluctant to give up comfortable habits and established ways of accomplishing tasks. Library staff may feel threatened by systems analysts, computer types, and others who do not speak their language and appear to have little sympathy with their problems. There may be feelings of being manipulated. "People resist being changed by other people . . . ,"[14] especially planners and innovators. Their resistance may be based on fear of change, threat of being manipulated, conflicting interests, constrained freedom of choice, or failure to see the value of the innovation. With technological innovation in libraries, users and librarians legitimately fear that the library will be more impersonal and the art of the book will die.

The organizational factors inhibiting change are both internal and external to the library. While most academic administrators believe that a library is essential to an educational institution, for some, the library has retained its "bottomless pit" image. Other administrators see innovation as a way to give the pit a bottom but either don't know how to stimulate and reward innovative thinking or don't want to invest the necessary capital. The lack of understanding and support leaves librarians in an impossible position of being "damned if they do and damned if they don't."

Planning and budgeting in publicly supported colleges and universities are not geared to investment and innovative activity. There is a tendency to allocate the budget on a "use it or lose it" basis rather than a planned basis leading to sufficient funding for academic services that are valuable to the institution. While many universities have obtained funds for the addition of audiovisual equipment and materials and computer-aided instruction, these innovative techniques remain underutilized in many instructional programs. The chalk and blackboard are comfortable and require little new thinking or activity.

Universities also create barriers to innovation because innovation may not be rewarded, especially in the library. Across-the-board salary increases and competitive promotion and tenure situations tend to inhibit rather than stimulate innovation.

The lack of output measures of value in library operations constrains innovation. Academic administrators are more concerned with the cost of input than the value of output. They may be unsympathetic to library innovation because of focus on input and fail to see the contribution to output. Information, knowledge, and reading produce social value that cannot be easily quantified. Measurements of input versus social output or costs versus social benefit are elusive and do not provide needed justification for capital investment.

Economic factors limiting innovation in the library relate to capital, investment, risk, and uncertainty. The "use it or lose it" approach to budgeting does not allow the library to accumulate capital to invest in technology or innovation. Capital appropriations generally are one-shot deals used for new typewriters, buildings, or stacks. The result of this practice is that not only are libraries technologically underdeveloped, they are also starved for capital.

University administrators appear unwilling to invest funds in innovation that will improve library staff and user productivity or make the library more efficient. Payoffs from investments in libraries are difficult to calculate. The value of the librarian is perceived in terms of the salary paid rather than the value produced. There is little consideration given to the value of user time in the library and how that time can be made more productive.

Risk and uncertainty are key factors in the process as well as the economics of innovation. Although innovation is a deliberate process, there is a risk that a particular project will fail or that results will be less than expected. "The most dramatic evidence of the risk involved in . . . innovation is the recent experience of Princeton University Library with 3M's automated circulation system. . . ."[15] This project ended in failure, the 3M system has been withdrawn from the market, and Princeton has returned to a manual method to charge out books.

This failure, however, is more than balanced by successful projects in many libraries; for example, the Ohio State University circulation system, a high-risk project at its inception, is a success. Implementation of shared cataloging and its by-products, involving hundreds of libraries, is another example of successful change.

Uncertainty is related to project success and failure as well as future conditions and investment. Academic institutions are facing an uncertain future with regard to enrollment, government funding, research activity, and endowment funding. In a highly uncertain economic environment, a natural tendency is to try to conserve what is at hand rather than invest for future gain. Project selection and the process of the individual projects also contain elements of uncertainty. With many projects from which to choose and fuzzy measures of payoff and benefit/cost, management has to live with the idea that the projects chosen may not turn out to have been the best selections. "Uncertainty resides at the level of the individual project, where the 'best' way to proceed seldom is apparent and the individuals involved instead have to be satisfied with finding a promising way."[16]

Until recently, librarians have had the luxury of living in a relatively certain and risk-free environment. An innovative environment calls for new skills in risk assessment, ability to understand uncertainty, and ability to manage increased entrepreneurial activity.

THE IMPACT OF INNOVATION

Innovation has changed and will continue to change everyone's life in dramatic ways. Downs and Mohr have identified three categories of benefits related to innovation: (1) programmatic, (2) prestige, and (3) structural.[17]

Programmatic benefits are greater efficiency or effectiveness in accomplishing organizational goals, such as increased profit or market share in the private sector and production of improved service at the same or lower cost in the public sector.

The prestige benefit is the recognition and approval that are associated with early adoption of a new program or technology.

Structural benefits are related to individuals in the form of greater worker satisfaction or some other internal value.

Innovation in libraries, thus far, has produced both advantages and disadvantages. Shared cataloging systems have resulted in programmatic benefits for libraries but have resulted in some disadvantages for the worker. While some catalogers may feel greater satisfaction at being able to share their knowledge and skill, others may feel that the value of their professional judgment has decreased because they are prisoners of the terminal.

The potential impact of technological and systems innovations on libraries is difficult to forecast. If libraries survive as viable organizations giving useful and valuable service, it is unlikely that their present forms of organization and operation will persist. It is likely that academic libraries will evolve in different ways. The small college library serving primarily instructional programs will not change in the same way as large university libraries serving research as well as instruction. There is not nor should there be uniformity among academic libraries. Each library should be encouraged to recognize the important factors and the unique elements within its own institutional setting. A "me too" approach should be used only when it is compatible with the goals and operations of the library.

As innovation proceeds, library staff and users will need to adapt to new ways of finding information and documents. The library's role in the information process will depend heavily on how quickly it adopts technology to make that process more efficient while retaining personal service.

Information technology is developing rapidly in the private sector. Libraries no longer are the sole sources of information for teaching and research faculties. Many librarians feel that this competition is unfair. In an era of tax revolts and taxpayer demands for spending limitations, competition is probably a fact of life. Competition from the private sector could reduce the importance of libraries in many areas.

IMPLEMENTING INNOVATION

Given the constraints, how can libraries adopt and implement innovative strategies? There is no recipe for transforming libraries into innovative organizations; however, experience in other kinds of organizations has identified some of the characteristics of innovators and innovating organizations.

The first characteristic is a positive attitude about the future and a belief that the future can be modified by decisions made in the present. Drucker has stated, "Innovative organizations spend neither time nor resources defending yesterday."[18] An innovator does not concern himself or herself with the past but focuses on a vision of the future. Within innovative organizations, the climate nurtures creative thinking and change.

The climate does not develop overnight but is built over a period of time. People with new ideas and the ability to develop those ideas are rewarded and recognized in innovative organizations. "Readiness for change gradually becomes a characteristic of certain individuals, groups, organizations and civilizations. They no longer look nostalgically at a golden age in the past but anticipate their utopia in days to come."[19]

The responsibility for creating readiness for change and innovative strategies rests with management. Daft points out that top managers bridge the gap between the organization and technological development. Their status places ". . . them in a position to introduce change into an organization."[20] They are exposed to new ideas from outside the organization and can stimulate new thinking within the organization. "The individual manager controls in large measure the kind and quality of ideas he will hear, by the questions he asks and the interest he shows in the answers. In that part of the job concerned with innovation, each manager must be responsible for stimulating the flow of ideas by appropriate questions and interest and by considerate screening of the idea he receives."[21] Most of the ideas received are likely to be rejected; however, acceptance or rejection must be based on standards and appropriateness and be in harmony with organizational goals. Only a few ideas will merit further investigation and careful evaluation.

Innovative managers recognize that innovation doesn't just happen. An idea without development remains an idea, good or bad. Innovation is deliberate, purposeful, and, in most cases, a planned process or program. There is an objective or goal to be achieved that requires resources to develop an idea into a program or innovation to be incorporated into library operations. "In . . . concentrating effort on the best ideas, the manager takes up the bare essence (which is the idea) and breathes life into it; he gives it form and dimension. He makes the idea his own, not in the sense of taking it from the originator, but in the sense of giving commitment, and adding the weight of his own recommendation to the request for additional development."[22]

Innovation and change require an organizational structure that facilitates the flow of communication up and down. Ideally, innovative ideas should originate at both ends of an organizational hierarchy. Administrative ideas originate at the top and move down while technical innovation originates near the bottom and moves up.[23] A great many words have been written about managerial styles and communication in libraries. McAnally and Downs suggest, "The director has to surrender some of his old authority and becomes more of a leader"[24] in a more participatory environment. The staff dissatisfaction discussed by McAnally and Downs in 1973 has not abated in 1979 despite the good faith efforts of many library directors and programs, such as MRAP.

Dickinson, in his review of participative management, concluded, "Some library managers are unwilling to admit that they want and need control over the operations for which they are accountable. . . . participative management or power sharing should not—and cannot, if it is to be successful—mean an abdication of responsibility for the library on the part of administrators and managers, in the name of democracy."[25]

Innovation and idea generation rarely occur in groups. Individuals have ideas. Management is the catalyst needed to bring an idea to the point of innovation. The usual library committee structures are not conducive to idea generation or innovative thinking. In using committees in the innovative process, managers should keep the words of L. J. Peter in mind: "No committee could ever come up with anything as revolutionary as a camel—anything as practical and as perfectly designed to perform effectively under such difficult conditions."[26] Committees are useful in studying specific issues and defining problems. A special task force drawn from appropriate departments of the library can be useful in drawing up plans to implement and integrate an innovation into library operations.

In the process of managing innovation, library users can be valuable. People responsible for developing new library programs should be sensitive not only to the user's needs but also to the user's wants. There may be substantial differences between needs and wants. If innovation is to succeed, users will need to be convinced that it is worthwhile.

A manager or library director may work at fine-tuning the climate of the library to produce innovation or new ideas and find that there is no response. He or she may proclaim in a loud voice that upward communications are welcome but find a quiet telephone or empty mailbox. If libraries are to implement significant change and staff is to be part of that change, library administrators will need actively to encourage change.

This encouragement should result in serious review of new ideas and innovation proposals as well as follow-through in development and feedback to the innovator. In addition, it may be necessary to alter the rewards and punishment system substantially so that innovators are recognized and rewarded with salary increases or perquisites.

Lastly, the library director desirous of closing performance gaps and shaping a meaningful role for the library in the future must present possibilities with enthusiasm, commitment, and confidence. He or she must communicate a sense of excitement and ability to make improvements in the future.

Conclusions

Innovation is purposeful economic and social change. If libraries are to continue their important contribution to the instructional and research missions of academic institutions, a climate conducive to change and generation of new ideas must be created. Library administrators must view innovation seriously and provide follow-through to develop ideas into innovations that can be integrated into library operations. Librarianship may be the fastest-changing and most exciting profession today. The potential to improve information service through technology is largely unrealized. Transforming potential into reality will require capital, innovation, perseverance, and leadership.

References

1. Gerald Zaltman, Robert Duncan, and Jonny Holbek, *Innovations and Organizations* (New York: Wiley, 1973), p.55.
2. F. Wilfrid Lancaster, "Whither Libraries? or,

Wither Libraries," *College & Research Libraries* 39:357 (Sept. 1978).
3. Joseph P. Martino, "Telecommunications in the Year 2000," *Futurist* 13:99 (April 1979).
4. Charles R. McClure, "The Planning Process: Strategies for Action," *College & Research Libraries* 39:459 (Nov. 1978).
5. Arthur M. McAnally and Robert B. Downs, "The Changing Role of Directors of University Libraries," *College & Research Libraries* 34:112 (March 1973).
6. Ibid., p.111.
7. Dennis W. Dickinson, "Some Reflections on Participative Management in Libraries," *College & Research Libraries* 39:254 (July 1978).
8. Lancaster, "Whither Libraries?" p.346.
9. Peter F. Drucker, *Management: Tasks, Responsibilities, and Practice* (New York: Harper & Row, 1974), p.67.
10. George C. Sawyer, "Innovation in Organizations," *Long Range Planning* 11:54 (Dec. 1978).
11. H. Brian Locke, "Planning Innovation," *Long Range Planning* 11:21 (Dec. 1978).
12. H. Brian Locke, "Innovation by Design," *Long Range Planning* 9:35 (Aug. 1976).
13. J. David Roessner, "Incentives to Innovate in Public and Private Organizations," *Administration & Society* 9:341–65 (Nov. 1977).
14. David E. Ewing, *The Human Side of Planning: Tool or Tyrant?* (London: Macmillan, 1969), p.44.
15. Miriam A. Drake and Harold A. Olsen, "The Economics of Library Innovation," *Library Trends* 28:98 (Summer 1979).
16. Richard R. Nelson and Sidney G. Winter, "In Search of Useful Theory of Innovation," *Research Policy* 6:51 (Jan. 1977).
17. George W. Downs, Jr., and Lawrence Mohr, "Toward a Theory of Innovation," *Administration & Society* 10:379–408 (Feb. 1979).
18. Drucker, *Management*, p.791.
19. Zaltman, Duncan, and Holbek, *Innovations*, p.103.
20. Richard L. Daft, "A Dual-Care Model of Organizational Innovation," *Academy of Management Journal* 21:193 (June 1978).
21. Sawyer, "Innovation," p.54.
22. Ibid., p.55.
23. Daft, "A Dual-Care Model," p.195.
24. McAnally and Downs, "The Changing Role," p.120.
25. Dickinson, "Participative Management," p.260–61.
26. Laurence J. Peter. *Peter's Quotations: Ideas for Our Time* (New York: Morrow, 1977), p.120.

Organizational Climate and Library Change
By Alan R. Samuels

ABSTRACT

Successful change in a library depends upon an adequate understanding of that library's organizational climate. A method of studying a library's organizational climate is presented and discussed. The importance of achieving perceptual agreement of current library functioning through modification of a library's organizational climate is stressed.

INTRODUCTION

Whatever else the American Library Association's comprehensive planning process for public libraries[1] will accomplish, it will certainly stimulate a flurry of activity among librarians. As a result, libraries are apt to be faced with strong forces impelling changes in many areas. Changes are likely to occur in leadership and managerial styles, in standard operating procedures, in services, and in the attitudes, perceptions, and values of librarians. The ability of a library to withdraw consciously and deliberately from repetitive, predictable, reactive, and normative ways of doing things will be called into question. This is not an ability easily acquired. In a scenario emphasizing innovation and change rather than the creeping incrementalism so characteristic of library activities in the past, a library's capacity for self-diagnosis and evaluation will be sorely tried.

Change is difficult even in the best of circumstances. The risks of failure are high. Yet it is possible to decrease these risks by determining whether or not the "climate is right" for change before, not after, substantial time and resources are invested in implementing major shifts from current modes of operation.

The central theme of this paper is that if change is to have lasting effects, people must agree that change is necessary. If such agreement is sought, then a common understanding of the problems facing an organization must be obtained by members of that organization. This common understanding can come about only in a climate emphasizing free exchange of ideas, perceptions, and information. But before such a climate can be created, the existing climate in the organization must be identified, analyzed, and modified if needed. Only then will a data base be provided from which directions for change can be derived.

The purpose of this paper is to suggest a methodology for diagnosing and modifying an organization's climate prior to implementing change activity. Utilizing such a methodology can increase the ability of an organization to withstand the potential disruptions in normal activities which any change process is likely to entail.

THE CONCEPT OF ORGANIZATIONAL CLIMATE

All of us have an intuitive grasp of what is meant by "climate." The term frequently appears in everyday speech. People speak of a "climate of consensus" or a "climate of learning." Often the term is used as a synonym for some other term such as "atmosphere" or "environment." In library literature, we occasionally use the term in such phrases as "climate for innovation."[2] In many organizational settings, we often hear that doing something at variance with established policy cannot be suggested because "the climate isn't right." Libraries can be typed as "cold," or "forbidding," or even "friendly" by users. But in whatever context the term is used, the notion of "climate" does have meaning to people, however uncertain that meaning might be.

A good analogy to climate, and one that is frequently used, is "weather."[3] For example, geographical localities are described in particular ways. They may be "temperate," or "cold," or "moderate." In this context, "climate" is used as a means of describing the average weather patterns characterizing regions. While individual days have different meteorological conditions, the overall weather pattern, the one that remains fairly consistent over time, remains the same. Further, this overall weather pattern affects the way people behave. Warm climates support outdoor activities: cold climates support the reverse. Climate, then, affects much of what people do, and how they go about doing it.

Organizations too have climates, hence the term "organizational climate." Librarians, for example, may perceive that participation in certain programs and services is not consistent with their own views of what libraries should do. These perceptions form part of a library's climate. In another context, librarians might not wish to engage in such highly touted activities as shared decision making in spite of the considerable support which this form of management has received in the library literature in recent years.[4] These attitudes also go into the making of a library's organizational climate. In any case, what constitutes an organization's climate has been debated, studied, measured, conceptualized, and analyzed over several decades. That no definite answers have yet been given or conclusions reached does not detract from the recognizable fact that an organization's climate does indeed affect the way people go about their business.

In order to understand the utility of organizational climate as a diagnostic tool, it is necessary to place it within the context of organizational research in general. What do researchers generally agree adequately defines "organizational climate?"

Among the earliest comprehensive reviews of studies related to organizational climate was the "state of the art" review by Forehand and Gilmer.[5] Describing organizational climate as "the set of characteristics that describe an organization and that (a) distinguish the organization from other organizations, (b) are relatively enduring over time, and (c) influence the behavior of people in the organization,"[6] Forehand and Gilmer identified five variables that researchers had thought important in studying an organization's climate. These were size of organization, organizational structure, the systems complexity of the organization, the type of leadership style in use within the organization, and the degree to which organizational goals were, in fact, motivating the behavior of organization members.

Tagiuri and Litwin provided an extensive discussion of the conceptual underpinnings of organizational climate.[7] Their definition of the term was more specific and described organizational climate as "a relatively enduring quality of the internal environment of an organization that (a) is experienced by its members, (b) influences their behavior, and (c) can be described in terms of the values of a particular set of characteristics (or attributes) of the organization."[8] To Tagiuri and Litwin, "climate" was essentially a unitary concept which reflected a very specific configuration of situational variables in an organization (such as leadership styles). While individual components of climate might vary as, for example, the type of decision-making practices used under different contingencies, its general meaning to the individual may remain the same (e.g., "is the climate participatory or not"). In addition to being relatively enduring, it is perceptually external to the individual, although the individual does interpret climate in terms of his or her own value systems. Finally, climate is based on external reality, a reality which exists among more than one individual. This is important in understanding the nature of organizational climate as distinguished from other climate-like concepts such as job satisfaction. If people *collectively*, not individually, believe that certain attributes do indeed characterize an organization, then those attributes become the property of the *organization* rather than of the individual. Hence those attributes join others similarly perceived and become part of that organization's climate.

In a later discussion of organizational climate, Hellriegel and Slocum further clarified the meaning of organizational climate by identifying and narrowing what could, and could not, be included in a definition of the concept. Their definition is worth quoting in full since it forms the basis of the author's own view of organizational climate. According to Hellriegel and Slocum, organizational climate "refers to a set of attributes which can be perceived about a particular organization and/or its subsystems, and that may be induced from the way that organization and/or its subsystems deal with their members and environments."[9] Hellriegel and Slocum continue by listing several implications of this definition:

1) Perceptual responses sought are primarily descriptive, not evaluative.
2) Units of analysis tend to be organizational attributes.
3) How people perceive organizational attributes tends to have behavioral consequences.

Other important and recent discussions of the concept include those of James and Jones,[10] Pritchard and Karasick,[11] Payne and Pugh,[12] Schneider and Bartlett,[13] Guion,[14] Lau,[15] and Samuels.[16] However, the role of organizational climate as a variable which intervenes between the individual and that individual's environment was stressed by Hellriegel and Slocum and generally accepted by those working in the field.

As libraries begin to doubt the validity of existing measures of library success, the development of new techniques for library evaluation seems particularly appropriate. The utility of organizational climate as a diagnostic tool for libraries lies in its ability to assess a group of currently unrecognized but potentially very valuable variables which can affect the library's administrative effectiveness, its daily activities, the value systems of its librarians, and its provision of service. In this paper, organizational climate is viewed as a means whereby potential change activities can be examined prior to their implementation. Evaluating potential reactions to such activities can enable administrators to take corrective action before any actual changes are implemented.

VIEWING ORGANIZATIONAL CLIMATE IN LIBRARY CONTEXTS

The role of organizational climate as an intervening variable which mediates between leadership processes within an organization and the behavior of individual workers is frequently stressed in the literature. However, organizational climate in libraries needs to be viewed from a wider perspective than merely as a reflection of what is occurring within the organization's boundaries.

Figure 1. The Role of Organizational Climate in Libraries

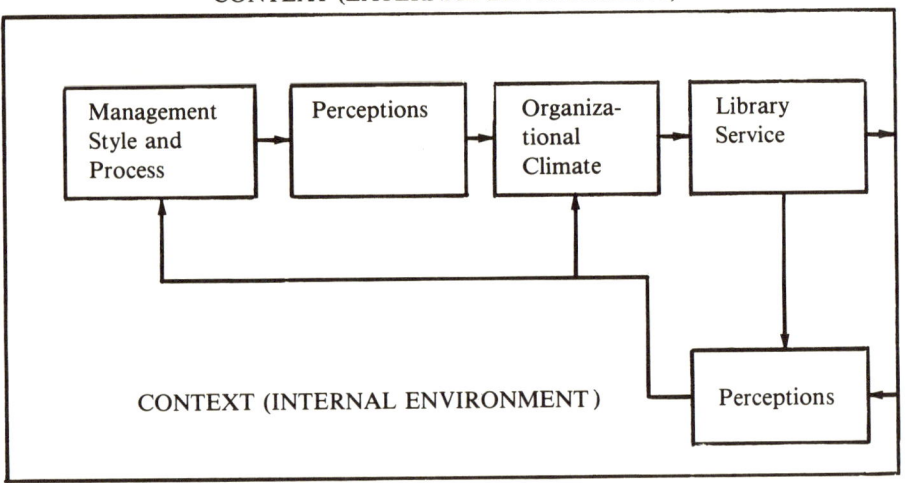

Figure 1 suggests that library organizational climate derives from the totality of perceptions held by individual staff members. These perceptions arise from how staff view current library functioning in four general areas: 1) management, or the type of control exercised by library administration over library affairs and library staff, 2) types of services and programs provided by the library and their perceived effectiveness in meeting client needs by library staff, 3) external environments within which the library must operate, such as budgetary constraints and governmental restrictions on library operations, and 4) organizational contexts, or internal environments within which the staff member must perform his or her job, such as departmental interrelationships or co-worker preferences.

Once an organizational climate is formed in a library, it then operates in two ways. As well as affecting the manner in which staff behave in the organization, it also affects the success of services provided by that organization. For example, librarians who perceive that services offered by the library are consistent with their own values and beliefs are likely to be more committed to these services than in situations where such consistency does not exist. The totality of librarian attitudes toward such services and the way in which they are perceived to be operating is one component of a library's climate. Similarly, if librarians perceive that management is operating in a way inconsistent with what it says it is doing, these perceptions will form part of that library's climate. The converse is also true: if management perceives that librarians are unwilling to accept the responsibilities of shared management, then such responsibilities will not be delegated. These perceptions also become part of that library's climate.

Externally imposed value judgments also give rise to climate perceptions. Such value judgments may take the form of "standards for college libraries, guidelines for school media centers, mission statements for public libraries," and the like. These documents form part of a library's external environment and can be perceived as either consistent or not consistent with the value systems of librarians within a specific library. It is not whether such documents are useful in themselves that is of concern in identifying a library's climate, but rather how they are perceived.

In summary, then, library organizational climate is a subjective representation of a library's functioning. In Tagiuri's words, climate is something which exists "out there" rather than solely within the mind of the perceiver.[17] Identifying the library's organizational climate provides a graphic and meaningful picture of the "psychological health" of that library at any given moment in time. It is that "psychological health"—that ability of a library either to encourage or to discourage goal integration of organization and individual—which can often determine whether or not more traditional library activities will have the effectiveness desired by those engaging in such activities.

CREATING A CLIMATE FOR CHANGE

Zaltman and Duncan have emphasized the need to develop a climate within an organization that is receptive to change and within which accurate problem recognition and problem definition can occur.[18] However, before such a climate can be developed, it is necessary to recognize clearly what climate actually characterizes the organization. Is, for example, the climate "open" and receptive to change and innovation, or is it "closed" and strongly committed to maintenance of the status quo?[19]

Change requires planning. However, very often planning in libraries, if done at all, is liable to be carried out in a climate that can impede such a process.[20] Individuals and groups participating in the planning process may not perceive the activities, events, programs, services, and interpersonal relationships of that organization's functioning in a like manner. This is not to mean that initial agreement on the appropriateness of any specific courses of action is necessary or even desirable, but merely that people should acquire the ability to agree on the nature of whatever problems exist. Such agreement is vital before solutions can be generated.

A convenient term for such mutual understanding is "perceptual agreement." As organization members begin to achieve a common understanding of current organizational functioning, perceptual agreement becomes increasingly characteristic of that organization's climate. In terms of the change process, organization members collectively, rather than individually, become aware of the extent to which that organization has become frozen in fixed patterns of operations. It is at the end of this awareness stage that an organization can be said to have achieved a climate of perceptual agreement.

Developing a climate stressing perceptual agreement is prerequisite to taking any change action. But to develop such a climate requires that the organization take the time necessary to study and evaluate its existing climate. Such a study is particularly critical in library contexts because of the library's failure to take advantage of techniques, such as marketing research, which can gradually produce an awareness of changing community conditions leading to a corresponding change in library operations. Because of the tendency for the library to remain within certain fixed boundaries of service, whether or not those services are actually desired by that library's clientele, a preplanning stage leading to increased awareness of environmental conditions is essential in helping a library increase, not decrease, the "fit" between that library and the community it serves. With awareness comes understanding, and it is that understanding which leads to effective planning for change.

DIAGNOSING THE LIBRARY'S CLIMATE

Although procedures for diagnosing the library's existing climate are likely to vary from one library to another, figure 2 suggests an overall framework within which such procedures can be developed. The goal of following such procedures is *not* agreement on goals, objectives, and courses of action, but rather the facilitation of the more normative planning process through creation of a climate within which organizational members are more readily able to perceive the need to plan for change.

There are several desirable outcomes of creating a climate emphasizing perceptual agreement. First, the library can develop an organizational climate which emphasizes the rapid reduction of perceptual gaps of current library functioning. Reducing these gaps increases a library's ability to perceive the need for, and desirability of, change. Second, dysfunctional aspects of current library operational and management policies become more visible to all library staff, both administrative and non-administrative. Third, the start-up dangers inherent in any program of planned change can be minimized through advance preparation. If people are able to agree that problems exist, and are able to perceive such problems similarly, then potential solutions can be developed quickly at a later time. Finally, diagnosing a library's climate, identifying perceptual gaps, and taking steps to eliminate these perceptual gaps, can bring into existence an organizational climate which encourages the testing and realistic evaluation of assumptions. It is this testing and evaluation of assumptions on a regular and continuous basis which can lead to the establishment of a planning culture in a library that stresses action research, policy modification, operational changes, and self-evaluation leading to lasting, not transitory, change.

Figure 2(a). Phase 1—Measuring the Library's Existing Climate

1. Management Conducts Context Assessment.
2. Management Prepares Context Assessment Document.
3. Using Variables Delineated Through Context Assessment, Management Prepares Climate Measuring Instrument.
4. Management Conducts Climate Assessment and Identifies Perceptual Gaps.
5. Management Evaluates Library Organizational Climate and Prepares Climate Evaluation Document Detailing Results. This Document Is Disseminated to Staff.

PHASE 2

Figure 2(b). Phase 2—Modifying Existing Climate Conditions

6. Management Conducts Problem Analysis and Disseminates Results.
7. Management and Staff Develop Perceptual Agreement Strategy.
8. Management and Staff Develop Plan for Achieving Perceptual Agreement.
9. Management and Staff Develop Plan for Monitoring Perceptual Agreement Plan.
10. Management Implements Perceptual Agreement Plan with Staff Assistance.
11. Management Implements Evaluation Plan with Staff Assistance.
12. Management Conducts Climate Assessment.
13. Management Prepares Written Document Detailing Results of Climate Assessment and Disseminates to Staff.
14. Management and Staff Jointly Decide Whether or Not Sufficient Perceptual Agreement Has Been Achieved. If Not, Revised Plan Is Developed and Implemented.

ASSESSING THE LIBRARY'S EXISTING CLIMATE

As figure 2 suggests, there are two distinct phases in conducting a climate study. Phase 1 is primarily measurement oriented and is the responsibility of library management. Phase 2 seeks to modify existing climate conditions. In phase 1 attempts are made to identify precisely what sort of climate actually exists in the library. Through this identification process, perceptual gaps are revealed. Care needs to be taken in order that accurate pictures of how different groups (such as public and technical services personnel), perceive the effectiveness of current library programs and services in meeting local needs, and the success of library management in dealing with employees. Library programs and services or library management processes are not in themselves the focus of such measurements, rather the attitudes of library staff.

In order to obtain a data base describing current library functioning to which librarians will be asked to react, it is necessary to conduct a context assessment prior to the actual measurement process. This context assessment should result in a document which lists and describes in one or two sentences programs and services offered in many areas, such as reference or outreach. Additionally, the document should provide information on what procedures exist for making library policy decisions. Senior management personnel should assume responsibility for writing this context assessment document. At this stage it is important that the document be as comprehensive as possible. Above all, the document must avoid any subjective judgments as to the success (or lack of success) of any of the items listed in achieving particular goals or objectives.

From this context assessment climate variables can be identified. It is important that this step be carried out with thoroughness because contexts are likely to differ from library to library. What may be relevant for one library may not be for another.

Most of the variables of the climate instrument that will be used to measure librarian attitudes toward current library functioning will derive from data obtained during the context assessment. For example, a particular service provided by the library might be defined in terms of what it is supposed to do. Librarians would then be asked whether or not that service is operating according to the definition provided. Similar services and programs would be evaluated by librarians as to whether they did, or did not, meet local needs.

In the case of the library managerial climate, five variables are of particular use in measuring organizational climate. These variables, exhibited and defined in table 1, can identify gaps which may exist between the way in which a library is said to be managed and the way in which it is perceived to be managed. In combination, the variables measure the "psychological health" of the library.[21]

Table 1. Managerial Climate Variables

Variable	Definition
INNOVATION	The readiness of a library to pursue innovative practices, policies, and services.
SUPPORT	The degree to which a library maintains mutually supporting relationships between different work groups within that library.
FREEDOM	The degree to which library staff feel co-opted by the organization in terms of the organization's rules, regulations, and "official" point of view.
DEMOCRATIC GOVERNANCE	The extent to which library staff feel that they have the opportunity to participate in library decision making.
ESPRIT	The level of morale and shared purpose among library staff.

The final state of phase 1 is formal evaluation of a library's climate. It is at this point that gaps in the perceptions held by different groups in the library can be delineated. The word "evaluation" is used in a wider sense than is currently fashionable. Here the term refers not only to the measurement process itself but also to the decision-making process.[22] The "decisions" to be made are what perceptual gaps of library functioning exist.

The product of this phase should be a document that clearly sets forth the variables that have been measured and the different perceptions of these variables held by various groups within the library. This document, which should be widely disseminated within the library, will serve as a basis for developing guidelines for closing whatever perceptual gaps may exist.

MODIFYING THE LIBRARY'S CLIMATE

Phase 2 begins at a point when the library has achieved a reasonable understanding of how groups perceive current library functioning in two general areas; internal management, and library service to the community. Perceptual gaps among staff should have emerged and become available for analysis.

As shown in figure 2, this second phase consists of nine steps. Initially, relationships are established among possible sources of perceptual misunderstandings through problem analysis. Figure 3 suggests one graphic way of conducting such an analysis, and is adapted from similar analytic tables presented by Goldhaber et al.[23] and Zaltman and Duncan.[24]

Figure 3. Problem Analysis Table

Problem Type	Levels of Analysis		
	Individual	Relational	Organizational
Unrecognized			
Continuing			
Emergent			
Current			

Each identified perceptual gap should be clarified by writing it down in the form of a problem statement. It may then be analyzed using a form similar to that of figure 3. An example of a problem suitable for analysis might be the lack of agreement between various groups in the library on the extent to which participation in decision making is emphasized by library administration. Another might be the perceived success of programs such as adult independent learning projects. Yet another may result from different views on the advisability of joining a bibliographic network.

When a list of these problem statements has been compiled, it is convenient to categorize them according to whether or not they are "continuing, emergent, current," or "unrecognized." Recognizing what *type* of problem is under scrutiny is useful in discovering root causes for the problem and removing them. A *current* problem might result from new circumstances in the library such as personnel displacements due to increased use of automation. *Emergent* problems, although also due to new circumstances, may not yet have reached the dysfunctional stage but have nevertheless emerged from problem analysis. *Unrecognized* and *continuing* problems can be related to past events in the library which, although no longer valid, may still be affecting library functioning. In addition to identifying root causes for problems, the categorization process serves to prevent repetition of past activities which have already proved dysfunctional and, indeed, may be the cause of current difficulties.

Once a problem has been categorized, it is then possible to continue analysis by searching for causes at three levels, the individual, the relational, and the organizational. For example, if it has been determined that different groups in the library perceive that they have varying impact on the library decision-making process, even though such participation has been vigorously encouraged by administration, such perceptions need to be analyzed in terms of existing climate conditions. Management and staff may perceive that delegation of responsibility is not encouraged (individual level). Interchange of differing views of current library policies may not be welcomed outside of the formal hierarchy (relational level). There may be no perceived need to engage in policy discussion because of excessive programming of decisions through a proliferation of written policies and procedures which are thought to cover all contingencies (organizational level). While the above situations will not exist in every library (they are given here for illustrative purposes only), analyzing these situations, not necessarily the situations themselves, is quite valuable. It is the analysis, not the solutions, which is important at this stage. And it is the dissemination of such analysis which is critical in increasing the chances for mutual understanding of current library functioning.

Once perceptual gaps have been identified and subjected to analysis, strategies and plans for closing these gaps can be developed and implemented. The processes for steps 7 through 14 do not differ significantly from similar steps in the normative planning process and are discussed elsewhere in this volume. Different alternatives are generated for achieving perceptual agreement, selection is made of appropriate alternatives, strategies and plans are developed, and steps taken to close the perceptual gaps. Throughout this process it is vital to assess carefully whether or not movement toward the desired perceptual agreement is being achieved. Without such assessment it is difficult to make necessary adjustments in procedures *at the point of impact*. This formative evaluation is necessary to ensure consistent and logical thinking throughout the climate modification process. It is only through such evaluation activity that the library is able to comprehend *what* is happening *while* it is happening.

Steps 12 through 14 are assessment. The climate of the library is again measured and the degree to which perceptual agreement has, or has not, been achieved is evaluated. While it is unlikely that such agreement will have been achieved to the extent desired, it is probable that all library staff, not just a few key individuals, will be better able to view needed change from a wider perspective than before. It is for each library to decide whether or not it is ready for the intensive activity essential in freeing that library from past assumptions and moving it in the direction of more meaningful service to the community it serves.

CONCLUSION

Conducting a climate study prior to implementing programs designed to change substantially library operations or services is not easy, nor is it likely to have immediate impact. However, results of the climate study will provide librarians with a realistic picture of what actually is occurring in the library and in the way that library serves its community. Many previously held assumptions will have to be discarded and replaced with more realistic appraisals. As the library begins to move through the change process, a climate of perceptual agreement can facilitate the rapid processing of information and its use in the decision-making process. The information nepotism that often characterizes library planning and decision making is likely to be substantially reduced.

Management and staff will have new responsibilities as the library's climate changes. Managers will need to exercise caution and patience in implementing a process that is apt to show little immediate result or impact. Employees must be willing to contribute to the climate modification process by assuming major responsibility for making use of the information that is given to them. Both management and staff have ultimate responsibility for seeing the climate modification process through. While management may guide the process, staff must participate in implementing it.

In the final analysis it is the library patron who will benefit from the approach suggested in this paper. The library's ability quickly to sense new directions in which it must go will be increased. Needed changes in library operations can be rapidly achieved with a minimum of disruption. The process of creating a climate for change is not a panacea for all that may trouble the library, but rather a means of self-discovery and increased awareness which will have cumulative effects on a library's success.

REFERENCES

[1] Vernon E. Palmour and Marcia Bellasai, *A Planning Process for Public Libraries* (Chicago: American Library Association, 1980).

[2] Miriam A. Drake, "Managing Innovation in Academic Libraries," *College & Research Libraries* 40 (1979): 508.

[3] Gary Dessler, *Organization and Management: A Contingency Approach* (Englewood Cliffs, NJ: Prentice-Hall, 1976), ch. 8.

[4] Louis Kaplan, "On Decision Making in Libraries: How Much Do We Know?," *College & Research Libraries* 38 (1977): 25-31.

[5] G. A. Forehand and B. von Haller Gilmer, "Environmental Variation in Studies of Organizational Behavior," *Psychological Bulletin* 62 (1964): 361-82.

[6] Forehand and Gilmer, "Environmental Variation," p. 362.

[7] Renato Tagiuri and George H. Litwin, ed., *Organizational Climate: Explorations of a Concept* (Boston: Division of Research, Graduate School of Business Administration, Harvard University, 1968).

[8] Renato Tagiuri, "The Concept of Organizational Climate," in Tagiuri and Litwin, *Organizational Climate*, p. 27.

[9] D. Hellriegel and J. W. Slocum, Jr., "Organizational Climate: Measures, Research, and Contingencies," *Academy of Management Journal* 17 (1974): 256.

[10] L. R. James and A. P. Jones, "Organizational Climate: A Review of Theory and Research," *Psychological Bulletin* 81 (1974): 1096-1112.

[11] R. W. Pritchard and B. W. Karasick, "The Effects of Organizational Climate on Managerial Job Performance and Job Satisfaction," *Organizational Behavior and Human Performance* 9 (1973): 126-46.

[12] R. L. Payne and D. S. Pugh, "Organizational Structure and Climate," in *Handbook of Industrial and Organizational Psychology*, Marvin D. Dunnette, ed. (Chicago: Rand McNally, 1976), pp. 1125-73.

[13] B. Schneider and C. J. Bartlett, "Individual Differences and Organizational Climate. I: The Research Plan and Questionnaire Development," *Personnel Psychology* 21 (1968): 323-33.

[14] Robert M. Guion, "A Note on Organizational Climate," *Organizational Behavior and Human Performance* 9 (1973): 120-25.

[15] A. W. Lau, *Organizational Climate: A Review of the Literature* (Bethesda, MD: ERIC Document Reproduction Service, 1975). (ED 130 359).

[16] Alan R. Samuels, "Assessing Organizational Climate in Public Libraries," *Library Research* 1 (1979): 237-54.

[17] Tagiuri, "The Concept of Organizational Climate," pp. 24-25.

[18] Gerald Zaltman and Robert Duncan, *Strategies for Planned Change* (New York: Wiley, 1977), pp. 78-79.

[19] William R. King and David I. Cleland, *Strategic Planning and Policy* (New York: Van Nostrand Reinhold, 1978), p. 274.

[20] Charles R. McClure, "The Planning Process: Strategies for Action," *College & Research Libraries* 39 (1978): 464.

[21] Samuels, "Assessing Organizational Climate," pp. 248-49.

[22] Edward A. Suchman, *Evaluation Research* (New York: Russell Sage, 1967), p. 31.

[23] Gerald M. Goldhaber et al., *Information Strategies: New Pathways to Corporate Power* (Englewood Cliffs, NJ: Prentice-Hall, 1979), p. 41.

[24] Zaltman and Duncan, *Strategies for Planned Change*, p. 57.

Contingency Theory, Values, and Change
By J. A. Millar

This paper represents a critique of the increasingly fashionable contingency theories, relating to such areas as organization, structure, management style, and orientation to work. Certain aspects of contingency theory represent a backlash effect against neohuman relations. The claim of contingency theorists that their approach is less value-laden than that of human relations appears doubtful. Only the contrast in values, rather than the absence, is apparent.

INTRODUCTION

This paper presents a critique of the increasingly fashionable contingency theories, relating to organization, structure, management style, and orientation to work. Certain aspects of contingency theory represent a backlash effect against neohuman relations. The claim of contingency theorists to be a less value-laden approach than that of the human relations school appears to be fallacious. Only the contrast of values, rather than the absence, is striking.

In Europe, the American-based human relations approach has always been viewed with a greater degree of scepticism: It has illustrated the pitfalls of "psychological universalism" (Lupton, 1971; Child, 1973) with one optimal type of organization, structure, and individual personality. Attempts have thus been made to move towards more diversified and allegedly less value-laden perspectives.

Early attempts to move away from this universalism appeared in those British studies emphasizing technological aspects and constraints on the

---

Reprinted from *Human Relations*, vol. 31, no. 10 (10 November 1978), pp. 885-904, by permission from Plenum Publishing Co.

social system at the Tavistock Institute (Trist & Bamforth, 1951). A further British development has been the concept of "best fit"—matching of organizational structure and technology (especially Burns & Stalker, 1961; Woodward, 1965), developing later as contingency theory. This has been complemented at the individual level by a move from "universal needs" towards more differentiated concepts of individual response, represented by typologies of differential orientations to work (e.g., Goldthorpe, Lockwood, Bechhoffer, & Platt, 1968; Ingham, 1970; Silverman, 1970). The latter is also associated with the "action approach" (Silverman, 1970). This increasing interest in differences at individual, environmental, and technological levels also reflects itself in situational or contingency theories of leadership.

Scepticism about universalism and neohuman relations has produced an approach allegedly avoiding prescriptive value assumptions, representing a new "breakthrough" to a more "scientific" method. (Lupton, 1971; Perrow, 1970; Lawrence & Lorsch, 1967).

I wish to question this latter assumption. My contention is that research is being impaired by the extremes on both sides—traditional human relations pursuing a behavioral utopia; the backlash, a pendulum swing in the opposite direction, to the determinism of structural "fit" relationships or the laissez-faire of "subjective meaning."

The first part of the paper will deal with contingency theories, followed by theories on individual orientation to work. The latter part of the paper is devoted to outlining an alternative model, which attempts to incorporate the advantages but avoid the pitfalls of both traditional models and more recent approaches.

A "SCIENTIFIC BREAKTHROUGH"?

"Managers have long recognized that different industrial environments have particular economic and technical characteristics, each of which calls for a unique competitive strategy. A set of marketing, manufacturing, and research policies that works well for a firm in the chemical industry will not meet the needs of a corporation producing steel. As obvious as these statements appear, their implications for organization theory have for too long been ignored" (Lawrence & Lorsch, 1967, p. 2).

A number of authors have become dissatisfied with earlier approaches to structuring complex organizations. In particular, they claim there is no "one-best" structure, but a number of different "best" structures suitable for differing situations. They reject the universalism of getting "human relations right and everything else follows" (Lupton, 1971, p. 18). Rather, getting technology to fit environment is the key variable.

Of particular interest in this fitting exercise is the recommendation for the "good old Weberian bureaucracy" (Perrow, 1970), or "tight formal structure, strong formal authority" (Lawrence & Lorsch, 1967), where conditions are stable and repetitive.

Such prescriptive statements on "fitting" the organization to its environment appear widely viewed as scientific breakthroughs, moves *away* from universalism, "loose talk," and generalization. Congruence of technology and structure is also regarded as a basis for revamping the more traditional "scientific management"-type approach (Argyris, 1972, critique of further reappearances of scientific management "through the back door"), an attempt to rectify the "*only* true deficiency of traditional scientific management which attempted to enunciate principles, laws, etc. which would apply to all organizations" (Perrow, 1970, p. 18). Contingency theories, in contrast, offer principles and laws which "best fit" the organization category in question.

In addition to prescribing "Weberian bureaucracy types" for stable conditions, the authors imply that the imposition of a people-oriented human relations approach in such conditions is both a "highly normative prescription" and "only realizable in certain conditions, unless we are willing to pay a high cost in terms of output" (Perrow, 1967, p. 116).

Thus, two clear statements emerge from the contingency approach: firstly, that tight authoritarian structures are optimally suited to stable conditions; secondly, that failure to impose such a structure will be damaging in terms of cost and output.

If those statements are not merely normative and prescriptive (as people-oriented approaches allegedly are!), then considerable hard data and empirical evidence should support them. This evidence, or rather its dearth, will be reviewed in the following section.

IDEAS AND EVIDENCE ON MATCHING TECHNOLOGY AND STRUCTURE

The major body of hard evidence rests with the Burns and Stalker study (1961) and the Joan Woodward study (1965). Later developments supporting contingency theories, such as Perrow's conceptual scheme (1967) and the Lawrence and Lorsch study (1967), tend to accept the bipolar model and Woodward's hypotheses as given, merely elaborating diverse sets of alternatives.

Lawrence and Lorsch (1967) develop an environmental classification system encompassing the market, research and development, degree of certainty, and feedback, as well as the more usual technology factors. They state that requirements for specialization and structure must differ (e.g., in an organization making chocolate from one making motor cars). Also, there may be sectional differentiation within the same organization. Perrow's scheme involves variables of search, uncertainty, and their fit with a number of structural and decisional variables.

The bipolar categorization of organizations in terms of mechanistic/organic structures was suggested by Burns and Stalker (1961). In the course of their investigation of a number of firms in Scotland, they observed difficulties experienced first by firms in rapidly changing environments who tried to retain a mechanistic structure; second by firms in a stable environment attempting to apply the newer "organic management"-type ideas.

Woodward's research of a number of firms in the Essex area lent confirmation to the Burns and Stalker hypothesis that organizational structures should correspond with their technological environment. The idea that some "matching" of structure and technology would correlate with organizational effectiveness was seized on with considerable enthusiasm. At first glance it appears to eliminate "messy value assumptions" and permit controlled testing and applicability. A number of researchers set out to confirm or disprove those first rather tentative ideas of Woodward and Burns and Stalker. The resulting evidence is conflicting in the extreme. It seems that structure may be correlated more closely to size than to technology (Hickson et al., 1969; Inkson et al., 1970. Technology, they suggest, is significant only when correlated with size), also that structure may be correlated closely with such factors as noise and task interdependence (Mohr, 1971) (which may also, in turn, correlate to some extent with technology). In addition, no support for the fit hypothesis that effectiveness of the organization is determined by the consonance between technology and social structure was found here. Further conflicting evidence relates to studies correlating effectiveness most strongly with style of supervision (e.g., Likert, 1967; Argyris, 1964) or with environmental background (Turner & Lawrence, 1965; Hulin & Blood, 1968).

The above represents only a small sample of the available evidence. It is both conflicting and controversial. It would seem to confirm the view that correlated measurements of structure and technology cannot take place until a great mass of evidence (and some tentative agreement) is achieved on how structure and technology may be defined. Each concept consists of many components. As a first step, it is essential to discover which of those components correlate with one another, e.g., technology with size, or noise with size with supervisory style, or age of supervisors, background, etc., with frequency of formal/informal interaction. As emphasized by Mohr, structure and technology are multidimensional concepts. Those dimensions must be examined in detail before one even attempts to make broader categorizations and groupings for comparison. I would like to make a (perhaps inappropriate) comparison with early science. It seems to me that dealing with such categories as fire, earth, air, and water is equivalent to dealing with broad variables such as "structure" or "technology," especially such groupings as "mechanistic" or "organic."

It is interesting to observe that the evidence of Burns and Stalker (1961) can be used to confirm both a fit theory of environment *and* a human relations-type theory of resistance to change, e.g., by a group of managers whose social background caused them to resist any loss of authority and privilege—except in the face of extreme external pressures! Also Woodward's work, in addition to serious methodological weaknesses such as crude categorization of technology, nonhomogeneity within organizations, problems of defining technology and structure, must by her own definition be invalid if one example could be found of a mass production organization functioning with high economic effectiveness and an organic-type structure.[2]

The Woodward prescription says organizations which wish to be economically successful should adapt the structure best fitted, e.g., mass production and "rigid authority structures," but, "on the contrary, it is perhaps this prescription that ought to be resisted, at least when considering the participatory structure of decision-making... hard evidence that assembly-line mass production is a special case in which movement towards organic structure cannot produce increased effectiveness [is required]" (Mohr, 1971, p. 454).

At this stage it is presumptuous to outline in a simple manner the relationship between these two concepts. Thus, the claim of contingency theory supporters that they (in contrast to human relations) base their theories on hard data rather than normative prescriptions seems open to doubt.[3]

THE QUESTIONABLE SUITABILITY OF THE "MECHANISTIC" ORGANIZATION FOR STABLE ENVIRONMENTS

Aside from empirical evidence, a number of other reasons for questioning the suitability of mechanistic/bureaucratic organizations for any kind of environment or technology exist. First, there is the question of how stable the allegedly "stable environment" is. Thus Woodward, Burns and Stalker, Lawrence and Lorsch, and Perrow offer prescriptive statements on

---

[2]This may already be the case today, e.g., work in Volvo, Saab.
[3]Similar problems are occurring in contingency theories of leadership. Both in the consideration—initiating structure and in the Fiedler models—it is "both conceptually and physically impossible to define and study all of the important variables which comprise the situation." Kerr, Schriesheim, Murphy, and Stogdill, 1974, p. 72.

which organizational structure is appropriate to which technology. However, no suggestions or prescriptions are offered for action in the face of change occurring, say, when stable technology, stable market, or research and development becomes unstable. To take the case of chocolate again, what would happen if a sudden shortage of cocoa or sugar occurred, or if legal pressure were exerted to switch to cyclamates, for example? The theories are prescriptive, but no prescriptions are offered to deal with change.

A further point of criticism lies in the definition of stable. Should an organization with fully stable technology, fully stable market, and research and development exist, would it not lend itself ideally to a program of full automation? Also, as mentioned previously, there is increasing evidence of stable technology functioning well with organic-type management structure. Present research in traditional mass-production organizations, especially in the car industry (Brown & Millar, 1974), would indicate strong possibilities that the "flexible structures, collegiate relations, and long-time horizons," etc., which Lawrence and Lorsch maintain are only suitable for rapid change and high uncertainty, function well when the latter conditions are not fulfilled.

A further aspect involves changes in attitudes in society at large. Thus, "tight formal structures and strong formal authority" may not be suitable for a society which is no longer rigidly authoritarian and stratified, a society whose schools and educational system are increasingly geared to encourage individual questioning, flexibility, innovation. Can mechanistic organizations, then, be adapted to society's and the organization's needs for greater flexibility, greater utilization of (increasingly expensive) human resources?

In conclusion, theories on the fit of technology and environment to structure also appear as normative and prescriptive. So-called psychological universalism is replaced by a form of structural determinism.

Signs of such developments appear not only in works on structure/ technology, but also in studies relating to orientation to work. There is a similar backlash against human relations universalism to forms of determinism or laissez-faire. In this case universalism is criticized due to its reliance on assumed a priori human needs and consequent neglect of individual differences. Both arguments hold validity in a certain context, but I believe them to be misapplied in this case.

MISUSE OF THE INDIVIDUAL DIFFERENCES ARGUMENT

A number of British studies have investigated different orientations to work. Both theoretically and empirically they have questioned the human relations assumptions on human needs and their influence on the work situation.⁴ This position can be summarized in the following statements (Silverman, 1970; Goldthorpe et al., 1968; Ingham, 1970). Assumptions on needs are highly questionable due to the difficulty of validating "assumed internal personality needs." Also, Silverman (1970) questions whether the subject of need "can be an object of systematic study" (p. 85). Difficulties in validating "assumed internal personality needs" as well as the issue of individual differences are stressed. Silverman further indicates that various means for the purpose of fulfilling needs (e.g., need for greater participation in decision-making by lower levels) could involve "an intolerable attack upon what management generally regards as its prerogative," and, as such, can neither be "efficient nor practical" (Silverman, 1970, p. 85).⁵

It has further been suggested by a number of authors (e.g., Silverman, 1970; Goldthorpe et al., 1968; Lupton, 1971) that, even assuming there are universal "personality needs," there is no reason why these should be fulfilled inside the work organization. Why not fulfill the needs outside the work organization, they ask?

I believe this deep scepticism about the existence of and evidence for human needs contrasts strongly with the easy acceptance of that scant evidence indicating the existence of "instrumental man," the view that "instrumental involvement .... coexists with work satisfaction." The existence (or nonexistence) of such instrumental involvement is thus a key area —and one which has been inadequately investigated.

EVIDENCE FOR THE EXISTENCE OF SO-CALLED INSTRUMENTAL MAN

The existence of instrumental orientations to work allegedly proves two points: first, the fallaciousness of the human relations argument about universalist needs for fulfillment in the work situation; secondly, it provides support for contingency theories in that a supply of instrumental people must exist to fit into "mechanistic organizations."

The major study quoted supporting the view that satisfaction may coexist in conditions almost totally devoid of possibilities for social fulfillment and/or self-actualization is that of Goldthorpe et al. (1968).⁶ Gold-

---

⁴With human relations, I mean those approaches advocating people-oriented systems, emphasizing the importance of interest at work, participation in work-related decisions, etc.
⁵Silverman apparently also shares views on congruence and matching: "When techniques for increasing satisfaction and efficiency succeed, this would be explained as a consequence of the congruence of the organizational changes with the role expectations and historical experiences of those concerned" (p. 86).
⁶See also: Turner and Lawrence, 1961; Hulin and Blood, 1968 on "city" workers.

thorpe's survey of car workers at Luton indicated that workers expressed satisfaction with their jobs, did not express negative attitudes towards their employers, and showed little interest in trade unions and social activities with fellow workers.

He thus concluded that ideas on alienation, discontent, etc., due to monotonous work must be erroneous. A type of worker existed, he claimed, who fitted neither into Marx's pattern of alienation and trade union activity, nor into the human relations concept of fulfillment at work and satisfaction. Here, according to Goldthorpe, was a worker who was both satisfied and contented with his employer, in spite of having a job without any kind of fulfillment in terms of social needs or self-actualization. Thus emerged "instrumental man." I am not satisfied, however, that Goldthorpe's conclusions can be accepted as valid. Three serious methodological weaknesses can be detected. First, with a view to perceived range of choice alternatives for the workers involved, Goldthorpe assumed but did not validate or even test that, at the time of choosing his work initially, the instrumental worker perceived acceptable level alternatives involving intrinsically interesting work.[7] Second, there is a dubious causal assumption: Since the workers did not actively seek for intrinsically satisfying work, Goldthorpe assumes this indicates that they did not desire such work.[8] Third, there is the "Ivan Denisovitch" phenomenon[9] of changing aspiration levels as an adaptation to the real situation. Goldthorpe and many others interested in "orientation to work" and stressing "individual differences" neglect the importance of this phenomenon. They assume that workers' emphasis on instrumental rewards results from a basic orientation to work, gained prior to the particular work situation in question. I would prefer to interpret instrumental orientation as an adaptation of aspiration levels in response to perceived opportunities of the situation. In contrast, Goldthorpe states: "Among the men we studied a particular orientation to work—one of a markedly instrumental kind—is predominant" (1964, p. 174). He concludes, in agreement with Dubin (1963), that workers no longer consider work as a central life interest and that satisfaction or happiness at work are irrelevant—a sweeping value judgment!

---

[7] Intrinsically satisfying jobs in, say, declining industries with high potential redundancy or in low wage situations are not acceptable level alternatives. Nor would be marginally more interesting jobs with 50% less wages.

[8] There is a contradiction in Goldthorpe's own work here. The Luton workers did express their belief in the importance of intrinsically interesting work. It would seem that a more rational causal explanation for their lack of search would be absence of perceived acceptable alternatives.

[9] This methodological critique may also be levelled at the "city" and "town" differences of Turner and Lawrence (1965) and Hulin and Blood (1968).

As with Burns and Stalker (1961), it seems that Goldthorpe's data may mean all things to all men. It could be reinterpreted to confirm a theory based on perceived acceptable alternatives and corresponding adjustment, or to confirm a human relations view on psychological withdrawal due to deprivation. Thus, it would confirm Argyris' predictions about the process by which workers suppress their expectancy for intrinsic satisfaction and change their focus to instrumental rewards. He states "employees in order to live with themselves must somehow devalue in the work situation the importance of human factors (such as self-esteem) and value material factors (such as money)" (Argyris, 1972, p. 144). A form of "Ersatzbefriedigung" occurs.[10]

Thus, an action-oriented approach, such as Goldthorpe et al. (1968) and Ingham (1970) have applied, has serious limitations. It emphasizes the importance of workers' own objectives and definition of the situation with regard to choice and behavior in work. Thus, action research by Goldthorpe led him to the conclusion that workers had chosen highly repetitive jobs because their primary orientation and satisfaction in work consisted of monetary rewards. Ingham's study (1970) of orientations to work indicated a similar pattern, that smaller plants with more interesting jobs had workers with less instrumental attitudes than the workers in highly bureaucratic, high-wage plants who tended to be highly instrumental in their orientation.

The interpretation of both authors seem open to question. Both results of the studies could be explained in common sense terms, i.e., regardless of which prior orientations workers had, they would probably adjust their attitudes and "satisfaction" to the rewards and opportunities available to them. Neither Goldthorpe nor Ingham made any control check for prior orientations previous to entering their present employment.[11]

It seems, without further evidence, to be a chicken-egg type argument: Do instrumental workes choose instrumental jobs? Or do people in jobs offering solely instrumental rewards adapt their attitudes accordingly?

In short, the evidence supporting the existence of the instrumental worker rests on the weak foundation of a momentarily observed status quo, whose interpretation is full of ambiguities.

---

[10] Note "instrumental orientation" should be used to explain satisfaction with employer, attitudes to trade union activities, and lack of involvement with fellow workers. But instead postwar recession worries would explain obsession with wages security and relative satisfaction with pay in comparison with other workers. It is obvious that while this feeling prevailed, trades unions, which are regarded mainly as wage-fighting units, would remain in the background. Lack of contact with fellow workers could be explained by the lack of on-the-job interaction on the assembly line together with noise and possibly the heterogeneous backgrounds of the workers involved. Further, work not providing fulfillment of any kind would not then be regarded as a source of satisfaction, identity-association, or status.

[11] A serious lack of longitudinal studies exists at present.

Whether one supports the view of instrumental man and the viability of mechanistic organizations, or deprived man and the promise of the organic organization is, on present-day evidence, a value judgment one way or the other. The latter view does at least incorporate a more optimistic view of the capacities of man, perhaps justifying more systematic study before rejection in favor of less optimistic though equally speculative approaches.[12]

CONTINGENCY VIEWS IN JOB ENRICHMENT RESEARCH

Another branch of social studies showing signs of a movement away from human relations, self-actualization needs, etc., and towards fit or contingency theories is that of job enrichment.

Here again generalistic human relations recommendations about allowing for more self-actualization at work, being more people-oriented, are discussed as over-generalizations. In particular, those assumptions which form the basis for job enrichment, and which link boring work with dissatisfaction and, in turn, with negative reactions in the form of high absenteeism and turnover and low output and quality of work, are heavily criticized. First, the linkage of boring work with dissatisfaction is questioned. It is indicated that, for some people, there is allegedly evidence that monotonous work can be actually pleasing (Baldamus, 1961, "traction" effect). A further argument cited, and I believe misapplied, is that of ethnomorphism. Here it is stated that, while boring work may dissatisfy academics and social scientists, it would be ethnomorphism to claim that it must dissatisfy all. This argument could easily be used by academics and social scientists to avoid all social responsibility. There is a further objection, due to serious lack of evidence on the prior orientations of workers involved and on shifts in orientation.

It seems now fashionable to criticize the human relations and people-oriented studies and ideas of the 1950s and 1960s.[13] The ideological bias of these studies is emphasized. Also they are criticized for assuming rather than proving that all human beings desire, and should have, opportunities

---

[12] A further point about action approaches on orientation to work, as well as congruency, is the inherent conservatism, the lack of predictive power of the approach. Action based on verstehen may be limited to an understanding of the status quo. Max Weber's verstehende approach to the organization mirrored the Prussian bureaucratic methods of his time and place. The human relations approach may have its pitfalls (and I would agree that there are many!), but it is at least based on the view that education, technology, etc., are changing society, offering new potentials. There is also the economic argument that human labor resources are too valuable to underemploy.

[13] E.g., studies on alienation, studies relating productivity and performance to people-oriented approaches

for self-actualization at work. Further criticism relates to arguments, which I believe again misapplied, on individual differences. It is pointed out here that studies of people with monotonous jobs have indicated varied patterns of response rather than a state of general discontent with nonenriched working lives.

Thus claim supporters of contingency and individual differences that specialization is not a major cause of job dissatisfaction (contrast Blauner, 1964; Shepard, 1971). Also *all* people will not react in the same way to the same jobs. Thus, some workers may have an instrumental orientation; some workers may compensate in their leisure time for work lacking intrinsic satisfaction (Goldthorpe et al., 1968; Silverman, 1970). Contrasting with middle class views it is felt that "many of the needs of workers would be more properly fulfilled outside the work organization." Experiments on job enrichment, satisfaction, and performance (Hulin & Blood, 1968; Turner & Lawrence, 1965) imply that enriching working life in terms of autonomy, responsibility, variety, etc. will gain positive response only from people with middle class values (or from rural backgrounds). Second generation, urban, working class people respond negatively. This the authors offer as evidence to support the "everyone-is-different" hypothesis. This is offered as another version of contingency theory, where ideas of fit and differentiation are substituted for universalist theories supporting self-actualization and interest for all at the work place. The view on individual differences is neatly summed up by MacKinney and supported by Hulin and Blood (1968): "The most compelling argument against specialization as a major cause of job dissatisfaction lies in the fact of individual differences. This is the central fact of life in the behavioural sciences..." (p. 47). I agree that to deny individual differences is absurd. But to deny shared human values and needs for some level of interest at work for all seems equally absurd.

Major social changes such as the introduction of education, health, and welfare problems have been based on the assumption of shared human needs. For the work situation it seems that such needs are disputed. The fallacy of the argument lies in the imputed assumption that all individuals must react in an identical manner to job redesign. Everyone does not react similarly to education or even like it or find it satisfying. This is not, however, used as an argument against education as another form of psychological universalism. It is strange that the work situation should be so sensitive to accusations of ethnomorphism—a sensitivity strangely absent with regard to most other social and political issues affecting the everyday problems of peoples' lives.

Apart from the argument about society defining its values and (especially within the welfare state) defining in particular basic minimal needs, there is a second weakness in the everyone-is-different hypothesis. This lies in the inherent conservatism implied in contingency theories on organization structure, defending the mechanistic organization, also in difference theories proposing the existence of instrumental man or a second-generation deprived urban working class (Hulin & Blood, 1968), who allegedly have no interest in intrinsic aspects of working life. A certain conservatism, pessimism, acceptance of the status quo, and neglect of opportunities and facilities to improve, develop, or change seems detectable here.

This neglect of the possibilities of change or guided change is further reinforced by concepts of matching the organization to the environment or the individual to the organization. Thus, Etzioni (1964) writes the "ultimate source of organizational dilemmas" is "the incomplete matching of the personalities of the participants with their organizational roles. If personalities could be shaped to fit specific organizational roles, or organizational roles to fit specific personalities, many of the pressures to displace goals, much of the need to control performance, and a good part of the alienation would disappear" (p. 75).

Such matching, Etzioni accedes, is extremely difficult to achieve, but this is what the goal researchers and practitioners should strive for, he claims (pp. 75-93). This view of the researcher's goal is widespread and implicit in matching and contingency theories. I would question it for two related reasons—its tendency to post factum rationalizations of what "is" and its use of crude categorizations, whereby multidimensional variables are treated as one. Ideas on change, improvement, and flexibility take second place.

TECHNOLOGY, STRUCTURE, AND WORK ORIENTATION AS MULTIDIMENSIONAL CONCEPTS IN THE TRADITION OF "GRAND THEORIES"

Contingency or "matching" and "action" approaches utilize categorizations and groupings. For example:

Work orientation is classified in terms of instrumental, expressive, city/town, intrinsic, Hawthorne, Marxian, etc. (Goldthorpe et al., 1968; Ingham, 1970; Silverman, 1970; Turner & Lawrence, 1965; Hulin & Blood, 1968).
Technology is classified in terms of type of production, or analyzability, stability/predictability of environment, etc. (Woodward, 1965; Perrow, 1967; Thompson & Bates, 1957; Lawrence & Lorsch, 1967).
Structure is discussed in terms of mechanistic, organic, polycentralized, decentralized, etc. (Burns & Stalker, 1961; Perrow, 1967; Thompson & Bates, 1957; Lawrence & Lorsch, 1967).

Can such comprehensive categorizations be truly applied as meaningful instruments of investigation? Each of those terms for structure, technology, and orientation are multidimensional variables.[14] To treat them as unidimensional represents, possibly, an attempt to fly before one can walk. I contend that analysis—studying the subdimensions of each category and its interrelations—is more appropriate. Contingency theories involving structure, technology, and orientation to work seem more in the tradition of grand theory and sweeping comparisons. The more modest, less dramatic approach (Dreyfus, 1965, "Alchemy and Artificial Intelligence") is less preferred.

ALTERNATIVE APPROACHES TO GRAND THEORY: WORKING HYPOTHESIS ON ORIENTATION SHIFT

Conflicting evidence exists as to the impact of the work situation on orientation to work. The two extreme positions are, on the one hand, prior socialization molding attitudes and orientation, thus the instrumental worker would choose an instrumental job; on the other hand, there is the idea that the work itself is the dominant influence, with background, education, and socialization being of much lesser import.

Goldthorpe's neglect of shift in orientation has already been pointed out by other British researchers. In particular Brown (1973) and Daniel (1973) take a first step towards emphasizing the importance of orientation shift. They do not, however, go far enough and do not question the validity of the action approach as such. Since action disclaims theories on shared human needs, it is poorly equipped to develop a testable working hypothesis linking orientation shifts to deeper causal variables. As has become apparent earlier in this paper, I am making a plea here for working hypotheses based on values. These hypotheses may be tested through a number of sources, such as interaction of personality types with certain work situations, more systematically controlled studies on job enrichment, possibly providing tentative predictions on desirable or undesirable learned reactions and adaptations.

Without such research on work orientation change, conclusions such as Goldthorpe, Ingham, Hulin and Blood, and others must remain without foundation. Is there homogeneity of orientation due to self-selection, a causal chain originating in the social situation, moving through orientation

---

[14]Mohr (1971) lists for example the following subdimensions of structure: "frequent-infrequent, vertical-lateral, formal-informal, authoritative-consultative, group oriented-individual oriented, task oriented-socially oriented, written-oral, political-rational" (p. 445).

to work and choice of job as Silverman (1970, pp. 184-185), Child (1973, p. 31), and Cotgrove and Box (1970) maintain? Or, is the dominant force the experience of the work itself, and such influences as that of self-direction on personality and development as Turner (1971), Kohn and Schooler (1969), and Nichols (1969) would have it?

Further exploration in the above field could be supplemented by research into the relative rate of change for different dimensions of orientation, e.g., relative stability, moderate change, rapid change—a model in some ways similar to the March—Simon (1958) concept of procedural and substantive programs may prove useful as also a model on the organizational learning process (Cyert & March, 1963).

Such factors as longer term shift due to changes in local information perception of realizability of goals could be examined as well as short-term shifts due to conflict, changing focus of attention, crises, etc. One could also examine the much-denigrated universalistic demands hypotheses as being caused by such factors as increased needs for flexibility and changing attitudes to authority. Shift could also be examined with respect to such factors as personality, age, prior education and background, and type of work, with reference to content, autonomy, and self-direction.

For purposes of comparison, it may also prove of value to have some taxonomy for assessment of relative change. This would be based on a scale outlining minimal levels of work content and self-direction.

One argument in support of human relations has been that of human rights; as education exists for all why not a humane kind of work situation with at least minimal opportunities for self-actualization for all workers.

A further, more economically oriented argument is that of efficiency —both as to increasing labor costs and the need for more flexible, innovative organizations.

It has been suggested by Faxén (1971) that organizations need a new flexibility or innovative capacity index. This would relate to the organization's flexibility, dynamism, capacity for change, and capacity for dealing with obsolescence and rigidity. The possibilities of operationalizing such an index are being explored; research presently being carried out at a cross national level is investigating this subject (Brown & Millar, 1974).

I previously mentioned the pendulum swings in social science from scientific management to neohuman relations, from conflict to systems, and the present swing towards a new form of scientific management, dressed up in contingency theory terms.

I would like to make some suggestions for an alternative, what I wish to describe as a sort of "maximum improvement" model based on values as well as ideas of improvement and increased opportunity, where technology is a variable rather than a constant.

As a beginning, one could start with the controversial topic of self-actualization and its role in motivation. The Maslow-Herzberg displacement and two-factor theories are (if one may use the term) unsatisfactory (Dunnette, Campbell, & Hakel, 1967; Heneman & Schwab, 1972; Waters, 1972). Further, due to their unspecific nature, who is self-actualized, when, and with what intensity?—they are open to a wide range of criticism.

Discussing motivation at work, a recent British publication stated: "In conclusion it must be stressed that the basis for all orientations to work is an instrumental one. If, in a situation of full employment, level of earnings in a given plant fails to rise above certain levels, high rates of labour turnover will occur whatever the orientation to work" (Ingham, 1970, p. 52).

I quote this statement partly to re-emphasize the British instrumental man extreme and partly to signify the meaninglessness of any statement on motivation, whether instrumental attitudes or self-actualization, without some definition on levels of actualization or instrumentality involved. Without a definition of "level of earnings" or level relative to whom, "what" or "when" statements on instrumental orientation say little. The above quote by Ingham would in fact imply that all workers must consciously strive towards that job with the highest level of earnings, regardless of any other factors.

Similarly little is conveyed by stating that all people are or are not motivated by self-actualization possibilities. Some basis of comparability is required.

It is obvious that such a scale cannot be measured in absolute terms. Thus, I would like to suggest defining in terms of minimal threshold value levels, to be adjusted and modified in light of experience and information feedback.

NEED FOR CHANGE IN METHODOLOGY

I would also at this point like to criticize research and methodology in testing ideas on motivation and related problems. Though recent developments have not supported Maslow-Herzberg, they have emphasized the importance of "higher-order needs." Thus, the more the latter are fulfilled, the more they are desired (Dunnette et al., 1967; Alderfer, 1969; Heneman & Schwab, 1972). Also with a view to career development stages, higher-order needs tend to increase in importance as career stages progress (Hall & Nougaim, 1968). Further, there is the emphasis on subjective utility and expectation (Lawler & Porter, 1967). These factors would point to a need for change in emphasis in methodology. Thus, there must be a shift from the cross-sectional studies to longitudinal studies, examining change over time. This does not just apply to ideas on motivation, but can also be extended as a further critique of contingency theory, which is also orientated to cross-sectional analysis. The dimension of change and potential for change is not assessed, since the contextual factors, once defined, dictate the organizational style.

MINIMAL LEVELS AND VALUES

In defining minimal levels, one could start by considering current values, e.g., as slavery is now unacceptable in Western society, as "beneath the dignity of the human being" or not permitting a sufficient degree of self-determination over one's life, so also may certain forms of assembly line work, short-term job cycles, and machine job pacing.

A further criterion for defining minimal levels could depend on willingness of workers to work in such circumstances—view the need for Western European industry to draw heavily on foreign sources of labor. Such minimal levels would also relate closely to "expectancy" (King, 1974) measurements. How expectancy levels change and are subject to influence would be investigated in relation to this minimal acceptable level: for example, differentials in expectations of workers in different countries, relationship to education, background, urban/rural differences, and socialization. One could also examine whether expectations for self-actualization shift at differential rates among workers and nationals, and how this is influenced by the degree of self-actualization permitted on the job.

Equipped with some basis for comparability with respect to threshold level and time one could then look anew at alternative authority structures and technologies, fitting the machine and the organization to the man rather than the vice-versa approach which is more usual.

A further possible area for investigating indices of shift in orientation involves the variable of "self-direction." The relationship of self direction to motivation and work task attributes, especially the two dimensions of intrinsic work interest and autonomy, could be further explored. It may also prove of value to split present RTA scales (Turner & Lawrence, 1965; Hackman & Oldham, 1975; Hackman & Lawler, 1971) into a number of subscales along which one could then rate greater variations in individual need, e.g., measured degrees of task variety and identity versus measured degrees of autonomy, responsibility and/or growth and social interactions (Cooper, 1973; Faxén, 1971).

Important variations exist in workers' wants and expectations. Assuming relative importance of aspects of the work situation, impact on orientation, etc. would be tested. It could also prove of value to test that set of characteristics called the instrumental worker (or select more suitable groupings of characteristics, if deemed necessary). In particular this would allow for testing of the "self-selection" hypotheses. One could mark out a new category rather analogous to the concept of the floating voter. This instrumental or floating worker would be willing to move geographically in pursuit of higher material gains (not because of unemployment or external pressures). Should one identify such a group and what percentage of the work force this constituted, then further tests could be made involving orientations of rural and urban dwellers. This would further highlight the influence of background on orientation, as well as shifting orientation due to the work situation.

CONCLUSION

I have attempted to outline the inadequacies of contingency theories on structure, technology, and orientation to work of the British action approach. Contingency theory shows signs of conservatism, and is not adapted to an approach involving flexibility, change, and improvement.

An alternative approach based on values and minimally acceptable value levels (as outlined in the previous section) could, I believe, serve as a basis for predictive theories and theories of change, levels being exploratory tools for adjusting change. Models of varying levels may counteract the major disadvantages of human relations, overstatement and lack of individual differentiation. Also, an approach based on values and minimally acceptable value levels would offer a useful basis to discuss problems of "intrinsic conflict between goals of workers and of the enterprises" (Daniel, 1973).

Such an improvement approach would include a further aspect, which I believe facilitates a move away from the static tendencies of action, contingency, best fit, and self-actualization. People would not have fixed perceptions or orientations but changing utilities accorded to the perceived nature of the situation (compare with changing expectations, aspiration levels, perceived alternatives, etc.). Further there would not be a fixed booty or reward to divide, nor fixed sets of needs and motivators. Instead this would be a result of social and situational interaction.

Forms of measurement for purposes of comparison are being developed based on modified and differentiated versions of RTA scales and indices of change, including some index of "innovative potential" (Brown & Millar, 1974; Hackman & Oldham, 1975). There are also relationships of this index to attitudes to work which could be explored.

Finally, the model avoids the pitfalls of maximization, the pursuit of optimal solutions for example, assuming "maximization of material rewards" as the motivating force (Goldthorpe)[15] or, assuming that motivation may be optimized through self-actualization (Maslow, Herzberg) or assuming that efficiency is maximized by optimal matching of technology and structure (Woodward, Burns, & Stalker, Perrow, Lawrence & Lorsch).

The assumption of minimal acceptable value levels, incorporated in the "improvement theory" would in contrast facilitate the use of a satisficing model rather than an optimizing one, thus permitting a simplification in the jungle of relevant variables, a reasoned focusing on a limited set.

In contrast to models implying fixed sets of priorities and optimization, a "pegged" satisficing model in combination with some index of innovative potential would contain both material and value components, thus forming a more useful tool to explore an organizational world of compromise, values, and mutual adjustment to needs in a background of economic and physical constraints.

REFERENCES

ALDERFER, C. P. An empirical test of a new theory of human needs. *Organizational Behavior and Human Performance*, 1969, *4*, 142-176.
ARGYRIS, C. *Integrating the individual and the organization*. New York: Wiley, 1964.
ARGYRIS, C. *The applicability of organisational sociology*. London: Cambridge University Press, 1972.
BALDAMUS, W. *Efficiency and effort*. London: Tavistock, 1961.
BLAUNER, R. *Alienation and freedom*. Chicago: University of Chicago Press, 1964.
BROWN, R. Sources of objectives in work and employment. In J. Child (Ed.), *Man and organisation*. Woking and London: Allen & Unwin, 1973.
BROWN, C., & MILLAR, J. *Job design change: An assessment of the potential for cross-national research on job redesign*. Report to SSRC, 1974.
BURNS, T., & STALKER, J. *The management of innovation*. London: Tavistock, 1961.
CHILD, J. (Ed.). *Man and organisation*. Woking and London: Allen & Unwin, 1973.
COOPER, R. Task characteristics and intrinsic motivation. *Human Relations*, 1973.
COTGROVE, S., & BOX, S. *Science, industry, and society*. Allen & Unwin, 1970.
CYERT, R., & MARCH, J. *A behavioral theory of the firm*. Englewood Cliffs, N.J.: Prentice Hall, 1963.
DANIEL, W. W. Understanding employee behaviour in its context: Illustrations from productivity bargaining. In J. Child (Ed.), *Man and organisation*. Woking and London: Allen & Unwin, 1973.
DREYFUS, C. *Alchemy and artificial intelligence*. Santa Monica, California: Rand Co. Mem. P-3244, 1965.
DUBIN, R. Power, function and organization. *Pacific School Review*, 1963, *6*.

---

[15]Daniel (in Child, 1973) summarizes Goldthorpe's "fixed priorities," "fixed booty" approach as follows:
  a. The worker has an overall, ordered consistent set of needs and priorities in what he wants from the job. This set of priorities is manifested in all aspects of his occupational behavior and choices.
  b. An increase in demands along one dimension must be at the expense of those along another ("fixed booty"). (Daniel is sceptical of both fixed priority and the view that say more extrinsic rewards implies less intrinsic.)

DUNNETTE, M. D., CAMPBELL, J. P., & HAKEL, M. D. Factors contributing to job satisfaction and job dissatisfaction in six occupational groups. *Organizational Behavior and Human Performance*, 1967, *12*.

ETZIONI, A. *Modern organizations.* Englewood Cliffs, N.J.: Prentice-Hall, 1964.

FAXÉN, K. *Research on self-developing forms of organisation.* Ravello Conference Paper, 1971.

GOLDTHORPE, J. *Social stratification in industrial society.* Sociological Review Monograph No. 8, 1964, pp. 97-131.

GOLDTHORPE, J., LOCKWOOD, D., BECHHOFER, F., & PLATT, J. *The affluent worker.* Cambridge: University Press, 1968.

HACKMAN, J. R., & LAWLER, E. Employee reactions to job characteristics. *Journal of Applied Psychology Monthly*, 1971, *55*, 259-286.

HACKMAN, J. R., & OLDHAM, G. R. Development of the job diagnostic survey. *Journal of Applied Psychology*, 1975, *60*, 159-170.

HALL, D. T., & NOUGAIM, K. E. An examination of Maslow's need hierarchy in an organizational setting. *Organizational Behavior and Human Performance*, 1968, *3*.

HENEMAN, H. G., & SCHWAB, D. P. Evaluation of research on expectancy theory. *Psychology Bulletin*, 1972.

HICKSON, D., PUGH, D. S., & PHEYSEY, D. C. Operations technology and organisational structure: An empirical reappraisal. *Administrative Science Quarterly*, 1969, *14*.

HULIN, C., & BLOOD, M. Job enlargement, individual differences and worker responses. *Psychology Bulletin*, 1968, *69*, 41-55.

INGHAM, G. *Size of industrial organisation and worker behaviour.* London: Macmillan Press Ltd., 1970.

INKSON, J., PUGH, D. S., & HICKSON, D. J. Organisation context and structure: An abbreviated replication. *Administrative Science Quarterly*, 1970, *15*, 318-329.

KERR, S., SCHRIESHEIM, C. A., MURPHY, C. J. & STOGDILL, R. M. Towards a contingency theory of leadership based upon consideration and initiating structure literature. *Organizational Behavior and Human Performance*, 1974, *12*.

KING, A. S. Expectation effects in organisational change. *Administrative Science Quarterly*, 1974, *19*, 221-230.

KOHN, M., & SCHOOLER, M. Class, occupation, and orientation. *American Sociological Review*, 1969.

LAWLER, E. E., & PORTER, L. Antecedent attitudes of effective managerial performance. *Organizational Behavior and Human Performance*, 1967, *2*.

LAWRENCE, P. R., & LORSCH, J. W. *Organization and environment: Managing differentiation and integration.* Boston: Harvard University Press, 1967.

LIKERT, R. *The human organization: Its management and value.* New York: McGraw-Hill, 1967.

LUPTON, T. *Management and the social sciences.* Manchester: Penguin, 1971 (Reprint).

MARCH, J., & SIMON, H. *Organizations.* New York: Wiley, 1958.

MOHR, L. Organisational technology and organisational structure. *Administrative Science Quarterly*, 1971, *16*, 444-459.

NICHOLS, T. *Ownership, control and ideology.* Allen & Unwin, 1969.

PERROW, C. A framework for the comparative analysis of organisations. *American Sociological Review*, 1967, *32*, 194-208.

PERROW, C. *Organisational analysis.* London: Tavistock, 1970.

SHEPHARD, J. *Automation and alienation.* Cambridge, Mass.: MIT Press, 1971.

SILVERMAN, D. *The theory of organisations.* London: Heineman, 1970.

STEERS, R. M. Effects of need for achievement on the job performance, job attitude relationship. *Journal of Applied Psychology*, 1975, *60*, 678-683.

THOMPSON, J. D., & BATES, F. E. Technology, organization, and administration. *Administrative Science Quarterly*, 1967, *2*, 325-343.

TRIST, E. A., & BAMFORTH, K. W. Some social and psychological consequences of the longwall method of coal-getting. *Human Relations*, 1951, *4*.

TURNER, A., & LAWRENCE, P. *Industrial jobs and the workers.* Cambridge: Harvard University Graduate School of Business Administration, 1965.
TURNER, B. *Exploring the industrial subculture.* New York: Macmillan, 1971.
WATERS, L. An empirical test of five versions of the two-factor theory of job satisfaction. *Organizational Behavior and Human Performance,* 1972, 7, 18-25.
WOODWARD, J. *Industrial organisations.* London: Oxford University Press, 1965.